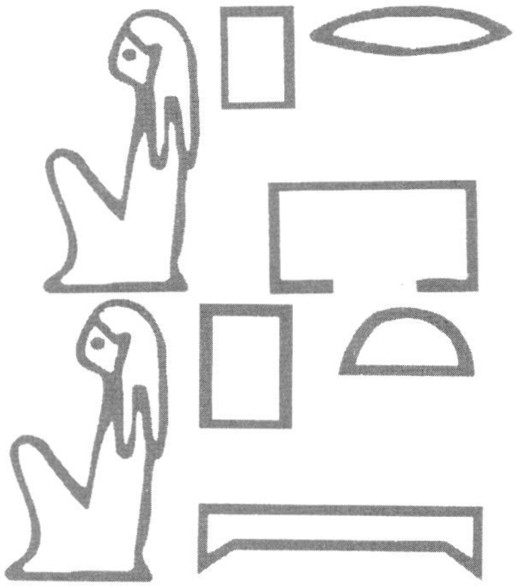

Mistress of the House Mistress of Heaven

WOMEN IN ANCIENT EGYPT

Anne K. Capel and Glenn E. Markoe, Editors

Essays by Catharine H. Roehrig, Betsy M. Bryan,
and Janet H. Johnson

Catalogue by Anne K. Capel and Glenn E. Markoe,
with Contributions by Richard A. Fazzini, James F. Romano,
David P. Silverman, and Donald B. Spanel

HUDSON HILLS PRESS, NEW YORK
in association with
Cincinnati Art Museum

Mistress of the House,
Mistress of Heaven:
WOMEN IN ANCIENT EGYPT

Cincinnati Art Museum
Cincinnati, Ohio
October 20, 1996, through
January 5, 1997

The Brooklyn Museum
Brooklyn, New York
February 21 through
May 18, 1997

FIRST EDITION

Published in conjunction with the exhibition organized by the Cincinnati Art Museum, Cincinnati, Ohio, October 20, 1996, through January 5, 1997, and also appearing at The Brooklyn Museum (February 21 through May 18, 1997).

Published in the United States by Hudson Hills Press, Inc., Suite 1308, 230 Fifth Avenue, New York, NY 10001-7704.

Distributed in the United States, its territories and possessions, Canada, Mexico, and Central and South America by National Book Network.
Distributed in the United Kingdom, Eire, and Europe by Art Books International Ltd.
Exclusive representation in Asia, Australia, and New Zealand by EM International.

Editor and Publisher: Paul Anbinder

Editorial Assistant: Faye Chiu

Proofreader: Fronia W. Simpson

Designer: Betty Binns

Composition: Angela Taormina

Manufactured in Japan by Toppan Printing Company.

Library of Congress Cataloguing-in-Publication Data
Mistress of the House, Mistress of Heaven : women in Ancient Egypt / Anne K. Capel and Glenn E. Markoe, editors; essays by Catharine Roehrig, Betsy Bryan, and Janet Johnson; catalogue by Anne K. Capel and Glenn E. Markoe with contributions by Richard A. Fazzini . . . [et al.].—1st ed.
p. cm.
Exhibition catalogue. "In association with Cincinnati Art Museum."
Includes bibliographical references and index.
ISBN 1-55595-129-5 (alk. paper)
1. Women in art—Exhibitions. 2. Art, Egyptian—Exhibitions.
3. Art, Ancient—Egypt—Exhibitions. I. Capel, Anne K. II. Markoe, Glenn, 1951– .
N5335.C56C566 1996
704.9′424′093207477178—dc20 96-9376
CIP

Contents

Foreword *7*
List of Lenders to the Exhibition *8*
Preface and Acknowledgments *9*

Woman's work: Some occupations of nonroyal women as depicted in ancient Egyptian art **13**
CATHARINE H. ROEHRIG

In women good and bad fortune are on earth: Status and roles of women in Egyptian culture **25**
BETSY M. BRYAN

Catalogue of the exhibition **47**
Notes to the catalogue *48*
Public and Private Lives **49**
Family *49*
Motherhood *59*
Adornment *75*
Occupations *91*
Female Royalty **103**
Goddesses **121**
Afterlife **145**

The legal status of women in ancient Egypt **175**
JANET H. JOHNSON

Notes *187*
Women's work 187
In women good and bad fortune are on earth 189
Catalogue of the exhibition 192
The legal status of women in ancient Egypt 215
Chronology *218*
Map *219*
Bibliography *221*
Journal and Monograph Series Abbreviations *225*
Index *227*
Photograph credits *235*

Foreword

People's fascination with the art of ancient Egypt is enduring and seems to transcend generation, gender, degree of exposure to art and art history, and other differences. Indeed, the fact that pyramids and mummies have become stock images of popular culture has apparently not diminished, but rather heightened, the public's desire to see original works of Egyptian art. At the same time, a new generation of scholars continues to find fertile ground for fresh interpretations and new discoveries in the study of ancient Egypt. This wonderful conjunction of public and scholarly interest has recently brought forth a number of extraordinary, complementary museum exhibitions, including the Cincinnati Art Museum's *Mistress of the House, Mistress of Heaven: Women in Ancient Egypt.*

All of us at the Cincinnati Art Museum are pleased that the original idea for *Women in Ancient Egypt,* advanced by Curator of Classical and Near Eastern Art Glenn Markoe and Guest Curator Anne K. Capel, has grown into a collaboration with a number of distinguished scholars and our esteemed colleagues at The Brooklyn Museum, which houses one of the world's foremost collections of Egyptian art. In the Preface and Acknowledgments Drs. Capel and Markoe express our gratitude to these colleagues and friends, but I would be remiss in not emphasizing our debt to the staff of The Brooklyn Museum and particularly its former director, Robert T. Buck, Jr., without whose encouragement and active participation this exhibition would not have been possible. Thanks also go to Roy R. Eddey, Acting President; Linda S. Ferber, Acting Director/Chief Curator; Ken Moser, Vice Director for Collections and Chief Conservator; and Deborah Schwartz, Vice Director for Education.

Our sincere thanks to Cinergy, and especially to James E. Rogers, CEO, and J. Joseph Hale, Jr., President of The Cinergy Foundation, Inc., for their early belief in the exhibition and the generous underwriting that allowed us to proceed with its organization. Three & Associates, *The Cincinnati Enquirer,* WKRC Channel 12, and the National Endowment for the Arts have all stepped forward with the assistance needed to share *Women in Ancient Egypt* with the widest possible audience.

The enthusiasm of Salem B. and Wafaa Foad encouraged us to seek the involvement of Jehan Sadat in our project. Her work on behalf of women everywhere brings a contemporary relevance to the exhibition's theme. We are grateful to the Foads and to Mrs. Mickey Kaplan for cochairing the opening gala and to the gala patrons whose support is also crucial to the exhibition's success.

The Cincinnati Art Museum staff and Board of Trustees comprise an extraordinary team of individuals whose combined energy, talent, and enthusiasm account for the museum's great achievements. My special thanks go to President Lawrence H. Kyte, Jr., and division heads Debbie Bowman, Pat Murdock, Diane Smith, and Anne el-Omami for their contributions to this project. Finally, tremendous gratitude is due to Glenn Markoe and Anne K. Capel for taking on a major project that brings great honor to this institution and makes lasting contributions both to the study of the art of ancient Egypt and to women's studies.

BARBARA K. GIBBS

DIRECTOR, CINCINNATI ART MUSEUM

MAY 1996

Lenders to the Exhibition

BALTIMORE, THE WALTERS ART GALLERY

BERKELEY, PHOEBE HEARST MUSEUM OF ANTHROPOLOGY, UNIVERSITY OF CALIFORNIA

BOSTON, MUSEUM OF FINE ARTS

THE BROOKLYN MUSEUM

THE ART INSTITUTE OF CHICAGO

CHICAGO, THE FIELD MUSEUM

THE ORIENTAL INSTITUTE OF THE UNIVERSITY OF CHICAGO

CINCINNATI ART MUSEUM

THE CLEVELAND MUSEUM OF ART

THE DETROIT INSTITUTE OF ARTS

KANSAS CITY, THE NELSON-ATKINS MUSEUM OF ART

OXFORD, OHIO, MIAMI UNIVERSITY ART MUSEUM

NEW HAVEN, YALE UNIVERSITY ART GALLERY

NEW YORK, THE METROPOLITAN MUSEUM OF ART

OMAHA, JOSLYN MEMORIAL ART MUSEUM

PHILADELPHIA MUSEUM OF ART

PHILADELPHIA, UNIVERSITY OF PENNSYLVANIA MUSEUM OF ARCHAEOLOGY AND ANTHROPOLOGY

PROVIDENCE, MUSEUM OF ART, RHODE ISLAND SCHOOL OF DESIGN

RICHMOND, VIRGINIA MUSEUM OF FINE ARTS

THE SAINT LOUIS ART MUSEUM

ST. LOUIS, WASHINGTON UNIVERSITY GALLERY OF ART

THE TOLEDO MUSEUM OF ART

Preface and Acknowledgments

The prominent social position occupied by ancient Egyptian women has long been recognized. In recent years, several books have been published on the subject, most notably, Gay Robins's excellent survey, *Women in Ancient Egypt.* The topic, however, has rarely been treated in exhibition form, a curious fact in view of the impressive number of objects relating to ancient Egyptian women that have survived throughout the world. The present exhibition, the first large-scale undertaking of its kind in the United States, explores the historical and artistic milieu of this topic.

The exhibition and accompanying catalogue are unique in another important respect: they draw exclusively on Egyptian art in American collections. Previous studies on ancient Egyptian women have focused, for obvious reasons, on the distinguished and often extensive Egyptian art holdings in Europe and Egypt. In planning this exhibition, however, the extraordinary richness and diversity of such collections in our own country became apparent. The decision was made to focus exclusively on this material, resulting in the present survey, which is drawn from more than twenty-five public institutions and private collections in the United States.

Appropriately, the scholars invited to contribute to this publication are all American Egyptologists. Their participation is fitting tribute to an exhibition designed to draw attention to the American contribution to continuing research on this subject.

The present catalogue is not intended as an exhaustive or comprehensive statement on women in ancient Egypt. Rather, it highlights a number of key works in this country and offers some new interpretations and discussions of these objects that may serve as a catalyst for further research on the topic of ancient Egyptian women. Although the catalogue entries have been written in a manner accessible to the general reader, it is hoped that students and scholars in the fields of Egyptology and women's studies will also find this publication to be an interesting and useful tool.

The title, *Mistress of the House, Mistress of Heaven,* was specifically chosen to connote the range and diversity of roles held by ancient Egyptian women—from household manager to priestess of Hathor, the Mistress of Heaven. Both titles, *nebet per* (Mistress of the House) and *nebet pet* (Mistress of Heaven), are commonly attested in ancient Egypt and appear on a number of works in this exhibition.

The present exhibition explores the spectrum of women's lives and activities throughout pharaonic Egypt's three-thousand-year history. In many ways the lives of ancient Egyptian women were unique compared with those of women from other ancient cultures. In other important respects, however, ancient Egyptian women shared many of the same experiences and concerns with household and family common to women of all times and places. Thus, both the mundane and the extraordinary aspects of ancient Egyptian women's lives are explored.

It has been our privilege to work with a diverse and highly respected group of scholars in the field of ancient Egyptian studies. An enormous debt of gratitude is due to Richard A. Fazzini, Chairman of the Department of Egyptian, Classical, and Ancient Middle Eastern Art at The Brooklyn Museum. His tireless and enthusiastic efforts in coordinating both Brooklyn's participation in the project and all aspects of the exhibition's development have contributed significantly to this project's success. His generosity not only in making available his own expertise but for checking and providing references from the Wilbour Library of Egyptology is deeply appreciated. Sincere gratitude is also due to Curator James F. Romano and Associate Curator Donald B. Spanel for their scholarly suggestions and contributions to the catalogue.

We would like to extend special thanks to the catalogue's three essayists: Betsy M. Bryan, Janet H. Johnson, and Catharine H. Roehrig. All have contributed thoughtful and thought-provoking essays on their respective areas of research. The time they devoted to this project in the face of otherwise demanding professional academic and museum responsibilities is greatly appreciated.

An especial debt of gratitude is due to Edna R. Russmann, Research Associate, Department of Egyptian, Classical, and Ancient Middle Eastern Art, The Brooklyn Museum, for her unflagging support and encouragement during this project. Throughout, she gave freely and unselfishly of her time and expertise on various matters connected with the catalogue and exhibition. Her input was crucial to the successful completion of this project.

This exhibition would not have been possible without the generous cooperation of the various lending institutions involved. Their willingness to lend these extraordinary works of art has made this exhibition a reality. Among the many individuals involved, we would like to extend particular thanks to Ellen Reeder and Carol A. Benson, The Walters Art Gallery, Baltimore; JoAnn Harris Smith, Bath, Ohio; Rosemary Joyce, Joan Knudsen, Tamsen Fuller, and Gene Prince, The Phoebe Hearst Museum of Anthropology, University of California at Berkeley; Rita Freed, Timothy Kendall, and Peter Der Manuelian, Museum of Fine Arts, Boston; Mary Greuel, The Art Institute of Chicago; Bennett Bronson, Janice B. Klein, and Nina Cummings, Field Museum, Chicago; Karen L. Wilson, Raymond D. Tindel, Emily Teeter, and John Larson, The Oriental Institute

Museum, University of Chicago; Walter I. Farmer, Cincinnati; Arielle P. Kozloff, Lawrence M. Berman, and Sharon Herene, The Cleveland Museum of Art; William H. and Elsie Peck, The Detroit Institute of Arts; Robert Cohon, The Nelson-Atkins Museum of Art; Edna Southard, Miami University Art Museum, Oxford, Ohio; Susan Matheson, Yale University Gallery of Art, New Haven; Dorothea Arnold, James P. Allen, Catharine H. Roehrig, and Marsha Hill, The Metropolitan Museum of Art, New York; Jack A. Josephson, New York; Marsha V. Gallagher and Theodore W. James, Joslyn Art Museum, Omaha; Felice Fischer and Sara Detwiler, Philadelphia Museum of Art; David O'Connor, David Silverman, Sylvia S. Duggan, Charles S. Kline, Denise Dokey, and Stacie Olsson, University of Pennsylvania Museum of Archaeology and Anthropology, Philadelphia; Florence Friedman, Museum of Art, Rhode Island School of Design, Providence; Margaret Ellen Mayo, Virginia Museum of Fine Arts, Richmond; Dr. and Mrs. W. Benson Harer, San Bernardino; Sidney M. Goldstein, The Saint Louis Art Museum; Joseph D. Ketner and Jane Neidhart, Washington University Gallery of Art, St. Louis; Patricia Whitesides, Lee Mooney, and the late Kurt T. Luckner, The Toledo Museum of Art.

The Museum would also like to extend particular thanks to the following professional colleagues who have generously lent their expertise in matters relating to the exhibition: James P. Allen, Carol Andrews, Dorothea Arnold, Kathleen Keller, Barbara S. Lesko, Geoffrey T. Martin, Malcolm Mosher, Barbara A. Porter, Patricia Podzorski, Martin Raaven, David P. Silverman, and Herman te Velde. Lastly, we owe a debt of gratitude to Jerome M. Eisenberg for his donation of the faience *shabti,* catalogue number 72.

The exhibition and the production of the accompanying catalogue could not have taken place without the participation of the Cincinnati Art Museum's capable staff. Our sincere appreciation goes to Mary Ellen Goeke, Head of Exhibitions and Registration, for her role in coordinating all the logistical arrangements for the exhibition. She and her support staff worked tirelessly to monitor every detail of the project's execution. An especial debt of gratitude is due to Designer/Preparator Patrick Brown for his thoughtful and innovative design and planning for this exhibition. Special thanks are also due to Chief Conservator Stephen S. Bonadies and Paper Conservator Cecile Mear for their diligent and expert conservation work on objects lent from the museum's own collections. Thanks are also due to Ellen Avril, Associate Curator of Far Eastern Art, for her advice, support, and encouragement throughout the project. Anne el-Omami, former Curator of Museum Education, and Assistant Curators Beverly Lamb and Julie Stevens are also to be thanked for their advice and input in developing the various educational components of the exhibition. Sincere gratitude is due to Môna Chapin and Cathy Shaffer of The Mary R. Schiff Library for their help in facilitating research on the catalogue. Lastly, Terrie M. Benjamin, Administrative Assistant to the Director, is to be commended for her help in coordinating communication among the various departmental offices.

On behalf of The Brooklyn Museum's Department of Egyptian, Classical, and Ancient Middle Eastern Art, we would like to thank again the members of The Brooklyn Museum's administration mentioned in the Foreword and the following staff members of The Brooklyn Museum: Diane Bergman, Librarian, Wilbour Library of Egyptology; Dean Brown, Chief Photographer; Faith Goodin, Museum Technician in Photography; Mary Gow, Assistant, Wilbour Library of Egyptology; Alison Lowey, Assistant, Department of Egyptian, Classical, and Ancient Middle Eastern Art; Ellen Pearlstein, Objects Conservator; Lisa Bruno, Associate Conservator; Irit Lev, Assistant Conservator; David Goldstein, Assistant Conservator; Elizabeth Reynolds, Registrar; Lisa Cain, Assistant Registrar; Cheryl Sobas, Exhibition Manager; Charles Froom, Chief Designer; Sally Williams, Public Information Officer; and Sallie Stutz, Vice Director for Marketing. Departmental Chairman Richard Fazzini extends especial thanks to Edna R. Russmann, Mary McKercher, and Herman te Velde for their gracious assistance.

The catalogue has benefited from the professional assistance of a number of individuals outside the institution. Our sincere appreciation goes to Karen Feinberg for her expert editing of the catalogue text; to Peter J. Gates and Ron Forth for their able photographic work on the Cincinnati Art Museum's objects; to Catherine L. O'Hara, Public Affairs Manager, Taft Museum, for her generous assistance in coordinating the final editorial work on this publication; and to the graduate students from the University of Cincinnati's Classics Department for their valuable and much appreciated assistance in this project: Regan Barr, Marguerite Prendergast, Tara Lygon, Eleni Hazaki, and A.J. Lyons. Others who have assisted and contributed in diverse ways include Jean Wellington and Mike Braunlin of the Blegen Classics Library of the University of Cincinnati; Renate Glenn, Cincinnati Art Museum volunteer; Chris Breyn; and Dawn Bellinger.

Finally, an enormous debt of gratitude is due to our museum Director, Barbara K. Gibbs, for her expert guidance and unflagging support of this exhibition.

ANNE K. CAPEL
Guest Curator

GLENN MARKOE
Curator of Classical and Near Eastern Art

CINCINNATI ART MUSEUM
SEPTEMBER 1996

Mistress of the House, Mistress of Heaven

Women in Ancient Egypt

Women's work: Some occupations of nonroyal women as depicted in ancient Egyptian art

CATHARINE H. ROEHRIG
The Metropolitan Museum of Art

Written evidence in the form of letters, tax records, and legal documents suggests that in legal status, the right to own property, and the ability to barter goods on their own terms, Egyptian women enjoyed a higher level of equality with men than did women in other ancient cultures. Yet, because Egyptian women did not, as a rule, hold high government office, either nationally or on a local level, they do not figure prominently in historical records. Nor have they left the kinds of autobiographical texts that are found in the tombs of their male contemporaries.[1] Because individual Egyptian women have left us few written records of their own, probably the richest source of information about their occupations and activities is to be found in the art, especially the artwork associated with tombs: wall paintings, reliefs, statuary, and funerary models.

In Egyptian art, representations of nonroyal women fall into two broad categories. One depicts women from the privileged classes, who are often (but not always) identified by name and title. The other portrays women from the lower ranks of society who are almost always anonymous. The first group of women includes the wives, mothers, and daughters of government officials and civil servants, priests and temple bureaucrats, army officers and military administrators.[2] These women sometimes have monuments of their own, such as the lovely seated statue of Enehy (cat. no. 35a),[3] but they are represented far more frequently in the tombs and on the funerary monuments of their male relatives.[4]

Women are often quite important figures in the funerary art of their husbands and sons. In most periods, the principal male and female figures are the same size in pair statues (cat. no. 93) and family groups (cat. no. 2), or else, as in the statue of Memy-Sabu and his wife (cat. no. 3a), the difference in size might appear normal in real life.[5] Unfortunately, one can tell little about a woman depicted in one of these statues except that she was a wife and/or mother and that she was "Mistress of the House," a title that precedes the names of most married women in the New Kingdom. These roles surely entailed a great deal of responsibility, but the specific duties are not enumerated clearly either in texts or in artistic representations. In tomb decoration and models, the tomb owner's wife is not shown directly supervising activities that certainly must have come under her authority as the mistress of a household.

Outside the home, upperclass women played an important role in the religious cults of various deities. Their positions are signaled both by title and by recognizable iconographic symbols. In the Old Kingdom, many women were priestesses of the goddess Hathor, and they are shown carrying her sacred symbols, the *menat* necklace (cat. no. 35c) and the sistrum (cat. no. 35b). These two instruments also were employed in the worship of other deities (both male and female) and became accoutrements of the chantresses, or singers, who were attached to various cults. In catalogue number 93, for example, Renenutet, whose titles include "Chantress of Amen" and "Chief of the Dance Troupe of Hathor of Madjet,"[6] is shown holding a *menat;* in catalogue number 35a, Enehy, who was "Chantress of the Mistress of the Southern Sycamore (Hathor)," holds a sistrum.

In painting and relief, wives, mothers, and daughters of the deceased are often prominent figures. As in statuary, they are usually the same size as their male relatives or only slightly smaller. The tomb owner is usually accompanied by his wife or his mother when he makes offerings to the gods. One of these women almost always sits with him

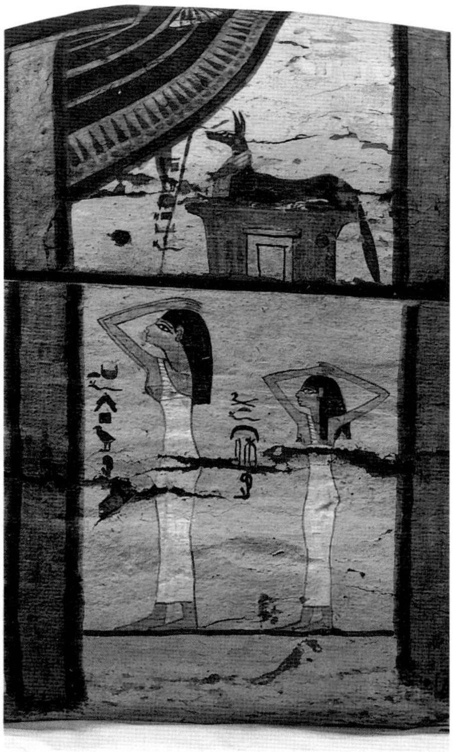

Fig. 1 Detail of the proper right side of the coffin of Ahmose. The Metropolitan Museum of Art. Gift of the Earl of Carnarvon, 1914. 14.10.2. Photograph courtesy of the Metropolitan Museum of Art.

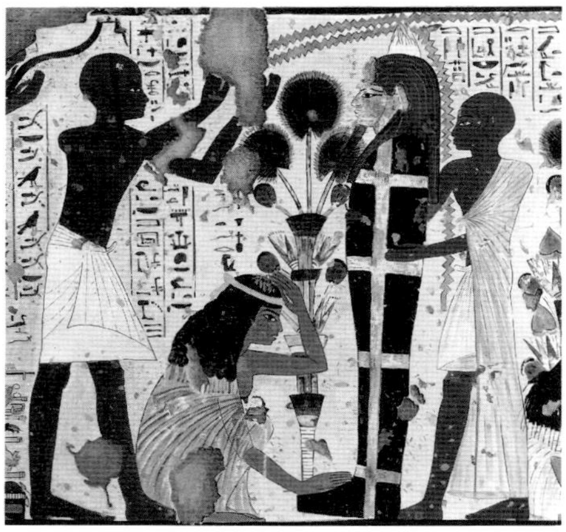

Fig. 2 Detail from the tomb of Nebamen and Ipuky (TT 181). Facsimile watercolor by Charles K. Wilkinson. The Metropolitan Museum of Art. Rogers Fund, 1930. 30.4.108. Photograph courtesy of the Metropolitan Museum of Art.

when he receives offerings in his tomb or on a stela. In marsh scenes, the wife generally appears with her husband as he hunts birds or spears fish.[7] In Old Kingdom tombs, wives and daughters are sometimes shown entertaining the tomb owner by playing the harp and singing. In the funerary context, this activity may be interpreted as having some ritual or symbolic function, but it probably also reflects reality. Some of these women were undoubtedly accomplished musicians who used their talents to entertain themselves and their families.[8]

Apart from the actions she performs with her husband or son, the woman in her role as wife and daughter frequently appears as an active participant in other situations. Occasionally a wife is shown offering to her husband, but far more frequently a daughter appears as the principal presenter of offerings to her parents. On the back of catalogue number 93, for example, Renenutet offers to her father and mother. While she pours a libation with her left hand, she holds a *menat* necklace in her right, as befits the title "Chantress of Amen," a title recorded in the text above her image.

Mourning is another function performed by the female relatives of a tomb owner. In the Old and Middle Kingdoms, mourning is treated very much as a ritual. The so-called *ḏryt*-mourners are usually interpreted as priestesses impersonating the goddesses Isis and Nephthys.[9] In both periods the *ḏryt*-mourners are usually unnamed. Even when they are named, it is hard to identify their relationship (if any) with the deceased. The other mourners in these scenes, though they may represent family members, are usually anonymous. In the New Kingdom, however, mourners at the funeral are sometimes identified as the wives and daughters of the deceased. Although they also probably fill a ritual function, they are now portrayed as human women mourning the death of a loved one. This may be seen in a vignette on an early New Kingdom coffin from Thebes inscribed for a man named Ahmose (fig. 1).[10] On either side of the coffin box, near the shoulder, his wife, Hapu, and his daughter, also named Ahmose, are shown in typical poses of mourning, their hands held up to their heads. A more poignant image appears in a later representation from the Theban tomb of Nebamen and Ipuky (TT 181). Nebamen's wife, Henutnofret, and his daughters are identified several times in various vignettes of the funeral procession. In one of these, Henutnofret appears crouched before her husband's coffin tears streaming down her face, one hand touching the foot of the coffin and the other rubbing dust into her hair (fig. 2).

Women from the privileged classes are usually designated by name and with one or more titles and epithets, but those from the lower classes are generally not identified as individuals. They appear in generic scenes on walls and in funerary models, and sometimes are accompanied by a short text describing their activity—servant, baker, weaver, spinner. These female figures, and their male counterparts, function more as hieroglyphs than as representations of real people. Some exceptions exist, of course. For example, in the Theban tomb of Djari, an official of the mid–Eleventh Dynasty, the women depicting food preparation are identified as the servant Sit-pep, the servant Senet, the servant Sit-henen, the servant Mekuty, and the servant Sit-in (fig. 3).[11] Although artistically the figures are merely generic representations, and quite crude at that, the addition of names makes them individual people. These women are known to us because their employer (or master) chose to name them in his tomb. This

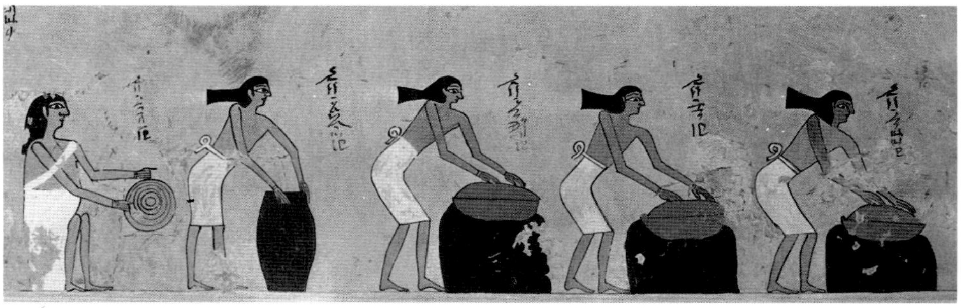

Fig. 3 Women preparing food, from the tomb of Djari (TT 366). Drawing by Lindsley Hall. 31.6.1. Courtesy of the Metropolitan Museum of Art.

may have been a way for a wealthy man to provide for his dependents. By being identified in the tomb, they could benefit from the funerary offerings.[12] Another example of this practice occurs in a scene on the back of catalogue number 93. In the lower register, Renenutet is followed by a woman identified as "her servant, Hathor."

Although the vast majority of the female figures in wall scenes and funerary models are anonymous, they give us at least some idea of the occupations that were considered women's work in ancient Egyptian society. In the Old Kingdom, and less frequently in later periods, groups of women are shown winnowing grain, although they are not seen cutting the stalks. They are also shown gleaning the fields, an activity represented more frequently in New Kingdom scenes. Women grind grain as well (cat. no. 28a), a task that seems to be theirs exclusively in all periods. They also bake bread, an activity they sometimes share with men. Beer is brewed more often by men, but women are also seen pressing the mash through sieves (cat. no. 28b) and preparing the ceramic storage containers. They probably even had a hand in making the pottery beer jars and bread molds used in brewing and baking, as suggested in a small limestone figurine of a woman burnishing or putting a handle on a pot (fig. 4). As a rule, however, men rather than women are shown as potters. Although the representations of these activities on tomb walls and in models usually reflect the large-scale production necessary to supply a big estate, we know that similar pursuits took place in the households of agricultural workers and artisans. These people were usually paid in measures of grain; their town sites have yielded numerous bread molds, grinding stones, and domestic hearths.

Apart from working with certain aspects of food production, women from the lower ranks perform a number of activities that might be interpreted as professions. They are represented as musicians, singers, and dancers (fig. 5), as mourners (cat. no. 31), and as servants of the wealthy. At one time or another, they share all of these occupations with men. However, women are also depicted participating in all phases of one industrial craft that seems to have been exclusively theirs, at least through the end of the Middle Kingdom. This is the manufacture of linen textiles. Because this is the only craft viewed clearly as women's work, and because it is also the only area of women's endeavor from which a tangible product survives (in the form of linen fabric), textile manufacture will be discussed below in greater detail.

This brief survey of the activities of nonroyal women as documented in art makes it clear that there is little overlap between the methods of portraying women of the elite classes and those of the lower ranks of society. However, women of both groups shared one activity in which both are occasionally represented in art, namely the nurturing of small children.

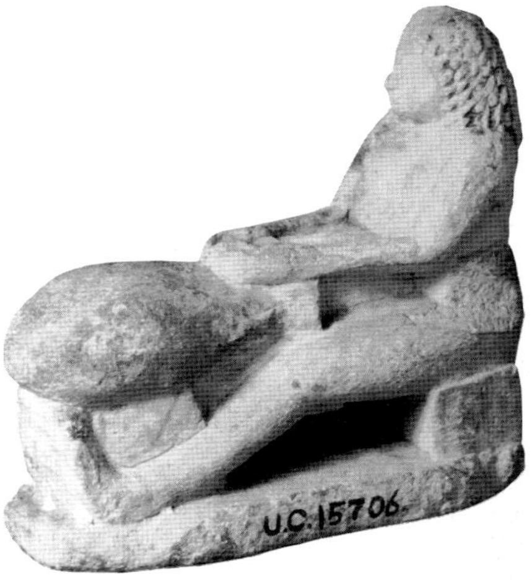

Fig. 4 Limestone figurine of a woman burnishing or adding a handle to a pot. New Kingdom. Courtesy of the Petrie Museum, University of London, UC 15706.

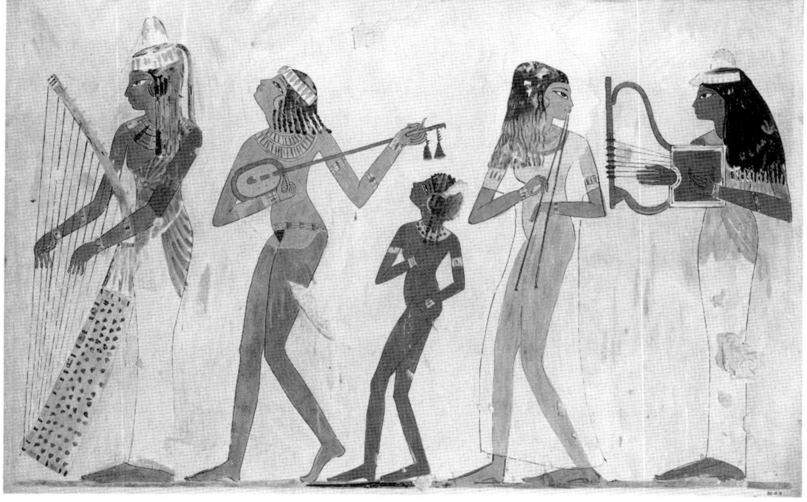

Fig. 5 Female musicians from the tomb of Djeserkarasonb (TT 38). Facsimile watercolor by Charles K. Wilkinson. The Metropolitan Museum of Art. Rogers Fund, 1930. 30.4.9. Photograph courtesy of the Metropolitan Museum of Art.

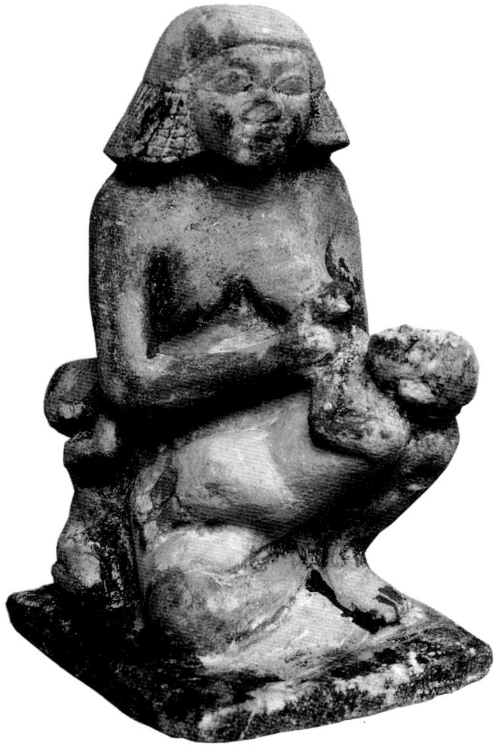

Fig. 6 Limestone statuette of a woman suckling her children. Old Kingdom. The Metropolitan Museum of Art. Purchase, Edward S. Harkness Gift, 1926. 26.7.1405.

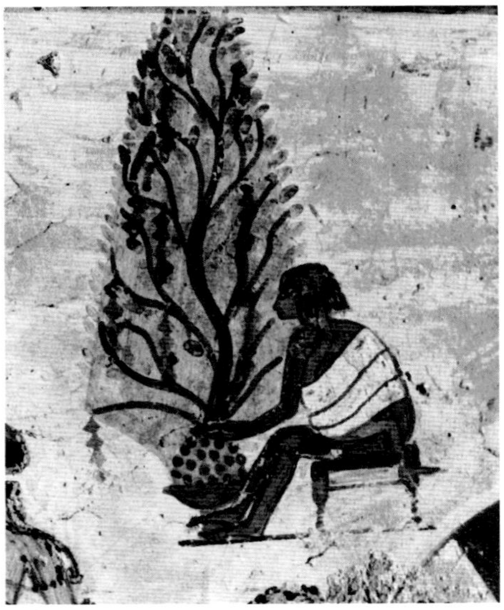

Fig. 7 Detail from the tomb of Menna (TT 69). Photo by Harry Burton. Courtesy of the Metropolitan Museum of Art.

Nurturing children

Regardless of their social status and their other occupations and responsibilities, the most important role of women in most societies is the bearing and rearing of children. The ancient Egyptian culture was no exception, and all Egyptian women, from the most powerful goddess to the lowliest peasant, are represented somewhere in Egyptian art as nurturers of the young.

Because most of the representations of daily life come to us from tomb walls and funerary models, whose main function was to provide for the continued maintenance of the tomb owner's spirit, infants and small children are far less numerous in art than they must have been in the population as a whole. Adult women are usually shown performing their duties unencumbered by toddlers and babes in arms even though Egyptian women seem to have suckled their children as long as three years.[13] There are representations from various periods, however, that give a somewhat more realistic idea of most Egyptian women's lives.

In the Fifth Dynasty tomb of Niankhkhnum and Khnumhotep at Saqqara a woman suckles her baby while tending a fire piled with bread molds. In the register above, another mother speaks to a young boy who clings to her shoulders while she grinds grain.[14] In several Fifth and Sixth Dynasty tombs a woman is shown seated on a cargo boat suckling a child, suggesting that the members of the crew and their families actually lived on the boats.[15] A limestone statuette (fig. 6), also dated to the Old Kingdom, shows a woman seated on the ground, her left leg raised to support the infant she suckles at her left breast. Just behind her at the right a second, slightly older child nurses from her right breast. The woman's pose, with one knee raised, is repeated in numerous representations of mothers nursing small children. In a delightful Middle Kingdom statuette, for example, a mother suckles her child while another woman braids her hair (cat. no. 8a). This pose is repeated in the Second Intermediate Period copper depicting a woman[16] suckling a small boy (cat. no. 9).

These examples of nursing mothers give some idea of the realities of domestic life, in which women tend their children while they occupy themselves in the home.[17] In the normal course of life, mothers must have found it necessary to take their children along when they needed to perform some task outside the home. Two scenes from New Kingdom Theban tombs seem to reflect this situation. In the tomb of Menna (TT 69), a woman is shown in an agricultural setting cradling a young child while she sits in the shade of a tree (fig. 7). This scene is reiterated in a relief fragment from the Twenty-sixth Dynasty tomb of Mentuemhat (cat. no. 8b). One assumes that at the height of the harvest, when every able-bodied person was needed, even nursing mothers probably participated.

The second New Kingdom scene comes from the tomb of Neferrenput (TT 133), who was "Foreman of the Weavers in the House of Usermaatre-Setepenre (Ramesses II) in the estate of Amen (the Ramesseum)." One wall bears a badly damaged representation of the weavers' workshop, which he oversaw.[18] In the two upper registers, several women and one man bring what appear to be skeins of spun thread to be weighed.[19] One woman in the top register leads a toddler by the hand; in the register below, the feet of two more children are preserved. In the third and lowest register, warping and weaving are shown taking place within the workshop. Two young children are depicted running near a doorkeeper, who holds a raised stick. Norman de Garis Davies, who published the scene, interpreted this vignette as showing the doorkeeper trying to control the children of the women seen at work in the room beyond.[20]

Although it is not surprising to find women at the lower levels of Egyptian society in the rather realistic scenes mentioned above, representations of elite women, queens, and even goddesses also depict the nurturing role of the female. In the divine realm, Isis, in her capacity as mother and protector of Horus, is the most famous nurturing deity, but images of the goddess holding her infant son do not become common in art until quite late in Egyptian history (cat. no. 59a,b). On the other hand, representations of a goddess suckling the king occur in Egyptian art as early as the Old Kingdom[21] and continue throughout Egyptian history, as seen, for example, in catalogue number 50. These images often appear in funerary contexts and symbolize the ruler's rebirth into the next world. In these scenes, the king is shown as a small adult dressed in full royal regalia, standing before the larger figure of the goddess, who offers her breast. The king was also thought to be suckled by a goddess at birth. This event is preserved in representations of the divine birth of Hatshepsut in her temple at Deir el-Bahri and of Amenhotep III in the temple of Luxor. In both scenes, the respective rulers and their *kas* are shown as infants, each seated on the lap of a kneeling goddess.[22]

In statuary, the earliest representation of a young child seated on the lap of an adult female is the late Old Kingdom statuette of Pepy II as a miniature king seated on the lap of his mother, Queen Ankhnesmeryra. We know that Pepy ascended the throne as a child, and this statuette may commemorate the fact that Ankhnesmeryra acted in some capacity as regent for her son. Pepy is shown as a miniature adult dressed as king. Mother and son sit quite rigidly at right angles to one another. Yet in spite of the formality of this pose, there is a suggestion of the intimacy between mother and child in the way the queen places her left hand on her son's back, as though supporting an infant or toddler. Her other hand lies across the king's knees, and he places his left hand on top of hers. A related grouping of royal mother and son occurs occasionally in Old Kingdom reliefs, where a seated queen places a protective or restraining hand on the arm of a young prince standing in front of her.[23] These types of representations seem to symbolize the nurturing relationship of mother and child, and such scenes are not preserved again in royal art until the Amarna Period. At that time it is quite common for the queen and even the king to be represented interacting in a very intimate fashion with their children, as seen in catalogue number 46.

Like royal women, nonroyal women from the elite class usually are not shown actively fulfilling their maternal role. Although their offspring are often represented with them in statuary and in tombs, elite women are not portrayed interacting with their own young children. In the Eighteenth Dynasty, however, a group of representations signal the special role filled by a small number of women with regard to the royal children. These women, who have the title "Royal Nurse" *(mn't nswt)*, seem to have been wet nurses to princes and princesses of the dynasty.[24] A few also record the title "One Who Nurtured the God" *(šdt nṯr)*, a designation that seems to have been given only to wet nurses of children who later became king.

Royal nurses are usually represented prominently in the tombs of their husbands or sons, and at least two received the signal honor of burial in the Valley of the Kings.[25] Sometimes an individual nurse is depicted holding and even suckling her royal nursling, who usually appears as a child, but occasionally is shown as a miniature king. The earliest of these representations that include the king is a statue of Hatshepsut seated on the lap of her nurse Sitra (fig. 8). The formal pose is the same as that of Pepy II on his mother's lap, but here the nurse is life-sized. Like Pepy and his mother, Hatshepsut and her nurse are seated at right angles to one another. Part of Hatshepsut's body is missing, but the preserved fragments show clearly that she is represented as a small adult dressed as a king. The fragmentary inscription indicates that she had already made herself coruler with Thutmose III when the statue was commissioned. Although Hatshepsut is depicted as ruler, it is clear that Sitra is not merely holding a statue of the reigning pharaoh.[26] Her broken left arm was originally around Hatshepsut's shoulders, and enough of Sitra's right arm remains to suggest that she was offering her breast to her nursling in the same gesture as seen in the much later representations of Isis and Horus (cat. no. 59a,b). Hatshepsut's head and upper torso are not preserved, but traces of her right arm can be seen wrapped around Sitra's waist in what appears to be an affectionate gesture.

The image of a nurse holding a small king also appears in relief and painting in the Eighteenth Dynasty. In the tomb

Fig. 8a Queen Ankhnesmeryra II with her son Pepy II on her lap. Dynasty 6. The Brooklyn Museum. 39.119. Photograph courtesy of the Brooklyn Museum.

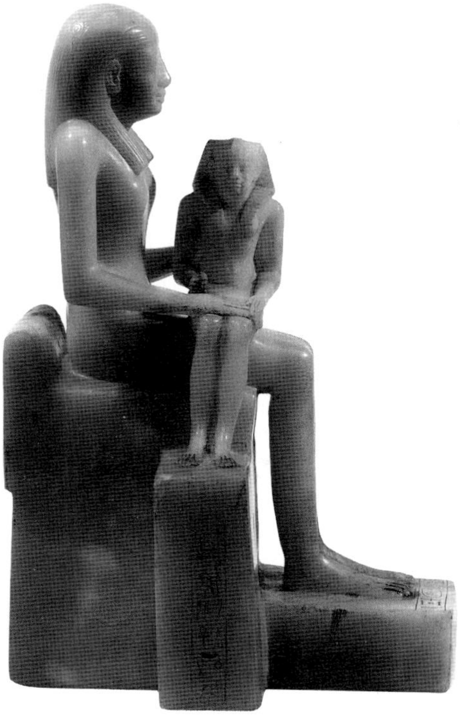

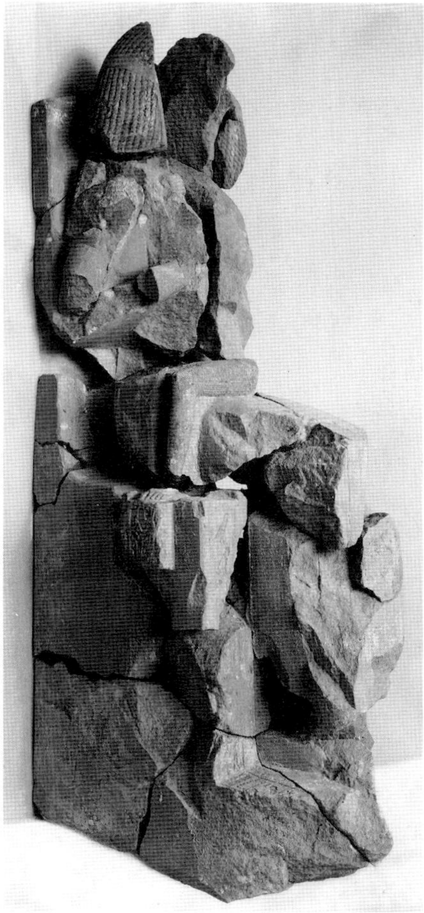

Fig. 8b Fragmentary statue of Hatshepsut seated on the lap of her nurse Sitra. Egyptian Museum, Cairo. JE 56264. Expedition photograph courtesy of the Metropolitan Museum of Art.

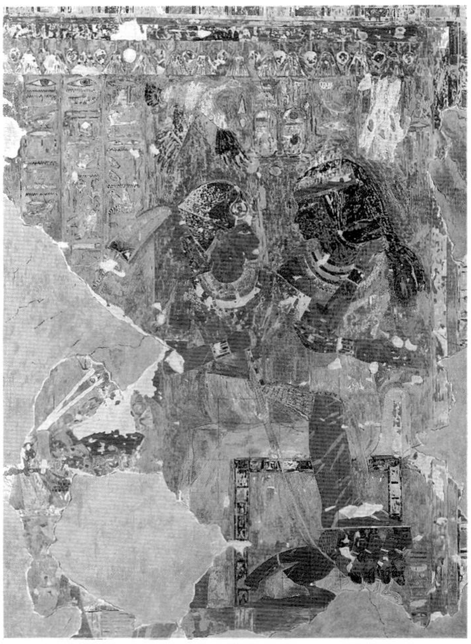

Fig. 9 Detail from the tomb of Kenamen (TT 93) showing the royal nurse Amenemopet with Amenhotep II. Facsimile watercolor by Nina de Garis Davies. The Metropolitan Museum of Art. Rogers Fund, 1930. 30.4.72. Photograph courtesy of the Metropolitan Museum of Art.

Fig. 10 Detail from the tomb of Hekarneheh (TT 64) showing the royal guardian Hekareshu with Thutmose IV. Photograph by Harry Burton. Courtesy of the Metropolitan Museum of Art.

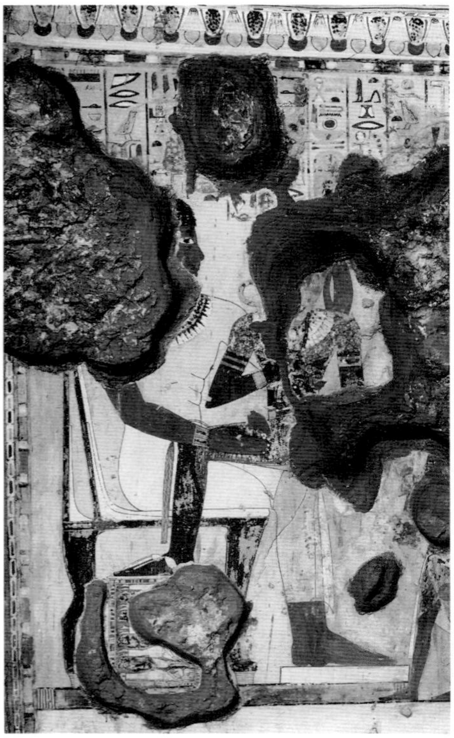

of Kenamen (TT 93), the owner's mother, Amenemopet, is shown holding the figure of Amenhotep II on her lap (fig. 9). The scene is beautifully composed. The nurse sits looking left, with the king seated facing her. His feet rest on nine bound captives, representing enemies of Egypt, who kneel beside the nurse's chair. Within the canonical formality of the pose, the two seem to exchange affectionate gestures.[27] Amenhotep reaches forward with his left hand to touch his nurse's shoulder, or perhaps to stroke her hair. Amenemopet's right arm is around his shoulders, and her hand rests on the back of his head as though supporting the head of a small child. Her left hand seems to support the king's left arm, but probably it is actually beneath her breast in the typical gesture of a woman nursing a child. Above the scene an inscription identifies Amenemopet as "Chief Nurse, Who Nurtured the God."

Because of the ritual significance of the king being suckled by a goddess at various stages of his existence, it is tempting to give a ritual interpretation to these representations of royal nurses. There is no evidence, however, that royal nurses in the Eighteenth Dynasty performed any ritual duties with regard to the pharaoh. They hold no titles that associate them with Hathor or any of the other goddesses who suckle the king at birth, coronation, or death. Royal nurses are shown holding young princes and princesses as well as small kings. This pose, whether in statuary or in painting, seems to commemorate, often retrospectively, the very human relationship between a child and his or her nurse. In cases where the nursling has already ascended the throne, he or she must be portrayed as pharaoh, not as a mere child.[28]

Another argument against reading a ritual meaning into these representations is the fact that men occasionally are shown in the same pose. These men, who are usually high officials, have a title similar to "Royal Nurse." The title is generally translated as "Royal Tutor" *(mn' nswt)*, though it might be rendered more correctly as "Royal Guardian." These officials included Senenmut, who was guardian to Hatshepsut's daughter, Nefrura. At least ten statues were commissioned in commemoration of Senenmut's position with regard to the princess. One is a unique seated statue in which Nefrura sits facing forward on Senenmut's lap and is enveloped completely in the cloaklike garment he wears.[29] Another statue, also unique, shows Senenmut seated on the ground with his left knee raised in a position reminiscent of the nursing mother in fig. 6 or catalogue number 8b. A young Nefrura is seated sideways on his lap, and he holds her protectively close to his chest, her head just under his chin.[30] Seven other images, many of them fragmentary, are block statues in which Senenmut sits with both knees drawn up in front of his chest, wrapped in a cloak.[31] Only Senenmut's head and the small head of Nefrura are visible, the body of the child being surrounded completely by that of her guardian. These nine statues are strongly expressive of a guardian protecting a young child. The tenth statue, catalogue number 43, is another unique type. Here, even though Senenmut shows a less protective stance, Nefrura's left arm passes around her guardian's left shoulder in what might be interpreted as an affectionate gesture similar to those found in the representations of royal nurses and their charges.

Like royal nurses, the male guardians of royal children of the Eighteenth Dynasty usually are shown holding their nurslings as children, but one exception exists. In TT 64 at Thebes, Hekareshu, guardian of Thutmose IV, holds the king on his lap (fig. 10). This painting is very similar to that of Amenhotep II and his nurse Amenemopet (fig. 9), and the artist who painted the scene in TT 64 may have used the earlier image as a model. Hekareshu, who is portrayed as an older man with folds of flesh on his chest, places his left hand behind the king's head, as with a child, and his right hand rests on the king's hip. Thutmose is dressed as a king, and his feet rest on a stool decorated with the crouching enemies of Egypt.

Although the scenes in TT 93 and TT 64 are essentially the same, there is one interesting difference. Whereas Amenhotep II interacts with his nurse by touching her shoulder, Thutmose IV does not make such a gesture toward his guardian.[32] This may reflect a difference between the understanding of a nurse's and a guardian's relationship with a former nursling who had become king.[33] As the child grew older, the role of the guardian seems to have developed into that of a mentor,[34] whereas the nurse's role probably remained that of an affectionate surrogate mother. This is not to say that one relationship was valued more or less than the other; they merely may have evolved in different ways as the nursling grew older.

These images form a special group, whether they depict a nurse or a tutor and whether the adult holds a child or a small king. They are the only works of Egyptian art in which a nonroyal person is shown in close physical contact with any member of the royal family, not to mention the reigning king. They also represent the only situation in which a nonroyal person is shown on a scale larger than the king. This departure from two basic rules of royal iconography emphasizes the special relationship that must have existed between the nurse/guardian and the royal child—a relationship that clearly extended throughout their lives.

Textile manufacture

During most of pharaonic history, linen was the basic material used for clothing, blankets, sheets, and other goods made of cloth. Because linen fabric and finished clothing were not perishable in the same sense as agricultural goods such as grain, they were also valuable commodities in the barter system on which the Egyptian economy was based.[35] Not surprisingly, linen cloth was one of the items included in funerary offering texts, beginning in the Old Kingdom. Intact burials from all periods have produced chests full of shawls, loincloths, blankets, tunics, shirts, dresses, and lengths of uncut cloth varying in texture from very coarse to superfine.[36] Linen was also an important component in the process of mummification, and in some periods phenomenal amounts of linen bandaging and padding were used to wrap the body.[37] Although much of the bandaging was made of strips of worn fabric, newly woven shrouds and lengths of cloth were also used. Clearly, the manufacture of linen was a major industry in Egypt throughout pharaonic times.

In view of the importance of linen in all aspects of Egyptian culture, it is surprising that so few representations of its manufacture have been preserved. The earliest of these is found on a decorated bowl discovered in a Predynastic cemetery at Badari by W.M.F. Petrie.[38] Two human figures are shown measuring warp threads, while two others appear near a loom. This horizontal loom does not differ substantially from those represented in wall paintings and models dating to the Middle Kingdom, more than one thousand years later. Although it is impossible to say with certainty who was producing linen cloth in prehistoric times, the fact that the bowl was found in a woman's grave suggests that weaving cloth was considered women's work even in that early period.

No representations of cloth manufacture appear in the tomb decorations of the Old Kingdom, but the Old Kingdom hieroglyph for "weaver" is a seated woman holding what is probably a shuttle or weaver's sword, used for beating in the weft threads.[39] Women also are shown accepting payment for finished cloth,[40] and a number of women have administrative titles such as "Overseer of the House of Weavers." This rather scanty evidence suggests that women not only made the cloth, but were also responsible for supervising its manufacture on a large scale in workshops attached to private estates, temples, and royal palaces.

During the Middle Kingdom, representations of cloth manufacture appear in wall paintings[41] and wooden funerary models.[42] The workers in these scenes are invariably women, who seem to have been involved in all aspects of production from harvesting the flax[43] to weaving the fabric.[44] The most complete scenes show women hackling and roving the flax fibers[45] and spinning them into thread. Others measure the warp by winding the thread around pegs on a wall or stakes set in the ground. The actual weaving is done on horizontal looms, each loom tended by two or sometimes three women. These weaving scenes often depict several looms and numerous workers supervised by an overseer, who is usually a woman. They probably document the mass production that would have been accomplished in a workshop attached

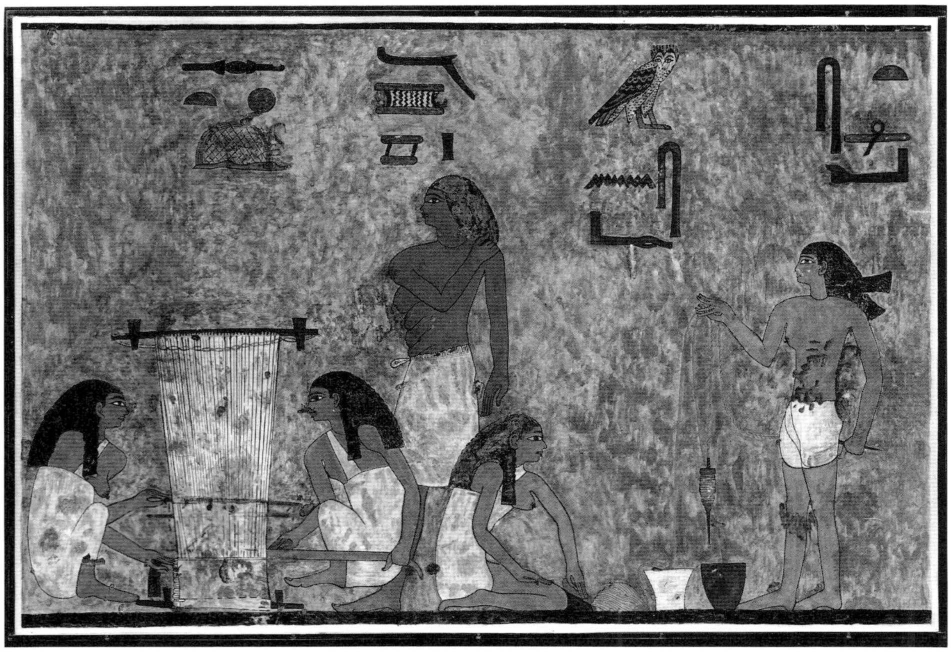

Fig. 11 Representation of spinners and weavers from the tomb of Khnumhotep at Beni Hasan. Dynasty 12. Facsimile painted by Norman de Garis Davies, 1933. Rogers Fund, 1933. 33.8.16. Photograph courtesy of the Metropolitan Museum of Art.

to a large private estate, one of the royal palaces, or a temple, but the tasks shown were undoubtedly repeated on a cottage-industry level in the villages of artisans and agricultural workers throughout Egypt.[46]

One well-preserved Middle Kingdom weaving scene is found in the Twelfth Dynasty tomb of Khnumhotep (Tomb 3) at Beni Hasan. Five women are shown occupied in different stages of linen manufacture (fig. 11). The woman kneeling at the center right is roving flax and has wound the loosely twisted fibers into a ball in front of her. The ball then would have been placed in one of the spinning bowls to the right, which probably kept the fibers damp and provided tension during spinning.[47] The spinner stands at the right, using two spindles simultaneously.[48] The second spindle is held in her left hand and is partially obscured by her body. At the center of the scene, a woman identified as the overseer supervises two weavers, who work at a horizontal loom. This loom appears to be upright because of the Egyptian artistic convention in which objects are depicted from their most recognizable angle. The warp threads are wound around two beams held apart by four pegs in the ground. The extra warp is wound around the upper beam, and finished cloth is rolled up around the lower beam. Along the left-hand side of the newly woven cloth, a short, looped fringe has been woven into the selvedge.[49] The wide, uncut lengths of linen from this period invariably have this supplementary or inlaid weft fringe.

In this scene, it is interesting to note that women of all ages are depicted. The overseer, with her drooping breasts and rolls of fat, is clearly meant to be old. The rover and the weaver seated at the left each have large, slightly drooping breasts and probably are meant to be mature, though perhaps not old. The other two figures, with their rather small breasts, seem to represent either girls or young women.

An even more highly detailed representation of linen manufacture is preserved in a weavers' shed from the Theban tomb of Meketra (TT 280), who lived into the early reign of Amenemhat I of Dynasty 12 (fig. 12).[50] The three rovers, three spinners, and five weavers in this model are accompanied by two women who measure out warp threads by winding them around pegs on the shed wall. The spindles, spinning bowls, shuttles, and other

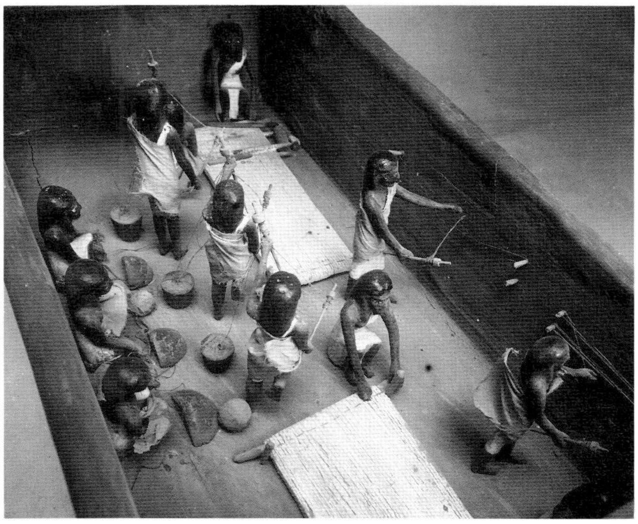

Fig. 12 Weavers' shed from the tomb of Meketra (TT 280). Now in the Egyptian Museum, Cairo. JE 46723. Excavation photograph courtesy of the Metropolitan Museum of Art.

implements are all reproduced. The loom is a solid block of wood onto which the warp threads and the finished cloth have been painted. Along the left-hand selvedge of the newly woven fabric on each loom, an inlaid warp fringe is visible.[51]

All of the representations of cloth manufacture from the First Intermediate Period and the Middle Kingdom suggest that this particular craft was exclusively women's province. This impression is reinforced by textual evidence. For example, the Middle Kingdom mortuary priest Hekanakhte negotiates with a woman about the processing of his flax harvest,[52] and a late Middle Kingdom papyrus listing servants includes twenty women who are designated as clothmakers.[53] By the New Kingdom, however, the situation seems to have changed somewhat, and men as well as women are employed in weaving linen cloth.

Only three representations of weavers have survived from the New Kingdom, all of which come from the tombs in the Theban necropolis.[54] In these scenes, two from townhouses or private estates and one representing a temple workshop, only upright looms are shown and all but one of the preserved weavers are male. On the basis of this scanty information, it has often been stated that in the New Kingdom men replaced women as weavers and/or that the upright loom replaced the horizontal loom as the mode of cloth manufacture.[55] The first of these statements is contradicted by one of the New Kingdom wall paintings. In the tomb of Neferrenput (TT 133), who was chief of weavers in the Ramesseum (the mortuary temple of Ramesses II), four upright looms are shown, one of which is worked by two persons. In the original publication, one of the five weavers is shown clearly as a woman.[56] Written sources also document that although men shared in the task, women were still very much involved in weaving cloth.[57]

The contention that the upright loom replaced the ground loom in the New Kingdom is difficult to support or to contradict.[58] Although many spinning and weaving tools have been preserved, such as spindles, spinning bowls, heddle-jacks,[59] and weaver's swords, no looms have been found.[60] From a purely industrial point of view it is not surprising that Egyptians began to use the vertical loom, because more looms could be set up in a smaller space.[61] Egyptian society was very traditional, however, and the Egyptians seldom completely abandoned an older, proven method in favor of a newer one. Instead they usually preferred to use both concurrently. One argument favoring the continued use of the ground loom is based on a study of the preserved textiles. It has been suggested that the supplementary weft fringe found along one selvedge of so many pieces of Egyptian linen was developed, at least in part, as a way of keeping the weft straight when weaving on a horizontal loom.[62] This theory is supported by the extant representations of looms. In Middle Kingdom scenes depicting horizontal looms, a weft fringe is always indicated along the left-hand selvedge of the finished cloth.[63] In the three New Kingdom representations of vertical looms, however, the finished cloth never has this feature. This evidence suggests that the large number of New Kingdom textiles that have inlaid warp fringes were woven on traditional horizontal looms rather than the newer vertical loom.

Authors frequently express wonder that the ancient Egyptians, using such simple equipment, were able to produce the fine fabrics that have survived from pharaonic times. In doing so, they fail to acknowledge that in most textile manufacture the quality of the cloth is determined by the skill and inventiveness of the spinners and weavers rather than by the sophistication of the tools. Because women played a major role in the production of textiles throughout pharaonic times, and since linen cloth is one of the few products of women's labor that survives today, a few examples of their handiwork deserve description.

Most of the textiles from ancient Egypt are executed in plain weave, the same simple technique that many of us (both male and female) learned as children in art classes at school. The apparent simplicity of this technique is deceptive. Depending on the type of thread and the openness of the weave, cloth of many textures and uses can be produced (fig. 13). Some surviving examples are woven tightly with two-

Fig. 13 Five sheets of linen of varying texture from the tomb of Hatnofer and Ramose at Thebes. Excavation photograph courtesy of the Metropolitan Museum of Art.

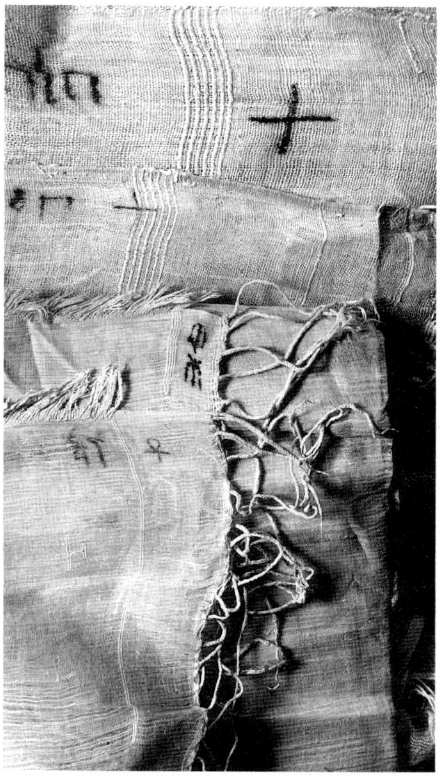

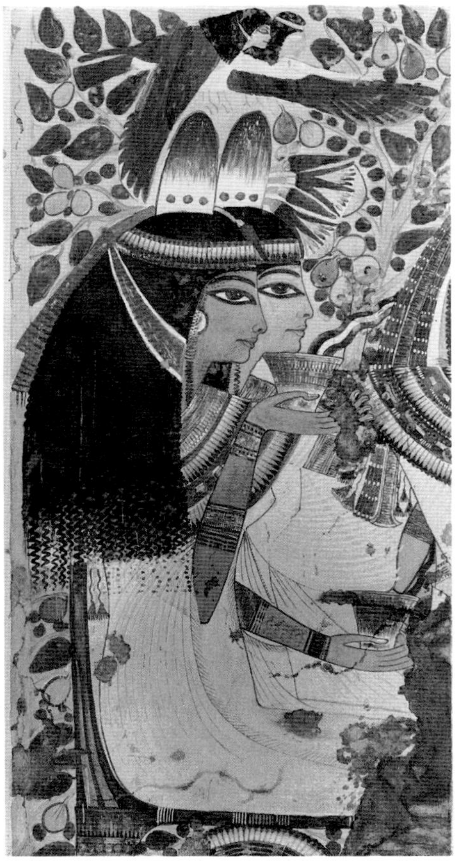

Fig. 14 Detail from the tomb of Userhat (TT 51). Watercolor facsimile, copyist unknown. Rogers Fund, 1930. 30.4.162. Courtesy of the Metropolitan Museum of Art.

or three-ply thread and have the softness of fine table linen. Others, using a coarser thread, are more akin to canvas or burlap. Still other examples, woven from single-ply thread, have the quality of the sheerest lawn.

Among the linen sheets found in the early Eighteenth Dynasty tomb of Hatnofer, Senenmut's mother, were two lengths of cloth made of this sheer fabric. The diaphanous quality is the result of a loose weave of superfine thread that must have been spun from flax harvested when the plants were very young.[64] One of these pieces of cloth, which is about sixty-three inches wide and almost seventeen feet long, weighs a mere quarter-pound.[65] Without knowing the particular artisans involved, one can only imagine the amount of time it would have taken to rove the fibers, spin the thread, warp the loom,[66] and weave a length of cloth this size. The sheerness of the featherweight fabric, with its silken softness, gives credence to New Kingdom representations of elaborately pleated outer garments that allow the contours of the body and even the color of the skin to show through. In figure 14, for example, the woman's upper right arm is visible through the cloth.

As on many of the preserved uncut lengths of cloth, one end of Hatnofer's sheet has a warp selvedge, the other end is finished with a plied fringe, and one weft selvedge is decorated with an inlaid fringe. These two types of fringe are visible on the garments shown in several statues of women in this volume. In the pair statue of Yuni and Renenutet (cat. no. 93), the latter is wearing a garment with a looped fringe along the selvedge that runs diagonally across her chest. The pleated garment worn by Enehy (cat. no. 35a) shows a similar short-looped selvedge fringe along the upper edge, and a longer warp fringe is visible down the front along the top of her left leg. Both types of fringe are also visible in figure 14. On the end of cloth directly behind the left arm of the woman in the foreground, one can see the very short weft fringe (above her arm) and the longer warp fringe (below her arm).

Although the only decoration on most preserved pieces of Egyptian linen consists of fringes and pleats, a few pieces of patterned fabric have survived. Three of the earliest examples come from Middle Kingdom Thebes and were found by the Egyptian Expedition of the Metropolitan Museum of Art. These are made with a simple pile technique in which supplementary weft threads are pulled out from the surface of the cloth at intervals during weaving

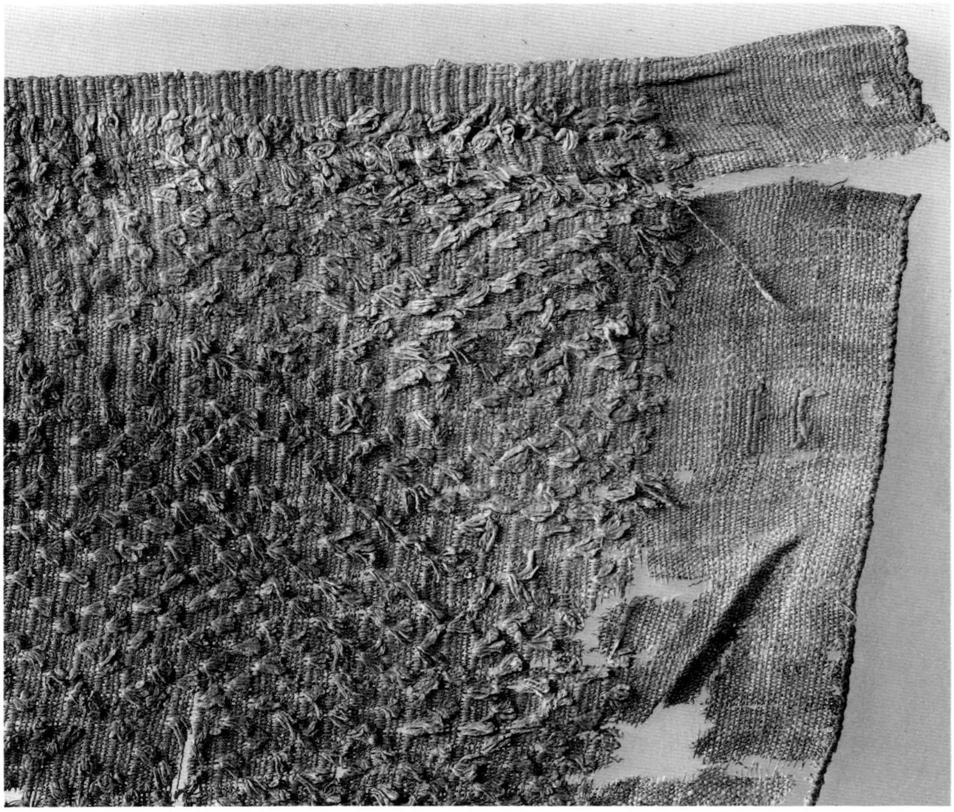

Fig. 15 Fragment of linen towel. Middle Kingdom. The Metropolitan Museum of Art. 31.3.62. Expedition photograph courtesy of the Metropolitan Museum of Art.

Fig. 16 Fragment of linen towel with pile decoration. Middle Kingdom. Egyptian Museum, Cairo. JE 56279. Expedition photograph courtesy of the Metropolitan Museum of Art.

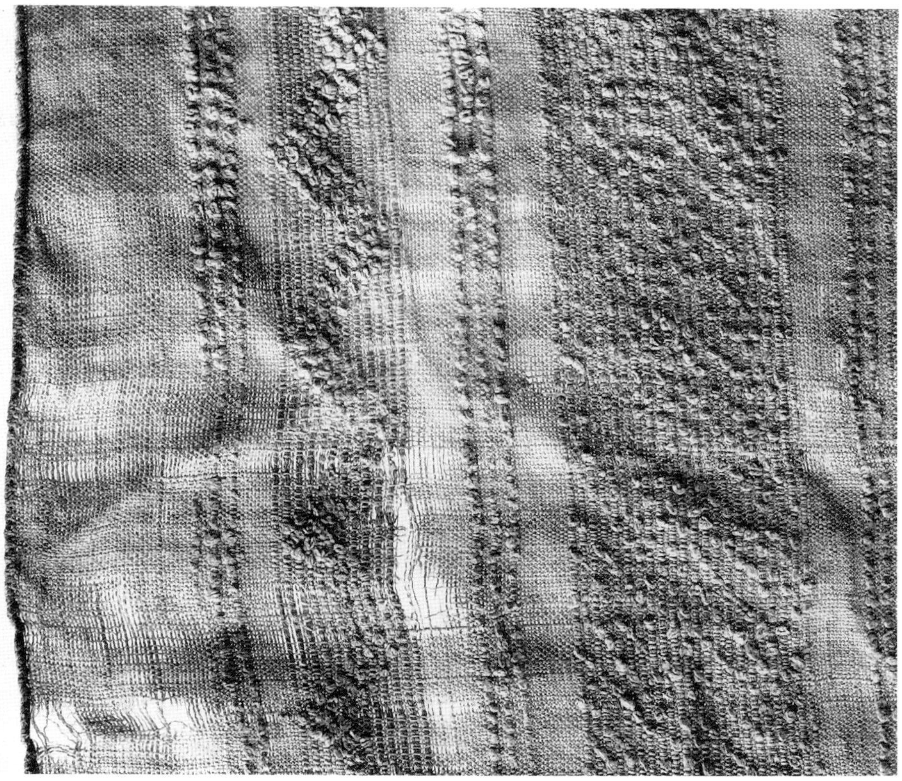

(fig. 15). Two of the pieces are often described as towels because they bear some resemblance to terry cloth and because the preserved width of one, about 17¾ inches, is more suited to toweling than to clothing.[67] The third fragment was woven with the same technique but has a more complicated geometric pattern of zigzags and stripes (fig. 16).[68] Because all of these fragments were made in the Middle Kingdom, it seems likely that they were woven by women using horizontal looms.

One final textile, perhaps the most interesting piece of fabric excavated by the Egyptian Expedition, deserves comment. It was discovered among the funerary offerings in the Eighteenth Dynasty tomb of Senenmut's parents.[69] Inside a basket, bunched together with a knotted pot sling, was a linen pad with rows of long pile on one side (fig. 17a,b). The woven section of the pad, measuring 26 x 19¼ inches, was

Fig. 17a,b Expedition photographs of a tufted pad from the tomb of Hatnofer and Ramose at Thebes. Egyptian Museum, Cairo. JE 66243. Expedition photographs courtesy of the Metropolitan Museum of Art.

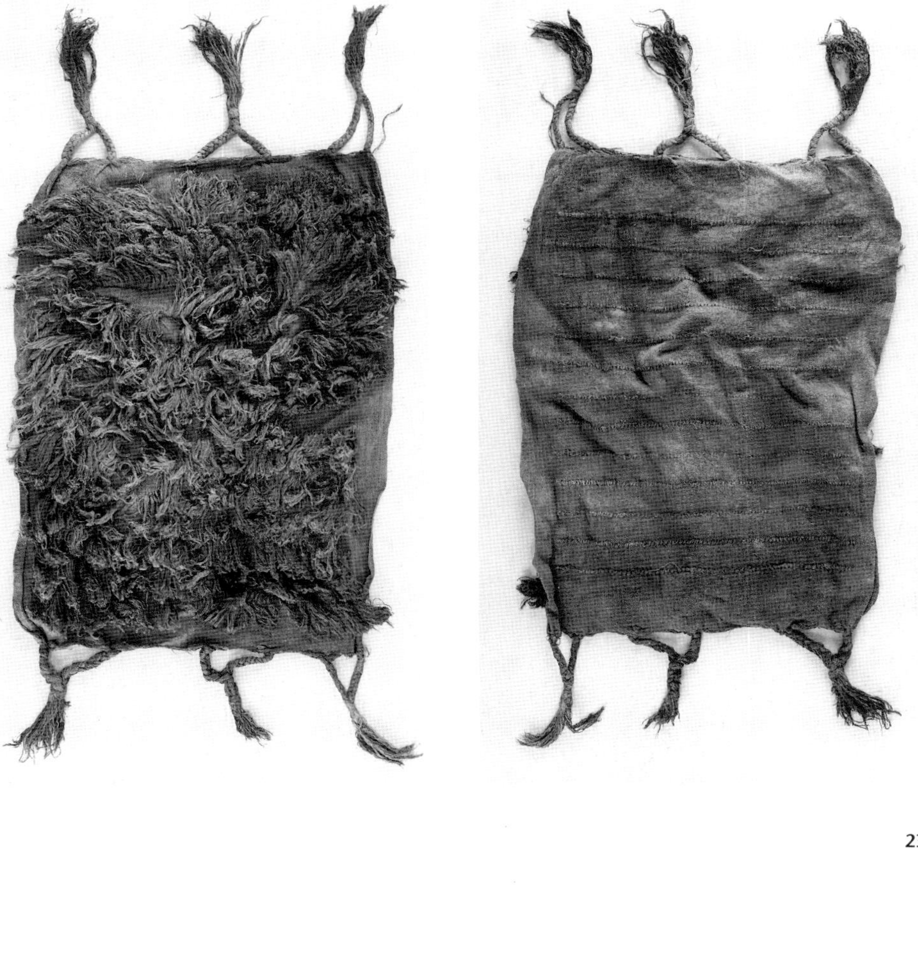

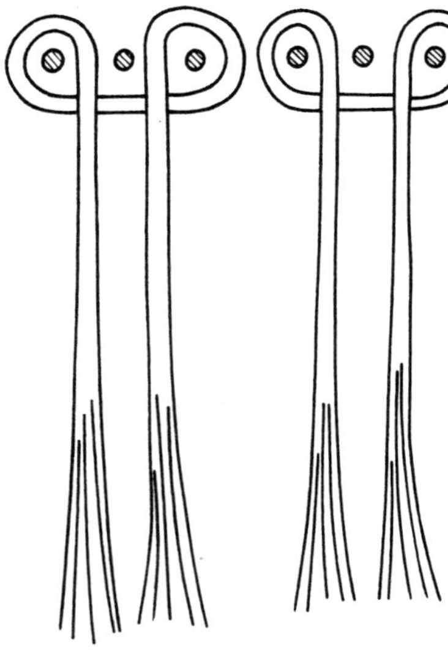

Fig. 18 Method of knotting used to make the pile of the tufted pad in figure 17a,b. Drawing by B. Girsh from MMA tomb card no. 4886.

executed in tight, plain weave and is described in the excavation notes as having a texture similar to burlap.[70] The selvedges are plain, and the warp threads are caught together in a braided fringe at either end.[71] The fascinating feature of this small piece of fabric is the method of making the pile. Unlike the Middle Kingdom examples mentioned above, in which the pile is created by pulling loops of the weft out from the surface of the fabric, this pile is made with a symmetrical rug knot, the so-called Turkish or Ghiordes knot, that is associated most frequently with the manufacture of carpets (fig. 18). This is not a unique example of this type of knotted pile. A similar textile from the Eighteenth Dynasty Theban tomb of Kha and his wife, Meryt, has ten rows of pile that appear, in available photographs, to have been made with the Ghiordes knot.[72]

In view of the many uses of linen cloth by Egyptians from all levels of society, both living and dead, its manufacture must have been a major industry in ancient Egypt, second only to the production of food. Unlike scenes of food production, however, which account for much of the decoration in most well-preserved tombs and funerary models, scenes of linen manufacture are quite rare. Such scenes are underrepresented even in comparison with depictions of other crafts.[73]

This underrepresentation is something that all types of women's work have in common. In Egyptian art, although women are portrayed frequently and quite positively, many of their occupations and day-to-day activities, from nurturing children to producing such a valuable commodity as linen cloth, seem to be taken for granted to the point of almost being ignored. This may be partly a function of the funerary nature of much of the art. Certainly it is also a result of the patriarchal nature of Egyptian society, which quite naturally placed more importance on the occupations of men than on those of women. After all, it was men who commissioned and created most of the art. In addition, however, the majority of women's work in ancient Egypt was done in the home, which, in most cultures, is considered a private place. Although this work was extremely important to the smooth running of the society, it was done in the background. Thus, we catch only glimpses of the activities that occupied the majority of ancient Egyptian women.

In women good and bad fortune are on earth

Status and roles of women in Egyptian culture

BETSY M. BRYAN

In the not-too-distant past it was common to describe women as especially privileged, indeed "equal" to men, in Egyptian society. Thanks largely to the contribution of Gay Robins, this view has been placed into appropriate perspective, coming as it did from scholars whose own culture had few women in the halls of power: "When the accepted ideal for a woman was that of a model wife and mother who did not go out to work or take part in public life, it is no wonder that scholars failed to notice the absence of women in public life in ancient Egypt."[1] As Robins implies, women did not regularly hold offices of royal managerial power in ancient Egypt (fig. 1).

This essay is less a catalogue of the roles played by women in ancient Egypt than an attempt to help the reader better understand those roles as they operated within ancient Egyptian culture. Our evidence derives from sources that must be evaluated in various ways. Royal monuments were carved in stone to immortalize a centralized state view; the information, although important, is often subsumed within political-religious ideology. Private monuments derived largely from the elite levels of society, and they reflect hierarchical and ideological motives similar to royal ones. Our least consciously controlled information comes from administrative documents, but letters also contain much information. Literary works, particularly in the New Kingdom, often represent less aristocratic societal norms. All of these types of sources must be combined to form something resembling a full picture. Crucial to an understanding is the fact that ancient Egypt was not a monolithic society in which all women were viewed in the same way and received the same respect or lack of it. It is certain from our various types of material that in all periods there were women of great influence and men who valued them; it is equally certain that in all periods elite women were expected to preside over the home but not over state offices. Within this overarching structure, however, individual male attitudes toward women were disparate; sometimes we are able to glimpse true marital partnerships and, at other times, unmistakable gender bias.

Our survey will include a discussion of the women who wielded royal power in Egypt. This first, long section contains a description of the royal family hierarchy, which is parallel to that of elite society. The second section summarizes the structure of Egyptian families generally, and a third outlines the societal roles performed by women of various classes.

Women as rulers

Egypt is famous not only for her great pharaohs but also for female rulers. Elite women throughout the Near East had the freedoms associated with affluence: servants, even entourages; involvement in family economics; status in formal religious worship—but not rulership.[2] Between 3000 and 1000 B.C., several females ruled Egypt as monarch. Hatshepsut's name as a female ruler is the best known outside scholarly circles, but the names of Nitokret (Dynasty 6), Sobeknefru (Dynasty 12), and Tauseret (Dynasty 19) also signify a true distinction in Egyptian society: the possibility, however infrequent and ideologically inconsistent, for women to assume the throne.

The phenomenon of female rulership, of course, was a product of the society, but in trying to explain how this occurred in Egypt it will be useful to examine another culture in which the same circumstance arose. There are not many comparative cultures to which we may look,[3] but a useful

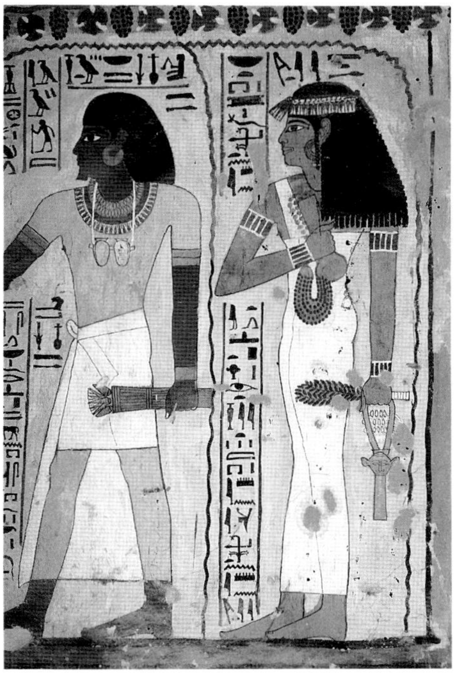

Fig. 1 A typical elite couple of the Eighteenth Dynasty. Mayor of Thebes Sennefer and his wife Meryt, a temple chorister. Theban Tomb 96 Lower, mid–Dynasty 18. Photograph courtesy of the author.

model exists from the Silla culture of Korea.[4] The Old Kingdom of Silla was situated in southeastern Korea between the first century B.C. and the late seventh A.D., but the actual formation of the state may have occupied only the latter half of this period. Silla was the outcome of six villages uniting and then conquering the peninsula they inhabited. Power was centralized thereafter over several centuries. Corvée labor, a clear indicator of state control, was well established in the mid–second century A.D.; a military leader and a land administrator were attested by the third century. An agricultural state, Silla also had iron resources and was therefore a strong trade power in the region. The land was considered the property of the state and could not be owned by individuals. Taxes were paid in both grain and labor, and the government kept granaries from which surpluses were used to meet emergencies such as famine. Both men and women were required to perform conscripted labor; for this purpose and for taxation, state censuses recorded all citizens by village, age, and sex, as well as all farm animals.

Religion in the Silla state was a decentralized system neither controlled by nor competitive with the state. Local gods were worshiped locally; there were no national deities.

The social structure of Silla was highly stratified. There was no chance to move between the ranks, and it has been presumed that the classes evolved and froze after the period of Silla's conquests. The government ranks were apportioned according to class status, so that the five highest-ranking offices were held only by members of the *Songgol* and the *Chin'gol*—that is, the Holy Bone and the True Bone classes. The next four ranks were held by the Sixth Head class, and the following two by the Fifth Head. Four more classes of commoners existed below the level of state service.

Rulers came only from the *Songgol* or Holy Bone class and were thought to have been descendants of gods. To belong to this group, both of one's parents must have been members. Rulers did not follow any specific pattern of patrilineality or matrilineality: "The relationships demonstrated by the king lists cannot be described by simple lineality. For instance, it was common for a ruler's daughter's husband to succeed to the kingship, and about equally common for the past ruler's brother or son to succeed, or both in no necessary order. Groups of endogamous families appear to have formed corporate descent groups without a unilineal principle at all, descent being reckoned bilaterally."[5] One scholar interpreted this to mean that "women play important connective roles in succession. A new king will have as wife a close female relative of the former king."[6] To another it meant that "the holders of the highest status [i.e., *Songgol*] . . . were eligible for the throne regardless of sex."[7] The Silla king lists include three female rulers, each without a husband who could have served simultaneously as king.[8]

In a number of ways the Silla case is helpful in examining female rulers in Egypt. The succession in Egypt has equally defied description as either patrilineal or matrilineal. A theory identifying princesses as "heiresses," through whom the kingship passed by their marriages,[9] has been criticized by Robins.[10] Robins states rightly that if this theory were correct, every king would have married a royal woman; however, in the Eighteenth Dynasty the wives who produced the heirs of Thutmose III, Amenhotep II, Thutmose IV, and Amenhotep III were all of nonroyal origins.[11] Clearly the "heiress theory" does not describe the succession of kingship.

Conversely, however, even in the Eighteenth Dynasty, kings more often than not married a royal family member, even if she was not the first wife or always a king's daughter. Only the last two rulers of Dynasty 18 did not marry into the ruling family.[12] From that dynasty Ahmose, Thutmose II, Thutmose III, Thutmose IV, Amenhotep III, Amenhotep IV/Akhenaten, and Tutankhamen all married princesses.[13] Thutmose I married a king's sister, and Amenhotep I took his own mother, Ahmose-Nefertari, as his official consort. She had the purest of all pedigrees: daughter, wife, and mother of a king. Daughters of the royal family in all periods, as Robins herself says, were "potential queens";[14] if this was the case, then the kingship at least was intended to belong to a dynastic family.

The Eighteenth Dynasty actually represents the royal succession as it had developed after 1,500 years, whereas the entire Silla state lasted only 725 years before the exclusive royal *Songgol* caste became extinct.[15]

Although the royal families in Egypt obviously did not depend entirely on specific family marriages for continuation, they equally obviously illustrate a *preference,* when possible, for dynastic purity. For example, the designation "King's Daughter" as "Princess" was sometimes applied to women whose royal family connection was far more tenuous than the literal translation of *sat ni-sut,* "King's Daughter"; in the Fourth Dynasty a prince's daughter could also be called "Princess"; similarly in the Eighteenth.[16] In the Old Kingdom, however, in the Middle Kingdom Eleventh through Twelfth Dynasties, and in the New Kingdom Eighteenth Dynasty, women who married kings and who had the title "King's Daughter" were, without exception, full-blooded kings' offspring.[17]

Most anthropological theory considers that state formation dismantles kinship principles and shifts them toward territorial ruling classes.[18] As Sarah M. Nelson points out, however, this destruction does not necessarily occur when the ruling classes are themselves kin groups.[19] Egypt's early state had a unique kinship connection for its dynastic lines: that is, the kingship itself preserved the line unbroken. This is implicit in the existence of the divine office of Horus, whose holders are the earthly embodiments of that god, deriving bodily of and from him. King Ny-Netjer of the Second Dynasty, for example, is "he belonging to the god," and King Neterikhet (Djoser) of the Third Dynasty is "he of the divine body." From the mid–Fourth Dynasty, the kings as Horus were also the offspring of the sun god Ra, and by the time of the Pyramid Texts, if not earlier, they were also acknowledged formally as sons of the deceased god Osiris.[20] The rulership need only be fed by unions with its surrounding female family to provide a single ruling family: the (last or reigning) king's family.[21]

The brother-sister marriage of Osiris and Isis supplied one useful divine model for the kingship, but it was the marriage of Horus to Hathor (as daughter and/or mother of Ra) or to Nekhbet (mother sky goddess) that first dominated royal ideology and continued to do so until late in Egyptian history (figs. 2a,b).[22] The queenship therefore was equated with sister, daughter, or mother of the king/god, perhaps depending on which was most appropriate. Thus the kinship relations of king and queen, predominant as they were throughout pharaonic history, no doubt interacted with cosmogonical accounts.[23]

There is much to suggest that the desire to preserve kinship lines in Egyptian ruling families could occasionally override gender preference, just as it did in the Silla state in three recorded instances. The royal women of the Old Kingdom were commonly characterized by their identities as members of the reigning king's family (as king's daughter, king's wife, king's mother). Their names and monuments are known to us from their tombs and those of their spouses, who were sometimes kings and sometimes members of the administrative class. An overview of the evidence for female royal family members reveals their role in the guarantee of dynastic continuity.

NEITH-HOTEP

The commonest form of female rule was that of regency, wherein a king's mother ruled on behalf of her son until he matured sufficiently.[24] The earliest example, however, was not of a mother ruling in place of her son. Early in the First Dynasty, Neith-hotep, the (probable) wife of Aha, is considered to have served as regent for Djer, possibly her nephew. This queen, whose name is known from tomb objects in both Nagada and Abydos, was buried in her own enormous niched mud-brick tomb at the site of Nagada, one of Egypt's most ancient centers. The name of Aha, one of the first kings of Dynasty 1, occurs with hers; objects naming her also stem from the royal tomb complex of Djer, ruler in the mid–First Dynasty. Although the titles of queenship were

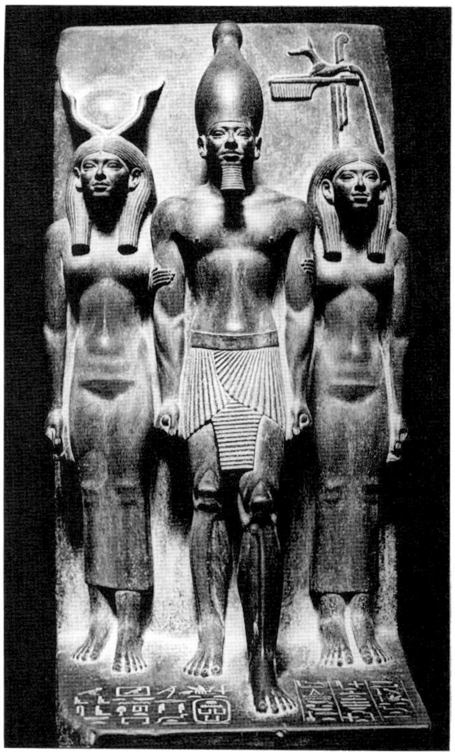

Fig. 2a Menkaura with the goddess Hathor as consort on his proper right and the personification of the Egyptian region of Cynopolis (17th Upper Egyptian nome) in Middle Egypt on his proper left. One of eight such triads, all with Hathor. From Giza, Dynasty 4. Cairo Museum, JE 40679. Museum photo.

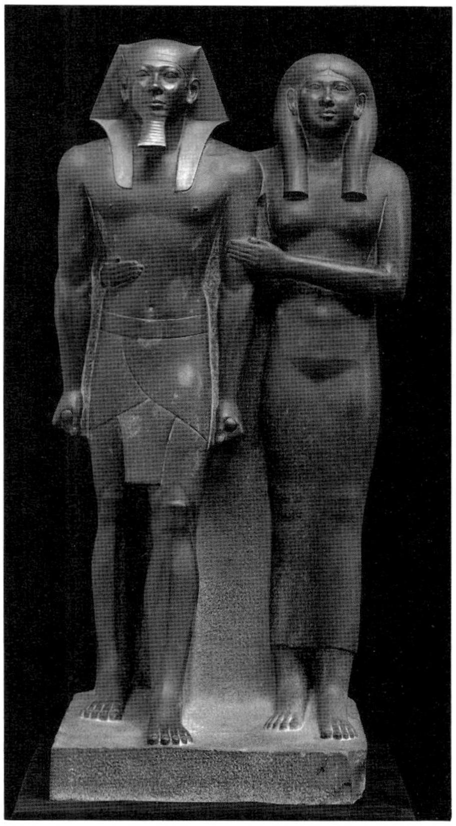

Fig. 2b Menkaura and Khemernebty. Dyad of Menkaura and Queen Khemernebty in the same material as the triads (see fig. 2a). The queen's position is here equated with Hathor's role in the triads as divine wife, mother, daughter. Photo courtesy Museum of Fine Arts, Boston.

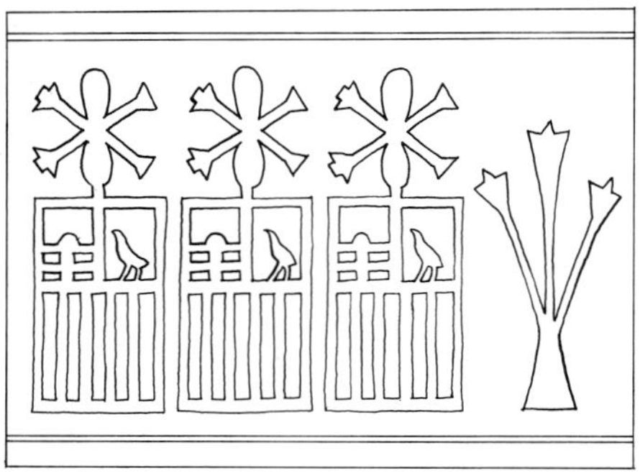

Fig. 3 Seal of Neith-hotep showing Neith emblem over the palace facade. Citation: Kaplony, *Inschriften* 3: pl. 54, no. 201.

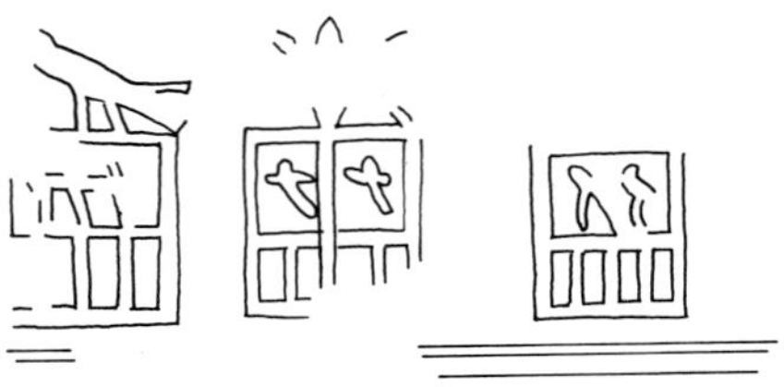

Fig. 4 Seal of Djer and Mer-Neith. Neith emblem over palace facade. Citation: Kaplony, *Inschriften* 3: pl. 122, no. 730.

not yet expressed by "King's Wife" or "King's Mother,"[25] Neith-hotep's importance may be assumed from a seal with her own name placed within a palace-facade hieroglyph (fig. 3). The emblem of her namesake goddess Neith was carved above the palace facade.[26]

This iconographic distinction was reserved, with only one other known exception, to the god whom the king embodied—in all but two instances Horus alone. (In the Second Dynasty a King Peribsen placed Seth atop the palace facade displaying his name, while a more conciliatory successor, Khasekhemuwy, celebrated his kingship under both Horus and Seth.[27]) The other instance, also in the First Dynasty, occurs on a seal of Djer, which shows Horus over the king's name on the palace facade, and Neith's over an uncertain name, perhaps Mer-Neith (fig. 4).[28] Neith-hotep's use of the palace facade for her name signals her importance and sometimes has been interpreted as indication of a dynastic union between Lower Egypt's Neith and Upper Egypt's (i.e., Aha's) Horus.

MER-NEITH

The regency of Mer-Neith is far better attested. It is now certain that she served, with the title "Queen Mother," as regent for King Den in the mid–First Dynasty. Her name appears on a seal found at Abydos amid a sequential list of rulers from Aha to Den (fig. 5). Mer-Neith is listed last.[29] She has her own royal tomb at Abydos from which are preserved two stelae identifying her as possessor of the complex. Mer-Neith's name has been associated with that of Djer, most probably as his daughter.[30] Her personal claim to royal prerogative is further evidenced in a label on a schist bowl from her tomb, which reads: "Merit-*Neith ḫntj pr-ḥḏ,"* "that which is from Mer-Neith's Treasury." As Peter Kaplony notes, this later example, unlike labels from Djer's time naming her as donor (and reading *simply Mr(t) Nt ḫntj,* "that which is from Mer-Neith"), means that she is providing offerings to her own burial not out of her personal storeroom, but directly out of the Royal Treasury.[31]

Mer-Neith also occurs in the Palermo Stone, a year-by-year list of kings compiled in the Fifth Dynasty, where her partially preserved name appears *([M]rt [Nt])* written horizontally above the year descriptions. It has been presumed for one hundred years that she was included as the mother of the king, although no title or filiation is present.[32] Since the Cairo fragment provides the name of Djer followed by that of his mother, Khen(s)et-hep, placed (as with Mer-Neith) in the horizontal band,[33] it is quite possible that Mer-Neith was described in the Fifth Dynasty list solely as "King's Mother."

The examples of Neith-hotep and Mer-Neith demonstrate clearly how the preference for male rulers gave way to the desire to preserve the dynastic succession. Nonetheless, the royal succession remained a male domain. It is unknown whether Neith-hotep ruled with any specific title, but Mer-Neith's rule was identified as that of "King's Mother" in the time of her son Den. This designation and her apparent exclusion as ruler from the Palermo Stone king list of the Fifth Dynasty inform us that her regency was not considered to have been kingship, despite its venerated status in the mid–First Dynasty. Thus, as in the case of the Silla, the fact of female rule was tolerated but publicly downplayed. Also, just as the Buddhist monks later appear to have suppressed some evidence of

Fig. 5. Seal with list of First Dynasty rulers, including King's Mother Mer-Neith. Citation: G. Dreyer, *MDAIK* 43 (1987): 36, Abb. 3.

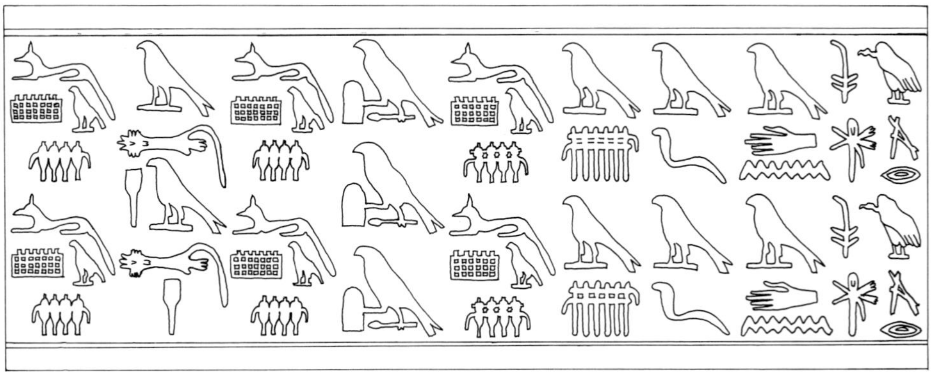

Silla female rulers, later Egyptian excerptors apparently omitted Mer-Neith's regency and included her only as mother of King Den. These revisions may have occurred intentionally or as the result of misunderstanding. In either case the later writers did not expect ruling queen mothers to be listed.[34]

NITOKRET

How the first female king emerged remains uncertain. Africanus, the late excerptor of Manetho, stated that in the reign of Ny-netjer of the Second Dynasty "it was decided that women might hold the kingly office."[35] Although it is difficult to believe that such a decision was ever made, evidence suggests that Queen Nitokret (Neith-ikret) assumed the actual rule of Egypt at the close of the Old Kingdom. The evidence, however, is not contemporary with the Sixth Dynasty period of Nitokret's presumed rule.[36] The earliest record of this woman as monarch comes from the Turin Canon, a list of kings of Egypt compiled in the reign of Ramesses II, about thirteenth century B.C. It places Neith-ikret, a king of [Upper and] Lower Egypt, after King Merenra of the Sixth Dynasty, about twenty-third and twenty-second centuries B.C. This kingship would have preceded the reign of Pepy II, which was so long that it all but ended the Old Kingdom. Traditions about this Nitokret from Herodotus, Manetho, and Eratosthenes cannot be relied upon for historical accuracy, but they contain some earlier reflexes.[37] The only certainty is that the king lists of later Egypt preserved the existence of this female ruler, at least as early as the Nineteenth Dynasty.

Merenra's successor, Pepy II, was a small child at his accession, and his mother, Queen Ankhnesmeryra, was fairly prominent as a result (fig. 6).[38] Perhaps Neith-ikret should be viewed as the female dynastic support between Merenra, the first son of Pepy I, and Pepy II, the other, younger son of Pepy I. Her identification with Neith, the daughter of Pepy I, wife of Pepy II, and sister of Merenra, is intriguing but undemonstrable.[39] The pyramid of Queen Neith is known but does not identify her as other than a princess, queen, and royal mother (of whom is unclear). Still, even this does not eliminate the possibility that Neith ruled as Neith-ikret, either as regent only or as king. Hatshepsut, too, had a tomb and burial goods naming her as "Queen" and "God's Wife of Amen"; Tauseret's tomb inscriptions referred to her as "King's Great Wife"; Sobeknefru of the Twelfth Dynasty ruled as king but left no known funerary monument of her own. Neith(-ikret), like Mer-Neith and Neith-hotep, might be seen as a ruler who was necessary to the moment but was suppressed in the aftermath.

These three examples from the first six dynasties illustrate four ways in which female rulers have been preserved in documentation: with both royal (Mer-Neith) and nonroyal (Neith-hotep, Neith[-ikret]?) types of tombs, with the title of "King's Mother," with the title of king (not contemporary), and with no title at all. This lack of pattern may represent the unusual nature of the female rule and the ambivalence toward it in the conventional dynastic culture.

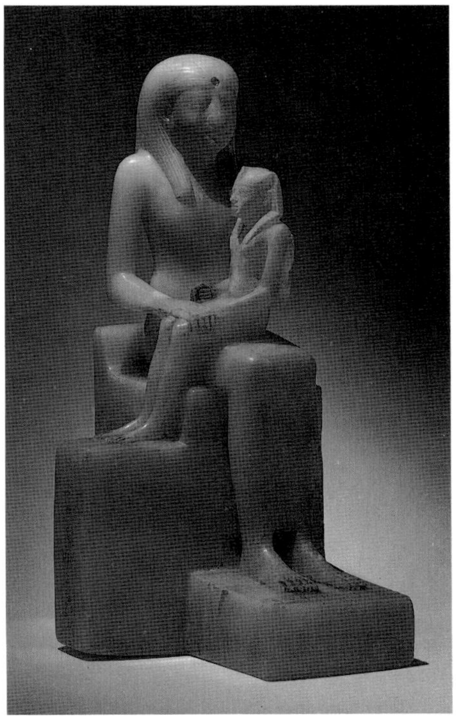

Fig. 6 Pepy II and Ankhnesmeryra. Statuette in calcite of Queen Ankhnesmeryra holding her son King Pepy II on her lap. Although she was not of pure royal birth herself, the queen's elevated position as King's Mother is stressed in Pepy's adult royal regalia. Charles Edwin Wilbour Fund. 39.119. Photo courtesy of the Brooklyn Museum.

SOBEKNEFRU

A somewhat different pattern may be identified for Sobekkara Sobeknefru, who ruled Egypt in the Middle Kingdom, although the circumstances that placed her in the kingship are quite analogous to those of the earlier periods. Sobeknefru[40] was the first female ruler to carry a full king's titulary: "The Horus, She Who Is Beloved of Ra, She of the Two Ladies, Powerful Daughter, Mistress of the Two Lands, the Golden Falcon, Enduring of Appearances, the King of Upper and Lower Egypt Sobekkara, the Daughter of Ra Sobeknefru." Sobeknefru was the daughter of Amenemhat III in the late Twelfth Dynasty.[41] Many scholars believe, perhaps on the strength of the Manethonian king list, that she was the sister and king's wife of Amenemhat IV: Africanus specifically calls her "his sister," referring to Ammenemes (Amenemhat IV), but there is no contemporary monument that refers to her as king's wife.[42] Although some scholars think that Amenemhat IV was coregent with Amenemhat III throughout his brief rule, and others believe that Sobeknefru was coregent with Amenemhat III

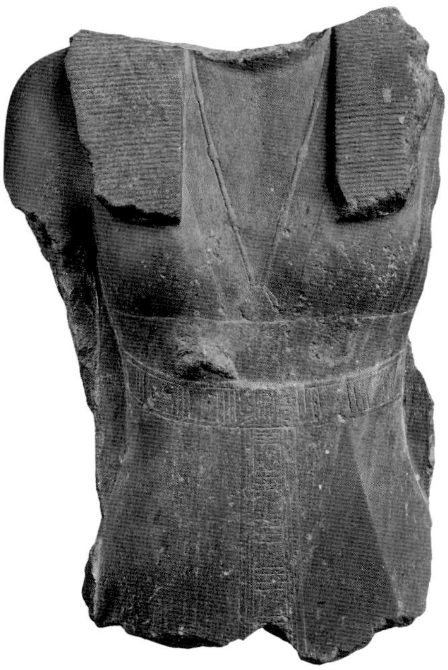

Fig. 7 Statue of Sobeknefru wearing king's headdress and kilt. Late Dynasty 12. Louvre E 27135. Copyright Maurice and Pierre Chuzeville, Musée du Louvre.

and/or Amenemhat IV, it is impossible to verify any of these joint rules. Upon the death of Amenemhat IV, apparently without issue, Sobeknefru assumed the throne for nearly four years, as the last ruler of the dynasty.[43] She left monuments in her own name, which are now in the eastern delta and Herakleopolis. She left her name in several places in her father's funerary-type temple at Hawara in the Fayum, but her own burial place remains undiscovered.[44]

The distinction between Sobeknefru and the female rulers cited earlier is her use of the titles of kingship and her adoption on statuary of the *nemes* headdress, uniquely a king's diadem (fig. 7).[45] On her statue in the Louvre, Sobeknefru wears a woman's dress with a king's kilt over it, along with *the nemes.* Despite her apparent break with tradition, Sobeknefru legitimated her right to rule, in a typically ancient Egyptian manner, with an inscription on a red granite column, probably from Hawara. There the Horus name of Amenemhat III offers the sign of life and stability to the Horus name of Sobeknefru, clearly indicating the deceased king's wish that she rule.[46]

We are entirely ignorant of the reasons why the dynasty ended with Sobeknefru's death. The fact of her acknowledgment as king, however, attests to the central role of the king's immediate family in perpetuating the ideology of a continuous kingship. Apparently the ruling elite regarded the kingship as interconnected sufficiently with Sobeknefru's ancestry to make her acceptable in the absence of a male heir. This was a distinct step beyond the First Dynasty regencies, and yet clearly derived from them.

Indeed, the fact that Sobeknefru assumed a full titulary and wore *the nemes* and royal kilt suggests that she unabashedly claimed rule as a female occupant of the kingship. It is uncertain whether this action was tantamount to the claim (as Nelson considered true in the Silla cases) that any member of the exclusive kinship group, regardless of gender, was eligible to assume rule. It should encourage our caution, however, in making the assumption that ancient Egyptians reacted monolithically to female rulers. The brevity of Sobeknefru's reign elicits the speculation that some persons may have taken advantage of the unusual circumstance of her monarchy, but her inclusion in the king lists (at Saqqara and Turin, as well as by Manetho) demonstrates the acknowledgment, however grudging, of female rule.

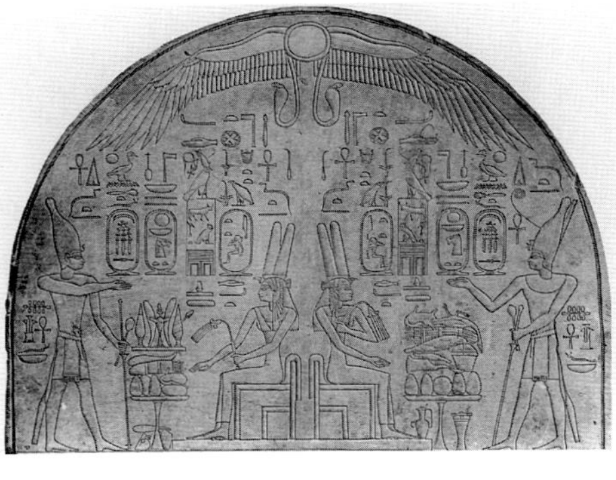

Fig. 8 Stela of Queen Tetishery, grandmother of Ahmose and Ahmose-Nefertari. From Abydos, early Dynasty 18. Cairo Museum, CG 34002. Photograph courtesy of the author.

HATSHEPSUT

Some three centuries after Sobeknefru's brief reign, a woman ruled again in Egypt. In contrast to the paltry monumental remains and contemporary references for Sobeknefru, however, Hatshepsut's reign is well documented, even in comparison with most male rulers. The model presented earlier, of female monarchs arising from a kinship pool that was defined by relation to the last reigning king, is illustrated again in Hatshepsut's case. She was the daughter of Thutmose I by a king's sister Ahmose, and she was the wife of her half-brother Thutmose II. Hatshepsut, however, was also a product of early New Kingdom royal ideology. A review of the period will place her in the historical context.

In the early fifteenth century B.C. the family that dominated Egypt was Upper Egyptian and as a result was devoted to Thebes. The immediately preceding era had been a time of strife and want: the southerners had been held economic hostage to Asiatic Hyksos rulers in the northeastern delta. Wars conducted by the southern kings Sekenenra, Kamose, and Ahmose eventually succeeded in defeating the Hyksos, establishing a reunified Nile valley and solidifying the Seventeenth Theban Dynasty as the Eighteenth Egyptian Dynasty.[47]

Already under the rulership of Ahmose, who is credited with the defeat of the Hyksos, a ruling family ideology was created for this new Eighteenth Dynasty. It elaborated the role of royal women in a manner reminiscent of Dynasty 1. Ahmose built monuments for his mother, Ahhotep, and he venerated his grandmother Tetishery (fig. 8) as well. On a stela left at the holy site of Abydos, Ahmose stated:

Fig. 9 Donation Stela of Ahmose and Ahmose-Nefertari transferring office of Second of Priest of Amen on behalf of the God's Wife of Amen. Early Dynasty 18. Photo from Ibrahim Harari, "Nature de la stèle de donation de fonction du roi Ahmôsis à la reine Ahmês Nefertari," *ASAE* 56 (1959): pl. 1.

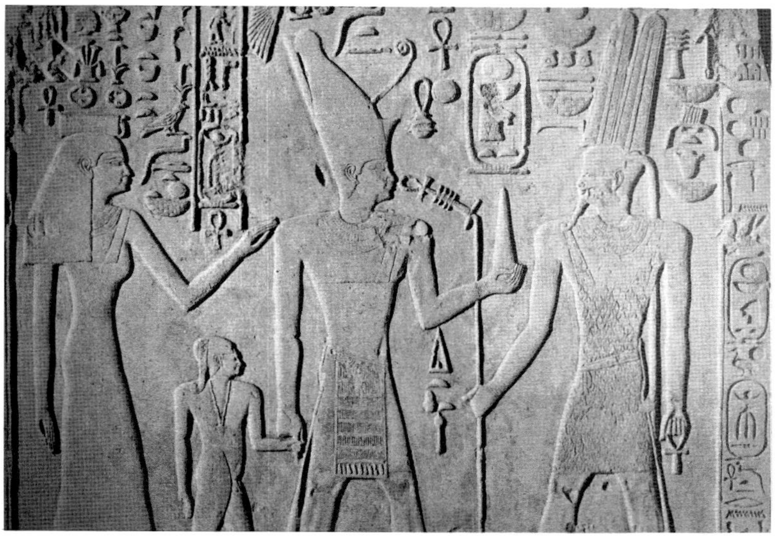

> I it is who have remembered the mother of my mother, and the mother of my father, great king's wife and king's mother Tetishery, triumphant. She has a tomb *(is)* and a mortuary chapel *(mꜥḥꜥt)* on the soil of Thebes and Abydos. I have said this to thee, in that my Person has desired to have made for her a pyramid and a house *(ḥwt)* in *Ta Djeser* as a monumental donation of my majesty.[48]

If we may accept Ahmose's genealogy as fact, then his parents were brother and sister, as were he and his wife, Ahmose-Nefertari. His mother, Queen Ahhotep, must have been left responsible in Thebes, at least for some time during the wars, because her active role is reflected on Ahmose's monuments and in the names of those who worked for her. A stela set up in Karnak Temple enumerated the royal gifts to Amen-Ra, almost certainly as a result of the capture of the Hyksos center at Avaris. On that stela Ahhotep was given the title "Mistress of the Two Lands," as well as other epithets.[49] Her own steward left the following inscription, proudly quoting a decree from the queen:

> Command of the king's mother to the hereditary prince, count, wearer of the royal seal, sole companion, overseer of the gold house, overseer of the silver house, chief steward of the king's mother Ahhotep, living; the herald Kares: "The king's mother has commanded to have made for thee a tomb at the stairway of the great god, lord of Abydos, . . . as the king's wife does for the one whom she has loved. . . . He [who is] before the people, the real [confidant] of his mistress to whom secret things are told, [experienced] in the plans of his mistress, transmitting affairs to the palace, finding solutions, making agreeable unpleasant matters, one upon whose word his mistress depends, approaching the truth, knowing the affairs of the mind, profitable in speech to his mistress, great in respect in the house of the king's mother. . . . "[50]

This inscription from Kares' tomb in Thebes informs us of Ahhotep's power to grant a chapel to a private person at the exclusive precinct of Abydos (a royal prerogative), and it demonstrates her active decision-making role as king's mother with respect to the court. Ahmose's sister and consort, Ahmose-Nefertari, continued the role played by his mother through the remainder of his lifetime (perhaps only after Ahhotep's death) and through the reign of her son Amenhotep I; perhaps she did not die until the beginning of Thutmose I's brief rule.[51]

Under Ahmose-Nefertari the religious office of "God's Wife of Amen" took on prominence (fig. 9). Ahmose purchased the second priesthood of Amen and its benefices to expand substantialiy the holdings of the God's Wife, and these priesthoods were deeded to Ahmose-Nefertari and her chosen successors in perpetuity.[52] Ahmose-Nefertari used the title "God's Wife of Amen" as her functioning designation on most of her monuments and those of her husband and son. Despite her claim to the purest of all royal pedigrees—king's daughter, king's sister, king's mother—she preferred to be termed "God's Wife." Perhaps she enjoyed the religious and economic power of the office, held solely in her own hands. That power came to rest in the hands of Hatshepsut.[53]

Like Ahmose-Nefertari, Hatshepsut was most often referred to as "God's Wife of Amen" during the reign of her brother-consort Thutmose II. They were half-siblings: Thutmose's mother had been a nonroyal woman named Mutnofret, and Hatshepsut's a king's sister Ahmose. It is entirely unknown whether Ahmose in fact was a full sister of Amenhotep I; she may have been only a collateral family member, for the title "Sister" could apply to a broad range of sisters, aunts, and nieces.[54] As Great Royal Wife and God's Wife of Amen, Hatshepsut was prominent in Karnak Temple on monuments in her husband's name. A limestone temple erected by Thutmose II showed her in cult performance with her daughter Nefrura behind her.[55] Recent study of this monument has confirmed that king and queen figured nearly equally and has left little doubt that Hatshepsut was recognized as an active priestess during her husband's reign.[56]

Peter Dorman has brought together the documents that illustrate the period of Hatshepsut's transformation from "God's Wife" to "King."[57] One important inscription came from the tomb of Ineni, who had served Thutmose II and died before Hatshepsut declared herself monarch. In his biography Ineni stated:

> His [Thutmose II's] son stood in his place as king of the two lands, he having assumed the throne of the one who had begotten him. His sister, the God's Wife Hatshepsut, settled the affairs of the land, the Two Lands in her governance. It was by Egypt with bowed head that she was served, the excellent seed of the god, who came forth from him. The prow-rope of the South, the mooring stake of the southerners; the excellent stern-rope of the Northland is she; the mistress of command, whose plans are excellent, the two banks being satisfied when she speaks.[58]

Ineni's inscription demonstrates that it was Hatshepsut's lineage and her prominence that gained the acceptance of all Egypt. Moving from her role as regent for the child, Hatshepsut carefully assumed the kingship as coregent to her stepson and nephew Thutmose III (son of Thutmose II by a nonroyal woman named Isis). This coregency persisted throughout Hatshepsut's reign, but she was so clearly dominant that it is often overlooked as a factor in her success. In addition, as monarch, Hatshepsut chose predominantly the image of male rulership toward which Sobeknefru had been moving. Although some statues portray her wearing female clothing and royal headgear, most of the sculpture from her temple at Deir el-Bahri represents her as a man, despite associated texts that sometimes use feminine endings and pronouns.

Hatshepsut handed on to her daughter Nefrura the power she wielded through her God's Wife office. Sometime after Thutmose II's death, she intentionally linked the economic holdings of the priestess office with those of the crown and the temple of Amen generally, as is borne out by the titulary of her close confidant Senenmut, who was steward for all three.[59]

Hatshepsut took on the titulary of king as "the Horus Powerful of Kas, She of the Two Ladies Flourishing of Years, the Golden Horus Divine of Appearances, the King of Upper and Lower Egypt Maatkara, the Daughter of Ra United-with-Amen Hatshepsut."[60] In the approximately fifteen years of her rule Hatshepsut pursued an active building program; most notably she erected a limestone mortuary temple in Thebes in the bay of Deir el-Bahri. The temple, now magnificently restored, was carved lavishly with relief sculptures exemplifying the ruler's deeds: among Hatshepsut's great sources of pride was her trading mission to Punt, an east African source for incense and central African products. She also represented the transport of her first pair of obelisks, dedicated in Karnak.[61] Hatshepsut's divine birth from the union of Amen and Queen Ahmose was the subject of one cycle of reliefs that also showed her presentation and acceptance before the gods as a child. Elsewhere in the temple she placed a scene of her father proclaiming her his heir, and she included scenes of military expeditions to Sinai, Nubia, and even the Levant to demonstrate her effectiveness as protector of divine order.[62] On the third terrace of the temple, Hatshepsut included rooms dedicated to her identification with the sun god in his daily and nightly celestial journeys, a shrine to the sun god with an offering altar, and cult rooms for Hatshepsut's statue rituals. The entire precinct was landscaped with incense trees brought from Punt, and large numbers of statues were made to inhabit the ritual setting. The chapel to Hathor at the south end of the temple housed the important festival of the Beautiful Feast of the Valley.

In emulating her predecessors, Hatshepsut left monuments at many of the traditional cult sites throughout Egypt and also in Nubia. Karnak, however, was the place of her heart: she installed two sets of obelisks in the temple and built a suite of rooms around the central sanctuary, in which she figured as the pious officiant of the daily cult. She dedicated a new pylon there, creating an emphasis on the north-south axis that had been long ignored. This pylon pointed the way to her chapel of Amen Kamutef on the south processional route toward the Mut precinct. She also left a gateway into that last temple area.[63]

Hatshepsut's best-known Karnak monument was a shrine of red quartzite made to house the boat that carried the statue of the god during processions. The boat, or bark, shrine of Hatshepsut, which may have occupied the central position before the temple sanctuary, was dismantled by Thutmose III, who built his own shrine late in his sole rule.[64] The Hatshepsut shrine blocks were reused several decades later, however, in the foundation of the Third Pylon. They constitute the best representations of two important festivals celebrated in Thebes over some 1,500 years, the Opet and the Beautiful Feast of the Valley.[65]

It is probably fair to say that Hatshepsut made her important contributions as king through her expansion of the cult of Amen, with the concomitant political and economic ramifications. Through Luxor Temple, where the Opet Festival was celebrated, Hatshepsut tied the renewal of kingship itself to Amen, and vice versa, because the god of that temple depended on the royal cult for survival. The Beautiful Feast brought Amen to the West Bank of Thebes to participate with the divine royal ancestors and Hathor of the cemetery region. Hatshepsut likewise established a cult for Amen at Medinet Habu.[66] The numbers of titleholders associated with the cult of Amen-Ra, women as well as men, increased sharply during her reign. Certainly the data are skewed by the relative absence of extant tomb chapels from the first four reigns of Dynasty 18. Even so, this author knows of only three "Singers" *(shemayit, ḥesyt)* from the first four reigns, out of 114 for all fourteen monarchies of Dynasty 18. Fifteen, however, are known for Hatshepsut alone, in addition to "God's Wife" and "Superiors of Amen's Entertainers."[67]

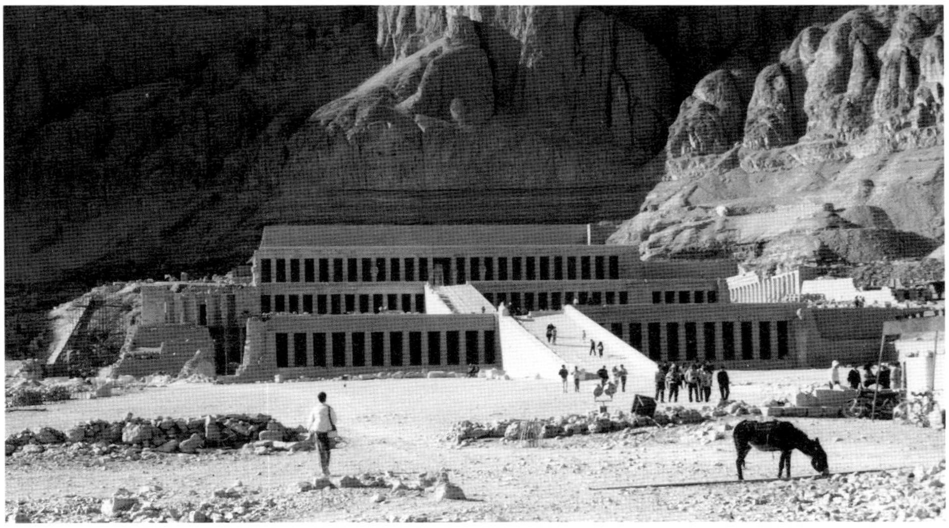

Fig. 10 Temple for the eternal cult of Hatshepsut at Deir el-Bahri, Thebes West. Dynasty 18. Photograph courtesy of the author.

These women, mostly wives and daughters of priests of Amen or high government officers, may be represented without their names on blocks from the Karnak quartzite chapel, where the Entertainers of Amen are shown singing and making music during festivals (see below).

Perhaps because of her ambitious building campaigns, Hatshepsut's officials were busy on her behalf throughout Egypt and Nubia. The names of her treasurer as well as those of local governors from north and south of Thebes appear in scenes from the Deir el-Bahri temple in whose construction they participated (fig. 10). We are fortunate also to have hieratic ostraca found around the temple with informal documentation of work organization.[68] Among the best-known officials of Hatshepsut's administration was Senenmut, her Steward of Amen, who also served as nurse and steward to her daughter Nefrura, the God's Wife of Amen (cat. no. 43).[69] Hapuseneb, the High Priest of Amen, was connected to the ruler through the God's Wife office as well: his daughter Senisonb was the Divine Adoratrice of Amen, a role second only to God's Wife. The position of this Senisonb in her family parallels that of royal females, for her marriage to Puyemra, the Second Priest of Amen, another highly influential man under Hatshepsut, helped to form a powerful aristocratic dynasty.

Recent discussions of Hatshepsut's reign have largely silenced an earlier argument that her disappearance in year 20 of Thutmose III was followed swiftly by a campaign to remove her name and memory from monuments.

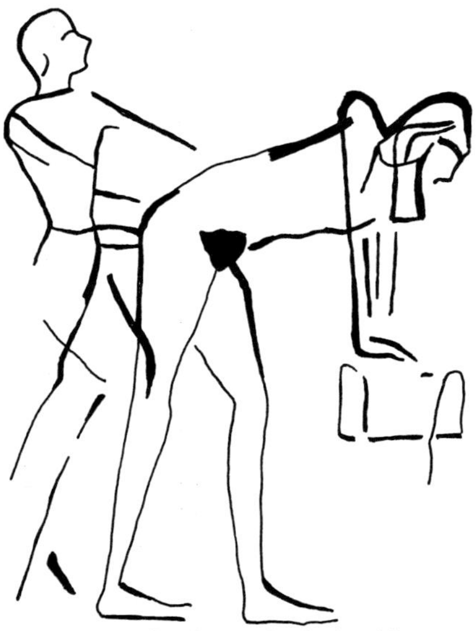

Fig. 11 Erotic graffito from unfinished Middle Kingdom tomb above Deir el-Bahri. After *Acta Orientalia* 38 (1977).

The overwhelming view now is that "the dishonoring of Hatshepsut" took place only in the last years of Thutmose III's life (post year 46), and perhaps not until he had already determined to associate his son Amenhotep II with him as coregent. This event, in his fifty-first year, may have signaled the beginning of an open attempt to destroy the memory of King Maatkara Hatshepsut. Amenhotep II took an active part in mutilating her monuments, and he profited by erasing her scenes and texts from the Eighth Pylon at Karnak and replacing them with his own. He also masked the bases of her obelisks and covered them with additional scenes and inscriptions.

At such an advanced age, Thutmose III could hardly have cared himself that Hatshepsut's monuments were sprinkled about Karnak. It is more likely that he attacked her memory in order to assure Amenhotep II's smooth transition to sole rule.[70] Although Hatshepsut had no living sons of whom we are aware, and although her daughter Nefrura was dispensed with soon after Hatshepsut's own disappearance, collateral members of the family line may still have been alive.[71] Certainly, too, the influence of Hatshepsut's powerful aristocratic allies was not to be ignored. Thus the same motivation that would have encouraged support for Hatshepsut's sovereignty—protection of the dynastic line—also supported her dishonoring. The royal ancestry was protected carefully by replacing Hatshepsut's name with those of Thutmose III, Thutmose I, and even Thutmose II.[72]

Was Hatshepsut's rule disgraced partly because of her gender? It would be rash not to conclude that this was a factor, for in all the 1,500 years of rulers who preceded Hatshepsut, we find no other widespread attempt to obliterate a king's memory.[73] On the other hand, the fact that Thutmose III and Amenhotep II waited some thirty years before acting against the queen suggests that her gender was as much a pretext as a motive, for public opinion against female rulers was likely strong. In the Eighteenth Dynasty the oldest known copies of a Middle Kingdom text, "The Instruction of King Amenemhat I," were penned, and perhaps revised. The words "Had any woman ever marshaled troops? Are rebels nurtured in the palace?" suggest that the fact of a woman in charge of the army was as unexpected as the attempt on Amenemhat's life made by his palace guard.[74]

Still there is no evidence, literary or otherwise, that female rulership was ideologically or theologically impossible. Nor does any known literary composition either parody the idea or present a cruel or wicked female monarch, although at least two stories present kings in a negative light.[75] The inhabitant of the office, by definition, was the god Horus, the Strong Bull, as well as the offspring of Ra. Would the ancient Egyptians have been any more offended by a woman termed "Strong Bull" than by the king's divine epithet *Ka-mut-ef,* "Bull of His Mother," which implies mother-son incest for procreative purposes? We cannot be sure, but we should not presume that the Egyptian culture can be understood according to modern notions of sexual dominance.

Hundreds of sketches of sexual acts have been preserved on ostraca, tomb walls, and papyrus. An uninscribed graffito of a standing male penetrating a naked woman from the rear has been interpreted as a political parody of Hatshepsut (fig. 11). The graffito, left in an unfinished Middle Kingdom tomb above Hatshepsut's mortuary temple, was found beneath a long funerary text on behalf of a man in charge of construction at Deir el-Bahri. Elsewhere on the same wall a second set of drawings shows a large male figure, and behind him (but not necessarily associated) a smaller male with an erect phallus.

In a first publication of the man and woman, the scene was used as an example of sexual practice; a second boldly labeled the woman in question as Hatshepsut and the man as Senenmut. The scene was labeled as political satire, "commenting upon the anomaly of having a female on the throne of Egypt in the person of Hatshepsut and upon her supposed affair with her chief steward Senenmut."[76] This rather strange interpretation of a scene that represents no royal iconography at all (the woman's wig is a common type from the mid–Eighteenth Dynasty)[77] and no text, was elaborated in a third publication. There it was suggested that the two male figures drawn elsewhere on the wall were to be understood as potential participants in homosexual relations and that Hatshepsut again was being parodied. In this case she was identified as the large male toward whom the excited smaller figure advanced.

Although this interpretation precluded the necessity of identifying Senenmut in the graffiti, the following conclusion was offered as a result of the observation that a rear approach is shown in both sets of drawings.

> The implication then is that the small male with an erect phallus at the right is the same individual as the male in the love-making scene at the left and that the large standing figure, depicted as a male, should be equated with the woman in the love-making scene. The only person of this period who could fill this dual gender role is Hatshepsut, who was universally represented as a male in two-dimensional depictions of her as king. . . .

In seeking to identify Hatshepsut's lover in these scenes, one might be missing the point of the political parody. The sexually active male may simply be an anonymous figure serving to provide the means for commenting pictorially upon the absurdity of Hatshepsut's acting as king, unable to be a "Mighty Bull."[78]

Surely more caution is demanded. The tolerance for female rulers exhibited throughout Egypt's first eighteen dynasties must be taken into account before we espouse such unsubstantiated opinions. After all, every woman upon death was transformed into the male deity Osiris and, from the New Kingdom, was provided (if resources allowed) with penises in the form of amulets for the necessary procreative acts leading to rebirth. Chapter 42 of the Book of the Dead iterates the parts of the body and the deities that preserve them. In the role of Osiris, all people assumed his bodily parts: "My eyes are Hathor, my ears are Wepwawet, my lips are Anubis, my teeth are Selket, my arms are the Ram of Mendes, my chest is Neith, my back is Seth, my phallus is Osiris."[79] Divine images often combined male and female, as, for example, when Mut appears with an erect phallus in Book of the Dead vignettes (fig. 12).[80]

NEFERTITI

The final two examples of female rulers, Nefertiti (fig. 13) and Tauseret, have much in common. Both lived in times of upheaval, in one case religious, in the other political. Nefertiti, whose name is well known today, was Akhenaten's Great Royal Wife and had no known genealogical connection to the royal family. Yet she played a profound role in the king's radical sun-worship religion, Atenism, insofar as she, like the other members of Akhenaten's nuclear family, were direct recipients of the Aten's benefices. In place of the proscribed national gods and goddesses, Nefertiti could intercede with the deity for members of the populace. Further, as the mother (with Akhenaten) of some six daughters, she provided the important royal offspring who could perpetuate the dynastic line. Akhenaten himself married at least two of the princesses in the hope of securing the purity of the lineage, while Nefertiti faded from public view. Some scholars believe she reemerged as a male coregent to Akhenaten, but this thesis lacks certainty.[81] Still, Nefertiti's visibility on the monuments and her varied royal regalia, which suggest more than queenship, imply that Akhenaten considered her role highly significant.

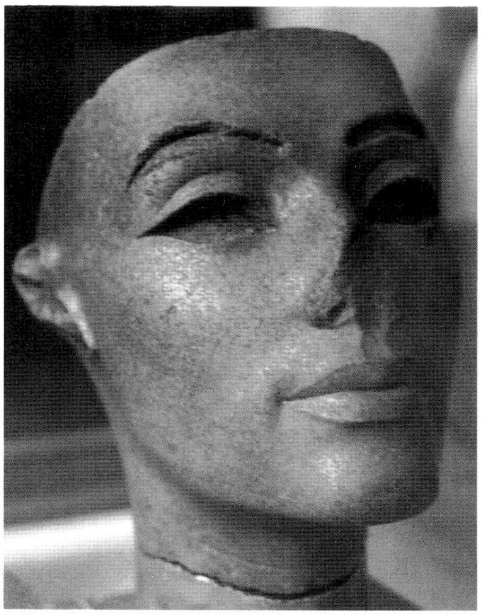

Fig. 13 Nefertiti. Part of a composite statue from Memphis. Late Dynasty 18. Cairo Museum, JE 45547. Photograph courtesy of the author.

TAUSERET

Tauseret (fig. 14), too, lived in a time of uncertainty. At the close of the Nineteenth Dynasty she was the Great Royal Wife of Sety II. Tauseret apparently attempted to assume the rule at her husband's death but was thwarted by the installation of the young Siptah, who was supported by the chancellor

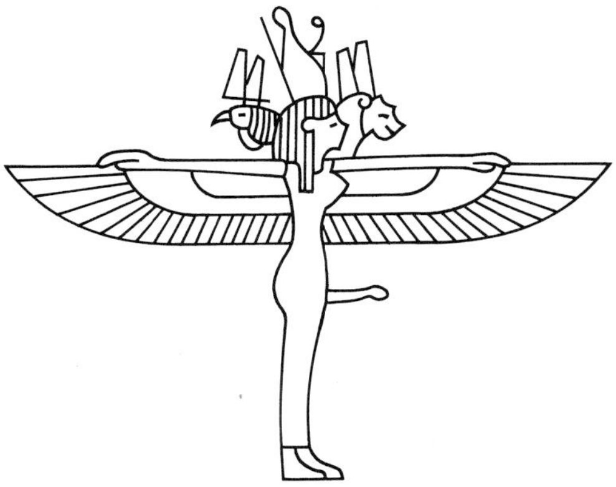

Fig. 12 Mut with three heads and a phallus. Dynasty 18. After drawing from the Book of the Dead in *Egypt's Dazzling Sun,* 217, fig. 7, 5.

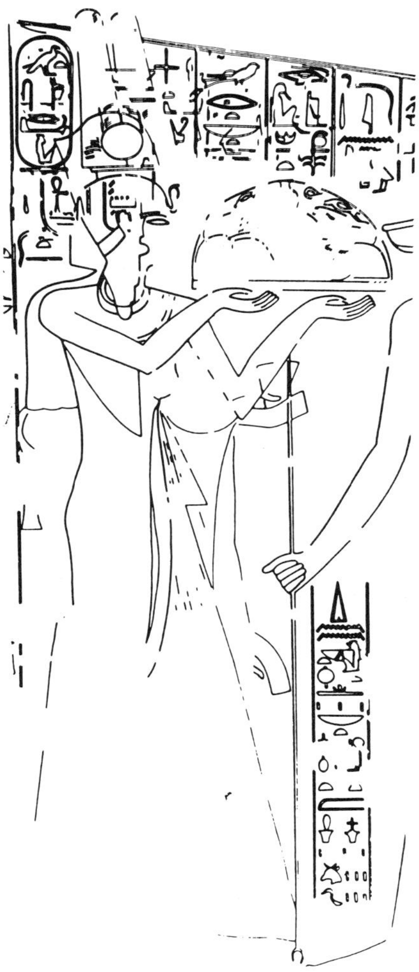

Fig. 14 Tauseret as woman ruler from her tomb in the Valley of the Kings. Her female form was later reworked for the tomb's usurper Setnakht. After H. Altenmüller in C.N. Reeves, ed., *After Tutʾankhamun* (London, 1992), 155, ill. 24.

Bay. The competition persisted through Siptah's brief reign, after which Tauseret may have ruled alone for a short time. Like Nefertiti, Tauseret appeared as Great Royal Wife, even in her tomb in the King's Valley, and always as a female. She too lacked the titles of lineage that would support a claim to rule, and, as with Nefertiti, her prominence as the king's wife implies a near-joint reign. The tomb of Tauseret in the Valley of the Kings was swiftly occupied after her death by Setnakhte, founder of the next dynasty.[82]

CONCLUSION

Egypt's dynastic families were motivated by self-preservation, and the kingship itself was a unique institution creating from divine embodiment a single kinship for all rulers. The families of reigning kings—mothers, daughters, and wives—served as spokes on a wheel with the monarch at the center. Women of the royal family normally acted to keep the king connected to the dynastic line and sometimes to join that line to powerful and affluent aristocrats. Nothing in the material suggests that the society entirely rejected the occasional royal woman at the center of the wheel. Indeed, the evidence demonstrates clearly that it tolerated such occurrences rather well, such that several of the female rulers, including Hatshepsut as Amessis, were remembered in the Manethonian king lists. After Hatshepsut's reign, however, kingship underwent some adjustments that resulted more often in joint husband-and-wife monarchies. Probably this represented the influence of an increasingly cosmopolitan world in which it was politic for queens to correspond with each other, as did kings. Occasionally a queen, such as Akhenaten's mother, Tiye, was even asked to intercede on behalf of a foreign ruler.[83] This model of rule is reflected in the visibility of Nefertiti and Tauseret. The joint rule did not support individual female reigns as successfully as did the desire for dynastic purity and survival.

Women within the family

FAMILY STRUCTURE

Oddly, marriage did not exist as a legal state in ancient Egypt. Marriages were economic and procreative unions that were often monogamous, enduring, loving. There was no marriage ceremony, however. The Egyptian family at all levels was based around a household that most commonly consisted of a husband and a wife, their children, the husband's widowed mother, and his sisters (see cat. no. 2). This nucleus could be extended to include sons- or daughters-in-law, their children, and numerous household servants. The artisan families at Deir el-Medina in the New Kingdom walled town were generally smaller than those whose livelihood came from the land. The family of Hekanakhte, an early Middle Kingdom funerary priest from Thebes, consisted of five sons, Hekanakhte's mother, his second wife, his sister or a collateral relative, a daughter, and a number of family retainers, totaling sixteen. Although Hekanakhte was not a highly ranked bureaucrat, he could support such a family from landholdings and their produce.[84]

In the wealthier families an image of the "Mistress of the *House" (nebet per)* was presented in Middle Kingdom and New Kingdom literature and continued on into Demotic instructions. That image encouraged the woman's superior status within the home but also encouraged the husband to keep ultimate control over the wife. "Ptahhotep's instruction" represents a view that is concerned above all with gaining promotion in society for the son whom he is educating. The advice is often less kind than efficient:

> When you prosper, then found your house. Love your wife according to her standard; fill her belly, clothe her back. Ointment soothes her body. Gladden her heart as long as you live, for she is a field fertile for her lord. Do not contend with her in court; keep her from power, restrain her—her eye as she gazes is a stormwind. This is how to make her stay in your house: restrain her. A female who is in her own hands is like the rainwater; she is sought, and she has flown away.[85]

The strong desire to keep control over a woman, which surfaces in Ptahhotep's instruction, is an economic theme not seen in later compositions. The New Kingdom "instructions of Any" praises the mother's active role in making sacrifices for her son and cautions him to take a wife, but also states:

> Do not control your wife in her house. When you know that she is efficient, don't say to her, "Where is it? Get it!" when she has put it in the right place.... If a man desists from strife at home, he will not encounter its beginning.[86]

Documents from the New Kingdom inform us about the result of marital strife, which often harms not the man but the woman. A Nineteenth Dynasty ostracon from the workman Horemwia to the Citizeness Tanetdjesere bears this inscription:

> You are my good daughter. If the workman Baki throws you out of the house, I will take action! As for the house, it is what belongs to Pharaoh, life, prosperity, health, but you may dwell in the anteroom to my storehouse because it is I who built it. Nobody in the world shall throw you out of there.[87]

Another ostracon—from a woman to her mother—demands that the older woman grind barley and emmer and make bread for the daughter. The daughter's husband had threatened to divorce her if her family did not contribute more foodstuffs.[88] It is quite possible that the difference between the early literary portrayal of marriage and the texts from Deir el-Medina lies in the social classes represented. Instruction literature was certainly intended for an upwardly mobile, if not elite, audience, in which an economically advantageous marriage might have been common. In Deir el-Medina, however, all of the families were probably of an artisan class without great wealth or aristocratic pretensions. Divorce may have been rather common in this population, but it, like marriage, had no state existence and was achieved simply by abandonment.[89]

POLITICS AND CHOICE IN MARRIAGE

By now it has become clear that the role of royal women was greatly circumscribed by biology and by chance position within the king's family. As potential mothers of monarchs, both king's daughters and king's wives were valued highly. As potential links in the dynastic chain, royal daughters were privileged by their brothers and fathers over those men's own wives; as mothers of reigning kings, even nonroyal women were venerated by their sons. So it is that we know much of Amenemhat III's daughter Nefru-Ptah (by objects bearing her name from six sites in Egypt), although apparently she was not married to her father.[90] Thus, too, Thutmose II's nonroyal mother, Mutnofret, was the object of her son's attention as king's mother, despite her absence as queen to Thutmose I.[91]

Royal women were important in securing the power of the royal family well beyond their ceremonial ties to the reigning king. From the Old Kingdom and the Second Intermediate Period comes evidence that kings' daughters married officials or local governors,[92] although in the Eighteenth Dynasty there is no certain evidence for this practice. Queen Khasnebu of the late Thirteenth Dynasty was the daughter of powerful southern aristocrats (fig. 15). Probably because she provided the king with children, her name has come down to us from monuments. The king himself was not named. Her daughter, one Khonsu, carried the title of "King's Daughter" and was married to the sealbearer and storehouse chief Ay. He later became vizier, and his family continued to be intertwined with the kingship. Anthony Spalinger summed up the historical situation in this way:

> The monarch had to rely upon his alliances with the powerful houses of his day and they in turn relied upon their king for the maintenance of their power.... It is significant that the name of the husband of queen *Ḫ*ᶜ.*s-nbw* [Khasnebu] is nowhere mentioned, almost as if he were a non-person. No doubt the monarch was quite weak at the close of Dynasty 13.[93]

The Middle Kingdom records of elite families contain indications that political marriages of the type mentioned above were common. The Twelfth Dynasty local governor Khnumhotep II stated in his autobiography:

> This my chief nobility is my birth, my mother having gone to be hereditary princess and countess as the daughter

Fig. 15 Stela of Queen Khasnebu. Dynasty 13. Louvre, C 13. Copyright Maurice and Pierre Chuzeville, Musée du Louvre.

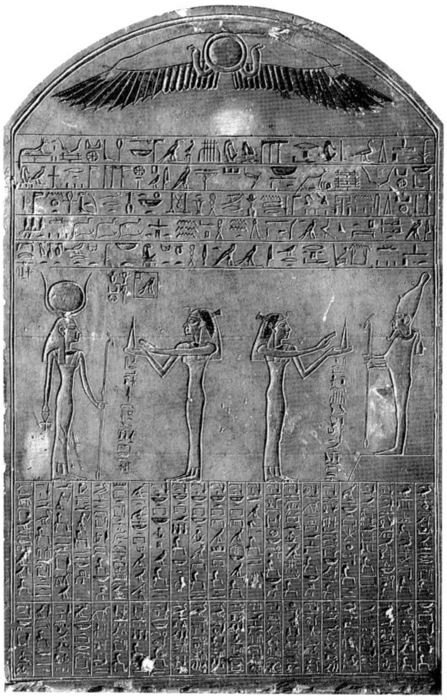

of the ruler of the Oryx nome to Hat Sehetepibre . . . to be the wife of the hereditary prince, count, ruler of the "new towns" . . . in his rank of governor of the residence city, Nehri, triumphant, revered.[94]

A daughter's marriage was so influential in making economic and political connections that it was used as a metaphor for agricultural wealth. A local governor of the First Intermediate Period stated: "I caused Gebelein to live during unfruitful years, there being 400 men [in trouble]. But I took not the daughter of a man; I took not his field."[95] Because Ptahotep's instruction refers to a wife as "a field fertile for her lord,"[96] the reading of "field" as a metaphor in this inscription appears warranted.

The early New Kingdom offers no evidence that kings' daughters married outside the court during most of Dynasty 18. Although the Egyptian rulers married princesses from other Near Eastern countries, it appears that they refused to send their daughters even to the Mitannian, Babylonian, and Hittite rulers.[97] The aristocracy of the Eighteenth Dynasty, as seen above with regard to Hapuseneb, Hatshepsut's High Priest of Amen, formed marital unions that created bureaucratic dynasties. The tombs from the first half of Dynasty 18 often listed detailed filiation for each person, so that a position within the family hierarchy was conveyed (fig. 16).

These aristocratic dynasties eventually gave way somewhat as military officers became a new type of elite. In the Nineteenth Dynasty the burial at Sakkara of Tia, the sister of Ramesses II, and her husband suggests that the practice of princesses marrying outside the royal family had been revived.[98] Tia's husband, also named Tia, was the overseer of the treasury for Ramesses II.

Unfortunately the names and titles of women and their husbands are often all that are left to us from ancient monuments. It remains unclear whether royal women could choose their own husbands or decide not to wed at all. Colloquial documents, however, such as letters and popular literature, give glimpses of the degree to which any women could determine their own lives. Very little information regarding royal women comes to us from letters, but literary settings describe some strong-willed princesses.

A princess who chose a mate for herself is found in the New Kingdom story "The Doomed Prince."[99] The princess in question was not Egyptian but was the daughter of the prince of Nahrin (Mitanni). In an ancient Egyptian version of the fairy tale "Rapunzel," the girl fell in love with an Egyptian prince (disguised as a soldier) who leaped up to the window of the seventy-cubit-high tower where she was secured.[100] Her father had announced a princely competition for his daughter's hand, to be won by the young man who reached the window.

> Now when many days had passed, the youth came to leap with the sons of the princes. He leaped, he reached the window of the daughter of the prince of Nahrin. She kissed him, she embraced him on all his body. . . . The daughter held him, and she swore by the god saying: "As Pre-Harakhti lives, if he is taken from me, I shall not eat, I shall not drink, I shall die right away!"[101]

After more threats by the father and more oaths by his daughter, the ruler allowed the Egyptian to marry the princess. "Then he gave him his daughter as wife. He gave him a house and fields as well as cattle and all sorts of good things."[102] Clearly the princess's role in persuading her father was the dominant theme in this section of the tale. At the same time, the prince *gave* his daughter to the Egyptian in the more formal sense, along with the wealth associated with her status. Although we have no information confirming that royal marriages ever were or were not love matches, it would be unlikely that many royal unions were

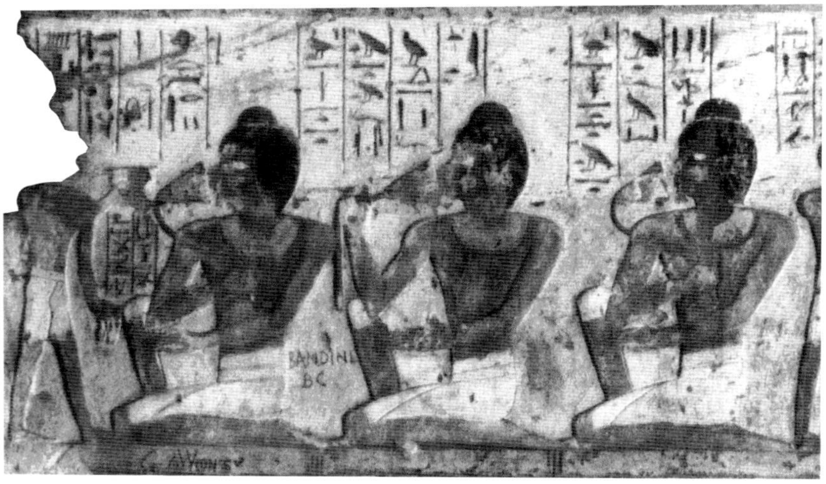

Fig. 16 Pahery's family members with specific intrafamily relationships detailed. At the banquet men and women are segregated. From El Kab, mid–Dynasty 18. Photograph courtesy of the author.

premised on affection, given the prominent roles of women in propagating and connecting the dynastic families. The carefully planned political unions described by Spalinger must have been more the norm.[103]

New Kingdom love songs are a source for popular views of love, and in one of them a girl plaintively recalls the home of her beloved. Between her and her lover stands his mother:

> If only the mother knew my heart, she would have understood by now; O Golden [an epithet of Hathor], put it in her heart, then will I hurry to my brother! I will kiss him before his companions, I would not weep before them; I would rejoice at their understanding that you acknowledge me![104]

Clearly love matches encountered social barriers, but the love songs reveal the strength of such feelings among young people in the New Kingdom.

The love songs also form a body of literature partially in "woman's voice," though not necessarily written by women. As a literary form the songs are gender-segregated—that is, they are sung by men to or about women, and they are sung by women to or about men. The setting may have been somewhat ritualized, as at weddings, funerals, or the like, with choruses of each sex singing to one another. Despite the strong sexual yearning expressed by the lyrics, the theme of inaccessibility dominates: "I passed by her house in the dark, I knocked and no one opened."[105] Although we can hear the emotion and desire in the words, we have little idea how often young people, even in simple villages, chose their mates.

Roles and offices of women

OCCUPATIONS

The Old Kingdom documents the largest number of elite women who possessed titles associating them with administration or court function. The majority of those either served royal women or were themselves royal. They include female stewards for queens and a princess, sealbearers (or treasurers), and a chief of funerary priests. Henry G. Fischer compiled and discussed administrative titles of women in the Old Kingdom, the First Intermediate Period, and the Middle Kingdom. William Ward surveyed the Middle Kingdom titles; Robins has summarized the materials in question, including the New Kingdom as well.[106]

Although Fischer concluded that both the number and the status of administrative titles held by women declined between the Old and the Middle Kingdoms, the differences in our sources for the periods must be kept in mind. Far more tomb inscriptions are available from the Old Kingdom than later; therefore the wall space was available for expanded titularies where appropriate. In addition, the large elite cemeteries near the Memphite capital provide records of men and women particularly connected to the court. In contrast, the bulk of evidence in the Middle Kingdom derives from votive stelae on which female servants and household members are identified. The space on such monuments is highly restricted; it allows only for a single designator, usually an occupation or kinship marker. The possibility that the comparison between the two eras could be skewed by our evidence is supported by the presence of fuller female titularies, including those with both "female patrician" and "countess," at provincial sites with Middle Kingdom tombs, such as Beni Hasan and Bersheh.[107] Nonetheless, it is not until the Twenty-sixth Dynasty that one can document, as in the Old Kingdom 1,500 years earlier, a few women with significant administrative titles in the service of female royalty.[108]

Only once in the Old Kingdom was the chief court function—that of vizier—ascribed to a woman.[109] Strong evidence suggests that this woman, one Nebet, never exercised the function, but rather was awarded the title, along with those corresponding to the highest court honors, after her granddaughter(s) became the mothers of Merenra and Pepy II respectively. Only once more, in Dynasty 26, is the vizierate title documented for a woman.[110] The normative pharaonic offices of chief treasurer, royal messenger, chief royal steward, city mayor, royal scribe, and general have never been attested for women. Nor did women fill the professions of artisanship at middling ranks of society: they were not chief draftspersons, nor were they sculptors, carpenters, or coppersmiths, employed by either the state or the temples. Even at the level of skilled workers, women did not perform certain jobs: they were not barbers; they were not professional gardeners (as opposed to caring for home gardens); nor do they seem to have done construction work, including brick-making. Even clothes washing was largely a male occupation, despite its tradition as a woman's profession in Western society.

Women were often conscripted as part of the government corvées to support the needs of large works projects. Papyrus Reisner I notes the presence of women brought to Thinis from a nearby town for a building project of Senusert I early in Dynasty 12. Apparently they were employed as servants, although their duties are not further specified.[111] In other Middle Kingdom documents, women appear as fugitives from corvée duty. In the reign of Amenemhat III the case of Tety, daughter of Sa-inheret, was closed by the Vizier's Scribe Dedu-Amen.[112] After Tety apparently had fled from doing agricultural work for the Scribe of the farmland of Thinis, her family was released from substitute service because she was found and returned. (The papyrus list of disposed cases included a column in which to indicate gender.)

Women employed as female domestic servants were very common (see cat. no. 29). Letters from all periods mention such employees in elite and middling households alike. The tendency for household servants to become emotionally connected with the family members they served was as strong in ancient Egypt as in Charlotte Brontë's or P.G. Wodehouse's England. Early in the Middle Kingdom, a letter inked in a bowl was written from a widow to her deceased husband, whose assistance in the next world she begged:

> As for this serving-maid Imiu who is ill—can you not fight for her day and night with any man who is doing her harm, and any woman who is doing her harm? Why do you want your threshold to be made desolate? . . . If there's no help from you, your house'll be destroyed; don't you know that it's this serving-maid who makes your house amongst men? Fight for her! Watch over her! Save her from all those doing her harm! Then your house and your children shall be established.[113]

An equally strong but opposite emotional reaction to a female house servant appears in the famous Hekanakhte letters, which were also written early in Dynasty 12. Apparently incensed at learning that the maid has been (we must suppose) taunting his second wife, Iutenheb, Hekanakhte writes to one Merisu, very likely his eldest son:

> Now make sure that the housemaid Senen is thrown out of my house—take great care—on whatever day Sahathor reaches you (with this letter). Look, if she spends one day (more) in my house—[watch it]! It is you who let her do evil against my new wife. Look, why must I nag you? What can she do against you, you five children?[114]

The latter text illustrates clearly how the emotional ties established between domestic employer and employee may often injure the social inferior: the maidservant receives the punishment that Hekanakhte believes his children deserve!

Female domestic servants did not constitute a single social rank. The girl Senen whom Hekanakhte wished to dismiss may have been of a status inferior to that of Imiu, the girl prayed for in the Letter to the Dead. Another maidservant was the subject of a letter (P. Louvre 3230b) written during the mid-Eighteenth Dynasty in the reign of Hatshepsut, by a man named Ahmose to Tey, the Chief Treasurer:

> Why is it that the maidservant who was with me has been taken away so as to be given to someone else? . . . Let payment for her be accepted for her to be with me because she is only a child and unable to work. Or let my lord command that I be made to bear her work load just like any maidservant of my lord because her mother writes me saying, "It was you who allowed my daughter to be taken away although she was there in your charge. However, it is only because she is a daughter to you that I haven't complained to my lord," so she says by way of complaint.[115]

It may be concluded that Ahmose is complaining to the Chief Treasurer because the maidservant was a servant of the state assigned by the treasury office and had been summarily reassigned. At the same time, the girl must have been handpicked by Ahmose, given that her mother considered her to be under his protection. A suggestion that the girl and her family were of a status nearly equal to Ahmose himself is evident in the mother's claim that she was a "daughter" to Ahmose and in his recognition of that claim.[116]

One final example of the ambiguity of roles and statuses among female (and no doubt male) domestic servants is found in a Dynasty 18 letter of the *wab* priest Userhet to his "sister" Resti. (The term "sister" meant female collateral relation, including both wife and true sister, as well as sister-in-law and cousin.[117]) The priest complains:

> I have noticed the woman Iupy's indifference toward me in the midst of my adherents. . . . Must I fetch for myself from [my own] house even though I have (?) no magazine [storehouse]? But [it is you who should] advise her properly so that she might be able to help you [in] whatever you [may do], for I have taken good care (of her). . . . Mind you reprimand her! Don't let her be indifferent in the midst of my adherents.[118]

The passage offers as much a clue to Iupy's social status as to Userhet's concern for his own: he views her as an inferior (to be reprimanded) and wishes his female relative to do the dressing down. Notably, however, he intends to modify the maidservant's behavior as a means of elevating his own status among fellow priests in service. The maidservant's "indifference" may be understood both as scorn for him and as evidence that his servants are ill-trained and inferior.

Textile production was a category of occupation commonly associated with females. (See the essay by Catharine Roehrig in this volume.) Scenes of female weavers are known from the Middle Kingdom tombs at Beni Hasan. From the New Kingdom there survives an exceptional letter from a female chief of entertainers to Pharaoh Sety II himself. The writer brags about garments made for the king and thanks him for sending to her a group of foreigners to be trained in weaving.[119] Nursing was also an important occupation, and women of every social class performed such duty. (See Catharine Roehrig essay and cat. no. 10b.) In the Eighteenth Dynasty, some wives of courtiers held the position of royal nurse; perhaps they wet-nursed children from the royal apartments. A male equivalent existed during this period, such that elder statesmen boasted of their title "Royal Nurse." Hatshepsut's steward Senenmut was the most famous of these tutors, having served as nurse and "Father of Nurture" to Princess Nefrura (cat. no. 43).[120]

WOMEN IN RELIGIOUS SERVICE

I have alluded here several times to female priests. At all periods in ancient Egypt women had opportunities to serve cults, and at least in the Old Kingdom they received income from priestly service in mortuary cults. It is unclear whether the most common cult role held by women of the Old and Middle Kingdoms—that of *hemet-netjer,* or servant, Priestess of Hathor (or other deities)—carried any recompense.[121] Certainly the women who held the title "Priestess of Hathor" could be of the highest social position, and elite women often chose to place this title on their tomb inscriptions (cat. nos. 5, 92). It is fair to say that it was a socially prestigious role, but the actual service performed is difficult to specify.[122]

Women of both higher and lower social classes also belonged to entertainment groups associated with temple cults, the king's own cult, and those of funerary endowments. Rhythmic chants accompanied by clapping, the hollow "choc-choc" sound of curved ivory wands knocked together, and even finger clicking characterized Old Kingdom music making. Slightly later, two musical instruments, the sistrum and the *menat,* were introduced (cat. nos. 35b,c,d; 55a). These objects were added as sound accompaniments; from the Middle Kingdom on, both instruments were particularly sacred to the goddess Hathor, although they were used in the ritual of all temples. The *menat* was a necklace of beads that was shaken to make clicking sounds; the sistrum was a frame with metal beads strung on horizontal wires. When shaken, the sistrum made a tinny rattle that complemented the clicking of beads. Clapping and singing were also part of the music, as was accompaniment by musicians on harp, double

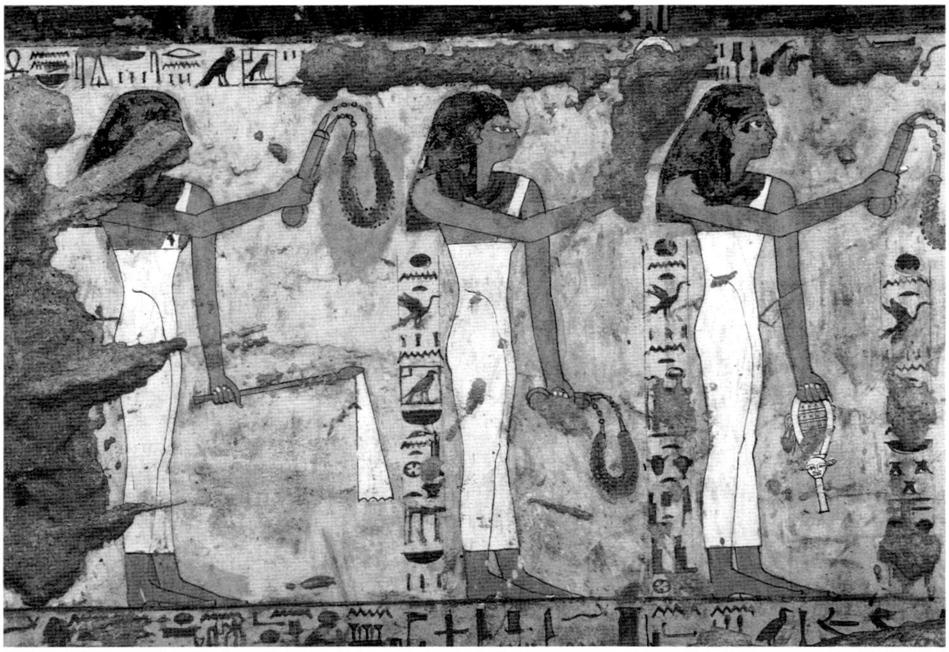

Fig. 17 The *kheneru* or *khenywt* of Hathor from Theban Tomb 82 of Amenemhat, mid–Dynasty 18, time of Thutmose III. Photograph courtesy of the author.

pipes, and lute (cat. nos. 32, 33). Dancers and acrobats of both genders also took part in the temple festivities, but these performers were probably professional entertainers, of a lower class than the women of the *kheneru*, or entertainment troupes.[123] Daughters of influential men of the Old Kingdom often belonged to these *kheneru* and performed for their fathers in banquets as well as in cult settings.[123]

In the New Kingdom the title "Servant Priestess" was abandoned, but the high-born women of Dynasties 18 through 20 served the cults as singers, either *shemayit* or *ḥesyt*. Both could be identified as members of *kheneru* (in some cases, perhaps with respect to Hathoric cults, called *khenywt)* (fig. 17).[125] The singers in the cult of Amen, the largest in the country, were called *shemayit* (cat. nos. 35a, 91); those in the cult of Hathor were termed *ḥesyt* (cat. no. 87), at least through the Eighteenth Dynasty. In the Nineteenth Dynasty, particularly in the Memphite cults, the priestesses of Hathor were called *shemayit*. Enehy (see cat. no. 35a) carried this last title.

The cults of Hathor in the New Kingdom, particularly that of the Theban goddess whose Thutmoside chapel was visited at the Beautiful Feast of the Valley, became increasingly popular with high-born women after the mid-Eighteenth Dynasty. Of 114 Eighteenth Dynasty women, only three or four held the title *ḥesyt* of Hathor during the combined reigns of Hatshepsut and Thutmose III; there were five under Amenhotep II, three under Thutmose IV, eight under Amenhotep III, and six (plus one *shemayit)* for the last reign of the dynasty.[126] The numbers, although quite incomplete, represent most of the elite tombs of Thebes and major monuments from elsewhere. An increase of participation in the Hathor cult during the time of Amenhotep III might reflect that ruler's devotion to solar cults and his celebration of Hathoric rituals at his first jubilee festival.[127]

Entertainment groups continued throughout ancient Egyptian history. The female chiefs of the *kheneru* in the New Kingdom were often wives of the high priests of the gods, and sometimes princesses.[128] Although the chief of an entertainment group was simply a choral leader, the prestige associated with the office and that of a simple singer was so great that women used these titles in daily life. For example, administrative and legal documents identify New Kingdom women as "Singers of Amen" or "Chiefs of the *khener* of Amen," and the like.

Perhaps the most infamous use of the last title appears in a group of letters from the end of the Twentieth Dynasty that concern a murder conspiracy by enemies of the ruler. There a general (perhaps Paiankh) writes in approximately the same words to Tjaroy, a scribe; to Payshuweben, an agent; and to Nodjme, Chief of the *khener* of Amen and wife of the High Priest and royal usurper Herihor:

> The general of Pharaoh, life, prosperity, health, to the chief of the *khener* of Amen-Ra, King of the Gods, the noble lady Nodjme: In life, prosperity and health and in the favor of Amen-Ra, King of the Gods! To wit: . . . I've taken note of all matters you wrote me about. As for the mention you made of this matter of these two policemen [and the charge] which you said they said [made]: join up with Payshuweben and Tjaroy, this scribe, and have these two policemen brought to my house and get to the bottom of their charges in short order and have [them] killed and have them thrown [into] the water by night. And write me about your condition. Farewell![129]

In his letter to Payshuweben, the general added at the end, "but don't let anybody in this land find out about them!"[130] Nothing at all indicates that Nodjme's functions as Chief of the *khener* of Amen were related to this politically motivated murder plot, but the social position of her office certainly does so.[131]

The office of God's Wife of Amen *(ḥemet netjer en Amen),* with its related cultic titles and administrative duties, was the largest and most powerful female priesthood in ancient Egypt. True priests as well as musicians, the God's Wives, along with the High Priest of Amen, officiated in daily rituals, approaching the sanctuary of the great god Amen-Ra himself. The God's Wife and the High Priest both burned effigies of the god's enemies, bathed in the sacred lake, and called the god to meals. At the door to the shrine, however, the king reached the doorway, and the God's Wife stood just behind with the priests (fig. 18).[132] From the beginning of Dynasty 18 through much of the New Kingdom, the holders of this office often represented the royal family, although after Hatshepsut's reign in the Eighteenth Dynasty, the role was removed from the hands of princesses and was given to kings' mothers during two reigns. From the reign of Amenhotep III through the end of Dynasty 18 the office of God's Wife was not filled. The secondary position, "God's *Hand (djeret netjer),"* was occupied, however, perhaps by Queen Tiye.[133] The functions of the God's Wife were also represented partially in the Divine Adora*trice (duat netjer);* she, as we have seen, could be a nonroyal woman, such as Senisonb, daughter of Hapuneseb, the High Priest of Amen.

The position of God's Wife was held again by royal women from the Nineteenth Dynasty. Before the Twenty-First Dynasty began, the office was held by princesses installed for the same motive of dynastic security as applied earlier to female rulers. Scholars have held for some time that the God's Wife, from the Third Intermediate Period on, was supposed to be celibate, if not a virgin. At least one woman, however, the princess Maatkara of the Twenty-First Dynasty, had a child, and indeed died in childbirth (cat. no. 77b). Therefore, if the office required celibacy, it must have done so only after Maatkara's tenure. The evidence for a "college of virgins," however, is not altogether convincing and perhaps should be reexamined.[134]

The God's Wives in Dynasties 23 through 26 were prominent in Thebes. During this time political disunity and often outright combat prevailed. The Kushite ruler Kashta installed his daughter Amenirdas I in Thebes (cat. no. 48) and had Shepenwepet, the daughter of Osorkon III, accept her as adopted heir. Through the Twenty-fifth Dynasty this method of transferring the office succeeded, such that Amenirdas I adopted Piye's daughter Shepenwepet II; she in turn adopted Amenirdas II, a daughter of Taharqa. In retaliation, the delta dynast Psamtik I, who established the Twenty-sixth Dynasty after the Assyrian defeat of the Kushites, caused Amenirdas II to adopt his daughter Nitokret. The line ended with Psamtik II's daughter Ankhnesneferibra.[135]

The God's Wives of Dynasties 25 and 26 left chapels in Karnak Temple and Medinet Habu on the West Bank at Luxor (fig. 19). Although these chapels

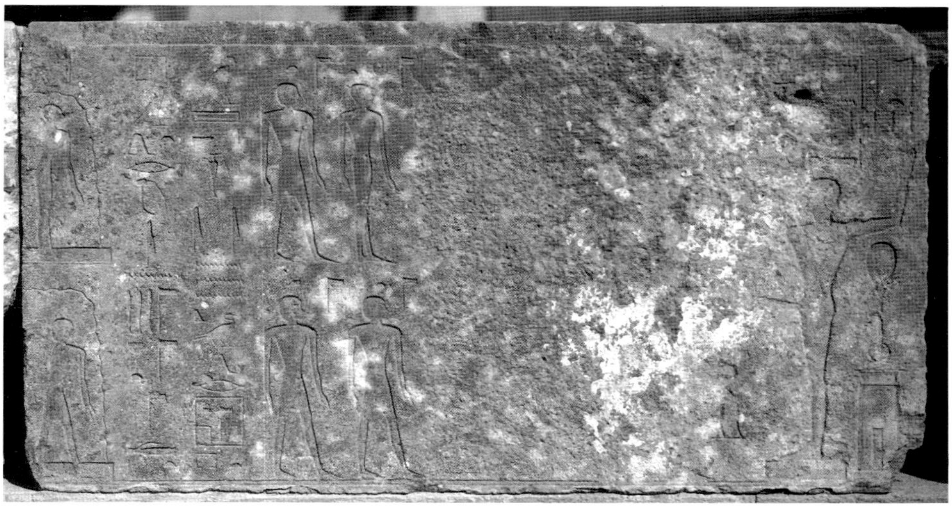

Fig. 18 God's Wife of Amen and God's Fathers (priests of Amen) bathe in sacred lake and approach sanctuary of Amen. Quartzite shrine of Hatshepsut, Karnak. Mid–Dynasty 18. Photograph courtesy of the author.

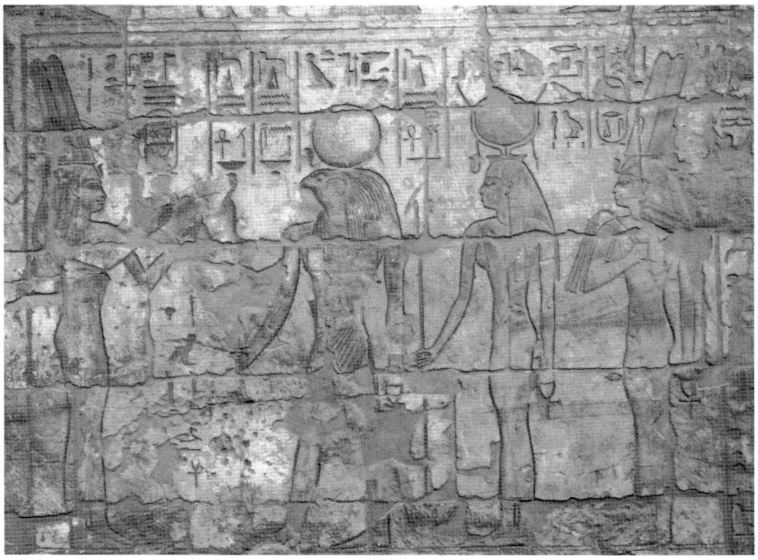

Fig. 19 Divine Adoratrice Shepenwepet II presents *maat* to deities Re-Horakhty, Isis, and the deified Amenirdis I. From Thebes West, Medinet Habu Chapel of Shepenwepet II, Dynasty 25. Photograph courtesy of the author.

have normally been termed the "tombs of the Divine Adoratrices," the scenes are often paralleled only in royal temples. In addition, the function appears to have been to memorialize deceased Adoratrices, perhaps paralleling the chapels at Karnak that honored deceased kings—and the kingship itself. Their regalia in the scenes from these monuments include a mace and the vulture headdress of queens. This same combination appears in the mid-Eighteenth Dynasty with the Queen Mother and God's Wife of Amen, Tiaa, who accompanies her son Thutmose IV in a scene of temple foundation from his sandstone court at Karnak. Nefrura also holds the mace as God's Wife, but the vulture headdress was not standard for her. Perhaps the Third Intermediate Period iconography was descended from the mid–Eighteenth Dynasty models.[136] Particularly in funerary chapels at Medinet Habu, the God's Wives appear in scenes performing rituals that had been purely royal prerogatives before this time, such as foundation ceremonies and the sacrifice of "first cuts." The institution over which they presided was enormous during these dynasties; they included employees such as bakers, brewers, goldworkers, storehouse keepers, treasurers, generals, and stewards.[137] The administration might well have been a shadow royal government that functioned in the absence of resident rulers. The Kushite kings faced military challenges from Assyria during much of the dynasty and also must have been required to spend time at home in the Sudan.

As the only royal family members resident in Thebes, these princess God's Wives were the local dynastic presence, but their individual control over the large holdings of the estates of God's Wife must remain in doubt. When Taharqa built an edifice in Karnak where the God's Wife appears as officiant, she was curiously unidentified. The stela marking Nitokret's arrival in Thebes to become the adopted daughter of Amenirdas II bore the formal language of an economic transaction providing wealth to the new officeholder. Yet the Donation Stela describing Ahmose's purchase to expand the holdings of the God's Wife of Amen for Ahmose-Nefertari had contained the guarantee that she, and she alone, could name her successor (see fig. 9). Since Psamtik I had forced the adoption on Amenirdas II, it is uncertain whether the last God's Wives wielded royal power or stood in its place.

WOMEN IN EGYPTIAN RELIGIOUS IDEOLOGY

A final topic concerns religious and cultural notions of the feminine aspect. A longer study would explore the various goddesses with whom women, particularly royal women, were associated in literary and temple texts. The most important information, however, is that in ancient Egyptian religion the female principle had several characteristics. (1) It was the second gender; the first deity had come into existence of itself and then had spewed out (or created by speech) principles of activity. The creator Atem first sneezed (or spoke) into existence the god Shu and then spit out the goddess Tefnut.[138] As twins, however, male and female were closely related, and the goddess was an energetic agent for her brother and/or father. (2) It was the protective and caring female body (or envelope) through which the sun traveled by day and night, to be reborn in the morning and swallowed up again in the evening. (3) It was the sky goddess bending over the male earth in the form of a naked young woman, a leopard with starry spots, a vulture with outstretched wings, or a heavenly cow.

The implications of the female characteristics described in cosmological texts can increase our understanding of women in Egyptian cultural terms. For example, women were primarily a vessel in the procreative process, receiving the seed and keeping it safe until the moment of birth. As evidence reveals, however, the female contributed to the successful outcome. Beliefs of the afterlife included an important sexual aspect that required copulation and impregnation of a female if any deceased person (male or female) was to have a continued existence:

> Every man who shall know this spell he shall copulate on this earth by night and day, the *ib* (heart, desire) of a woman being under him at each time of his copulating. Words to be spoken over a bead of carnelian or amethyst which is placed on the beatified deceased on his right arm.[139]

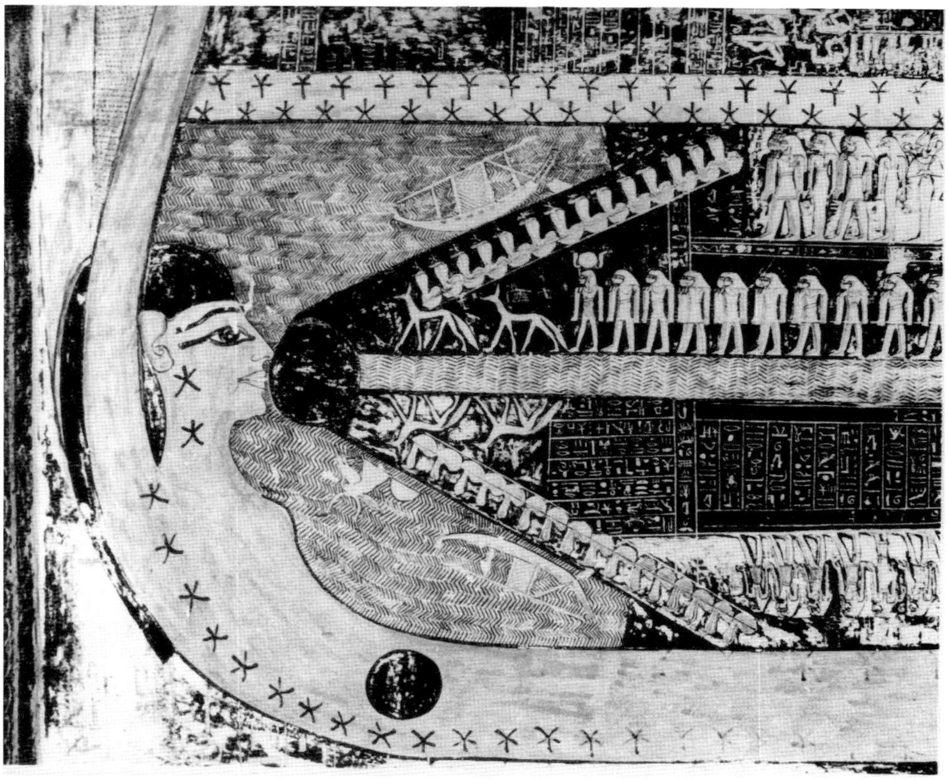

Fig. 20 Detail of ceiling depicting the birth of the sun as a winged scarab beetle from the womb of Nut, the sun as a red ball swallowed by Nut at sunset, and the consequent movement of the sun through her protective body during night. From Tomb KV 9 of Ramesses VI, Thebes West, Dynasty 20. Photograph courtesy of the author.

The result of such copulation was "that his semen might be intact on earth and that his heir might survive eternally."[140] The offspring of any procreative act was not simply the grown seed of the father kept by the woman; he or she had the *mot*her's *ib,* for it had been summoned as in Coffin Text, Spell 576. Apparently the successful sexual union combined the hearts (the organ of will, intelligence, and emotion) of both father and mother, but the *ib* with which a child was born was contributed by the mother.[141] Throughout one's life the heart was to be treated with care: when it was in balance, one could use it as a pilot (the conscience), but when it was out of place, it might lead one astray. The capacity of the heart to act for or against the person was encapsulated in a spell (Book of the Dead 30) and inscribed on large beetle-shaped amulets (cat. no. 81). These amulets, called "scarabs" after the beetle of the same name, were placed over a mummy's heart at the time of wrapping.

The following spell from chapter 30 of the Book of the Dead is intended to prevent the heart from opposing the deceased in the netherworld:

> O my heart of my mother, my heart of my mother, my heart of my transformations. Do not oppose me; do not witness against me, and do not go against me before the tribunal. Do not show yourself to be hostile to me before the keeper of the balance; for you are my Ka who is found in my body, the god Khnum who makes my limbs safe and well.

Several of the goddesses with whom these female aspects were associated (e.g., Nut, Nekhbet, Mut, Hathor) were identified with the sky through which the sun made a difficult journey by day and by night (fig. 20). The terrors of the dark sky were sometimes associated with and transformed into a protective vulture with outstretched wings who carried the sun god safely over the waters of heaven; another connection was with a large feline who docilely carried the sun on her back. The motherly aspects of these frightening beings were harnessed in the cosmology to keep order in the universe, but the potential for eruption by the violent side (as with the disord*ere*d *ib)* was always present. In the story of the Destruction of Mankind, Hathor in the form of a lioness became bloodthirsty and was bent on killing all humans.

Fig. 21 Good and bad Hathors in the form of lion-headed snake goddesses. From the birth house of Hathor at her temple in Dendera. Roman period. Photograph courtesy of the author.

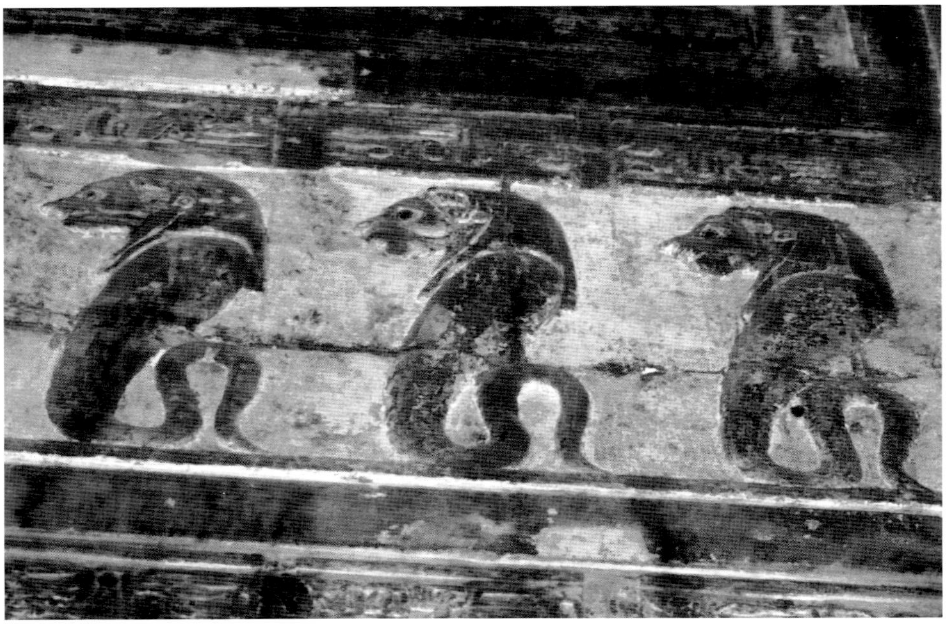

The fundamental fear of uncontrolled behavior was characteristic of Egyptian culture generally, as attested by the king's role as the keeper of order. A number of religious and literary compositions, however, amplified the dualistic character of female deities and used them as large motifs. For this reason Egyptian literature contains archetypes of the good and efficient mother, which are set beside those of the cruel and seductive stepmother. Probably these archetypes were recognized as such by the ancient Egyptians, just as they are today. Therefore literary and religious texts should be used to help us understand the entirety of Egyptian culture, but no texts or groups of texts should be taken as representing the attitude toward women. A fine example of literary amplification appears in "The Instructions of the Demotic Insinger" Papyrus:

> A good woman who does not love another man in her family is a wise woman. The women who follow this teaching are rarely bad. Their good condition comes about through the god's command. There is she who fills her house with wealth without there being an income. There is she who is the praised mistress of the house by virtue of her character. There is she whom I hold in contempt as an evil woman. Fear her on account of the fear of Hathor. . . .
>
> The work of Mut and Hathor is what acts among women. It is in women that good fortune and bad fortune are upon earth. Fate and fortune go and come when he (the god) commands them.[142]

Mistress of the House, Mistress of Heaven

Women in Ancient Egypt

CATALOGUE OF THE EXHIBITION

Notes to the catalogue

CATALOGUE SEQUENCE

The catalogue is arranged according to the four sections of the exhibition: *Public and Private Lives, Female Royalty, Goddesses,* and *Afterlife.*

MEDIUM

The term *terracotta* has been used to describe objects of fired clay. Whenever possible, all stones are listed by proper geological terms, e.g., *limestone, granite, schist,* etc. The one notable exception is the term *alabaster,* which, according to Egyptological convention, has been used to describe a lustrous white or cream calcite (calcium carbonate). The term *faience* here refers to the colored, glazed composition typically used by the ancient Egyptians in the manufacture of beads, amulets, and pendants. The term *gesso* refers to a paste prepared by mixing whiting (powdered calcium carbonate) with size or glue. The term *cartonnage* refers to a material used in the production of mummy cases, which is composed of linen or papyrus glued together in many thicknesses and usually coated with stucco; the term is also used to designate the actual mummy case.

PROVENANCE

Those objects with securely recorded provenance are recorded in one of two ways. Those known to have come from a particular site or monument are listed accordingly, e.g., "from Deir el-Bahri, Thebes, Tomb of Queen Nofru." Those objects with recorded excavation histories are qualified by the term "excavated at. . . ." Those objects whose origins may be assigned on the basis of recorded parallels or compelling circumstantial evidence are qualified by the term "probably from. . . ." Those objects with unconfirmed provenance information from museum records are qualified by the terms "reportedly from," or "said to be from." For those objects with no indication of source or origin, the term "provenance unknown" has been employed. All sites recorded in the catalogue entries are listed on the map of Egypt located on page 219.

DATE

Dating of works in the exhibition is based on the following criteria: archaeological find–context, inscriptional evidence, style, and dated comparanda and adheres to the following sequence: general chronological period (e.g., Old Kingdom), dynasty, and regnal period (e.g., reign of Amenhotep III). Absolute dates have not been used in the catalogue text; for an absolute chronology, see the chronological chart on page 218.

DIMENSIONS

All dimensions are recorded in centimeters.

INSCRIPTIONS

All ancient Egyptian texts in the catalogue proper are recorded in transliteration. The following spellings have been used in the rendering of certain ancient Egyptian names: *Ra* (for Re) and *Amen* (for Amun).

PUBLISHED REFERENCES

The published references listed under most catalogue entries are selective and are not meant to constitute exhaustive publication records for those objects. These references represent the primary and/or most recent publication(s) of those works.

CATALOGUE AUTHORS

The authors of the catalogue entries are identified by the initials at the end of each entry or group of entries:

AKC Anne K. Capel
RAF Richard A. Fazzini
GEM Glenn E. Markoe
JFR James F. Romano
DBS Donald B. Spanel
DPS David P. Silverman

Public and Private Lives

FAMILY

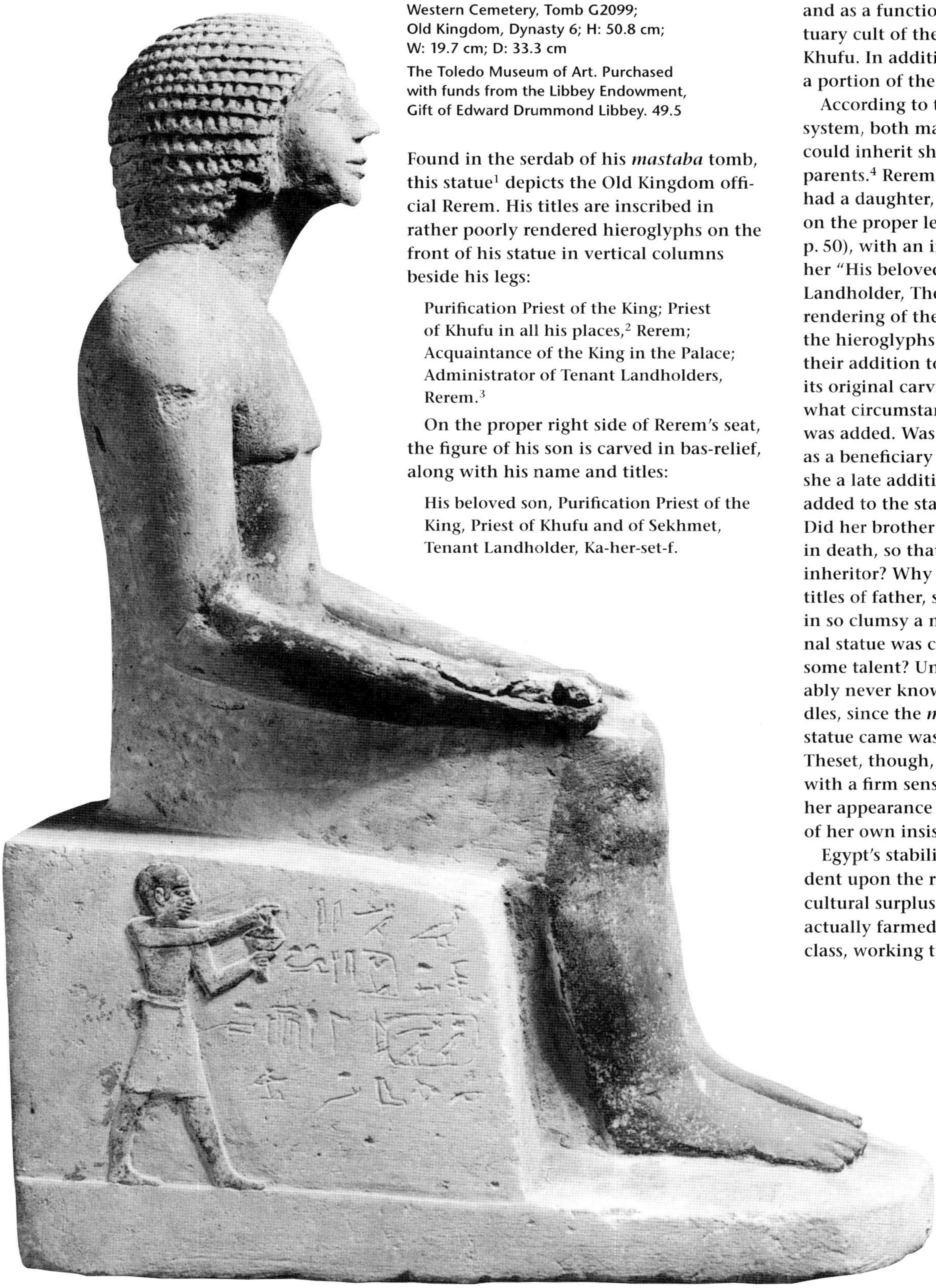

1 Statue of Rerem

Limestone with pigment; from Giza, Western Cemetery, Tomb G2099; Old Kingdom, Dynasty 6; H: 50.8 cm; W: 19.7 cm; D: 33.3 cm

The Toledo Museum of Art. Purchased with funds from the Libbey Endowment, Gift of Edward Drummond Libbey. 49.5

Found in the serdab of his *mastaba* tomb, this statue[1] depicts the Old Kingdom official Rerem. His titles are inscribed in rather poorly rendered hieroglyphs on the front of his statue in vertical columns beside his legs:

> Purification Priest of the King; Priest of Khufu in all his places,[2] Rerem; Acquaintance of the King in the Palace; Administrator of Tenant Landholders, Rerem.[3]

On the proper right side of Rerem's seat, the figure of his son is carved in bas-relief, along with his name and titles:

> His beloved son, Purification Priest of the King, Priest of Khufu and of Sekhmet, Tenant Landholder, Ka-her-set-f.

Ka-her-set-f seems to have inherited his father's offices as *wab* priest of the king, and as a functionary in the royal mortuary cult of the Fourth Dynasty king, Khufu. In addition, Ka-her-set-f received a portion of the land held by Rerem.

According to the ancient Egyptian legal system, both male and female offspring could inherit shares in the estates of their parents.[4] Rerem, in addition to his son, had a daughter, Theset. She is depicted on the proper left side of this statue (see p. 50), with an inscription that names her "His beloved daughter, Tenant Landholder, Theset." The extremely crude rendering of the figure of Theset and of the hieroglyphs seems clearly to indicate their addition to the statue sometime after its original carving. One wonders under what circumstances the daughter's figure was added. Was she not originally named as a beneficiary of her father's estate? Was she a late addition to the family and added to the statue as an afterthought? Did her brother soon follow their father in death, so that she became the sole inheritor? Why were her figure and the titles of father, son, and daughter added in so clumsy a manner, though the original statue was carved by a craftsman with some talent? Unfortunately, we will probably never know the answer to these riddles, since the *mastaba* from which this statue came was otherwise uninscribed. Theset, though, must have been a woman with a firm sense of self-respect—surely her appearance on the statue was a result of her own insistence in the matter.

Egypt's stability and wealth were dependent upon the reliable production of agricultural surpluses. Most of the people who actually farmed belonged to the lower class, working the land for a percentage

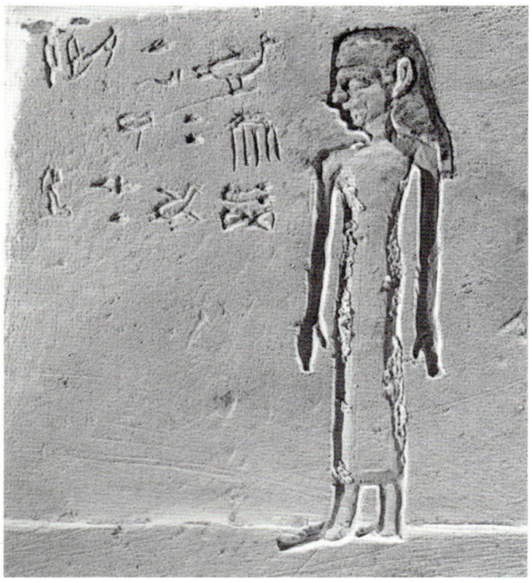

of the harvest.[5] Above them were the wealthier "managers," the *ḫntyw-š*, who administered the lands belonging to the king or to a temple.[6]

> One large group—priests, scribes, herdsmen, cultivators and (rarely) artisans—presumably worked for the owning institution [royal or religious] and each was also allotted a dues-paying farm for his subsistence. . . .[7]

Rerem probably obtained his property in this manner, due to his service to the king, or in the cult of Khufu. At his death, control of the property was passed by inheritance to his son and daughter. They did not engage in the manual labor of farming; rather, they managed the estate and collected a percentage of the harvest remaining after the owning institution received its share. The peasants who worked the land were "inherited" with the land itself, or perhaps drafted to work through the corvée system.[8]

Fischer, in his study of feminine titles of the Old and Middle Kingdoms, notes "many examples" of women who held the title *ḫnyt-š*, "Tenant Landholder."[9] Unfortunately, this frequent title gives us no indication of the size of the estate, the number of people employed to work it, and at least in this case, the wealth and status of the person to whom the title was attached. The poor rendering of Theset's figure and of the inscriptions on this statue may imply that the family's assets had diminished to a considerable degree since the time that her father had managed the estate.[10] AKC

Published: Frédérique von Känel, *Les prêtres-ouâb de Sekhmet et les conjurateurs de Serket* (Paris, 1984), 11–13, pls. I–V; Fischer, *Egyptian Studies*, 72–73, n. 25 (incorrectly cited as 49.4); Kurt T. Luckner, "The Art of Egypt, Part I," *Toledo Museum News* 14, no. 1 (Spring, 1971): 13, fig. 13.

2 Family group: Couple with granddaughter

Limestone with pigment; probably from Thebes; New Kingdom, Dynasty 18; H: 30 cm

The Metropolitan Museum of Art. Gift of Mrs. S.W. Straus, 1925. 25.184.8

The family was the basic social unit in ancient Egypt, and parents expressed love for their children and grandchildren by representing offspring on funerary monuments[1] so that the family might remain together throughout eternity. Family statues are known beginning in Dynasty 5[2] and continue through pharaonic history.

Here Ked-Amen, an official in the cult of the deity Amen, is depicted with his wife, the Mistress of the House Nebet-Yunet, and their granddaughter Mutnefret. Ked-Amen and Nebet-Yunet are seated on a chair with a high back. He wears a wig with elaborate undercurling at the neck and a long, simple kilt with an inscription[3] requesting a share from the offerings of Amen:

> May everything that comes from the altar of Amen be for the *ka* of the hall-keeper of Amen, Ked-Amen.[4]

Nebet-Yunet, whose name means "Lady of Dendera"—a reference to the goddess Hathor—wears a long, heavy wig. A broad collar is indicated in relief on her chest, and her dress is a long, straight sheath with straps. The inscription on her garment mentions her wish to have a portion of the offerings made to Hathor:

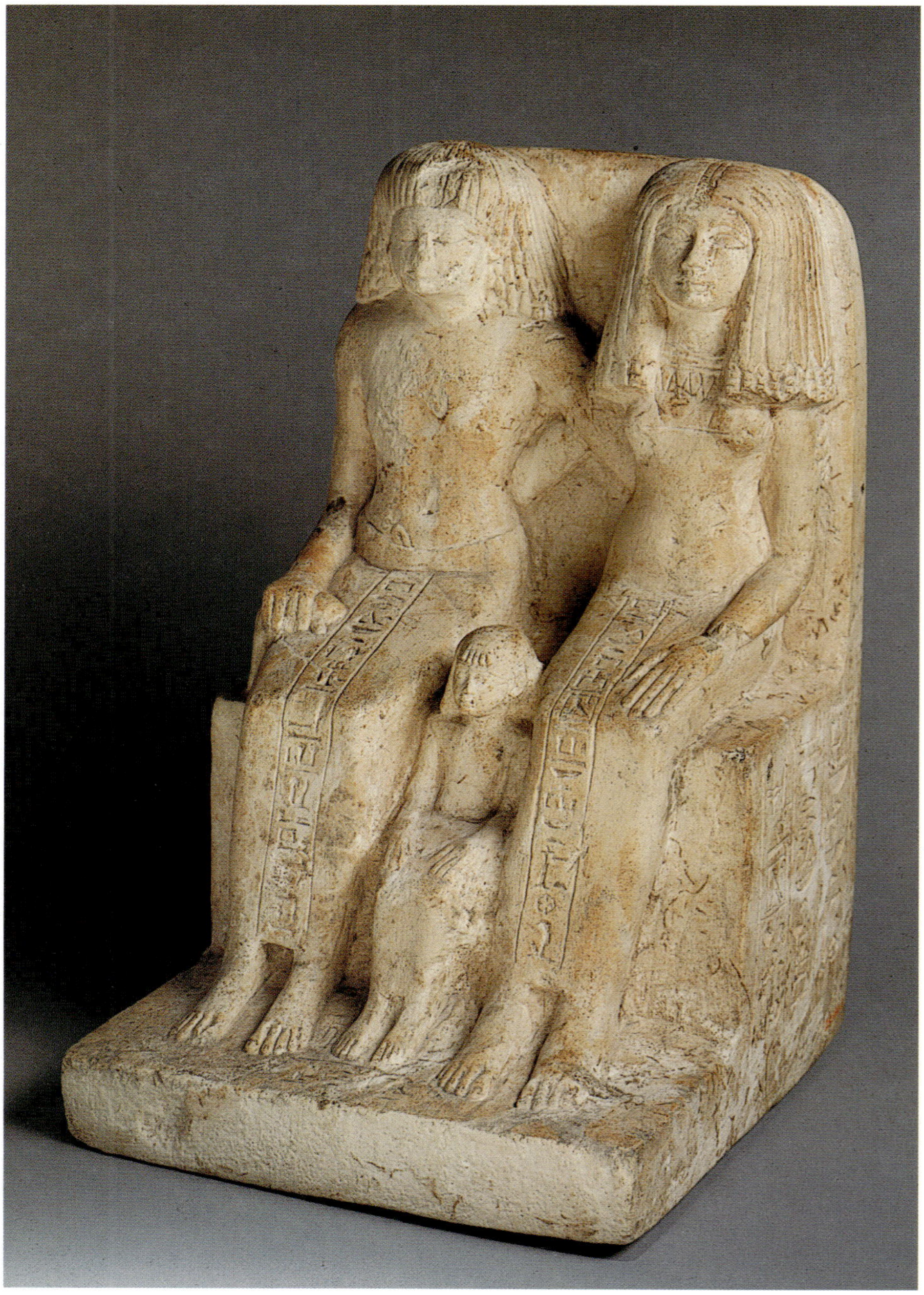

> May everything that comes from the offering-table of Hathor be for the *ka* of the Mistress of the House, Nebet-Yunet.[5]

Husband and wife hold one another about the waist; their free hands rest on their knees.

Mut-nefret is seated on her own little chair between her grandparents' legs. Before her, on the base of the statue, is this inscription:

> The daughter of her [Nebet-Yunet's] daughter, Mut-nefret.

Like her grandmother, Mut-nefret wears a long, simple dress, but without inscription. Her hair is gathered into a sidelock, a convention for depicting young children in Egyptian art;[6] on her forehead rests a row of curls similar to that worn on occasion by the goddess Bat.[7]

In ancient Egypt, parents hoped for the births of many healthy children. Though sons are virtually always specified in instructional literature,[8] or depicted (where sex can be determined) with votive female figurines,[9] it is clear that daughters and granddaughters were also desired and esteemed.[10] In ancient Egyptian society, where the home was the center of production for all of the food and clothing required by a family, parents must have greatly valued daughters' assistance in performing the numerous household chores: fetching water, grinding grain, preparing bread and other foods, weaving and sewing garments and linens, attending to livestock, and watching over younger siblings. Not only did daughters help with the family work, they were also expected to help support their parents in old age,[11] to arrange for their proper burial,[12] and to aid in their parents' and ancestors' continued existence in the afterlife with offerings and prayers at the tomb.[13] In return, women expected a share in the division of their parents' property and offices.[14]

This family statue portraying Ked-Amen and Nebet-Yunet was dedicated, in fact, by their daughter, Duat-nefret:

> A royal offering of Amen and Osiris, the great god, ruler of eternity, giving bread, water, incense on the fire, cool water, wine, milk, fowl, forelegs, and choice cuts of meat for the *ka* of the Hall-Keeper of Amen, Ked-Amen, justified, and the Mistress of the House, his beloved, Nebet-Yunet, justified. Their daughter, Duat-nefret, justified, is the one who has caused their name[s] to live [by commissioning this statue].

It is not unusual that a woman would want to immortalize her deceased parents and the child, who quite possibly was her own daughter, in a funerary statue that would enableem, according to Egyptian belief, to continue in the next life.[15] It is noteworthy, however, that Duat-nefret was able financially (perhaps through inheritance) to commission the statue according to her wishes, and apparently to do so without the approval of a male, whether husband or relative. This is a clear indication of women's economic and legal status in ancient Egypt.[16] AKC

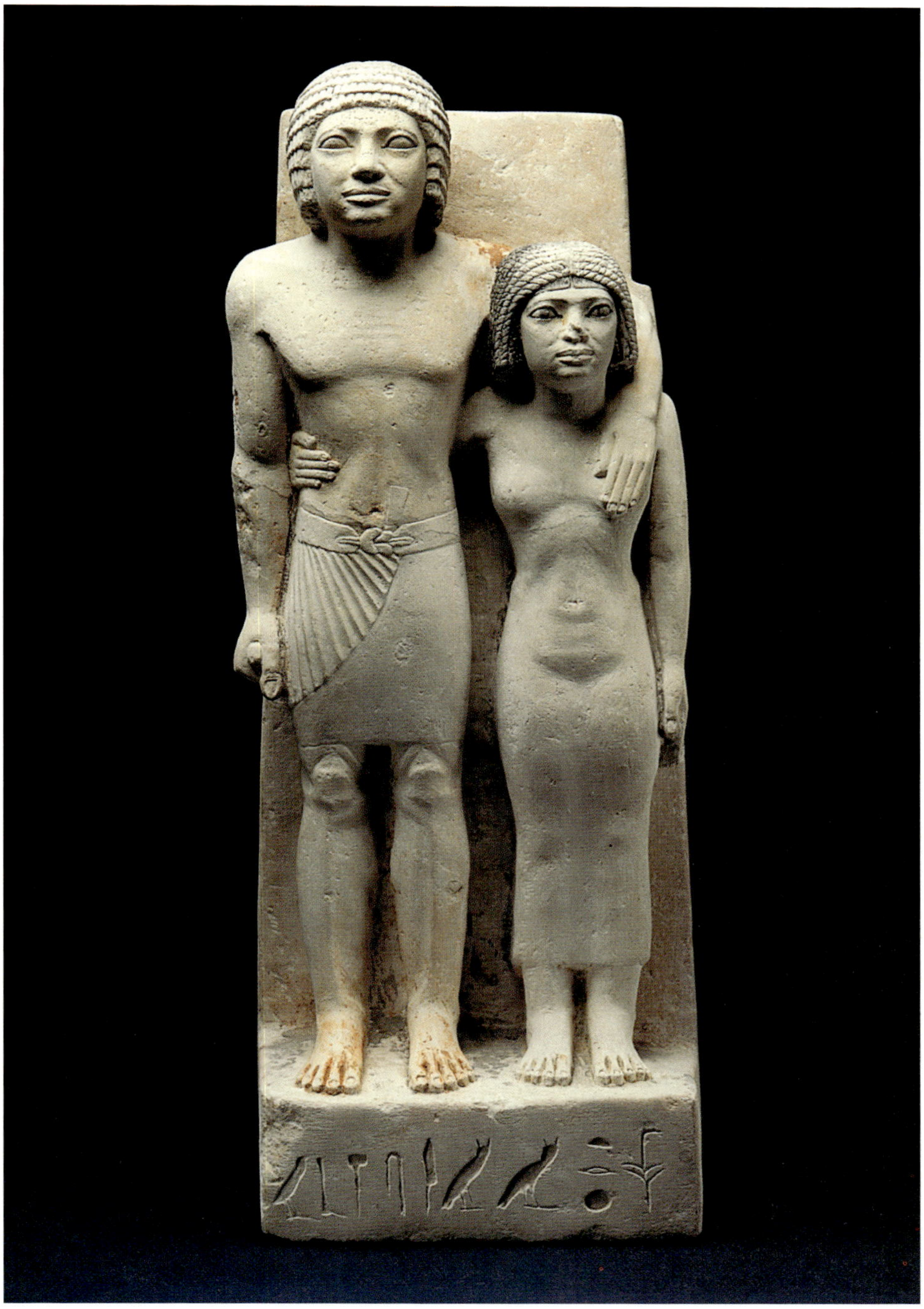

3 a Pair statue

Limestone with pigment; provenance uncertain; said to be from Giza; Old Kingdom, Dynasty 5 or 6; H: 62 cm

The Metropolitan Museum of Art. Rogers Fund, 1948. 48.111

3 b Seated statue of Sabu

Limestone with pigment; provenance uncertain; said to be from Giza; Old Kingdom, Dynasty 5 or 6; H: 48.2 cm

Philadelphia Museum of Art. Louis E. Stern Collection. 1963.181.257

A popular artistic composition during the Old Kingdom, the group sculpture or so-called family statue most often features a man and a woman, usually his wife, and sometimes also their children. The exam-

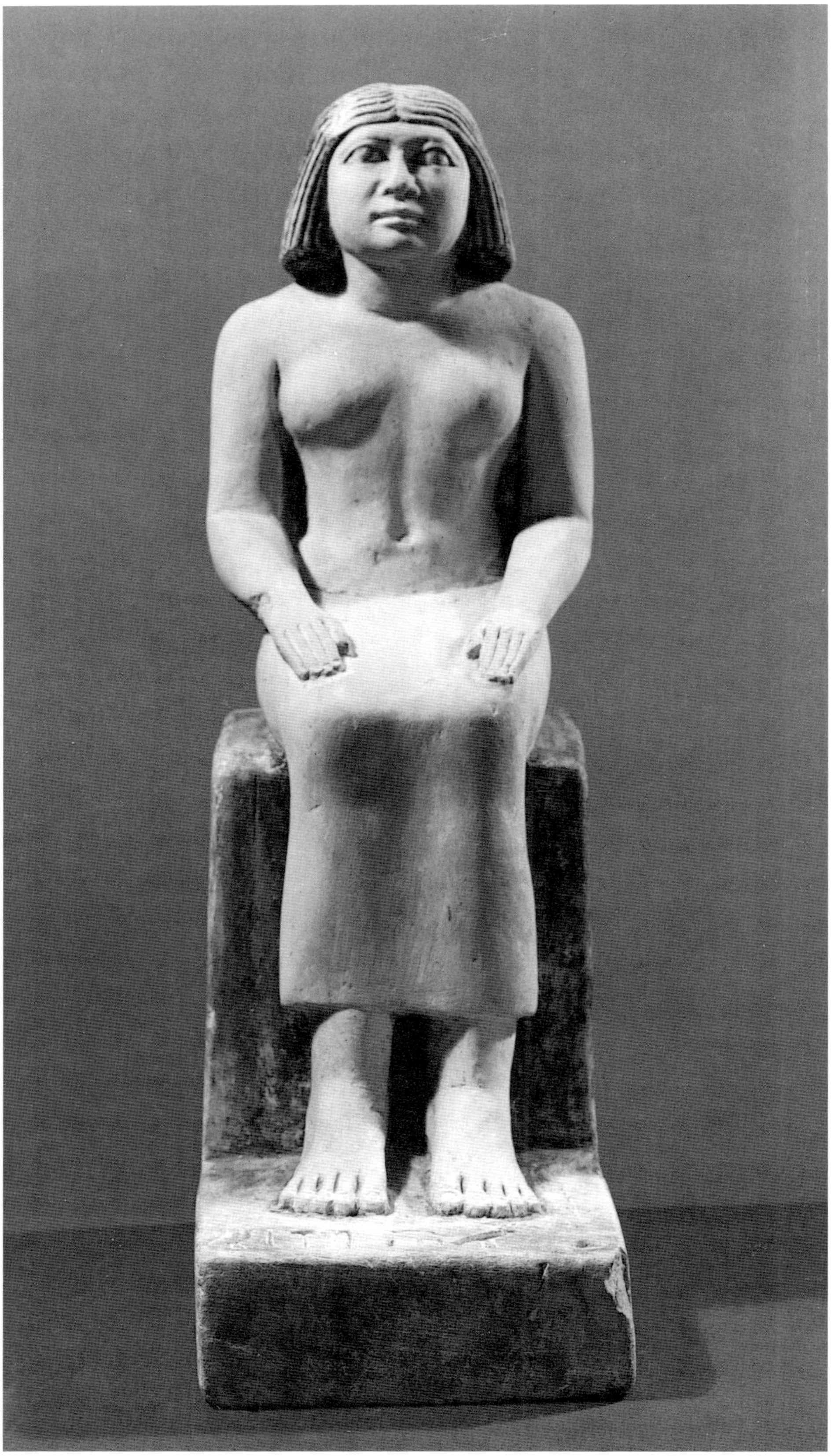

ple in the Metropolitan Museum of Art, New York, is highly significant not only for its aesthetic qualities but also, together with the statue of the seated woman from the Philadelphia Museum of Art, for the issues concerning gender equality in the Old Kingdom that it raises.

On the New York statue, a man who appears to have been named Memy-Sabu and who held the common title "King's Acquaintance" stands to the proper right of an unnamed woman, who is often said to be, but is not necessarily, his wife.[1] Many other group statues show the same configuration. In general, the right side was the more prominent position, not only in ancient Egypt but also in other cultures. Nonetheless, women sometimes also occupy the right side in Old Kingdom group sculptures; hence, the importance of the right side is not completely clear.[2]

The issue of disparities in stature is perhaps less equivocal.[3] Although the man and the woman are often depicted at the same height in Old Kingdom group sculptures, the man is frequently taller, as in the Memy-Sabu composition. The difference in height may be no more than an accurate reflection of the particular people involved. In at least one case, the woman is taller than the man.[4] On the other hand, seated male figures are at least as tall as the female figure(s) or taller.[5] An important adjustment in height is found in the famous Old Kingdom statue of the dwarf Seneb and his family.[6] Because Seneb's wife was not a dwarf, she would have been much taller than her husband had both been depicted standing. Consequently, the artist cleverly seated both figures on a high pedestal, raising Seneb to his wife's elevation. He is also considerably larger than his son and daughter. Therefore, during the Old Kingdom, the treatment of height appears to have been a gender disparity.

The most significant aspect of the Memy-Sabu statue is its display of requited affection, which is extraordinarily rare in Old Kingdom group statues and underscores a second area of inequality between the sexes in Old Kingdom representations. Until the Middle Kingdom, the female almost always clasps the male around the waist or holds his arm, shoulder, or hand but to no avail, because the man keeps his hands to himself. His restraint reverses the hierarchy of sentiment dominant elsewhere in Egyptian thought.[7]

Until the latter half of the New Kingdom, love was extended from a superior to an inferior. Deities loved kings, who loved mortals. In the opposite direction, lesser beings "adored" and "praised" their higher-ups. During the Ramesside Period, the strictures loosened, and love was reciprocated. Old Kingdom pair statues of private persons—and of some royal persons—invert the prevailing ethos because males are embraced ("loved") by the female.[8] Thus, the Memy-Sabu pair statue and a very few other remarkable sculptures are double reversals, in effect, because the man, as the superior figure, extends gestures of love or intimacy.[9] The social dynamic behind this configuration becomes circular. Although Memy-Sabu's attitude is highly unusual for Old Kingdom pair statues of nonroyal individuals, it is otherwise completely normative for Egyptian protocol.

Memy-Sabu's embrace—as endearing as it is unexpected—and the absence of identification for the woman may indicate that the statue comes from her tomb or from her section of the family's tomb. Apparently her name would not have been necessary because it was self-evident from the context of her burial.[10] If the pair statue came from the woman's own tomb, decorum perhaps dictated that Memy-Sabu extend a gesture of appreciation because he was the "guest."[11] Etiquette possibly also determined Memy-Sabu's posture. Although men are very often shown in a striding pose, Memy-Sabu stands with both feet together, as does the woman. The significance of his stance is not clear. In other pair statues, the man has his feet together but does not embrace the woman; conversely, when the man requites the woman's affection, he takes a stride.[12]

In examining the question about the origin of the Memy-Sabu statue, the sculpture from the Philadelphia Museum of Art should be considered. Although both statues are said to come from the same tomb at Giza at "the extreme north edge of the West Cemetery," no proof is forthcoming.[13] The Philadelphia sculpture depicts only a woman and only the name "Sabu." In addition to "King's Acquaintance," which is written on the New York statue, the Philadelphia sculpture bears the title *imy-pr* ("Steward," "Chamberlain"). Three possibilities exist: First, the simplest explanation is that Sabu is a short form of Memy-Sabu. Second, the name may refer to a different man altogether, perhaps a relative of Memy-Sabu.[14] Third, because a statue of a woman inscribed only for a man is rather unusual, both the title and the name may belong to the woman.[15] Although women did not frequently hold the position of *imy-pr,* Old Kingdom examples are known.[16] In the inscription on the Philadelphia statue, neither title has the feminine declension *-t,* but orthographical exactitude was never observed strictly or consistently in ancient Egypt.[17]

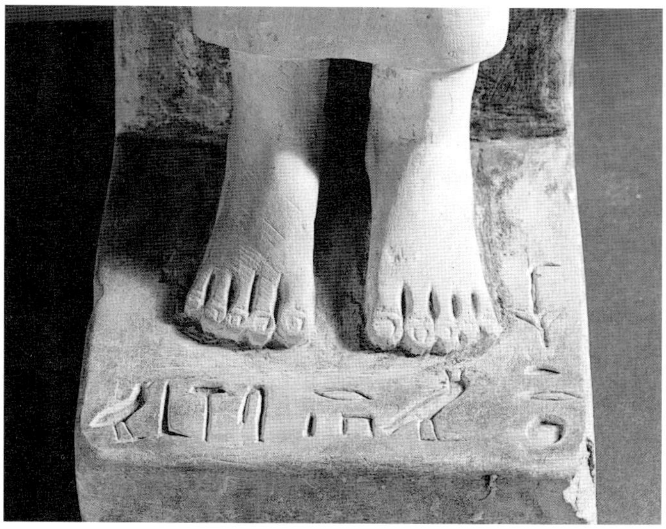

Whether one or both of the sculptures come from a woman's burial is uncertain. If a person's name could be omitted from a sculpture because it was "redundant" in the ambience of the burial, why do countless inscriptions on tomb statues and tomb walls include the name of the tomb owner? Furthermore, many group sculptures from men's tombs include the names of both the male and the female.[18] If the woman in the New York sculpture is the tomb owner and hence the more important person, it is perhaps noteworthy that she is of smaller stature than the man and stands to his left.

Counterarguments are possible. Regardless of context, many group sculptures have no names at all. Memy-Sabu's greater height—again—may mirror reality. The sculpture in the Metropolitan Museum may have been part of a pair positioned symmetrically around some architectural feature of the tomb such as a doorway, corridor, or false-door stela. In the other sculpture, the woman would have stood to Memy-Sabu's right, and in both, she would have been closer to the central item that the statues flanked. The woman's diverted gaze—to her left—perhaps relates to its original position in the tomb.[19]

Sufficient traces of pigment indicate that both sculptures were painted in the traditional gender-specific hues—red or red-brown for men and yellow for women. According to one explanation for this distinction, Egyptian men worked outdoors and thus developed deeper tans than women, who stayed around the house. Some Old Kingdom representations show yellow-skinned Egyptian men whose bulky proportions indicate less stressful work performed indoors. Furthermore, in several instances men who have just had haircuts are shown with yellow- or light-skinned scalps, which contrast with the red flesh of the body.[20] Under Egypt's fierce sun, however, few persons would have remained pale-faced; therefore the representation of skin color may have been more symbolic than accurate. Among several values, red had connotations of vitality, and yellow suggested immortality and possibly also beauty.[21] DBS

Published: Nadine Cherpion, "Sentiment conjugal et figuration à l'Ancien Empire," in *Kunst des Alten Reiches,* 37d and pl. 8c; Henry G. Fischer, "Anatomy in Egyptian Art," *Apollo* 82 (Sept. 1965): 173, fig. 6; Fischer, "Redundant Determinatives in the Old Kingdom," *MMJ* 8 (1973): 14 and fig. 12; Fischer, "An Elusive Shape within the Fisted Hands of Egyptian Statues," *MMJ* 10 (1975): 16, fig. 9; Fischer, "The Protodynastic Period and Old Kingdom in The Metropolitan Museum of Art," in *Kunst des Alten Reiches,* 84–85, 86; Hayes, *Scepter,* 1: 110; Howard Hibbard, *The Metropolitan Museum of Art* (New York, 1986), 36, no. 56; *The Metropolitan Museum of Art: Ancient Egypt and the Near East* (New York, 1987), 20; Nora E. Scott, "Memy-Sabu and His Wife," *BMMA* 7 (1948–49): 95–100.

4 Double *shabti* of Bener-merut and Ikhem

Gabbroic rock, possibly serpentine; provenance unknown; New Kingdom, Dynasty 18, reign of Thutmose III; H: 22.4 cm

The Metropolitan Museum of Art. Rogers Fund, 1944. 44.4.73

This handsome sculpture belongs to a class of double *shabti,* popular in the mid– to later Eighteenth Dynasty, which depicts double mummiform figures of a male and a female positioned against a stela-shaped back tablet.[1] Most of the surviving examples depict a husband and wife, who are rendered separately, with their arms crossed on their chests. Occasionally the wife embraces her husband.[2]

The present example is relatively rare because it depicts a mother and a son: Ikhem and Bener-merut. In physical appearance the two figures are quite similar. Bener-merut wears the Osirian false beard, while Ikhem is beardless. Ikhem's face also appears somewhat softer and fuller than her son's.[3] Hieroglyphic texts recording the traditional *shabti* spell, drawn from Chapter 6 of the Book of the Dead, are inscribed over both figures. The texts are identical save for the owners' names and the use of the feminine pronoun and feminized form of the word *shabti* in Ikhem's text.[4] The vertical inscription between the two figures furnishes the names, titles, and familial relationship of the two individuals. It reads: "The Overseer of Works and Chief of the Royal Crafts, Bener-merut, born of the Lady of the House, Ikhem."

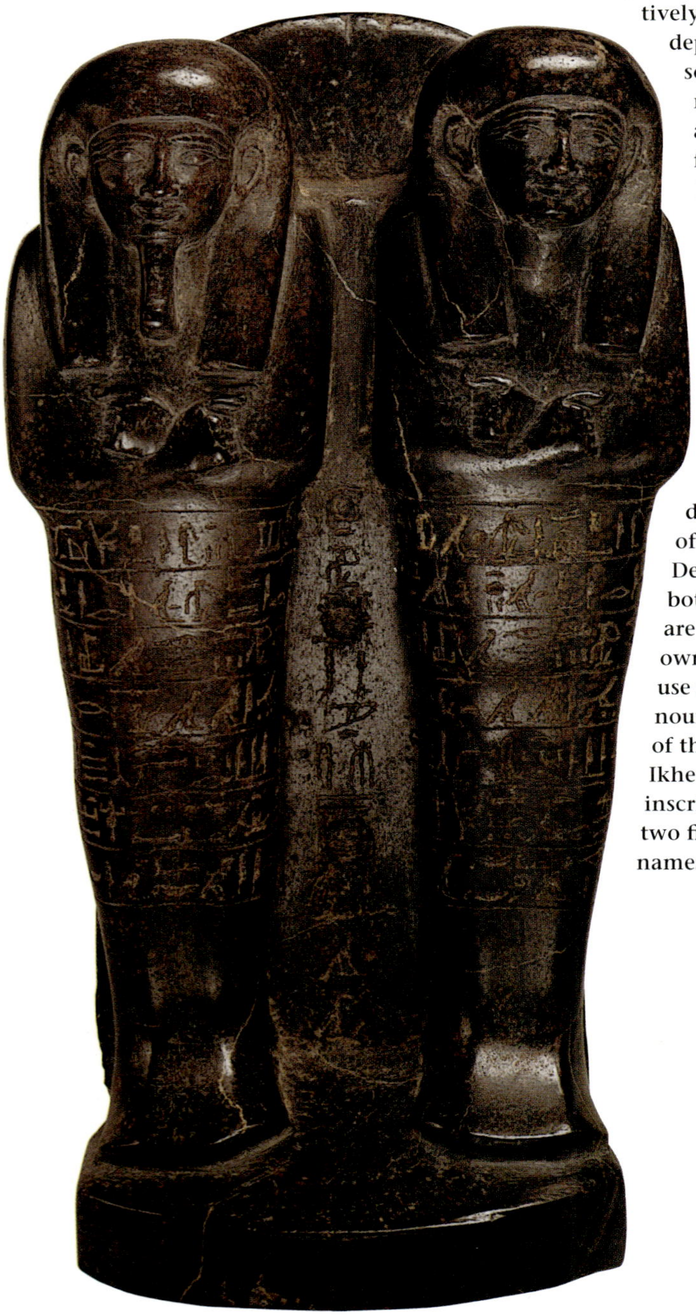

Bener-merut, as recorded on other monuments and inscriptions, was a high-ranking official who served as Overseer of the Treasury and Overseer of All Works of the King under Thutmose III.[5] His close relationship to Thutmose is reflected in one of his subsidiary functions: he served as tutor of Thutmose's daughter, the Princess (later Queen) Meryt-Amen.[6] The fact that a prominent official elected to have himself depicted on his *shabti* alongside his mother underscores the respect in which he held her.

Unfortunately we know nothing of Ikhem beyond her title *nbt pr,* "Mistress of the House." Interestingly, her name, as it occurs in the *shabti* spell and the central inscription, is a secondary addition, apparently written over the name Tekh-em-sha ("Intoxicated in the Field"), which is preserved elsewhere on the *shabti* inscription. The shortened version "Ikhem" apparently is the owner's nickname; the reason for the insertion of the shortened name is unclear. GEM

Published: Hayes, *Scepter,* 2: 130, fig. 68.

5 Statuette of a noblewoman

Limestone; provenance unknown; Middle Kingdom, Dynasty 12; H: 16.5 cm

The Saint Louis Art Museum. Purchase. 30:1924

In the Middle Kingdom, individual portrayals of women of nonroyal rank were relatively rare.[1] In most instances, women were depicted in the company of their husbands or fathers. Many of the extant statues from this period that depict an unaccompanied female represent women of elevated status or social standing. Such was apparently the case with the present statuette, which depicts a woman named Itef.

In conventional fashion, Itef wears the archaic dress of the Old Kingdom, consisting of a tube of linen supported by two broad straps over the shoulders and breasts.[2] Her attenuated proportions typify the style of the Twelfth Dynasty. Her

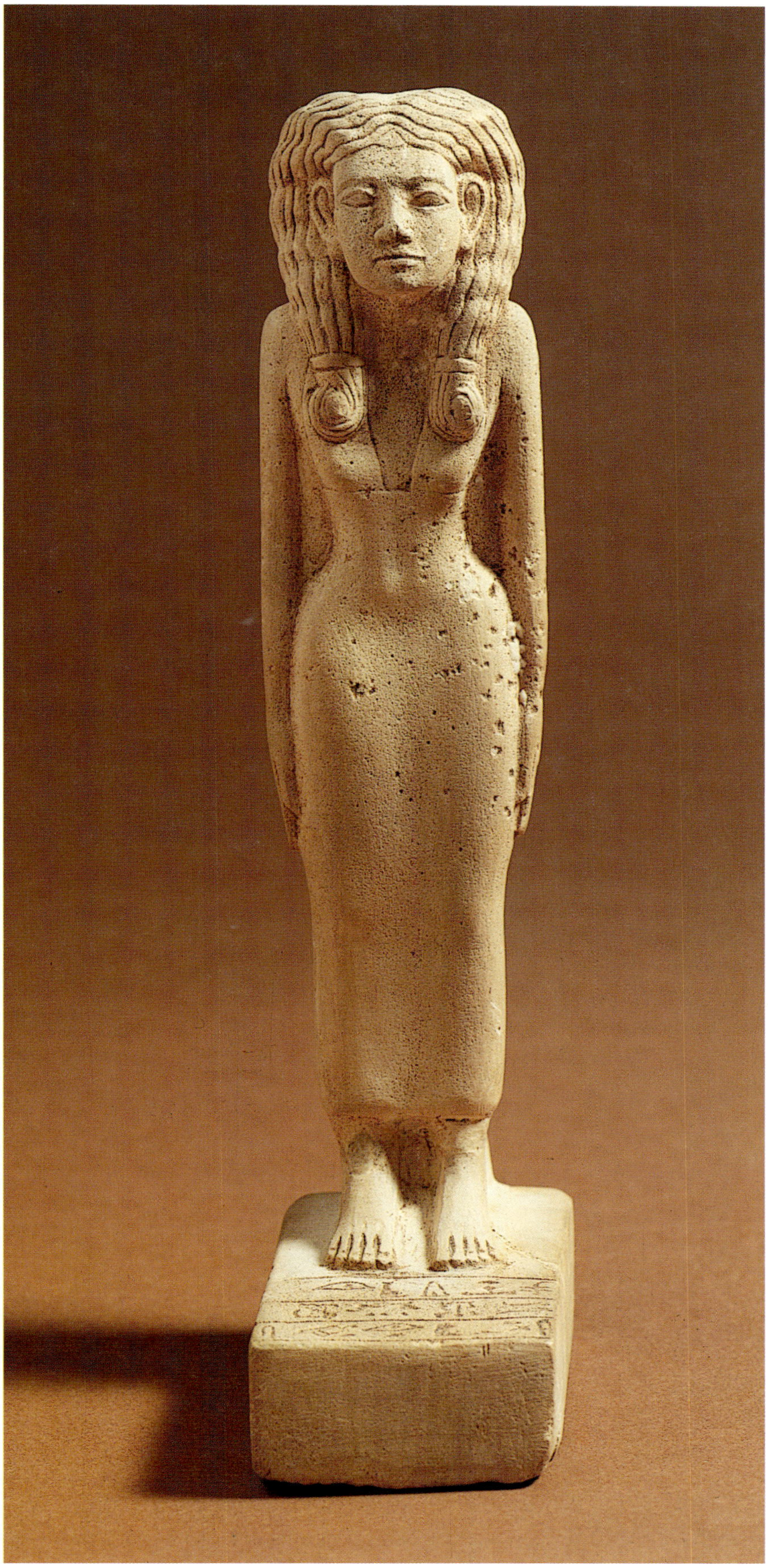

small breasts and narrow waist are characteristic of the Middle Kingdom. Like most nonroyal female sculpture, she is small in scale; the fine quality and vigor of the carving, however, are reminiscent of works of a larger size.

Itef's sober gaze reflects the austerity of the Middle Kingdom sculptural style.[3] Her facial features are framed by a massive wig of undulating locks that drape over her back and fall forward over her shoulders. Her hair in front is bound into two thick tresses, drawn behind the ears, which terminate in large, ribbon-bound spirals wrapped around disk-shaped ornaments.[4] Prominently associated with representations of the goddess Hathor (cat. nos. 54a,b and 55a,b),[5] this scroll wig makes its first appearance at this time in depictions of female royalty and aristocracy.[6] In all likelihood, Itef's hairstyle is worn in imitation of the goddess'.[7]

The inscription on the base reads: "An offering which the king gives to Osiris, that he might give an invocation-offering of bread and beer, oxen and fowl to the *ka* of Itef." The offering to Osiris is formulaic and conventional. The name of the deceased, It or Itef,[8] a man's name, which means "[his] father," is unexpected here. The inscription ends by stating that the statue was made by "his" mother.[9] Thus, we have a rather uncommon instance of a funerary statuette commissioned by a mother for her daughter.[10] GEM

Published: S.M. Goldstein, *St. Louis Art Museum Bulletin*, n.s. 19, no. 4 (1990): 11.

6 Painting of the Lady Tjepu

Paint on gesso over mud plaster; Thebes, Tomb 181 ("The Tomb of Two Sculptors"); New Kingdom, Dynasty 18, reign of Amenhotep III; H. of figure: 30.2 cm

The Brooklyn Museum. Charles Edwin Wilbour Fund. 65.197

The subject of this tomb painting fragment is the Lady Tjepu, whose name is partially preserved behind her head.[1] As the tomb records, Tjepu, who held the title "Mistress of the House," was the mother of Nebamen, one of two sculptors commemorated in this unusual tomb setting at Thebes.[2] The present fragment preserves the upper torso of Tjepu, who was originally represented in attendance behind Nebamen. As the tomb paintings on the site originally revealed, she assisted her son in worship during the annual ritual of the Beautiful Feast of the Valley celebrating the god Amen's annual visit to the Theban necropolis.[3] In this capacity,

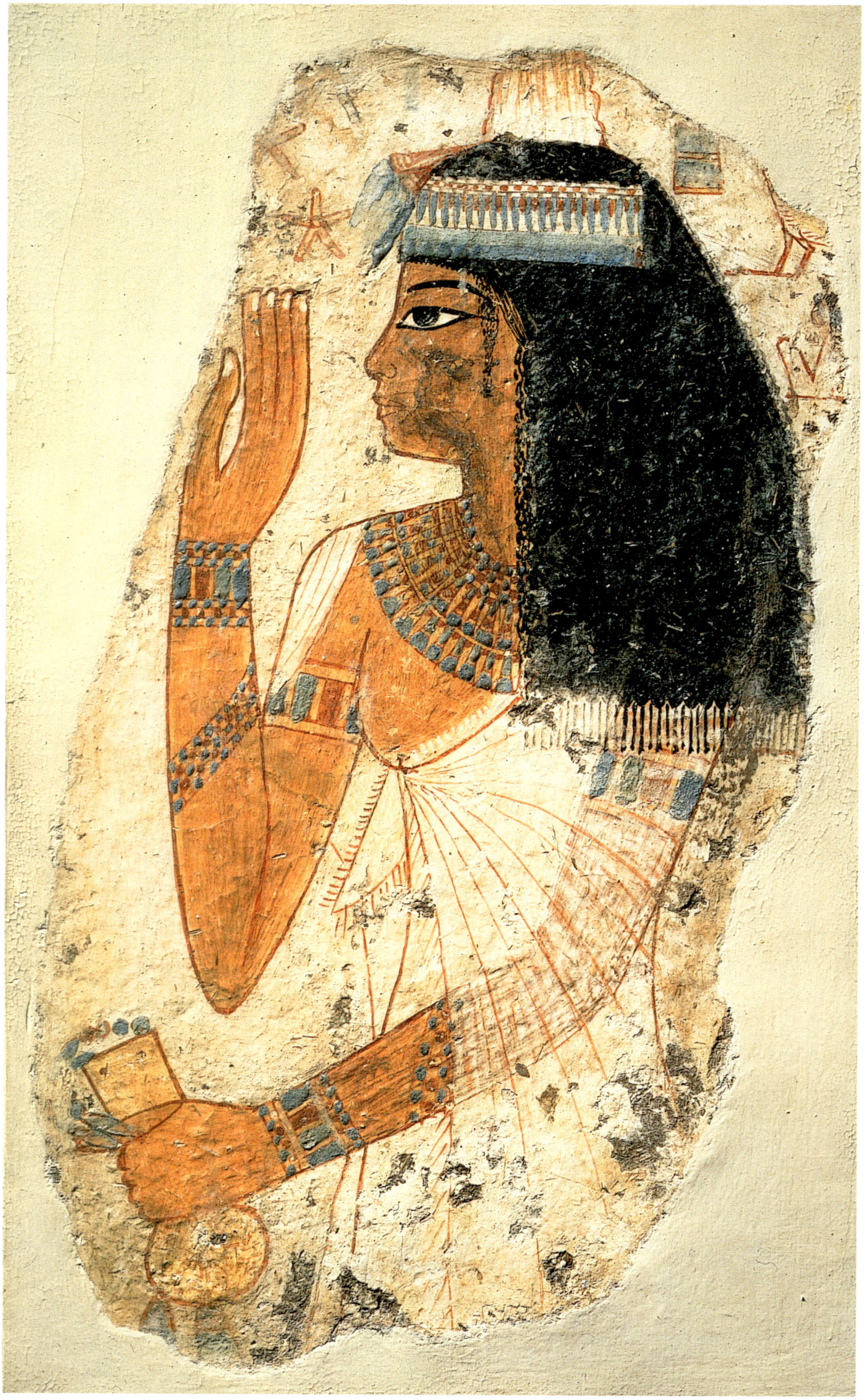

she stands with her right hand upraised in a gesture of blessing or salutation; in her left hand she holds a *menat* necklace and counterweight (cat. no. 35c,d).

Despite her mature age, Tjepu is idealized, according to contemporary fashion, as a young woman. Dressed in a diaphanous white linen gown and mantle, she is elaborately coiffed and outfitted with an *usekh* collar and a variety of armlets.[4] On her head she wears a beaded chaplet and a perfumed cone of fat, which cooled and scented the body as it melted. Tjepu's face is framed by fine wavy strands of hair; these and the little wisp at the brow represent her own hair escaping from under her wig.

The prominent place occupied by Tjepu in the present scene underscores the esteem in which she was held by her son, Nebamen.[5] Tjepu's motherly appearance here as companion of the deceased is relatively unusual; normally it is the wife who appears at the tomb owner's side in such tomb scenes.[6] The situation in Tomb 181 is further complicated by another unusual situation: two men of identical title and occupation share a single tomb chamber. In addition, both men are associated pictorially with a single woman, Henetnofret, who is identified as *senet,* a term denoting both sister and wife. The tomb's excavator, Norman de Garis Davies, speculated that Henetnofret served successively as the wife of each tomb owner, Apuki and Nebamen, and that she may have supervised the decoration of this joint tomb for her husbands.[7] Another possible explanation is that Henetnofret was Apuki's wife and Nebamen's sister.[8] In any case, the tomb illustrates the influential roles that both wives and mothers played in the funerary cult of the deceased. GEM

Published: Davies, *Tomb of Two Sculptors,* 29–31, pls. 3, 5, 8; Fazzini et al., *Ancient Egyptian Art,* no. 43.

7 Lady with a large wig

Schist; provenance unknown, reportedly from modern Benha (near ancient Athribis), about 50 km north of Cairo; Late Period, fourth century B.C.; H: 56.5 cm; W: 22.9 cm; D: 26 cm

Virginia Museum of Fine Arts, Richmond. The Adolph D. and Wilkins C. Williams Fund. 55.8.13

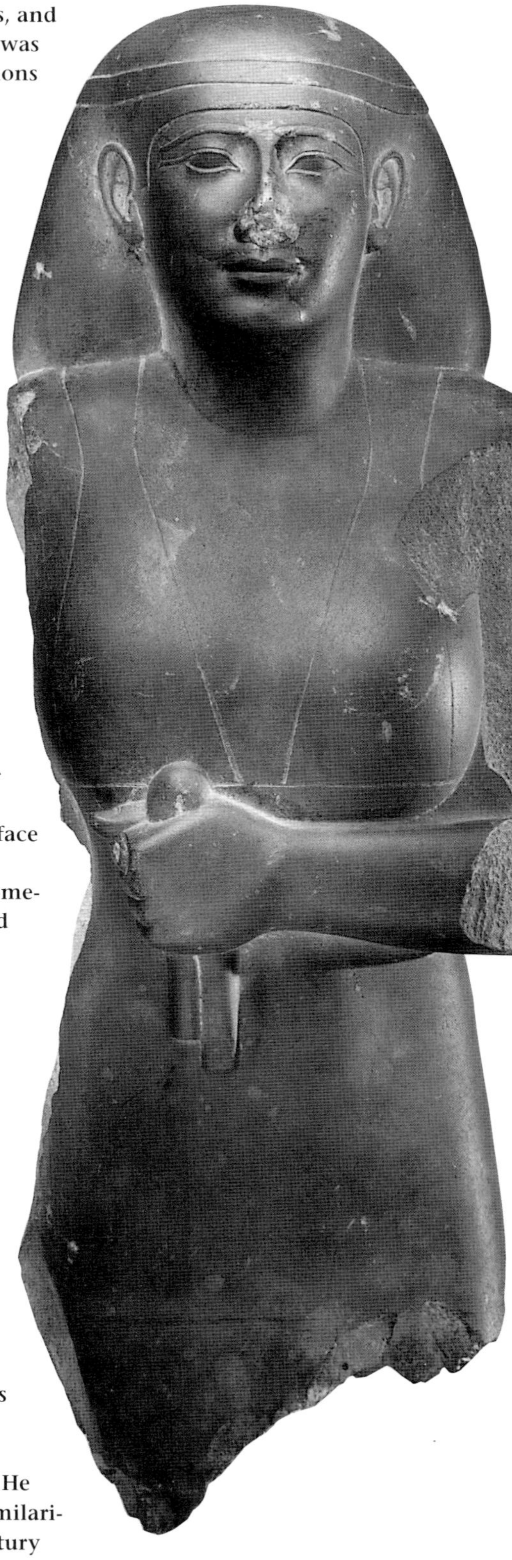

This sculpture represents a woman holding a kerchief to her chest. She wears a broad wig encircled by a fillet bound in the back so as to leave two streamers, and a dress supported by two halters. As was very often the case with representations of elite women in ancient Egyptian art—and almost always before mid–Dynasty 18—the dress is sufficiently formfitting to suggest that it was intended to emphasize the figure's sexuality, did not necessarily reflect actual clothing, and surely would not facilitate movement.[1] Nevertheless, the figure is shown with her left leg advanced, the pose of most upright statues of royal and private men since before the Old Kingdom. Although statues of queens and goddesses in this pose exist as early as Dynasty 4 (female servants were so depicted somewhat later), upright statues of elite, private women made before mid–Dynasty 18 normally show them standing with legs together.

The Richmond statue was surely made much later than Dynasty 18. Even though the mouth, nose, lower right cheek, and part of the chin are modern restorations, enough of the face and body are preserved to allow the attribution on stylistic grounds to sometime after Egypt's First Persian Period (Dynasty 27). The question that remains is "How much later?"

In the first publication of the Richmond figure,[2] Bernard V. Bothmer attributed it to the Macedonian Period, in part because the figure lacks both the supple modeling of some sixth century B.C. female sculptures and the more full-bodied modeling of Ptolemaic times. Moreover, he believed that the sculpture displayed "a modesty not found in representations of the female form in either pre-Persian or Ptolemaic times": the dress "conceals more than it reveals," the nipples are not indicated, and the navel and abdomen are suggested only faintly. He also noted the sculpture's stylistic similarities to two other possibly fourth century

B.C. female sculptures: a bust in the British Museum that he thought might be somewhat later, and a statue of a queen in Berlin that he felt might, with the Richmond figure, prove to be works of Dynasty 30 if more comparable material were available for study.[3] Bothmer may prove to have been correct: in recent years the London bust and the Berlin queen,[4] as well as a few other female heads,[5] have been attributed to Dynasty 30, albeit with reservations. Yet the number of truly comparable pieces, none securely dated, remains very small.

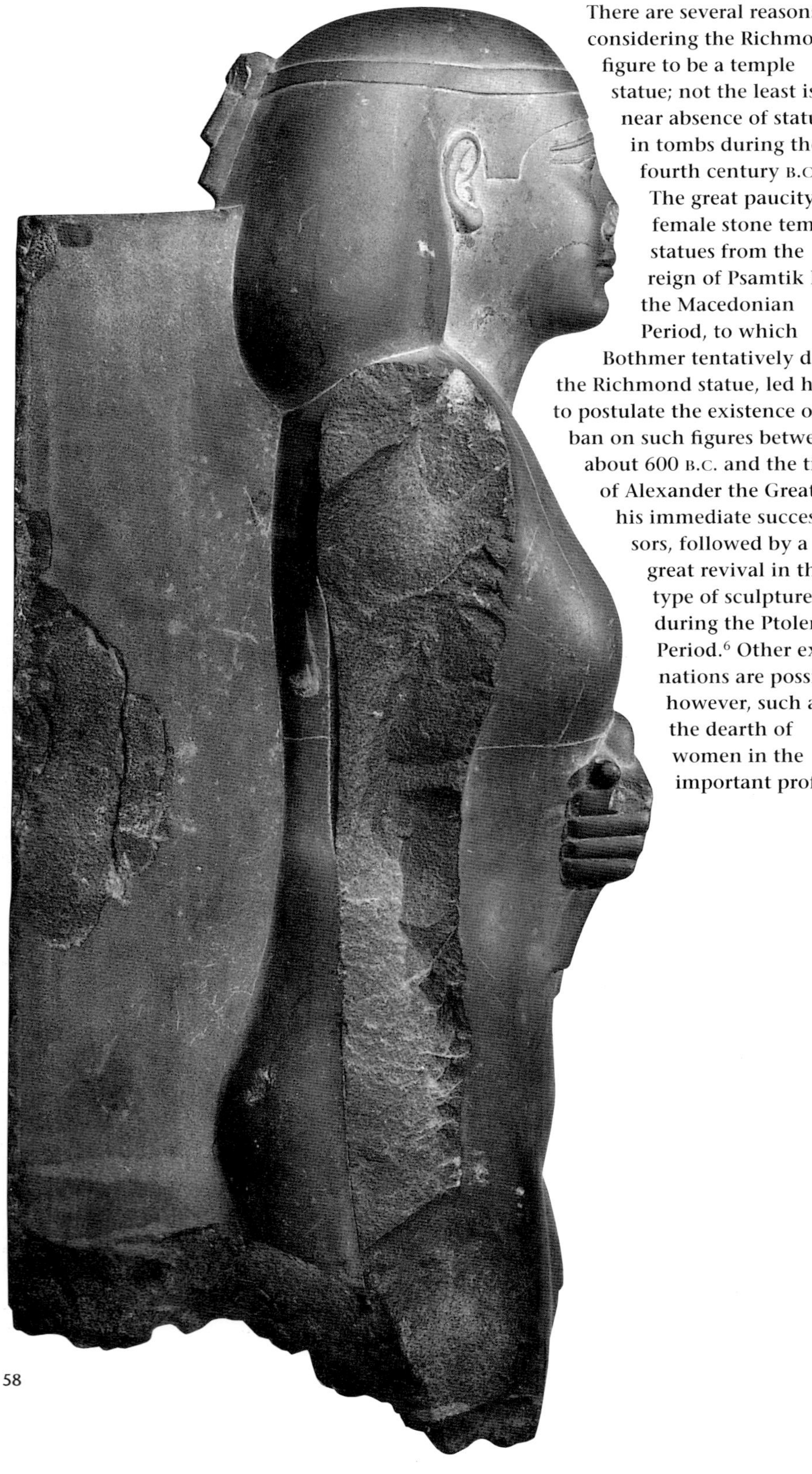

There are several reasons for considering the Richmond figure to be a temple statue; not the least is the near absence of statues in tombs during the fourth century B.C. The great paucity of female stone temple statues from the reign of Psamtik II to the Macedonian Period, to which Bothmer tentatively dated the Richmond statue, led him to postulate the existence of a ban on such figures between about 600 B.C. and the time of Alexander the Great or his immediate successors, followed by a great revival in this type of sculpture during the Ptolemaic Period.[6] Other explanations are possible, however, such as the dearth of women in the important professional positions reflected in most stone temple statuary.[7] Moreover, the possible attribution of some works to Dynasty 30 has begun to improve, slightly, the picture of female statuary in hard stone during the fourth century B.C. It may be, however, that one should not expect the picture to change dramatically: even in earlier times, private temple statuary was largely a male prerogative[8] in both numbers and the variety of statue types. For example, of a group of statues dating mainly from the New Kingdom to early Late Period primarily from the Amen Temple at Karnak, only four (1.69 percent) depict private women; three more show such women in a group with a male relative.[9] Even if female sculptures were not as scarce as this sampling suggests, it seems that they may have been significantly less numerous than in the Ptolemaic Period.

The later Ptolemaic sculptures include several images of striding women (one holding a handkerchief, although at her side[10]) whose wigs may differ but who wear fillets with streamers. Some of these statues hold one hand to the chest; some are inscribed for songstresses or musicians of Amen and are certainly from the god's temple at Karnak.[11] Both the pose and similar fillets had long been used in images of women with other titles, but perhaps it is worth asking if the Richmond sculpture might depict a somewhat earlier and more northerly songstress or musician, perhaps for the goddess Khuyt ("the Protectress") at Athribis. RAF

Published: Bothmer et al., *ESLP,* no. 92, 116–17 and pl. 86; Bothmer, "Living Gifts from the World of the Dead," *Arts in Virginia* 3, no. 1 (1962): 22–29, esp. p. 28, fig. 10, and p. 29; *Ancient Egyptian Art in the Virginia Museum* (Richmond, 1973), no. 66, p. 57 (illus.); P. Vernus, *Athribis: Textes et documents relatifs à la géographie, aux cultes, et à l'histoire d'une ville du Delta égyptien à l'époque pharaonique, BdE* 74 (Cairo, 1978), no. 156, p. 189.

MOTHERHOOD

8a Statuette of woman dressing hair of nursing mother

Limestone with traces of pigment; provenance unknown; Middle Kingdom, Dynasty 12–13; H: 7.2 cm; L: 7.5 cm

The Metropolitan Museum of Art. Rogers Fund, 1922. 22.2.35

8b Relief of woman and child between trees (Tomb of Mentuemhat)

Limestone; from Thebes, Tomb of Mentuemhat (TT 34); Third Intermediate Period–Late Period, Dynasty 25–26; H: 23.9 cm; W: 28.7 cm

The Brooklyn Museum. Charles Edwin Wilbour Fund. 48.74

As with all mothers of any country or era, ancient Egyptian women were especially concerned with safe pregnancy and delivery, and with adequate nourishment for their infants following birth. A statuette in The Metropolitan Museum of Art depicts a nursing mother having her hair coiffed. Similar scenes found on ostraca and on the walls of village houses[1] have been interpreted as part of the ritual ending the period of purification[2] following childbirth.[3]

Women gave birth in a kneeling position or while squatting on two bricks.[4] Midwives attended the laboring mother and were equipped with magical spells and amulets as well as medical prescriptions, which were used to lessen the pain of contractions and speed delivery.[5] The Ebers Papyrus includes oral and topical prescriptions for hastening birth.[6]

Evidence from the New Kingdom suggests that birthing took place in a special light, perhaps temporary, structure (the "birth arbor," in modern terminology), where the mother and baby remained secluded during the period of purification.[7] This airy structure may have been erected in the courtyard or on the roof of the house. Enclosed platforms in the main rooms of the village houses at Deir el-Medina may also have been used for the seclusion of the mother and infant.[8]

Following purification, women returned to their usual duties, accompanied by their infants, who were carried in a sling across the front or side of their bodies.

On a relief from The Brooklyn Museum, a woman rests after picking fruit in an orchard with her child supported in a sling worn across her right shoulder. The child (who is shown disproportionately large) wears the sidelock of hair representing youth and reaches up to caress its mother's hair.[9] The mother's legs are crossed at the ankles with a sense of relaxation uncommon in Egyptian art.

Breast milk, especially that of a woman who had borne a boy, was believed to have special qualities and was a frequent ingredient in prescriptions for treating purulent wounds,[10] eye ailments,[11] burns,[12] and sinus infections (ozena).[13] According to an ancient Egyptian fertility test, if vomiting occurred after a woman drank the milk of a mother who had given birth to a boy, she was, or could become, pregnant.[14]

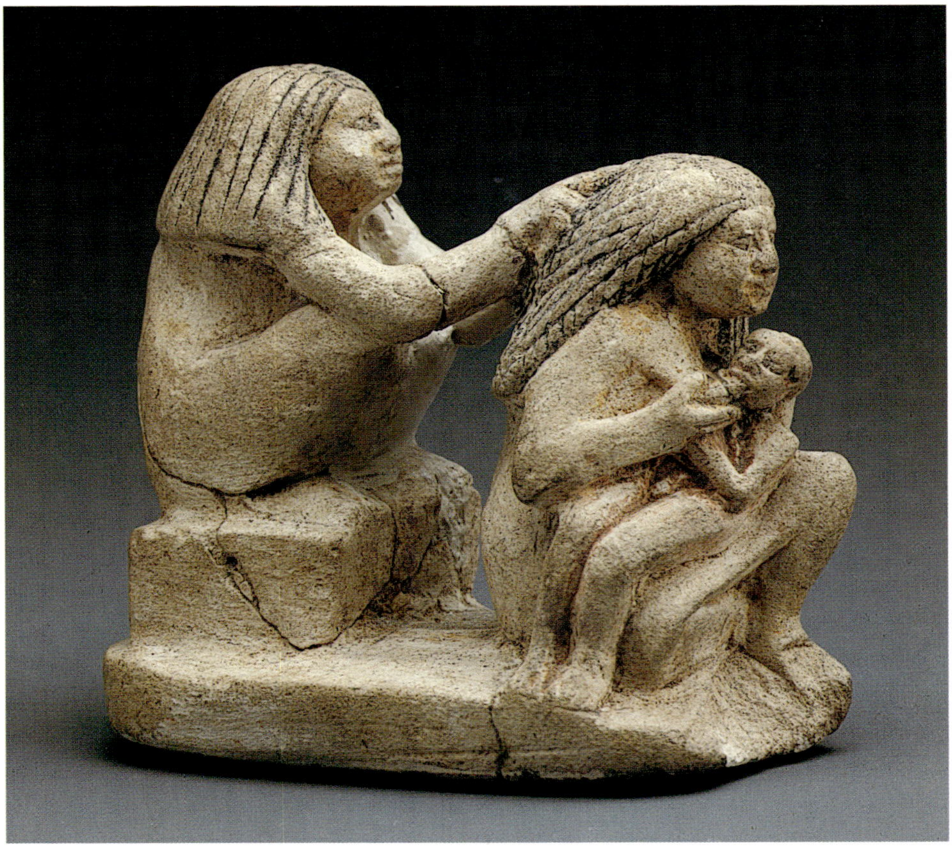

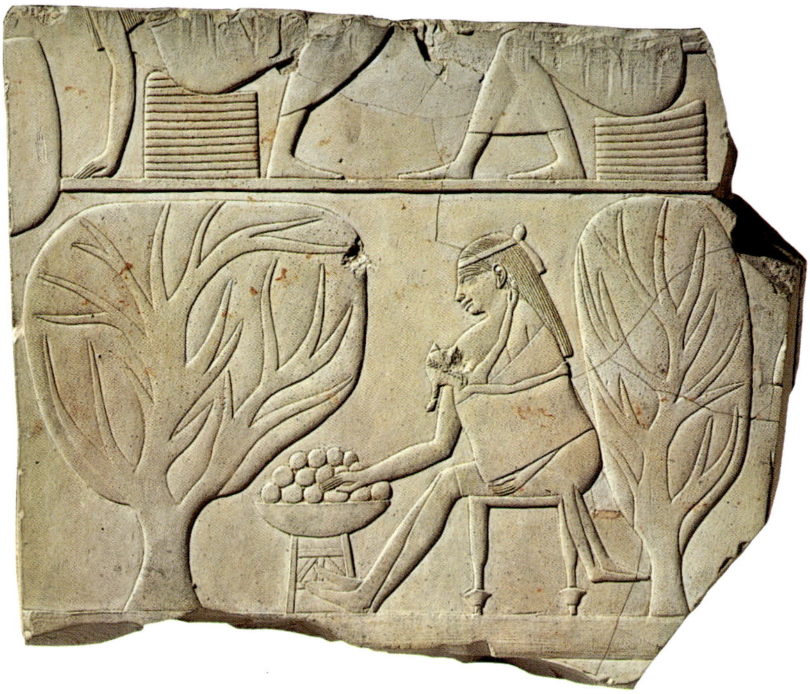

Breast milk was stored in special containers shaped as a woman with a child (cat. no. 10b) or as a woman holding the nipple of her breast.[15] Spells and amulets magically ensured an adequate supply of breast milk,[16] and various tests were performed to judge its quality.[17]

Women nursed their children for up to three years. According to "The Instructions of Any": "When you were born after your months, she [your mother] was yet yoked [to you], her breast in your mouth for three years."[18] Wet nurses were employed when a mother's own milk supply was inadequate. Evidence suggests that noblewomen preferred to hire a wet nurse; legal contracts have survived that enumerate the responsibilities of both parties.[19] AKC

Statuette: Published: Hayes, *Scepter* 1, 222, fig. 138.

Relief: Published: J.D. Cooney, "Three Early Sarte Tomb Reliefs," *JNES* 9 (1950): 193–203; Fazzini et al., *Ancient Egyptian Art,* no. 71.

9 Statuette of Princess Sobek-nakht nursing a prince

Copper; provenance unknown;
Second Intermediate Period, mid–late Dynasty 13; H: 10.5 cm; W: 6.9 cm; D: 8.1 cm

The Brooklyn Museum. Charles Edwin Wilbour Fund. 43.137

Egyptian artisans of Dynasties 12 and 13 fashioned a series of copper statuettes reflecting the highest standards of the metalworker's art. Among the most important of these creations is a figure, today in The Brooklyn Museum, representing a woman suckling a male child. The crudely incised inscription on the statuette's base identifies the lady as Sobek-nakht and mentions that she is a "Hereditary Noblewoman," a highly unusual feminine version of a common male title.[1] She sits with her left leg perpendicular to the ground and offers her right nipple, held between her thumb and index finger, to the boy in her lap. Sobek-nakht wears a fillet and *uraeus* atop her long tripartite wig; the hem of her simple dress stretches across her knees; her lively face is framed by large, stylized ears. The boy is naked. A *uraeus* appears on his forehead, and a sidelock, symbolizing youth, hangs from his right temple.

Although the text on the Brooklyn statuette merely identifies Sobek-nakht as a "Hereditary Noblewoman," several factors suggest that she was also a princess. Her fillet and *uraeus,* for example, are normally associated with members of the royal family. In addition, a stela discovered at Edfu and today in the Cairo Museum represents the "Hereditary Noblewoman Sobek-nakht" who is also called "the King's Daughter."[2] Because the boy of the Brooklyn sculpture also has a *uraeus,* we may safely assume that he is a prince, most likely Sobek-nakht's son.

Two objects help to date the statuette. First, the hieroglyphic text on a glazed steatite scarab in the Cairo Museum mentions the "Hereditary Noblewoman Sobek-nakht."[3] Given the extreme rarity

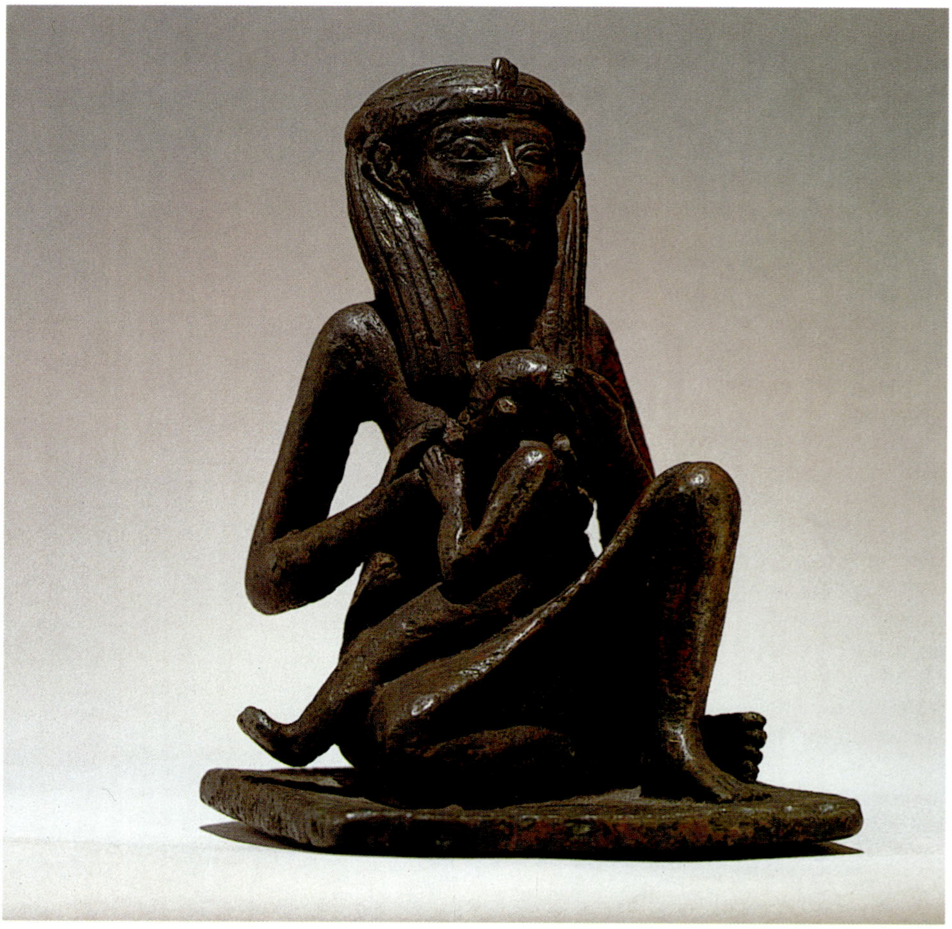

of this title, the inscriptions on both the Brooklyn copper figure and the Cairo scarab probably refer to the same woman. The scarab belongs to a type restricted to the Thirteenth Dynasty, thus providing a general date for the statuette. Second, the abovementioned Edfu stela refines this attribution. On stylistic grounds it can be assigned to the later part of Dynasty 13, a period understood only imperfectly by historians. The obscurity of the era prevents us from knowing the identity of either Sobek-nakht's father (the king) or the prince she suckles. Egyptologists cannot even be certain whether the Brooklyn statuette commemorates the actual birth of a prince or represents Sobek-nakht's plea for divine intervention in producing a royal heir.

Whether Sobek-nakht was the prince's mother in fact or only in expectation, the Brooklyn piece seems to represent her and the prince as more than mere humans. Another Thirteenth Dynasty copper statuette, in the collection of the Ägyptisches Museum in Berlin, shows a mother nursing a tiny male figure.[4] The Berlin sculpture has many features in common with the Brooklyn statuette, including the female's coiffure and costume, a similar rendering of the ears, a nearly identical metallic composition, and the same iconographic theme of a mother suckling a child. The text on the base of the Berlin figure, however, suggests that the "mother" is the goddess Isis and the "child" is her son Horus.[5] The similarity between the Brooklyn and the Berlin groups implies a common theme: the mother's responsibility for providing her offspring with physical and psychological nourishment. By consciously invoking the theme of Isis and Horus, Sobek-nakht underscored her role as mother, nurturer, and guardian of the future ruler of Egypt. JFR

Published: James F. Romano, "A Statuette of a Royal Mother and Child in The Brooklyn Museum," in *MDAIK* 48 (1992): 131–43 (with earlier references).

10 a Vessel in form of a kneeling woman

Green glazed steatite; provenance unknown; New Kingdom, late Dynasty 18–early Dynasty 19; H: 9.7 cm; D: 5.1 cm

The Brooklyn Museum. Charles Edwin Wilbour Fund. 49.53

10 b Figure vase: Woman holding a swaddled infant

Red burnished terracotta; provenance unknown; New Kingdom, mid–Dynasty 18; H: 14.0 cm

Museum of Fine Arts, Boston. Frank Bemis Fund. 1985.336

A lack of visual evidence has seriously hindered attempts to understand the rituals and activities relating to childbirth in ancient Egypt. Although countless thousands of scenes from daily life survive from antiquity, we have no detailed illustrations of an actual human birth.[1] Representations of postpartum rituals are known, but they deal with only a single theme—caring for the new mother immediately after delivery.[2] With so few visual references available, scholars can only speculate on how the Egyptians used many objects whose iconography demonstrates a relationship to pregnancy, delivery, and the health of the mother and child. Two such enigmatic pieces are a glazed steatite container in The Brooklyn Museum and a pottery vessel from the Museum of Fine Arts, Boston.

The Brooklyn object represents a kneeling figure holding or offering a round pot and a curved object. John D. Cooney, who purchased the piece while curator at Brooklyn, recognized no association with birth. Instead, he interpreted it as a representation of an itinerant male barber or a "surgeon" holding the tools of his profession.[3] Subsequently Elizabeth Riefstahl, Cooney's colleague at Brooklyn, suggested that the container served as a votive object and represented a woman dedicating gifts to a deity.[4] More recently, H. Rand proposed that the object depicts a midwife. According to Rand, the figure holds in her left hand a pot containing oil or salt for rubbing on a newborn infant and, in her right, a surgical instrument for an episiotomy or embryotomy.[5]

Rand further related the object's function to the Egyptian practice of gynecology. Several Egyptian papyri, for example, provide instructions for conducting a

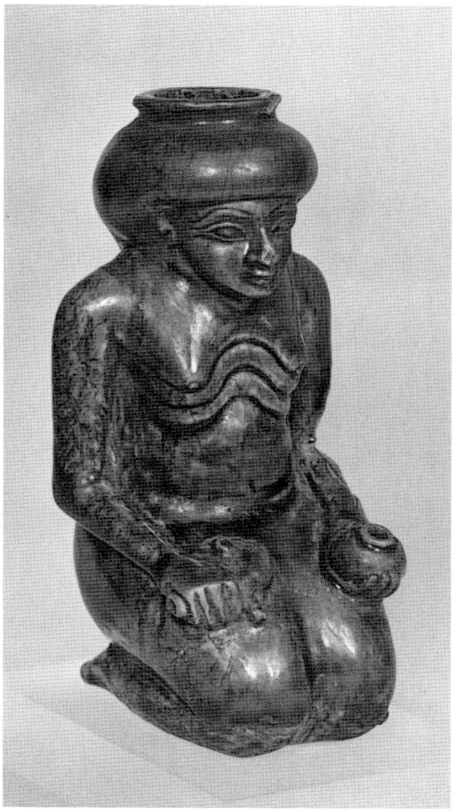

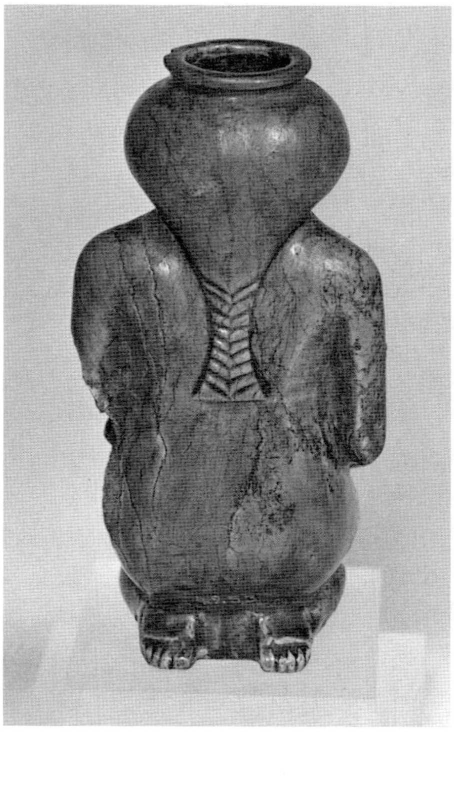

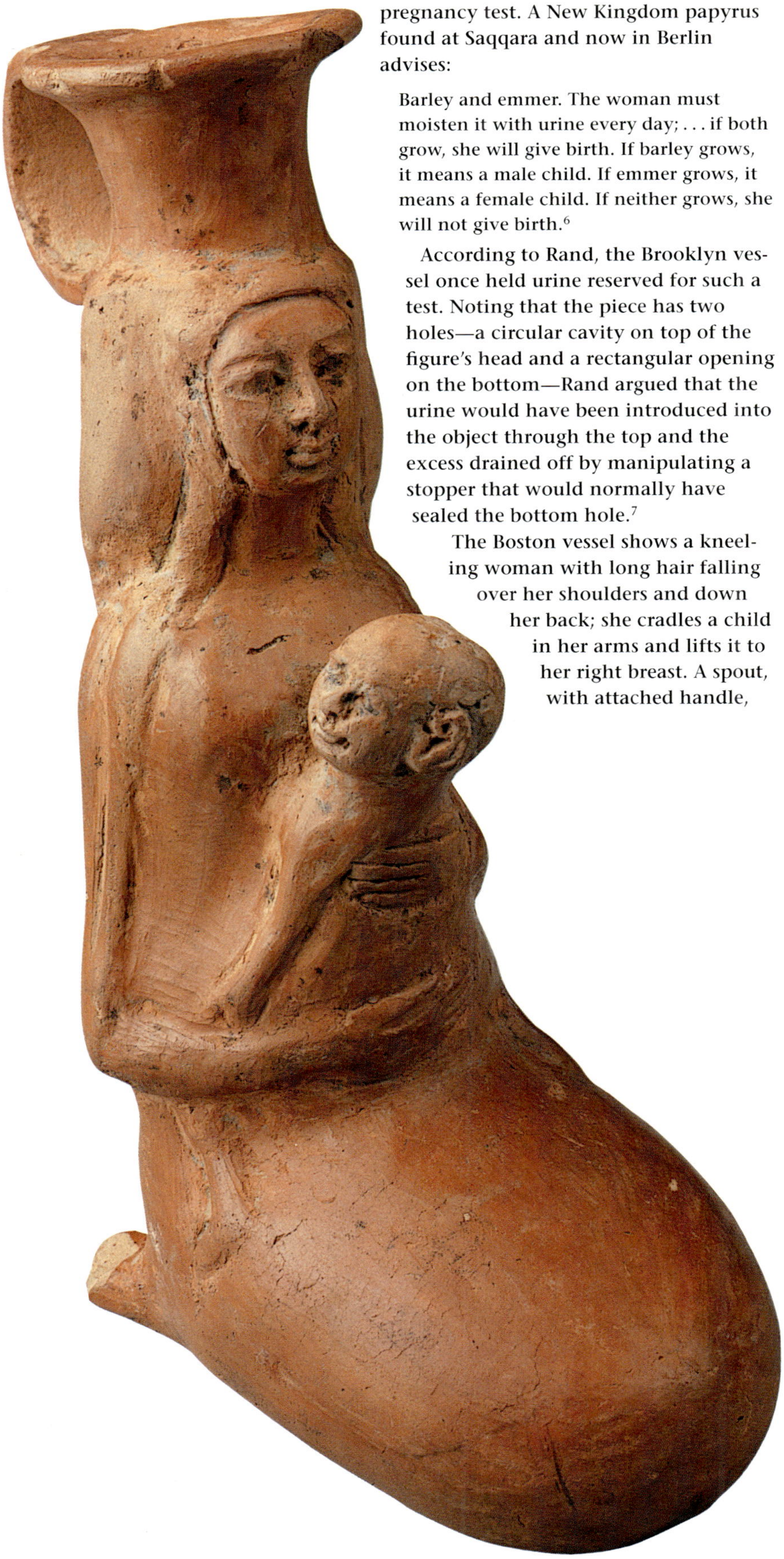

pregnancy test. A New Kingdom papyrus found at Saqqara and now in Berlin advises:

> Barley and emmer. The woman must moisten it with urine every day; . . . if both grow, she will give birth. If barley grows, it means a male child. If emmer grows, it means a female child. If neither grows, she will not give birth.[6]

According to Rand, the Brooklyn vessel once held urine reserved for such a test. Noting that the piece has two holes—a circular cavity on top of the figure's head and a rectangular opening on the bottom—Rand argued that the urine would have been introduced into the object through the top and the excess drained off by manipulating a stopper that would normally have sealed the bottom hole.[7]

The Boston vessel shows a kneeling woman with long hair falling over her shoulders and down her back; she cradles a child in her arms and lifts it to her right breast. A spout, with attached handle, rises from the woman's head.[8] The Boston piece belongs to a class of beguiling objects conveniently called "nursing woman vases."[9] All of these vessels were made over the course of forty years, from late in the reign of Thutmose III to early in Amenhotep III's kingship. They may have been the product of one highly inventive workshop or even of a single master potter.[10]

Egyptologists have long debated the iconography and ancient use of these vessels. General consensus exists on only one point: the woman is a wet nurse.[11] The child's nature is far more problematic. It has been suggested, for example, that the infant is dead. Milk poured into a vessel fashioned with an image of a dead child would acquire magical properties and could be used to cure an ailing baby.[12] Most scholars, however, interpret the child as alive and hungry. Christiane Desroches-Noblecourt believed that the child's good health provided the key to understanding this class of containers. She averred that milk supplied by a wet nurse in one of these vessels would magically impart strength and vigor to a sick baby.[13] Emma Brunner-Traut offered a different interpretation. To her, the "nursing woman vases" originally held the breast milk of mothers who had delivered a male child.[14] The Ebers Medical Papyrus of the early Eighteenth Dynasty describes the curative power of such milk. To relieve pain, for example, this papyrus advises taking the milk of a woman who has borne a son, leaving it in a jar overnight until cream appears, and then applying that cream on "all the sick places."[15] JFR

Vessel: Published: Susan K. Doll, in *Egypt's Golden Age*, 292, no. 401 (with earlier references).

Figure vase: Published: Janine Bourriau, "Pottery Figure Vases of the New Kingdom," in Pascale Ballet, ed., *Cahiers de la céramique égyptienne* 1 (Cairo, 1987), 94, n. 66, pl. 31, 5; and William Kelly Simpson et al., *A Table of Offerings: Seventeen Years of Acquisitions of Egyptian and Ancient Near Eastern Art by William Kelly Simpson for the Museum of Fine Arts, Boston* (Boston, 1987), 34–35 (illus.).

11 Jar in the form of a woman

Alabaster;[1] provenance unknown; New Kingdom, mid–Dynasty 18; H: 14.8 cm
The Oriental Institute Museum, University of Chicago. 11313

Archaeologists have long believed that the unusual, consciously evocative iconography of certain antiquities must reflect their ancient function. The Egyptians' facility for merging the appearance with the purpose of an object can be documented as early as the Predynastic Period.[2] This tendency continued for millennia. A group of New Kingdom bottles in the form of nursing women, for example, seems to have contained human breast milk (cat. nos. 23o,p,q,r).

Another class of objects may also demonstrate the association of form with function. This rare group comprises approximately a dozen Egyptian alabaster containers carved in the form of naked women;[3] a fine example of the type, from the collection of the Oriental Institute Museum, is included in this exhibition. The subject stands facing front, her hands resting on her torso just below her flat, pointed breasts and above her huge stomach. The stone carver drilled a wide cavity at the top of her head; the woman's hair is pulled back from her ears and extends behind her head, forming a curved handle that falls onto her back.

Although the figure has a woman's face, the torso probably belongs to the divine rather than the human realm. Emma Brunner-Traut has convincingly demonstrated that the figure's distended abdomen must indicate pregnancy, but the swollen proportions of her torso are too exaggerated, her limbs are too thick, and her breasts are too flaccid to convey realistically the appearance of a pregnant human.[4] Rather, the underlying theme of all the jars in the group is the goddess Taweret, protector of pregnant women and the newborn, who appears with the body of a pregnant hippopotamus, leonine paws, and flat, pointed breasts (cat. no. 63a,b).[5]

Thus, the iconography of these jars strongly implies a role in birth or birth-related activities. To clarify this role, Brunner-Traut observed the similarity between the natural banding of Egyptian alabaster, from which all of these vessels were made, and the stretch marks that appear on the bodies of many pregnant women, particularly during their last trimester.[6] Brunner-Traut suggested that in antiquity these jars contained an unknown substance which, when mixed with behen oil from the moringa tree, produced a soothing ointment used for relieving a pregnant woman's discomfort, especially as she approached delivery.

When discussed in print, these vessels customarily are assigned a general Eighteenth Dynasty date.[7] This attribution can be refined further. One of the vessels was discovered in a tomb at Abydos that also contained a variant of the so-called nursing woman vase (cat. no. 10b). Because this class of pottery vessels can be dated with reasonable certainty to the period from the end of Thutmose III's reign to the early years of Amenhotep III, a similar time span for at least some of the stone jars of pregnant women seems tenable.[8] Of course, some may have been manufactured earlier, and others well into Amenhotep III's reign. JFR

Published: Emma Brunner-Traut, "Gravidenflasche: Das Salben des Mutterleibes," in A. Kuschke and E. Kutsch, eds., *Archäologie und altes Testament: Festschrift für Kurt Galling* (Tübingen, 1970), 37, pl. 7a.

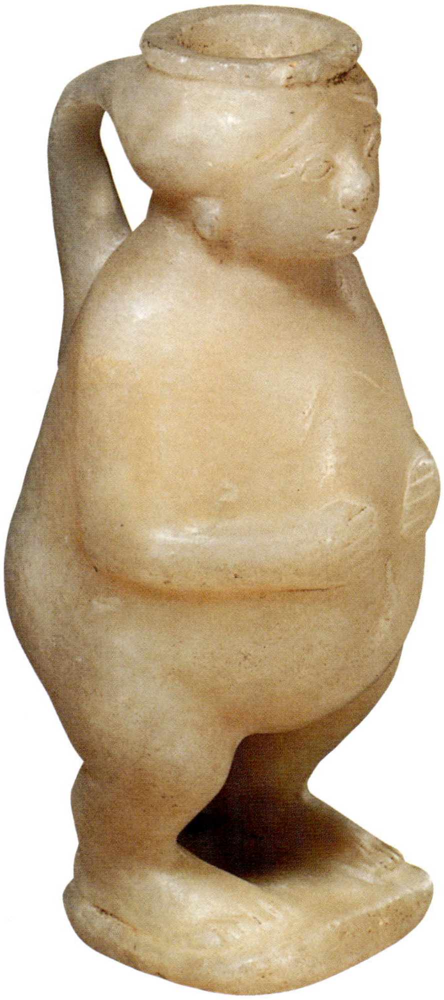

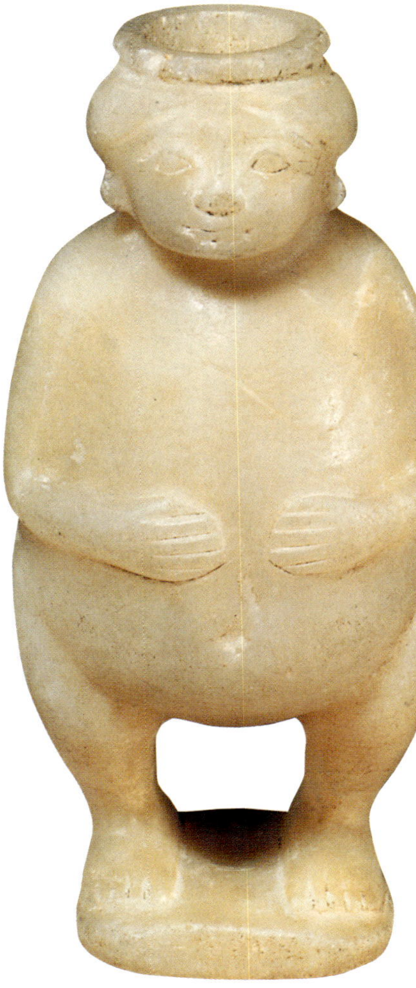

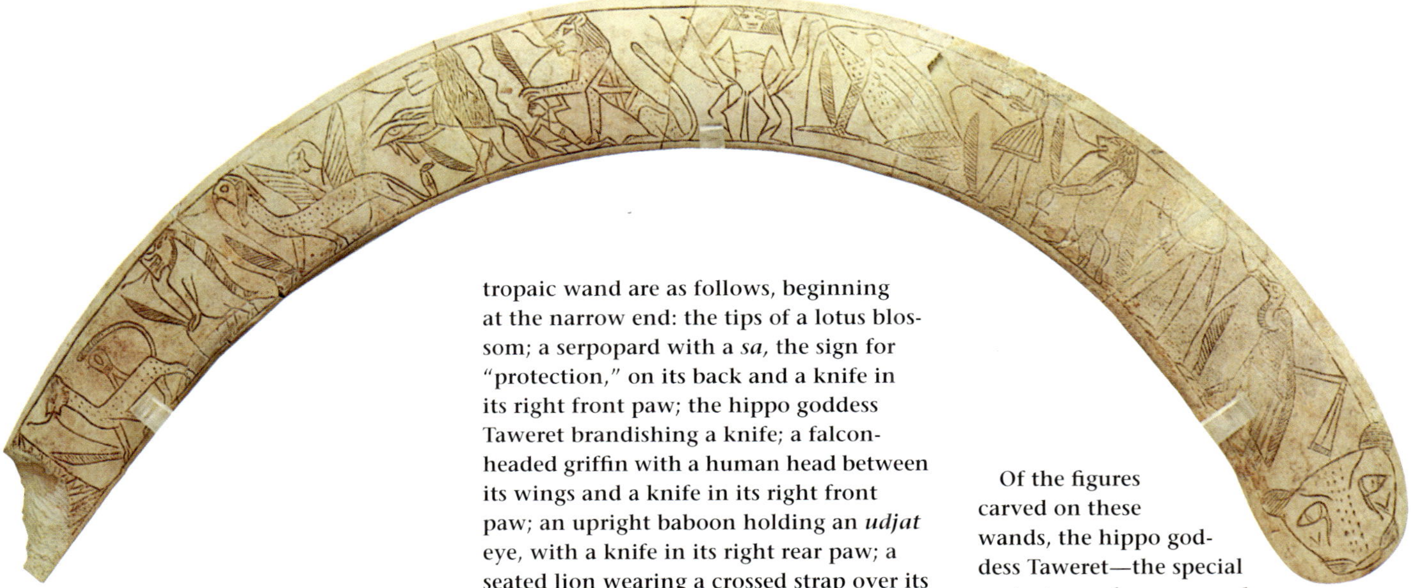

12 Magic (apotropaic) wand

Ivory; provenance unknown;
Middle Kingdom; L: 36.8 cm

Courtesy of The Walters Art Gallery, Baltimore. 71.510

During the Middle Kingdom and Second Intermediate Period, curved wands were used for the protection of women and children. They were most commonly made of hippopotamus ivory,[1] as is this example. The hippo's tusk was split lengthwise, resulting in the characteristic curve; one or both sides were incised, or sometimes carved in relief.[2] Examples of wood,[3] faience,[4] and calcite[5] are known as well; these also incorporate the curved shape.

Though no two of the known apotropaic wands bear identical decoration, most have the same elements at the ends: an incised panther head at the broad end, and a jackal head, either incised or carved in relief,[6] at the narrow tip.[7] Sometimes the jackal's ears merge with the petals of a lotus flower carved directly above the animal's head.[8]

The figures incised on these wands represent a mix of malevolent and protective elements. A study by H. Altenmüller[9] suggests that the owners of the wands—mothers and their children[10]—were identified with the young sun-god Ra and his divine mother. With the aid of benevolent deities, the youthful Ra battled the forces of chaos. As Ra had emerged victorious over his enemies, so, through the use of one of these wands, would a child be magically protected against the demons of childhood.[11]

The figures and signs incised on the obverse of the Walters Art Gallery's apotropaic wand are as follows, beginning at the narrow end: the tips of a lotus blossom; a serpopard with a *sa,* the sign for "protection," on its back and a knife in its right front paw; the hippo goddess Taweret brandishing a knife; a falcon-headed griffin with a human head between its wings and a knife in its right front paw; an upright baboon holding an *udjat* eye, with a knife in its right rear paw; a seated lion wearing a crossed strap over its chest, and grasping the hair of an enemy and the handle of a knife in its left front paw; the god Aha depicted frontally, holding two snakes in each hand, with the tail of a panther skin (his usual apparel) hanging between his legs; a frog representing Hekat, the goddess of childbirth, with a knife; the canine head, which represents *wsr,* the word for "powerful," emerging from the upper edge of a pleated kilt over leonine legs, with a knife in its right paw; an erect lion (or lioness)[12] whose right paw holds an upraised knife and a pendent *ankh;* a solar disc encircled by the *uraeus* serpent, supported on a pair of human legs, with the right foot brandishing a knife and an *ankh* hanging from the *uraeus;* and the vulture goddess Nekhbet grasping a knife in her right claws, with a flail emerging from her back. Each of these figures, except Aha and the solar disc, holds a snake in its jaws.

In the center of the reverse side are three vertical lines forming two registers, though these were never inscribed. At either side of these registers and facing inward[13] is a winged cobra. Incised in the areas created by the undulating serpents' bodies are (to the left of the registers): an *udjat* eye; Taweret standing erect, holding a knife and the *sa* sign in her front paws; a seated lion with a knife, holding a serpent in his mouth; the frog goddess Hekat; and the *wsr*-canine head supported on a kilt and lion's legs. The usual panther's head is incised at the broad end. To the right of the registers, within the curves of the serpent's body, are an *udjat* eye; the frog goddess Hekat; a sphinx holding an *ankh;* again, the Hekat frog; and the *wsr* sign supported on kilt and lion's legs, with a knife in the right paw. The lotus blossom and part of the jackal's face are preserved at the narrow tip.

Of the figures carved on these wands, the hippo goddess Taweret—the special protectress of women and children—is the most common. Also frequently depicted on these apotropaic wands are the god Aha and his female counterpart,[14] whose name means "fighter" and who shared Taweret's protective role. Other elements that appear on these wands, though not on this example, include the divine cow standard, an upright lion devouring a human, the double sphinx, the double bull, the Seth animal, the scarab beetle, the head of a hippopotamus or an ass (?) within the *ḥwt* enclosure,[15] deities in various forms, the incense sign,[16] the flame sign,[17] cats brandishing knives, crocodiles, and turtles. Some apotropaic wands bear inscriptions. "Protection by night; protection by day" is a clear reference to their function. One inscribed example reads, "Cut off the head of the enemy . . . who enters into the chamber of the children born to the lady. . . . "[18] Some examples are inscribed for the "Mistress of the House"; others name the "Daughter of the King," indicating that they were used by people of all classes.

The wear patterns on these apotropaic wands indicate that they were used to "draw" a magical circle of protection around a child.[19] One example[20] shows signs of ancient repair. Clearly these wands were intended to protect the living; their presence in burials suggests a belief in their power to protect the deceased on the dangerous journey to rebirth.[21] AKC

Published: G. Steindorff, "The Magical Knives of Ancient Egypt," JWAG 9 (1946): 41ff., figs. 1, 2.

13 Fertility figurine

Faience; provenance unknown; Middle Kingdom, Dynasty 12; H: 20 cm

Lent by JoAnn Harris Smith

Like the so-called paddle dolls (cat. no. 14), female faience figurines have often been described as "concubines of the dead," that is, as sexual accessories for dead men. Although the tattooing and especially the nudity are erotic,[1] the sexual component of these figurines is very likely one aspect of the larger issue of fertility,[2] which was essential both in this life and in the next. Consequently, female figurines have been found in different contexts and surely served several purposes. By no means made exclusively as funerary equipment for men, they have been found in temples, in houses, and in burials of women and children. In the world of the living, some figurines may have been magical guarantors of fertility both to mothers and to children who had reached the age of puberty. As burial equipment, the figurines represented the potential for rebirth and procreation, thus assuring continuity and immortality in the afterlife for both sexes.

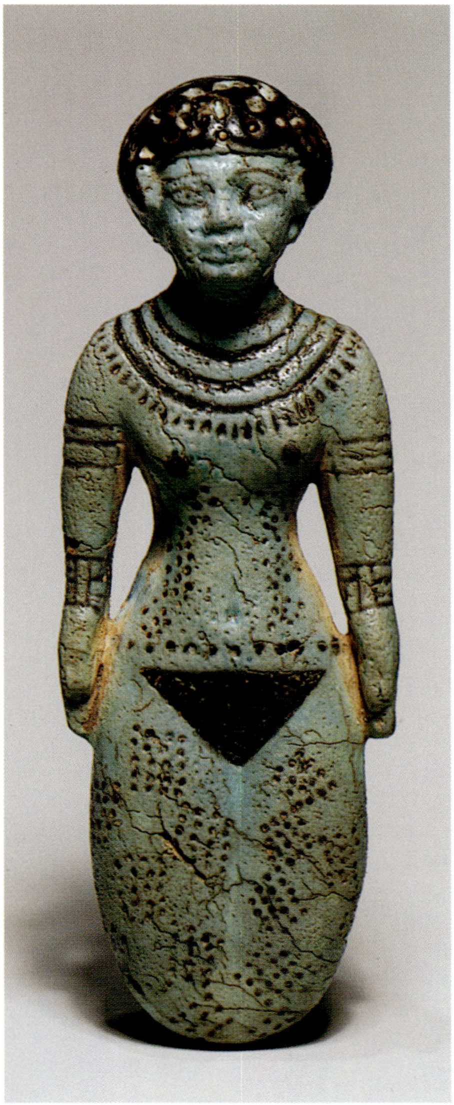

Unlike the "paddle dolls," which have neither feet nor legs and sometimes no arms, the faience figurines have truncated, stumpy legs. Some scholars have compared this curious modeling to the intentional mutilation of hieroglyphs of humans and animals in inscriptions of the Old Kingdom and the First Intermediate Period, continuing sporadically thereafter. Occasionally the heads and limbs are severed or omitted, supposedly to negate the potential harm to the deceased caused by humans and animals were they to be activated.[3] In the case of the female figurines, the incomplete or absent legs supposedly prevented them from running away from the deceased or reinforced their submissive role as objects of sexual desire.

Although these interpretations may be valid in certain contexts, they presuppose that all figurines were made as playthings for the deceased, particularly men, and conjure a male bondage fantasy. Since the Predynastic Period, however, Egyptian artists had created highly abstract forms of the human body, male as well as female, that either lack limbs altogether or have simple forms at best,[4] no doubt for reasons other than constraint. Female fertility figurines with rudimentary or missing arms and legs but large breasts and genitalia are perhaps analogous to the models of vulvae and phalli, which clearly had a sexual purpose.[5] The artists probably chose to emphasize the figurine's value in revitalizing the dead without necessarily worrying about the figurines and the models running away or causing any harm. DBS

14 Paddle-shaped female figure with bead-hair

Wood, thread, mud, pigment; provenance unknown; Middle Kingdom; H: 22.8 cm

The Brooklyn Museum. Charles Edwin Wilbour Fund. 37.102E

Dating primarily to the Eleventh Dynasty and the Middle Kingdom and possibly through the early Eighteenth Dynasty,[1] female figurines of this intriguing type—the so-called paddle dolls—have been found in large numbers in the Theban area in southern Egypt and at Beni Hasan in the central part of the country.[2] The emphasis on the genitalia has inspired interesting, even fanciful, conjectures about the purpose of the figurines. Were they "concubines of the dead," that is, male sexual paraphernalia that provided

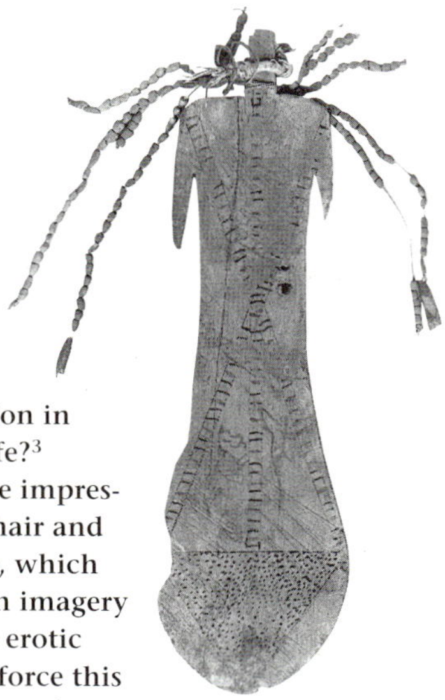

revitalization in the next life?[3] Perhaps the impressively big hair and the tattoos, which in Egyptian imagery often have erotic value, reinforce this interpretation.[4] Then, too, the very summary modeling of the face and head and the abstraction of the body—the absence of the legs and sometimes also of the arms—may indicate that the sexual aspect of the "dolls" was most important.[5] Nonetheless, the "concubine of the dead" theory is not the only, and probably not even the primary, explanation for the paddle dolls. Although female figurines of various types may occasionally have served sexual purposes for men in the underworld, many other examples have been found in contexts (temples, houses, and burials associated with women[6]) that subvert this hypothesis.

Fertility was probably the more important underlying purpose. Some paddle dolls bear images on the reverse of the deities Bes or Taweret (Thoeris), who were associated with pregnancy.[7] Furthermore, because some of the figurines have been found with magical implements, they may have been part of a magician's kit and may have guaranteed fertility for both the living and the dead.[8] Whether the paddle dolls were children's toys is not clear; some of them may have had an amuletic purpose, guaranteeing fertility to a young female upon reaching puberty.[9]

These hypotheses are not incompatible; in ancient Egypt sexuality and fertility were intimately connected,[10] and one and the same object often had multiple purposes. The dual possibilities are revealed in a fascinating study on the shape of the paddle dolls.[11] Their pyriform bodies have been likened to the counterpoise (counterweight) of an Egyptian necklace known as the *menat* (see cat. no. 35c,d). Supposedly both are highly stylized representations of the goddess Hathor's body. By their Hathoric association, the "dolls" acquired connotations of both sexuality and fertility through the various myths in which the goddess not only appeased the solar god by exposing her genitalia but also nursed the infant Divine Child.

In addition to the large genitalia, the other striking features of the "dolls" are the elaborate coiffure, the abstract treatment of the face, and the colorful patterns on the body. Made of cord, seeds, faience beads, or tiny mud pellets, the "hair" on these Middle Kingdom figurines has a parallel on a fascinating linen-cord "doll" from Beni Hasan that much resembles a ginseng root topped by dreadlocks.[12] This hairstyle is found on several mummies of the early Eighteenth Dynasty.[13] The facial area on the present figurine and catalogue number 13 has no modeling at all; a small rectangular area that protrudes from the middle of the shoulders is the sole indication of the head. Occasionally the face is rendered abstractly as a beak with eyes,[14] somewhat analogous to certain Predynastic female figurines.[15] The widely varying geometric designs probably denote clothing, although some patterns, particularly stippling, may indicate tattoos.[16] DBS

15 Nude female figure

Wood; from Deir el-Bersheh; Middle Kingdom; H: 27 cm

Museum of Fine Arts, Boston. Harvard University–Museum of Fine Arts Expedition. 20.1120

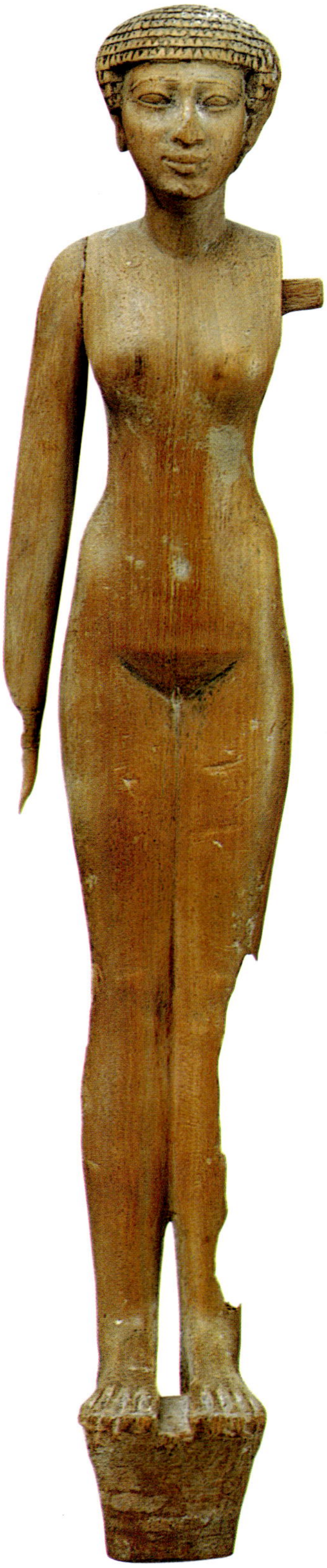

Discovered in the tomb of Djehutynakht at Deir el-Bersheh, which has yielded a rich inventory of important early Middle Kingdom funerary equipment such as coffins, models of boats, and statuettes of offering bearers,[1] this finely rendered statuette of a female was most likely a fertility figure, as suggested very generally by its nudity. The loss of the left arm, however, precludes certainty about its function. Usually, but not always, when fertility figures have complete arms, they extend straight by the side.[2] On the other hand, because some statuettes of female offering bearers not only have one arm straight and the other arm extended but are also naked,[3] this statuette may perhaps have represented a servant carrying an offering either on its head or in front of its chest. No marks or other traces on the head suggest an attachment of an offering, but the other configuration remains possible.

Likewise, the position of the feet is not conclusive evidence. In contrast to the striding posture of some of the offering-bearer statuettes from Djehutynakht's tomb, the side-by-side arrangement of the woman's feet indicates a lack of movement and hence might be interpreted as a submissive attitude. However, other naked female figurines that are clearly offering bearers have both feet together.[4]

The sensuality of the statuettes does not necessarily provide a clue about their function because several of the offering bearers from Djehutynakht's tomb are just as attractively modeled.[5] Equally subjective would be a judgment based on the similarity in style between this figure and another from Djehutynakht's tomb that represents a naked woman with abbreviated legs and no arms at all,[6] a configuration that is well attested among fertility figurines.[7]

In spite of these uncertainties, the statuette is more likely a fertility figurine than an offering bearer. The sensual quality is not merely a modern aesthetic judgment but a characteristic that was surely appreciated in ancient times. Sexuality may have been one aspect of the figurine, but connotations of fertility both in this life and in the next were just as important and perhaps more so.[8] DBS

Published: Breasted, *Servant Statues,* 84, pl. 89a; Dows Dunham, *The Egyptian Department and Its Excavations* (Boston, 1958), 70, 72 (fig. 46a); William Stevenson Smith, *Ancient Egypt as Represented in the Museum of Fine Arts, Boston,* 4th ed., rev. (Boston, 1960), 97, fig. 60 (left); Edward L.B. Terrace, "The Entourage of an Egyptian Governor," *BMFA* 66 (1968): 19, fig. 19; Terrace, "An Age of Reflection: The Egyptian Middle Kingdom in Boston," *The American Connoisseur* 168, no. 678 (1968): 270, fig. 11 (right)

16 a Stela: Woman and boy adoring Taweret

Limestone with pigment; New Kingdom, Dynasty 18, reign of Akhenaten; excavated at Amarna, Main City, House N.49.21; H. 15.24 cm; W. 12.7 cm

Cincinnati Art Museum. Gift of the Egypt Exploration Society. 1921.279

16 b Female figurine with model bed

Terracotta with pigment; New Kingdom, Dynasty 18, reign of Akhenaten; excavated at Amarna, Main City, House N.49.21; H. of figurine: 12.5 cm; L. of bed: 16.5 cm

Cincinnati Art Museum. Gift of the Egypt Exploration Society. 1921.280, 281

This group of objects[1] was found together in a cabinet under a staircase in House N.49.21, a modest home in the main city of Tell el-Amarna.[2] In another corner of the same room—the "central hall" of the house—was a wall niche set above a raised platform reached by a series of four steps. This raised dais was interpreted by the excavators as a "little shrine."[3]

The stela depicts a woman and a young boy[4] adoring Taweret, the protective goddess of pregnant women, women in childbirth, and children (cat. no. 63a,b). The woman wears a long, pleated dress, large round earrings, and an incense cone on top of her full wig. The boy behind her wears a sidelock, a broad collar, and a white kilt. Both offer lotus flowers to Taweret. The woman also has one hand raised in a gesture of reverence before the goddess. Three vertical lines above these two figures form columns for the insertion of the names of the worshippers and perhaps a short prayer to the goddess. The registers were never filled in, however, suggesting that stelae of this type were mass-produced with columns left blank for personalized inscription by the purchaser. The rather hasty manufacture of this stela is evident in the unsmoothed back and sides of the stone.

The figurine's frontal features were formed by pressing moist clay into an open mold. The back of the figure is slightly convex and unmodeled. The legs and headrest of the model bed were hand-shaped and were applied to the bed before firing. Red and brown stripes in criss-crossed bands suggest the woven fiber support of an actual bed. Evidence from Amarna indicates that such female figurines and model beds were mass-produced. During excavations in 1987, the remains of a pottery factory were discovered near the main city. Along with sherds of pottery vessels, the refuse pits associated with the factory held fragments of these female figurines.[5]

Since the discovery of these objects, scholars have interpreted the niche, dais, and objects from the cabinet in House N.49.21 as the focus of domestic prayer and worship. Whether as votive offerings in temples or as objects of devotion in private homes, female figurines of this variety expressed the desire for children and perhaps magically ensured rapid conception.[6] More than sixty of these figurines have been found in excavations at Amarna; numerous additional examples have been found at other New Kingdom town sites as well.[7] The stela depicting the mother and child adoring Taweret visually represents the thankful prayer offered to the goddess for her assistance through successful pregnancy and delivery.

Objects such as these illustrate the importance of offspring in ancient Egypt. Bearing healthy children ensured that property, and sometimes titles and offices,[8] remained within the family. Children were expected to bury their parents in a fitting manner[9] and to maintain continued offerings and prayers at the tomb to sustain their parents and ancestors in the afterlife.[10]

Infertility was considered adequate grounds for divorce in ancient Egypt.[11] A childless couple had the option of adopting a child or even an adult to ensure that they would be cared for in their old age, given a proper burial, and pass their property on to their designated heirs.[12] AKC

Published: T. Eric Peet and C. Leonard Woolley, *The City of Akhenaten, Part I: Excavations of 1921 and 1922 at El-ʿAmarneh* (London, 1923), 24–25, pls. 12, 19; Janssen and Janssen, *Growing Up,* 10; Pinch, *Votive Offerings,* 216; Tyldesley, *Daughters of Isis,* 257–58; Gay Robins, "Women and Children in Peril: Pregnancy, Birth, and Infant Mortality in Ancient Egypt," *KMT* 5, no. 4 (1994–95): 31.

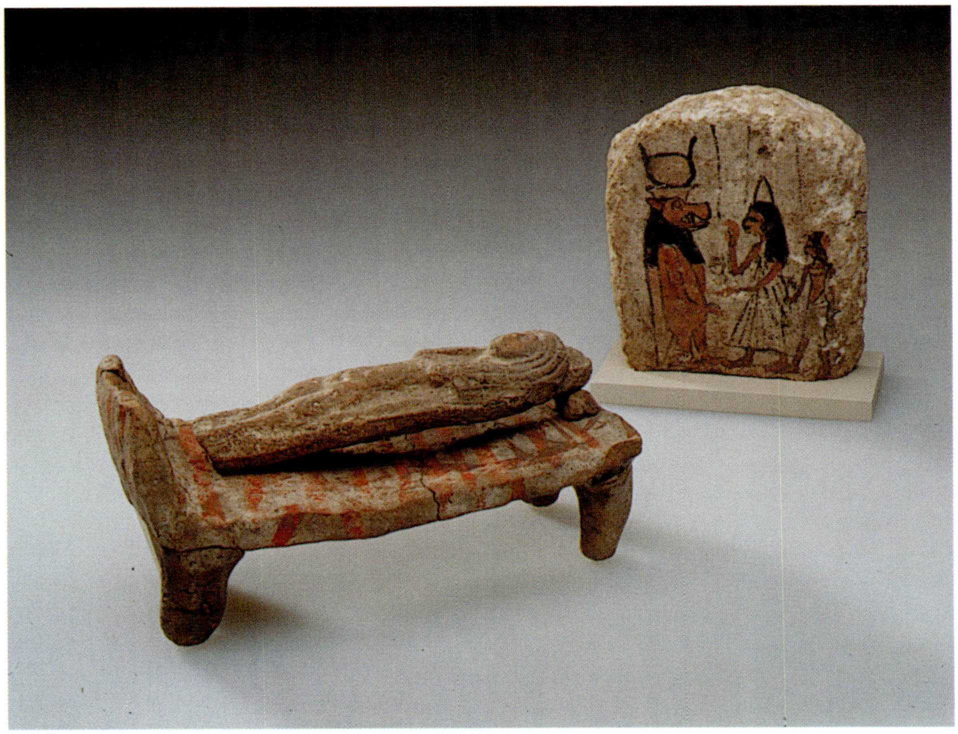

17 Plaque with Bes image

Faience; provenance unknown; Third Intermediate Period, Dynasty 21–25; H: 21.5 cm

The University Museum of Archaeology and Anthropology, Philadelphia. E 14358

The ancient Egyptians had only a perfunctory understanding of the human reproductive system, and their obstetrical and gynecological practices often approached the level of folk medicine. Not surprisingly, the months of pregnancy, the hours of delivery, and the weeks immediately following parturition were most perilous times for mother and child alike. Probably the mortality for both was always quite high.

Unable to rely on adequate medical care, the Egyptians called on a roster of deities to protect the vulnerable mother and child. The two most common were the goddess Taweret (cat. no. 63) and her male companion, frequently called Bes. "Bes" is a convenient term encompassing nearly a dozen gods—including Aha, Hayet, Tetetenu, and Bes himself—all represented by very similar or even identical images. Previous attempts to distinguish among these deities have proved unsatisfactory; thus, unless a figure is identified by inscription, it is impossible to know whether it represents Bes or one of his counterparts.[1] To avoid confusion the term "Bes-image" is employed here to designate a visual form applied to several deities, one of whom was Bes.

The Bes-image changed markedly over time.[2] By the beginning of the Third Intermediate Period, most Bes-images had a huge head with stylized facial features including a furrowed brow, thick eyebrows running obliquely over the forehead, deeply set eyes, a flat nose with flaring nostrils, and a long moustache extending past the corners of the god's wide mouth. The mouth is often open, exposing huge, menacing teeth.[3] Artisans of the time rendered the Bes-image with a thick torso and flat chest, distended abdomen, enlarged buttocks, muscular limbs, and bowed legs.[4] The resulting figure has a feral, forbidding quality accordant with his apotropaic role.[5]

Perhaps the most dramatic manifestation of the Bes-image in the Third Intermediate Period appears on a series of flat objects, sometimes called plaques, showing the god standing on a papyrus capital and feeding a second, much smaller Bes-image.[6] On the present example, two frogs can be seen beneath the god's feet, and a troop of monkeys scampers over his body. Two of these simians

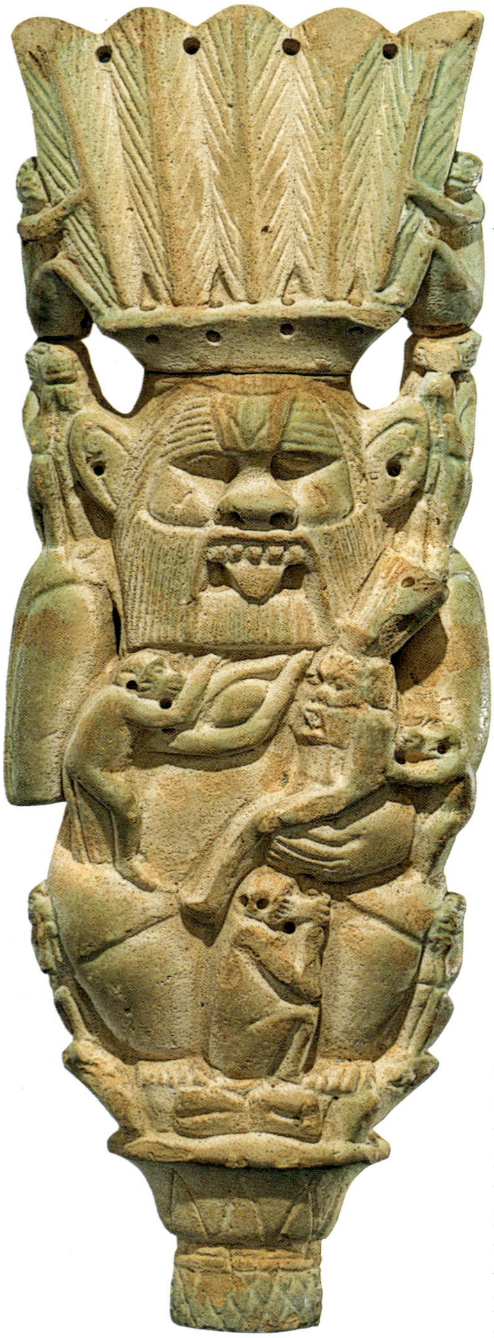

hang from his headdress, and two others grasp his tail.[7] One monkey even tries to steal the object—probably a date[8]—that the god offers to the smaller deity.[9] On the back of the Bes-image's perforated five-plumed headdress, we see the raised relief representation of a cat using a stick to drive a pair of birds.[10]

These plaques combine several potent symbols of nourishment, protection, and birth. The dominant figure, the Bes-image, safeguarded nursing children, beginning at least in the Middle Kingdom.[11] According to a late papyrus, the fruit of the date palm contains a divine liquid that enabled the god Thoth to bring himself into being.[12] Aside from their natural association with dates and palm trees, monkeys also served as agents of the sun god, who experienced the daily cycle of birth, death, and rebirth. The frogs on the present piece allude to the goddess Hekat, another deity who assisted at delivery (cat. no. 12).[13]

Several of these plaques were discovered in the remains of houses at Tanis, suggesting that they served in domestic rather than cultic activities.[14] The plaques themselves may provide a clue to how they were used. Most feature a series of tiny holes, usually at the top of the plumes, at the base of the headdress, and through the god's ears and nose. In antiquity these holes probably accommodated metal rings.[15] By gently shaking one of these plaques, a servant or the mother would have produced a soft, soothing rustle that calmed a fractious infant while placing the child under vigilant divine protection.
JFR

Published: Lionel Casson, *Ancient Egypt* (New York, 1965), 75; Bulté, *Talismans Égyptiens*, 23, no. 29.

18 Vessel in form of Bes-image

Faience; provenance unknown; Late Period, early Dynasty 26; H: 14.1 cm; W: 9.5 cm

Virginia Museum of Fine Arts, Richmond. The Adolph D. and Wilkins C. Williams Fund in Memory of Bernard V. Bothmer. 93.110

At the beginning of Dynasty 26, Egyptian artisans abandoned the stylized form of the Bes-images made in the Third Intermediate Period. The older model had relied extensively on severe lines to create a formidable countenance (cat. no. 17); the "new" Bes-image placed much greater emphasis on curvilinear details. Massive eyebrows rise from the wrinkled bridge of the god's nose and extend over his furrowed forehead before tapering to a fine point. The eyes are usually wide open; a pair of thin, plastic ridges runs from the nasal alae past the corners of the mouth; and the god's cheek whiskers are rendered as long individual strands, each ending in a tight curl. This preference for soft, rounded forms tempers the god's earlier ferocity with a new accessibility and calm.[1]

It is impossible to know whether this change signaled a fundamental shift in beliefs concerning the birth gods. Perhaps the appearance of the "new" Bes-image reflected another, nonreligious factor such as rejection of a style associated with the Libyans of Dynasty 22 and the Kushites of Dynasty 25. It is certain, however, that in the Late Period the Bes-image appeared on most of the same types of objects as it decorated in earlier eras, including amulets, bronze and terracotta statuettes, cosmetic containers, furniture attachments, and reliefs. The style of the Bes-image had changed; its decorative context had not.

The present faience vessel—one of the five or six finest Bes-images in the world—shows all the hallmarks of the "new" style. The details of the face are so strikingly similar to those on a faience plaque datable to the reign of Psamtik I[2] that the Richmond piece can be assigned with reasonable certainty to the first five or six decades of Dynasty 26. The vessel belongs to a small group of high-quality faience containers modeled in the form of the Bes-image; all appear to be roughly contemporary.[3]

The precise function of the vessel, however, is far more difficult to define. It may have contained a preparation for curing a sick infant. Alternatively, it could have held a medicine or a cosmetic used by the mother. Either just before the birth or immediately thereafter, the mother was removed to a temporary enclosure called a maternity or birth arbor. This place of seclusion contained a bed, numerous cosmetic objects, and an array of attendants who served the new mother until she was ready to return to society. Before she could return, she had to be cleansed of her impure state.[4] Inscriptions mention that women underwent some form of washing, but we have no textual evidence documenting the specific rituals.

A series of painted ostraca of the Ramesside Period from Deir el-Medina provides some visual clues, however. They tell us that during the mother's isolation,

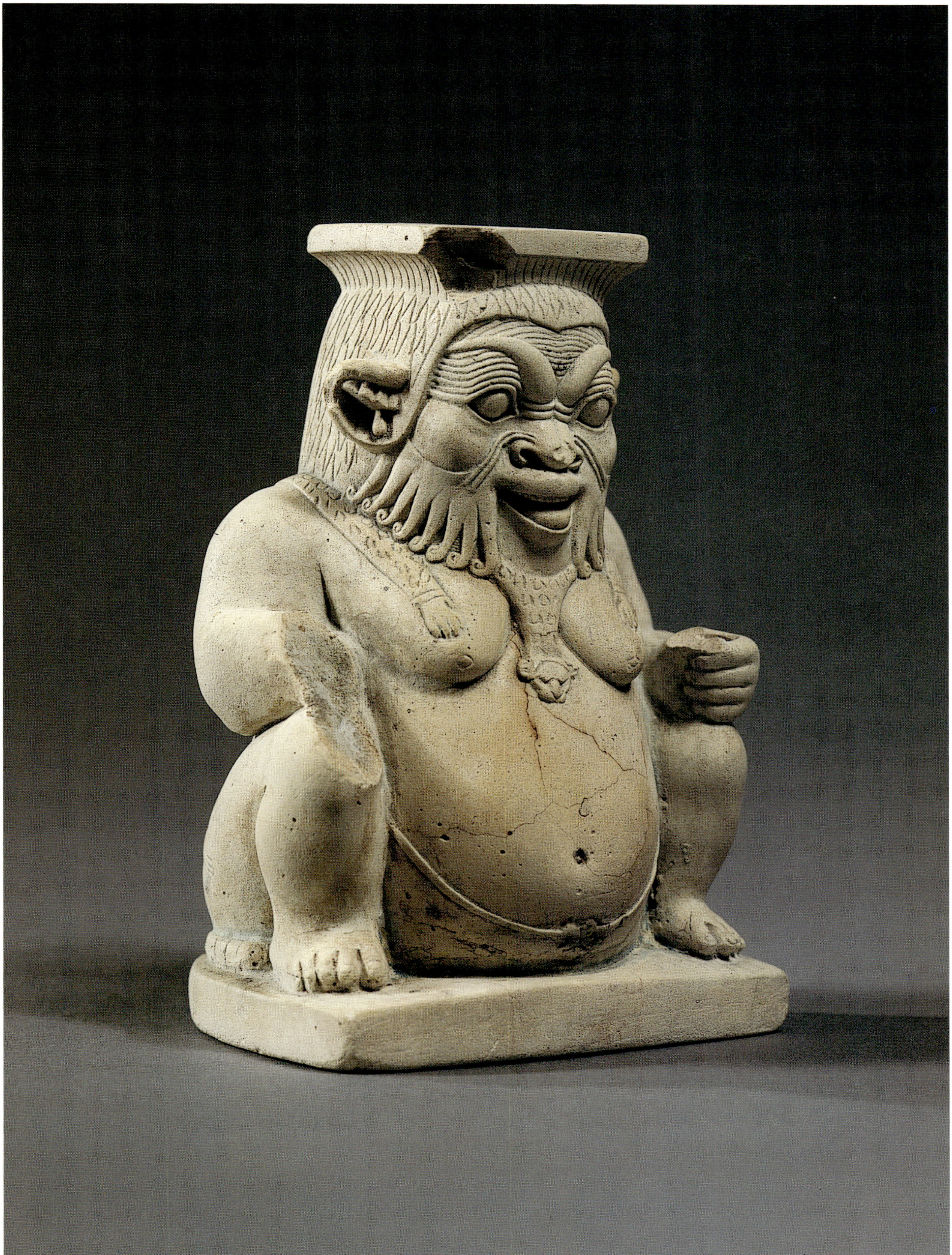

great care was given to her physical appearance and to reinforcing her sense of sexual attraction. Servants arranged her hair, applied her makeup, washed her feet, and adorned her in the most fashionable clothing of the day, often while she nursed her baby.[5] (See cat. no. 8a.) Such ceremonial attention almost certainly had erotic implications: before the new mother could resume her place as mistress of her house, she had to be restored to her former state as a vibrant, sexually attractive, and thus potentially fertile woman.

Archaeologists have no idea how long these rituals continued after the Ramesside Period. However, belief in the necessity of secluding the new mother from society can be documented in many cultures far removed chronologically and geographically from ancient Egypt.[6] We have no reason to believe that such a widespread practice did not continue well beyond the late New Kingdom in Egypt. If it did so, the Richmond vessel may have contained a medicine or cosmetic used during the new mother's isolation. JFR

Amulets

From the earliest times, ancient Egyptian men and women wore a variety of amulets or charms that provided them with magical protection.[1] Such amulets served their wearer in both life and death. Many of those worn by the living could be taken to the grave; others were made expressly for the tomb—to safeguard and protect the deceased on his or her journey to and sojourn in the next world.

The use of amulets in ancient Egypt dates back to Predynastic times. The earliest amulets focused primarily on animals known for their strength, ferocity, and speed, such as the hippopotamus, lioness, bull, gazelle, and falcon. These were rendered in their entirety or by their heads alone. Natural objects, such as shells, also functioned as amulets; their popularity—especially for women—continued through Dynastic times.

While many amulets served both men and women equally, others reveal clear gender distinctions in usage. Early associations with the concerns of women are already revealed in Egypt's early historical period. A woman's burial from the First Dynasty at Nag ed-Deir, for example, contained three gold amulets—in the form of a beetle, oryx, and bull—associated with the goddesses Neith, Isis, and Bat (later associated with Hathor), respectively.[2] The late Old Kingdom saw the emergence of a variety of animal-shaped amulets, including the frog, female hippopotamus, locust/grasshopper, and monkey, which appear to have been favored by women. Owing to their reproductive abilities, the frog and locust were favored early on as fertility-inducing charms.[3] A potent symbol of sexual fulfillment in ancient Egypt, the monkey, too, probably served as a procreative aid.[4]

In the Middle Kingdom, a greater variety of female deities associated with childbirth and maternity were represented in amuletic form, most notably, Taweret, Hathor, and Isis.[5] The hippopotamus goddess Taweret, protectress of women in childbirth, was perhaps the earliest and most potent of such amuletic symbols. Her origins may be sought in amulets of Old Kingdom date depicting an upright female hippopotamus.[6] By the New Kingdom, amulets of Taweret formed a ubiquitous feature of women's jewelry (cat. nos. 20v2 and 25). Likewise, amulets of Bes were worn by women and children for protection against the perils of childbirth and infancy (cat. no. 72j).

Concern with childbirth is reflected in a number of other women's amulet types, beginning in the Middle Kingdom. One prominent variety was a container in the form of a tube of gold or silver (cat. no. 19). Cowrie-shell-shaped pendents in precious metal (cat. no. 24d) now occurred exclusively in association with women's jewelry, imitating the actual shells that had been worn since Predynastic times (cat. no. 72i). The cowrie's amuletic significance for expectant mothers may have derived from its resemblance to the female genitalia.[7] During the Middle Kingdom, it became a standard feature on women's girdles, positioned to protect the wearer from harm.[8] From the Middle Kingdom onward, the oyster-shell amulet appears to have served a similar protective function. (Its name in Egyptian was *wedja,* meaning "sound" or "healthy").[9]

Beginning at the end of the New Kingdom, goddesses appear with greater diversity in amuletic form, either in animal or fully human guise.[10] Isis, the archetypal protective mother goddess, may be identified by the hieroglyph that she wears upon her head (cat. no. 58). In the Late Period, Isis and her sister Nephthys (cat. nos. 20h,i), who is likewise identified by her hieroglyphic headdress, are often paired together with Isis's son, Horus. Together with Neith and Selket, these two goddesses formed the four protectresses of the dead.

In her maternal aspect, Isis often appears in seated posture, holding or suckling the infant Horus. From the Third Intermediate Period onward, amulets of Isis suckling Horus often depict her with the Hathoric headdress consisting of cow's horn and disc (cat. no. 20j). Other deities, such as Mut (cat. no. 61) and Selket (cat. no. 60), also assumed the guise of a nurturing mother goddess.[11]

A protective funerary amulet closely associated with Isis is the *tyet,* or Girdle of Isis, which was placed on the neck of the deceased (cat. no. 20g). The amulet's lower portion depicts a long sash with folded loops, which may represent a cloth actually worn during menstruation.[12] Many of these amulets were made of red jasper, the color denoting Isis' blood, as prescribed in Chapter 156 of the Book of the Dead.[13]

A variety of feline goddesses were also popularly represented in amuletic form. One of the oldest to appear is the goddess Bastet, patroness of the city of Bubastis in the Nile delta. As an amulet, she typically appears in late Dynastic Egypt as a seated cat, often accompanied by her kittens.[14] Like the frog, hippopotamus, and cow amulets, cat amulets were almost certainly worn by women for their fertility-enhancing powers.[15] Along with a number of other female deities, Bastet was often represented as a maned lion-goddess.[16] Sekhmet, the Memphite goddess often associated with war and pestilence,[17] is similarly depicted. As with other leonine goddesses, Sekhmet had a maternal aspect as well; amulets often depict her as mother goddess suckling a child god.[18] GEM

19 Cylindrical amulets

Gold and amethyst; excavated at Lisht (51.199.1); said to come from Dahshur (51.226); Middle Kingdom, Dynasty 12; L: 5.9 cm (51.226); 5.3 cm (51.199.1)

The Brooklyn Museum. Charles Edwin Wilbour Fund. 51.226, 51.199.1

These amulets are typical of two types of cylindrical pendents[1] popular during Egypt's Middle Kingdom.[2] The first consists of a hollow tube of precious metal, usually decorated with granulation or designs of twisted or braided wires, also of precious metals.[3] This type is sometimes fitted with an inner sleeve of copper or bronze.[4]

The second type is made of segments in the shape of stone beads alternating with beads of gold. In some cases, the latter are bead-shaped cores covered with precious metal.[5] The stone beads of these examples are of amethyst. The bead-shaped seg-

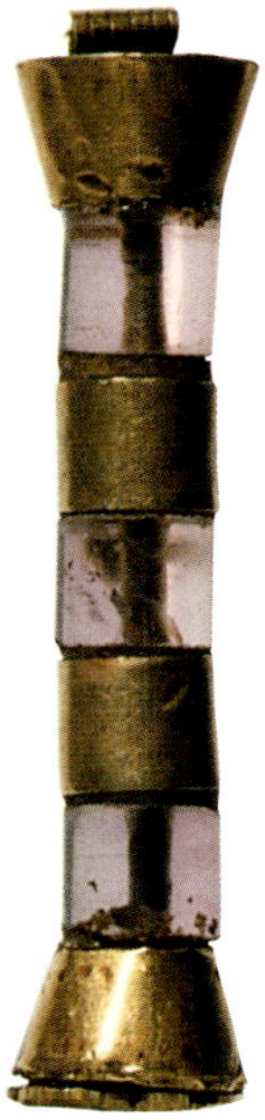

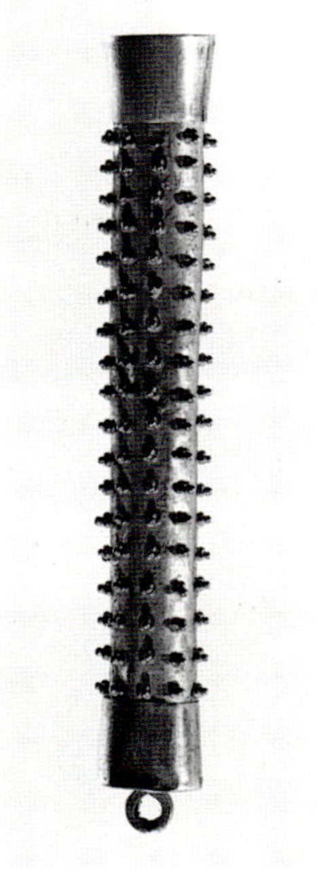

ments of this latter type are pierced so that they can be connected by a wire passing through their centers; they are not, however, hollowed fully enough to accommodate another object inside. Both types have straight or slightly flared end caps and a loop for suspension, and have been found in royal and nonroyal burials.[6]

The hollow cylindrical amulet obviously functioned as a container for another material. This example contains a carnelian stone; another from el-Haraga contains two copper beads (apparently in place of more expensive gold beads, as mentioned below) and unidentified organic material.[7] These contents have been compared[8] to those listed in the instructions for preparing an amulet for a child, described in Papyrus Berlin 3027:

> This spell is to be said over pellets of gold, balls of garnet(?), a seal [with(?)] a crocodile and a hand. To be attached to a piece of fine linen. To be made into an amulet, applied to the throat of a child.[9]

All excavated examples of cylinder pendents have come from the tombs of women or children.[10] A New Kingdom example excavated at Semna was found in an infant's burial.[11] The exact magical significance of these materials in protecting women and children is not yet understood. Red stones seem to have reminded the ancient Egyptians of blood, particularly the blood of Isis.[12] In Chapter 156 of the Book of the Dead, red jasper was specified as the material to be used for *tyet* amulets to be placed on the neck of a deceased person: "The power of Isis will be the protection of his body."[13] Gold was the color of divine flesh[14] and must have carried powerful protective significance. Cylindrical amulets of the solid type have been termed "dummy" cases;[15] their structures, however, incorporate gold and stones with colors symbolic of power and protection.[16] The same materials are contained in hollow cylindrical amulets in which the original contents have been preserved.[17] AKC

Published: Wilkinson, *Jewellery,* 209, A1 (51.226); 208, A1 and pl. IE (51.199.1).

20 a Figurine of Taweret

Faience; provenance unknown; Third Intermediate or Late Period; H: 7.62 cm

Cincinnati Art Museum. Gift of Millard F. and Edna F. Shelt. 1947.32

Taweret here wears the cylindrical *modius* and leans for support on a protective *sa* sign. Her pendulous breasts and swollen abdomen, characteristic features of the goddess, resemble those of a pregnant woman.

20 b Frog amulet

Glass; provenance unknown; New Kingdom; H: 0.95 cm

Cincinnati Art Museum. Gift of Millard F. and Edna F. Shelt. 1947.283

The frog was especially favored by women as an amulet. Known for its regenerative and reproductive powers, it was particularly abundant in Egypt's marshes, where

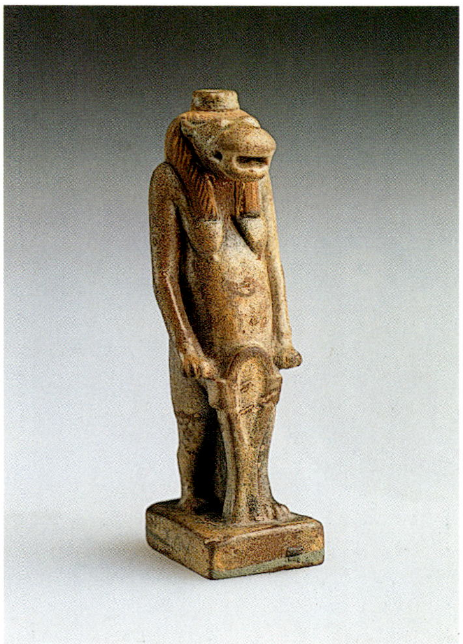

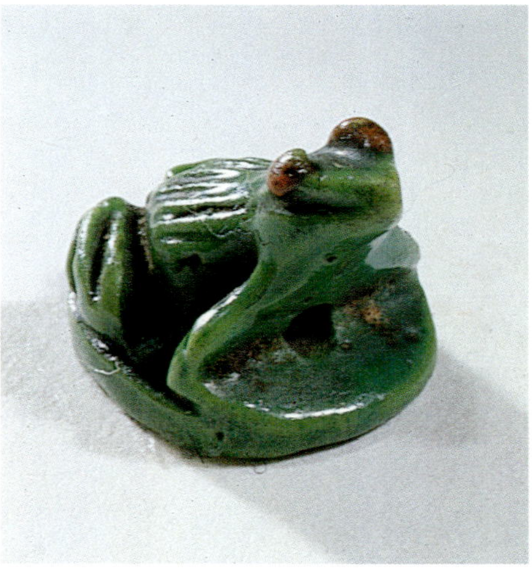

it bred voraciously. (The tadpole, in fact, served as the hieroglyph for "100,000.") The annual reappearance of frogs each year with the retreat of the Nile's waters led to the mistaken belief that they had powers of self-creation. As a result, the frog served in amuletic form as a symbol of rebirth in the hereafter.[1] For women, the frog also served as a powerful symbol of fecundity during life. It has been suggested that frog amulets may depict the birth goddess Heket, whose worship extended back to Predynastic times.[2] Amulets, such as this one, were probably worn by women to ensure fecundity and to protect them during childbirth.[3]

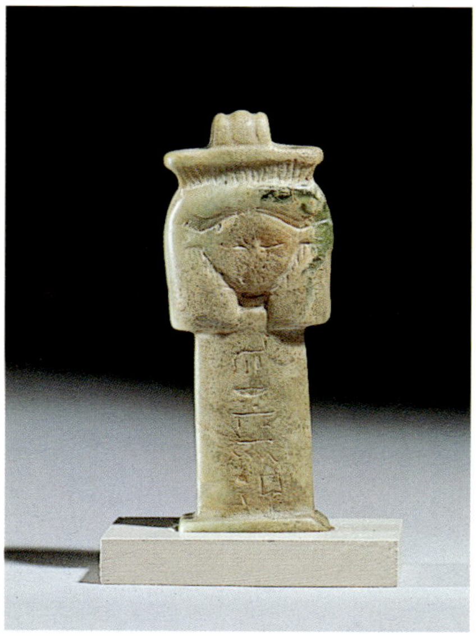

20 c Hathor head on pillar

Green magnesite marble or porphyry; provenance unknown; Late Period; H: 6.9 cm

Cincinnati Art Museum. Gift of Millard F. and Edna F. Shelt. 1947.33

One of the most ancient of maternal deities to appear in amuletic form was the goddess Hathor; from the New Kingdom onward, she was represented as a woman with heavy plaits and cow's ears.[4] Hathor is frequently depicted by her head alone, which often surmounts a column or pillar. The present amulet bears an inscription to Hathor, *Nebet hetepet,* "Lady of Hetepet," an ancient Heliopolitan goddess whose cult was widespread.[5] Beginning in the New Kingdom, Nebet Hetepet became assimilated with a number of goddesses, Hathor most prominent among them.[6] The term *hetepet* has several meanings: contentment or offerings as well as vulva or uterus.[7] In all likelihood, it is in the latter capacity—as Mistress of the Vulva—that Hathor is propitiated on this amulet, which probably served as a woman's fertility charm. (See cat. nos. 8a, 34, and 39.)[8]

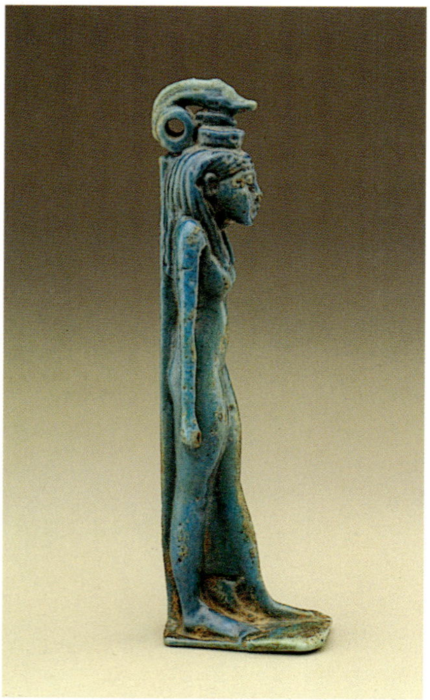

20 d Hatmehit amulet

Faience; provenance unknown; Third Intermediate Period; H: 8.2 cm

The Detroit Institute of Arts. Gift of Dr. and Mrs. Irving Burton. 68.67

Attested by the Fourth Dynasty, the fish goddess Hatmehit (Foremost of Fishes) was one of the principal deities of the nome of Mendes in the Nile delta.[9] Her fish symbol, which she wears upon her head, appeared early as an emblem of this region. The precise identification of this fish has been debated. It may represent a dolphin or a Schilbe, the sacred fish of the region, which appears early in depictions of the standard of Mendes.[10]

Little is known of Hatmehit's cult and divine nature. She was paired with Banebdjed, the sacred ram of Mendes with whom she bore a local manifestation of Horus the Child. The three formed the so-called Mendesian triad.[11] One of her associated activities may have been the local production of precious unguents; her epithets included that of "Queen of Punt, Mistress of Myrrh . . . whose perfume is diffused throughout the Two Lands."[12] According to later Osirian tradition, along with the goddess Nephthys, she helped to recover the dismembered limbs of Osiris.

With the exception of the Mendes standard, depictions of Hatmehit are not known before the Third Intermediate Period, when she occurs in amuletic form, either fully human or as a fish.[13] In the former instance, she appears either seated or standing, wearing her fish emblem on her head.

20 e Seated monkey

Faience; provenance unknown; Third Intermediate or Late Period; H: 7.3 cm

Cincinnati Art Museum. Gift of Millard F. and Edna F. Shelt. 1947.30

Amulets depicting squatting monkeys and baboons accompanied by their offspring may have served as fertility charms for women.[14] The present subject assumes the typical squatting pose with its head resting on its paws. Broken at the base, it is missing the diminutive figure of the baby that originally stood at its feet.[15]

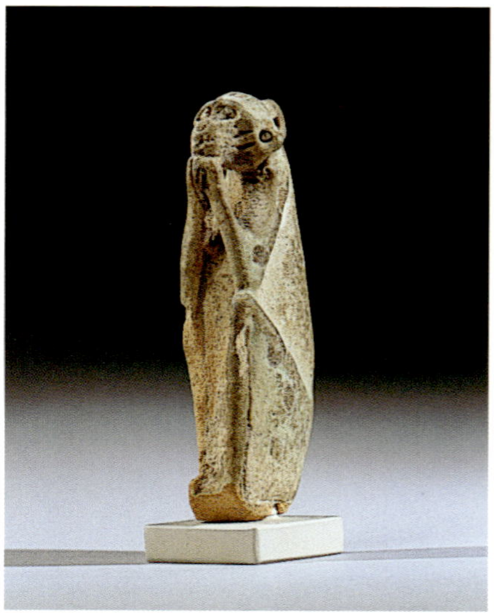

20 f–q Assorted amulets favored by women

Provenance unknown; New Kingdom–Late Period; dimensions range: H. 2.2–4.8 cm; W. 1.3–2.7 cm

Cincinnati Art Museum. Gift of the Egypt Exploration Society; Gift of Millard F. and Edna F. Shelt.

f Isis, faience, Late Period, 1947.292
g girdle of Isis, jasper, New Kingdom or later, 1947.219
h Nephthys, faience, Late Period, 1947.294
i triad of Isis, Horus, and Nephthys, faience, Late Period, 1947.290
j seated Isis–Hathor with Horus, faience, Late Period, 1947.304
k seated lion-headed goddess, Bastet or Sekhmet, faience, Late Period, 1947.437
l seated lion-headed goddess, Bastet or Sekhmet, faience, Third Intermediate Period or later, 1947.302
m standing lion-headed goddess with lotus scepter, Bastet or Sekhmet, faience, from Abydos, Dynasty 22, 1912.386
n Neith, faience, Late Period, 1947.291
o seated cat, faience, Late Period, 1947.423
p seated cat, lapis lazuli, New Kingdom, 1947.444
q Nut as sow with young, faience, Late Period, 1947.440

Amulet q depicts the sky goddess Nut as a rooting sow accompanied by her piglets; the latter symbolized the heavenly stars, which Nut bore each evening and consumed the following dawn.

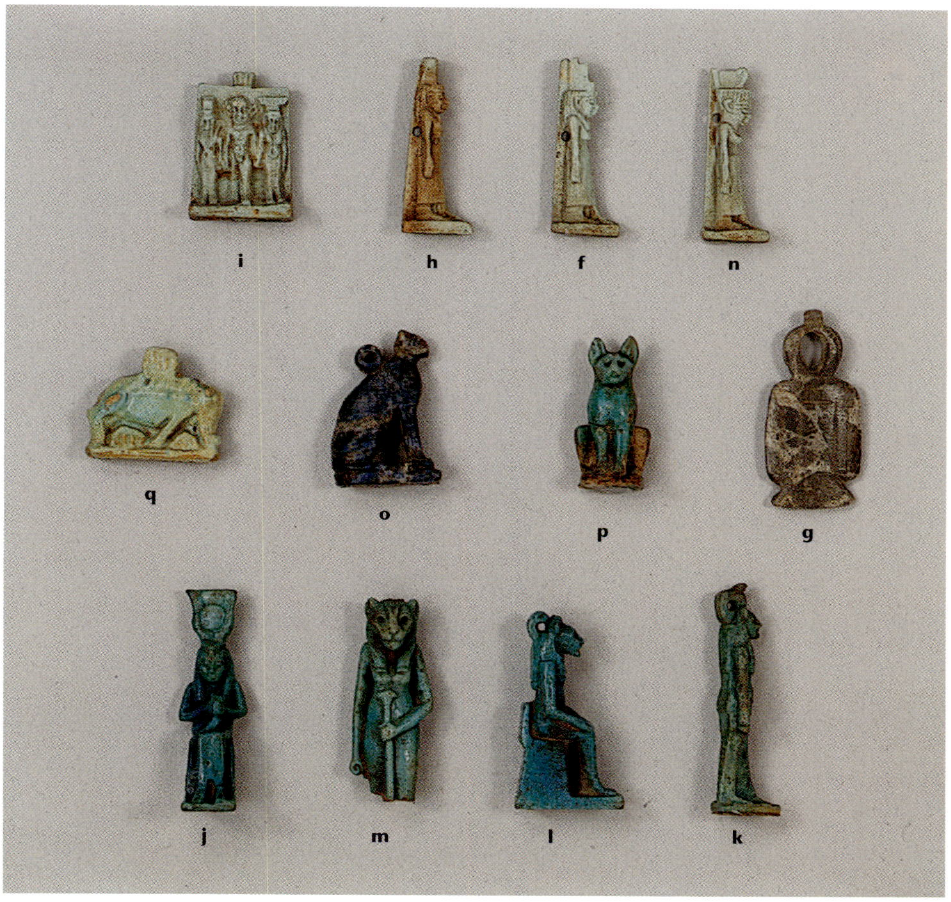

20 r–u Amulets with Bes-image

Excavated at Amarna, Abydos, and Antinoe; New Kingdom–Roman Period; dimensions range: H. 3.8–4.5 cm; W. 1.3–3.2 cm

Cincinnati Art Museum. Gift of the Egypt Exploration Society; Gift of Millard F. and Edna F. Shelt.

r Bes-image, blue faience, from Amarna, late Dynasty 18, 1921.307
s head of Bes-image, faience, Late Period, 1947.471
t mold for Bes-image amulet, terracotta, from Antinoe, late Roman Period, 1914.576
u Bes-image, green faience, from Abydos, Dynasty 18, 1914.402

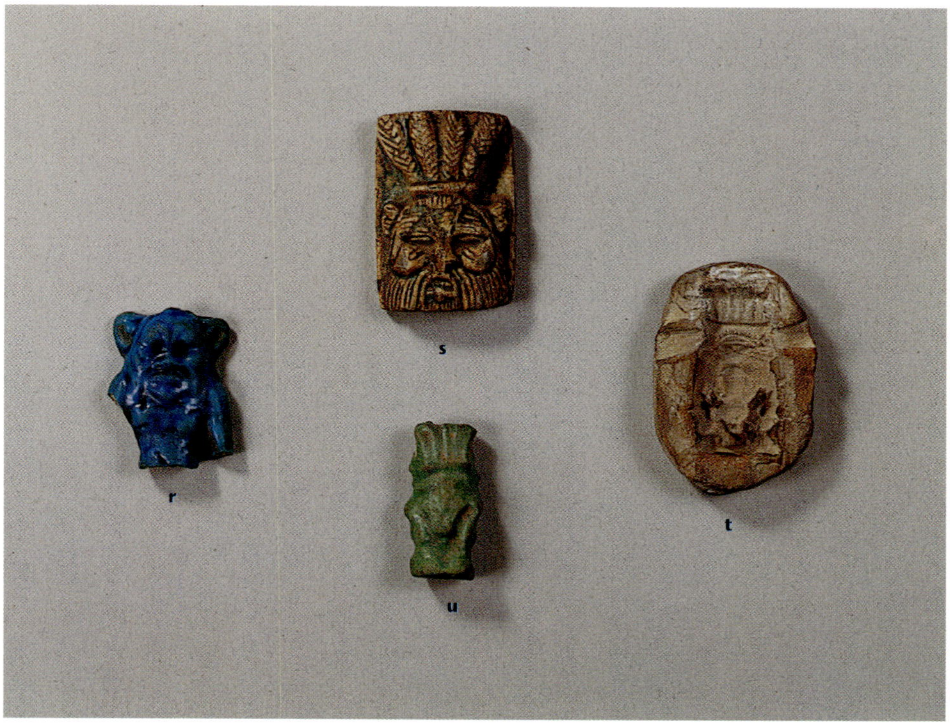

The Egyptians worshipped a large number of gods—Bes among them—who assumed the image of a bandy-legged, leonine-headed creature. (See cat. no. 20k,l,m.) Without an identifying inscription, it is often impossible to determine which of them is depicted. This is particularly true of amulets, which rarely identify their subject by inscription. While the major roles occupied by such Bes-image deities were that of domestic, household gods, they also performed other functions, especially in *mammisis,* or birth-houses centered around child gods, such as Horus.[16] The common occurrence of such Bes-image amulets in houses at Amarna (cat. no. 16) reflects their usage in daily life; more than likely, they belonged to women or children. Their presence reveals the continuing popularity of such household deities, even during the reign of Akhenaten.

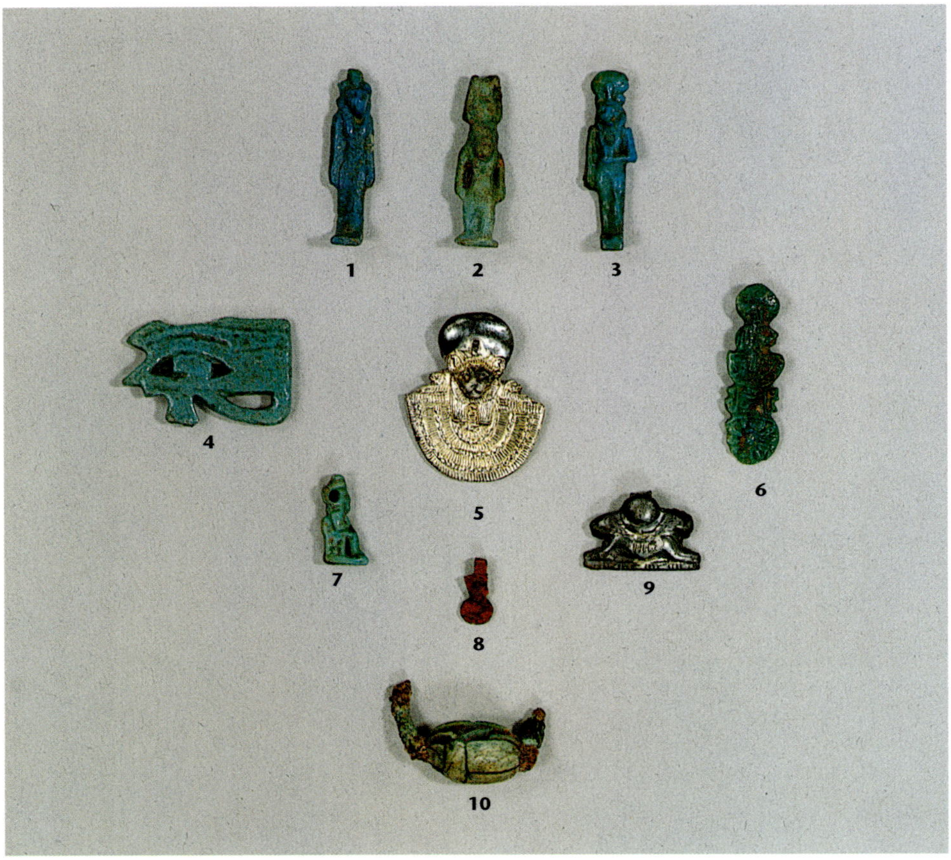

20 v1–v10 Group of amulets from a woman's burial

Excavated at Abydos, Cemetery S, Tomb 49; Third Intermediate Period, Dynasty 22 or later; dimensions range: H. 1.9–2.5 cm; W. 1.3–1.9 cm

Cincinnati Art Museum. Gift of the Egypt Exploration Society

v1 lion-headed goddess, faience, 1912.377c
v2 Taweret, faience, 1912.377a
v3 lion-headed goddess, faience, 1912.377d
v4 *uadjet* eye, faience, 1912.378
v5 lion-headed aegis, silver, 1912.381
v6 aegis with counterpoise, faience, 1912.377e
v7 seated Isis, faience, 1912.377b
v8 *menat*, jasper, 1912.380
v9 addorsed lions, silver, 1912.382
v10 bronze ring with blue faience scarab, 1912.379

This group of faience and silver amulets was found at Abydos in the burial of a woman in a wooden anthropomorphic coffin. As expected, a number of maternal goddesses are represented, including Taweret, Isis, and Bastet. The presence of Hathor is also evidenced by a jasper amulet in the shape of a *menat*, a form of collar closely associated with Hathor (cat. nos. 54, 55, and 56). This burial also contained two amulets in the form of an aegis with a feline-headed goddess (cf. cat. no. 66). One example in faience is equipped with a counterpoise, while a second, in silver, has two flanking falcon-headed terminals.[17] As the excavations revealed, a protective *uadjet* eye was placed over the deceased's mouth, while a bronze scarab ring with the name of Senuser was found on her hand.

Published: Peet and Loat, *Abydos*, 2: 47. The female identity of the deceased, who was buried alongside a man (presumably her husband), is noted in the unpublished notes of the burial's excavation. A network of minute blue-glazed discoid beads and small shells was found on the deceased's chest.

Hair ornaments and accessories

The attention that ancient Egyptians devoted to coiffure and hairdressing is well documented, both pictorially (cat. nos. 8a, 34, 39) and by the evidence of hair implements and accessories found in tombs. Entire cosmetic sets, consisting of items such as razors, tweezers, hair curlers, mirrors, and kohl tubes, were frequently buried with their owners, often in their original containers; these included baskets, leather cases, and inlaid wooden boxes.[1]

To the ancient Egyptians, abundant facial and body hair were signs of uncleanliness: the face, neck, limbs, armpits, chest, and pubic regions were shaved regularly. Men and women of the upper classes typically wore their hair close-cropped and adorned themselves with wigs on public occasions.[2] Consequently, implements for shaving and hair removal, such as razors, knives, and tweezers, were used widely from an early period.

The razor had a long history in Egypt, extending back to late Predynastic times. Throughout its long evolution, it took a variety of shapes and forms: copper and bronze implements served the well-to-do, while chipped flint tools were undoubtedly used by the poor.

Tweezers are documented from the beginning of Egypt's Dynastic era. They are found in abundance in tombs, often in multiple pairs. Although they were used for a variety of tasks, one of their primary purposes, especially among women, was the removal of unwanted facial hair. It has been suggested that the blunt-tipped variety was designed expressly for this purpose (cat. nos. 21b,c).[3]

Eighteenth Dynasty "shaving" sets also contained small bronze toilet implements of uncertain function, composed of two parts hinged together: a straight pin slotted at one end and pointed at the other, and an upper element with a flat blade in front and a rounded blade in back. This second element was often shaped decoratively in human or animal form (cat. no. 21d). (On both examples in the exhibition, the blade end of the upper element is shaped like a papyrus flower.) Such implements probably served a variety of purposes, but one function clearly was that of a razor. It probably also functioned as a hair crimper or curler. In this capacity, it was apparently intended for curling small amounts of hair without heat.[4] Like the razor and tweezers, the hair curler enjoyed a long use extending from the Old Kingdom to the Late Period.

Beginning in Predynastic times, attention to the dressing of hair is documented amply by numerous hairpins and combs carved of bone, wood, and ivory. The two implements are often found together in baskets with cosmetic items.[5] Occasionally they were combined into a single multipurpose implement: a straight pin with a comb-headed terminal.[6]

Most ancient Egyptian combs were utilitarian in nature and design; they consisted of a plain wooden horizontal grip with parallel rows of teeth. Double-sided examples displayed fine and coarse teeth back to back (cat. nos. 21f,g). Although most of these combs were straight-edged, occasional examples were curved, suggesting their secondary use as hair ornaments.[7] The comb had a clear (although not exclusive) funerary association with women. At Deir el-Medina, for example, all of the combs were found in women's tombs.[8]

Like combs, straight hairpins were a frequent feature of women's burials at Deir el-Medina and elsewhere. The use of the straight pin as a lock fastener in hairdressing scenes is well documented on reliefs of the Middle Kingdom (cat. nos. 8a, 34, 39).[9] As reliefs and actual examples show, the canonical hairpin of Dynastic times was a long, tapering straight pin of bone, ivory, or hardwood, often embellished with incised linear decoration and a round, knoblike finial (cat. nos. 21h,i). The simplest variety, used by the poorer classes, consisted of a bit of fine reed with a head of pinched clay.[10] In the New Kingdom, elaborate examples often bore tiny, carved terminal figures of animals, most frequently seated cats (cat. no. 21i) and crouching monkeys.[11] Associations with the maternal concerns of birth and fertility are evident in the inclusion of the goddess Taweret and the theme of a cow suckling a calf.[12] GEM

21a Razor

Bronze; excavated at Amarna; New Kingdom, late Dynasty 18, reign of Akhenaten; L: 6 cm

Cincinnati Art Museum. Gift of the Egypt Exploration Society. 1924.278

Such knife-shaped razors typically were part of "shaving" kits in the Eighteenth Dynasty. In addition to its principal rounded cutting edge, it has a convex chisel-like edge at the base of the handle.

For the type, see *Egypt's Golden Age,* no. 223; Hayes, *Scepter,* 2: 64, fig. 33.

21b Blunt-edged tweezers

Bronze; excavated at Abydos, Tomb D229; New Kingdom, Dynasty 18; L: 5.4 cm

Cincinnati Art Museum. Gift of the Egypt Exploration Society. 1914.382

These tweezers, one of several from an Eighteenth Dynasty tomb at Abydos, were found with other cosmetic items such as a bronze kohl stick and a bone pin. The type—with pinched top—apparently originated in the Eighteenth Dynasty.

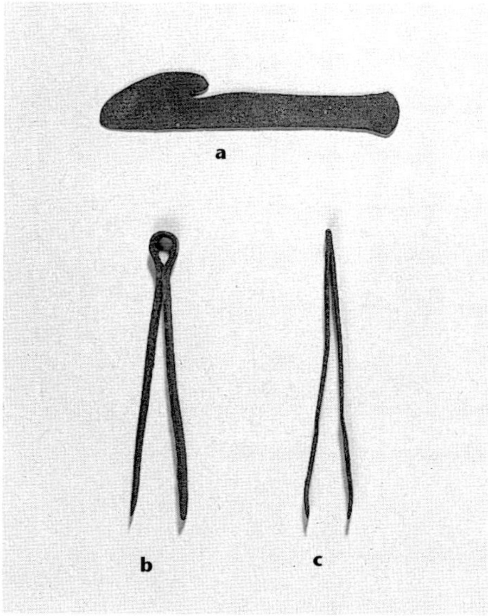

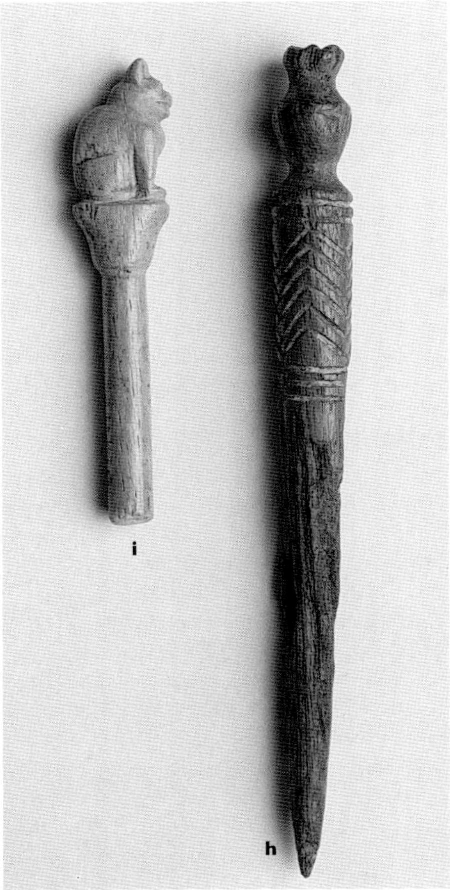

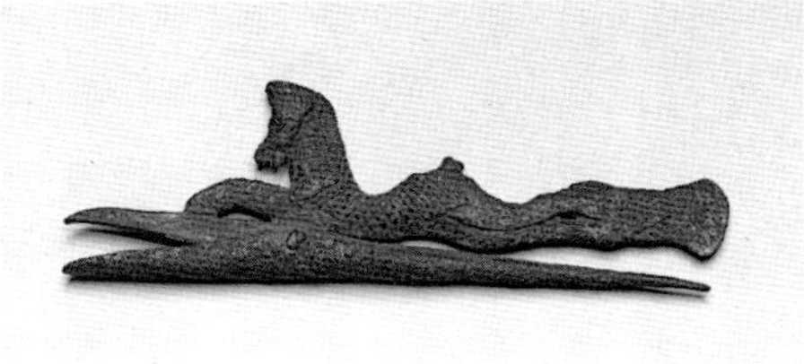

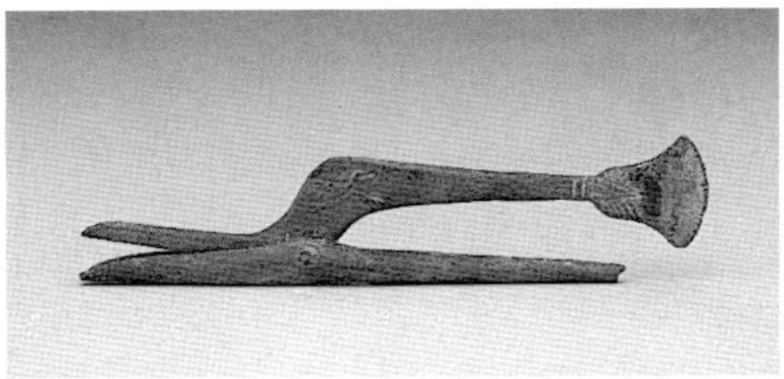

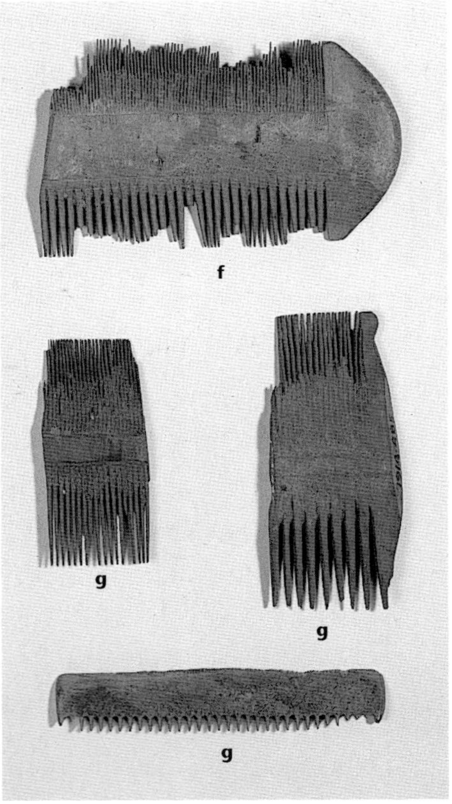

21 c Blunt-edged tweezers

Bronze; excavated at Antinoe;
Late Roman or Byzantine Period;
L: 5.7 cm

Cincinnati Art Museum. Gift of the
Egypt Exploration Society. 1914.568

21 d Toilet implement with horse-shaped handle

Bronze; provenance unknown; New
Kingdom, Dynasty 18; L: 12.2 cm

Art Institute of Chicago. Gift of Henry H.
Getty and Charles L. Hutchinson. 1894.963

For a discussion of horse-shaped implements of this type, see *Egypt's Golden Age*, no. 227.

21 e Toilet implement with papyriform blade

Bronze; provenance unknown;
New Kingdom; L: 6.4 cm

The Detroit Institute of Arts. Gift of
Frederick K. Stearns. 90.1S12435

21 f Double-sided comb

Wood; excavated at Abydos; Middle
Kingdom, Dynasty 12; L: 10.5 cm

Cincinnati Art Museum. Gift of the
Egypt Exploration Society. 1912.397

21 g Fragmentary combs

Wood; excavated at Antinoe; Late
Roman or Byzantine Period; L: 2.9 cm;
3.8 cm; 9.5 cm

Cincinnati Art Museum. Gift of the
Egypt Exploration Society. 1914.484,
485, 492

21 h Hairpin with pomegranate-shaped terminal

Wood; excavated at Amarna;
New Kingdom, late Dynasty 18, reign
of Akhenaten; L: 10 cm

Cincinnati Art Museum. Gift of the
Egypt Exploration Society. 1921.299

Cf. Petrie, *Objects of Daily Use*, 24 and pl. 19, 20, 21, 23.

21 i Fragmentary hairpin with seated cat

Wood; provenance unknown; New
Kingdom; Preserved L: 6 cm

Cincinnati Art Museum. Gift of Millard
F. and Edna F. Shelt. 1947.146

22 a Mirror with double Hathor face

Bronze; provenance unknown; New
Kingdom, early Dynasty 18; H: 28 cm

Cincinnati Art Museum. Gift of
Millard F. and Edna F. Shelt. 1947.366

22 b Mirror with handle in form of a woman

Bronze; provenance unknown; New
Kingdom, early to mid–Dynasty 18;
H: 24.6 cm

The Brooklyn Museum. Charles Edwin
Wilbour Fund. 37.635E

The mirror was an indispensable accessory for applying cosmetics and arranging coiffure and jewelry. In the Middle Kingdom, the typical hand mirror consisted of two pieces: a metal disc and a wood or ivory handle. The latter traditionally was shaped as a papyrus column with a gracefully spreading umbel (cat. no. 24a). On more elaborate examples dating to the Eighteenth Dynasty, the papyriform column was ornamented with flanking falcons (perched on the umbel) or images of Bes or a double Hathor head (cat. no. 22a). Elsewhere the papyriform-column handle was modified to include a nude female figure with upraised arms (cat. no. 22b).

The mirror disc itself—of copper, bronze, or silver polished to a highly reflective shine—was attached to the handle by a rivet. The rivet was fabricated from a variety of materials including wood, ivory, stone, faience, and bronze.

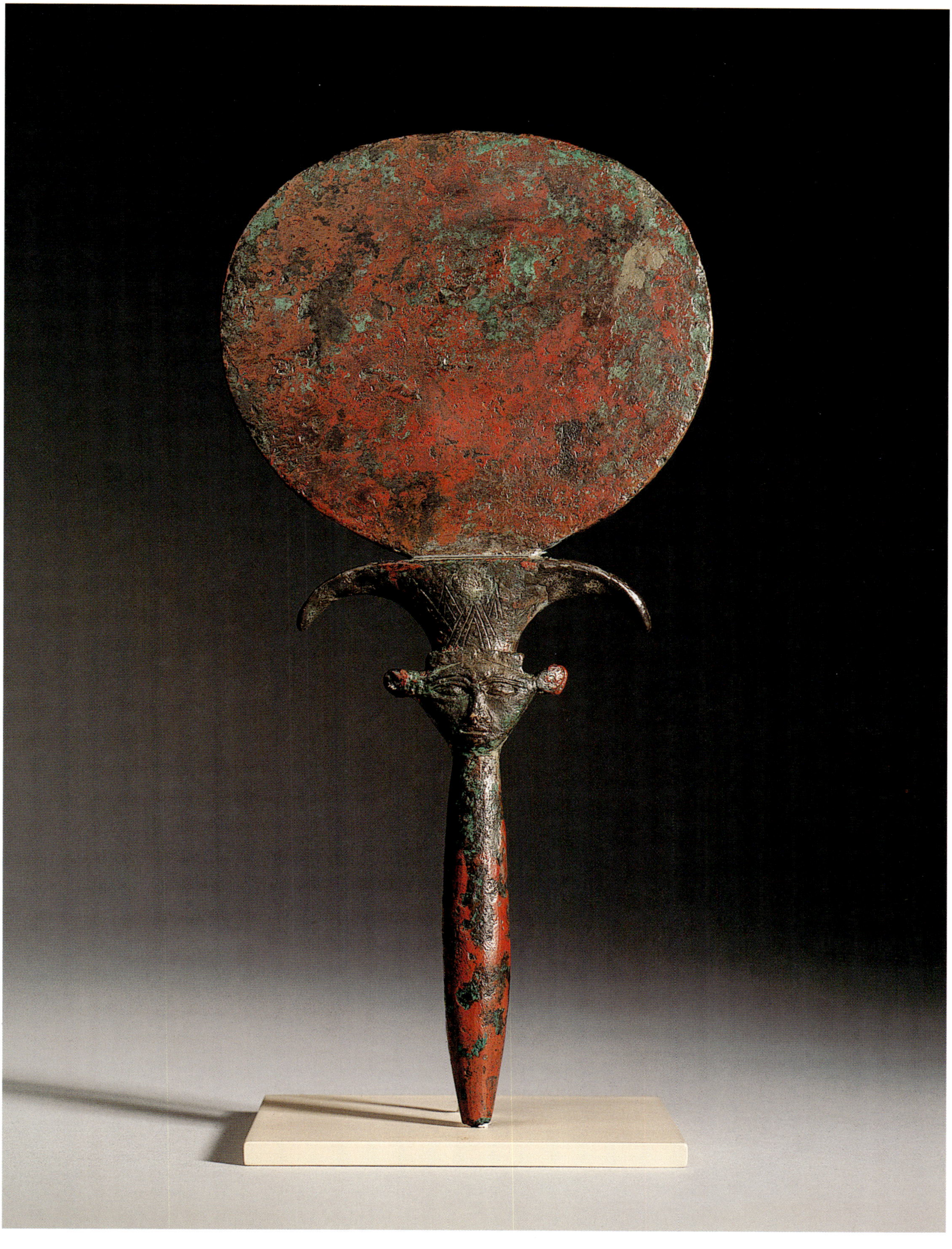

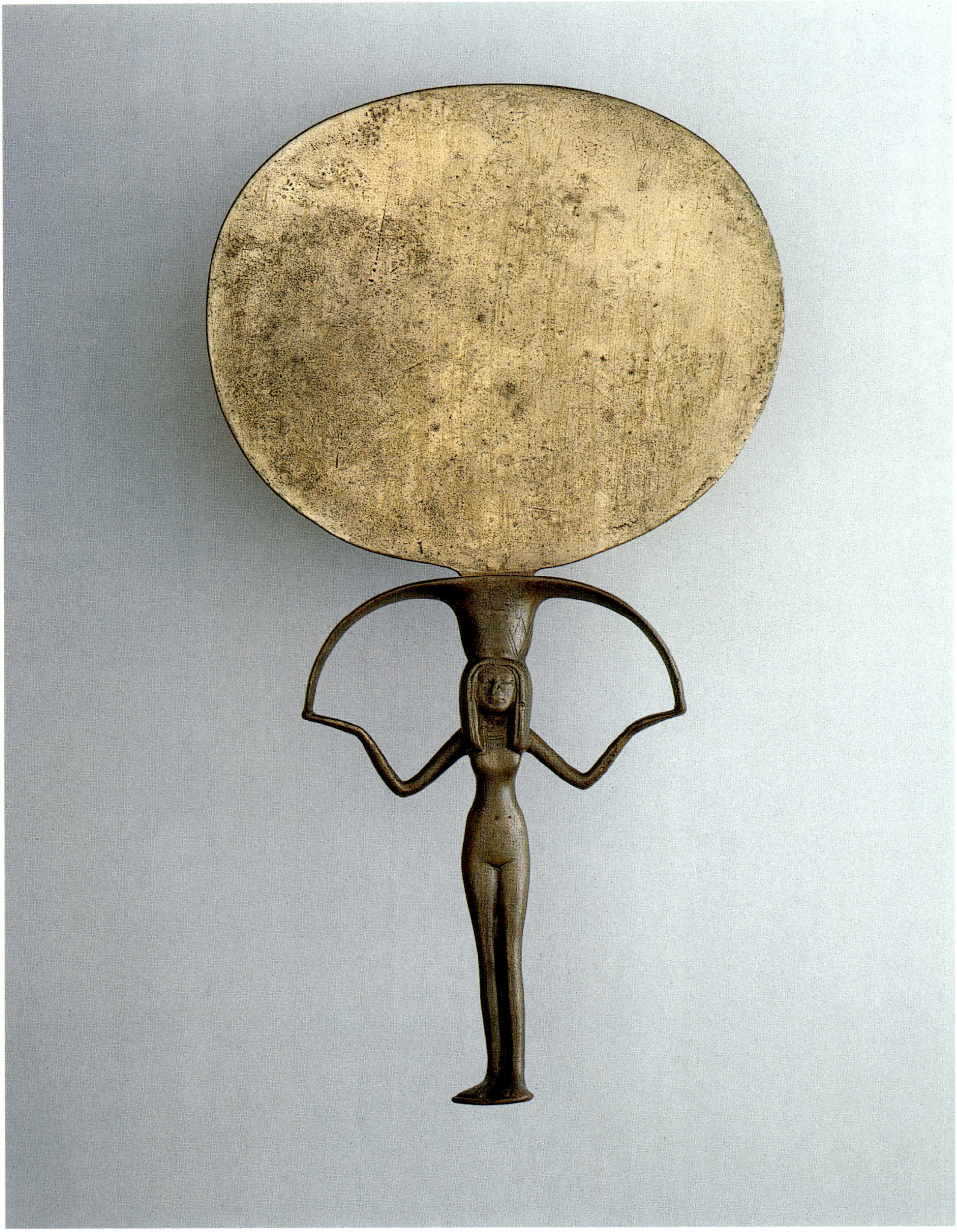

Used in Egypt from at least the Old Kingdom, the mirror served a funerary and religious purpose as well as a practical function. Mirrors were endowed with great magical potential because they had the power to hold the user's image. This power is embodied in the Egyptian word for mirror, *ankh,* which is also the ancient Egyptian word for "life." The mirror disc itself, whose poles—top and bottom—intentionally were flattened like those of the sun, symbolized the solar orb. The image of the sun disc, in fact, was used in Egyptian hieroglyphic writing to indicate the word *sun.*

The goddess Hathor's face on catalogue number 22a displays the usual triangular shape and protruding cow's ears.[1] In view of Hathor's association with fertility and procreation, this mirror type was probably favored by women, and perhaps was used in cultic worship of the goddess.[2]

The subject of catalogue number 22b is a nude woman with arms upraised typical of bronze mirrors dating to the mid–Eighteenth Dynasty.[3] The nudity and youthfulness of such figures and their use as mirror supports suggest that they may have been intended to represent servants or household attendants of the owner.[4] Indeed, female servants are depicted in contemporary tomb paintings holding mirrors for their masters. Alternately, these figures may have represented the goddess Hathor, whose association with physical beauty and procreation rendered her an ideal ornament for mirror handles.[5] GEM

Published: Fazzini et al., *Ancient Egyptian Art,* no. 45.

Cosmetic vessels[1]

Kohl-rimmed eyes, elaborately coiffed and perfumed wigs, and miniature stone pots filled with scented unguents—all of these conjure up exotic images of ancient Egyptians. Indeed, they were all part of the daily lives of the upper classes. As early as Predynastic times, both men and women used cosmetics to enhance their appearance. Health concerns as well as religious and magical beliefs prompted the use of many types of paints, oils, and medical remedies.[2]

The use of facial cosmetics in the West today is associated primarily with women, but in ancient Egypt both sexes employed them regularly. The use of eyeliner and shadow was particularly common. Eyes were outlined with pigments produced from a variety of minerals. A black colorant known as kohl *(mesdemet* in ancient Egyptian)[3] was produced from powdered galena; green and red were produced respectively from malachite *(wadj*[4]) and hematite. Both black and green were commonly used to outline the rim of the eye, and the latter was also used to color the eyelid. The use of green eye paint was particularly widespread in the Old Kingdom, when it was applied liberally from the eyebrow to the base of the nose.[5] In addition to enhancing appearance, kohl served a practical function: it prevented damage to the eyes both from disease and from the sun's glare, a constant concern in the Egyptian desert.

Ancient Egyptians, both men and women, bathed often; upperclass Egyptian homes frequently had rooms equipped with stone slabs, where water was poured over the bather.[6] In Egypt's hot, dry climate, frequent appplications of oils were necessary to prevent the skin from drying. The Egyptians made copious use of various ointments, chiefly vegetable oils and fat, applied to the skin and the hair either as salves or in liquid form. In fact, more than thirty types of oils and unguents were commonly used in ancient Egypt. These ranged from linseed and castor-bean oil to expensive varieties scented with costly imported aromatics such as frankincense and myrrh. Other commonly used oils included moringa, balanos, sesame, safflower, almond, and olive. For perfumes, scents were extracted by steeping various plants, flowers (the essence of lily was highly esteemed), or splinters of fragrant wood in oil. In Egypt's hot climate, durability of scent was a practical consideration. As the Greek scientist Theophrastus stated in the third century B.C., "A lasting perfume is what women require."[7]

Early in Egypt's history, the number of essential ointments and perfumes was established at seven.[8] The seven sacred oils, in fact, became standard equipment for affluent Egyptian men and women in the Old Kingdom. In addition to their ceremonial and ritual use in anointing statues in both temples and tombs, these oils and unguents were doubtlessly employed by living Egyptians in their daily lives.[9] AKC/GEM

PALETTES

In the Prehistoric and Early Dynastic periods, cosmetic palettes in geometric and animal shapes were used by both men and women to prepare eye paint. Ores or minerals were ground directly on the stone; the resulting powder was applied dry, or mixed with resin or oil to form eye paint. The remains of dry pigment on palettes[10] as well as extensive surface wear indicate that they were objects of frequent use in daily life.

23 a Cosmetic palette in the shape of a fish

Slate; provenance unknown;
Predynastic Period, Naqada II;
H: 6.4 cm; L: 12.9 cm

Cincinnati Art Museum. Museum Purchase. 1962.700

Published: *Sculpture Collection,* 13 (illus.).

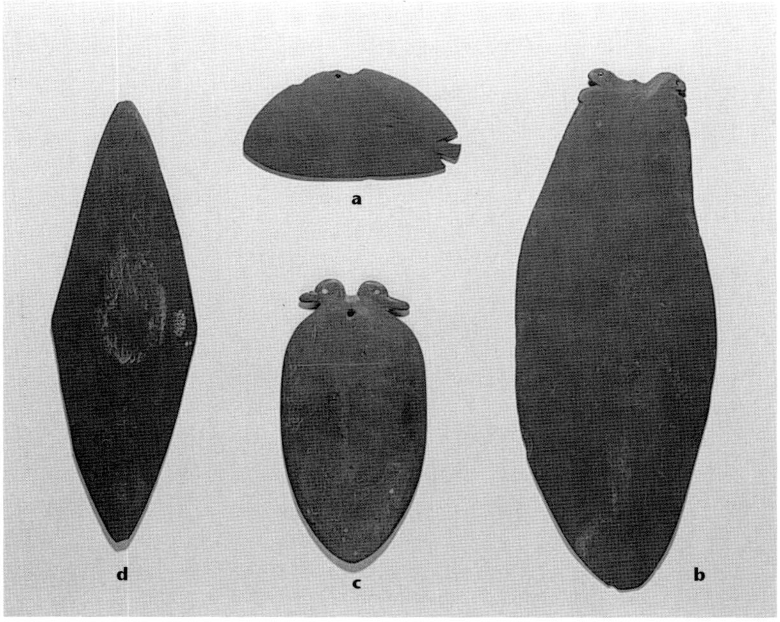

23 b Double bird-headed cosmetic palette

Slate; provenance unknown; Predynastic Period, late Naqada II–Naqada III; L: 30.4 cm; W: 12 cm

Cincinnati Art Museum. Museum Purchase. 1962.701

Published: *Sculpture Collection*, 13 (illus.)

23 c Double bird-headed cosmetic palette

Argillite; provenance unknown; Predynastic Period, late Naqada II–Naqada III; L: 15.5 cm; W: 8.8 cm

Cincinnati Art Museum. Gift of the Cincinnati Museum of Natural History and Louis E. Bryant. 1990.1919

23 d Rhomboidal cosmetic palette

Slate; provenance unknown; Predynastic Period, Naqada I; L: 25.5 cm; max W: 8.7 cm

Cincinnati Art Museum. Gift of the Cincinnati Museum of Natural History and Louis E. Bryant. 1990.1918

23 e Cosmetic palette in the shape of a hippopotamus

Slate; provenance unknown; Predynastic Period, Naqada II; L: 16.3 cm

The Toledo Museum of Art. Gift of Edward Drummond Libbey. 06.176

Published: *Museum News. The Toledo Museum of Art* n.s. 14, no. 1 (1971): 5, fig. 3.

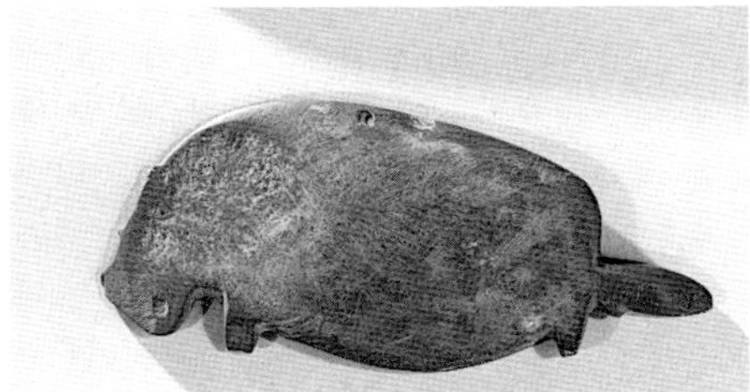

KOHL CONTAINERS AND APPLICATORS

Ancient Egyptian eye paint was stored in a variety of containers. In the Old Kingdom, a wide range of materials—from glazed ceramics to colorful, variegated hard stones—were employed. During the Middle Kingdom, the kohl pot assumed a standardized shape—a small squat jar with a flat bottom, a wide, flat rim, and a flat, disc-shaped lid. Occasionally these pots were mounted on small, four-legged stands, either made separately or carved in one piece with the jar.[11]

In the New Kingdom, kohl containers varied in shape and material. Because of the ease with which they were carved as well as their attractive veining, alabaster and, to a lesser extent, anhydrite ("blue marble") became popular for cosmetic vessels. During the late Eighteenth and Nineteenth Dynasties, faience and core-formed glass were employed increasingly in the manufacture of kohl containers; glass kohl tubes in the form of palm columns were especially favored (cat. no. 23m). Kohl and other cosmetics were also commonly stored in cut tubes of hollow reed, which were often tied together in bundles.[12] For the affluent, imitations of reed tubes were produced in faience.

In the Middle Kingdom, kohl applicators—slender sticks made of hard wood, stone, or bronze with a bulbous tip at one end—were introduced. One variety of applicator had a chisel-shaped end designed expressly for mixing pigment with oil or resin to form eye paint (cat. no. 72p).

23 f Kohl pot

Gabbro; provenance unknown; Old Kingdom, Dynasty 4; H: 4.2 cm

Cincinnati Art Museum. Gift of Millard F. and Edna F. Shelt. 1947.65

23 g Kohl pot

Alabaster; excavated at Abydos, Tomb 1009; Middle Kingdom, Dynasty 12; H (with lid): 4.5 cm

Cincinnati Art Museum. Gift of the Egypt Exploration Society. 1926.58

23 h Kohl pot

Travertine or anhydrite; provenance unknown; Middle Kingdom; H: 6.7 cm

Cincinnati Art Museum. Gift of the Egypt Exploration Society. 1947.63

23 i Kohl pot

Dried mud; excavated at Balabish, Tomb B20; New Kingdom, Dynasty 19; H: 4.5 cm

Cincinnati Art Museum. Gift of the Egypt Exploration Society. 1915.415

This small, lidded kohl pot of dried mud was found, together with the alabaster kohl pot (cat. no. 23j) described below, in a Nineteenth Dynasty grave at Balabish.

23 j Kohl pot

Alabaster; excavated at Balabish, Tomb B20; New Kingdom, Dynasty 19; H (with lid): 3 cm

Cincinnati Art Museum. Gift of the Egypt Exploration Society. 1915.416

This vessel contains remnants of kohl.

23 k Kohl tube with names of Amenhotep III and Queen Tiye

Faience; provenance unknown; New Kingdom, Dynasty 18, reign of Amenhotep III; H: 13 cm; Diam: 1.7 cm

Phoebe Hearst Museum of Anthropology, University of California at Berkeley. 5–2100

Published: *Egypt's Golden Age*, no. 277.

23 l Quadruple kohl set

Faience; provenance unknown; New Kingdom, Dynasty 18; H: 4 cm; W at base: 6.1 cm

University of Pennsylvania Museum of Archaeology and Anthropology, Philadelphia. Gift of Mrs. John Harrison. E 597a–d

Multiple kohl tubes such as this were clearly intended for different varieties of eye preparation. On several examples, three of the tubes were inscribed with the names of the seasons; the fourth contained the label "eye paint for every day." (See *Egypt's Golden Age*, 216, and no. 280).

23 m Kohl tube in form of palm column

Core-formed glass; reported to have been found at Alexandria; New Kingdom, late Dynasty 18 or Dynasty 19; H: 11.2 cm; D: 3.5 cm

The Toledo Museum of Art. Gift of Edward Drummond Libbey. 66.114

Published: Grose, *Ancient Glass*, no. 10.

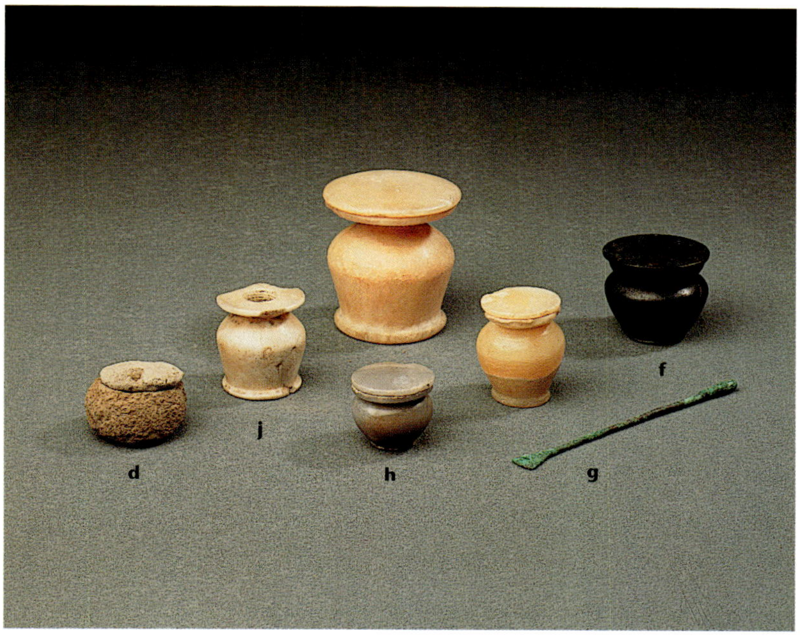
f
j
d
h
g

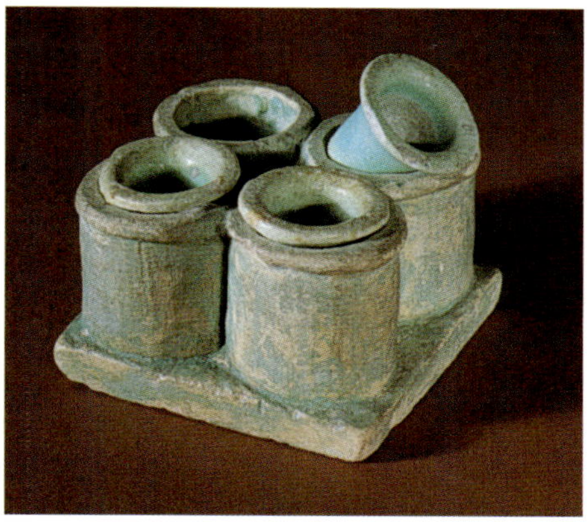

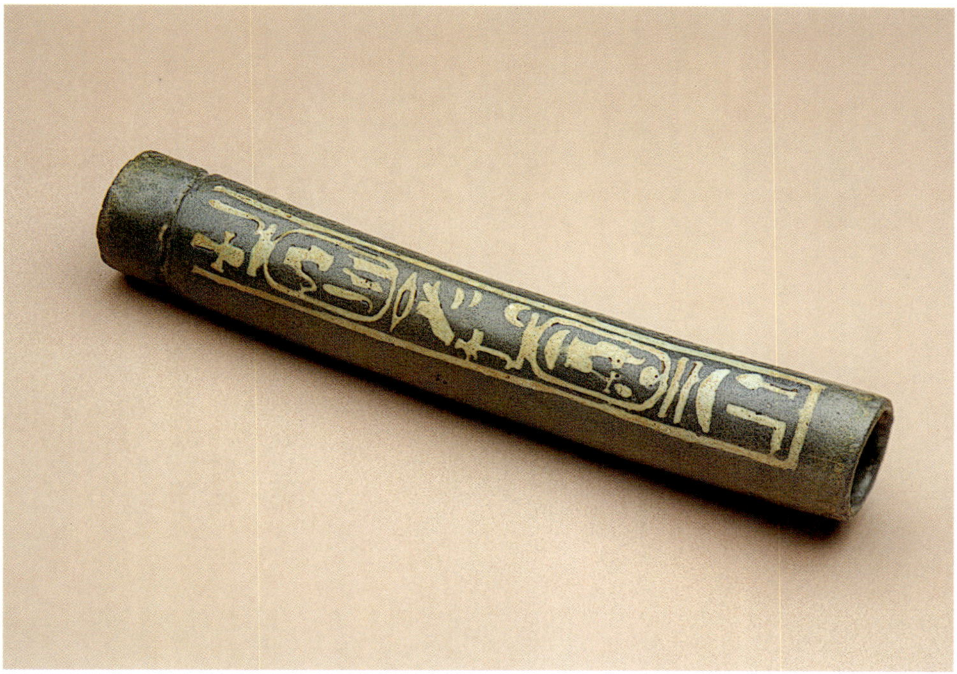

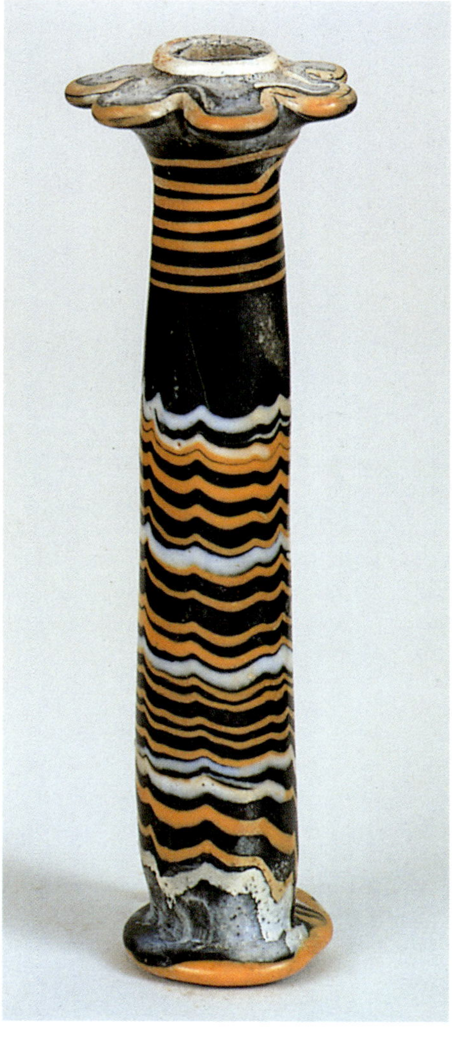

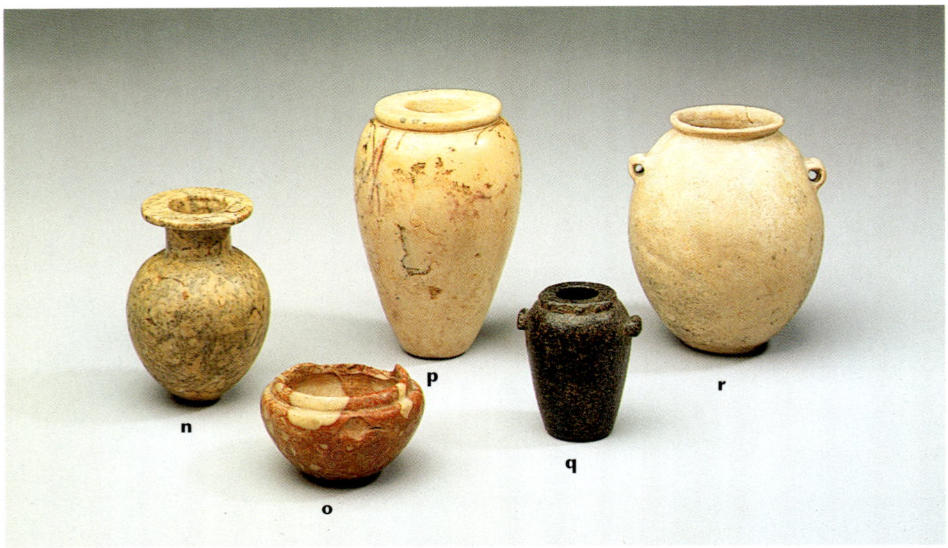

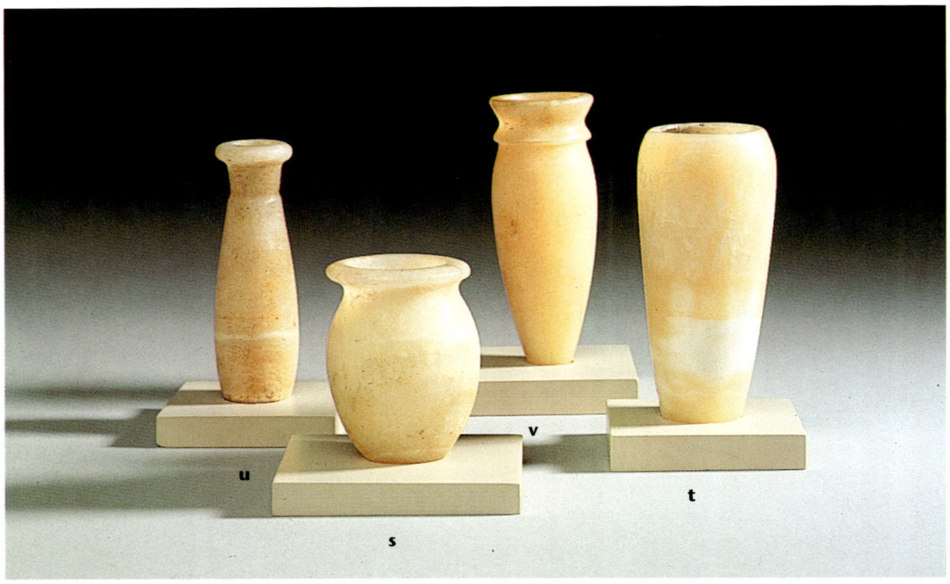

COSMETIC AND UNGUENT VESSELS

Beginning in Early Dynastic times, precious unguents were stored in small jars. In the Early Dynastic Period and the Old Kingdom, these miniature vessels were frequently carved from hard conglomerate stones such as travertine and diorite. In the New Kingdom, alabaster, long prized for its translucency, became the material of choice for ointment vessels. Tall, narrow bottles tapering at the neck or base were preferred. Such vessels were originally equipped with stoppers to prevent the scent from dissipating. When not in use, unguent jars were commonly stored with other cosmetic items (such as mirrors and razors) in small wooden caskets specially outfitted with drawers or compartments.

23 n Ovoid jar

Stone; provenance unknown; Old Kingdom; H: 7.9 cm

Cincinnati Art Museum. Gift of Millard F. and Edna F. Shelt. 1947.348

23 o Jar

Limestone pebble conglomerate; provenance unknown; Early Dynastic Period, Dynasty 1 or 2; H: 6 cm

Cincinnati Art Museum. Gift of Millard F. and Edna F. Shelt. 1947.79

23 p Jar

Limestone; provenance unknown; Early Dynastic Period, Dynasty 1 or 2; H: 11.6 cm

Cincinnati Art Museum. Gift of Millard F. and Edna F. Shelt. 1947.84

23 q Jar with lug handles

Diorite; provenance unknown; Early Dynastic Period, Dynasty 1 or 2; H: 5.7 cm

Cincinnati Art Museum. Gift of Millard F. and Edna F. Shelt. 1947.385

23 r Jar with tubular string holes

Limestone; provenance unknown; Early Dynastic Period, Dynasty 1 or 2; H: 9.8 cm

Cincinnati Art Museum. Gift of Millard F. and Edna F. Shelt. 1947.347

23 s Jar with everted lip

Alabaster; provenance unknown; New Kingdom, Dynasty 18; H: 5.7 cm

Cincinnati Art Museum. Gift of Millard F. and Edna F. Shelt. 1947.87

23 t Jar

Alabaster; provenance unknown; New Kingdom, Dynasty 18; H: 8.6 cm

Cincinnati Art Museum. Gift of Millard F. and Edna F. Shelt. 1947.89

23 u Jar

Alabaster; provenance unknown; New Kingdom; H: 7.9 cm

Cincinnati Art Museum. Gift of Millard F. and Edna F. Shelt. 1947.90

23 v Jar

Alabaster; provenance unknown; New Kingdom, Dynasty 18; H: 8.9 cm

Cincinnati Art Museum. Gift of Millard F. and Edna F. Shelt. 1947.94

23 w Cosmetic shell

Anhydrite; provenance unknown; Middle Kingdom, Dynasty 12; L: 5.5 cm

Yale University Art Gallery. Anonymous Gift. 1936.37

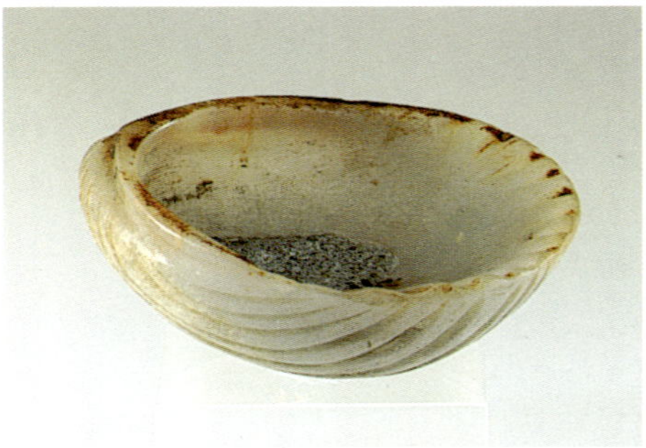

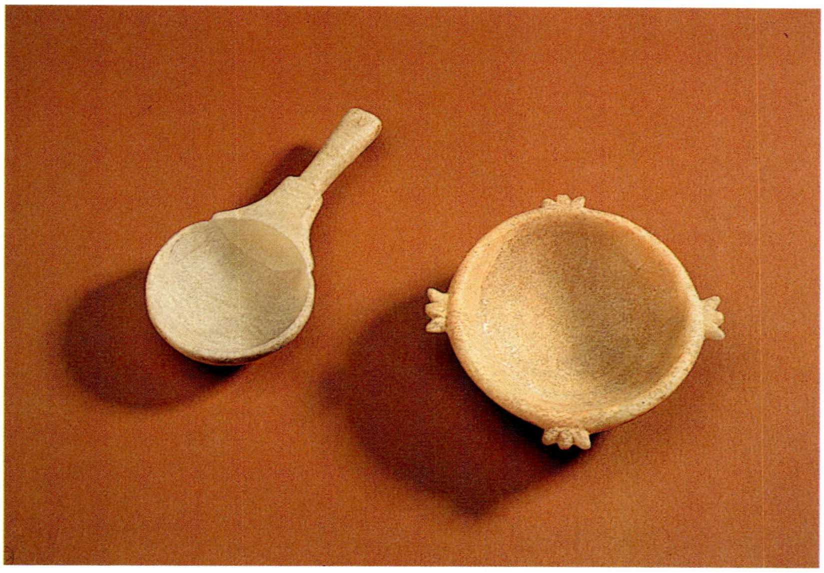

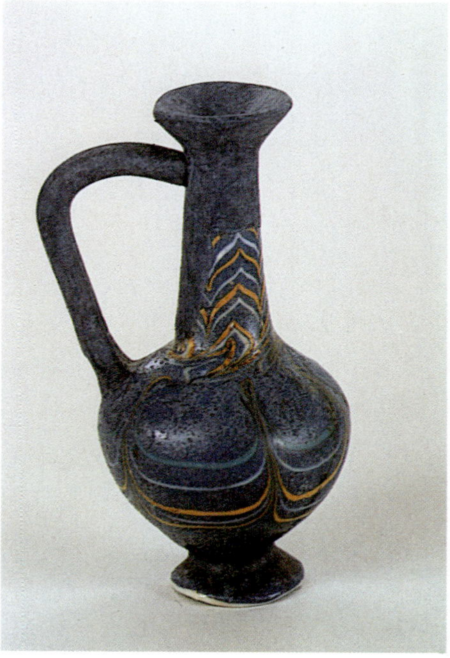

From earliest times, shells were used to prepare eye pigment. Remains of ground malachite and galena have been found on examples dating to the Old Kingdom (Brovarski in *Egypt's Golden Age,* 216, nn. 15, 16). The present container, carved from anhydrite in the form of a half shell, retains traces of the eye paint that it originally held.

Published: Scott, *Egyptian Art at Yale,* no. 35.

23 x Cosmetic spoon

Onyx; provenance unknown; New Kingdom, Dynasty 18; L: 11 cm

Cincinnati Art Museum. Gift of Millard F. and Edna F. Shelt. 1947.77

23 y Cosmetic dish

Alabaster; provenance unknown; probably Ptolemaic era; max Diam: 7.9 cm

Cincinnati Art Museum. Gift of the Cincinnati Museum of Natural History. 1990.1921

GLASS UNGUENT BOTTLES

23 z Amphoriskos

Core-formed glass; provenance unknown; New Kingdom, later Dynasty 18; H: 12.3 cm

The Toledo Museum of Art. Gift of Edward Drummond Libbey. 51.405

Published: Grose, *Ancient Glass,* no. 5.

23 aa Base-ring jug

Core-formed glass; provenance unknown; New Kingdom, later Dynasty 18; restored H: 10.2 cm

The Toledo Museum of Art. Gift of Edward Drummond Libbey. 23.330

Published: Grose, *Ancient Glass,* no. 6.

23 bb Krateriskos

Core-formed glass; provenance unknown; New Kingdom, later Dynasty 18; H: 8.2 cm

The Toledo Museum of Art. Gift of Edward Drummond Libbey. 48.16

Published: Grose, *Ancient Glass,* no. 9.

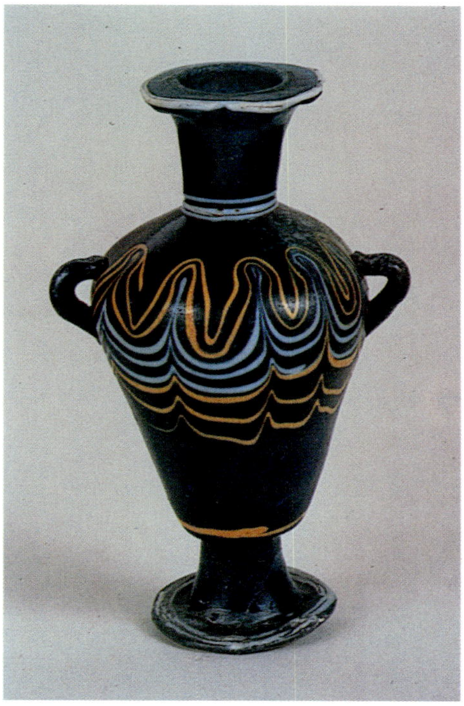

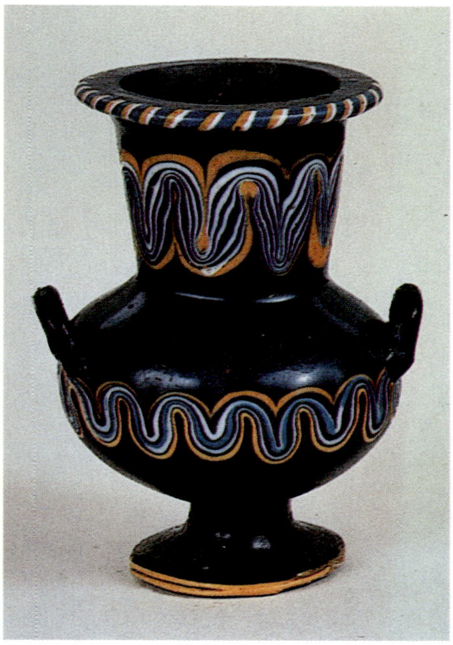

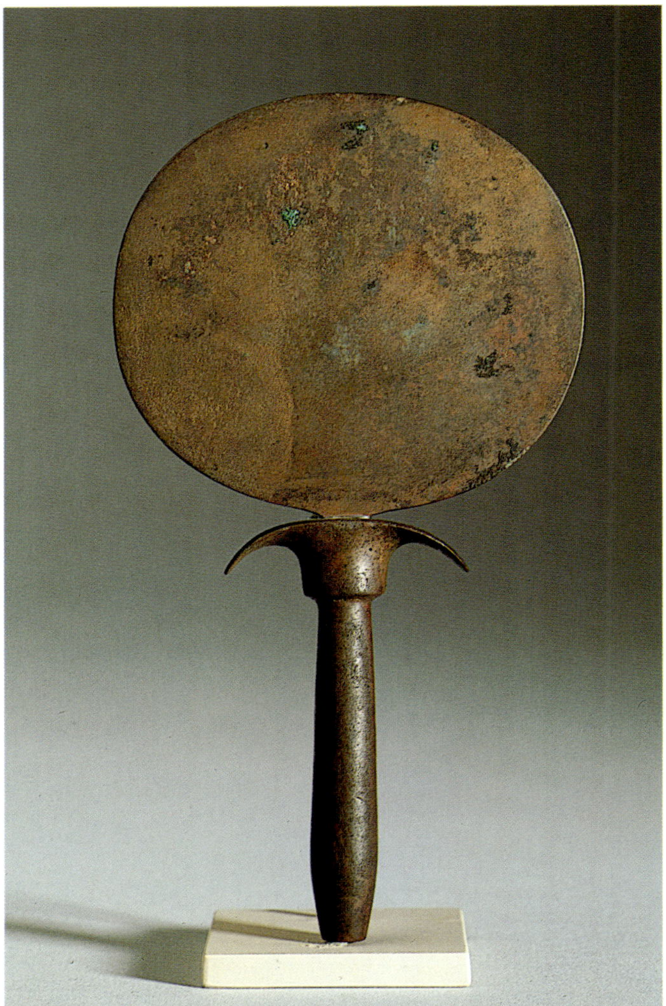

a

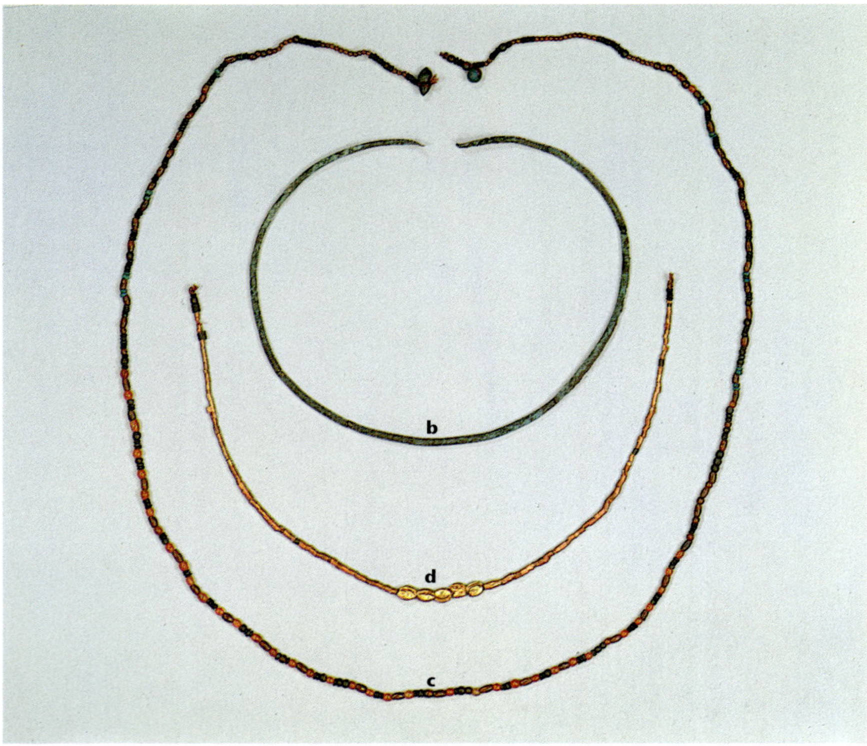

b

d

c

24 a–d Woman's burial assemblage

Gold, silver, bronze, garnet, carnelian; excavated at Abydos, Tomb 1008; Middle Kingdom, Dynasty 12; various dimensions

Cincinnati Art Museum. Gift of the Egypt Exploration Society

a bronze mirror, 1926.57a
b silver torque, 1926.57b
c necklace of garnet and carnelian barrel beads, 1926.57c
d necklace of gold cylindrical beads with gold cowrie-shell pendents, 1926.57d

This burial assemblage belonged to a young woman of considerable wealth, to judge from her tomb belongings. These included a finely cast bronze mirror with papyriform handle[1] as well as two beaded necklaces, one with cylindrical shells of gold and silver leaf and five gold cowrie-shell pendents. The most remarkable item, however, was a silver torque, which was found, along with the two necklaces, around the neck of the deceased. An ornament indigenous to the Caucasus and central Europe, it represents one of only a small number of examples known from Dynastic Egypt.[2] In all likelihood, the present torque was an import from the Near East, where similar examples have been found.[3]

Bronze mirrors, along with kohl pots, were standard items in women's as well as men's burials (cat. no. 22a,b). Typically, they were placed on the body of the deceased—on the chest, behind or near the head, at the hands, or between the knees. The standard variety in the Middle Kingdom was a simple bronze disc with rivet insertion for a club-shaped handle in alabaster, bone, wood, or ivory.[4] GEM

Published: H. Frankfort, "Cemeteries of Abydos: Work of the Season 1925–26," *JEA* 16 (1930): 219, pl. 27.

25 Woman's burial assemblage

Electrum, silver, lapis, carnelian, amethyst, turquoise, marble, faience; from El-Assassif, Thebes, Tomb 840; Middle Kingdom, Dynasty 12; various dimensions

The Metropolitan Museum of Art. Rogers Fund, 1913. 13.180.1–18

During attempts to determine the boundaries of the causeway of the mortuary temple of King Mentuhotep of the Eleventh Dynasty, a collapsed portico tomb of the Twelfth Dynasty was discovered on the southern side of the ancient cutting of the causeway.[1] The collapsed tomb contained three burials, two of which were empty. A third shaft, however, contained jewelry and vessels of pottery and stone. Though the body was not present in the tomb (the body perhaps had been removed by thieves, who expected the most valuable objects to be included in the mummy wrappings), the nature of the jewelry indicates that this was a woman's interment. Of the known caches of Middle Kingdom jewelry,[2] those from the burials of both royal and nonroyal women include the same types of objects as those found in this Tomb 840, including cowrie-shell girdles, pendents in the shape of acacia seedpods and oyster shells, barrel beads, and a variety of amulets.

The girdle from Tomb 840 consists of twelve silver cowries and one silver acacia-seedpod pendent strung with 129 amethyst and carnelian ball beads. Andrews notes that beaded girdles were worn only by males until the Twelfth Dynasty; at that time they became frequent adornment for preadolescent girls and women[3] and were commonly included in females' burials.[4] The girdles found in the burial of the noblewoman Senebtisi are the earliest known complete girdles; one was made of faience beads, and the other was made of tiny beads of semiprecious stone and gold.[5] Certain vessels and fertility figurines in the form of females are represented as wearing cowrie-shell girdles.[6] Hollow cowrie shells were sometimes fashioned with metallic beads inside to produce a tinkling sound as the wearer moved.[7] Cowrie-shell girdles were worn low about the hips and apparently had protective significance for that part of a woman's body, perhaps because the shells resemble the outer female genitalia.[8]

Beads in the shape of the acacia seedpod were popular amuletic ornaments during the Middle Kingdom. These pods were frequently an ingredient in ancient Egyptian remedies; the Ebers Papyrus contains several recipes in which acacia is to be used for uterine complaints.[9] The long, indented seed pods of the acacia contain about 30 percent tannin[10] in addition to phenol. Tannin acts as an astringent,[11] and phenol has antibacterial properties.[12] These qualities would have been invaluable to ancient Egyptian women who had just given birth: the tannin helped to shrink the tissues and thus prevent hemorrhage, and the antibacterial action of the phenol aided in preventing infection. Thus the pods of the acacia tree were powerful protection in the dangerous period immediately following childbirth, and it is not surprising that females of childbearing age would have worn amulets in that shape.[13] Even in the recent past,

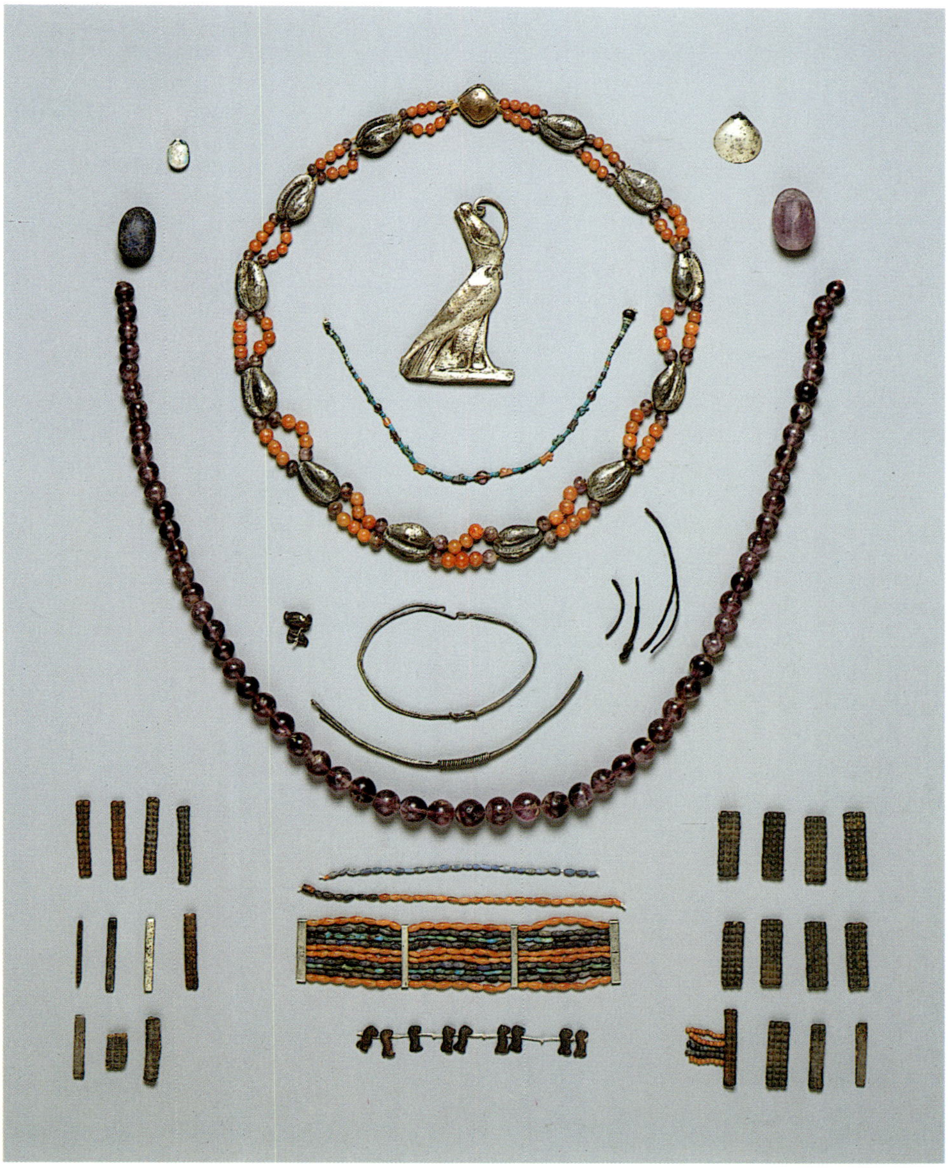

women in Egypt and other parts of Africa bathed in the hours following childbirth in water in which acacia seedpods had been steeped.[14]

A large silver pendent in the shape of an oyster shell was also found in Tomb 840 (MMA 13.180.3). A popular type during the Middle Kingdom, and apparently a protective amulet for women,[15] the oyster shell was called *wedja* in Egyptian, meaning "healthy" or "sound." Examples also have been found in gold[16] and electrum;[17] some have elaborate inlays in stone[18] or are decorated with techniques such as filigree or granulation.[19] The Munich Egyptian collection contains a shell pendent dated to the Middle Kingdom, with a repoussé design of a *naos* sistrum with the head of Hathor, animated by the addition of human arms. Each hand holds a *menat* with a double counterpoise, beneath an inlaid butterfly flanked by lotus flowers.[20] (See cat. nos. 35b and 35c,d for sistrum and *menat*.)

The Horus pendent (MMA 13.180.2) found with this group of jewelry is of sheet electrum over a core of undetermined material and depicts the royal falcon wearing the Double Crown. A loop for suspension on the reverse indicates that it was to be worn as a pendent. It is unclear why these ornaments depicting Horus wearing the double crown were included in the burials of nonroyal persons. It has been suggested that such crowned falcon pendents endowed the wearer with Horus power against the evil influences of Seth.[21]

Thirty *seweret* (barrel-shaped) beads of lapis lazuli and carnelian were found in Tomb 840. These beads were believed to provide powerful magical protection, as is made clear by their placement on the throats of mummies;[22] their function seemingly was to preserve the name of the deceased.[23]

Taweret, the popular household deity invoked for the protection of women and children, was represented in the Tomb 840 jewelry group by ten amulets, nine of silver (MMA 13.180.4A–I) and one of lapis (MMA 13.180.7). Each was pierced through the shoulder for suspension. A small lapis amulet in the form of a Horus falcon is pierced at the back. Other amulets from the tomb include four couchant lions and one lion's (lioness'?) head in lapis, carnelian, and turquoise; six *udjat* ("healthy") eyes in the same materials as well as faience; three flat ovoid beads in carnelian and amethyst; acacia-seed beads of amethyst; and one silver ball bead. This group of amulets and beads was strung together with tiny disc and ball beads from Tomb 840 by H.E. Winlock in 1933.[24] An amethyst necklace of ball beads in graduated sizes presents an elegantly simple and quite contemporary appearance (MMA 13.180.12).

The unnamed woman of Tomb 840 possessed a circlet of silver wire (MMA 13.180.1), now in fragile and fragmentary condition. Two bracelets (MMA 13.180. 13–14) of double strands of silver wire with knot medallions may have formed a set with the circlet. Another set of wide bracelets (MMA 13.180.16A–D) consists of tiny lapis, carnelian, and turquoise barrel beads with bar spacers (reconstructed from the originals) of silver.

Three scarabs were recovered from Tomb 840, one each of amethyst, lapis, and glazed steatite. The last has a stylized design on the flat side representing *sm3 t3wy*, "the Uniting of the Two Lands."[25] The others are uninscribed.

Other grave goods found in Tomb 840 include a vase and a small pot. The smaller vessel, of blue marble, was probably intended to hold kohl. This pot is made in three separate pieces: the body, a separate rim, and the lid (MMA 13.180.19A–C). The vase (MMA 13.180.20), also of blue marble, may have contained oil for the skin. AKC

Published: Herbert E. Winlock, "Excavations at Thebes in 1912–13, by the Museum's Egyptian Expedition," *BMMA* 9:1 (1914): 16, fig. 8; Hayes, *Scepter,* 1: 237 and fig. 153.

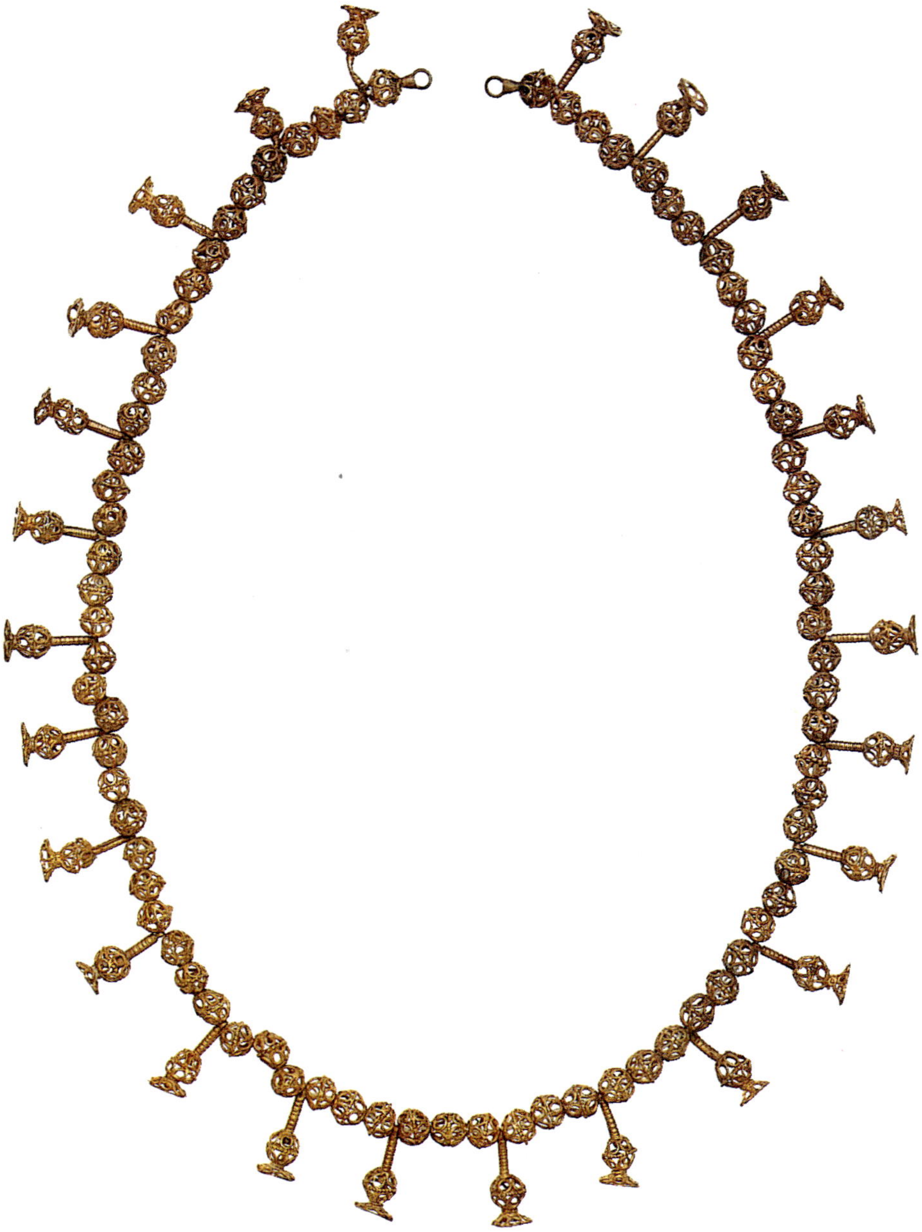

26 Necklace

Gold; from Thebes, Valley of the Kings, Tomb 56 ("Gold Tomb"); New Kingdom, Dynasty 19, reign of Sety II; L: 61 cm

The Metropolitan Museum of Art. Theodore M. Davis Collection, Bequest of Theodore M. Davis, 1915. 30.8.66; Purchase, Edward S. Harkness Gift, 1926. 26.7.1346, 1348

This elegant gold necklace was found in a cache of Nineteenth Dynasty objects uncovered in a small uninscribed tomb (56) in the Valley of the Kings in western Thebes.[1] Its workmanship is particularly refined and recalls the delicate technique of Middle Kingdom jewelry models (in contrast to the heavier, more ostentatious style of the New Kingdom). The necklace was reconstructed entirely from loose gold elements in *ajouré* filigree and is composed of seventy-seven openwork spherical beads and twenty-six pendents in the form of cornflowers.[2] Both the beads and the pods of the cornflowers are made from openwork shells formed from wire rings of various diameters soldered together. Additional elements in the form of a flared rim and a striated tube make up the flower head and the stalk, respectively.[3] As strung, the necklace measures twenty-four inches in length.

Based upon the quality of its workmanship and its archaeological context, the Metropolitan Museum of Art's necklace and the associated finds from Tomb 56 probably belonged to a female member of the royal court under King Sety II, perhaps even to Queen Tauseret herself.[4] As the names of both Tauseret and Sety II occur on objects from the burial, it has been suggested that the finds represent a cache of material that had been salvaged from Tauseret's own tomb (14) in the Valley of the Kings at the time it was appropriated by Sethnakhte, founder of the Twentieth Dynasty. Like Hatshepsut before her, Tauseret actually assumed the titulary of a reigning pharaoh, a relatively unusual circumstance in Egyptian history.[5]

Alternately, it has been suggested that the finds of Tomb 56 represent the scattered remains of an intact burial that had been destroyed by silting in antiquity. According to this interpretation, the burial may have been prepared for a child of Sety II and Tauseret, probably sometime during the reign of the former.[6] GEM

Published: Hayes, *Scepter,* 2: 361, fig. 227; Andrews, *Jewellery,* 127, fig. 110.

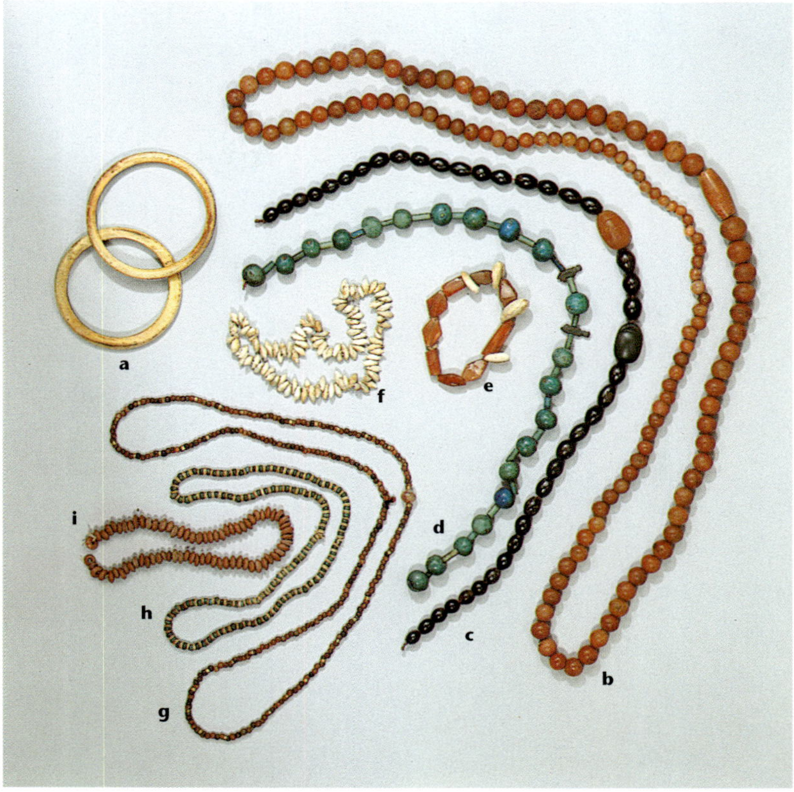

Jewelry

From the earliest times, jewelry figured prominently in the body adornment of Egyptian men and women. Already in Predynastic times, numerous burials dating back to the Badarian Period have yielded elaborate beaded jewelry of shell, bone, clay, and various stones. This period marked the beginning of the Egyptian penchant for single-string beaded necklaces, a practice that continued through the Dynastic Period and beyond. The tradition of stringing pierced, unworked shells also began at this time (cat. nos. 27f, 72i).[1]

As dynastic burials reveal, the circlet, collar or necklace, girdle, and bracelet formed the primary components of a woman's jewelry assemblage (cat. no. 25).[2] Head adornment for both men and women often consisted of a simple circlet of gold or silver sheet or wire (cat. no. 25). The diadem's occurrence as an item of female adornment predates the Dynastic Period; a single string of colored stone and gold beads graced the head of a woman from a Predynastic burial of the Naqada II Period at Abydos.[3] By the Middle Kingdom, ornately decorated diadems in both sheet gold and wire openwork marked the burials of female royalty.[4]

One of the most distinctive elements of both male and female adornment was the broad collar known as the *usekh* ("the broad one"). By the early Old Kingdom, the *usekh* had assumed its canonical shape, with multiple rows of tubular beads terminating below in an outer row of drop beads.[5] The decorative format of the *usekh* underwent a major change in the late New Kingdom, when a varied repertoire of floral elements replaced the tubular beads of the earlier type (cat. nos. 92, 93). A more unusual form of female neck ornament in Egypt was the metal torque (cat. no. 24b), which is attested in women's burials beginning in the Middle Kingdom.[6]

Another recurrent item of female adornment was the cowrie-shell girdle (cat. no. 25), which was worn slung low around the hips. Aside from its occurrence in the grave, it is rendered frequently in paintings and on reliefs depicting female dancers, musicians, and servants. Worn exclusively by males until the Twelfth Dynasty, it became a frequent ornament for women from that time forward.[7]

The bracelet (and anklet) assumed a variety of forms, ranging from simple beaded strands to inlaid gold cylindrical bands. One of the most common and longest enduring forms was the bangle (cat. no. 27a), a solid hoop designed to be slipped over the hand. Examples in bone, shell, horn, and stone have been found in graves dating from the Predynastic Period onward.[8] GEM

27 a–i Assorted jewelry

Faience, gold, shell, bone; excavated at Abydos and Balabish; Predynastic–Third Intermediate Period; various dimensions

Cincinnati Art Museum. Gift of the Egypt Exploration Society (1912, 1915, 1926); Millard F. and Edna F. Shelt (1947); and Mrs. Mary Eva Keyes (1915.485)

a pair of bone bangles, Predynastic or Early Dynastic Period, 1947.170, 171; provenance unknown

b carnelian spherical beads, Middle Kingdom, 1915.485

c hematite scaraboid beads strung with two uninscribed scaraboids in carnelian and green jasper, from Abydos, Tomb 613, Dynasty 12, 1926.64

d green faience ball and tubular beads with two faience Taweret amulets, from Abydos, Tomb 1631, Dynasty 12, 1926.66

e red carnelian rhomboidal beads and cowrie-shell pendents, from Abydos, Tomb S62, Dynasty 12, 1912.388

f shells *(columbella rustica),* from Abydos, Tomb S49, Third Intermediate Period, 1912.373

g, h carnelian spherical and gold collar beads, shell disk beads, and faience spherical beads, from Balabish, Tomb B181, Second Intermediate Period, 1915.410, 411

i red stone lenticular beads, from Balabish, Tomb 50, Dynasty 19, 1915.452

The beaded strand remained the most common element of jewelry throughout Egypt's long history and frequently was

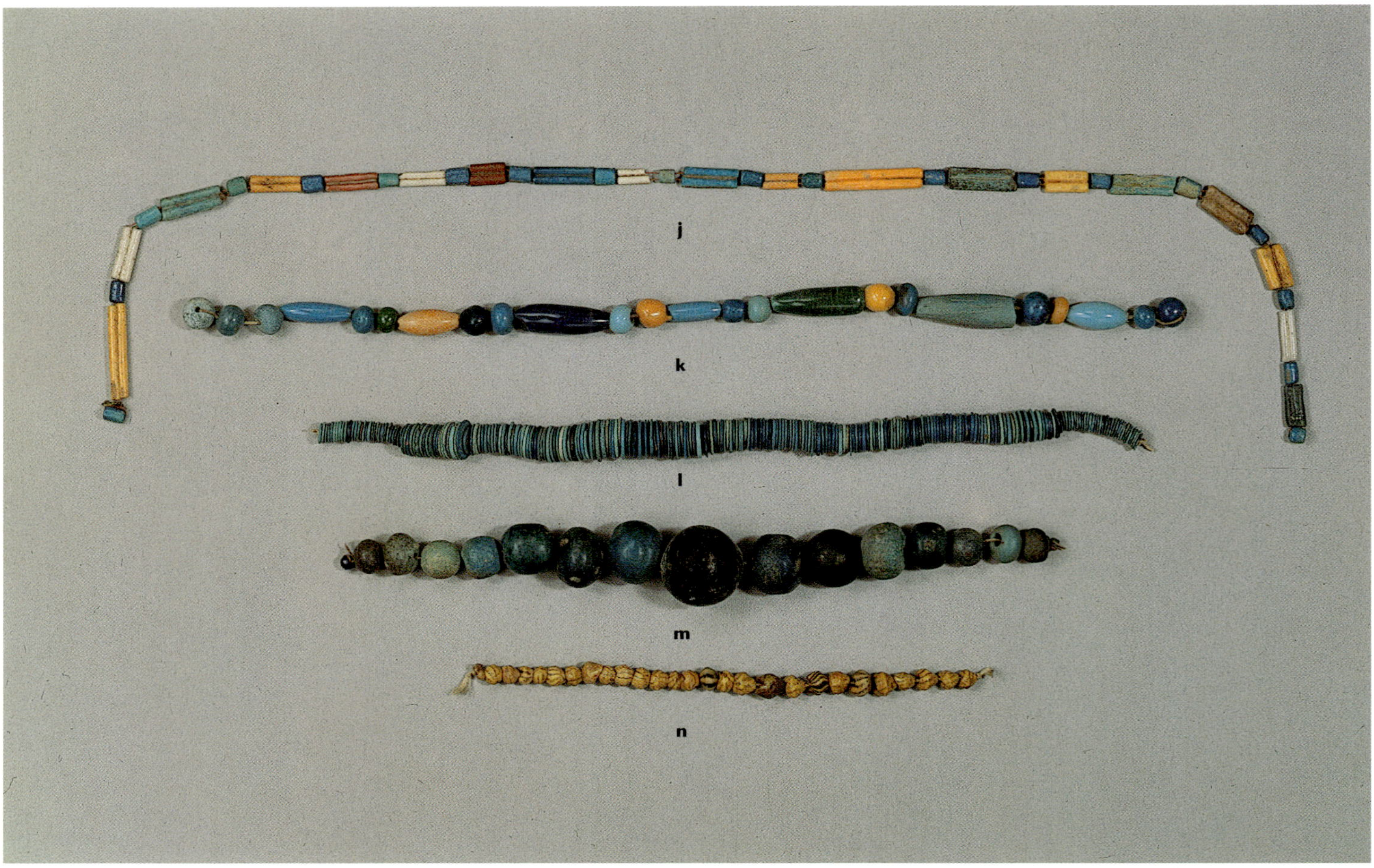

the sole form of decoration in burials of the poor and lower middle classes. Composed of various shapes and materials (faience, stone, shell, bone, metal), it often fulfilled a variety of functions—as necklace, girdle, armlet, bracelet, and even diadem.[9] The Egyptians used a wide variety of decorative formats, characterized by alternating shapes and materials (e.g., carnelian and shell [e]; faience and shell [h]). When beads of the same shape and material were used, they were often arranged in order of size (b). On more elaborate strands, the beads were often capped with gold and silver collar elements (g).

Several of the above specimens (d and f) were recovered from documented women's burials. Beaded strand d, with its two Taweret amulets, was found around the neck of an adult female in an undisturbed shaft grave at Abydos.[10] Strings g and h were found on the neck and chest of the deceased in an undisturbed pit burial of the Second Intermediate Period at Balabish. This grave was the richest in jewelry at Balabish and the only one to contain gold.

27 j–n Beaded jewelry from Amarna

Faience, glass; excavated at Amarna; New Kingdom, late Dynasty 18; various dimensions

Cincinnati Art Museum. Gift of the Egypt Exploration Society

j polychrome faience tubular beads, 1924.292
k polychrome faience ball and drop beads, 1924.293
l blue faience disk beads, 1927.362
m graded blue faience spherical beads, 1927.368
n yellow glass beads, 1927.372

The beaded jewelry reproduced here is characteristic of the late Eighteenth Dynasty, when multicolored faience came into vogue and replaced stone and shell as the primary material for beads. The advantage of faience production lay not only in the wide range of colors achievable, but also in the potential for low-cost, large-scale production. All of the above examples—which represent articles of costume jewelry designed for the middle class—were uncovered in the urban quarters of Amarna.

27 o–v Penannular earrings

Silver, lead, ivory, bone, stone, glass; excavated at Abydos, Amarna, and Balabish; New Kingdom–Third Intermediate Period; various dimensions

Cincinnati Art Museum. Gift of the Egypt Exploration Society

o white glass, from Amarna, late Dynasty 18, 1924.452, 453
p jasper, provenance unknown, New Kingdom or later, 1947.358, 359
q stone, from Amarna, late Dynasty 18, 1921.283
r carnelian, from Abydos, Dynasty 21, 1914.359, 360
s lead, from Abydos, Dynasty 21, 1914.388
t silver, from Abydos, Third Intermediate Period, 1912.383
u bone, from Balabish Tomb T50, Dynasty 19, 1915.454
v ivory, from Amarna, late Dynasty 18, 1922.137

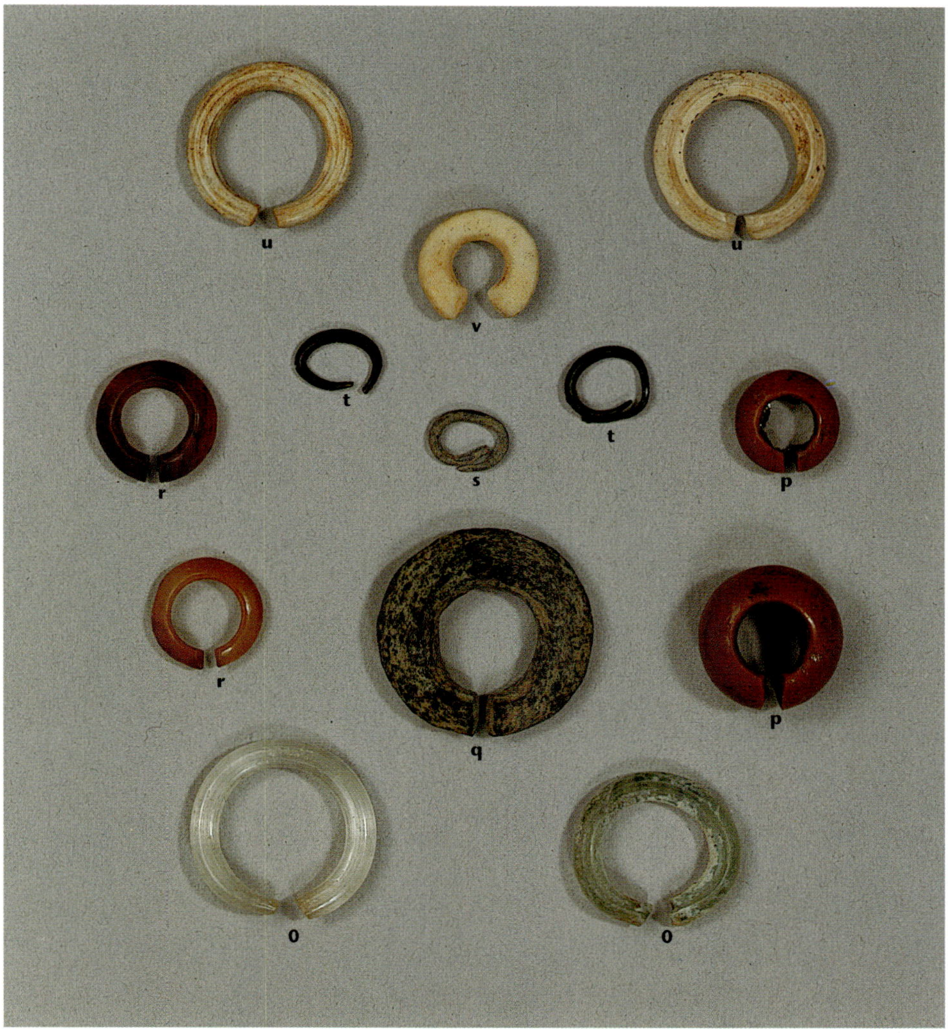

Penannular hoop earrings are ubiquitous in Egyptian burial assemblages of the New Kingdom. A Nineteenth Dynasty grave at Balabish contained a mummy (sex not identified) with three stone penannular earrings in place: one earring in white hard stone in one ear and two earrings (in white stone and carnelian) in the other. The simultaneous use of two pairs of earrings is attested elsewhere.[11] The earrings worn by the deceased at Balabish were clearly inserted through the earlobes, revealing that the ears had been pierced.[12] The bone examples displayed in u formed part of a group of nineteen such earrings from a Nineteenth Dynasty tomb at Balabish.[13]

27 w Penannular earring

Electrum; provenance unknown; New Kingdom, Dynasty 18–19; Diam: 2 cm

The Brooklyn Museum. New-York Historical Society, Charles Edwin Wilbour Fund. 37.744 E

Published: *Egypt's Golden Age,* no. 292.

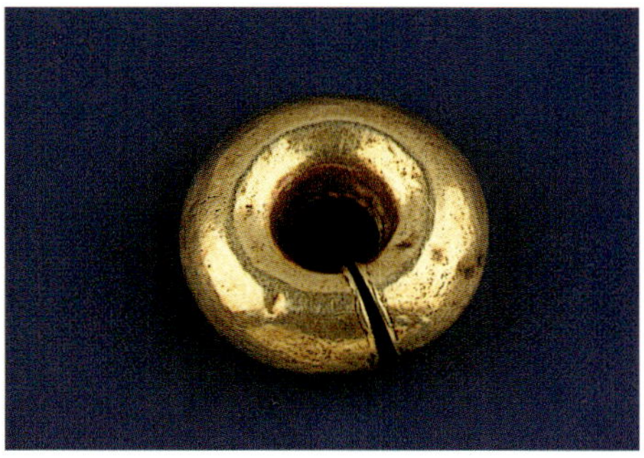

This electrum example illustrates the more expensive variety of hoop earring worn by both men and women of the upper classes.

27 x Lotus-flower earrings

Red glass; provenance unknown; said to come from Thebes; New Kingdom, Dynasty 18–19; H: 3.3 cm; W: 3.3 cm

The Brooklyn Museum. Anonymous gift. 52.149a,b

Published: *Egypt's Golden Age,* no. 306.

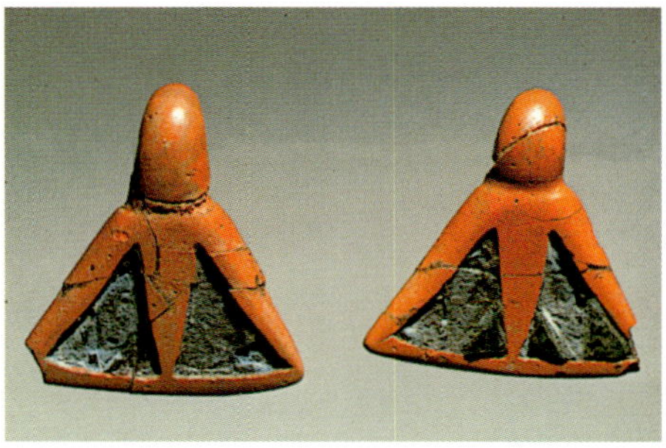

As depictions from the late New Kingdom reveal, earrings in the form of pendent lotus flowers were worn frequently by female royalty; both Queen Tiye and Nefertari, wife of Ramesses II, are shown with such earrings.[14]

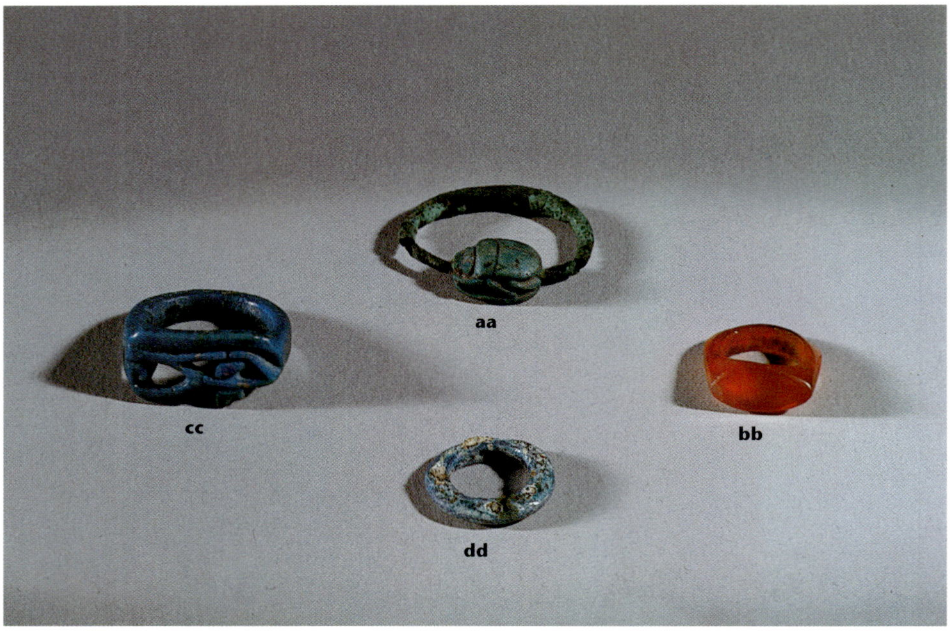

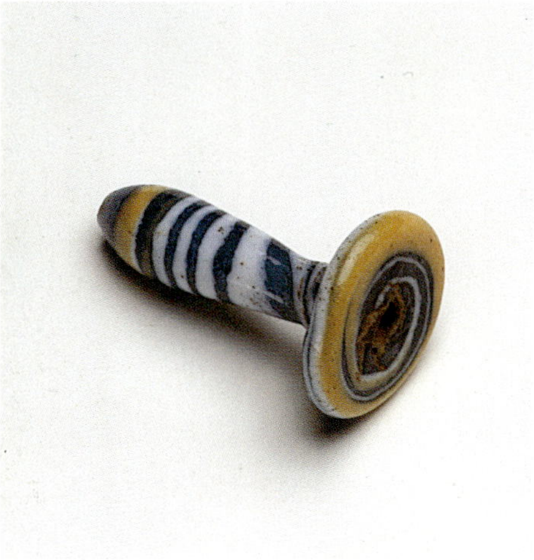

27 y Ear stud in the form of a papyrus column

Glass; from Thebes, Palace of Amenhotep III; New Kingdom, late Dynasty 18; H: 2.4 cm; Diam. at top: 1.5 cm

The Brooklyn Museum. Gift of Mrs. Lawrence Coolidge and Mrs. Robert Woods Bliss. 48.66.31

Ear studs of this variety were designed to be inserted through a hole in the earlobe with the circular head facing out. In typical fashion, two twisted glass threads of different colors are employed for decorative effect.

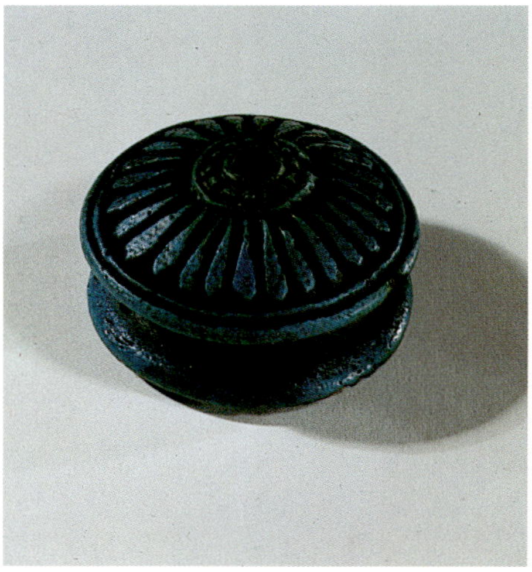

27 z Openwork ear plug in the form of a rosette

Faience; provenance unknown; New Kingdom, Dynasty 18; Diam: 4 cm

Miami University Art Museum, Oxford, Ohio. Gift of Walter I. Farmer. 78.J.2.5

Rosette-ornamented ear plugs such as this one were worn by women in the late Eighteenth Dynasty.[15] The large diameters of such disks (up to 6.5 cm) reveal the extent of the earlobe's distortion. This practice is confirmed by the presence of female mummies with enormous earlobe piercings.[16]

27 aa–dd Finger rings

Bronze, carnelian, faience, glass; excavated at Amarna; New Kingdom–Late Period; various dimensions

Cincinnati Art Museum. Gift of the Egypt Exploration Society (1924, 1927); Gift of Millard F. and Edna F. Shelt (1947)

aa scarab ring, bronze, from Amarna, 1924.434
bb child's ring, carnelian, provenance unknown, 1947.258
cc *udjat* eye ring, faience, from Amarna, 1924.440
dd ring, glass, from Amarna, 1927.378

Rings uncovered from burials of the Predynastic and Early Dynastic periods were simple bands of stone, shell, or precious metal. The tradition of scarab rings originated in the Middle Kingdom; the more elaborate examples of the New Kingdom allowed the scarab to swivel on a mount, facilitating its use as a signet ring. Although rings are rarely depicted in ancient Egyptian paintings or reliefs, the archaeological evidence attests that both sexes commonly wore them (cat. no. 20v10). Mold-produced in the New Kingdom, faience rings were a ubiquitous jewelry component of middle-class burials, along with penannular earrings.[17]

28 a Servant statue: Woman grinding grain

Limestone with pigment; excavated at Giza, Tomb G1213; Old Kingdom, Dynasty 5 or 6; H: 18 cm; W: 11.9 cm; L: 34 cm

Phoebe Hearst Museum of Anthropology, University of California at Berkeley. 6–19766

28 b Servant statue: Woman straining mash for beer

Limestone with pigment; excavated at Giza, Tomb G1213; Old Kingdom, Dynasty 5 or 6; H: 23 cm; W: 9.3 cm; L: 30.3 cm

Phoebe Hearst Museum of Anthropology, University of California at Berkeley. 6–19811

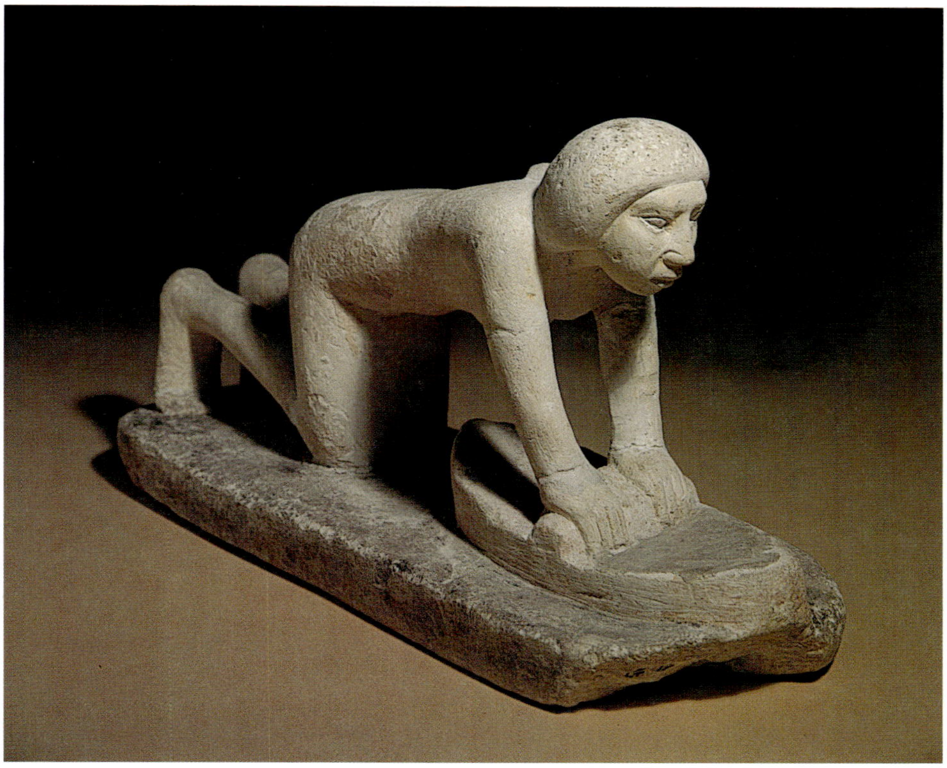

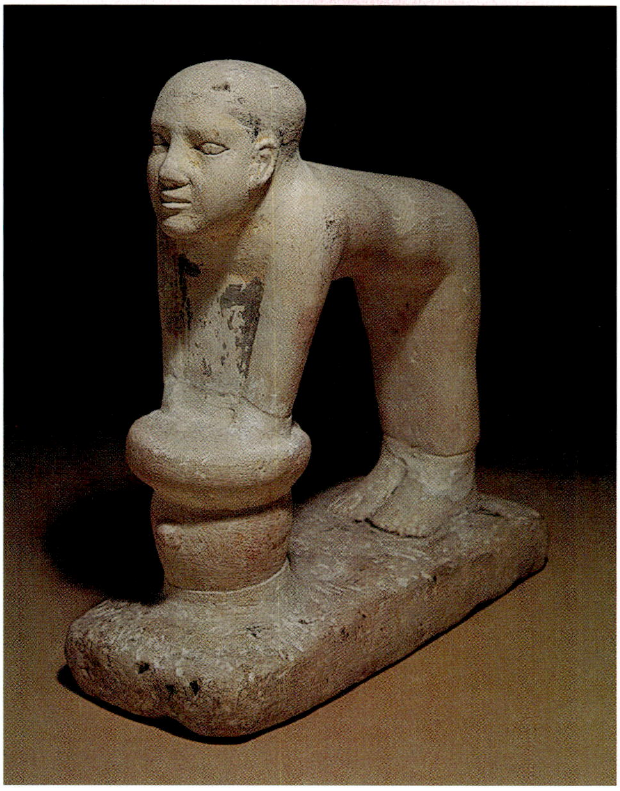

Ancient Egyptian women performed many necessary tasks in the domestic sphere. One important activity was weaving; until the New Kingdom, in fact, this occupation was associated exclusively with women.[1] Another vital activity was the making of bread, a staple of the ancient Egyptian diet. In the Old Kingdom, women undertook virtually all of this work; as Henry Fischer observes, "they are seen pounding and grinding the grain, making dough and heating the moulds for the loaves."[2] Of these various processes, the most frequently represented is grinding; it is this arduous activity that predominates among the many surviving servant statuettes of the Old Kingdom from Giza.

An Old Kingdom servant figure exemplifies the type. The figure kneels forward and pushes a grinding stone over a flat, slightly concave stone slab that slopes from either end toward the middle.[3] The woman rocks forward on her toes, her head bowed in concentration. (The concavity of the grinding slab may be an artistic device to indicate the many hours of toil in which she has been engaged.) As in other examples of the type, her attire is simple, consisting of a short skirt that extends from below the breasts a little beyond the knees; a plain cloth, knotted at the neck, covers the head.[4]

Closely allied with the making of bread was the production of beer, another activity that frequently involved women. Both men and women are depicted in the act of straining the fermented mash made from barley bread. (Barley, the principal food crop in Egypt until the Ptolemaic Period, was the primary ingredient of bread and, therefore, beer.) The second servant statue depicts a woman leaning over to pour material into a sieve placed over a large vat with a base rendered to indicate wicker.[5] She wears a tightly fitting apron that extends to the ankles. Her hair is closely cropped;[6] traces of the black pigment that originally decorated it are visible on the forehead and neck. Although the present example is uninscribed, several female beer makers have their names and titles recorded, including the woman Ni-Inpw-kauw, who carried the title "Mistress of the House."[7]

These two servant statues originally formed part of a group of three female servant figures found in the chapel corridor of *mastaba* G1213 at Giza.[8] With their thick lips, broad noses, large eyes, and full cheeks, the faces of both figures typify the sculptural style of the Old Kingdom. GEM

Published: Lutz, *Egyptian Statues*, 27–28 and pl. 41 a,b; Fazzini, *Images*, no. 27 (6–19766 only).

29 Tomb model: Female servant or offering-bearer

Wood with pigment over gesso; provenance unknown, possibly from Asyut; Middle Kingdom, late Dynasty 11 or early Dynasty 12; H: 52 cm

Cincinnati Art Museum. Gift of Millard F. and Edna F. Shelt. 1947.273

The practice of placing model servant figures in tombs originated in the late Old Kingdom (Dynasty 6) and reached the height of its popularity in Dynasties 11 and 12 of the Middle Kingdom. Like the painted scenes depicting servants in later tombs of the New Kingdom, they served to ensure the future well-being of the deceased by magically providing the products and services required in the afterlife.

Like other tomb models (i.e., depicting boats and scenes of daily life), the presence of model offering-bearers was a mark of the tomb owner's relative affluence.[1] Rendered singly or in rows of two or more, they depicted both males and females; during the Middle Kingdom, the figures of women became much more common than those of men.[2]

This tomb model illustrates the conventional female type. She strides forward with her left foot advanced, carrying a

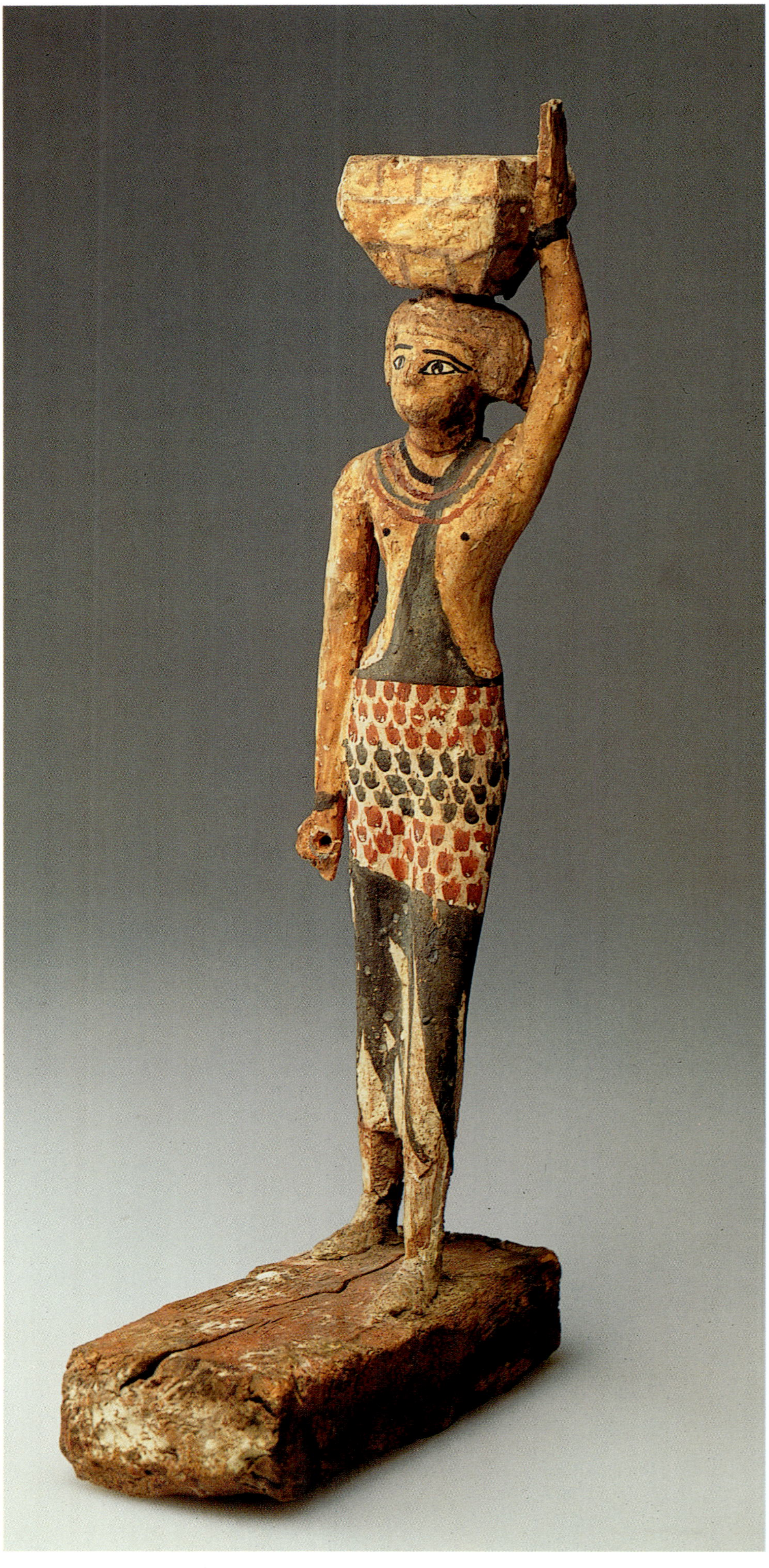

basketful of objects on her head (which she steadies with her left hand) and holding a bird (as usual, a duck) by the wings in her pendent right hand.[3] She wears an elaborately decorated garment consisting of a long, tight skirt supported by a single strap that crosses over her left shoulder.[4] The painted decoration on her kilt represents a beaded overskirt with a feather pattern and free-swinging strands that swirl over a white linen underskirt. A broad collar is suspended around her neck, and bracelets are worn on each wrist. The figure's small bared breasts reveal her youthfulness.[5] As in other examples, her mouth has been omitted. This is an intentional feature that may have been designed to prevent her from partaking of funerary offerings left for the tomb owner.[6] AKC/GEM

30 Statuette of a serving girl

Terracotta; provenance unknown; New Kingdom, late Dynasty 18–Dynasty 19; H: 28.4 cm; W: 9.2 cm

The Cleveland Museum of Art. John L. Severance Fund. 91.107

This model of a young serving girl conforms to an interesting category of hand-modeled burial figurine of late New Kingdom date.[1] Stylistically, the type is a distinctive one. The subject is a standing nude female who cradles a large pot or jar in her left arm; the single lock of hair that hangs down to one side of her head—a characteristic mark of youth in ancient Egypt—clearly identifies her as an adolescent.

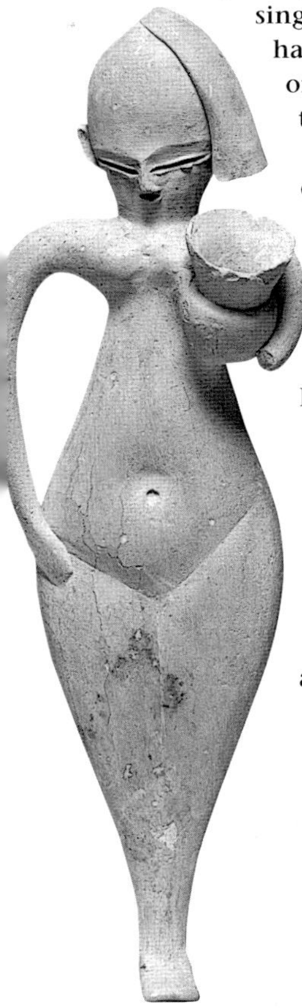

Characteristic of this category of figurine is the distinctive cone-shaped head and swelling torso with narrow chest, broad hips, and tapering legs. The stylized face, with slit eyes and diminutive mouth, and the long, spindly curving arms are typical as well.[2]

Various features of hand finishing, such as the slit treatment of the eyes, the triangular delineation of legs and pubis, and the depressed navel, suggest a single center or workshop for the group as a whole. Unfortunately, very few of the known examples have recorded contexts; little can be deduced about the production source of these figurines.[3]

The marked nudity of these figurines and their exaggerated hips and delineated pubic areas suggest their possible function as fertility figures.[4] Several examples are marked by a pair of flowering, vinelike tassels that pass between the breasts and extend to the level of the navel.[5] Features of the head and face (sidelock, eyes, ears, mouth) on the present example were originally highlighted in black and red. GEM

Published: *Cleveland Museum of Art Bulletin* 79, no. 2 (1992): no. 3, p. 66 (illus.).

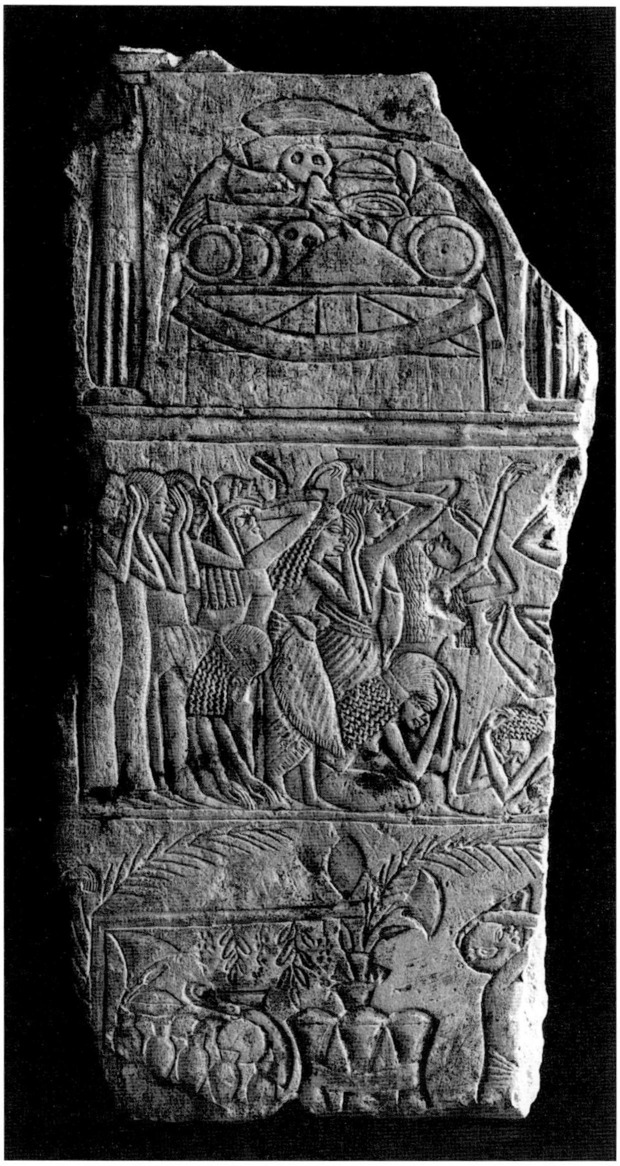

31 Relief of mourners and funerary repast

Limestone; provenance unknown, possibly from Memphis; New Kingdom, late Dynasty 18–early Dynasty 19; H: 52.7 cm; W: 26.7 cm

The Detroit Institute of Arts. City of Detroit Purchase. 24.98

This limestone fragment carved in sunk relief preserves portions of three registers depicting funerary ceremonies. In the lower register, wine jars are sheltered from the sun's heat by a light kiosk decorated with palm fronds and flowers. A male mourner clutches his head, thrown back in sorrow, with both hands. Depicted in the upper register is a table piled high with food between two columns at the tomb's entrance. The food and wine were left as offerings for the deceased in the tomb, or consumed by the mourners and officiants at a funerary banquet.

Mourners (also see cat. no. 78) in eloquent attitudes of grief are depicted in the central register. Two mourners, one male and one female, kneel on the ground sorrowfully holding their heads in their hands. Another woman bends over to touch the ground, perhaps gathering dust to throw over her head. The other mourners claw the air in their grief or cover their faces or foreheads with their hands. The sculptor of this relief has devoted much attention to the detailing of the waving wigs and wraparound kilts[1] worn by the women and to the expressive gestures of the mourners' arms and hands.

One of the few public occupations[2] open to women was that of professional mourner. These women were hired to follow the funerary procession while

> ... making an ostentatious display of grief which included loud wailing, beating exposed breasts, smearing the body with dirt and tearing at dishevelled hair; all signs of uncontrolled behaviour, the 'disorder of sorrow.'...[3]

These women wore certain types of hairstyles and garments, which evolved over time, as did the specific poses and attitudes.[4] A stela from Deir el-Medina inscribed for a mother and daughter specifically terms these women "mourners," suggesting professional status for the title.[5] Particularly important were the two women who impersonated the goddesses Isis and Nephthys,[6] who had mourned at the death of Osiris, the god of the afterlife with whom a deceased person was identified. These women were called *ḏryt*-mourners, and this title may reflect a specialization among professional mourners.[7]

The Detroit relief directly joins another fragment from the same tomb now in the Pushkin Museum of Fine Arts, Moscow.[8] The central register of the Pushkin relief continues the theme of mourning, although there the mourners are all male, and they are dressed in the type of kilt worn by soldiers.[9] This suggests that the tomb from which these fragments came was that of an important military officer.[10] AKC

Published: J. Walther, *Bulletin of the Detroit Institute of Arts* 6, no. 4 (1925): 41 (illus.); Capart, *Documents* 1, 42, pl. 58; P. Pavlov, *Proceedings of the Puschkin Museum of Fine Arts* (Moscow, Leningrad, 1939), pl. 41; Werbrouk, *Les pleureuses*, 86.

32 Relief: Female attendants clapping hands

Limestone and pigment; from Deir el-Bahri, Thebes, tomb of Queen Nefru; Middle Kingdom, Dynasty 11, reign of Nebhepetra Mentuhotep; H: 32 cm
Anonymous loan

This scene comes from the tomb of Queen Nefru,[1] wife of the Eleventh Dynasty king Nebhepetra Mentuhotep.[2] Two women are depicted, with fragmentary representations of two others, clapping their hands.[3]

Music was an essential part of ancient Egyptian life.[4] Singers and musicians performed for royal and religious rituals and festivals, at banquets, and in military and funerary processions; sometimes, in agricultural scenes, a musician plays a tune for the workers' enjoyment.[5] Though wealthy private households probably retained their own musicians, temples and the royal palace were the largest employers of musicians, singers, and dancers.[6] The terms *ḫny* and *ḫnr,* formerly believed to refer to a "harim" attached to a temple or the palace, are now commonly translated as "a troupe of musical performers."[7]

A wide variety of instruments were played in ancient Egypt, including the harp, lute, lyre, flute, oboe, and trumpet. Percussion instruments included drums, cymbals, and tambourines. Though not precisely percussion instruments, sistra and *menat* necklaces (see cat. nos. 35c,d and 35b) were employed in a rhythmic way during religious rituals. Rhythm also was kept by finger clicking and handclapping, as in this relief from Nefru's tomb. Clapping and sistrum playing required a high degree of skill: a Middle Kingdom tomb at Kom el-Hisn depicts a priest instructing young women in those arts.[8]

As evidence of the prestige enjoyed by skilled musical performers, their figures and names sometimes were included on the funerary monuments of others. As early as the Fifth Dynasty, for instance, the official Nikaura had the names and likenesses of his favorite musical duo carved on the false door in his tomb: these were the harpist Hekenu and the singer Iti, both women.[9]

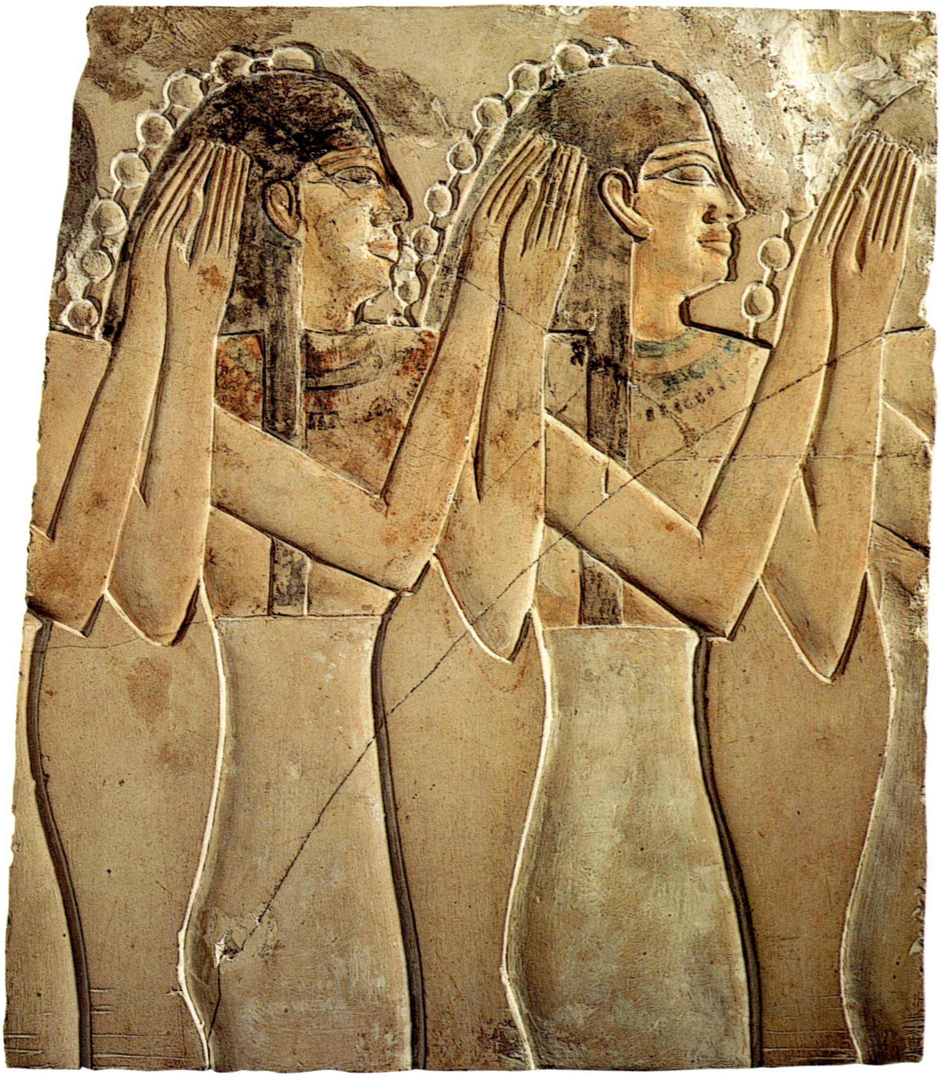

The unnamed women depicted on this relief orginally clapped in a procession that decorated the corridor[10] of Queen Nefru's tomb. Each woman wears a white sheath dress; their broad collars are indicated by traces of blue, red, and green paint. The long wigs, with locks pulled forward to rest on the chest, are a style favored during this period.[11] Unique to this scene, however, are the ornaments worn attached to the hair—strings of large round balls held apart by some means along the length of the strand. Traces of white paint on these globular beads suggest that they were painted to represent silver.[12] Two similar strands of hollow balls made of precious metal and separated by spacer beads have been found in tombs dating to the same period as Nefru's. From the tomb of Wah comes a string of very large, hollow balls of silver.[13] A similar strand, but of hollow gold beads, was found in the burial of Mayet,[14] a young girl who died sometime in the reign of Nebhepetra Mentuhotep, and whose tomb was incorporated in that king's mortuary temple.[15] Though these have always been interpreted as necklaces,[16] perhaps they were also used as hair adornments. AKC

Published: E. Riefstahl, "Two Hairdressers of the Eleventh Dynasty," *JNES* 15 (1956): 10–17; Aldred, *Jewels*, pl. 23.

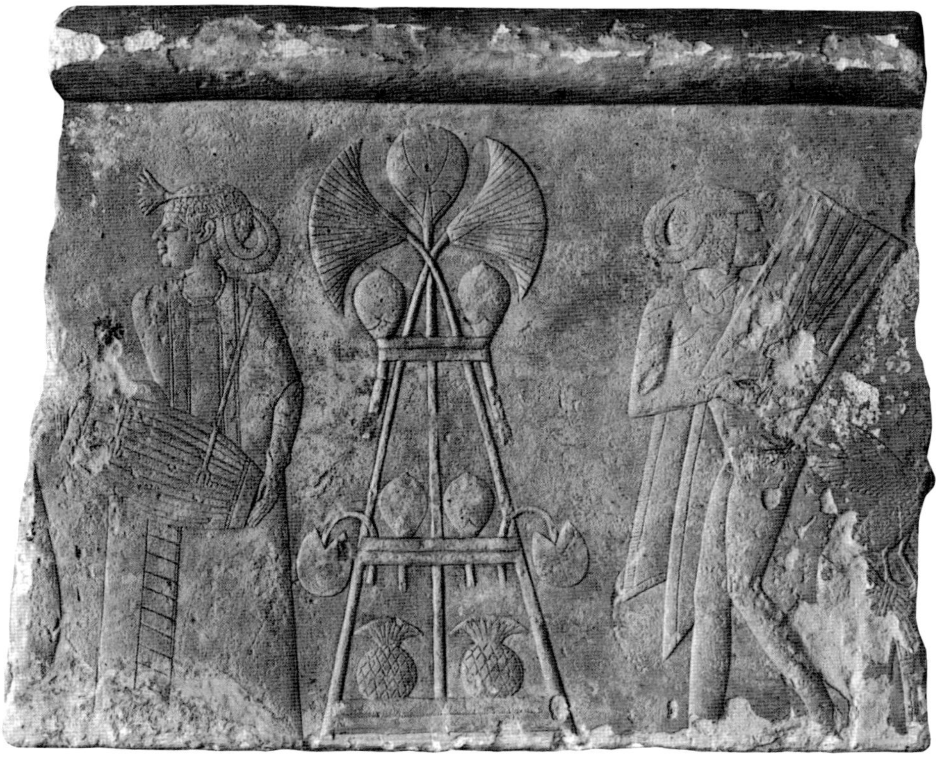

33 Relief depicting Hap-iu's lady musicians

Limestone; provenance unknown, probably from Heliopolis; Late Period, Dynasty 30; H: 27.3 cm; W at bottom: 34.5 cm
The Cleveland Museum of Art. Gift of the John Huntington Art and Polytechnic Trust. 14.542

As tomb scenes illustrate, music making formed a regular part of the ancient Egyptian funerary banquet. Entertainment was frequently furnished by women, who served as singers and dancers. The music itself was often provided by an ensemble consisting of a trio of female instrumentalists: a harpist, a lutist, and a double-oboe player.[1] The present relief, which comes from the lintel of a private chapel datable to the Thirtieth Dynasty, illustrates a portion of one such musical ensemble. Although its exact provenance is uncertain, the context of the scene is clear: it depicts two members in a larger orchestral procession directed toward the seated figure of the tomb owner, named Hap-iu. On an adjoining fragment in Berlin,[2] Hap-iu, seated right, is approached by a male harpist who leads the procession; traces of his rounded back are preserved at the left-hand margin of the Cleveland relief.

The two female musicians on the relief in Cleveland are of considerable interest. The woman at the left plays a barrel drum suspended from a cord around her neck. The instrument, of probable Kushite origin, provided a common form of accompaniment in military processions; women are rarely depicted playing them until the Late Period.[3] The female drummer in the Cleveland relief wears an ankle-length, fringed tunic;[4] her closely cropped curly hair is adorned with a lotus flower and is augmented by a wig insert attached by the two ends.[5] She wears a beaded necklace equipped with an exceptionally large, barrel-shaped pendent or *seweret* bead.[6] Her earrings, with their crescent-shaped stem and multisectioned vertical pendents, are typical for the period.[7]

The female musician on the right plays a rectangular lyre of a type well known in ancient Egypt.[8] Lightly clad in a diaphanous garment pinned at the neck, she wears a shoulder-length curled coiffure with a rosette-decorated headband and wig attachment.[9] With left leg bent and head turned back, she dances or sways to her own accompaniment; the motif itself apparently derives from artistic models of the mid–Eighteenth Dynasty.[10] Contemporary parallels suggest that this musical troupe included a third female participant: a lutist.[11]

The fragment in Cleveland belongs to a series of lintel reliefs from Heliopolis depicting musical processions.[12] A close parallel to the Hap-iu fragment may be found in a lintel relief in Baltimore, which also depicts a seated tomb owner entertained by a male harpist and three female musicians (including a drummer and lyre player as on the Cleveland relief). As its inscription reveals, both the host and approaching male attendant represent Divine Wine Stewards in the service of Hathor, "Goddess of Drunkenness." The attendant female musicians on the Hap-iu relief may likewise have been associated with the Hathor cult.[13] GEM

Published: C.R. Williams, "The Egyptian Collection in the Museum of Art at Cleveland, Ohio," *JEA* 5 (1918): 280–84 and pl. 39; Bothmer et al., *ESLP*, no. 82, pl. 78, fig. 203.

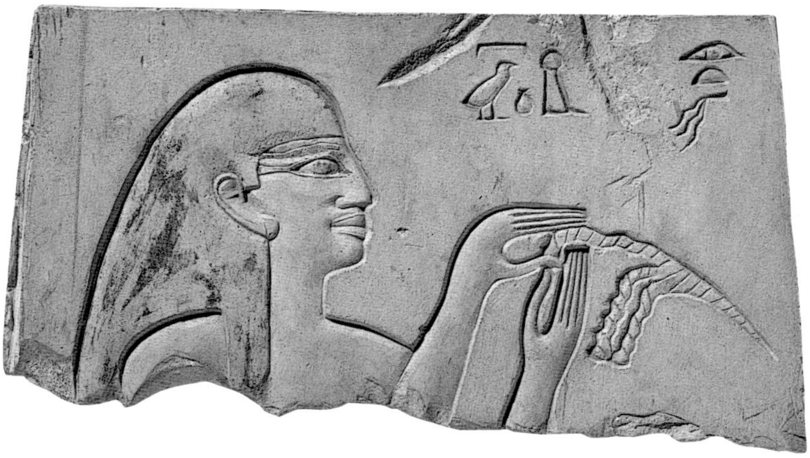

34 Relief of the hairdresser Inu

Limestone with pigment; from Deir el-Bahri, Thebes, tomb of Queen Nefru; Middle Kingdom, Dynasty 11; H: 13.2 cm; L: 24.5 cm

The Brooklyn Museum. Charles Edwin Wilbour Fund. 51.231

Because of the divinity of Egypt's monarch, only the most trusted attendants were allowed to touch the person of the king and his wife.[1] Beside hairdressers, other attendants who were permitted close physical contact with the king and his family included manicurists,[2] those in charge of the royal chambers and garments,[3] and of course the royal physicians.[4] Those who served in these capacities must have enjoyed very high social status.[5]

In this relief, the hairdresser Inu, whose name and title are carved above her figure, holds a lock of hair ready to insert into the coiffure of her mistress, Queen Nefru (cat. no. 39). Actual hairpieces of this type have been found in burials of women, including that of Queen Meryet-Amen,[6] whose tomb yielded two types of hairpieces. Triple braids ending in a single strand for fastening to the coiffure were found at the back of the queen's head and are precisely like the one held by Inu. Long, single braids of varying thickness were also found in Meryet-Amen's tomb; these had long, thin strands at the top for tying into the natural hair near the roots. Numerous braids were found attached to the head of Meryet-Amen's mummy, and extra braids were found coiled in a basket.[7]

Though it is commonly believed that the Egyptians shaved their heads, evidence from mummies and from medical texts proves that this was not necessarily the case.[8] Both women and men seem to have valued their natural hair. Recipes for preventing hair loss, covering gray hair, and making the hair grow longer are known from the Ebers medical papyrus, as in these examples:

> ... to make the hair of a bald-headed person grow: fat of lion, fat of hippopotamus, fat of crocodile, fat of cat, fat of serpent, fat of ibex, are mixed together, and the head of a bald person is anointed therewith.[9]

> ... to expel grizzling and to treat the hair: blood of a black calf is boiled with oil and (it) is anointed therewith.[10]

> ... Another remedy to make the hair grow, prepared for Shesh, the mother of his Majesty the King of Upper and Lower Egypt Tety, the justified: leg of hound, *njt* of dates, hoof of ass, are boiled thoroughly with oil in a *d3d3w*-vessel and (it) is anointed therewith.[11]

For the vengeful, there was even a recipe to make a rival's hair fall out: "... Another to cause the hair to fall out: burnt chaetopod (?), boiled with oil and balanites-oil, is applied to the head of a hated woman."[12]

In the lower socioeconomic classes, neighbors or relatives probably assisted one another with their hairstyles (cat. no. 8a). Women (and men) of middle income probably received this service from household servants. Presumably, royalty and the upper class were able to employ people whose sole duty[13] was to dress the hair of the family and to make and care for wigs and hairpieces.

Little is known about the training of hairstylists in ancient Egypt. Like most craftspersons, novices probably learned and practiced skills through apprenticeship. A title held by a woman of the Old Kingdom, "Overseer of the Wig Workshop,"[14] and the recent excavation of such a workshop at Deir el-Bahri[15] indicate that wigmaking was quite a profitable industry in which people were employed in a centralized setting. AKC

Published: E. Riefstahl, "Two Hairdressers of the Eleventh Dynasty," *JNES* 15 (1956): 10–17.

35 a Seated statue of Enehy

Limestone; provenance unknown, probably from Memphis; New Kingdom, Dynasty 19; H: 1.32 m

The Walters Art Gallery, Baltimore. Museum Purchase. 22.106

(Removed from exhibition because of conservation problems)

This is one of two nearly identical statues depicting Enehy, who served in the cult of Hathor (see cat. no. 85 for an Old Kingdom Hathor priestess). The statues have an interesting history; they were probably acquired by Champollion,[1] who travelled in Egypt in 1828–29. He sent them to an estate in France, the Château des Egalades. At an undetermined date, the statues were sent by art dealers in Paris to New York, where they were purchased respectively by the Walters Art Gallery and by the Reverend Theodore Pitcairn. The statue in the Pitcairn collection was acquired in 1976 by the Matsuoka Museum of Art in Tokyo (fig. 1).[2]

On both statues, Enehy is seated on a chair with leonine legs. (The chair's horizontal and diagonal support struts are indicated carefully.) The roughness of the stone on the sides of the chair reveals that the statue had not yet received its final polishing when it was placed in the tomb.

Enehy wears the long, heavy wig and elaborately pleated garment popular at this period of Egyptian history and holds a sistrum in her left hand. This statue (as well as its mate in Japan) allegedly came from Memphis; indeed, it is virtually identical to another statue[3] originally from that site depicting the priestess-musician Meryt (now in the Rijksmuseum van Oudheden, Leiden). The noblewoman Meryt, whose husband, Maya, was treasurer for King Tutankhamen,[4] must have been so greatly admired as the ideal of feminine beauty and religious piety that her statue was unabashedly copied by other upperclass women, such as Enehy, who served in temple ritual.

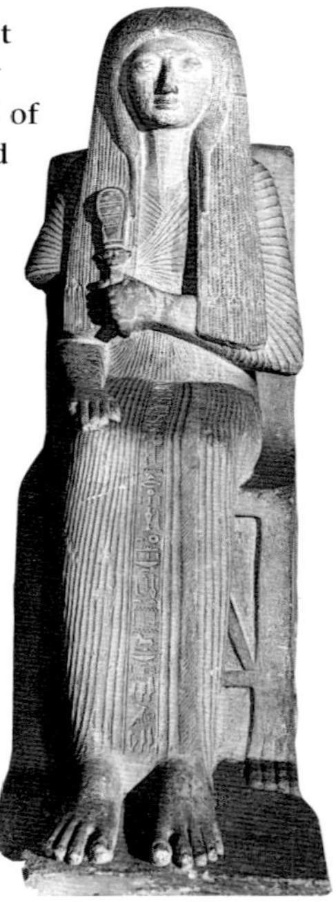

Fig. 1 Statue of Enehy. Photo courtesy of Matsuoka Museum of Art, Tokyo.

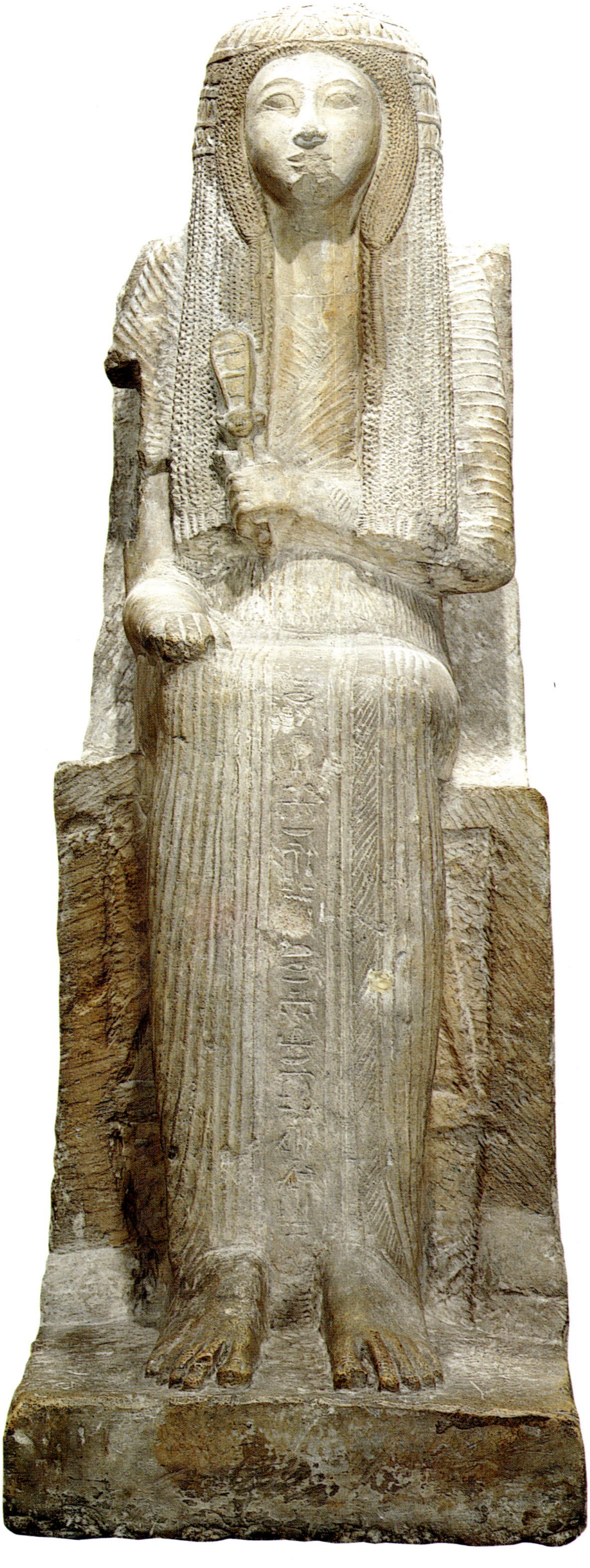

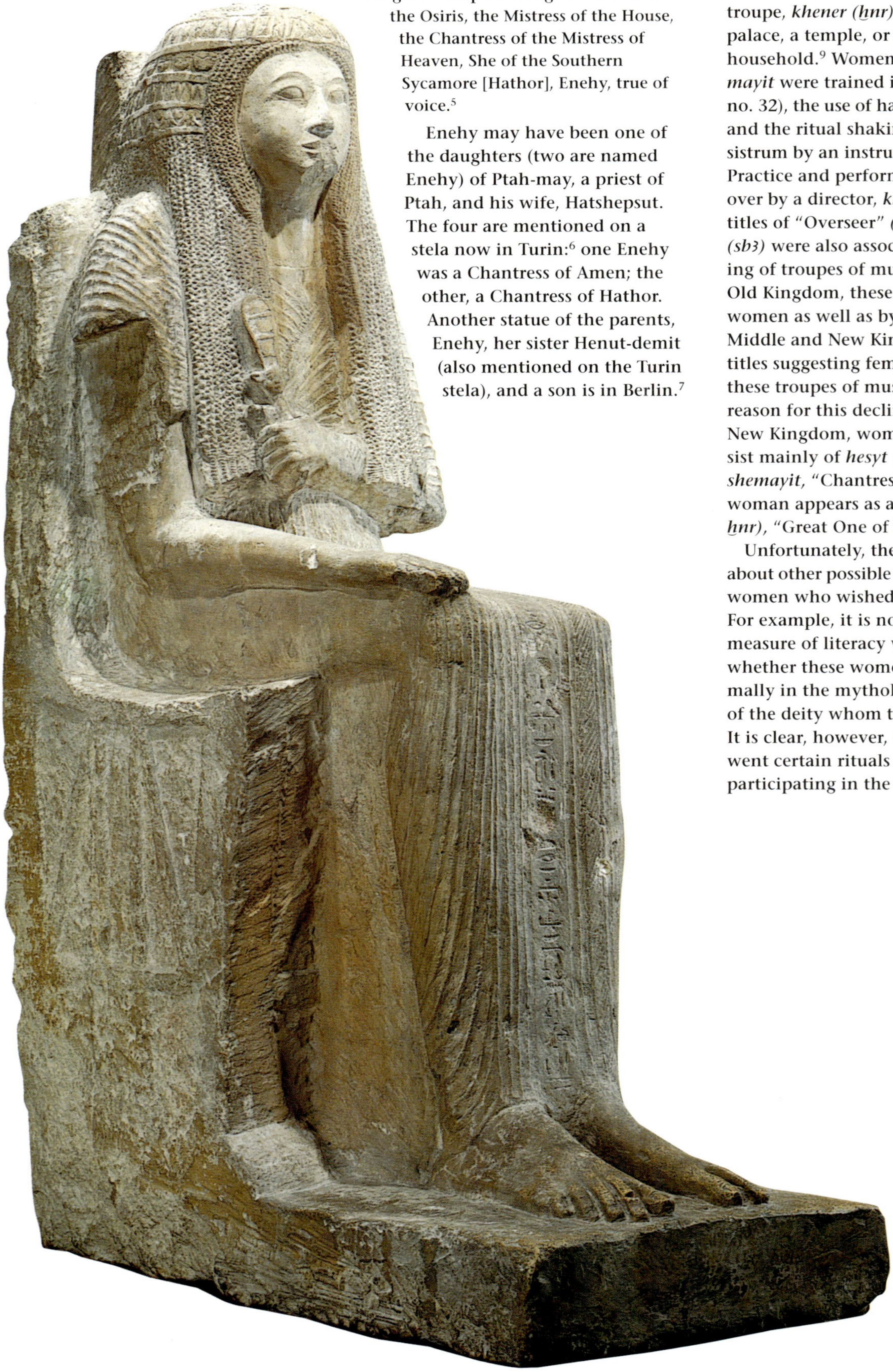

An inscription running down the front of the gown reads:

> Everything which goes forth before the Lords of the Necropolis: bread, beer, oxen, fowl, wine, incense, libation-water, and all good and pure things for the *ka* of the Osiris, the Mistress of the House, the Chantress of the Mistress of Heaven, She of the Southern Sycamore [Hathor], Enehy, true of voice.[5]

Enehy may have been one of the daughters (two are named Enehy) of Ptah-may, a priest of Ptah, and his wife, Hatshepsut. The four are mentioned on a stela now in Turin:[6] one Enehy was a Chantress of Amen; the other, a Chantress of Hathor. Another statue of the parents, Enehy, her sister Henut-demit (also mentioned on the Turin stela), and a son is in Berlin.[7]

During the New Kingdom, women of the upper classes served in the temple of one or more gods as *shemayit (šmꜥyt)*, variously translated as "Singers" or "Chantresses."[8] Apparently, these women were considered part of the musical troupe, *khener (ẖnr)*, attached to the palace, a temple, or to a large private household.[9] Women who served as *shemayit* were trained in handclapping (cat. no. 32), the use of hand wands (cat. no. 36), and the ritual shaking of the *menat* and sistrum by an instructor, *sehedj (sḥḏ)*. Practice and performances were presided over by a director, *kherep (ẖrp)*.[10] The titles of "Overseer" *(imy-r)* and "Teacher" *(sb3)* were also associated with the training of troupes of musicians.[11] During the Old Kingdom, these titles were held by women as well as by men.[12] During the Middle and New Kingdoms, we find fewer titles suggesting females' authority over these troupes of musician-priestesses; the reason for this decline is not clear. By the New Kingdom, women's cultic titles consist mainly of *hesyt (ḥsyt)*, "Singer," and *shemayit*, "Chantress"; occasionally a woman appears as a *weret khener (wrt ẖnr)*, "Great One of the Musical Troupe."[13]

Unfortunately, there is little information about other possible training procedures for women who wished to serve as priestesses. For example, it is not known whether a measure of literacy was required,[14] or whether these women were schooled formally in the mythology and iconography of the deity whom they wished to serve.[15] It is clear, however, that priestesses underwent certain rituals of purification before participating in the cult.[16]

Two particularly important cultic implements[17] were used by priestesses of Hathor during worship of the goddess: the sistrum and the *menat* necklace.[18]

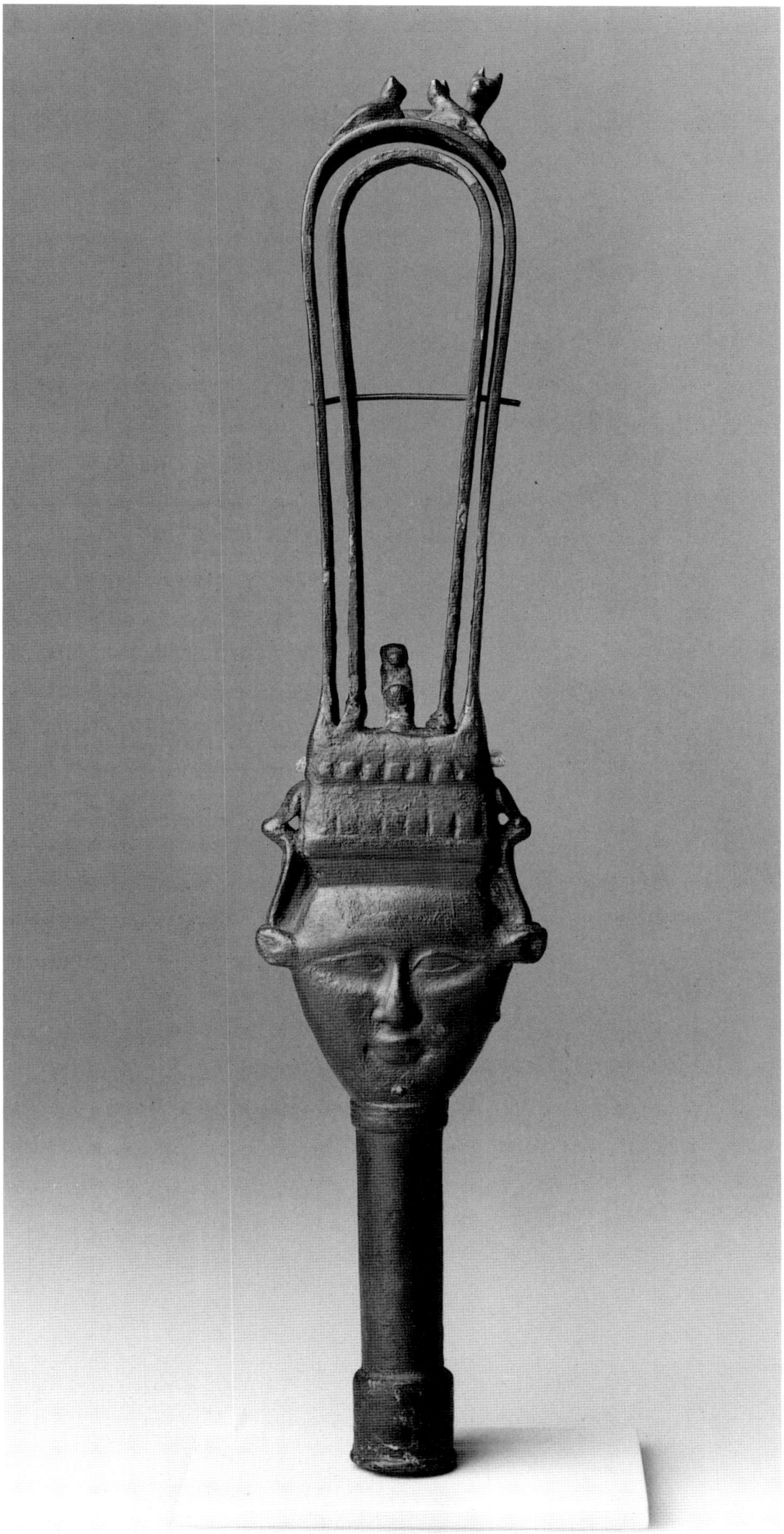

35 b Sistrum with Hathor head

Bronze; provenance unknown, possibly from Bubastis; Late Period; H: 47 cm

Cincinnati Art Museum. Gift of Millard F. and Edna F. Shelt. 1947.403

Of the two types of sistra used in ancient Egypt, the earlier form, known from the Old Kingdom,[19] was the *naos* sistrum (which may have been a development of the *sekhem* scepter[20]), with metal rods and disks (see cat. no. 36b). The later type of sistrum incorporated an arched loop through which passed the rods threaded with discs. The ancient Egyptian name for sistra, *sesheshet,* is perhaps an onomatopoetic echo of the swishing sound made by a sistrum as it was shaken. Two sistra are included in this group: the one depicted in Enehy's hand, and the Cincinnati Art Museum's bronze sistrum. Both incorporate the mask of Hathor[21] with its bovine ears, which appears under the arched loops. The bronze example also depicts the goddess Bastet reclining with her litter of kittens at the top of the arch. A great mother goddess, Bastet was associated in the Late Period with Hathor. Inside the bronze loop, Hathor's son Ihy, the god of music and dance, is represented as a young child.

35 c *Menat* necklace

Bronze, faience, stone, and glass; from Thebes, palace of Amenhotep III; New Kingdom, Dynasty 18, reign of Amenhotep III; L. of counterpoise: 14.7 cm

The Metropolitan Museum of Art. Rogers Fund, 1911. 11.215.450

Published: Aldred, *Jewels,* pl. 114; Hayes, *Scepter,* 2: 253, fig. 153.

The *menat* was another object that was shaken during the worship of Hathor.[22] The "necklace" part of the *menat* consists of numerous strands of small beads gathered together at the ends and attached to single strands of larger beads. Originally each end of the necklace terminated in a counterpoise—a keyhole-shaped pendent

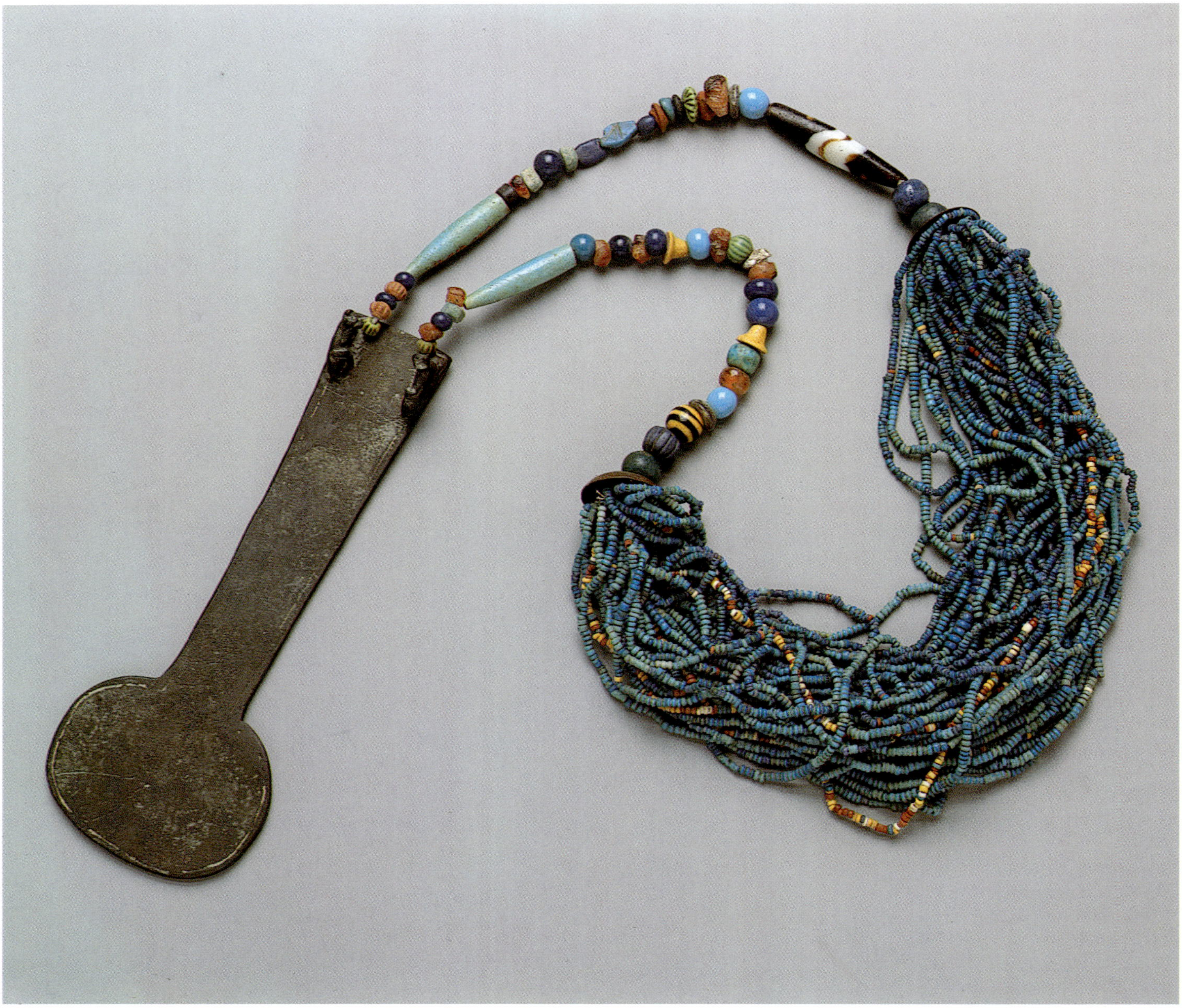

that was worn at the back to balance the weight of the necklace. By the New Kingdom, a single counterpoise joined together the ends of the beaded strands.[23] *Menat* necklaces are depicted in a variety of ways: worn hanging about the neck,[24] worn about the neck with the counterpoise held extended horizontally (during actual worship),[25] and held in the hand (see cat. no. 93, where Renenutet holds a *menat* necklace).

Most Egyptian deities had dual natures: the raging, destructive persona and the benevolent aspect that might be persuaded to bestow blessings upon mortals.[26] The soothing swishing and tinkling noises produced by the shaking of sistra and *menats* were believed to pacify the violent aspects so that one might safely approach the deity[27] without incurring his or her wrath.

These cultic implements sacred to Hathor and her priestesses were also viewed as instruments capable of bestowing the goddess' favors: life, health, and rebirth. The daughters of Senusert I, for example, requested full pardon (i.e., life) for Sinuhe by shaking their sistra and *menats* before the king.[28] During the Festival of Hathor, the priestesses of the goddess went from house to house, shaking their sacred implements for the benefit of the populace.[29] In tomb scenes,[30] the deceased may be offered sistra and *menats* as a way of indicating his or her successful "spiritual transition"[31] from this life to the next.

35 d *Menat* counterpoise

Bronze; excavated at Semna, Sudan; New Kingdom, Dynasty 18; H: 13.8 cm; W: 4.5 cm

Museum of Fine Arts, Boston. Harvard University–MFA Expedition. 29.1199

Published: Dunham and Janssen, *Semna Kumma,* pl. 128a; *Egypt's Golden Age,* no. 418; *Egypt's Dazzling Sun,* no. 90.

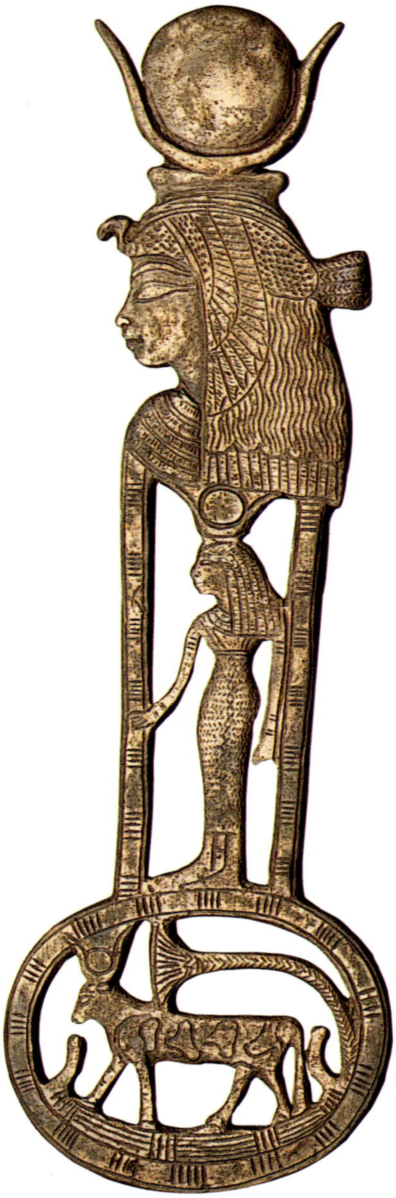

The openwork counterpoise from the Museum of Fine Arts, Boston, portrays Hathor three times: twice in the form of a human female and once as a bovine. The top of the counterweight is formed by the goddess' head, neck, and shoulders. She wears a wig of long, wavy locks ending in tightly curled ringlets,[32] which is partially covered by the vulture headdress. As in the other two depictions, she wears a horned solar disc atop a *modius* crown. A broad collar encircles her shoulders. Hathor is next depicted on the counterweight in full human form. She holds in her hand a *was* scepter, symbolic of her dominion as Mistress of the Sky. This role is emphasized again by the third portrayal: the goddess in bovine form standing in a papyrus skiff, a reference to her daily travels with the sun god Ra in his solar barque.[33]

The connection of the *menat* with the goddess was so intimate that the counterpoise could be anthropomorphized as a depiction of Hathor[34] (fig. 2). At her temple at Dendereh, Hathor was given the epithet "Mistress of the Counterpoise"; that temple was called House of the Counterpoise.[35] The New Kingdom provides evidence that Hathor's musician-priestesses, *shemayit* and others belonging to the *khener,* actually were identified with Hathor. In an inscription from the reign of Ramesses II, referring to the worship of Hathor at the temple of her consort, Ra, at Heliopolis, certain priestesses of the goddess are specifically termed Hathors.[36] At Dendereh, too, the titles accorded to Hathor's priestesses are those borne by the goddess herself, including "Divine *Menat*-Necklace, Great *Menat*-Necklace, and Mistress of the *Sesheshet*- and *Sekhem*-Sistra."[37] Like the sacred cult objects, these priestesses embodied the essence of Hathor. So great was their devotion to the goddess that women such as Enehy had themselves portrayed in their tomb statues in their cultic roles, so that they might continue to serve Hathor through eternity. AKC

36 a Hand wands (pair)

Carved wood; provenance unknown; New Kingdom, Dynasty 18; L. of l. hand: 29.9 cm; L. of r. hand: 30.3 cm

The Toledo Museum of Art. Gift of Edward Drummond Libbey. 1925.145a,b

36 b Hand wand

Ivory; from Deir el-Ballas; New Kingdom, prob. Dynasty 18; L: 18 cm

Phoebe Hearst Museum of Anthropology, University of California at Berkeley. 6–8436

Wands such as these, with tips in the shape of human hands,[1] had several functions in ancient Egypt. Dancers clacked them together to keep time to music[2] and to punctuate certain movements. They also had protective significance. A pair was found in the Thirteenth Dynasty tomb under the Ramesseum, with other objects having magical protective import, such as an apotropaic wand (cat. no. 12) and a Beset statuette.[3] The noise produced by clacking the wands together was

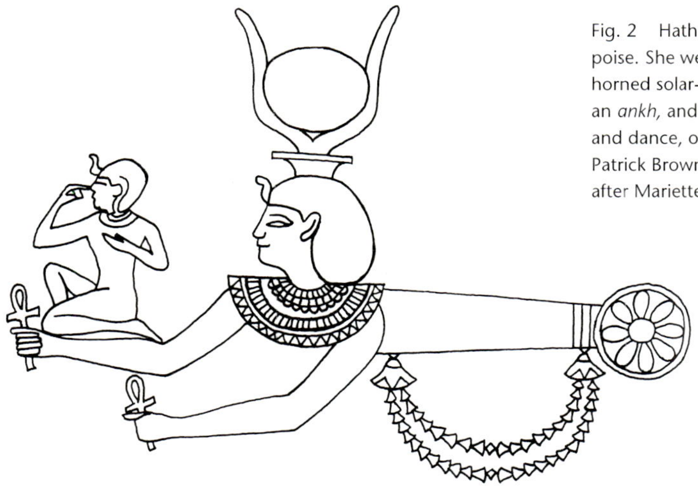

Fig. 2 Hathor as an anthropormorphized counterpoise. She wears the *uraeus* on her brow, and the horned solar-disc headdress. In each hand she holds an *ankh,* and supports her son Ihy, the god of music and dance, on her outstretched arm. Rendering by Patrick Brown. Originally published in *JNES* 7 (1921), after Mariette, *Denderah,* II, pl. 80.

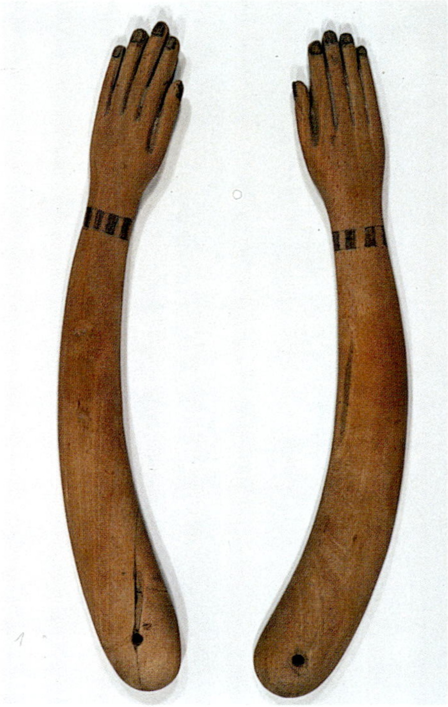

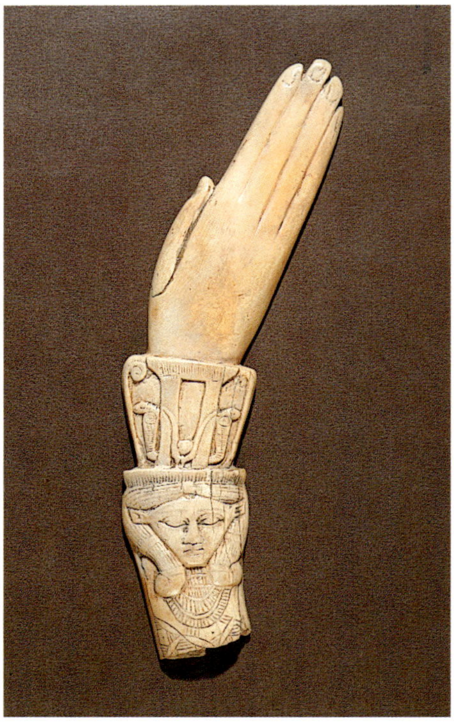

believed to keep malevolent spirits at bay during critical moments such as childbirth,[4] or during puberty rituals.[5] Their protective power accompanied the ritual renewal of the king's vigor during the *Heb Sed* and assisted in the rebirth of a deceased person into the afterlife.[6]

Hand wands were most commonly carved from ivory, though examples in bone and wood are also known.[7] A bracelet often encircles the wrist, as on the Toledo pair, where the decoration is incised and stained with pigment. The fingernails are carefully carved and stained as well. The butt ends of the wands were pierced so that they could be strung together with a cord.[8] Some hand wands are inscribed; for instance, the pair from the tomb of Tutankhamen bear the inscription, "The great royal wife, Tiye, may she live! The king's daughter, Meritaten."[9] A wand in the Oriental Institute at the University of Chicago is inscribed for the "Maidservant of the Princess Sithathor."[10]

The elaborate Hearst hand wand[11] also has the carefully rendered fingernails, though the fingertips exhibit wear to the carved ivory surface. The thumb is naturally positioned against the inner side of the hand, and the hand itself curves outward rather sharply at the wrist. Directly below the wrist is a bovine-eared Hathor mask surmounted by a shrine flanked by cobras; these elements are common to the *naos*-type sistra used in the worship of Hathor.[12] It is not known whether this wand was pierced; the butt end of the wand has been broken away and lost.

Erotic connotations are expressed in the combination of the mask of Hathor with the hand. Hathor's epithets included "Mistress of the Vulva"[13] and "Hand of Atum" (also applied to other goddesses[14]), a reference to that god's creation of the world through masturbation. As G. Pinch has observed, "The divine hand could be a symbol of creative energy as well as protective power."[15]

In a dance exclusive to Hathor worship, a single hand wand was used in conjunction with a mirror (cat. no. 22a).[16] During the dance movements, the hand wand was held so that it was reflected in the mirror. It has been suggested that this dance refers to Hathor's role as the Eye of Ra, with the image of the solar disc echoed in the shape of the mirror.[17] AKC

Female Royalty

37 Pair statue of Queen Hetepheres II and her daughter Meresankh III

Limestone; from Giza, Tomb of Meresankh III, G7530; Old Kingdom, Dynasty 4; H: 59.3 cm

Museum of Fine Arts, Boston. Harvard University–Museum of Fine Arts Expedition. 1927.30.1456

Hetepheres II[1] and Meresankh III[2] witnessed Egypt's great pyramid age from the choicest of vantage points. Hetepheres was the daughter of King Khufu—builder of the Great Pyramid at Giza. She married her half-brother, the crown prince Kawab, who died before ascending to the throne.[3] Hetepheres then became the principal wife of King Djedefra, Khufu's immediate successor. Meresankh, Hetepheres' daughter by Kawab, was the wife of King Khafra, for whom the second great Giza pyramid was constructed. Hetepheres and Meresankh held similar titles, including "King's Daughter"[4] and "King's Wife." Both served as priestesses of the bull deities Tjasep and Bapef;[5] Meresankh was also a priestess of Hathor, "Mistress of Heliopolis."[6]

The tomb chapel of Meresankh was discovered on what was intended to be the final day of the 1927 Harvard–MFA Expedition.[7] While clearing debris from the face of *mastaba* G7540 in the Eastern field at Giza, a doorway was found at ground level.[8] Upon investigation, this entrance led to the three-room tomb (G7530) of Meresankh III. The tomb was decorated with painted reliefs depicting the queen and her family, the preparation of funerary goods and statuary, and agriculture and marsh scenes.[9] Hetepheres' prominent presence in the tomb suggests that she had this rock-cut chapel and its contents prepared for her daughter who had predeceased her.[10] Along one wall, life-size statues of Hetepheres and Meresankh and her daughters were carved from the standing rock.[11] In the burial shaft of the tomb, a black granite sarcophagus was found with its heavy lid propped up by rocks just as the ancient robbers had left it. The sarcophagus was originally inscribed for the burial of Hetepheres; an added text commemorates Hetepheres' donation of the sarcophagus to her daughter: "I have given (it) to the king's daughter and wife, Meresankh."[12] In a corner of the tomb was found a disjointed skeleton—the remains of Queen Meresankh.[13]

A number of fragmentary statues were found in the tomb of Meresankh, including the

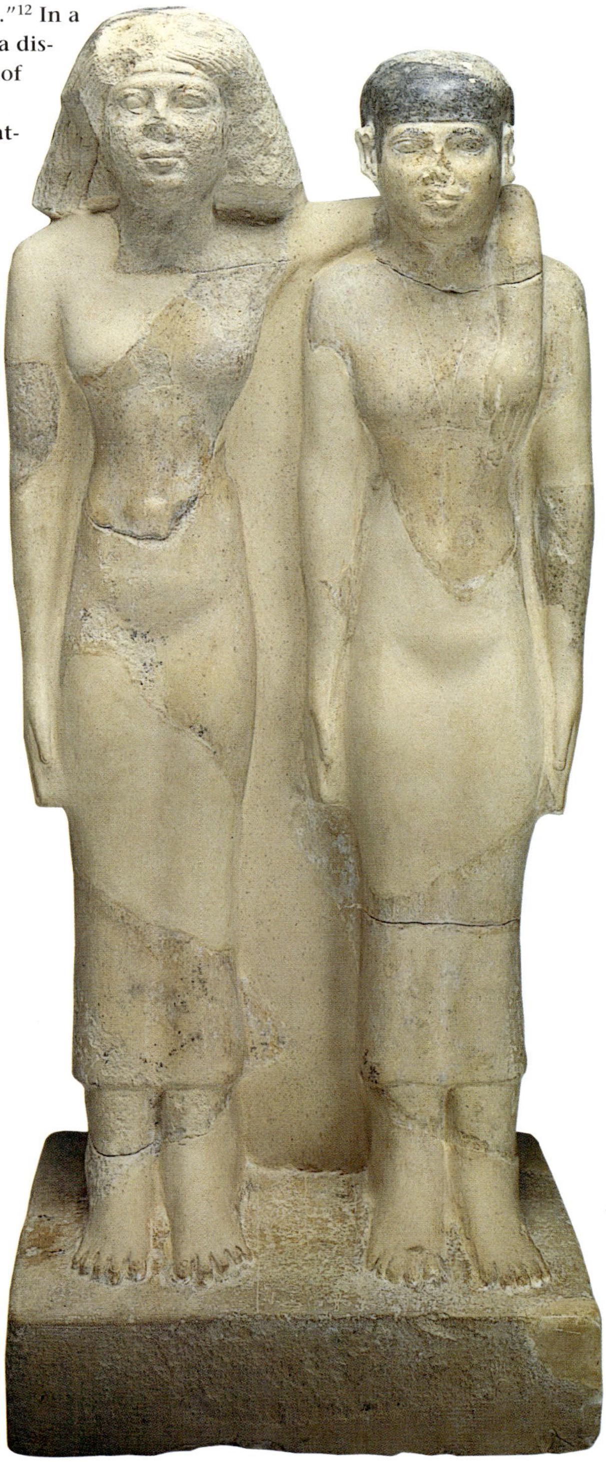

reconstructed example featured here.[14] Hetepheres stands on the proper right, with her left arm across the shoulders and her left hand on the breast of her daughter. Meresankh's arms rest at her sides. Both women wear the female costume popular in the Old Kingdom: a tightly fitting sheath dress, which reveals the musculature of the women's bodies. Meresankh's hair is close-cropped; her mother wears a heavy, shoulder-length wig with her natural hair indicated at the front. On the base of the statue is an inscription, which reads: "She Who Sees Horus and Seth, United with the Two Ladies, Hetepheres; Her Daughter, Wife of the King, Her Beloved, Meresankh." The only remaining pigment on the statue consists of traces of black on the eyes and wig(s).[15]

The statue's similarity in pose to that of the well-known pair statue of Memy and Sabu[16] in the Metropolitan Museum of Art (cat. no. 3a) has often been observed. In Egyptian pair statuary, it is typical for the person of higher status to be embraced; usually, a wife holds her husband, and a child holds his or her parent. In these two examples, however, the younger queen is embraced by the elder, and the woman Sabu is embraced by Memy (though Sabu reciprocates by clasping Memy—who may have been her husband—about the waist). Donald Spanel suggests that this pose indicates that the embracer was a "visitor" in the tomb of the person embraced,[17] as Hetepheres was in the tomb of Meresankh.

Inscriptions on a doorway in Meresankh's tomb record the dates of both her death and her burial.[18] The span between the two dates is 272 days. It was once thought that this was the period necessary for mummification,[19] though recent experiments indicate that much less time was actually required for the preservation of a corpse in natron.[20] More likely, Meresankh died unexpectedly, and the nine-month interval was used to prepare not only her mummy, but her tomb and funerary goods as well.[21]

There is disagreement over the burial place of Hetepheres II. G. Reisner was convinced that *mastaba* G7530[22] contained the burial shaft of the queen,[23] though such a shaft was never found. W.S. Smith identified the double *mastaba* of Kawab (G7110 and 7120) as the tomb of Hetepheres II.[24] Though that *mastaba* may originally have been designed to hold her burial, the part prepared for her was unfinished and never used. A third tomb seems to have been prepared for Hetepheres II in the Eastern field at Giza (G7350); this tomb too was largely unfinished and apparently unused.[25] Once she had become the wife of King Djedefra, it seems likely that a more fitting tomb would have been planned for Hetepheres, perhaps near her husband's pyramid at Abu Roash (though his tomb also seems never to have been completed).[26]

Hetepheres II prepared the tomb chapel of her daughter Meresankh in the reign of Menkaura.[27] Hetepheres herself died at an advanced age in the reign of Shepseskhaf;[28] her remains have not been found. It seems, however, that her descendants continued to rule Egypt in the Fifth Dynasty. It is possible that King Niuserra of the Fifth Dynasty was the son of Meresankh III;[29] a young boy by that name is depicted with Meresankh in her tomb.[30] AKC

Published: *Worcester Art Museum Annual* 1 (1935–36): 18, fig. 3; Wenig, *Woman*, pl. 8; Capart, *L'art égyptien* 2:2, pl. 259.

38 Relief: Queen Wedjebten with lotus

Limestone with pigment; excavated at Saqqara, pyramid of Wedjebten; Old Kingdom, Dynasty 6, reign of Pepy II; H: 42.2 cm; W: 25.6 cm

Cincinnati Art Museum. Anonymous gift in honor of Mrs. John J. Emery. 1974.413

The pyramid of the Sixth Dynasty Queen Wedjebten was excavated by the French Egyptologist Gustave Jequier in the 1925–26 season at Saqqara.[1] This relief fragment comes from the proper left-han jamb of the "false door" that was set abov the offering table in the west wall of the pyramid's funerary chapel.[2] When the wa was dismantled in antiquity for reuse, a section of the false door fell away and cracked. When this fragment was discovered, there were two vertical registers on the left jamb; each depicted the queen facing to the left with her name written twice in vertical registers above each representation.[3]

In her depiction on the Cincinnati frag ment, Wedjebten wears a close-fitting sheath dress with straps fitting over her breasts and shoulders. Her jewelry consis of a pair of wide bracelets and a broad co lar. Her short hair (or wig) is held in plac by a diadem with a bow and streamer at the back.[4] Wedjebten holds to her nose a lotus blossom, a symbol of resurrection.

Wedjebten was one of the wives of Pepy II. In addition to those titles expres ing her status as the king's wife, her title include *ht ḥr* ("Follower of Horus"), *wrt ḥts* ("Great One of the *hts* Scepter"), and *iryt-pꜥt* ("Hereditary Noblewoman").[5] She is not called *sꜣt nisw*, "Daughter of a King," or *mwt nisw* "Mother of a King," but her marriage to Pepy II and her title "Hereditary Noblewoman" indicate her family's political importance.[6]

Wedjebten's pyramid was constructed near the southeast corner of the pyramid of Pepy II. Her edifice, like those of Neith and Iput,[7] two other wives of Pepy II, included most of the elements of a major pyramid complex: the pyramid itself, a funerary chapel with the offering table and false door, tombs of the queen's retainers, and an enclosure wall. The pyramid of each of these queens had a base of about twenty-four meters.[8] Two of the upper courses of Wedjebten's pyramid were discovered during Jequier's excavations;[9] together with the preserved blocks of the lower courses, they indicate that the slope of the pyramid's sides was about 65 degrees. According to texts found on fragments in the funerary chapel, these upper courses were topped with a pyramidion covered with electrum.[10]

The burial chamber in Wedjebten's pyramid was dug into the ground surface and held the queen's sarcophagus and canopic box.[11] The ceiling was decorated with hundreds of stars.[12] Most significant, however, are the walls of the burial chamber.[13] Like those in the tomb chambers of

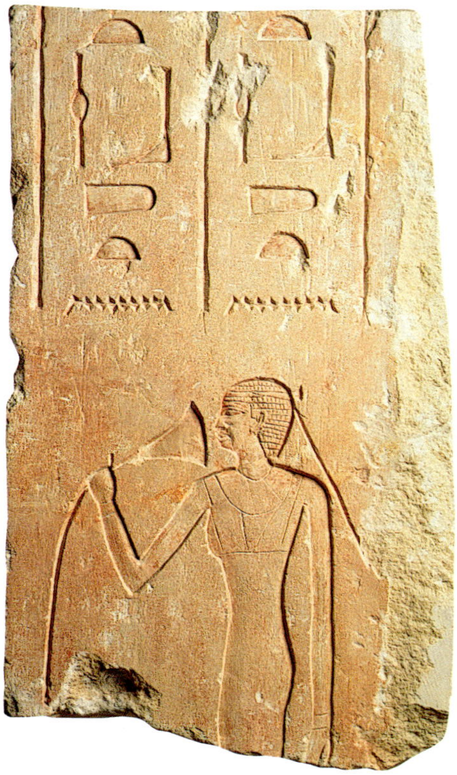

Neith and Iput,[14] they were covered with prayers and magical spells to aid the deceased through the journey to rebirth—the Pyramid Texts.

The earliest known burial chamber inscribed with the Pyramid Texts is that of King Unas, the last king of the Fifth Dynasty. From that time until the reign of Pepy II,[15] the Pyramid Texts remained the exclusive prerogative of kings. It is unclear why, during Pepy's reign, the royal wives were permitted to use this body of magical texts.[16] In doing so, however, they began the "democratization" of religion that eventually led to the use of these texts by nonroyalty, beginning in the late third millennium B.C.[17] AKC

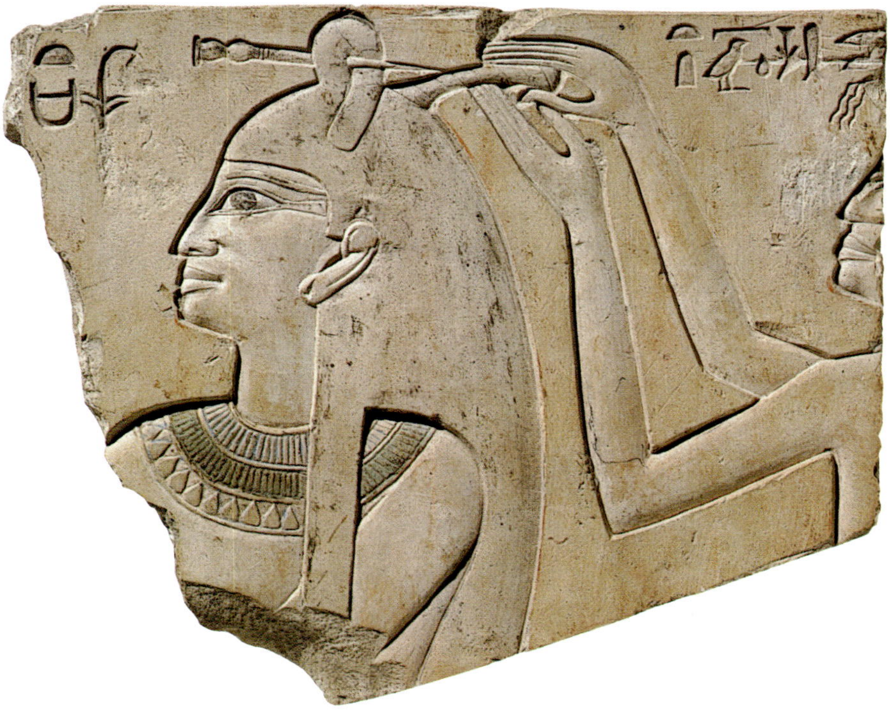

39 Relief: Queen Nefru and the hairdresser Henut

Limestone; from Deir el-Bahri, Thebes, tomb of Queen Nefru, Middle Kingdom, Dynasty 11, reign of Nebhepetra Mentuhotep; H: 19 cm; L: 23.6 cm

The Brooklyn Museum. Charles Edwin Wilbour Fund. 54.49

Nefru was the wife of Nebhepetra Mentuhotep, the Eleventh Dynasty Theban ruler who succeeded in reuniting Upper and Lower Egypt, thus inaugurating the Middle Kingdom.[1] Along with her title "Wife of the King," Nefru bore the title "Daughter of the King."[2] Archaeological evidence shows that her tomb (TT 319) was built before the final phase of construction of the mortuary temple of Nebhepetra, suggesting that she died during the middle part of his long reign.[3]

This relief and those of catalogue numbers 32 and 34 come from Nefru's tomb, which consists of a short passageway leading to a small underground chapel. From there a longer corridor leads to a false burial chamber, and finally to the actual crypt.[4] The tomb was plundered in antiquity,[5] and the fine limestone relief of the chapel (sunk) and the corridor (raised) was stolen for reuse.[6]

In several of the surviving fragments, Queen Nefru's hair is being dressed by the hairdressers Henut and Inu (for the latter, see cat. no. 34). In this scene, Henut, whose name and title are carved above her figure, holds a lock of Nefru's hair. Perhaps Henut is preparing to twist the strand and pin it out of the way with another hairpin like the one depicted,[7] or to fasten to it a lock of false hair.[8]

Scenes of royal and noblewomen having their hair dressed became part of the funerary iconography, especially in the Tenth and Eleventh Dynasties.[9] They appear on sarcophagi,[10] stelae,[11] and on tomb walls,[12] as in Nefru's tomb. Often the woman being coiffed holds a mirror[13] or a lotus flower,[14] and/or an attendant offers her a beverage from a small bowl.[15] It is obvious that these scenes possessed important funerary significance. One scholar has suggested that these scenes were erotic euphemisms indicating a woman's preparations for sexual relations, and therefore necessary for inclusion in tomb contexts so that the deceased might enjoy lovemaking in the afterlife.[16]

A more plausible theory connects these scenes to the cult of Hathor[17] because most of the women being coiffed bear the title of priestess of that goddess.[18] Hathor masks and pillars often depict a hairstyle that was particularly associated with the goddess, with the hair bound about two roundels that rest on the shoulders.[19] Hathor bore the epithet, "She of the Beautiful Hair,"[20] and a legend surrounded a lost lock of her hair.[21] Women who served as priestesses of Hathor likely underwent some sort of purification, including an appropriate coiffure, before serving the goddess.

Some years ago, the Egyptologist Aylward Blackman wrote about the "House of the Morning," the *pr-dw3t*, and the religious ritual surrounding the performance of the king's morning toilette.[22] Titles connected with this royal/divine purification held great importance in the Old Kingdom, but the ritual seems to have lost its significance during the First Intermediate Period.[23] Perhaps the royal women of the Eleventh Dynasty, especially those connected with the cult of Hathor, adopted this ritual, in which they were offered beer,[24] were freshly coiffed, and were presented with a mirror[25] as a symbol of their religious purity.

The interpretation of these hairdressing scenes as purification rituals is also supported by recent studies of scenes termed *Wochenlaube*,[26] "birth arbor," which indicate that following childbirth, women underwent a period of purification, during which they lived in a special light structure apart from the rest of their family.[27] Barry Kemp, who has also studied extensively the depictions of the *Wochenlaube*, suggests that the scenes in which the new mother is offered a drink and a mirror depict the purification ritual that ended the period of uncleanliness.[28] This ritual was so well known that it became the subject of satire.[29]

Rather than being preparations for sexual encounters, these scenes of the ritual toilette of royal and noblewomen were meant to express religious purification. The presence of such scenes in funerary contexts was intended to allow the deceased woman to be ritually prepared throughout eternity for the purpose of worshipping Hathor, the goddess whom she had served in life. AKC

Published: E. Riefstahl, "Two Hairdressers of the Eleventh Dynasty," *JNES* 15 (1956): 10–17; Fazzini et al., *Ancient Egyptian Art*, no. 17.

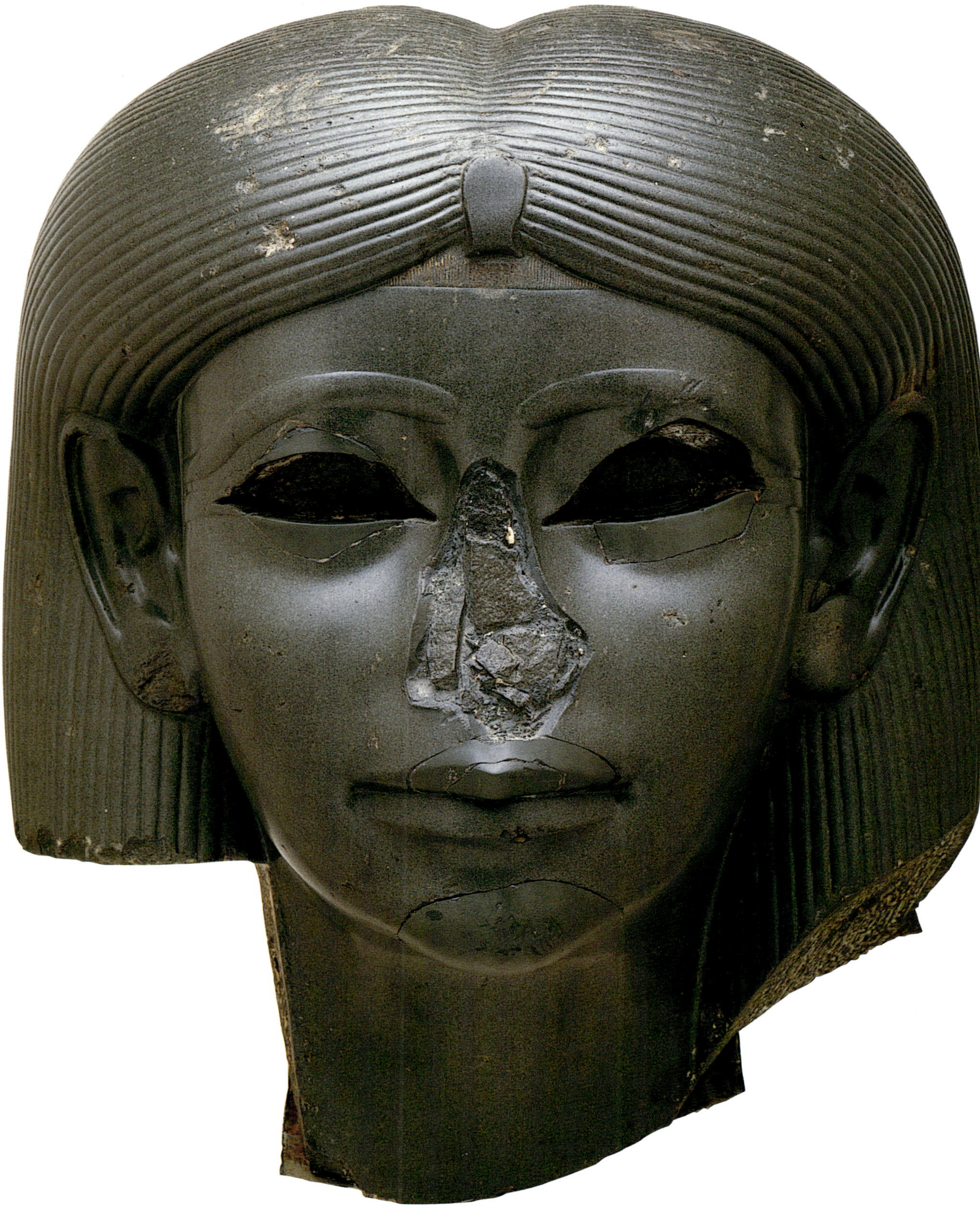

40 Head of a queen or princess

Chlorite; found near Rome, perhaps in Hadrian's Villa at Tivoli; Middle Kingdom, mid–Dynasty 12; H: 38.9 cm; W: 33.3 cm; D: 35.4 cm

The Brooklyn Museum. Charles Edwin Wilbour Fund. 56.85

Since the Brooklyn Museum purchased this colossal head in 1956, nearly every historian of Egyptian art has acknowledged it as one of the finest works of stone sculpture to survive from antiquity. Most Egyptian statuary was intended to *represent* a figure, not to *reproduce* its living form in all its details. The Brooklyn head, however, far surpasses the level of mere representation. The facial surface has been polished to an extraordinary sheen, giving the stone not only the look but also the feel of soft, supple human flesh. Great care was also taken to model the surface to convey, most naturalistically, the feel of the skull beneath the skin.

Great works of art such as this example can be appreciated on an aesthetic level, but they must also be understood. Learning a sculpture's date, function, and history is essential to such an understanding. When dating sculptures, archaeologists often rely on the object's inscription, which may relate when it was made, or they may analyze the archaeological context in which the piece was discovered. If a figure is uninscribed, however, or if its original provenance is not known, the Egyptologist must use stylistic analysis to establish a precise attribution.

John D. Cooney, who purchased the head for Brooklyn, had to apply just such a stylistic approach. He realized that this sculpture's gently arching eyebrows, the shape of its eyes, the large ears, and the long, horizontal mouth are all stylistic hallmarks of the middle reigns of Dynasty 12.[1] He also recognized that the long, striated wig and the smooth contours of the face proved that the subject was a woman. The presence of a tiny *uraeus* cobra on the subject's forehead indicated that she was of the blood royal—a queen or princess. Because the back of her wig trails off toward the horizontal, the head could have come only from a sculpture of a sphinx, a figure with a human head and a leonine body.

One of the objects used to define the style of royal sculpture of mid–Dynasty 12 is a small, badly damaged sphinx statue from the Syrian site of Qatna. That piece, discovered in 1927, does not represent a king; it depicts a princess named Ita, daughter of King Amenemhat II, who ruled in the middle of the Twelfth Dynasty.[2] The faces of the Qatna sphinx and the Brooklyn head are strikingly similar in style, suggesting that the two sculptures were produced very close in time. Both may represent the same individual. The Brooklyn head was one of the first works of ancient Egyptian art to be published in Europe; it was seen and described in 1764 while in the Villa Albani at Rome.[3] Although there is no account explaining how the head came to the villa, we might reasonably suppose that it was transferred there after its discovery in or near Rome sometime in the eighteenth century. Quite probably it was unearthed at Hadrian's Villa at Tivoli. That emperor displayed a marked predilection for the finest Egyptian art, and imperial agents exported major works directly from the Nile Valley to Tivoli. Yet a large number of Middle Kingdom royal statues have been excavated in western Asia, including the Qatna sphinx.[4] The sphinx from which the Brooklyn head derives may have been sent from the court of Amenemhat II in the Middle Kingdom to an unknown site on the Syrian coast from where it was brought to Tivoli two millennia later.

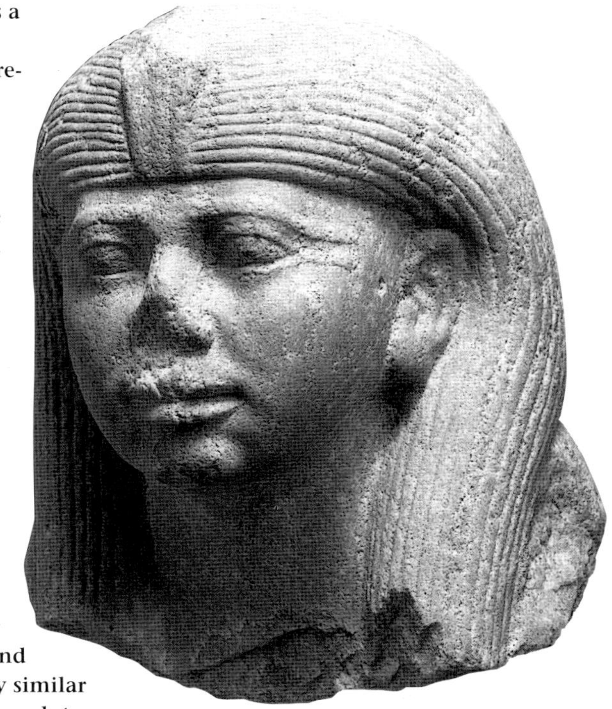

The present condition of the head camouflages its original, beguiling appearance. The eyes, made of metal and stone, were pried from their sockets in antiquity, and the nose, lips, and chin all suffered from disfiguring vandalism. At some time, probably while the sculpture stood at Tivoli, the mouth and chin were repaired in an effort to restore some of the grandeur of the head. JFR

Published: For the most recent publications, see Fay, *Louvre Sphinx*, 28–30, no. 3, pls. 55–57.

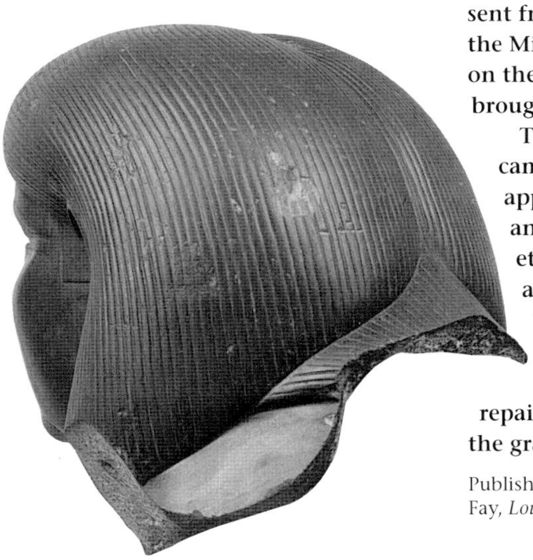

41 Head of a female sphinx

Quartzite; provenance unknown; reportedly from modern Matariya, by the ancient site of Heliopolis; Middle Kingdom, early Dynasty 12; H: 27 cm; W: 24 cm; D: 22 cm

Lent by Jack A. Josephson.

Quartzite is a stone that can be carved very finely, as this superb, approximately life-size female head demonstrates. The striated lappet wig set low on the brow is adorned with a *uraeus* (cobra), which identifies the woman as a princess or queen;[1] the shape of what is preserved of the shoulders indicates that the head came from a sphinx. The particularly striking modeling around the nose and mouth may have been intended to indicate maturity in contrast to the more youthful appearance of most women in ancient Egyptian art.[2]

The cosmetic lines of the eyebrows and eyelids are rendered in relief; the broad face has a wide and straight mouth, a thickset nose, small eyes, and high, prominent cheekbones. For the head's first publisher, these features were sufficiently individualistic and different from those of other female faces of Dynasty 12 to suggest that they are portraitlike.[3] This is not impossible. There are great problems, however, in determining the extent and nature of what might be called portraiture in ancient Egyptian art, especially when we do not know the identity of a sculpture's subject and have no other images of him or her.[4] Even many sculptures that appear somewhat individualistic also display features that reflect a style of their time, including styles established by royal workshops. Hence it is not surprising that one can find parallels for many of the features of this head from a sphinx in a number of images of kings of the earlier part of the Middle Kingdom. Indeed, the chronological attribution of the head depends basically on comparisons with such pieces.

If the presence of a *uraeus* identifies the sculpture's royal subject as a queen or princess, the arrangement of the cobra's body in numerous curves as it runs back over the head relates it to many more royal images of Dynasty 6[5] and later Dynasty 11–early Dynasty 12 than of later Dynasty 12.[6] The sculptures of kings of late Dynasty 11 and early Dynasty 12 also provide some parallels for elements of the facial features,[7] the reason the Josephson head is attributed to early Dynasty 12.[8] This is not to say, however, that the head lacks stylistic affinities with some mid-Dynasty 12 sculptures, including catalogue number 40, another head from a sphinx.

Egyptian sphinxes represent deities or certain members of royalty. The most common composite human-leonine form characterizes its subject as more than human and symbolizes religious concepts concerning the subject and his or her office.[9] Although most sphinxes of royalty represent kings, the earliest known Egyptian sphinx may be a statue of a queen or princess of King Radjedef of Dynasty 4.[10] No other Old Kingdom female sphinxes are yet known, but there are a reasonable number of such statues from the Middle Kingdom, of which the Josephson head may be the earliest.

At least two explanations have been proposed for the occurrence of female sphinxes in the Middle Kingdom. One associates them with the importance of at least some royal women as transmitters of royal legitimacy to their husbands.[11] The other suggests that their leonine aspect relates them to the concept of the daughter and eye of the solar deity (cf. cat. nos. 56, 65, and 67) and that they probably all represent princesses.[12]

The true floruit of female sphinxes occurred in Dynasty 18, from which we have a significant number in both statuary and relief. Although not limited to the middle part of the dynasty, an avenue of sphinxes may have existed at this time in Thebes, in which sphinxes of Amenhotep IV/Akhenaten alternated with those of his chief queen, Nefertiti. This presence, it has been argued, reflects Nefertiti's cultic role as the terrestrial image of Hathor.[13] In mid–Dynasty 18 we also find Nefertiti and her mother-in-law, Tiye, King Amenhotep III's principal queen, represented as sphinxes trampling female foreign enemies. Such images are part of the extraordinary prominence of these two queens in the art of their era. This prominence has been viewed, in part, as a new emphasis on the divine aspects of queenship, corresponding to an even greater new stress on the divinity of the kingship.[14] Also, whereas Middle Kingdom female sphinxes have been associated with the Eye of Ra, Dynasty 18 images of queens as sphinxes defeating symbols of hostile forces have been associated with that solar daughter (identified with many goddesses) as defender of Egypt and the Egyptian kingship.[15] RAF

Published: Wildung, *Sesostris und Amenemhet*, 86, fig. 75, and p. 88; Fay, *Louvre Sphinx*, 64, no. 16 and pl. 84f in an appendix on sphinxes.

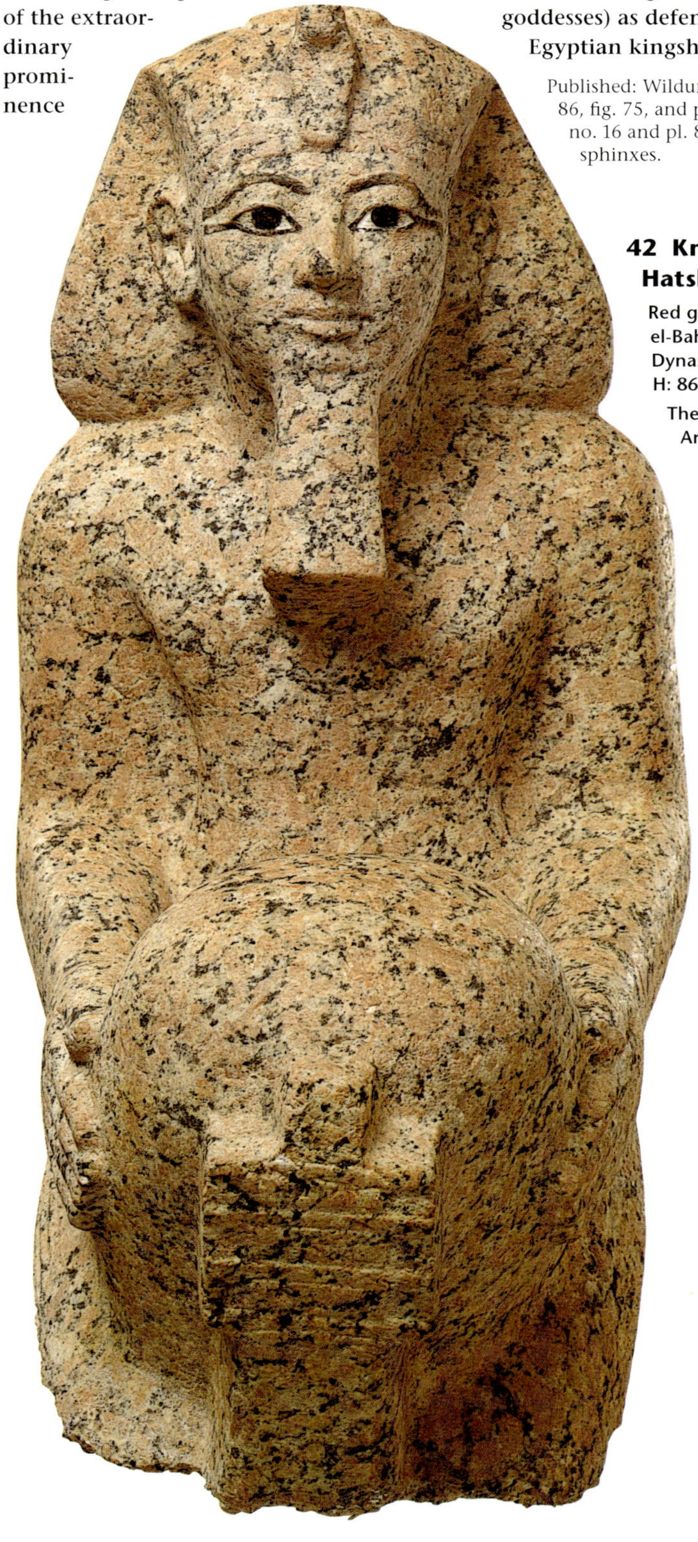

42 Kneeling statue of Hatshepsut

Red granite; excavated at Deir el-Bahri, Thebes; New Kingdom, Dynasty 18, reign of Hatshepsut; H: 86 cm (restored)

The Metropolitan Museum of Art. Rogers Fund, 1923. 23.3.1

This statue depicts the female king Hatshepsut kneeling, her hands supporting a libation vessel.[1] It is one of a series of statues probably erected between the columns of the third terrace of her famous mortuary temple at Deir el-Bahri.[2] In these statues, Hatshepsut is depicted with a "male" body and an idealized, rather aloof, countenance. She wears the royal *shendyt* kilt, a false beard, and a *khat* headdress.[3] The inscriptions on these statues vary in reference to Hatshepsut's gender.[4] On the present example, as king she is called the "Daughter of Ra, Khnum-Amen-Hatshepsut," the latter element being her Horus name.

Hatshepsut was the daughter of Thutmose I and his principal wife, Ahmose. Inscriptions on two of Hatshepsut's monuments relate that Thutmose I declared her as his intended successor, although many scholars have dismissed this claim as a myth invented after the fact to legitimize her eventual rule as king.[5] It is possible, however, that this ceremonial declaration took place late in his reign before the birth of a son, Thutmose II, to the king and a secondary wife.[6] With Thutmose II's birth, the usual male succession was reinstated.

Hatshepsut eventually became the King's Principal Wife of Thutmose II, her half-brother, with whom she had a daughter, Nefrura (cat. no. 43). Hatshepsut also bore the title "God's Wife of Amen,"[7] a high priestly title that she seems to have regarded as more important than her queenly title, since she used the former far more frequently.[8]

When her husband died after a relatively short reign of only fourteen years, Hatshepsut was declared regent for her young stepson, Thutmose III, the son of Thutmose II and a secondary wife.[9] Around year 7 of Thutmose III's reign,[10] Hatshepsut declared herself co-king, ruling jointly with her stepson. Her success in attaining the throne suggests that she had the firm backing of powerful and loyal courtiers[11] whom she had cultivated through her tenures as King's Daughter, King's Principal Wife, and God's Wife of Amen. As co-king, Hatshepsut adopted a full titulary of five names and was depicted with kingly garments, crowns, and other regalia. Of young Thutmose III's opinions regarding the actions of his stepmother, we have no record.[12]

Throughout Egypt's history, other kings had taken co-regents.[13] This practice was intended to ensure that the elder king's chosen successor would inherit the throne and presumably to prepare the younger co-regent for his sole rule.[14] On occasion, other women, too, had taken the throne:[15] Nitokret at the end of the Sixth Dynasty,[16] Sobeknefru at the end of the Twelfth Dynasty,[17] and Tauseret at the end of the Nineteenth Dynasty.[18] These women assumed control when their family lines were dying out and seem to have been chosen as a "last resort."[19] Hatshepsut, however, assumed the role of the dominant partner in the co-regency in spite of the fact that there was already a legitimate (though younger) ruler on the throne. This was a unique occurrence in Egypt's long history.[20]

In spite of her unorthodox accession, the joint rule of Hatshepsut and Thutmose III was a period of prosperity for Egypt. Hatshepsut undertook ambitious building programs,[21] led troops on military campaigns,[22] and sent a trading expedition to Punt to obtain luxury goods.[23]

In his twenty-second regnal year, Thutmose III appeared as sole ruler of Egypt.[24] We do not know if Hatshepsut died (whether of natural causes or assassination) or if she lost her political backing and disappeared from public view. No trace of her mummy was found in her tomb in the Valley of the Kings.[25] AKC

Published: Vandier, *Manuel,* 3: 301–2, pl. 99; Tefnin, *Statuaire d'Hatshepsout,* 89–90, fig. 4, pl. 23a; Suzanne Ratier, *La Reine Hatchepsout, sources et problèmes* (Leiden, 1979), 126; Hayes, *Scepter,* 2: 97.

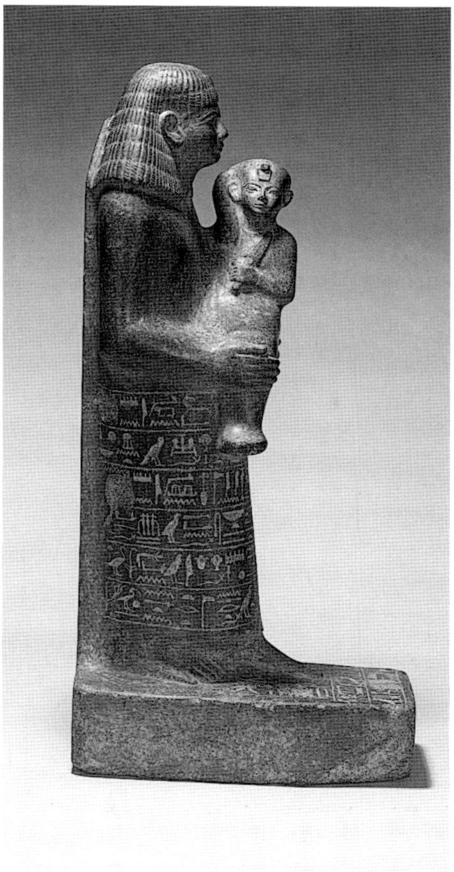

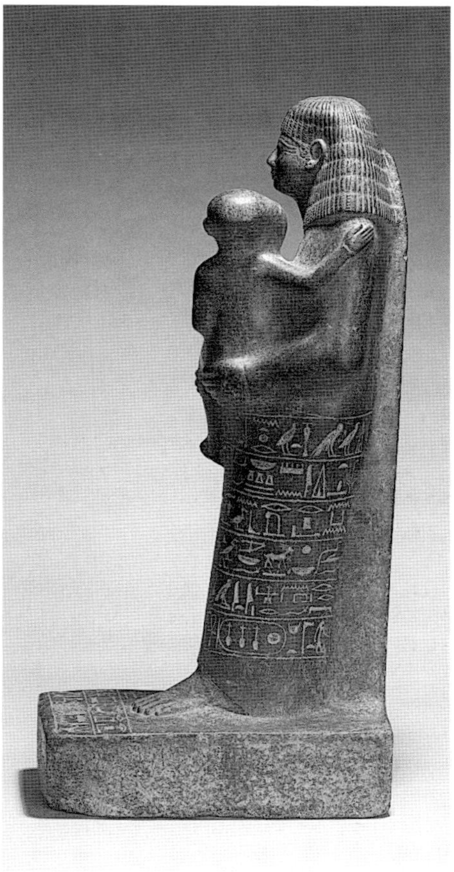

43 Statue of Senenmut holding Nefrura

Black granite; provenance unknown, probably from Karnak; New Kingdom, Dynasty 18; H: 53 cm

Field Museum of Natural History, Chicago. 173800

Nefrura was the daughter of Thutmose II and his chief queen, Hatshepsut. Prior to assuming the kingship (cat. no. 42), Hatshepsut held the office of God's Wife of Amen and apparently considered it her most important title, as she used it more frequently than "King's Wife."[1] When she became "king," it was necessary to pass the title of "God's Wife" to Nefrura.[2] Images of an unnamed God's Wife of Amen depicted on Hatshepsut's barque shrine (the "chapelle rouge") at Karnak are generally identified as the youthful Nefrura.[3] There, the God's Wife is depicted undergoing purification in the temple's holy lake, ritually destroying the names and images of enemies and presenting offerings to deities.[4]

In this statue, Nefrura is held by the court official Senenmut—a man of humble origins[5] who began his career in the royal palace probably during the reign of Thutmose II.[6] He would rise to become the favorite of the female king, Hatshepsut, the overseer of the estates of the god Amen, and the tutor and steward of Nefrura.[7]

Ten[8] known statues depict Senenmut with Nefrura. In this example, both fig-

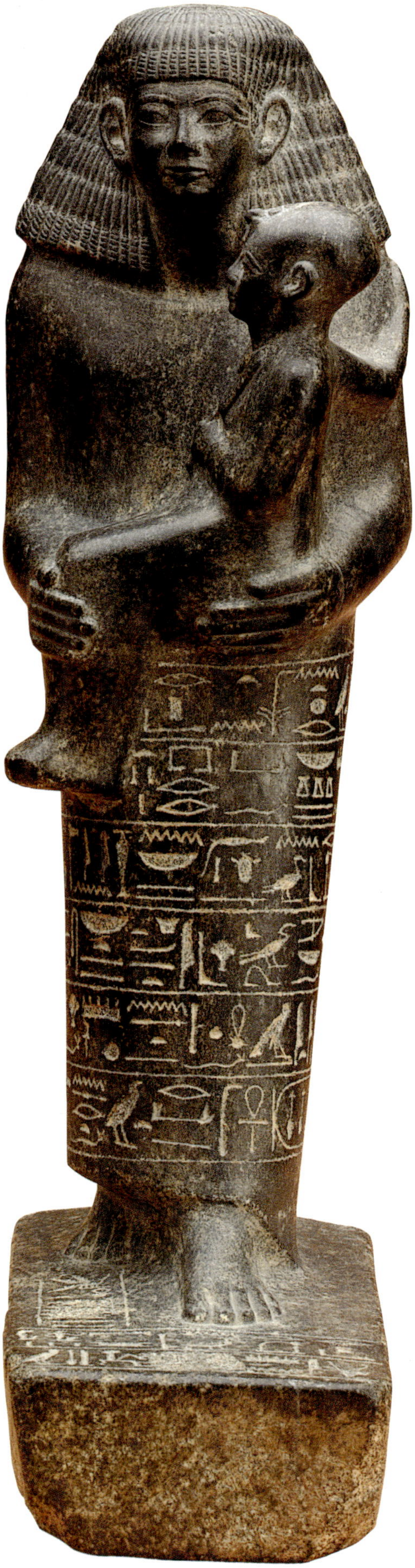

ures are enveloped in cloaks, resulting in simple planes that invite inscription. Senenmut strides forward with his left foot, as is typical of standing male statuary in ancient Egypt. His heavy, shoulder-length wig and large, prominent ears echo the earlier fashion of the Middle Kingdom.[9] Senenmut holds Nefrura rather awkwardly in a seated position. In her left hand, the princess holds the *hetes* scepter[10] against her chest. Her right arm curves up and back to embrace Senenmut's shoulder. She wears the sidelock of youth and the royal *uraeus* on her forehead.

The inscription on the statue is nearly identical to that on another in Berlin,[11] also depicting Senenmut and Nefrura. The text reads, in part:

> [Funerary offering] to the *ka* of the hereditary prince . . . great confidant of the lord of the two lands, praised by the good god, overseer of the granaries of Amen, Senenmut. He says: I am a dignitary beloved of his lord, who has entrée to the marvelous character of the mistress [*sic*] of the two lands; he ennobled me in front of the two lands and made me the chief spokesman of his estate and judge in the entire land. . . . I educated the eldest king's daughter, the god's wife Neferura, may she live; I was given to her to be the "goddess' father," because of my excellence on behalf of the king.[12]

It has often been suggested that Hatshepsut was grooming her daughter to succeed as the next female king, though this was not to be the case. For reasons we may never fully understand, Senenmut seems to have fallen from royal favor, and his name was carefully erased from many of his monuments,[13] including this statue. Hatshepsut herself disappeared from the historical record around year 22, when Thutmose III appeared as sole ruler of Egypt.[14]

It used to be thought that Nefrura had died by year 16 of the coregency; however, a stela dating to the early period of Thutmose III's sole rule may have been made for Nefrura.[15] It depicts a woman with the title "God's Wife of Amen," but was recarved with the name of Satiah, a wife of Thutmose III. Satiah never bore this title, and the stela may have been recarved for her upon Nefrura's death. It has also been suggested that Nefrura was Thutmose III's queen, and that she bore his son, but the evidence is inconclusive.[16] Whether or not Nefrura became his queen, Thutmose III seems to have stripped the office of God's Wife of Amen of much of its power in order to prevent the accumulation of influence and authority that had fueled Hatshepsut's rise to the throne;[17] there were no prominent holders of this title during the remainder of the Eighteenth Dynasty. AKC

44 Head of Queen Tiye

Magnesite marble; probably from Sedeinga, Sudan; New Kingdom, Dynasty 18, reign of Amenhotep III; H: 20.3 cm; W: 11.5 cm

Museum of Fine Arts, Boston. Gift of George A. Reisner. 21.2802

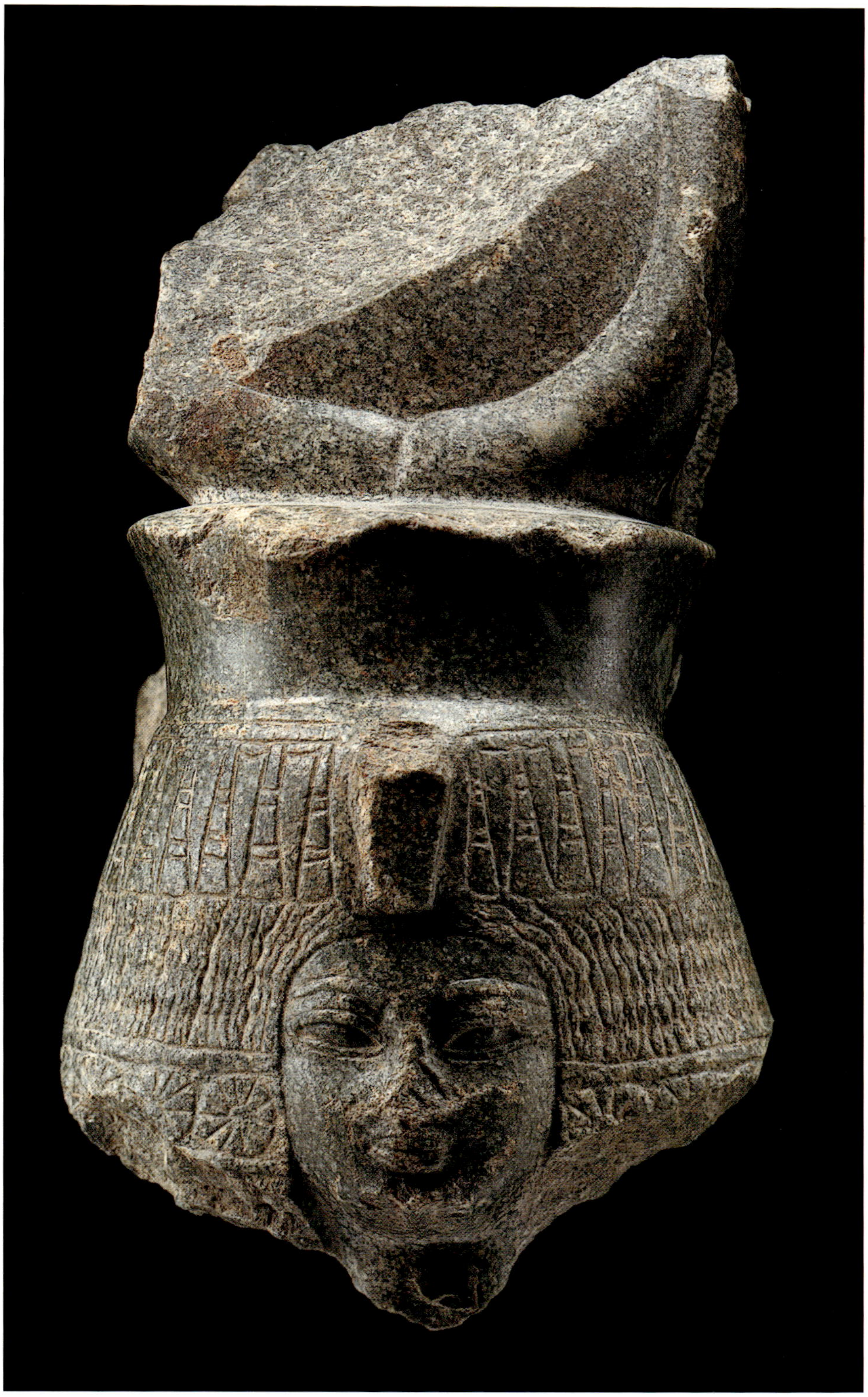

This head comes from a statue depicting Tiye, one of a line of powerful and influential queens of the Eighteenth Dynasty.[1] The fragment was originally part of a pair or group statue, as indicated by the inscription on the back; only the top of one in a row of vertical registers has been preserved.[2] Queen Tiye wears a heavy wig, with careful indication of the wavy locks, held in place by a diadem with *uraeus*. A second band is wrapped around the hair at ear level. Her headdress consists of a *modius* surmounted by the horned solar disc. Much of the latter element has been broken away and lost.

Queen Tiye's extremely youthful appearance here is also found in certain statues depicting her husband, Amenhotep III.[3] Statuary of this style—with the round face, the small, full, slightly pursed lips, and the long, narrow eyes—dates to the last part of Amenhotep's reign and symbolizes the rejuvenation of the king's power and authority through celebration of the *Sed* festival in his thirtieth year of rule.[4] Queen Tiye figures prominently in the scenes depicting the *Heb Sed*;[5] apparently the effects of this ritual of rebirth and renewal were extended to the queen, because after this period she was depicted in the same youthful manner as the king.[6]

Tiye is one of the few queens of nonroyal origin[7] whose parentage is known. Certain commemorative scarabs—those believed to date from the very beginning of the reign of Amenhotep III,[8] and those announcing his marriage to a foreign princess[9]—give the names of her father and mother, Yuya and Thuya,[10] of the town of Akhmim.[11] Tiye, in fact, is mentioned on all of the commemorative scarabs from the reign.[12] Her name, enclosed within a cartouche, and her titles follow the king's titulary and the regnal year; this arrangement suggests that the reign was regarded as the queen's as well as the king's.[13]

Tiye's unprecedented appearance on these scarabs and in the scenes depicting the *Heb Sed* indicates her political, cultic, and religious status. She is mentioned in the Amarna letters, and correspondence from the king of Mitanni is addressed to her, requesting her to intercede on his behalf with her son, Amenhotep IV/ Akhenaten.[14] Throughout her reign, she appeared in the guise of various goddesses,[15] and she was the first queen to employ the divine Hathoric headdress, consisting of bovine horns and the solar disc, as an element of her own queenly iconography.[16] In recognition of her religious role as her divine husband's female counterpart, prayers were addressed to her by her courtiers.[17]

During her lifetime and afterward, Tiye was worshipped at a temple devoted to her at Sedeinga in Nubia.[18] There she appears in the roles of Hathor and Tefnut; in one aspect of the latter goddess, she is depicted as a guardian female sphinx.[19] Tiye's divine preeminence set the stage for the next chief queen of Egypt—Nefertiti, wife of Tiye's son, King Amenhotep IV/Akhenaten.[20] (See cat. nos. 45 and 46.)

This statue fragment was acquired in Nubia (modern Sudan) and probably came from Tiye's temple there.[21] The stone has been identified as peridotite, probably quarried in that region.[22] A fragment of a statue of a god dating to this reign, and made of the same material, may have been a part of the same pair or group statue from which the Tiye fragment came.[23] AKC

Published: Vandier, *Manuel* 3: 429–31, pl. 137; Bryan, in *Egypt's Dazzling Sun*, no. 15.

45 Relief: Nefertiti offering to the Aten

Nummulitic limestone; from Amarna, Boundary Stele N; New Kingdom, late Dynasty 18, reign of Akhenaten; H: 48.2 cm; L: 62.2 cm

The Nelson-Atkins Museum of Art, Kansas City, Missouri. Purchase: Nelson Trust. 44-65

In about the fifth year of his reign,[1] the Pharaoh Akhenaten decided to move his court from Thebes to a new city to be devoted to the worship of his god, the Aten. The site chosen by Akhenaten had never been part of any other deity's estates. The boundaries of the new city, called Akhetaten, "Horizon of the Aten" (now more commonly known by its modern name, Tell el-Amarna), were delineated by a series of stelae set up in the cliffs surrounding the site.[2]

This fragment, from the boundary stela designated "N,"[3] is part of a scene depicting Akhenaten, his chief wife, Nefertiti, and their two eldest daughters worshipping before a table piled high with offerings. The disc of the Aten, with its rays ending in human hands, offers *ankhs* to the noses of the king and queen.

Much has been written about the status of Nefertiti,[4] for she is depicted in a manner unlike any other Egyptian king's wife. In fact, scenes depicting Akhenaten alone are much less common than those in which she and one or more of their daughters appear. One building at the Aten temple complex at Karnak, the *ḥwt-bnbn*, depicts *only* Nefertiti worshipping the deity with her daughters,[5] an indication that she could act as the religious officiant for temple ritual.[6]

At some point before Akhenaten's fifth regnal year, Nefertiti was given an epithet, Neferneferuaten ("Exquisite Beauty of the Sun Disc"),[7] and her names were written in two cartouches, as were those of the king. Also, in at least three instances, the decoration of nobles' tombs at Amarna employed an artistic device to indicate a sense of "near" equality[8] between Akhenaten and Nefertiti: rather than the conventional depiction of the wife seated behind her husband, a set of double lines was used to express their bodies seated (twice)[9] or standing (once)[10] side by side. In at least one tomb scene, Nefertiti appears wearing a crown almost identical to that of Akhenaten,[11] and they present the same types of offerings to the Aten.[12] On the cabin of her royal barge, Nefertiti is depicted in the pharaonic stance of smiting the enemy (fig. 3).[13] At Karnak she appears as a rampant sphinx.[14] The Aten always offers the *ankh* equally to Nefertiti and to the king, and prayers are addressed to her as they were to Akhenaten and the Aten.[15] On the basis of this and other evidence, some scholars have theorized that Nefertiti became co-regent at some point in her husband's reign and possibly succeeded him as pharaoh.[16] Much controversy surrounds this proposition, however; until definitive evidence is recovered, Nefertiti's ultimate royal status at the time of her death remains a mystery.

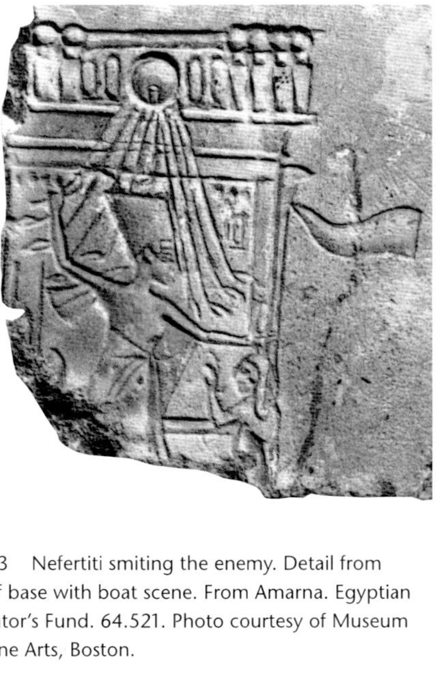

Fig. 3 Nefertiti smiting the enemy. Detail from relief base with boat scene. From Amarna. Egyptian Curator's Fund. 64.521. Photo courtesy of Museum of Fine Arts, Boston.

Nefertiti's divine status also must be considered. The intimate scenes of Nefertiti, Akhenaten, and their daughters are believed to express the royal couple's assumption of the role of fertility deities.[17] (See also cat. no. 46.) As noted above, she was portrayed as Akhenaten's religious equal, both in regard to her approaching the Aten and in the deity's response. Moreover, at the *ḥwt-bnbn* at Karnak, Nefertiti's cartouche was juxtaposed with that of the Aten, without the presence of the name of Akhenaten.[18] To some scholars,[19] this suggested an "equality of divinity." Prayers addressed to Nefertiti[20] indicate her perceived ability to act not only as a liaison between common people and the Aten but as a deity herself, able to satisfy the petitioner's request.[21]

As noted, the stela from which this fragment comes dates to the early part of Akhenaten's reign. At no other time in ancient Egyptian history had a king had himself depicted in such a manner, with features exaggerated nearly to the grotesque. Akhenaten's heavy hips and thighs; his spindly calves, upper torso, and arms; and his long, narrow face with its protuberant jaw, thick lips, and elongated eyes are reflected in the depictions of Nefertiti, their daughters, and even his courtiers.[22] As the reign progressed, this artistic style[23] was gradually softened to present a more natural depiction of the face and body.

Here the face of Nefertiti, whose beauty is apparent in many of the extant statues that depict her,[24] exhibits the qualities of the exaggerated style, with pendulous jaw, thick lips, and long, thin arms and fingers. Her tall cap crown[25] is surmounted with the solar disc and double feathers, a *uraeus* is at the brow, and streamers are attached at the back. The pleats of her transparent gown are visible on her arms, which she raises in a gesture of worship before the Aten.

On the intact stela, Meritaten, the eldest daughter of Akhenaten and Nefertiti, stands behind her parents. The second daughter, Maketaten, whose figure is preserved in this fragment of Stela N, stands on her own higher ground line; apparently she was added after the original design of the stela had been executed.[26] Her body reflects the early style of Amarna art, with exaggeratedly plump hips and thighs and spindly chest, arms, and lower legs.

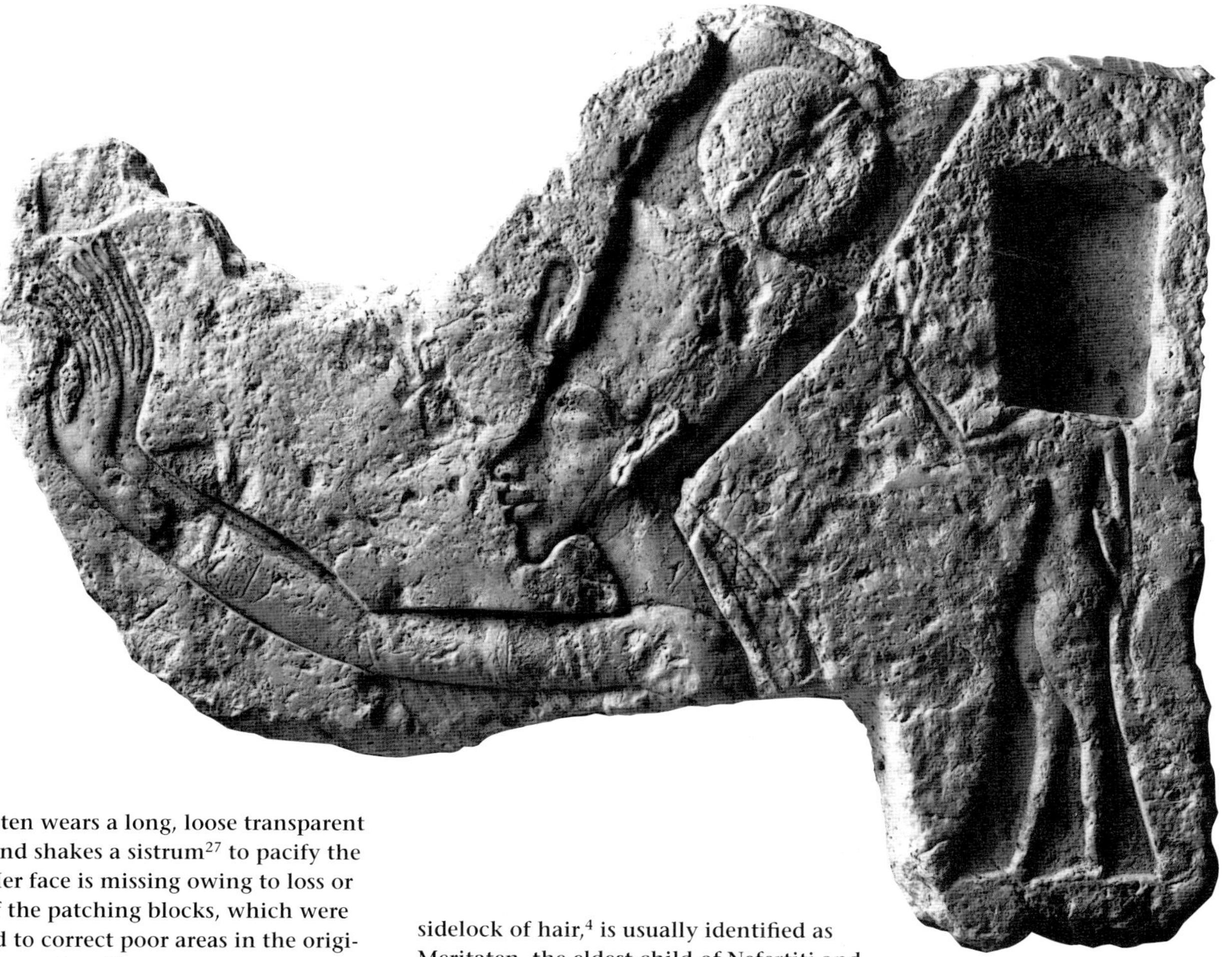

Maketaten wears a long, loose transparent gown and shakes a sistrum[27] to pacify the Aten. Her face is missing owing to loss or theft of the patching blocks, which were inserted to correct poor areas in the original stone surface.[28] AKC

Published: Aldred, *Akhenaten and Nefertiti*, no. 28.

46 Relief of Queen Nefertiti kissing daughter

Painted limestone; found at Hermopolis, but originally from El Amarna; New Kingdom, Dynasty 18, reign of Akhenaten; H: 23.2 cm; L: 45.2 cm

The Brooklyn Museum. Charles Edwin Wilbour Fund. 60.197.8

Nefertiti, whose name means "a beautiful one is come," is probably the most widely recognized ancient Egyptian woman. Nefertiti was the chief wife of the Pharaoh Amenhotep IV/Akhenaten, who built a new city[1] devoted to the worship of his god, the solar deity Aten, at a previously uninhabited site in Middle Egypt. This relief, which depicts Nefertiti kissing one of her six daughters, probably comes from that city, usually known by its modern name, Tell el-Amarna.[2]

Though Nefertiti's name is not preserved in the (intentionally) damaged inscription, she can be identified by the *uraeus* on her brow and the *ankh* held to her nose by a hand of the Aten.[3] The daughter, whose youth is expressed by her sidelock of hair,[4] is usually identified as Meritaten, the eldest child of Nefertiti and Akhenaten, because part of her name can be detected in the inscription. It has also been suggested, however, that the fourth daughter, Neferneferuaten-Tasherit, is depicted, with the other princesses represented elsewhere in the scene.[5]

During Akhenaten's reign, revolutionary changes occurred in art, especially in the manner in which the king and his family appeared. Egyptian monarchs previously had been depicted in a formal, aloof, godlike manner, in a seemingly standardized set of scenes: offering to or receiving blessings from the gods, performing rituals in the temples or during festivals, receiving tribute, and so forth. Occasionally the king was shown being clasped about the waist in a decorous manner by a goddess or his wife. In Akhenaten's reign, however, apparently according to his direct desire and command, the king, Nefertiti, and their children were portrayed (in addition to the more formal attitudes of worship) in scenes of extraordinary familial intimacy: Nefertiti bending to fasten a collar around Akhenaten's neck,[6] Akhenaten bouncing his wife and children on his knee,[7] one of the princesses caressing her sister's chin,[8] or the entire family sitting down together to a meal.[9] At Tell el-Amarna, such scenes dominated the walls of the royal palace,

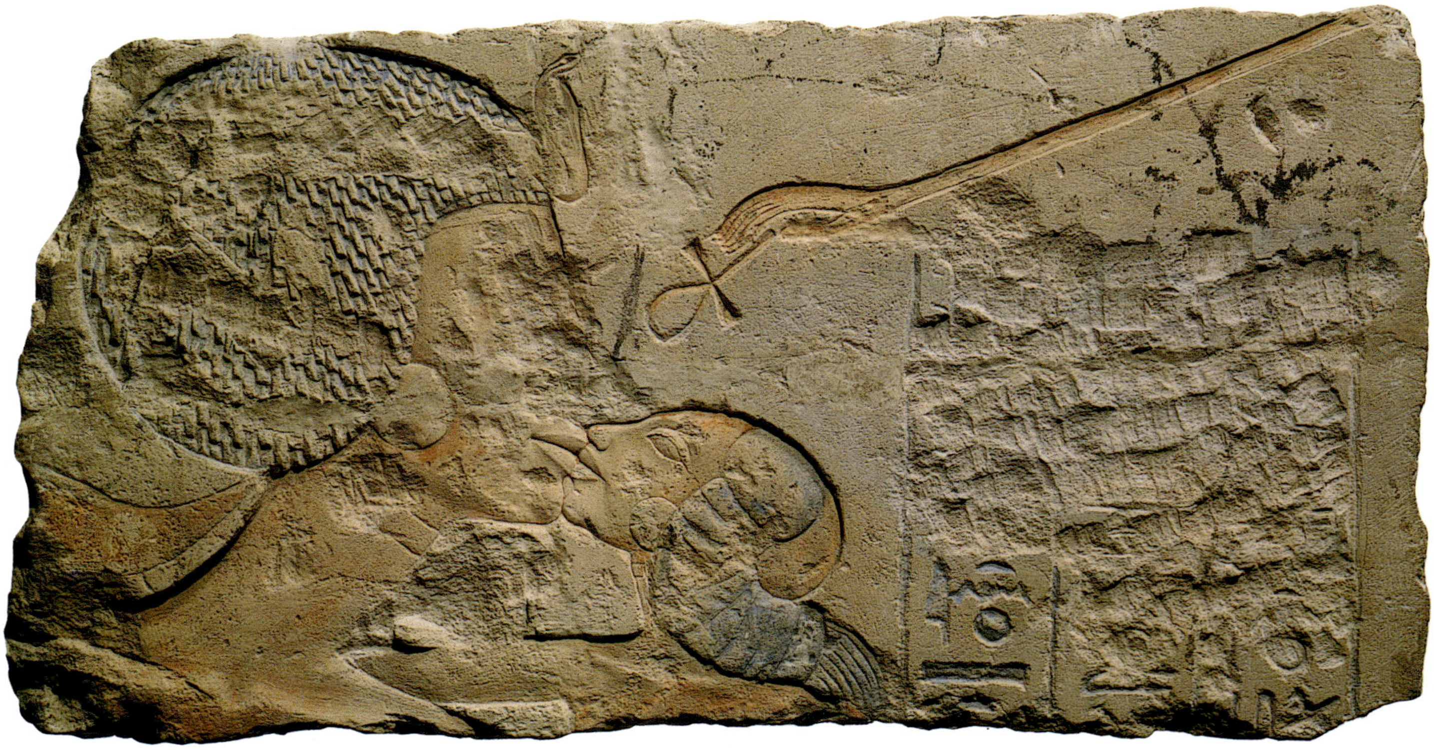

the nobles' tombs, and the stelae set up for private worship of the royal couple.[10]

Why did Akhenaten and Nefertiti have themselves depicted in such a familiar manner? The Aten, the physical disc of the sun, was an abstract principle, deified and anthropomorphized by the addition of rays ending in human hands. In these intimate scenes of the royal family, the disc of the Aten is always present, located prominently at the top of the composition.[11] Unlike the gods of Egypt's past, no myths surrounded the divine attributes of the Aten or referred to any relationships of the Aten with other deities, such as a divine consort. Therefore, these scenes of the royal family's private life substituted for depictions of the deities of Egypt's old religion.[12] The Aten offered the *ankh* equally to Nefertiti[13] and to Akhenaten, and prayers were addressed to her, as to a goddess.[14] The personal, familial nature of these scenes emphasized the relationship of the king and queen with the deity, and their own divine status.[15] Thus the Aten, Akhenaten, and Nefertiti together formed a divine family triad to replace those of the past, such as the Theban triad of Amen, Mut, and Khonsu.[16]

In the latter half of the Eighteenth Dynasty, the daughters of kings began to appear more frequently in ritual and festival scenes,[17] but young royal children were not featured so prominently until the Amarna Period. The constant presence of the royal couple's offspring may represent the adoption of the role of fecundity deities[18] by the king and queen, now that the old fertility gods and goddesses had been suppressed. It has also been suggested that, just as the Aten bestows life in the form of an *ankh* to Nefertiti and Akhenaten, so the king and queen in turn transmit life and other royal and divine properties to their daughters through an intimate physical gesture—a kiss.[19] AKC

Published: Cooney, *Amarna Reliefs,* no. 12; Aldred, *Akhenaten and Nefertiti,* no. 92; Aldred, *Akhenaten,* pl. 36; Fazzini et al., *Ancient Egyptian Art,* no. 50.

47 Standard bearing statue of queen

Black granite; provenance unknown; New Kingdom, Dynasty 19, reign of King Ramesses II; H: 94 cm; W: 28 cm; D: 28.2 cm

The Harer Family Trust.

The subject of this statue wears an elaborately pleated gown with knotted tie,[1] a broad collar necklace, a bracelet on her right wrist, sandals, disc-shaped earrings, and a heavy wig. She is identified as royalty by the vulture headdress over her wig, a headdress worn by queens beginning no later than Dynasty 5. It appears to have originated with Nekhbet, the protective goddess of Upper Egypt, who is often shown as a vulture, and came to be worn by other goddesses as well.[2] Although such goddesses included Mut in the New Kingdom and later, the standard held by the queen's left hand and arm (her right hand holds a folded handkerchief) bears no vulture headdress on its terminal. This terminal is a bust of Mut[3] wearing the double crown of Upper and Lower Egypt, which became closely associated with her (cf. cat. no. 61), and a *uraeus*.

This queen in the Harer collection has sometimes been claimed as a work of Dynasty 18 and possibly as an image of Amenhotep III's Queen Tiye.[4] Certain aspects of its style, however, indicate that it is a work of Dynasty 19. These include the forms of the facial features and, as G. Scott noted, the higher polish on skin surfaces than on the costume. Such polish focuses attention on the skin, this tendency to contrast levels of polish being a feature of Ramesside sculpture.[5] Moreover, the inscription on the standard's shaft reads, "The good god, the son of Amen, born of Mut in order to rule all that the sun's disc encircles, the lord of the Two Lands, User-Maat-Ra Setep-en-Ra [i.e., Ramesses II]. . . ."[6] In part because of this inscription identifying Ramesses as the son of the goddess Mut, the statue sometimes has been assigned to Ramesses' terrestrial mother, Queen Tuya, also known as Mut-Tuya during her lifetime.[7] Admittedly the statue's face bears some formal resemblances to a known sculpture of Tuya.[8] On the other hand, and to paraphrase G. Scott, the text need not contain the specific reference asserted; various queens of Ramesses II were associated with Mut; stylistic parallels with depictions of other of his queens can be found; and the statue could just as well represent one of Ramesses' own queens as his mother.[9] Indeed, in his most recent publication of the statue, Scott has suggested that it is "most probably" an image of Ramesses' Queen Nefertiry.[10]

Whatever the identity of the statue's subject, she is the only ancient Egyptian woman known for certain to be depicted in a statue as the bearer of a divine standard; this sculptural type was almost totally restricted to the New Kingdom and was attested in significant numbers first for kings and then for other men.[11] The interpretation of this statue type is a complex question. In brief, it includes concepts of standards both as independent powers and as aspects of the gods they depict, which grant royal aspects to the king and link private persons to the deity depicted and to the cult of the king.[12] Whatever the specific meaning of the statue for the queen (presumably once identified on the now-missing base), it related her to both Ramesses II and Mut.

It was once suggested that the Harer standard-bearing queen may have come from the temple precinct of Mut at South Karnak on the east bank of the Nile,[13] the goddess' main cult place. This is hardly impossible. Indeed, given the mention and depiction on the statue of deities associated with Thebes, that ancient southern Egyptian metropolis is a likely provenance. The statue, however, just as possibly could have come from the great temple of Amen at Karnak, normal resting place of the divine standards of Amen and the deities in his following, or from one of the other Theban temples to which the standards were brought in religious processions.[14]

Regardless of the statue's provenance, not only is it unique in being an image of a woman as standard bearer, it is also a relatively rare statue of a queen. If the queenship was divine, it was not the equal of the divine office of kingship. Although queens played important cultic roles, they were mainly linked to maintaining and renewing the kingship. Thus, it is not very surprising that the evidence available suggests that there were far fewer statues made of queens than of kings. RAF

Published: G. Scott, III, *Temple, Tomb and Dwelling: Egyptian Antiquities from the Harer Family Trust Collection*, exh. cat., University Art Gallery, California State University, San Bernardino (San Bernardino, 1992), 132–34, 136, no. 82, with references to earlier literature; to which add *In the Tomb of Nefertari: Conservation of the Wall Paintings*, exh. cat., the J. Paul Getty Museum and the Getty Conservation Institute (Malibu, 1992), 76–77, no. 23; C. Desroches-Noblecourt, "Abou Simbel, Ramses et les dames de la couronne," in Bleiberg and Freed, eds., *Shattered Visage*, 129; and G. Scott, III, *Dynasties: The Egyptian Royal Image in the New Kingdom*, exh. checklist, San Antonio Museum of Art (San Antonio, 1995), no. 38.

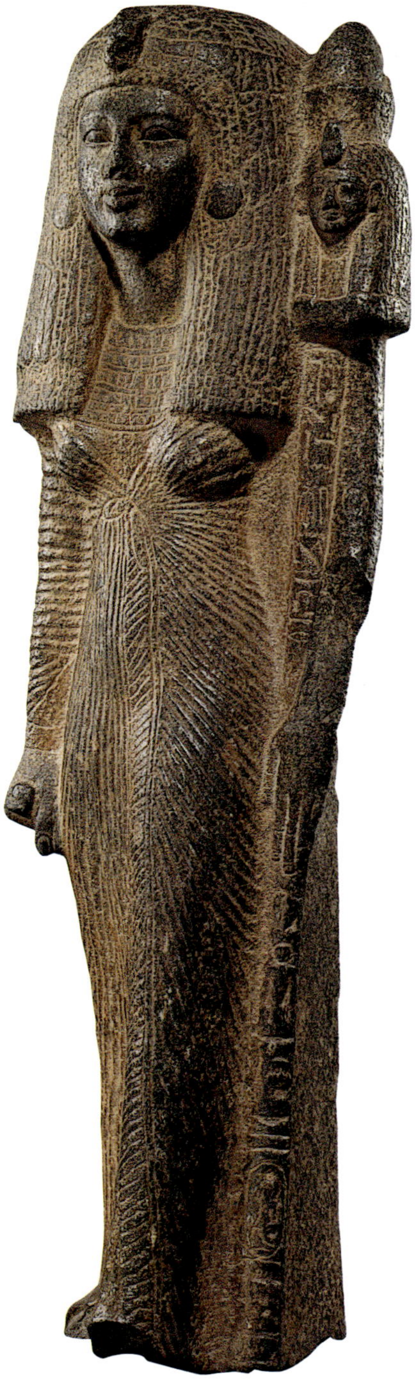

48 Statue of Amenirdas I, God's Wife of Amen

Granite; probably from Thebes;
Late Period, Dynasty 25; H: 64.3 cm

Joslyn Art Museum, Omaha, Nebraska.
1953.80

During the Third Intermediate Period, which lasted about 450 years, Egypt was fragmented politically. The land was controlled by rival dynasties in the north, while a series of military priests ruled the southern part of the country from Thebes.[1] During this period, the rulers in the north attempted to maintain a degree of influence in the south by having their sisters or daughters appointed as God's Wives of Amen at Thebes.

The high priestly title "God's Wife of Amen" is first attested in the Middle Kingdom.[2] The Eighteenth Dynasty queen Ahmose-Nefertari is the earliest God's Wife for whom much documentation survives.[3] This office, which was richly endowed with goods and property, was bestowed on royal women during the first half of the Eighteenth Dynasty through the reign of the female king Hatshepsut, who passed the title to her daughter, Nefrura (cat. no. 43). Thereafter, the title "God's Wife of Amen" is attested sporadically[4] through the New Kingdom.

During the Third Intermediate Period, the office of the God's Wife assumed increasing political and religious importance. Unlike the God's Wives of the New Kingdom, who were married to the king and bore his children, the God's Wife of the Third Intermediate Period remained celibate,[5] passing her office to an adopted heir. This arrangement prevented the development of dynastic control over the office.[6]

During the first half of the seventh century B.C., a powerful family[7] arose in Kush, Egypt's southern neighbor. The Kushite King Kashta, who was devoted to the worship of Amen, took advantage of the fragmented political situation in Egypt and invaded the country. His sons Piankhy and Shabako continued his efforts. Shabako eventually succeeded in reuniting all of Egypt under his rule, thus inaugurating Egypt's Late Period.[8]

At the time of the Kushite invasion, Shepenwepet I, daughter of the Twenty-Second Dynasty King Osorkon III, reigned as God's Wife of Amen in Thebes.[9] She was compelled to adopt Amenirdas, a daughter of Kashta, as her successor to the office of God's Wife.[10] Amenirdas was the

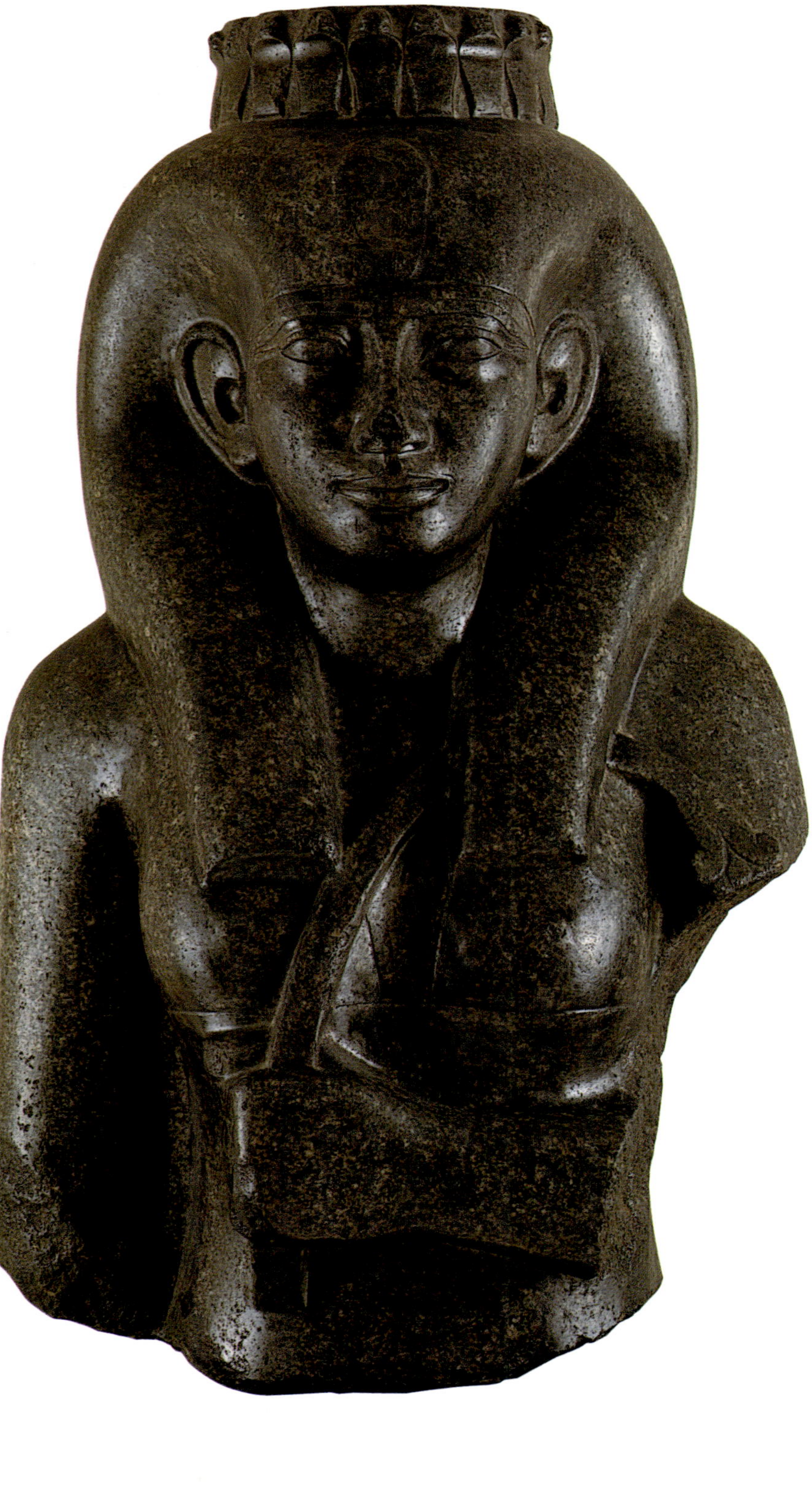

first woman of Kushite descent to hold this priestly title.[11] During the years of Egyptian domination over her native country, many temples to the god Amen and his consort, Mut, had been erected.[12] While Egypt was divided by warring petty kings, the Kushite monarchy remained devoted to Amen.[13] When the Kushites occupied Egypt, the common people may have welcomed their sovereignty as benefactors and supporters of the state god Amen and as restorers of peace and unity.[14]

According to later documentary materials, successors to the reigning God's Wife may have been adopted at a fairly young age.[15] We do not know how old Amenirdas was when she was accepted by (or perhaps forced upon) Shepenwepet I. An inscription dating to the twelfth regnal year of Piankhy (brother of Amenirdas) mentions her succession to the office of God's Wife at Thebes.[16] Certainly Amenirdas had reached adulthood by this time and was completely aware of the wealth and power that were attached to the office. She built a tomb and mortuary temple for herself at Medinet Habu and embarked on other building projects.[17] A stela commemorating the arrival at Thebes of Nitocris, a later God's Wife of Amen, gives us an idea of the wealth (and therefore the political power) that attended the office.[18] Nitocris' dowry, given upon her acceptance and adoption by the incumbent Wife of Amen, included more than 2,200 acres of land and its produce;[19] thus it augmented the property already attached to the office of the God's Wife, who must have controlled enormous wealth.

During the Third Intermediate and Late Periods, Amen's wife was depicted in scenes more commonly reserved for male monarchs: she celebrated a *Heb Sed;* she wore the double crown; her crown was touched by the god; and she was suckled by a goddess.[20] Her ritual duties included pouring libations before images of deities and offering *maat* to Amen.[21] The names of the God's Wives—prenomen and nomen—were written in cartouches, like those of a king.[22]

Sculpture of the Kushite Period tends to be more truly portraitlike than statuary from earlier periods in Egypt. Amenirdas' Nubian heritage is evident in her slightly broadened facial features and in the elegant bone structure of her face. The statue exhibits the "Kushite fold," a curving line that extends from the nostrils to the corners of the mouth, emphasizing the fleshy pad that forms the cheek.[23] Here Amenirdas is depicted wearing a close-fitting sheath dress[24] with halter straps that cover her breasts. Her tripartite wig[25] is topped by a *modius* crown formed of *uraeus* serpents. The *uraeus* that once adorned her brow has been broken away. In her left hand Amenirdas holds a lily.[26] The hieroglyphic signs for Upper and Lower Egypt on the back of the statue probably formed part of a title proclaiming Amenirdas Mistress of Upper and Lower Egypt.

Amenirdas began her reign as God's Wife of Amen in about 736 B.C.[27] In 710 B.C., she adopted as successor her niece, Shepenwepet II, daughter of her brother Piankhy. The two women apparently shared the office of God's Wife for about ten years until Amenirdas retired in 700 B.C.[28] AKC

Published: Bothmer et al., *ESLP*, no. 1, pls. 1, 2.

49 *Shabti* of Nebseni

Wood (tamarisk) and pigment; provenance unknown; New Kingdom, early Dynasty 18; H: 28.2 cm

The Art Institute of Chicago. Gift of Henry H. Getty and Charles L. Hutchinson. 1892.28

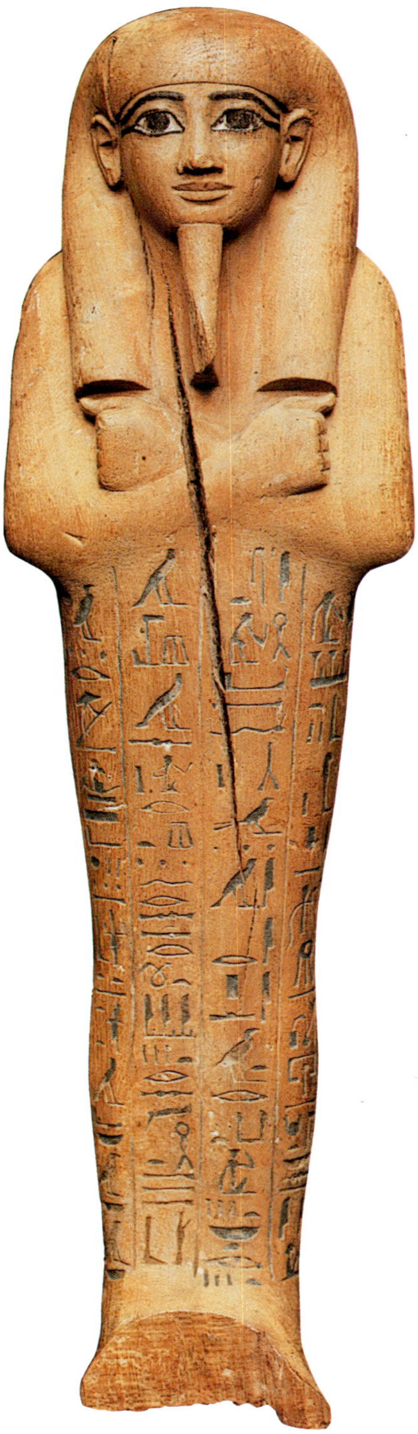

As its inscription indicates, this *shabti* belonged to Nebseni,[1] who served as scribe for a woman who held the title "God's Wife of Amen." In type, it may be assigned to the sequence of God's Wives of the early Eighteenth Dynasty,[2] which originated with Ahmose-Nefertari, wife of King Ahmose, founder of the Eighteenth Dynasty. In the absence of a specific genealogy for Nebseni himself, it is impossible to tell which of these female dignitaries Nebseni served, but the list, in all likelihood, can be narrowed to three candidates: Ahmose-Nefertari herself, Hatshepsut, and Nefrura.[3]

In view of the various powers and duties associated with the office of God's Wife,[4] numerous administrators, including scribes, must have been employed in its service.[5] The size of the estate and administration associated with the office are reflected in the large number of extant scarabs with this title that are attested for Ahmose-Nefertari and Nefrura.[6] In all probability, the royal women who occupied this position had acquired sufficient skills in reading and writing to administer this important position and to supervise the scribes in their employ.[7]

In typical fashion, Nebseni's *shabti* bears the standard spell drawn from Chapter 6 of the *Book of the Dead*. It is depicted with the false beard, the male mark of divinity that associated the deceased with Osiris, god of the underworld. GEM

Published: *Ancient Art at the Art Institute of Chicago*, The Art Institute of Chicago, *Museum Studies* 20, no. 1 (1994): no. 6.

50 Ostracon: Ramesses II suckled by a goddess

Limestone with pigment; provenance unknown; Dynasty 19, reign of Ramesses II; H: 31.2 cm; W: 18 cm

The Cleveland Museum of Art. Given in Honor of James N. Sherwin, Trustee 1957–1971. 87.156

51 Goddess suckling a queen

Silver; from El-Kurru, tomb of Neferukekashta (Ku. 52); Third Intermediate Period, Dynasty 25, reign of Piankhy; H: 5.1 cm; W: 1.8 cm

Museum of Fine Arts, Boston. Harvard University–Museum of Fine Arts Expedition. 24.928

The royal women of the Kushite Twenty-Fifth Dynasty enjoyed extraordinary religious and political status in their roles as queens and as God's Wives of the god Amen. Nefrukakashta, who is depicted on this silver plaque, was one of the five daughters of King Kashta and his queen, Pebatma.[1] Another of their daughters, Amenirdas I, was placed in the office of Divine Wife of Amen (cat. no. 48). Nefrukakashta and her three other sisters—Abar, Khensa, and Peksater—were married to their brother, Piankhy, a common practice of the Kushite and Egyptian royal families.[2]

Amenirdas, as the God's Wife, was a major presence in the city of Thebes in Upper Egypt.[3] Khensa,[4] too, apparently visited Egypt, because several objects bearing her name have been found there.[5] Less is known about the presence of Piankhy's other three queens in Egypt. All four royal women, however, were furnished with pyramidal tombs[6] in the Kushite royal necropolis at El-Kurru.[7]

This silver plaque, found in the tomb of Nefrukakashta (Ku. 52), depicts the queen being embraced and suckled by a goddess. Before the Third Intermediate Period, only kings were depicted as receiving the divine milk of the mother goddess.[8] On the ostracon from the Cleveland Museum of Art, Pharaoh Ramesses II stands within a shrine suckling from the breast of an unnamed goddess.[9] The king is depicted as an adult, with the blue crown, the crook and flail, and the *devanteau*. Behind him, his prenomen, User-ma'at-Ra Setep-en-Ra, is written in a cartouche. The scene on this ostracon may commemorate the accession of Ramesses II to the throne, an event also depicted in the temple at Beit el-Wali.[10] There the goddess who offers her divine milk to the new king is Anuket.

The scene on Nefrukakashta's silver plaque is very similar. Here the physical proximity between the royal personage and the goddess is expressed even more intimately. Nefrukakashta grasps the wrist of the hand that offers the divine breast. The goddess's left arm encircles the queen's shoulders; her hand rests on the queen's breast.[11] The goddess depicted here may represent Mut, who, as consort of

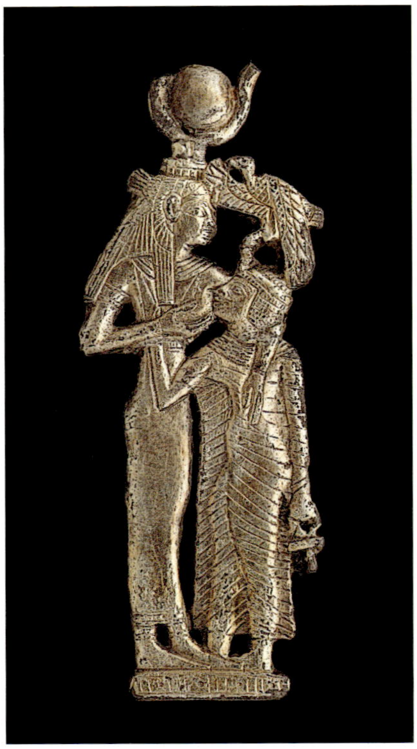

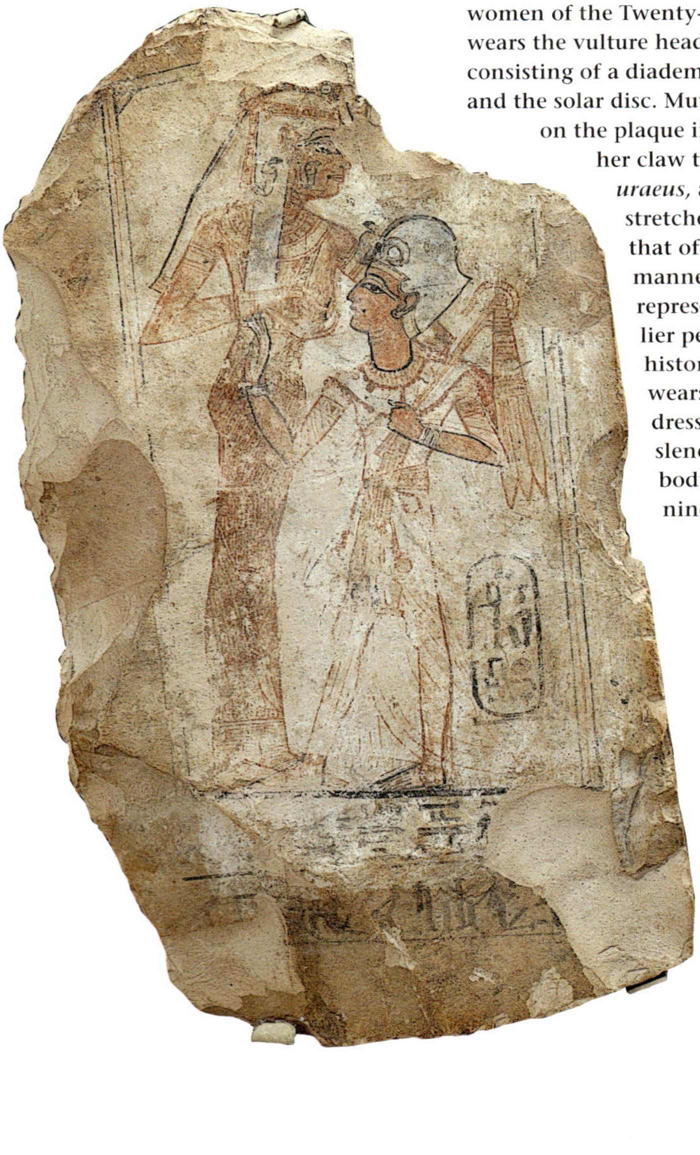

Amen, was the patron goddess of the royal women of the Twenty-Fifth Dynasty.[12] She wears the vulture headdress and a crown consisting of a diadem with bovine horns and the solar disc. Mut is also represented on the plaque in her vulture form; her claw touches the queen's *uraeus*, and her outstretched wing caresses that of the goddess. In a manner typical of female representations from earlier periods of Egyptian history, the goddess wears a tight sheath dress that reveals the slender lines of her body. The Kushite feminine ideal is expressed in the figure of Nefrukakashta, whose plump curves are indicated under a diaphanous gown.[13]

A study by J. Leclant[14] shows that the king was suckled by a goddess on three occasions: at birth into this world; at coronation—his "birth" into kingship; and after his death, when he was reborn in the afterlife. T. Kendall suggests that these scenes depicting Twenty-Fifth Dynasty queens suckled by the goddess may commemorate their coronations.[15] An inscription on a vessel from the tomb of King Aspelta,[16] which was used for drinking "divine" milk, reads: "Hail to you, O beautiful liquid, O good produce which averts every evil. . . . May you drive away every evil and ward off every abomination. . . ."[17] This milk-drinking ritual evidently was believed to purify a person of sin as he or she underwent a crucial rite of passage.

A similar vessel, uninscribed but with two spouts reminiscent of breasts, was discovered in the tomb of Queen Khensa,[18] sister of Nefrukakashta. This vessel was one of a set of objects apparently used during Khensa's coronation to purify her for her birth into queenship.[19] The plaque of Nefrukakashta and the vessel of Khensa were undoubtedly placed in their tombs to ease them through the next rite of passage, when they would be reborn in the afterlife, nourished by the divine milk of the mother goddess.[20] AKC

Published: Dunham, *El Kurru*, pls. 60C, 70B; Kendall, *Kush*, 26–27, fig. 23 (24.928).

52 Bust of a queen

Hard green stone; provenance unknown; Late Period, Dynasty 30; H: 28.5 cm

Courtesy of The Walters Art Gallery, Baltimore. 22.405

Although uninscribed, the regal identity of this sculpture is affirmed by its distinctive headdress formed by a vulture's wings extended downward along the sides of the wearer's head. Known from the Old Kingdom, this cap was originally worn by the vulture goddess Nekhbet, patron deity of Upper Egypt. From the Fifth Dynasty onward, the vulture headdress was a potent emblem of queenship that persisted throughout pharaonic history.[1] The fact

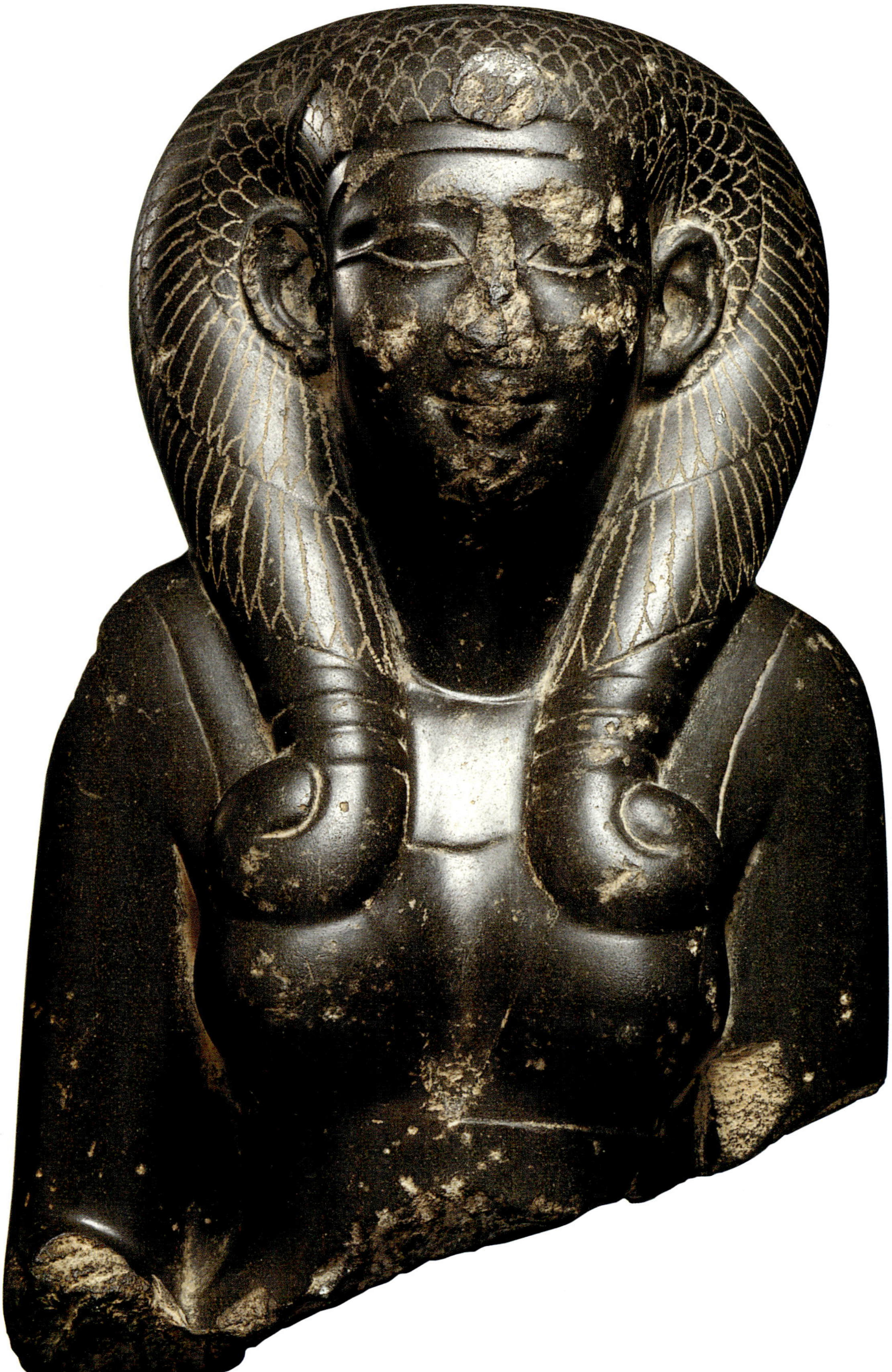

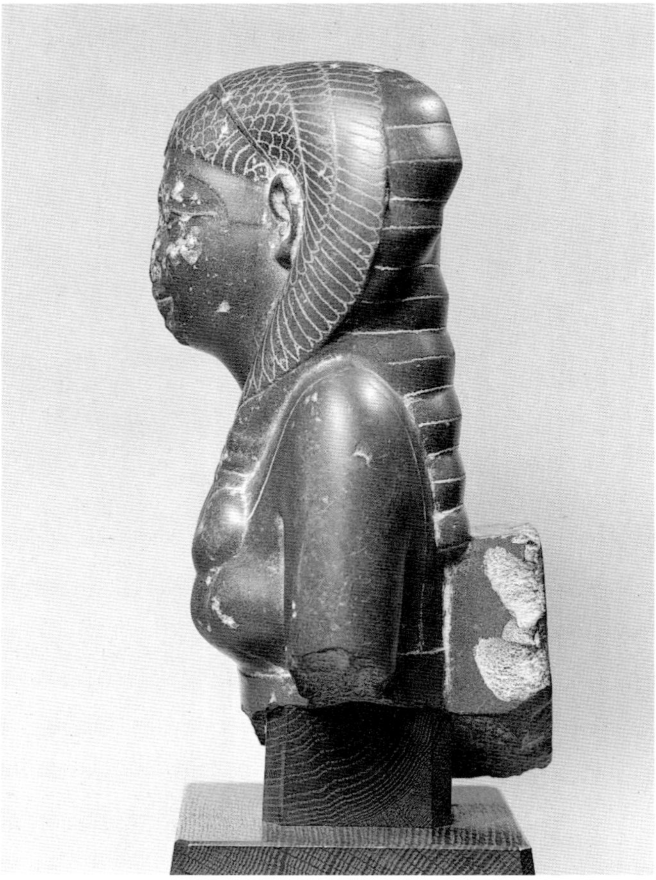

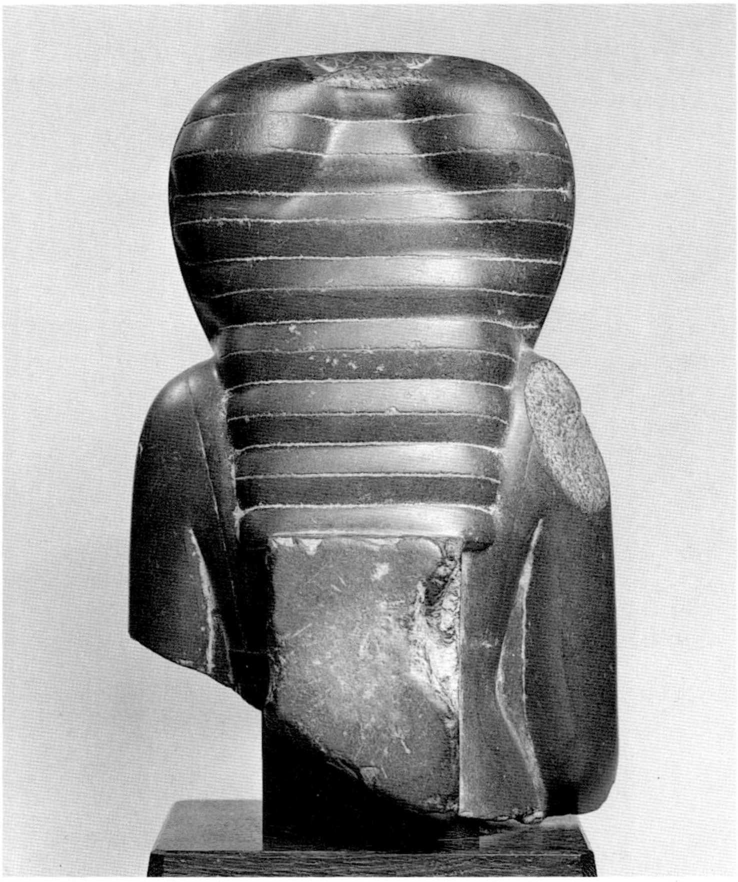

that it originated as a divine emblem, and was later transferred to female royalty, suggests that it may have marked a divine aspect of queenship.[2]

On the present example, the vulture cap is bound above the forehead by two bands; the projecting vulture's or cobra's head that originally served as its central emblem has been lost. The heavy wig with stylized Hathoric curls worn by the Baltimore queen is distinctive and may indicate the wearer's possible association with the cult of the goddess.[3] Attention may also be drawn to the hair, which falls in back in six undulating waves.

Stylistically, the Baltimore queen may be assigned an advanced date within the Late Period, specifically in the fourth century B.C.[4] This late dating is particularly apparent from the formation of the eyes and eyebrows; the latter, as well as the plastic cosmetic lines that enhance the eyes, are extremely long and thin, a distinguishing feature apparent also in the contemporary bust in Richmond (cat. no. 7).[5] The Baltimore queen's features in general recall those of the Virginia fragment, which likewise has been dated to the end of the fourth century B.C.[6] Like the Richmond bust, the Baltimore queen exhibits a sense of modesty or restraint in the modeling of the torso, a feature especially apparent in the subtle rendering of the breasts.[7]

As with other works of the Late Period, the Baltimore bust reveals strong archaizing or, more properly, "archaistic" tendencies, which hark back to antecedents in Middle Kingdom sculpture.[8] Such tendencies may be seen, above all, in the archaic sheath dress with shoulder straps, the protruding ears, and the Hathor wig.[9] The bust fragment in Baltimore originally belonged to a full seated statue depicted with forearms resting on the thighs. GEM

Published: Steindorff, *Catalogue*, no. 31 and pl. 7.

Goddesses

53 a Female figurine with incurving arms

Terracotta; excavated at El Ma'mariya; Predynastic Period, Middle Naqada II; H (to top of head): 31.4 cm

The Brooklyn Museum. Museum Collection Fund. 07.447.502

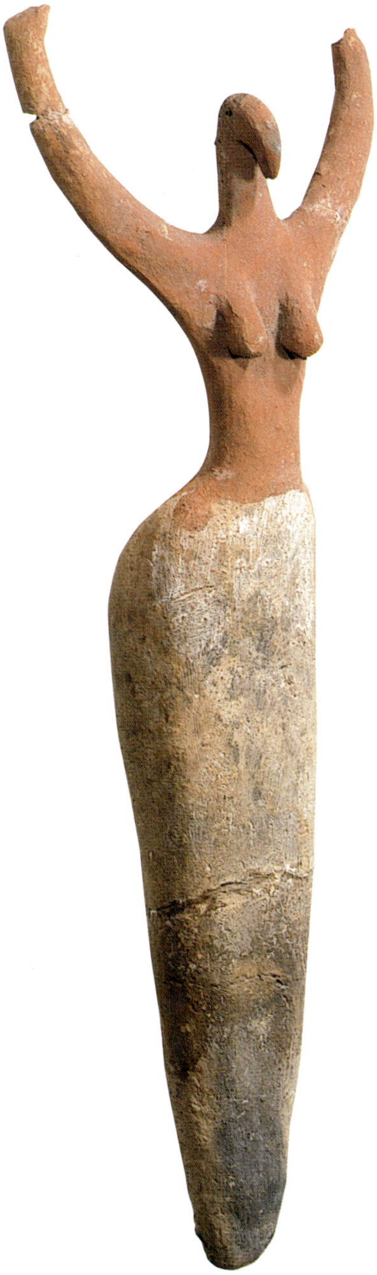

53 b Jar with female and attendants on boat

Terracotta; excavated at El-Adaima; Predynastic Period, Middle Naqada II; H: 17.5 cm

The Brooklyn Museum. Museum Excavation. Charles Edwin Wilbour Fund. 09.889.400

This female figurine is one of two[1] found together in Burial 2 at El Ma'mariya during H. de Morgan's 1906–7 season of excavations.[2] Fragments of sixteen similar figurines were found together in Burial 1 at the same site.[3] This figurine, and the decorated pot that depicts a female in similar pose, date to the Naqada II phase of Egypt's Predynastic Period.[4]

A pointed pinch of clay forms the figurine's face, and dark resinous material remains on the head where hair originally was attached. The exaggerated size of the buttocks and thighs is highlighted by the slender waist. The rather pendulous breasts apparently were modeled separately and attached; clearly, the figure's sex was emphasized deliberately. Only a shallow groove differentiates the two legs; no feet are indicated. The lower half of the body was originally painted white to represent a long skirt. These figurines sometimes have been interpreted as early examples of servant figures (cat. nos. 29, 30) or fertility figurines (cat. nos. 13, 16b).

On the decorated pot, three boats are depicted, each equipped with oars, a palm branch, and two cabins. The artist distinguished the boats from one another; each flies a different standard. Atop the cabins are female figures accompanied by one or more male attendants.[5] The female figures are larger than the males and, according to

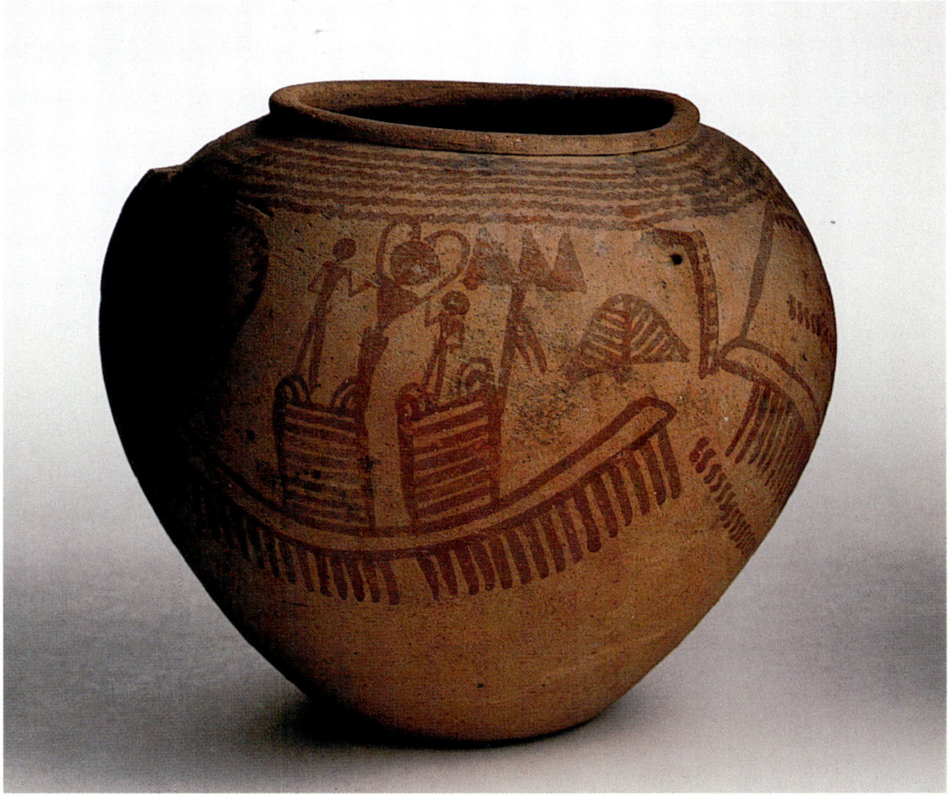

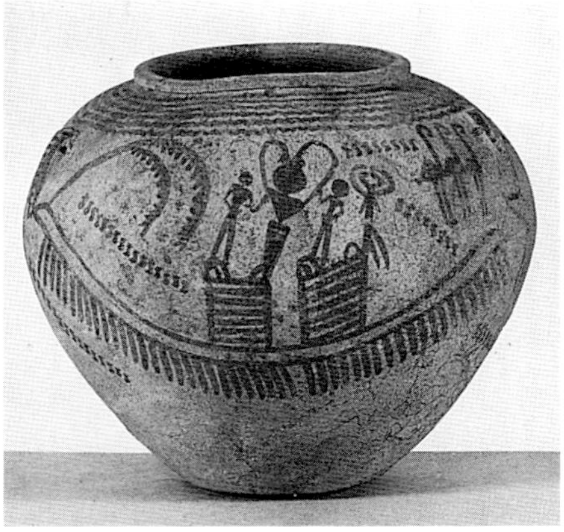

the conventions of Egyptian art, seem to be more important—perhaps goddesses.[6]

The females' arms are curved up and back with the palms of the hands apparently held upward, if we may judge from the position of the thumbs of the terracotta figurine in Brooklyn,[7] where the hands are largely intact. This pose has generated several theories regarding the function of this type of female figurine: that they represent dancers,[8] worshippers,[9] or mourners;[10] are symbols of resurrection;[11] mimic the bovine horns of the goddess Hathor or Bat;[12] symbolize the protective, nurturing arms (and breasts) of a mother;[13] or, as noted above, depict the ritual stance of a deity. The pose with the palm turned upward is precisely that of the *ib3*-dance depicted in later periods.[14] It is curious, however, that some of the similar figurines from Burial 1 have stub arms. One would suspect that this position of the arms was symbolic in some important way, and it is odd that in some instances the arms have been reduced to stubs (fig. 4).

Equally perplexing are male figures that have many points in common with the female statuettes. One, also in Brooklyn,[15] has the same beaky face, stub arms, and resin on the head for attachment of a long wig or headdress. The figure is clearly male; it wears a penis sheath. An example in Boston (fig. 5)[16] and another in the British Museum[17] have downpointed heads and penis sheaths, as well as arms curving out and upward, like those of the female figurines. If the females may represent goddesses, might the male figures represent gods? It is tempting to see a link between these birdlike heads and the Horus falcon.

A recent study[18] suggests that ancient Egyptian kingship emerged through the assimilation by males, both human and divine, of the powers of the primeval mother goddess. With this emergence of male control, according to this theory, myths were developed that attributed control over the formerly female powers of fertility, birth, and regeneration to the male god Osiris. Similarly, the god Ra assumed solar creative powers formerly associated with goddesses. One wonders whether these Predynastic male figurines represent an early usurpation of the female goddesses' powers.

The precise significance of these figurines probably will never be understood completely. Yet their emphasis on fertility and (by extension) rebirth, their ritualistic poses, and their inclusion in burial contexts all point to a connection with the supernatural.[19] AKC

Published: Needler, *Predynastic*, no. 268 and pl. 63 (07.447.502); no. 58 and pl. 16 (09.889.400). D. Spaniel in Thomas et al., *American Discovery*, cat. no. 22.

Fig. 4 Female Predynastic figurine with stub arms. 07.447.501. Photo courtesy of The Brooklyn Museum.

Fig. 5 Male Predynastic figurine. Emily Esther Sears Fund. 04.1802. Photo courtesy of Museum of Fine Arts, Boston.

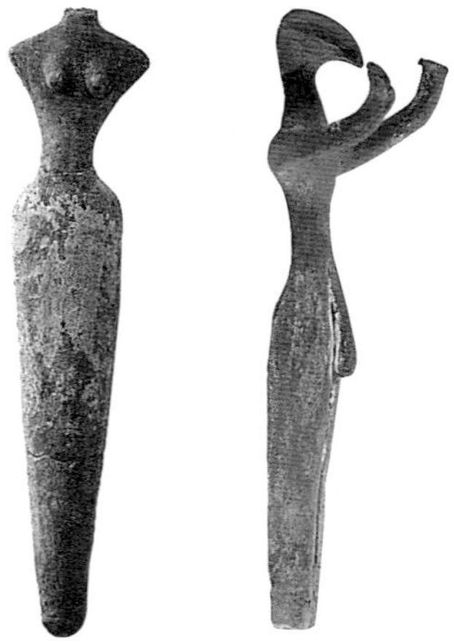

54a Fragment of statue of bovine-headed Hathor

Porphyritic diorite; provenance unknown, probably from Thebes; Dynasty 18, reign of Amenhotep III; H: 50.8 cm

The Metropolitan Museum of Art. Rogers Fund, 1919. MMA 19.2.5

Brooklyn venue only

54b Statuette of bovine-headed Hathor

Bronze with inlays of gold and electrum; from Memphis; Ptolemaic era; H: 19 cm

The Brooklyn Museum. Charles Edwin Wilbour Fund. 37.356E

The goddess Hathor took numerous forms. She was a tree goddess, the Mistress of the Southern Sycamore;[1] as the Eye of Ra, she assumed the form of a raging lioness.[2] Sometimes she appeared as a falcon.[3] In the famous triads of Menkaura of Dynasty 4, Hathor appears in fully human female form, with her characteristic headdress consisting of a sun disc resting between the horns of a cow.[4]

Beginning in the Middle Kingdom, Hathor assumed the iconography of the ancient bovine goddess Bat, who is known from the very beginning of ancient Egypt's historical period.[5] Other cow goddesses with whom Hathor was associated include Mehet-weret, a primeval sky deity who was mother of the sun god Ra;[6] Sekhat-Hor, "She Who Remembers Horus," who nourished the infant Horus in the papyrus swamps;[7] and the seven sacred Hathor cows, who determined a child's destiny at its birth.[8] In her bovine form, Hathor was revered as the Mistress of the West, goddess of the deceased,[9] and was frequently

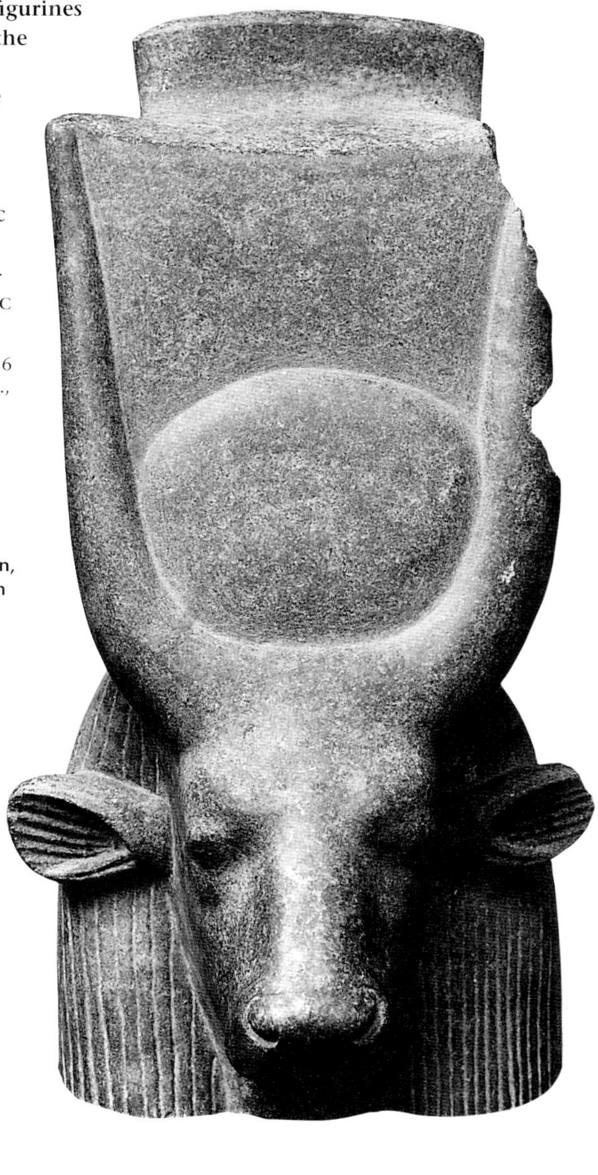

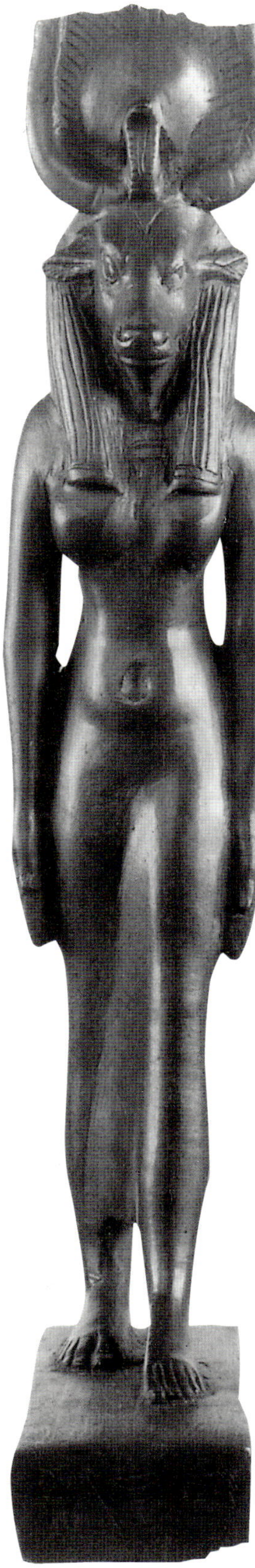

depicted on the walls of tombs[10] and on funerary papyri.[11]

This statue fragment from the Metropolitan Museum of Art depicts Hathor in fully bovine form and dates to the reign of Amenhotep III. A slightly earlier, intact statue in the Cairo Museum twice depicts Amenhotep II with the cow goddess—once suckling from the deity, and again under the goddess's head.[12]

During the Late Period, depictions of Hathor in her cow-headed and female-bodied form became more common. It has been suggested that these statuettes of the goddess, such as the bronze example from the Brooklyn Museum, depict a form of the goddess especially revered at Memphis,[13] where Hathor was worshipped with her consort, here the god Ptah.[14]

At least eight examples (five in bronze and three in faience) of the bovine-headed Hathor are in the Cairo Museum, as noted by C.R. Williams.[15] Other cow-headed Hathor statues are of glass or stone.[16] The example from Brooklyn has a *menat* counterpoise at the back of the headdress, which supports the crown, and Williams observes that the heavy lappet wig aids in the transition between the bovine head and the human neck.[17] An example in Berlin depicts the goddess with a gold-inlaid collar.[18]

At least one example of the bucephalic deity in Cairo[19] carries an inscription naming the goddess as Mehet-weret. The Brooklyn statuette, however, bears an inscription clearly identifying the deity as Hathor: "Hathor, Mistress of the Sycamore, May she give life to Aset-reshty and Pa-en-Ptah. Made by the Mistress of the House, Nefer-awy-Aset-[ ]."[20] This inscription apparently was not the original dedication. Markings made by a flint scraper indicate that the statue was reused. AKC

Published: Hayes, *Scepter,* 2: 239, fig. 144; Roeder, *Ägyptische Bronzefiguren,* 265, para. 326b (with references to earlier publications).

55 a Sistrum fragment with Hathor mask

Faience; provenance unknown; Ptolemaic era; H: 15.2 cm

The Walters Art Gallery, Baltimore. 48.465

55 b Hathor mask

Bronze and glass; provenance unknown; Ptolemaic era; H: 15 cm; W: 13 cm

The Saint Louis Art Museum. Gift of Mr. and Mrs. Alvin S. Novack. 545:56

This faience sistrum originally depicted the mask of Hathor on either side; one side, however, has been broken away and lost. The goddess's head is surmounted by a shrine of a type frequently termed a *naos.*[1] Within the *naos* is a cobra serpent before a rectangular structure, perhaps an altar. On either side, volutes extend up to the cavetto cornice. It has often been suggested that these volutes represent the incurving horns of the very ancient bovine goddess Bat, who is depicted twice on each side of the famous Narmer Palette.[2] By the beginning of the Middle Kingdom, the iconography of Bat had been assumed by Hathor.[3]

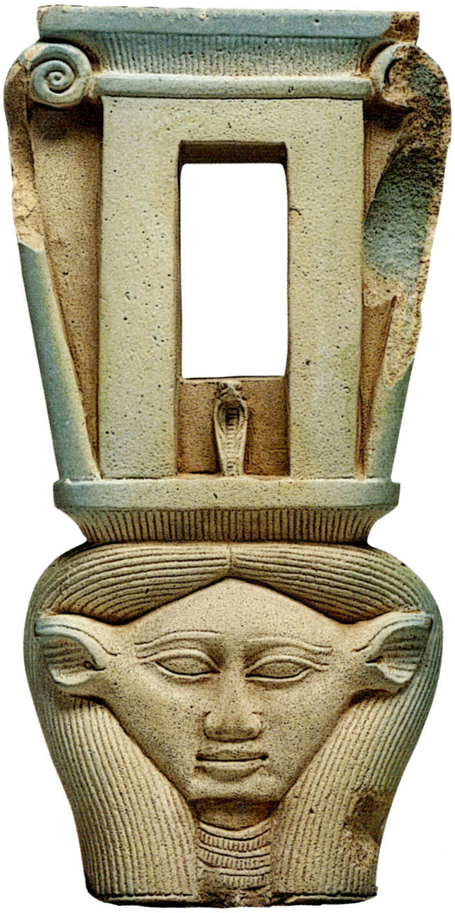

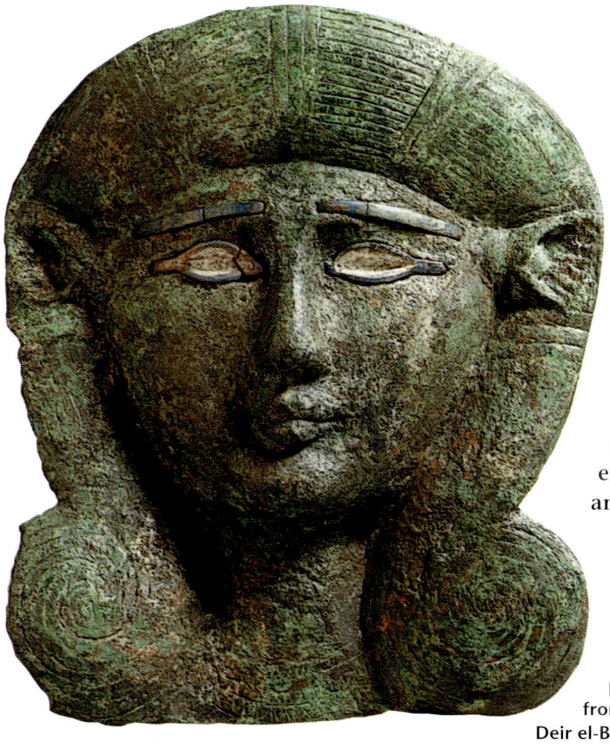

On this sistrum (which is missing its handle), Hathor wears a long, straight wig parted in the center and a broad collar around her neck. As is typical of such Hathor masks, the ears of the goddess are bovine.

The sides and volutes of this *naos* shrine are pierced by three holes. Metal rods (possibly in the shape of snakes) threaded with discs passed through these openings and created a swishing sound when shaken. The handle, had it been preserved, might have borne an inscription providing the name of the sistrum's owner.[4]

The bronze mask of Hathor from the Saint Louis Art Museum depicts the goddess's face in a manner similar to that on the faience sistrum. Here the Hathoric wig, with the ends of the hair wound in tight curls, is held in place by bindings radiating outward from the face. The bovine ears and broad collar are indicated in the usual manner. The eyebrows and the corneas of the eyes are blue glass inlays. The central inlays that formed the iris and pupil were probably also made of glass but have been lost.[5]

These images were not intended to portray the actual head of the goddess; rather, they were masks that duplicated Hathor's iconographic features. The masks were incorporated as elements in a number of ancient Egyptian objects, including mirrors (cat. no. 22a), actual and votive architectural columns, vessels, textiles, stelae, jewelry, *menat* counterpoises, and sistrophorous and naophorous statues.[6] Likewise, at Hathor's temple at Dendera, a large mask of the goddess carved in relief on the outer rear wall was an object of devotion.[7] These occurrences suggest that the mask of Hathor was considered to be a form of the goddess and was venerated as such. AKC

56 Votive stela to Hathor

Limestone, with traces of blue pigment preserved in the texts; from Thebes, Deir el-Medina, or Deir el-Bahri; New Kingdom, mid- to late Dynasty 18; H: 19.5 cm; W: 15.1 cm; D: 4.7 cm

The Brooklyn Museum. Gift of the Estate of Charles Edwin Wilbour. 16.92

A curved hieroglyph for "sky" or "heaven" surmounting a winged sun disc adorns the upper part of this stela. Below stands a figure of a king labeled as Nebhepetra, one of the names of Mentuhotep II of Dynasty 11, whose reunification of the country ushered in the Middle Kingdom. Unlike most kings, he enjoyed more-than-human status and veneration long after his death. A potential intermediary to the divine, Nebhepetra is shown making a gesture of invocation before a statue of a cow on a pedestal bearing offerings. Labeled "Hathor, Chieftainess of Thebes," the divine image bears a sun disc with *uraeus* and two tall ostrich plumes between her horns (a headgear not unique to Hathor); a Bat/Hathor symbol is suspended from her neck.[1] Below the scene the stela is inscribed for An, a priest of Amen.

An's stela was purchased in 1887 at Medinet Habu on the West Bank at Thebes, but it probably came from one of the two nearby sites of Deir el-Medina or Deir el-Bahri. Deir el-Bahri is perhaps the more likely provenance because Nebhepetra, also associated with Hathor outside Thebes, built his funerary temple at that site and was particularly venerated there. Hathor played a role in that temple, which is associated with the earliest definite image of Hathor in cow form suckling a king.[2] Both Hatshepsut and Thutmose III also built chapels to Hathor at Deir el-Bahri.

Hathor was such an important and complex deity throughout most of ancient Egyptian history that her many aspects and forms can be summarized only briefly here.[3] Like many goddesses, Hathor could be the sun god Ra's daughter, his mobile and powerful eye who protected Egypt and the equilibrium of the ordered universe (cat. no. 69), but she was also a potential threat to that which she should protect. Embodiment of the sexual excitement necessary to creation, and associated more closely with biological than with sociological motherhood, Hathor could be not only Ra's daughter but also his spouse and celestial mother. The latter, sometimes in the form of a cow[4] and like the goddess Nut,[5] bore and gave (re-)birth to the rejuvenated Ra each dawn. Hathor means "House/Temple of Horus." Another of her names, "the Golden," also relates her to the solar; thus it is not surprising that Hathor could be both wife and mother of a form of Horus, who could himself be related to Ra.

Given this pharaoh's links to Ra and Horus, it is not odd that he could be viewed as Hathor's son, or that in celebrations, such as the *Sed* Festival of royal rejuvenation, he could at least eventually play the role of both her spouse and her son. In the *Sed* rituals, with which Hathor was intimately connected, and in other contexts, queens also came to play various

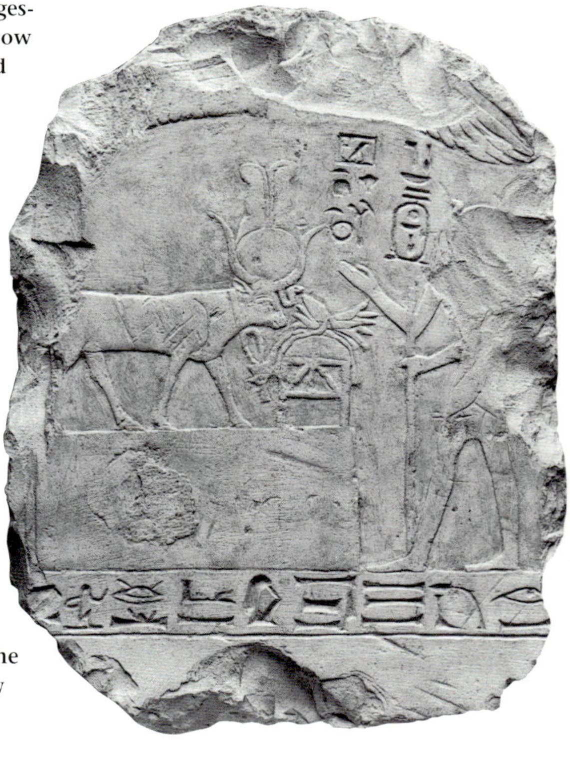

divine roles, such as Maʾat[6] (another daughter of Ra) or Hathor.[7] Indeed, it has been suggested that Hathor was a major divine prototype for the queenship.[8]

For the Egyptians, a deity's true form was hidden from the living. Thus Hathor, a goddess with many aspects, could be envisaged in many forms, such as a lioness, *uraeus*, hippopotamus, "tree nymph," "Hathor" column or pillar (cat. no. 20c), sistrum (cat. no. 35b), or *menat* (cat. no. 35c). Each conveyed a nuanced message about some facet of her being.[9] One familiar image is that of a wild cow of the desert fringes and marshes, such as the Hathor, "Chieftainess of Thebes," depicted on this stela. Like many other manifestations of Hathor, however, the "Chieftainess of Thebes" could also be shown as a woman crowned with cow's horns and sun disc or, eventually, as cow-headed. These bovine and mixed human-bovine forms are often associated with Hathor's maternal aspect.

As eternal life could be viewed either as rebirth or as cyclical rebirth in the next world, Hathor could also be a mother for the deceased. This was certainly true at ancient Thebes; at that city's West Bank cemeteries Hathor became a major funerary goddess for both royalty and private persons.[10] Yet even on the West Bank of Thebes, Hathor was not just a funerary deity; her chapels there received numerous votive offerings from the living as well.[11] Strongly associated with sexuality, fertility, pregnancy, and birth, Hathor was particularly significant to women, who are well represented by West Bank Theban votives to her. That Hathor was not worshipped solely by women is demonstrated by the priest An's stela, among many others. RAF

Published: PM 1,2[2]: 798; James, *Corpus*, 1: no. 433, pp. 176–77 and pl. 85; Richard Fazzini, "Two New Kingdom Stelae from the Collection of Charles Edwin Wilbour in the Brooklyn Museum," in C. Van Siclen, III, ed., *Iubilate Conlegae: Egyptological Studies in Memory of Abdel Aziz Sadek, Varia Aegyptiaca* 10, nos. 2–3 (1996).

57 Statue of winged Isis and Osiris

Schist; provenance unknown;
Late Period, Dynasty 26 or later;
H: 35.8 cm; W: 6.7 cm; Depth: 14.1 cm

Courtesy of The Walters Art Gallery, Baltimore. 22.199

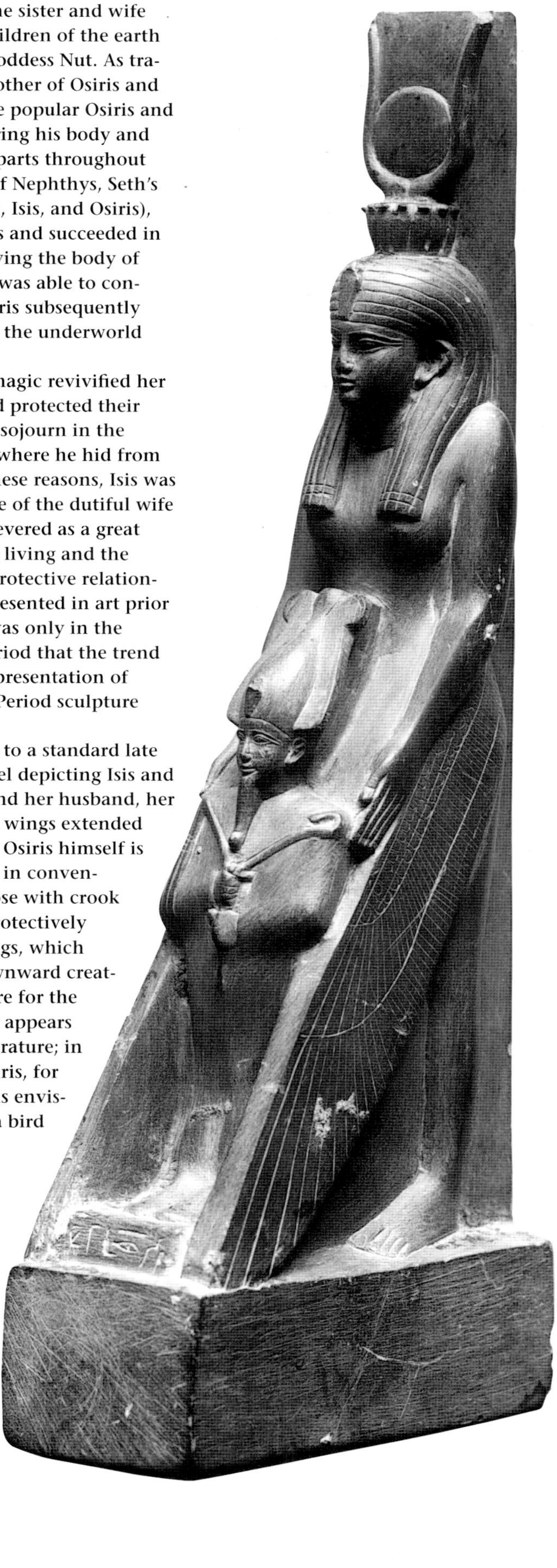

The goddess Isis was the sister and wife of Osiris; both were children of the earth god Geb and the sky goddess Nut. As tradition relates, Seth, brother of Osiris and Isis, grew jealous of the popular Osiris and killed him, dismembering his body and scattering the various parts throughout Egypt. With the help of Nephthys, Seth's wife (and sister of Seth, Isis, and Osiris), Isis retrieved the pieces and succeeded in reassembling and reviving the body of Osiris with whom she was able to conceive a son, Horus. Osiris subsequently descended to rule over the underworld as king of the dead.[1]

Isis's knowledge of magic revivified her murdered husband and protected their son, Horus, during his sojourn in the marshes of Chemmis, where he hid from the jealous Seth. For these reasons, Isis was considered the epitome of the dutiful wife and mother and was revered as a great protectress of both the living and the dead. Although Isis's protective relationship with Osiris is represented in art prior to the Late Period, it was only in the Third Intermediate Period that the trend toward the popular representation of Osiris and Isis in Late Period sculpture began.[2]

The statue conforms to a standard late period sculptural model depicting Isis and Osiris: Isis stands behind her husband, her outstretched arms and wings extended on either side of him.[3] Osiris himself is depicted on a pedestal in conventional mummiform pose with crook and flail. He stands, protectively enveloped in Isis's wings, which extend diagonally downward creating a niche or enclosure for the god. This iconography appears rooted in Egyptian literature; in the Great Hymn to Osiris, for example, the goddess is envisaged as a kite *(djeryt*, a bird

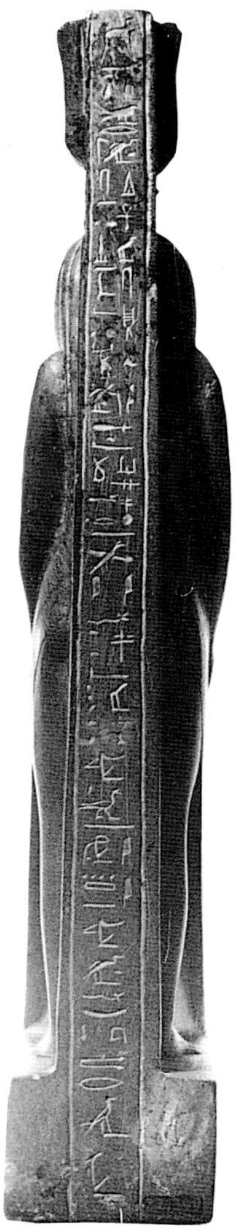

in the hawk family) who protectively shades the god with her wings. Here Isis is described as one "who made a shade with her plumage, created breath with her wings."[4] Her headdress consists of a horned solar disc atop a *modius*, one of the goddess's conventional Late Period crowns.

The dedicatory inscription on its back pillar reveals that this statue was an offering to Isis, "the Great One" *(wr[t])*, "Mother of the God" *(mwt nṯr)*, by a man named P(y)f-tȝw-ʿwy-(m)-sẖmt.[5] A roughly contemporary, more monumental version of the same statue was dedicated in the Temple of Amen at Karnak by Sheshonq, chief steward of the God's Wife Ankhnesneferibra in Dynasty 26.[6] GEM

58 Bust fragment of a goddess, probably Isis[1]

Indurated limestone; provenance unknown; Third Intermediate Period, Dynasty 22 (?); H: 8.4 cm; W: 5.5 cm

Cincinnati Art Museum. Gift of Millard F. and Edna F. Shelt. 1947.383

Dating back to the Old Kingdom, the venerable cult of Isis remained popular throughout Egyptian history.[2] Like most other Egyptian deities, she was depicted in a number of forms, including that of a tree-goddess, a mother goddess in the form of a cow, and a kite.[3]

Isis's most common form, however, was fully human.[4] In this context, she was often depicted opposite the goddess Nephthys with arms outspread in a protective manner (cat. nos. 90 and 91).[5] She is most readily identified by the hieroglyphic sign for "throne," which she wears upon her head.[6]

The cult of Isis achieved its greatest popularity and geographic spread under the Ptolemies, the dynasty with Macedonian Greek origins that ruled Egypt after Alexander.[7] Because of her royal associations, Isis was especially favored by the Ptolemaic queens. Arsinoe II, the wife of Ptolemy Philadelphos, was instrumental in popularizing Isis's worship to the Greek population of Egypt.[8]

What became the largest cult establishment devoted to the goddess was founded no later than Dynasty 26 on the island of Philae in Upper Egypt.[9] Here and at other shrines throughout the country,[10] Isis became associated increasingly with the Egyptian goddess Hathor as well as other (often foreign) deities with whom she was assimilated. Her cult survived until A.D. 537, when Justinian closed her primary temple at Philae.[11]

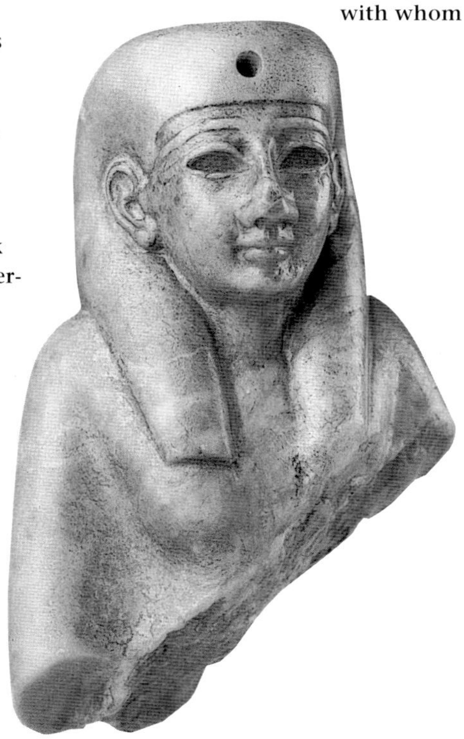

Stylistically, this delicate bust fragment of a goddess, which may have come from a seated figure of nursing Isis, may be dated to the Third Intermediate Period, thus placing it early in the production sequence of such votive statuettes.[12] A cylindrical drilling at the top of the head served for the insertion of a headdress—a solar disc between bovine horns—Isis's conventional Late Period crown (cat. nos. 54 and 59). A small perforation on the forehead originally held a *uraeus*. The eyes of the goddess, enhanced by fine cosmetic lines, were originally inlaid with a dark stone. AKC/GEM

59 a Isis nursing Horus[1]

Bronze; provenance unknown; Late Period, Dynasty 26 or later; H: 39.5 cm

University of Pennsylvania Museum of Archaeology and Anthropology, Philadelphia. Gift of Mrs. D. Parrish. E 12548

59 b Isis nursing Horus

Bronze; provenance unknown, reportedly found at Zagazig; Late Period, Dynasty 26 or later; H: 12.7 cm; W: 3.3 cm

Cincinnati Art Museum. Gift of Millard F. and Edna F. Shelt. 1947.97

59 c Horus the Child

Bronze; provenance unknown; Late Period, Dynasty 26 or later; H: 13.6 cm; W: 2.6 cm

Cincinnati Art Museum. Gift of Millard F. and Edna F. Shelt. 1947.99

Following the murder and mutilation of Osiris, Isis, with the aid of other Egyptian deities, reassembled and mummified the dead king.[2] Through her efforts, Osiris was thus sufficiently animated to enable Isis to conceive their son, Horus.[3] To conceal his existence from the vengeful Seth (the murderous brother of Osiris), Isis hid Horus during her pregnancy and during Horus's childhood in the papyrus marshes of Chemmis near Buto. She used her magical skills to protect him from the dangers of the marshes, which included poisonous snakes and scorpions (cat. no. 60).[4] When Horus reached adulthood, Isis continued to assist him (he was the rightful heir) in his effort to inherit Osiris's role as divine king.[5]

Because of her fierce devotion to and protection of her son, Isis came to be regarded in Late Dynastic Egypt as the paradigm of the devoted mother. As mother goddess par excellence, she was often invoked for the protection of children; in recognition of her magical skills, women frequently addressed prayers to her on behalf of their offspring.[6]

From an early period, Isis's suckling of Horus symbolized her pivotal role in the transmission of divine kingship. Each new king who succeeded to the throne was considered to be the "living Horus," the incarnation of the son of Isis and Osiris. Isis was thus the symbolic mother of each king and one of his links to the divine world.[7]

The two bronze statuettes in Philadelphia and Cincinnati depict Isis in her typical Late Period manifestation as mother goddess: seated, suckling the infant Horus on her lap. Supporting him by the shoulder with her left hand, she offers him her left breast. The extraordinary number of surviving statuettes and amulets of Isis and Horus offers vivid testimony to the widespread importance of the cult of Isis in Late Dynastic Egypt.[8]

The first millennium, in fact, witnessed a rise in prominence of cults of both goddesses and child gods such as Horus.[9] Among the temples in which the latter were venerated are those known today as *mammisis (pr-mst,* "House of Birth" in ancient Egyptian).[10] Normally closely associated with the temple of a goddess, a *mammisi* was the setting for rituals celebrating the birth/renewal of the child god with whom the king identified.[11] The increasing importance of such cults, and those of divine family triads, beginning in the Third Intermediate Period, is reflected in the newly prominent cultic role that certain royal women enjoyed in connection with child gods.[12]

Beginning in the New Kingdom, Isis began to absorb many of the attributes and functions of other goddesses. Her cult became assimilated with that of Hathor, who was long associated with kingship; as was the case with Isis, the king was described as Hathor's son.[13] On both figures, Isis wears the queenly vulture headdress with *uraeus* ornament.[14] Her crown, consisting of cow horns and a solar disc atop a *modius,* was originally that of Hathor, from whom it was borrowed.[15]

Both statuettes, which probably served as votive offerings in shrines to Isis, are delicately modeled; with its inlaid gold eyes and delicate features, the Cincinnati figurine (cat. no. 59c) exhibits exceptional detail for such a small-scale statuette. Both figures are missing their original bases, which probably consisted of simple block thrones.[16] AKC/RAF/GEM

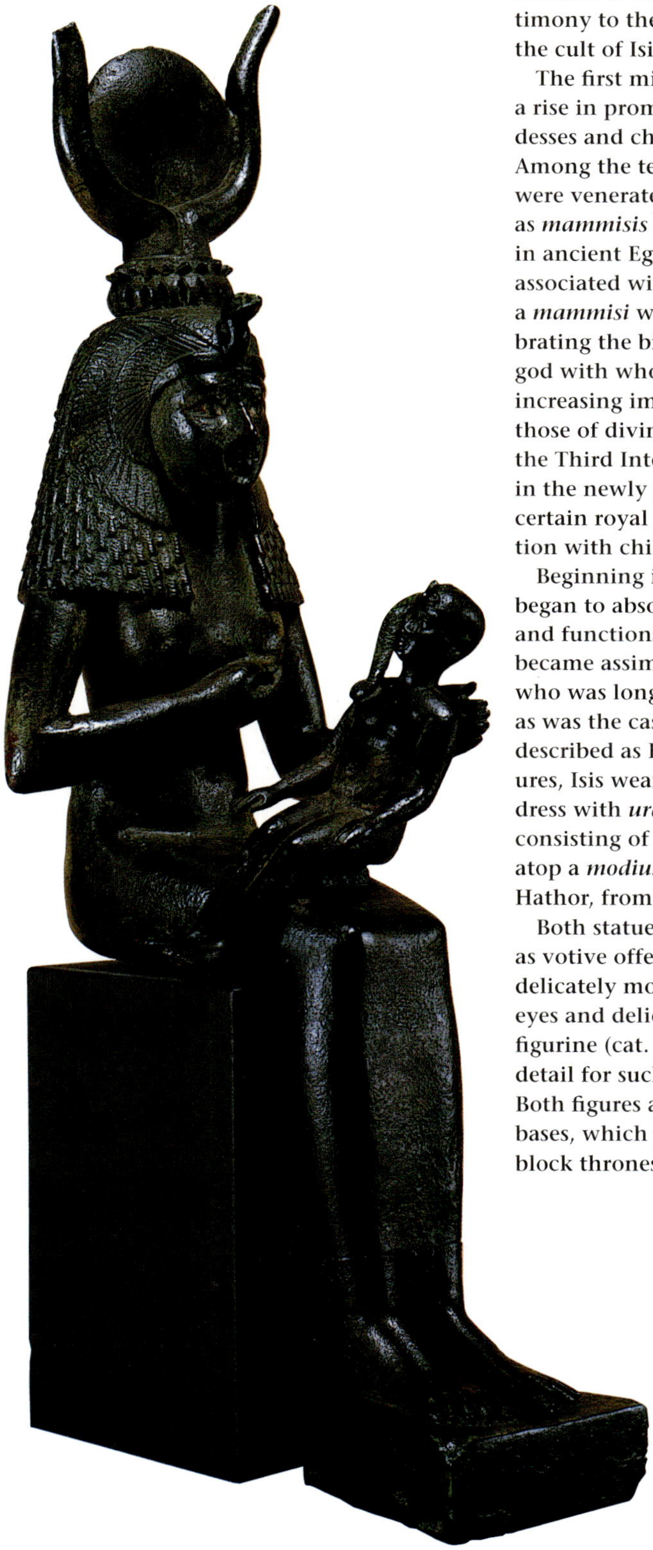

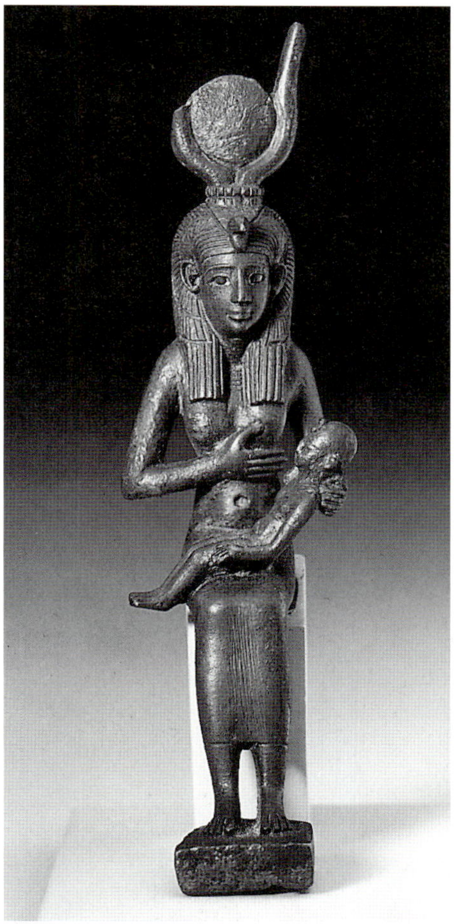

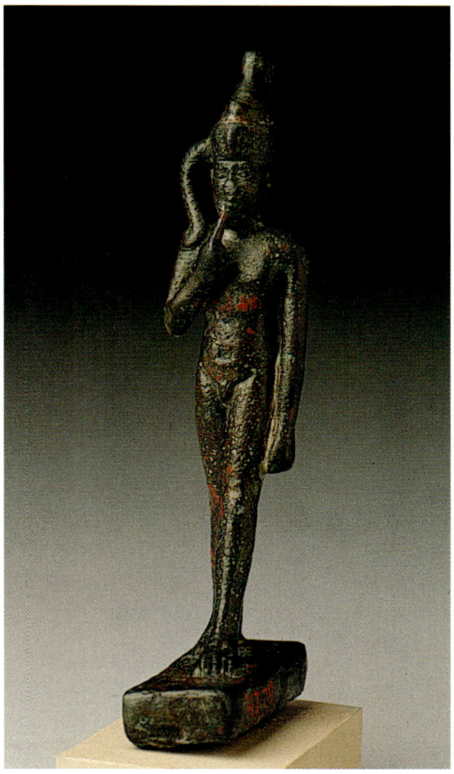

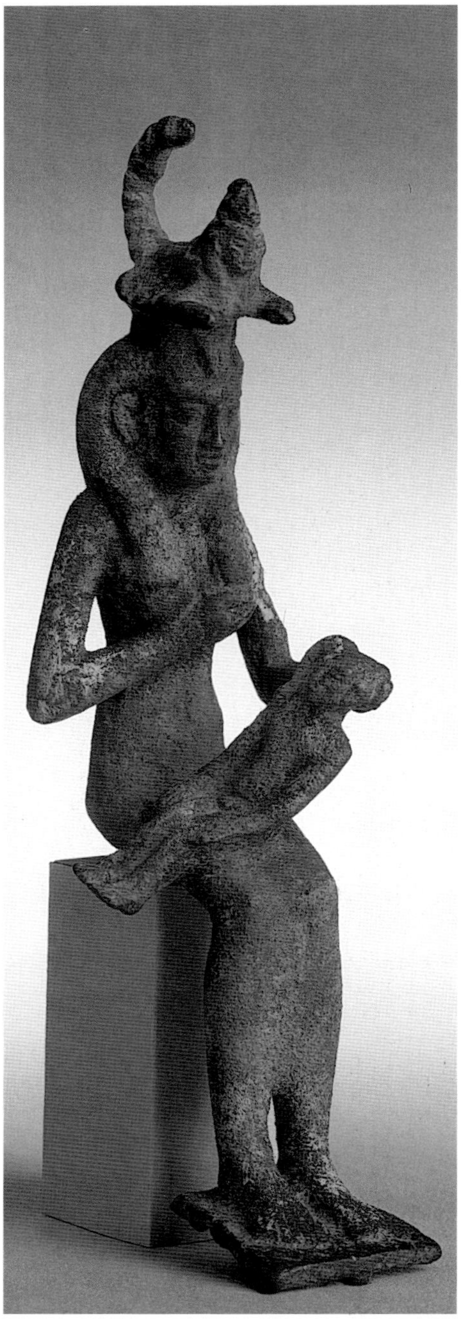

60 Isis/Scorpion nursing infant Horus

Bronze; provenance unknown;
Late Period, Ptolemaic era; H: 16 cm
Field Museum of Natural History, Chicago. 173236

The ancient Egyptian divine pantheon included a number of protective goddesses associated with the scorpion, an inhospitable creature omnipresent in Egypt's desert environment. The most prominent and ancient of these deities was Selket, whose cult is already attested in the First Dynasty.[1] Her name, apparently an abbreviation of *serket hetyt* ("She Who Causes the Throat to Breathe"), refers to her ability to neutralize the threat of asphyxiation posed by the toxic venom of the scorpion; in magical texts, she often served to cure or avoid venomous snake bites. In the Old Kingdom, Selket played a protective role around the king.[2] Her most prominent function, however, was in the funerary sphere. Here, along with Isis, Nephthys, and Neith, she served as tutelary guardian of the sarcophagus and of the four canopic jars that held the viscera of the deceased.[3]

The scorpion goddess Selket was one of a group of beneficent deities (Hathor among them) who attended the birth of the god Horus at Chemmis in the Nile Delta. Through her magical powers, she helped to protect Horus from the dangers, in the form of scorpions and snakes, inherent in the marshes.[4] Isis herself was revered for her magical healing powers, which included the cure of venomous snake bites;[5] one of her most frequent epithets was *weret heka* ("Great of Magic"). The association of Isis and Selket was a natural one, in that both goddesses shared similar protective roles as guardians of the deceased.[6]

Isis was associated with another scorpion goddess named Hededet, who is first mentioned in the Coffin Texts and is later attested at the end of the Eighteenth Dynasty at Edfu, her primary cult center.[7] Like Selket, Hededet was a guardian goddess who protected against venomous creatures. Hededet's association with Isis in the Late Period is well attested;[8] at Edfu, Isis-Hededet was regarded locally as the mother of Horus.[9]

It is this assimilated goddess—Isis-Selket or, perhaps, Isis-Hededet—who is depicted in this figurine, which probably served as a votive offering in a Ptolemaic-period cult center.[10] In the manner of Selket or Hededet, she wears a rearing scorpion on her head, its tail poised, ready to sting. The goddess is depicted in the standard pose of Isis as mother goddess, suckling the infant Horus on her lap (cat. nos. 59 a,b).[11] GEM

61 Statuette of the goddess Mut

Schist; provenance unknown;
Late Period, Dynasty 26; H: 16.2 cm;
W: 3.8 cm; D: 4.8 cm
The Brooklyn Museum. Charles Edwin Wilbour Fund. 76.38

This statuette represents the goddess holding an *ankh* in her left hand. Her left leg is advanced in the pose that is generally called "striding" but actually represents a state of repose; perhaps it symbolizes the potential for motion. The remains of a hemline demonstrate that the figure was not nude but was depicted wearing a tightly clinging dress. Although nudity was highly unusual for images of most goddesses and for the vast majority of elite women, their clothing generally emphasized their figures and often revealed as much as it concealed.[1]

That the statuette represents the goddess Mut (pronounced "Moot") is all but certainly indicated by the presence, atop the striated wig with *uraeus*,[2] of the double crown of Upper and Lower Egypt. This crown was worn by kings and by some male deities, most notably Atum and Horus, but not by queens.[3] Among goddesses it was worn almost exclusively by Mut from Dynasty 18 until the Third Intermediate Period and was restricted mainly to her even thereafter.[4] This is one reason Mut recently has been interpreted as having a special link to the kingship as some sort of heavenly queen-regnant, whose earthly manifestation (according to some ancient texts) is the kingship.[5]

More important for the goddess's identification is the inscription on the back pillar. The two epithets used here for Mut make this one of a small number of images of a form of Mut, connected mainly with Heliopolis, on whose braziers were burnt the bodies of human sacrifices identified by particular biological characteristics as incarnations of forces inimical to the king, as well as to Ra and Osiris.[6]

Goddesses with the name Mut are known from several cities, including Heliopolis, Memphis, and Thebes. Even if they were not related originally, they became so closely identified over time that only the text of the Brooklyn figure distinguishes it from images of other forms of Mut. If forms of Mut were venerated in the Memphite-Heliopolitan region, she is far more familiar to us from the southern Egyptian metropolis of Thebes, where her temple precinct at Karnak is located just south of that of Amen, her spouse.[7]

That the statuette is Mut of Heliopolis does not necessarily mean it is from that city, although there is reason to believe that it came from the region of Egypt between and around Heliopolis and Memphis. The piece bears both iconographic and stylistic resemblances to a Late Period statuette from Saqqara.[8] Its figural style is also related to two works of Dynasty 25, one Memphite and the other possibly Heliopolitan.[9] All of these works are archaizing; that is, they reflect the style of a former era or eras. Compare, for example, the figural style of this Mut statuette with that of catalogue number 3a, an Old Kingdom sculpture. Indeed, the archaizing tendencies reflected in the Mut statuette's figural style arose in the region of Memphis sometime in Dynasty 22 and appear to have spread to other

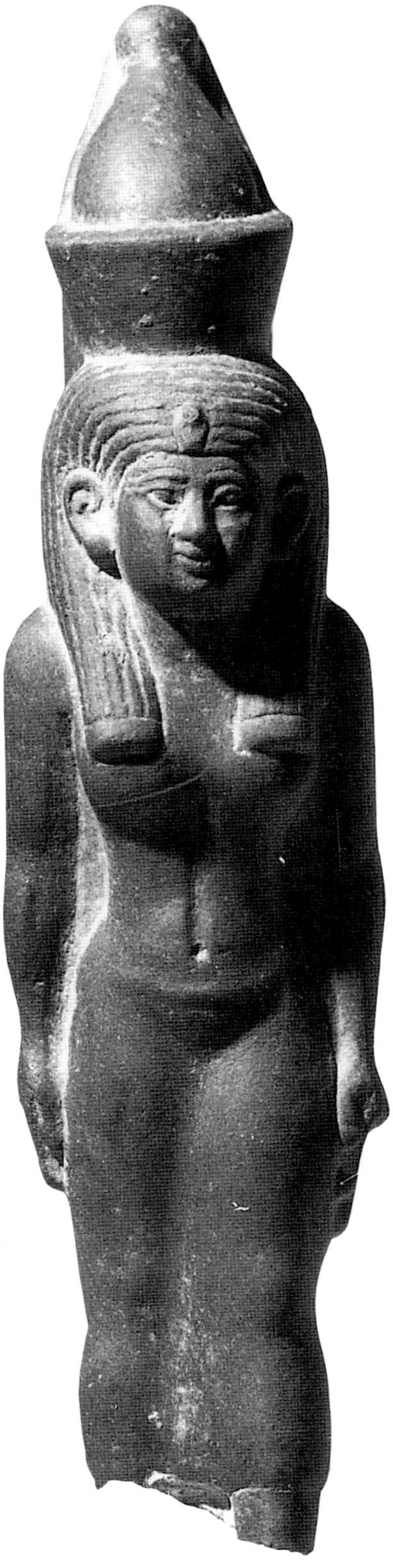

regions of the country and to have grown stronger.[10] Less closely linked to the past are the particular forms of its full face, curved brows, tilted eyes, and small mouth, which help date the figure to Dynasty 26 (cf. cat. no. 57). The form-fitting dress, which in this period is archaizing when worn by mortal women, may simply reflect goddesses' greater freedom from changes in fashion.

Almost all goddesses could embody the varied aspects of wife and mother. Many functioned variously as daughter, wife, and mother of a god, a metaphor in the form of a goddess for the ongoing renewal of divine life. At Thebes and elsewhere, Mut played this role in the relationship with Amen-Ra and their son, the lunar deity Khonsu, with whom pharaohs could be identified. Renewal of divine life thus became renewal of the kingship. Indeed, actual royal mothers, wives, and daughters may have played the same symbolic role as the goddess in relation to the king.

As mother, Mut is normally depicted anthropomorphically, but she can also appear in other guises, such as a *uraeus,* a leonine-headed woman, or a cat. As with many goddesses, these diverse forms help express concepts of the powerful protectress and the dichotomy of uncontrolled rage and appeased beneficence that are often associated with the Eye of Ra, daughter of the sun.[11] Catalogue numbers 56 and 65–68 also express these ideas.

RAF

Published: R. Fazzini, "The Art of the Ancient World," *Apollo* 115, no. 242 (April, 1982): 235, 236 and figs. 12, 13; R. Bianchi in Fazzini et al., *Neferut net Kemit,* no. 60, with pl. 60.

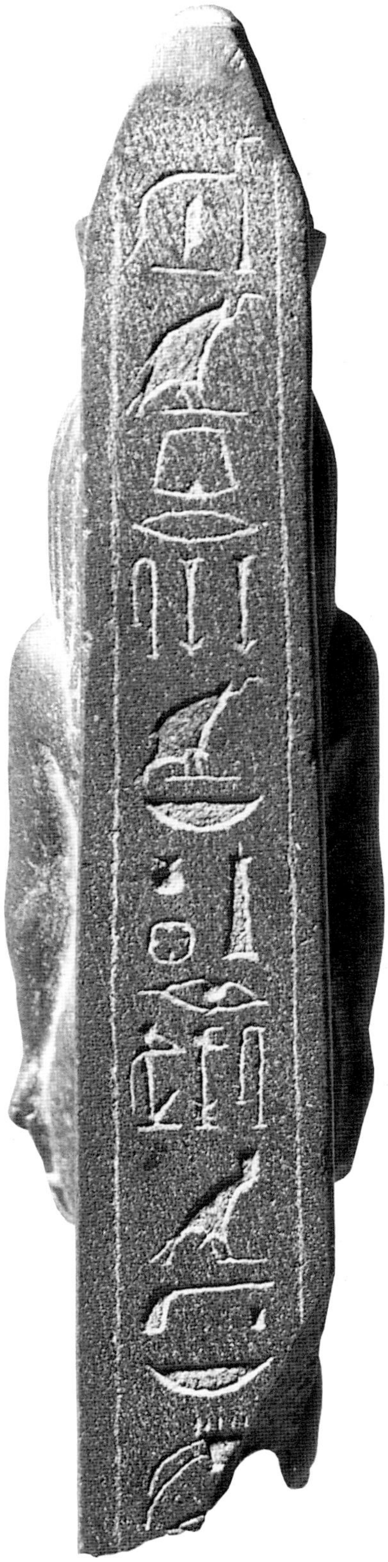

62 Votive stela with Taweret and Mut

Limestone; reportedly from Deir el-Medina, Thebes; New Kingdom, Dynasty 18–19; H: 17.7 cm; W: 14.3 cm

The Metropolitan Museum of Art. Dodge Fund, 1947. 47.105.4

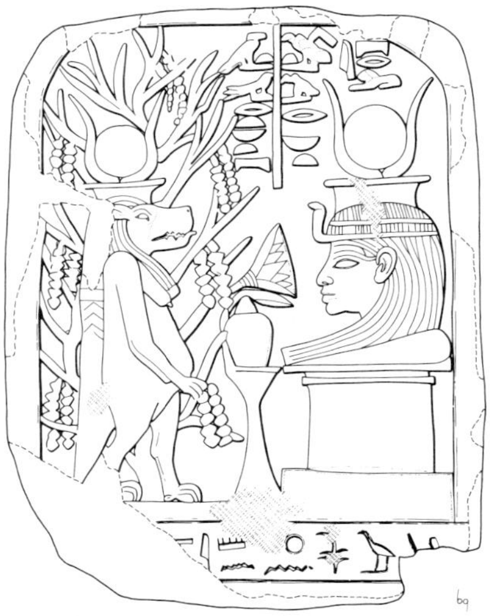

This unique stela, which was discovered around 1932, is believed to have come from the Theban area, possibly from the workmen's village at Deir el-Medina.[1] A trade item, the stela was made in advance and personalized for the purchaser, whose name and title, "The [. . .][2] of Amen, Khonsu," were added rather hastily in the bottom register.

Two goddesses are depicted: one in the form of a hippopotamus, and identified in the text as Taweret ("the Great One"); the other, "Mut, the Great One, Mistress of Isheru," represented by the likeness of her head atop an altar.[3] Taweret holds a stalk of papyrus and the stem of a lotus flower over the libation vase on an offering stand, and so seems to take on the role of a worshipper. Both goddesses wear a flat *modius* crown topped by the horned solar disc; a *uraeus,* however, is added to Mut's diadem, perhaps to signify that her rank is more highly divine than that of Taweret.

Both Taweret and Mut were revered as mother goddesses. Mut, together with her divine husband, Amen, and their son, Khonsu, was worshipped in her own temple precinct at Karnak. Because of her role as a mother goddess, Mut came to be identified with other divine mothers such as Isis and Hathor. Taweret was popular among people of all social classes in ancient Egypt, and her likeness was worn in amuletic form (see cat. nos. 20a, 20v2),[4] especially by pregnant women and women in childbirth.

It has been suggested that the hippo goddess depicted on this stela is Ipet[5] rather than Taweret,[6] with the words *t3-wrt* serving as an epithet ("the Great One") rather than a name. Ipet was a celestial deity[7] and the embodiment of the city of Thebes.[8] The goddess depicted here, however, stands beside an acacia tree, clearly identified by the pods hanging from the branches. Ipet is not known to be a tree goddess,[9] nor does there seem to be any reason to associate her specifically with the acacia tree.

The physicians of ancient Egypt recognized the beneficial qualities of the acacia tree, and the medical texts give recipes that include acacia for uterine complaints.[10] Acacia[11] contains phenol and tannin, thus providing both antiseptic and shrinking properties, which help to prevent infection and hemorrhage.[12] In recent times in Egypt, newly delivered mothers were bathed in water in which acacia seed pods had been steeped.[13] One ancient Egyptian recipe from the Ebers Papyrus that incorporates acacia has been shown to produce lactic acid, a chemical used in modern contraceptives.[14] The women of ancient Egypt wore strings of amulets in the form of acacia seed pods (see cat. no. 25) about their hips so that they might be surrounded magically by these protective qualities of the acacia. The presence of the acacia tree on this stela suggests that the hippo goddess should be identified as Taweret, the protectress of pregnant women and women in childbirth.

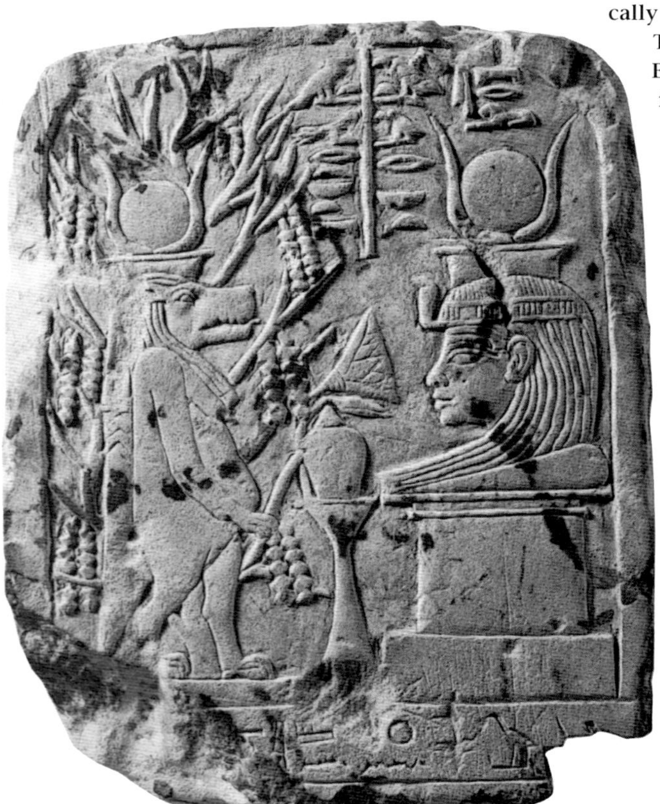

James P. Allen's recent reanalysis of the damaged areas of the stela's inscription[15] shows that the title of the person who dedicated this stela, "The [. . .] of Amen, Khonsu," is not "[Sculptor] of Amen," as was suggested by William C. Hayes,[16] but *šmʿyt] nt imn,* "[Chantress] of Amen."[17] The name "Khonsu" was given to females[18] as well as males. It is now clear that this stela, which incorporates powerful magical and medical symbols appropriate for the protection of a pregnant or newly delivered woman, was dedicated to Taweret and Mut by a woman who served in the temple of Amen, and who was named for Khonsu, divine son of Amen and Mut. AKC

Published: Hayes, *Scepter,* 2: 385, fig. 242; Kozloff, in *Egypt's Dazzling Sun,* 403 and fig. 105a.

63 a Statue of Taweret

Basalt; provenance unknown; Late Period; H: 41.5 cm

Field Museum of Natural History, Chicago. 30822

63 b Statuette of Ipet/Taweret

Bronze; provenance unknown, reportedly from Mitrahina; Late Period; H: 21.5 cm

Courtesy of The Walters Art Gallery, Baltimore. 54.2067

Taweret, whose name means "the Great One" in ancient Egyptian, was a protective deity revered by people of all social classes.[1] Her upright form combines the head[2] and body of a hippopotamus, the back and tail of a crocodile, the mane and paws of a lion, and pendent human breasts. Often she is depicted with a swollen belly mimicking pregnancy. This composite appearance seems to have served an apotropaic function, frightening off evil spirits. Taweret was invoked, often along with the deities Hathor and

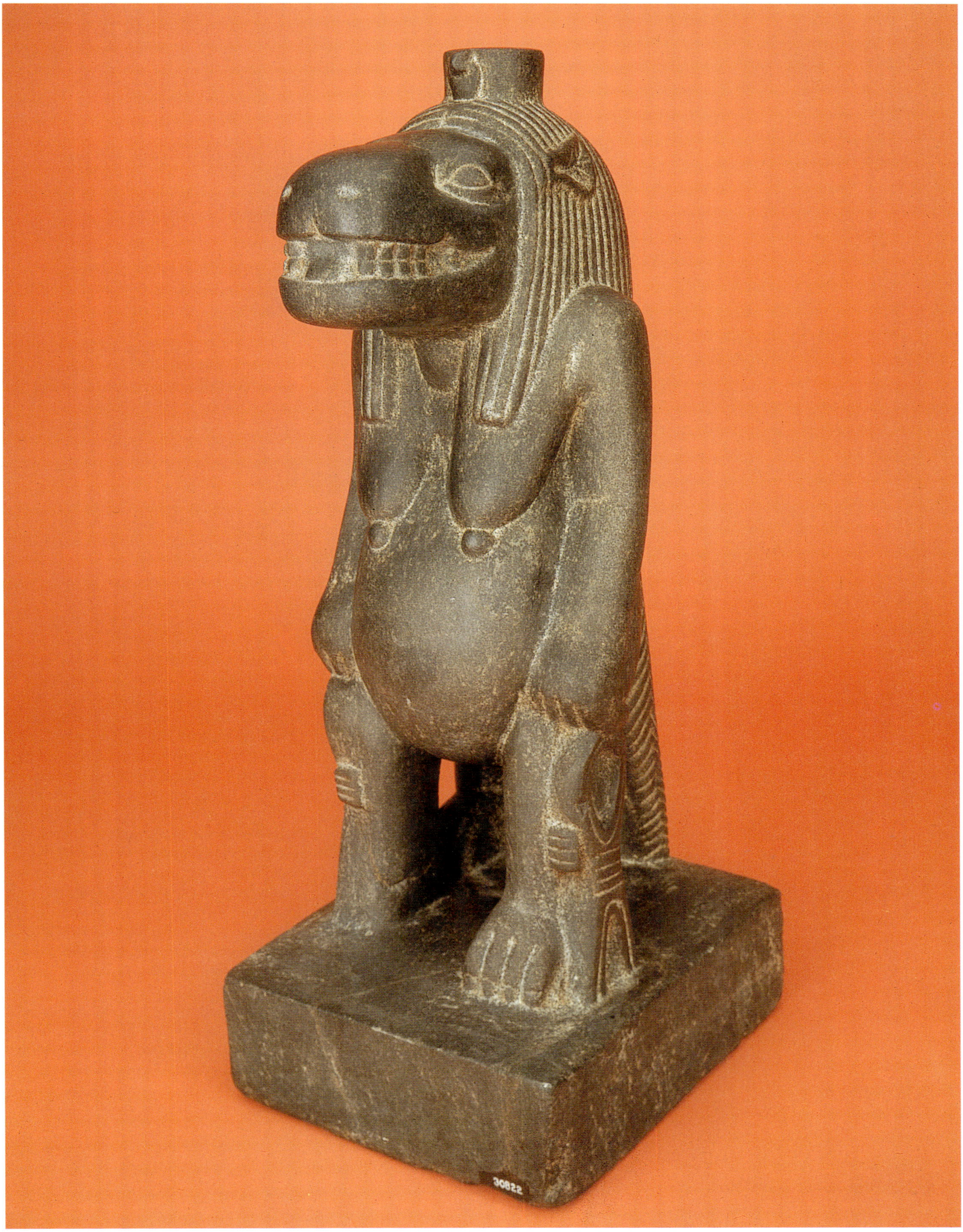
30822

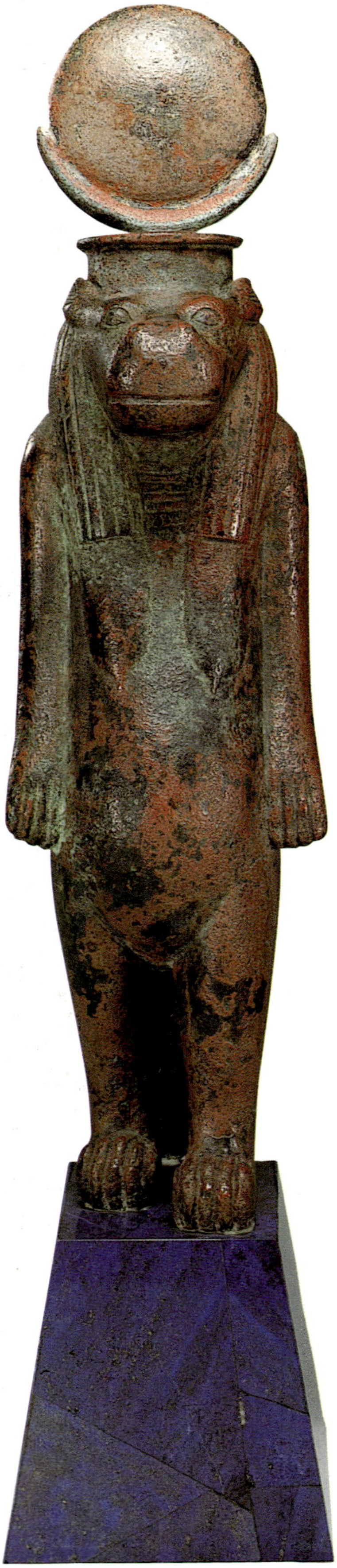

Bes, to protect women during pregnancy and childbirth and to safeguard the health of children.[3] Similarly, these three goddesses presided over various rites of passage, such as the maturation rituals for adolescents or the rebirth of a deceased person into the afterlife.[4]

This Taweret statue depicts the goddess striding forward with her left foot. Her large, threatening teeth are visible in her opened mouth. Taweret wears a rather abbreviated *modius* crown with a *uraeus* at the front; usually this platform is topped with the solar disc and plumes of the Hathoric headdress. Perhaps these elements were originally present in bronze or another metal.[5] The paws of the goddess rest on *sa* signs, symbols of protection. Alternately, Taweret may hold an *ankh,* the sign for life; in two-dimensional representations she often brandishes a knife or torch, emphasizing her protective function.

This bronze statuette depicts the hippopotamus goddess in a similar fashion. Here, however, a lunar disc resting on a crescent moon surmounts the *modius* platform.[6] This symbol identifies the goddess as Ipet, to whom a temple at Karnak was dedicated.[7] In an utterance from the Old Kingdom Pyramid Texts, Ipet is considered to be the mother of the deceased king.[8] As a celestial,[9] she is depicted in the astronomical ceiling of the tomb (KV 17) of Sety I.[10]

In addition to her numerous extant statues, Ipet/Taweret's likeness is also found on tomb,[11] temple,[12] and house walls,[13] and on stelae (cat. no. 62), furniture,[14] apotropaic wands (cat. no. 12), vessels,[15] jewelry and amulets (cat. nos. 20a, 20v2), and votive objects, including the present figurines.[16] Two statuettes of the hippopotamus goddess have human female faces, which are believed to reflect the features of Queen Tiye of the Eighteenth Dynasty.[17] During the Ptolemaic and Roman Periods, images of Taweret adorned and protected the temples of other deities,[18] extending her role as guardian to the gods themselves. AKC

Published: Walters Art Gallery figurine: Steindorff, *Catalogue,* no. 606, pl. 93.

64 a Standing figure of Neith

Bronze, with gold inlay; provenance unknown; Late Period, Dynasty 26 or later; H: 22.7 cm

The University of Pennsylvania Museum of Archaeology and Anthropology, Philadelphia. E 14309

64 b Standing figure of Neith

Bronze; provenance unknown; Late Period, Dynasty 26 or later; H: 27.7 cm

Cincinnati Art Museum. Gift of Millard F. and Edna F. Shelt. 1947.57

The Egyptian cult of the goddess Neith was of great antiquity; her most ancient symbol—two crossed arrows, often overlaid on a shield—is attested as early as the Late Predynastic Period.[1] This symbol often occurs in connection with another emblem of the goddess: the coleoptera beetle, symbol of Neith's regenerative powers; a gold amulet in this shape from a First Dynasty woman's grave at Nag ed-Deir bears the crossed arrows-and-shield motif.[2]

By the Early Dynastic Period, Neith's emblem occurs in clear association with both male and female royalty.[3] Her early dominance finds reflection in the large number of theophoric names of the period that incorporate that of the goddess.[4]

Neith's early association with female royalty is evidenced by the fact that her name is incorporated by two prominent royal women of the First Dynasty: Neithhotep and Mer-Neith.[5] The goddess's standard, in fact, surmounts the *serekhs,* or palace facade hieroglyphs, of these two queens. That Neith occupies the position held by Horus in the kingly *serekh* speaks to her early symbolic importance in the divine hierarchy and suggests that Early Dynastic royal women may have held certain powers comparable to those of the king.[6] Neith's association with queenship continued into the Old Kingdom. The coleoptera beetle and the crossed-arrows-and-shield emblem appear prominently in the decoration of a chair found in the tomb of Queen Hetepheres of the Fourth Dynasty.[7]

Neith's worship was centered at her cult establishment at Sais in the western delta, which may already have been established by the reign of King Aha in Dynasty 1.[8] During the Old Kingdom Neith became associated with the Red Crown, her sym-

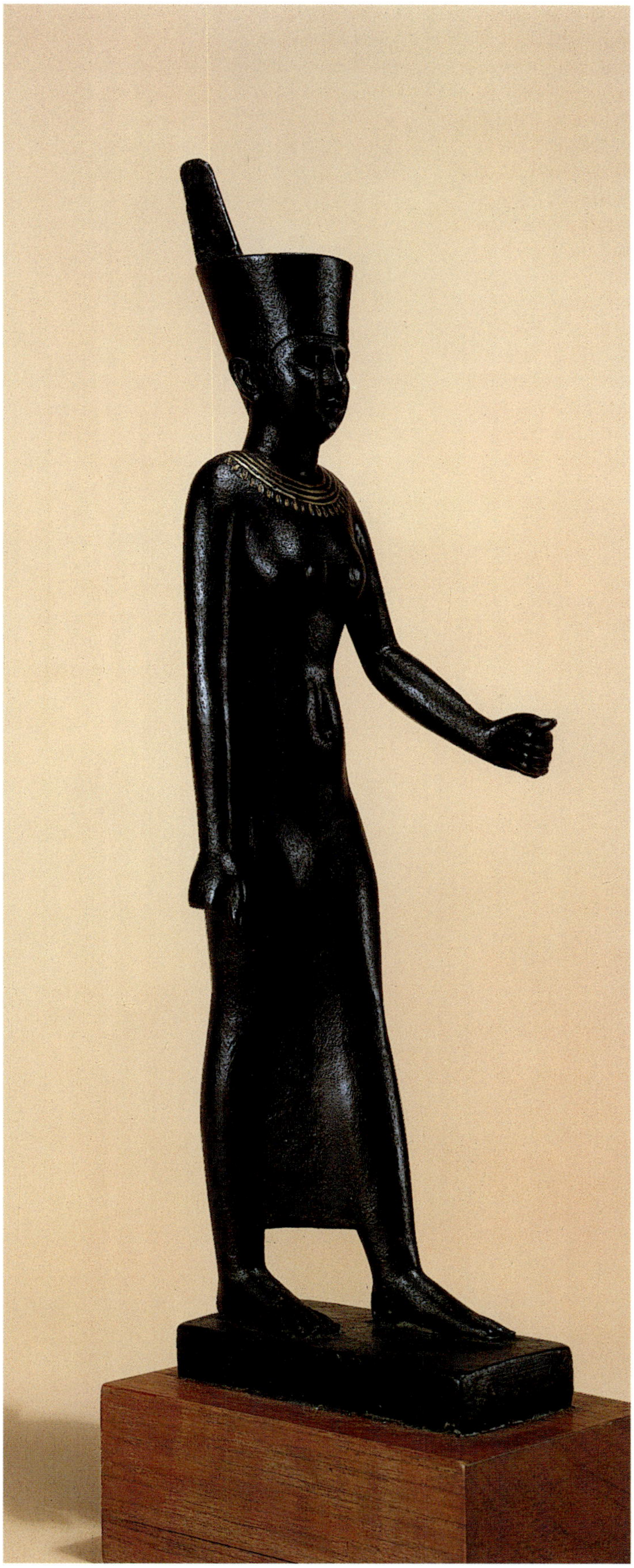

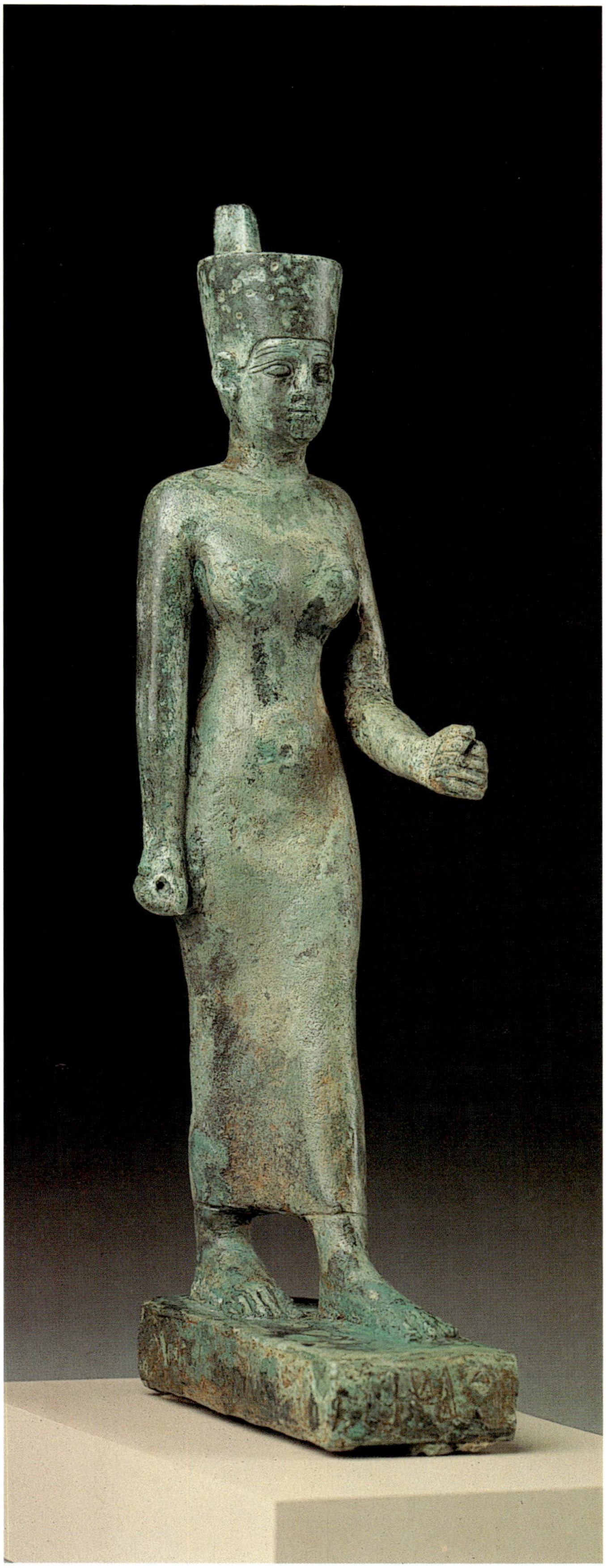

bol of sovereignty over Lower Egypt, which identified her as the protectress of the royal crown and monarchy.[9]

Neith's aggressive, warlike nature—embodied in her crossed-arrows symbol—stands in opposition to the goddess' creative nature. Her dual aspect is reflected in the epithet "Father of Fathers, Mother of Mothers" recorded in the Roman Period Esna cosmology.[10] Neith's antiquity is reflected in her vital role as creator goddess and deity of primordial floodwaters.[11] Her association with the inundation of the Nile Delta led to her early identification as mother of the crocodile god Sobek and her assimilation with the goddess Mehet-weret.[12]

One aspect of Neith's creative domain was weaving, a profession served exclusively by women in Egypt's early history.[13] Neith's maternal aspect is evidenced in her close and early association with the goddess Hathor.[14]

These two statuettes depict Neith in one of her early manifestations—a standing woman garbed in a tight-fitting, ankle-length dress.[15] Outfitted with the Red Crown,[16] she strides forward with her left foot advanced.[17] Her left, scepter-bearing arm is extended, while her right hangs pendent at her side; the latter may have held an *ankh* sign.[18] The prototype for both statuettes may be sought in models of the Twenty-sixth Dynasty, when Neith's cult enjoyed a renaissance at her capital at Sais. The Philadelphia statuette, with its inlaid gold *usekh* collar, is particularly well modeled.[19] The Cincinnati figure bears a standardized inscription on its base requesting long life, health, and happiness from the goddess for its dedicant, a man.[20] RAF/GEM

65 Bust from a statue of the goddess Sekhmet

Granodiorite; provenance unknown, presumably from Thebes; New Kingdom, Dynasty 18, reign of Amenhotep III; H: 72.3 cm; W: 51.4 cm; D: 44.7 cm

Cincinnati Art Museum. John J. Emery Fund. 1945.65

In the nearly four decades of King Amenhotep III's prosperous reign, a significant number of large-scale statues of deities were created (e.g., cat. no. 54a),[1] including hundreds of Sekhmet, both seated and standing.[2]

The present bust of Sekhmet is most probably from a seated statue on a human scale, the most common (although not the only) size for such statues.[3] The goddess's face is a combination of strong modeling and geometric detail; the latter is also found on the ears, the leonine ruff, and the striated lappet wig. Such wigs were worn by gods and goddesses, by the noble dead of both sexes (as on coffins and *shabtis),* and by mortal women, both earlier and later than Amenhotep III's time. A slot in the top of the head is presumably intended for the attachment of the sun disc with *uraeus* that is found on virtually all complete statues of Sekhmet (fig. 6). The goddess wears a broad collar necklace and a tightly fitting dress of a type (evident on complete statues) that by now was somewhat out of style for mortal women but not necessarily for goddesses. More contemporary are the floral motifs over the breasts on the shoulder straps of the dress. These are among the details that have been viewed as marks of the best sculptural workshops of the reign;[4] they have a partial prototype in the rosettes over the breasts on a sculpture of Thutmose IV's mother.[5] The necklace, dress straps, and certain other parts of the statue may once have been painted.[6]

The inscriptions on the completed Sekhmet statues from Amenhotep III's reign make statements about Sekhmet's nature and relate her to other deities and to various geographical locales.[7] Each also indicates that Amenhotep III is beloved and blessed by the manifestation of Sekhmet named.

It has often been theorized that Amenhotep III's dedication of so many statues of Sekhmet reflected dental and health problems

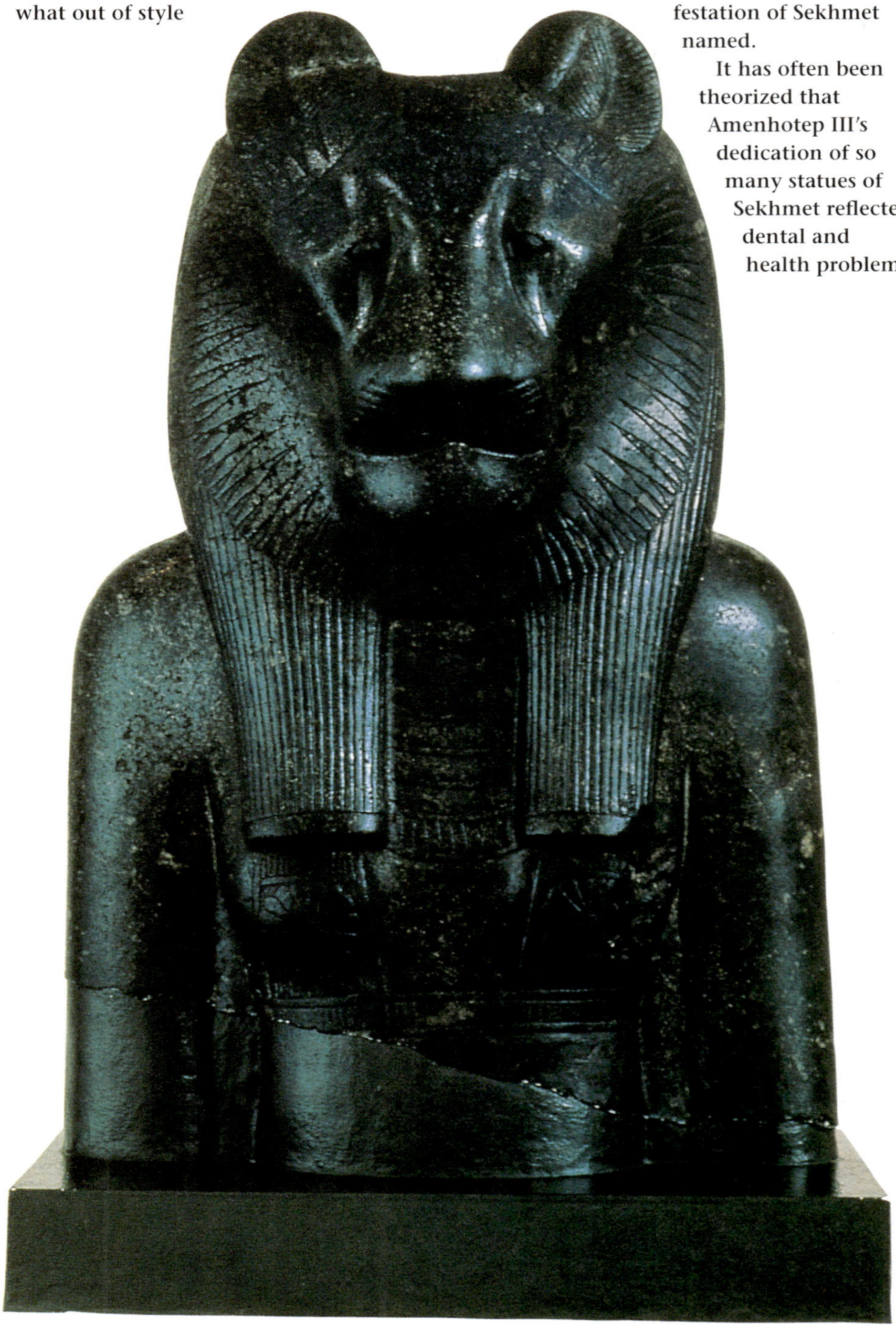

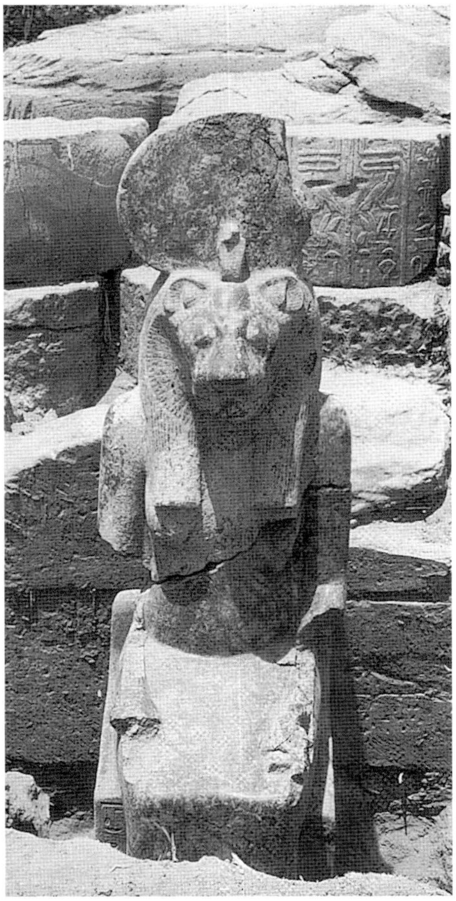

Fig. 6 A statue of Sekhmet in the Mut precinct wearing the sun disc and *uraeus*. Photo courtesy of The Brooklyn Museum.

that he hoped the goddess might alleviate.[8] Indeed, Sekhmet, who could unleash emissaries of disease and pestilence—but who could also recall them—had long since become linked to medicine and the healing arts. These arts themselves were linked to magic, the *wab* ("pure") priests of Sekhmet being a type of ritualist and medical specialist.[9] Whether or not Amenhotep III's Sekhmet statues were related to his health, however, they certainly invoked for him the goodwill of a deity whose ill-will could spell disaster.

"Sekhmet" is a word in feminine form meaning "The Powerful" or "The Power," an idea expressed by her leonine head. She was also one of the goddesses identified with the daughter and eye of the solar creator (cf. cat. nos. 41, 61, 66, and 68), who could defend the kingship, Egypt, and Maʾat (cat. no. 69). Sekhmet could also attack what she should protect and, according to myth, once abandoned Egypt, refusing to return until pacified by the gods. These aspects of the goddess, who could also take the form of a *uraeus* and has been called the "ultimate female warrior,"[10] once would have been expressed by this sculpture's now-missing *uraeus* and sun disc and by her leonine head. As one Egyptologist has noted, a number of protective goddesses are represented in a leonine form expressive of fury and the power to destroy enemies because "image and name combine in every instance to form a differently nuanced expression of one central theme, the protective power of dangerous force."[11]

The varied epithets on the Sekhmet statues make each of them a nuanced expression of this dangerous goddess' multiple manifestations and her syncretistic links with other goddesses. These epithets have been associated with others known from later temple inscriptions. The statues themselves have been viewed as the embodiment in stone of a litany invoking Sekhmet "in all her names and in all her places." It is entirely possible that once there were 365 seated and 365 standing statues (two for each day of the year), which conjured the goddess daily not to unleash her dreadful powers against the king and Egypt.[12]

Hundreds of Amenhotep III's Sekhmet statues were found in the Theban temple precinct of the goddess Mut at South Karnak (cf. cat. nos. 47, 61). Many Egyptologists now believe, however, that they were all made for the king's funerary temple on the West Bank of the Nile and were dispersed to other sites at Thebes and elsewhere beginning in the reign of Dynasty 19's King Ramesses II.[13]

Although it may be that none of Amenhotep III's Sekhmet statues stood in and around the Mut Temple during Dynasty 18, evidence of links between Sekhmet and the site exists even before his reign. One example is a statue excavated there of Hapuseneb, vizier under Hatshepsut, on which Sekhmet is one of the deities invoked.[14] Moreover, Mut was at home in Thebes by sometime in Dynasty 17.[15] By Amenhotep III's reign her precinct had long been the site of an "architectural" feature related to leonine goddesses: a sacred lake named Isheru,[16] an ancient term for a lake associated with some leonine goddesses. The Isheru could also be viewed by this time as the place to which Ra's Eye returns and within which she is appeased. Mut's Isheru, which seemingly encloses the temple (fig. 7), reinforces the idea of containment and appeasement.

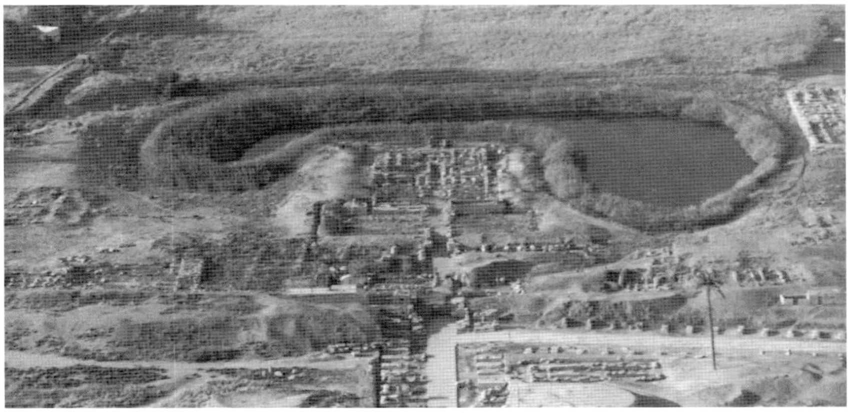

Fig. 7 Aerial view of the Mut precinct showing the Isheru surrounding the Mut Temple on three sides. Photo courtesy of The Brooklyn Museum.

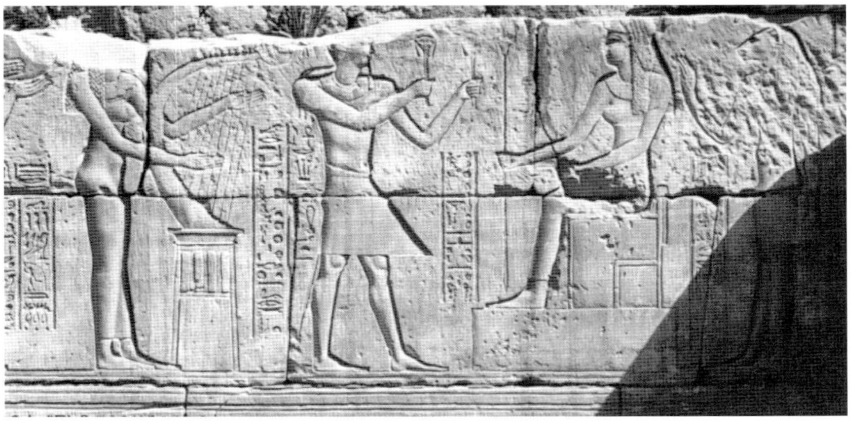

Fig. 8 Relief at the front entrance to the Mut precinct showing a king playing sistrum for Mut and Sekhmet. Photo courtesy of The Brooklyn Museum.

To be sure, it seems that Mut was only rarely called "The Eye of Ra" until the reign of Ramesses II. This may be, in part, because it was during his reign that the ritual navigation of the Isheru (related to the cult of the Eye of Ra and her return[17]) began at the Mut precinct. If Sekhmet statues had not been present in the precinct before Ramesses II's reign, the possible arrival of many of these statues of Eye of Ra Sekhmet at this time may reflect or may have enhanced Mut's identification as "Eye of Ra." But even before she gained that epithet, Mut could also be shown leonine-headed. By late Dynasty 18, however, she was occasionally called Eye of Ra and from this time, as well, could also be called a "Lady of Terror" who must be pacified.[18] Moreover, in the New Kingdom, Mut, like Hathor, is one of the few goddesses who can appear as a cat, among whose meanings is the dangerous goddess appeased; Bastet (cat. no. 68) is a later addition to this group.[19]

Rituals to appease some goddesses could entail song, music, and dance, as is apparent, for example, in a scene on the entrance to the Mut precinct built in the Ptolemaic Period (fig. 8). Here the lead musician before Mut and Sekhmet is a king whose inscription states, "I am the perfect sistrum player for the Golden Lady, who pacifies the heart of my mistress every day."[20] Such ideas date back to earlier times, as demonstrated by a hymn from the Third Intermediate Period relating to Mut's daily temple ritual, which reflects a still earlier situation. The hymn links Mut and Sekhmet in various ways, including as Eye of Ra, and refers to Mut's return and her appeasement, which includes rituals of music and dance. These rituals may have formed a more important part of the daily cult at the Mut Temple than in other temples.[21]

The close relationship between Mut and Sekhmet may also have had a "political" aspect. As Mut had become the spouse of Amen-Ra, chief god of the southern metropolis of Thebes, so Sekhmet was the spouse of Ptah, chief god of the northern metropolis of Memphis. Together the two goddesses could symbolize the unity of Egypt conceived as a duality.

Sekhmet and Mut could be described as "united" on one of Amenhotep III's Sekhmet statues,[22] but by the Ptolemaic Period they could sometimes be viewed as "two different functions of one goddess, . . . one the image of destruction and danger, the other that of joy and serenity."[23] The distinction between the two can be shown, as in figure 8, by Mut's anthropomorphic form and Sekhmet's leonine head.

To be sure, the leonine can also signify powerful protection, as in a lioness protecting her young; thus the leonine-headed Sekhmet can be represented as a mother and as nursing a child or a king. Mut's more common role, on the other hand, despite her leonine associations, is as mother of the god Khonsu and of kings, and normally she is shown as a woman rather than a lioness. Yet the potential for sudden, uncontrollable rage remained. Perhaps the ancient Egyptians would have appreciated, on more than one level, the late Frank Stockton's once widely read short story "The Lady or the Tiger." And it is certain that ancient Egyptian men could sometimes think of their wives alternatively as enraged lionesses and as gentle cats.[24] RAF

Published: *Sculpture Collection,* 22 (illus.).

66 Aegis and *menat* with head of lion-headed goddess

Gold; provenance unknown; Third Intermediate Period, probably Dynasty 22; H: 7 cm; L of *menat:* 6.8 cm

Courtesy of The Walters Art Gallery, Baltimore. 57.540

The end of the New Kingdom witnessed the introduction of a cultic ornament, known as an aegis, consisting of an *usekh,* a broad beaded collar, surmounted by the head of a deity.[1] Depicted often as an amulet, several large examples in bronze have survived that probably served as votive offerings or attachments to large-scale divine statuary.[2] As on the present example, the aegis is often combined with a secondary element: a *menat* counterpoise.[3] Like the aegis, the *menat* served a protective and regenerative function; both ornaments assured their possessor of the blessings of rebirth and eternal life in the hereafter.[4]

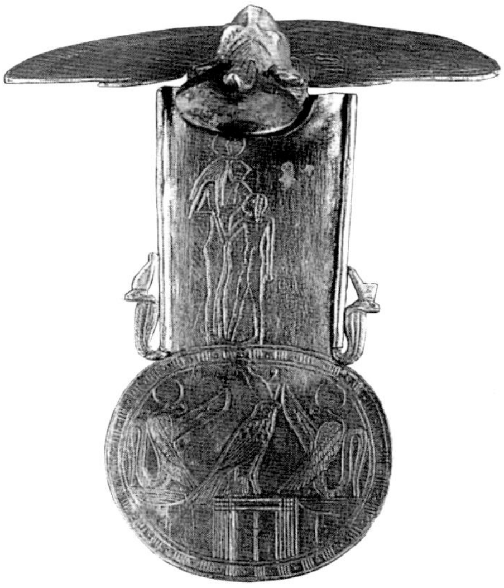

The aegis and *menat* were most frequently associated with a series of female deities, including the feline goddesses Sekhmet, Bastet, and Tefnut.[5] Because of its *uraeus* and solar disc head ornament, the present feline head is thought to represent Sekhmet, the fierce Memphite goddess who symbolized the burning heat of the sun and the sun god's vengeful eye.[6] Like other deities, Sekhmet had a dual nature. In addition to her vengeful side, she had a protective, beneficent aspect. It is to this aspect of the goddess that the present ornament appeals.[7]

The hinged *menat* counterpoise on the reverse illustrates this point. Its upper portion depicts the figure of the solar lion goddess suckling the child Horus, who is depicted below in the form of a falcon flanked by winged *uraei.* The act of suckling reflects the goddess' nourishing, life-generating capabilities.

The precise function of the present gold ornament is unclear. It may have served as a large amulet,[8] as a votive offering, or as an actual cult object used in the worship of the goddess.[9] The aegis's broad collar—with its beaded rows of dates, papyrus blossoms, leaves, and lotus blossoms, and its flanking falcon-headed terminals—accurately reproduces the jewelry ornament commonly worn by Egyptian men and women. The hinged *menat* on the ornament's reverse echoes the actual *menat* counterpoise that was worn on the back to balance the heavy necklace. On the Baltimore attachment, Sekhmet herself wears a similar *usekh* collar to which a shrine-shaped pectoral has been attached. GEM

Published: J.V. Canby, *Jewelry: Ancient to Modern* (Baltimore, 1979), 22, no. 31.

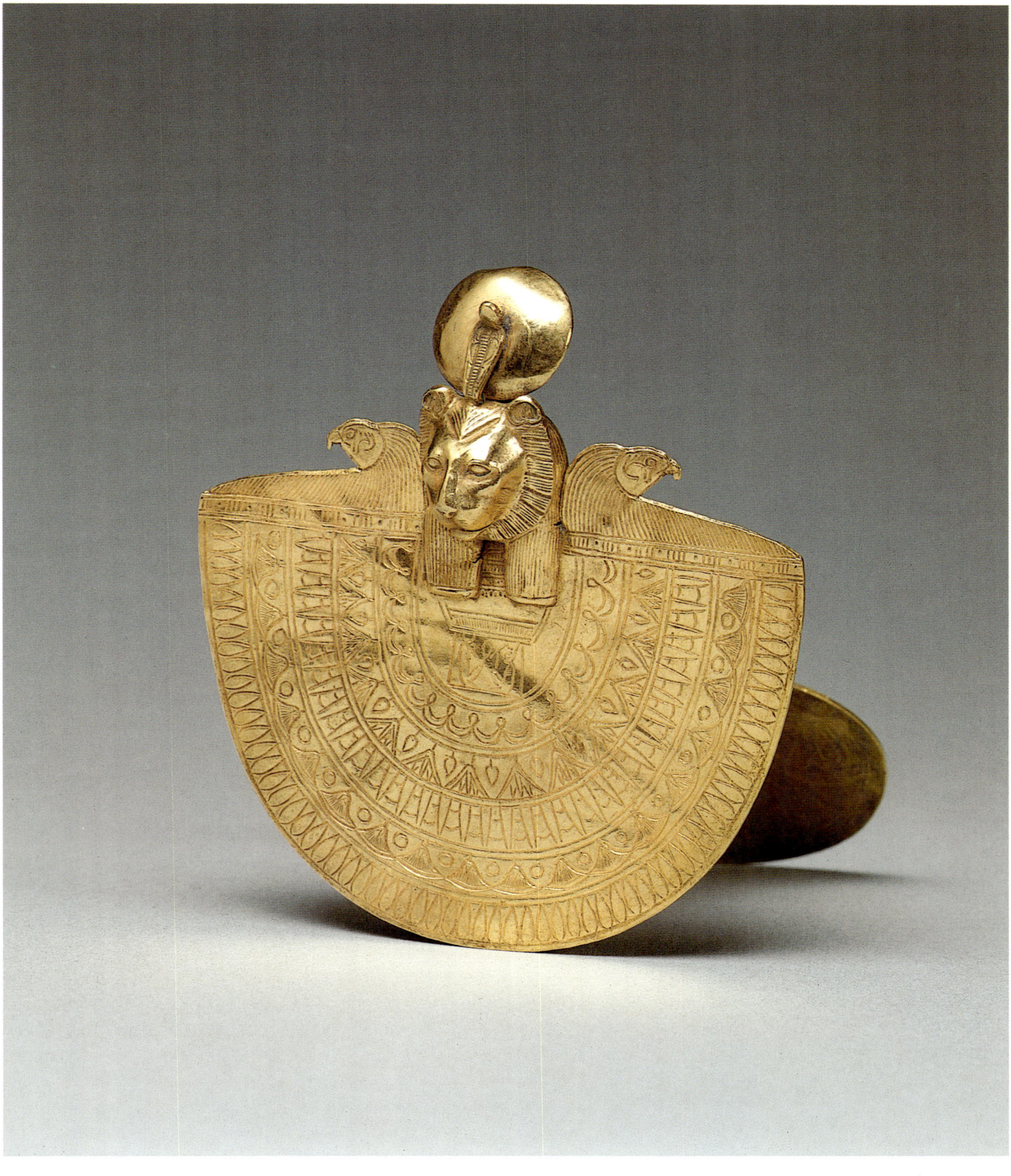

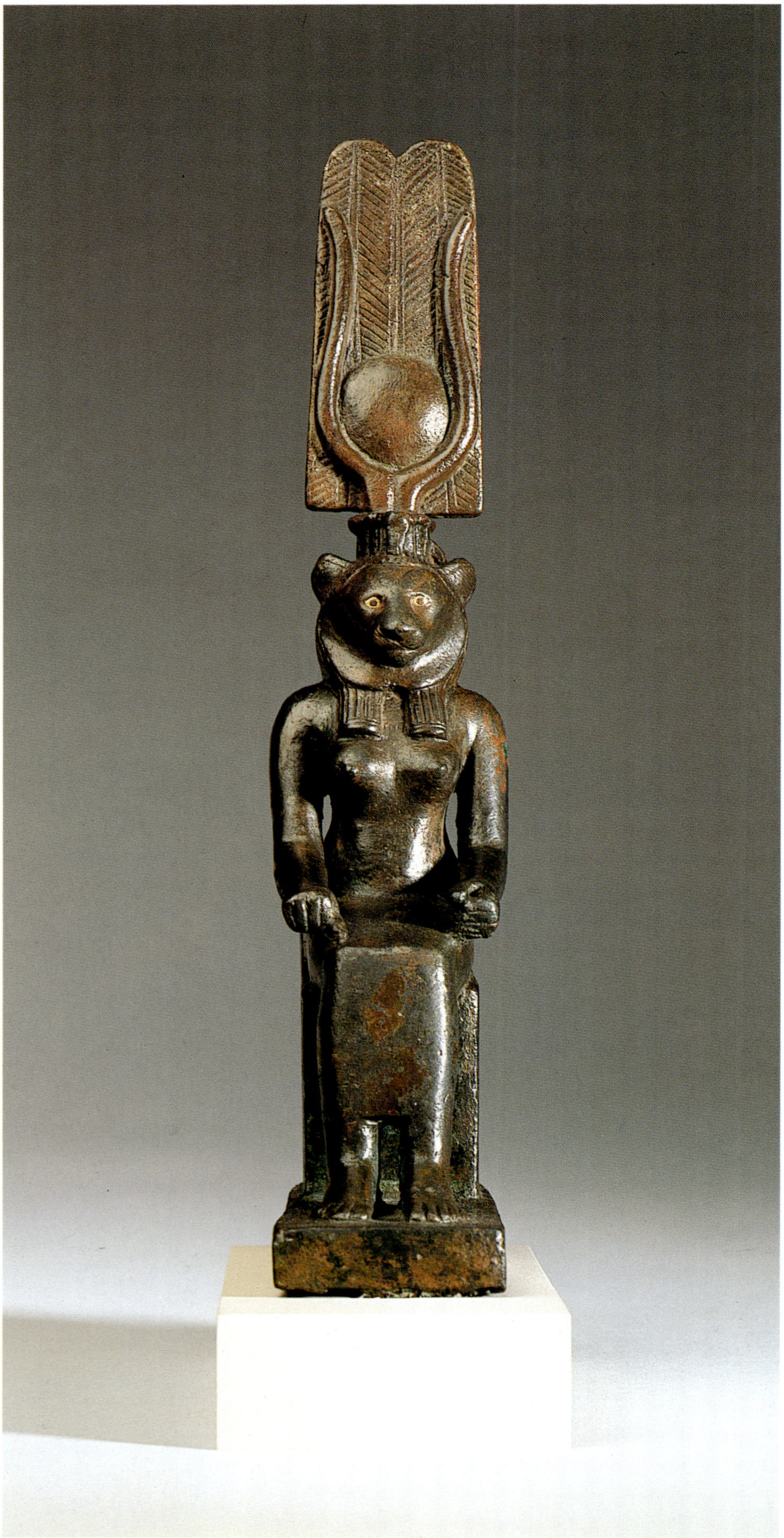

67 Statuette of lion-headed goddess

Bronze, with gold overlay in eyes; provenance unknown, reportedly from Bubastis; Late Period, Dynasty 26 or later; H: 29.7 cm; W: 5.9 cm; D: 11.4 cm

Cincinnati Art Museum. Gift of Millard F. and Edna F. Shelt. 1947.297

One of the long-lived and widespread features of ancient Egyptian art is the composite theriomorphic-anthropomorphic image that associates or identifies its subject with the other-than-human and may convey more specific messages. The most common type has a "human" body and an animal head.[1] Goddesses with a leonine head and a woman's body are known in relief as early as the Old Kingdom[2] and in three dimensions (e.g., cat. no. 65) from the New Kingdom. Yet, although a few bronze images of deities are confidently dated to the Third Intermediate Period,[3] they do not appear to have been made in large numbers until Dynasty 26 and later,[4] the period of this entry's subject.

This bronze leonine-headed goddess is depicted seated on an unadorned throne. As is often the case in Egyptian art, the transition between animal head and human body is obscured by a lappet wig, here partially hidden by a leonine ruff.[5] The goddess's left hand holds the remains of a separately made object, probably the papyrus scepter long associated with goddesses and with ideas of protection and renewal. Atop her headdress is a *modius* (platform crown) with a circlet of *uraei* (cobras) surmounted by two tall, straight plumes, cow's horns, and a solar disc. This headdress, with or without the *modius*, is associated with Hathor and with other goddesses and queens of the New Kingdom and later.[6]

One side of the statue's base bears the badly damaged remains of an inscription. Known to me through a copy,[7] it appears to preserve parts of a genealogy but, unfortunately, not the name of the deity. This makes a certain identification of the goddess problematic: almost forty goddesses can be associated with the leonine; a leonine head is a "mark of the forces of destruction."[8] Indeed, as noted in a publication of a similar bronze whose inscription identifies it as the goddess Mut (cf. cat. no. 61), the names of some goddesses connected with the leonine—Sekhmet ("The Powerful"), Matit ("The Dismemberer"), Mehit ("The Seizer"), and Pasht (Pakhet: "The Mangler")—reflect the terror they could inspire.[9] Because the present bronze is reportedly from Bubastis, one might suspect that it represents Bastet, known to be shown with a lioness's head from the Old Kingdom onward, even after the Third Intermediate Period when she began to appear cat-headed or as a cat (cat. no. 68). However, the provenance of Bubastis is hardly certain.

The figure of Mut mentioned above demonstrates that not all seated, bronze, leonine-headed goddesses with a sun disc or the type of crown worn by this figure depict Wadjet, as once proposed. The majority, however, appear to do so,[10] probably including the present figure.

Wadjet, tutelary deity of Lower Egypt, is normally shown as a *uraeus*. The reason usually given for her leonine-headed appearance in Late Period bronzes is that she is one of the goddesses identified with the Eye of Ra, some of whom had long been associated with the leonine[11] (cf. cat. nos. 41, 61, 65, 66, and 68). The eye of the solar creator—the first female being in the ordered universe—could be viewed in a number of ways, some of the ideas about her being present as early as the Middle Kingdom. She could be dangerous and destructive, attributes often expressed by leonine forms, or beneficent and contented, aspects eventually represented by feline forms. Reflecting the ancient Egyptians' male-oriented and particularly dualistic view of the female, either mortal or divine, myths of the goddess[12] underscore her importance as a protector of the king, Egypt, and the ordered universe. Yet, they also emphasize her ability to unleash her terrible powers against, or to abandon, that which she should protect.

In ancient Egypt, natural phenomena normally were perceived as deities and were associated with the divine. The annual movement of the sun southward and its return northward came to be considered as both the death and the rebirth of the sun god, and the departure of the furious goddess and her return when appeased. That return, at the Egyptian New Year, was accompanied by the revivifying flood of the Nile—also sometimes identified with the goddess. The flood (perhaps like water breaking at childbirth) signaled the annual rebirth of the sun from the Eye, now his mother. As his spouse, the Eye could also be the cooling water that tempered the sun's burning but vital heat.

Symbols can have several layers of meaning, and the leonine form of the figure is more indicative of protective power than of uncontrolled rage. Moreover, many bronzes of this type are containers for mummified ichneumons,[13] animals associated with a form of Horus identified as son of the sun, his seeing, daytime eye, and his power to defend against the enemies of order. Wadjet, by means imperfectly understood, came to be associated with the child Horus as protective "mother" and/or "nurse."[14] RAF

68 a Bastet cat

Bronze; provenance unknown;
Late Period, Dynasty 26; H: 26.3 cm

The Detroit Institute of Arts. Gift of Mrs. Lillian Henkel Haass and Miss Constance Haass. 31.72

68 b Standing figure of Bastet

Bronze; provenance unknown;
said to have been found at Bubastis;
Late Period, Dynasty 26 or later;
H: 12.5 cm

Cincinnati Art Museum. Gift of Millard F. and Edna F. Shelt. 1947.14

The domesticated female cat in ancient Egypt[1] was noted for her fecundity, and her seated image was long associated with the notion of fertility and sexuality in women.[2] It is not surprising, then, that the cat in its female form ultimately achieved divine status as the embodiment of several goddesses, one of whom was Bastet (literally, "she of Bast")[3], who was known and revered for her procreative powers.[4]

Despite her longstanding prominence in ancient Egypt, Bastet's origins remain obscure.[5] Her name, derived from the

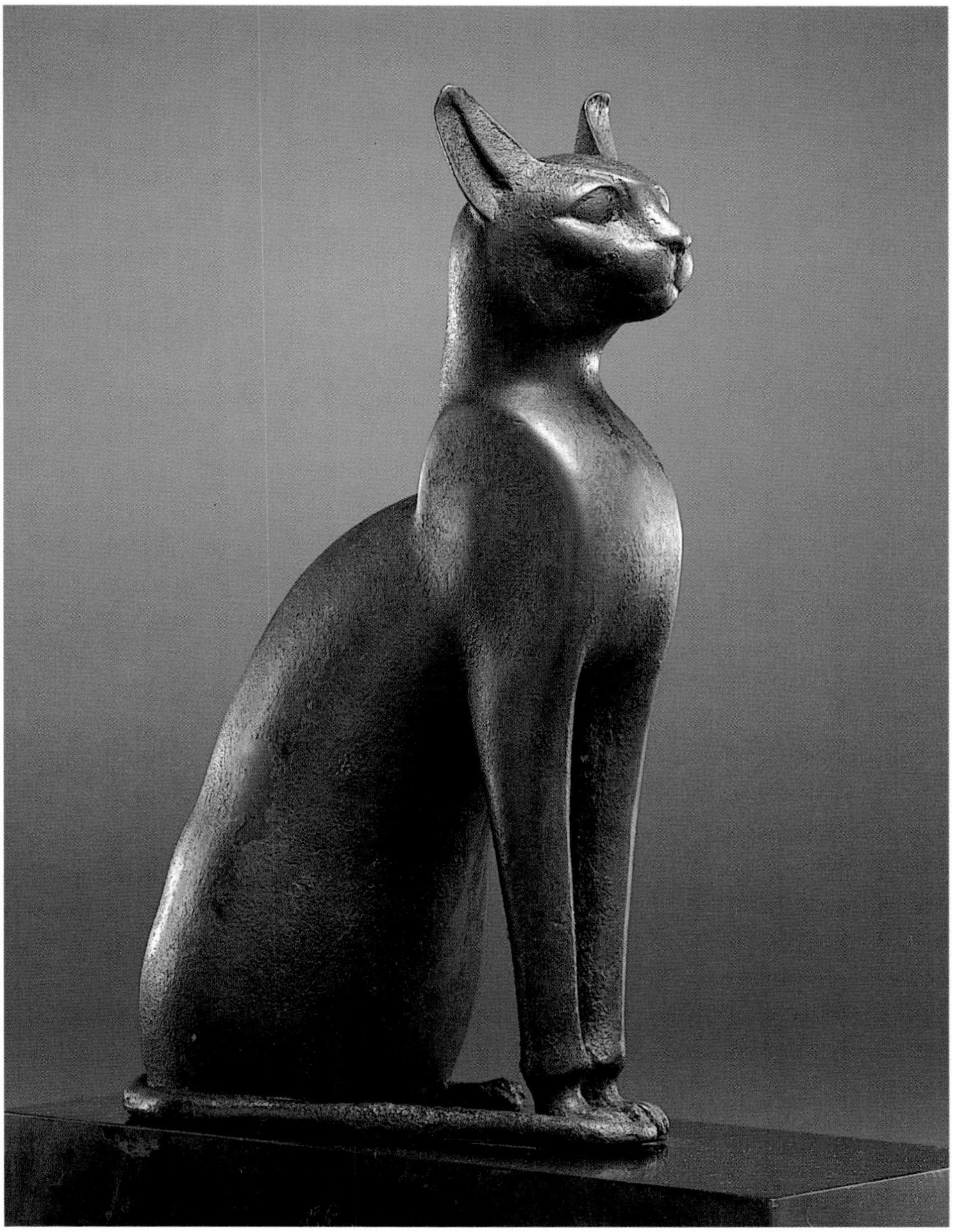

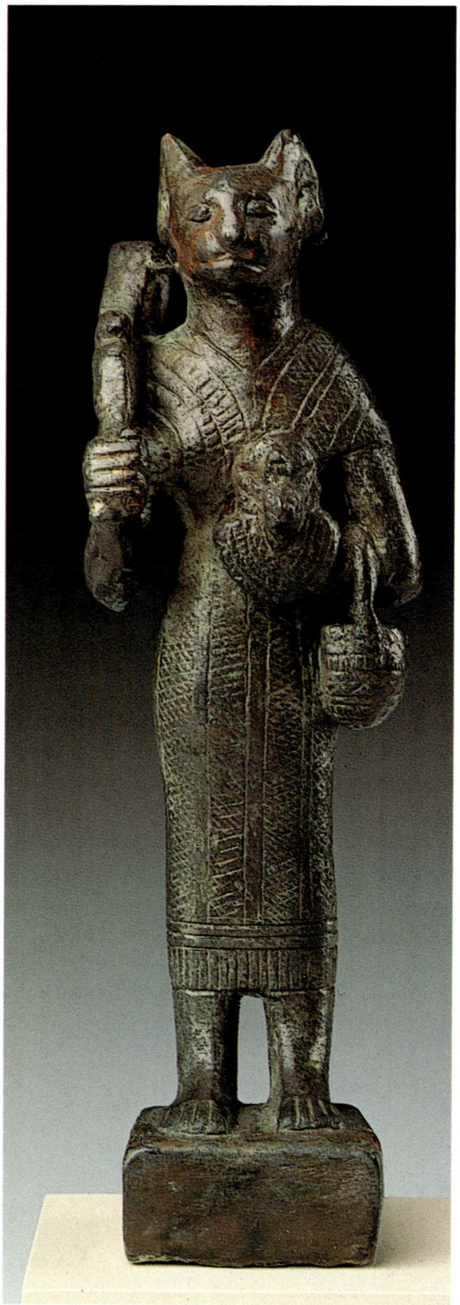

goddess's cult center at Bubastis (Bast in ancient Egyptian) in the western delta, is attested early in Egypt's Dynastic history. Her cult was an ancient one; mention of a "Priest of Bastet" occurs on the fragment of an inscribed bowl dating to the Second Dynasty.[6]

By the Old Kingdom, Bastet was closely linked with the Egyptian monarchy. The Pyramid Texts invoke Bastet as the "mother and nurse of the king." She is, in fact, one of only two goddesses mentioned on Khafra's valley temple at Giza. Bastet's association with royalty later reached a peak with the Libyan kings of the Twenty-second Dynasty, who elevated Bastet to a position of prominence at Bubastis.[7] It was also in this general period of time that Bastet is first known to have been represented as a cat.

While revered for her beneficent, procreative powers, Bastet's appeal to the Egyptian monarchy probably stemmed from her aggressive, militant nature. The Eighteenth Dynasty pharaoh Sety I, for example, described himself as "valiant in the very heart of the fray, a Bastet terrible in combat."[8] The dual nature of the goddess finds reflection in Bastet's close association with the goddess Sekhmet (cat. no. 65), who may be understood to represent the feline goddess's fierce or violent side.[9] In contrast to her counterpart Sekhmet, Bastet represented the life-giving rather than the destructive powers of the sun. The distinction between the two deities is made clear in a late text from the temple of Philae; there Hathor is referred to as "gracious or peaceful as Bastet and raging as Sekhmet."[10] In the fifth century B.C., Bastet's festival at Bubastis was described as a jubilant one, accompanied by singing, dancing, and unrestrained drinking.[11]

These two bronze figurines depict Bastet in two of her primary manifestations beginning in the Third Intermediate Period—as a cat-headed female and as a seated cat. The seated cat from Detroit shows her poised—in a manner befitting the goddess—in a stately, dignified manner with head erect and front legs together. With her graceful contour and lustrous finish, she represents one of the finest and most elegant of surviving bronze statuettes of the goddess. Many depictions of the sacred cat show it heavily decorated—with patterned gold inlay and jewelry: gold rings through the ears and nose, collars with *udjat* eye amulets and scarab pendents, and scarab-shaped forehead ornaments.[12] The Detroit Bastet, by contrast, is distinguished by her unadorned elegance. As for her function, the Detroit cat's diminutive size suggests that she was intended as a votive offering in a temple or household shrine of the goddess. Other larger, similarly posed cat statuettes in wood or bronze served alternately as coffins for cat mummies.[13]

The votive bronze in Cincinnati depicts Bastet as a feline-headed woman dressed in a tight-knit, clinging robe.[14] As the elaborate hatched vertical patterns on her garment indicate, she wears the long, fringed dress of striped material characteristic of Late Period representations of the goddess.[15] As in depictions of the sacred cat, she is adorned with a pair of plain hoop earrings. (The original bronze earring is still in place in the left ear.) In typical fashion, Bastet carries a pair of cultic implements in either paw: an aegis in the left paw and a Hathor-headed sistrum in the right.[16] The sistrum, originally an emblem of the goddess Hathor (cat. no. 35b), underscores Bastet's association with the Lady of Dendera. Since the sistrum served to pacify Hathor in cultic ritual, its association with Bastet may be taken as reference to the goddess's fearsome aspect, which required appeasement.[17] The aegis (cat. no. 66) is frequently associated with Bastet; its beaded collar is here surmounted by the cat head of Bastet herself equipped with solar disc. The empty round-bottomed basket that Bastet carries on her left arm is a typical attribute of the goddess. The presence of kittens in some renderings of these containers reveals that the basket served as a carrier for Bastet's sacred animals.[18] Numerous votive offerings and amulets of Bastet depict her accompanied by kittens, an obvious allusion to the goddess's fecundity.[19] GEM

Published: *The Detroit Institute of Arts: A Visitor's Guide* (Detroit, 1995), 108.

69 Maat

Bronze; provenance unknown;
Late Period, probably Dynasty 26;
H: 22.8 cm; W without base: 5 cm

Museum of Art, Rhode Island School of Design, Providence. Helen M. Danforth Fund. 1989.088

Maat occupied a relatively unique position among the many female deities in the Egyptian pantheon.[1] Unlike other Egyptian divinities, her character was not so much that of a goddess but of an abstract entity. Maat was the moderator of all things in the universe, the source of equilibrium in the natural realm. She represented the deified concept of world order, balance, and harmony. Her powers extended beyond the realm of the purely cosmic; she regulated not only the seasons and the movement of the stars but relations between the gods and men. Consequently, she served as the embodiment of truth, justice, and moral integrity.[2] As mortal representative and spokesman of the gods, it was, in fact, the king who had the responsibility to maintain Maat and preserve Egypt's social order.[3]

> Ra has placed the king on the earth of the living for forever and eternity to judge humanity and to pacify the gods, to realize *Maat* (Right) and to annihilate Wrong. He gives divine offerings to the gods. . . .[4]

Not surprisingly, the goddess Maat is often depicted in a direct (and supportive) relationship with the king;[5] her image was the supreme offering given by the pharaoh to the gods. On temple reliefs, the king is often shown in the ritual act of presenting a small image of Maat to the temple deity (fig. 9).[6]

In the New Kingdom, several prominent royal women were associated with Maat in an effort to validate their authority. Queen Tiye, wife of Amenhotep III, was represented standing alongside the king as the personification of Maat.[7] As reigning monarch, Hatshepsut adopted the prenomen Maatkara ("Maat is the *ka* of Ra"); on one of her colossal kneeling figures in her temple at Deir el-Bahri, she elected to have herself described as offering up Maat to Amen.[8] Likewise, Nefertiti, wife of Akhenaten, was represented offering Maat to Amen.[9] In adoption of the kingly custom, the Divine Wife of Amen was also depicted presenting the image of Maat before the god.[10]

This statuette may have served as such a votive offering in a royal presentation.[11] Maat is depicted in canonical pose—squatting with her hands on her knees, an ostrich feather (her attribute) perched atop her head. (The ostrich feather, in fact, served as the hieroglyph for the word *maat*.) She wears the striated, tripartite wig conventional for female deities. Her adornment consists of a broad collar and a plain head fillet.

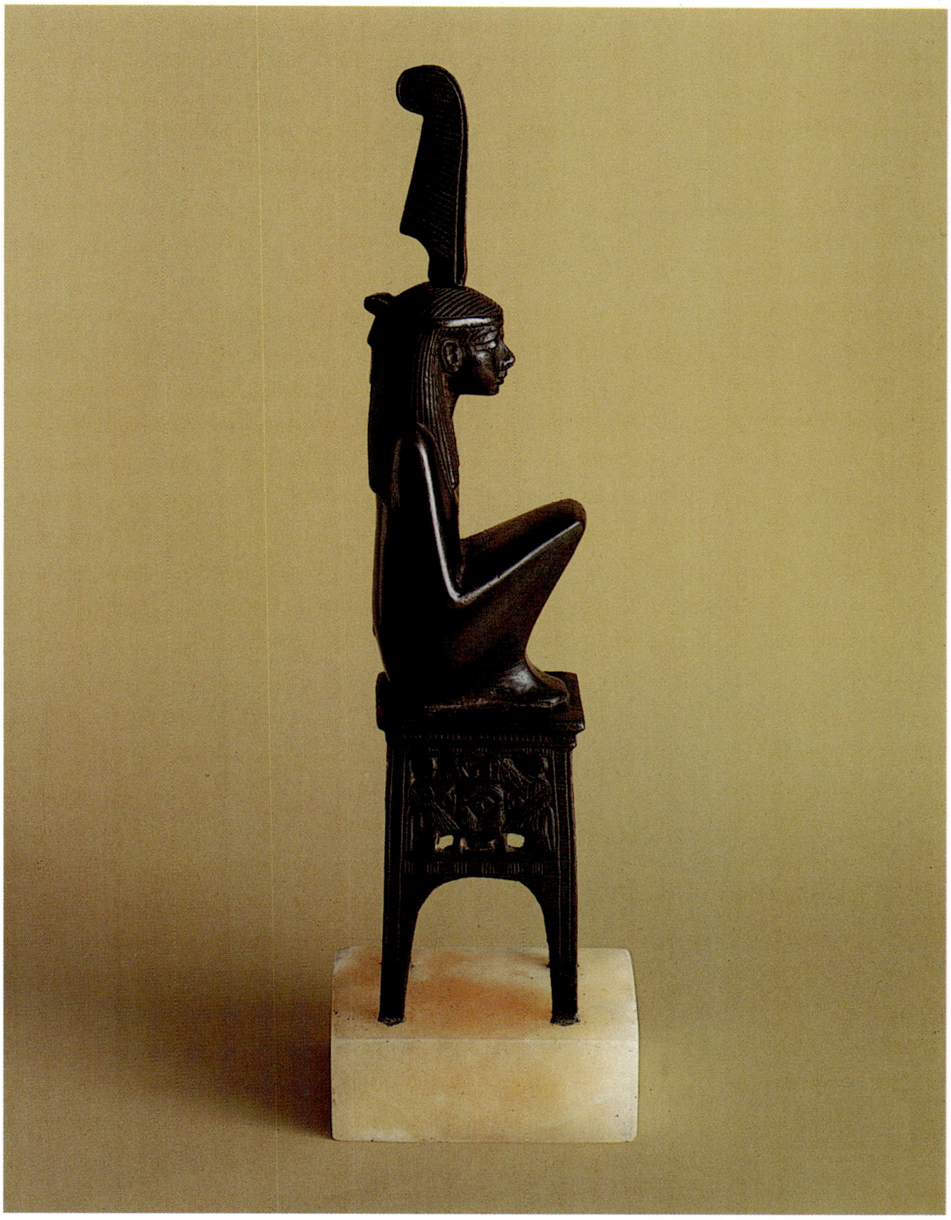

A conspicuous and integral feature of the statuette is its supporting openwork altar, which is decorated on both sides with the image of a Hathor mask with *naos* headdress on a pedestal flanked by winged solar *uraei*.[12] The two short ends of the altar bear royal cartouches flanked by solar *uraei*. These were originally inscribed with the name of the king in whose reign the statuette was probably produced; his name, unfortunately, has been erased, possibly by a later king.[13]

GEM

Published: F.A. Friedman, *Rhode Island School of Design. Museum Notes* 77, no. 1 (1990): 10.

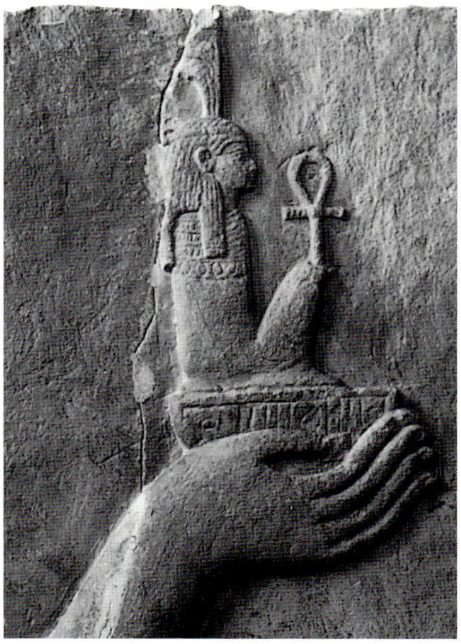

Fig. 9 Figure of Maat. Detail from relief depicting king offering Maat to Thoth. 1945.64. Photo courtesy of the Cincinnati Art Museum.

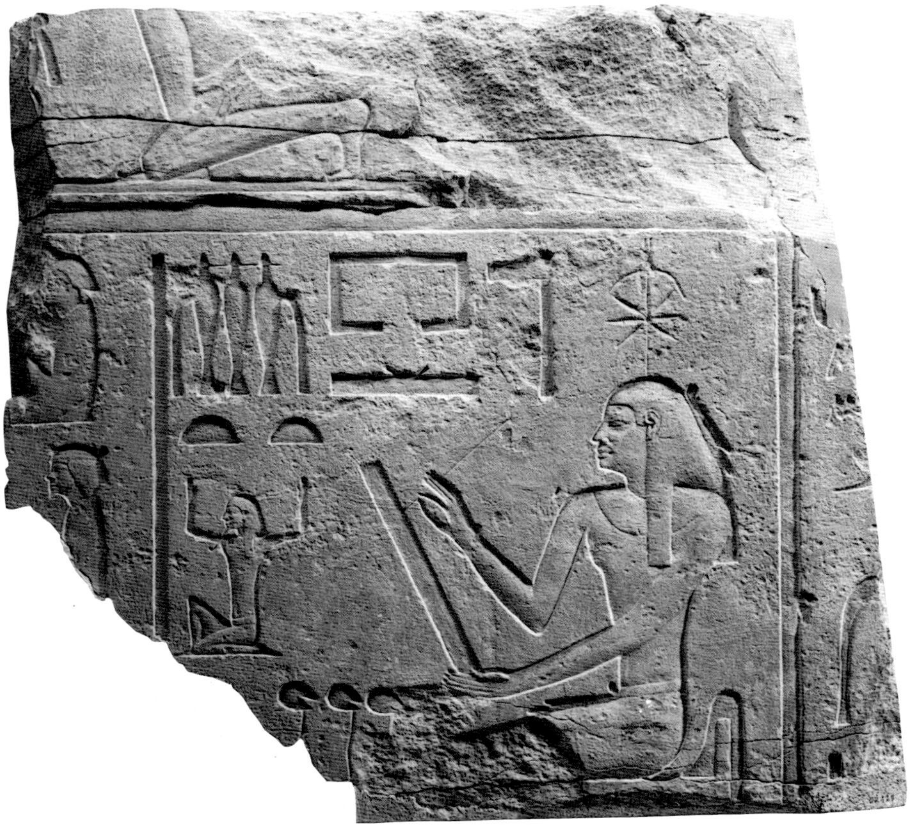

70 Relief of the goddess Seshat

Limestone; excavated at Lisht, Pyramid Temple of King Senusert I; Middle Kingdom, Dynasty 12, reign of Senusert I; L: 59 cm; H: 52.5 cm

The Brooklyn Museum. Charles Edwin Wilbour Fund. 52.129

Although rather infrequently depicted in art, the goddess Seshat, patroness of writing and measurement, played a significant role in the Egyptian divine pantheon.[1] As the goddess of records, she was responsible for the oversight of royal accounts and kingly annals; in the latter capacity, she kept count of regnal years and royal jubilees. From Ramesside times forward, Seshat participated in the ritual recording of the king's name on the leaves of the *jšd* (Persea?) tree.[2] In this task, she used the measuring stick with which she is often depicted: a notched palm branch (the sign for "years") terminating (in the New Kingdom and beyond) in a tadpole (the number 100,000) atop the symbol for eternity.

Unlike most other female deities, there is little evidence for the existence of a local cult to Seshat.[3] As a divine symbol, she occurs at the beginning of Egypt's dynastic history; as early as the Second Dynasty, she assists King Khasekhemwy in the hammering of boundary poles in the temple foundation ritual of the "stretching of the cord."[4] By the Old Kingdom, Seshat was known as the "Mistress of Builders"; architects numbered among the goddess's divine attendants.[5]

Seshat's role in the divine hierarchy raises interesting speculation about the education of women in ancient Egyptian society. While her name denotes a female scribe, there is no evidence that women ever fulfilled this role professionally in the ancient Egyptian bureaucracy.[6] This does not preclude the fact that certain women of rank and social standing may well have acquired literacy; the evidence to support this assumption, however, is unfortunately lacking.[7]

In this wall-relief fragment, which comes from the funerary temple of King Senusert I,[8] the goddess Seshat is shown in the act of recording prisoners and booty taken by Senusert during his military campaigns. The role fulfilled by the goddess is an old one. Its prototype may be found in the reliefs of the Fifth Dynasty funerary complex of King Sahura; there the goddess records herds of domestic animals (cattle, sheep, goats, and donkeys) seized as booty from Libyan tribes.[9]

On the present relief the goddess sits, surrounded by kneeling and squatting captives, before a papyrus roll, entering her accounts for the king with a long-handled brush. The hieroglyphs for "one million" and "three thousand" are recorded above her; these probably formed part of the enumeration of prisoners and tribute acquired by the king. Seshat is entitled "The One Foremost in the House of Divine Writings"—a reference to her long-standing role as scribe of divine books and patroness of the House of Life, where sacred books were written.[10] She wears her conventional headdress, consisting of a headband with a seven-pointed star or rosette surmounted by a moon-shaped symbol or pair of horns. This head ornament and her long panther-skin robe served as her primary identifying features.[11]

The fragment originally formed part of a much larger relief illustrating King Senusert smiting his enemies; it was once brightly colored, although no trace of pigment survives.[12] GEM

Published: Hayes, *Scepter,* 1: 188 and 189, fig. 115; James, *Corpus,* 1: no. 92 and pl. 33 (drawings of text); Fazzini, *Images,* no. 36a; Cooney, *Five Years,* 25, no. 28; M. Eaton-Krauss, in *Aegyptische Kunst aus dem Brooklyn Museum,* exh. cat., Ägyptisches Museum (Berlin, 1978), no. 19; J. Quaegebeur, in H. De Meulenaere et al., *Egypte Eternelle: Chefs d'oeuvre du Brooklyn Museum,* exh. cat. Organized by the Service de la Diffusion des Arts du Ministère de la Culture, Belgium (Brussels, 1976), 47, no. 19.

71 Statuette of cobra goddess

Limestone; provenance unknown, possibly from Buto; Late Period, Dynasty 26, reign of Psamtik I; H: 43 cm; W: 11 cm; D: 28 cm

The University of Pennsylvania Museum of Archaeology and Anthropology, Philadelphia. 57-18-1

The focus of the statue is a human-headed cobra goddess, the upper part of whose body is erect, while its lower part is in coils upon a rectangular base.[1] The back is in the form of a stela decorated in raised relief that may never have been completed. An inscription on both sides of the piece, between the figure and the back, includes the name of the second pharaoh of Dynasty 26, Psamtik I.

Framing the face of the female figure is a tripartite wig with an equal portion of tresses on either side, while the third falls down the back. She has plastic eyebrows that are squared off at the end and cosmetic lines that extend beyond the end of the eye, almost like narrow slits. She wears a broad collar, the horizontal strands of which parallel the markings of the underside of the serpent's hood. Upon her head is a composite crown consisting of a diadem with encircling *uraei*, a sun disc set within upraised horns, and two feathers side by side. Such headgear is usually associated with queens as well as goddesses—Hathor in particular and, less often, Isis.[2]

Anthropomorphic deities with such regalia as that depicted here appear fairly frequently on votive sculptures and reliefs.[3] Inscriptions on the votive reliefs often identify the image either as the goddess Meretseger (a Mistress of the West, who protected and aided her worshippers and offered help and nourishment to the deceased)[4] or the goddess Renenutet (a deity associated with the harvest, who could also provide aid and nursing to those who offered to her).[5] Ordinarily, images of these two goddesses and stelae depicting them are not uncommon as votive objects dedicated in temples by private citizens, placed in small shrines, or occasionally kept at home. Artifacts made with or in the image of these goddesses can have royal inscriptions, although such examples may not be as common as those dedicated by private citizens.[6] Both of these deities have associations with each other and with several other goddesses including Hathor and Isis. It may be more usual to find the latter two deities (especially Hathor) represented as human-headed serpents, but such iconography is also known for Meretseger and less so for Renenutet.[7]

The area between the serpent and the back of the stela is decorated with both raised and sunk relief of a fairly low quality. At the top, carved in moderately detailed raised relief—again, of rather poor workmanship—is a vulture whose outspread wings extend downward on each side and reach the level of the *uraeus modius*. In each of its claws are the *shen* sign, meaning "infinity," and a feather. A similar image is often depicted on the ceilings of temples and royal tombs from the New Kingdom onward. It also appears on the upper parts of royal furniture of the same period.[8] It is perhaps only coincidental that the image of the vulture (rendered in two dimensions on the upper part of the composition) and that of the cobra in three dimensions are also the representations of the tutelary goddesses of ancient Egypt, Nekhbet and Wadjyt.

These two divinities appear in low sunk relief on either side of the serpent figure, in the area between the snake and the back stela. On the serpent's left side are three lines of hieroglyphs in sunk relief, of which only the uppermost has register lines. The quality of the carving is mediocre, and the text contains some grammatical peculiarities;[9] such a situation would not be unusual in a sculpted piece of this period. The inscription is a quotation by the goddess Wadjyt, pictured below, who is referred to as the "Mistress of Pe and Dep,[10] who has given all life, endurance, and dominion, like Ra forever, to Wahibra [the birth name of the king]." Underneath the text is a representation in sunk relief of the serpent goddess who wears the Red Crown of Lower Egypt. She is coiled on a basket that "floats" above the hieroglyph representing a cluster of papyrus, plants symbolizing Lower Egypt, the area with which Wadjyt was associated. To the left of the plant is a falcon with double plumes, below which is a figure of a striking man. It is possible that this grouping represents one of the five names of the king, "The Horus of Gold, Kenu (The Valiant One),"[11] but it could simply be a reference to the falcon deity—"Valiant Horus"—whose epithets and image appear on the back stela.

On the serpent's right side is a corresponding text of the speech of the tutelary deity of Upper Egypt, Nekhbet, whose image is below the inscription. Only two lines of text appear here, and the crudity of carving suggests haste in the preparation. Both lines have registers and can be translated: "Words said by Nekhbet who has given all life, endurance, and prosperity, like Ra forever, to the Son of Ra, Psamtik."[12] Like her counterpart on the other side, the goddess is fully animal in form and is perched upon a basket. The vulture goddess Nekhbet wears the *atef* crown rather than the more common White Crown of Upper Egypt, the latter being more usual in paired representations such as that in this example.[13] Below the goddess is a hieroglyph representing a cluster of plants, which should be lotuses (or lilies), signifying Upper Egypt but which, in actuality, resemble a simplified form of the sign on the other side.[14]

The stela at the back is decorated in raised relief, and the quality of the carving is mediocre. The lack of many fine inner details as well as the absence of any decoration on the lower half of the stela suggests that it was never completed. That the whole piece was left in an "unfinished" state is supported by the cursory carving and peculiarities of the horizontal inscription on the sides of the serpent and the accompanying vertical sunk relief designating the tutelary goddesses of Egypt. On the upper part of the rounded top stela, a winged sun disc appears with a *uraeus* on either side of the orb. The desig-

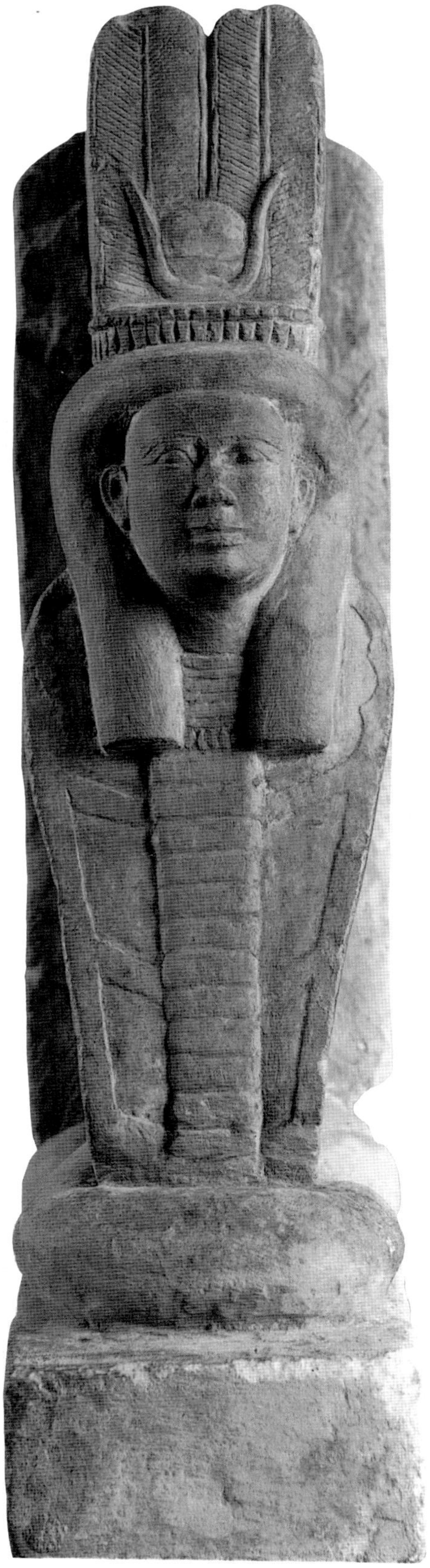

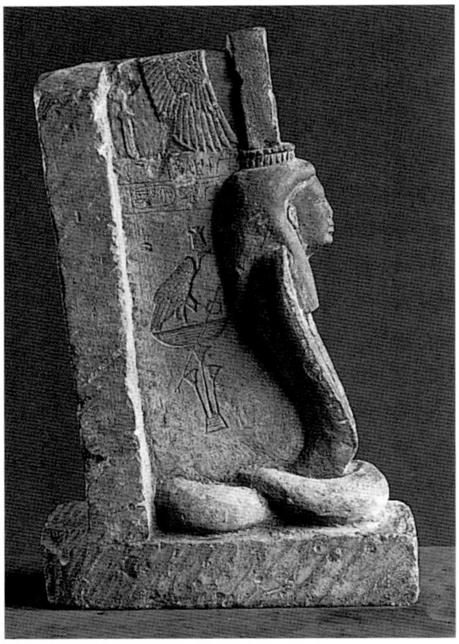

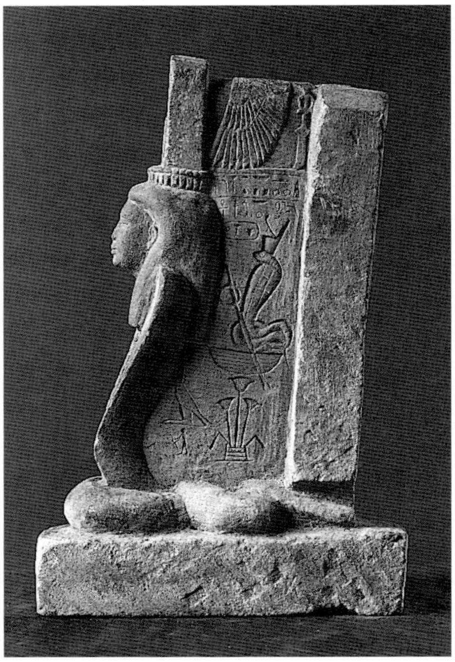

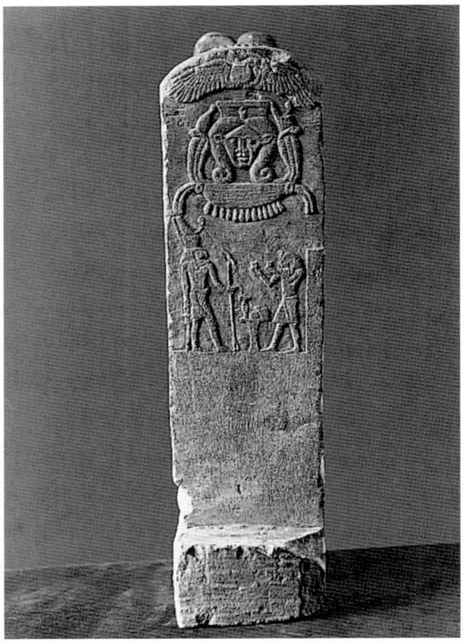

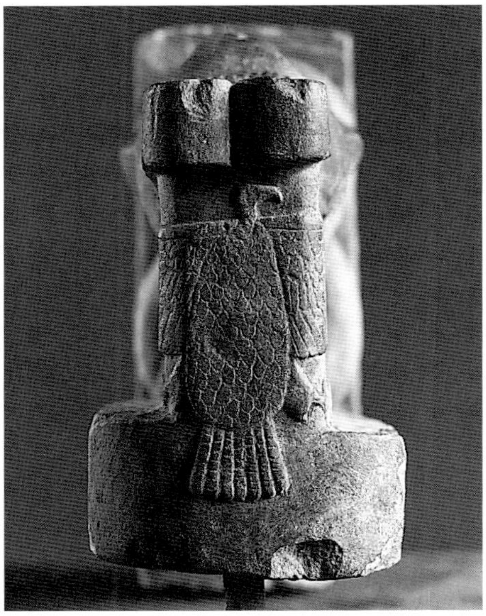

nation of the Behdedite, a common epithet of Horus of Edfu, is carved in sunk relief below the end of each wing.[15] The image of Hathor—a human head with bovine ears—is below the disc, and twin *uraei,* one on each side, wear crowns representing Upper and Lower Egypt (Nekhbet and Wadjyt respectively).[16] These images are above the hieroglyph for gold, perhaps indicating Hathor's epithet, "The Golden One."[17] The serpent at the top of her head may represent the *uraeus* ordinarily projecting from the forehead of Hathor and other deities.[18]

The central portion of the stela is devoted to a scene depicting the pharaoh, identified by the inscriptions on the side as Psamtik I, making an offering to a deity. Between the king and the god is a table with more offerings. The god is in composite form, with a human body and the head of a falcon. He wears the double crown of Upper and Lower Egypt and holds a *was* scepter in his left hand and an *ankh* in his right. Considering the imagery, iconography, and the designation at the top of the stela, the deity is likely to be Horus.[19]

While this object has its share of unusual features, the unfinished state and its late date may account for some of these details. The uneven quality and care given to different parts of the figure suggest that several hands may have contributed to the final product and that perhaps some time may have elapsed during the different phases of work (the serpent may well represent the work of the original sculptor, while areas of the crown and the relief on the remainder may be a later, secondary recarving). No provenance is known for the sculpture, but the accession notes suggest that it may have originated from Buto. Such a conclusion may be unlikely, considering that the low quality of carving on the stela's back is somewhat similar to that found on contemporary Saite reliefs at Karnak.[20] DPS

Afterlife

72 Woman's burial assemblage

Bronze, stone, terracotta, faience, wood, shell; excavated at Abydos, Cemetery D, Tomb D229; Third Intermediate Period, Dynasty 21; see below for pertinent dimensions

Cincinnati Art Museum. Gift of the Egypt Exploration Society.

a terracotta feminoform vase (H: 23 cm) 1914.336
b terracotta female figurine (H: 17.5 cm) 1914.337
c alabaster kohl pot (H: 6.7 cm) 1914.340
d bronze kohl stick, 1914.378
e alabaster cup (H: 10 cm) 1914.341
f cosmetic shell, 1914.396
g bronze model of shell (D: 6.2 cm) 1914.380
h faience *ushabti*, 1914.342
i string of mussel and cowrie shells, 1914.348
j and k two strands of bronze and faience amulets and pendents, 1914.349, 355–57, 362–66, 389
l bronze figurine of Nefertum (H: 11.5 cm) 1914.379
m carnelian earrings, 1914.359–60
n and o faience scarabs, 1914.354, 361
p bronze tweezers, 1914.382
q wooden spindle shaft, 1914.397

The present burial grouping comes from a shaft tomb with a rock-cut chamber at Abydos dating to Dynasty 21. Like other chamber tombs from the cemetery, this one was plundered in antiquity; consequently the burial itself was not found intact.[1]

Even though the tomb has been robbed of its more precious belongings,[2] the surviving objects give a general idea of the more common personal items included in the burial inventory of an upper-middle-class Egyptian woman of the Third Intermediate Period. These include a wooden headrest,[3] a set of pottery vessels,[4] an alabaster cup, a wooden spindle, and a molded faience *shabti*. Cosmetic items include an alabaster kohl pot with bronze applicator, several pairs of bronze tweezers, and a mussel shell, which proba-

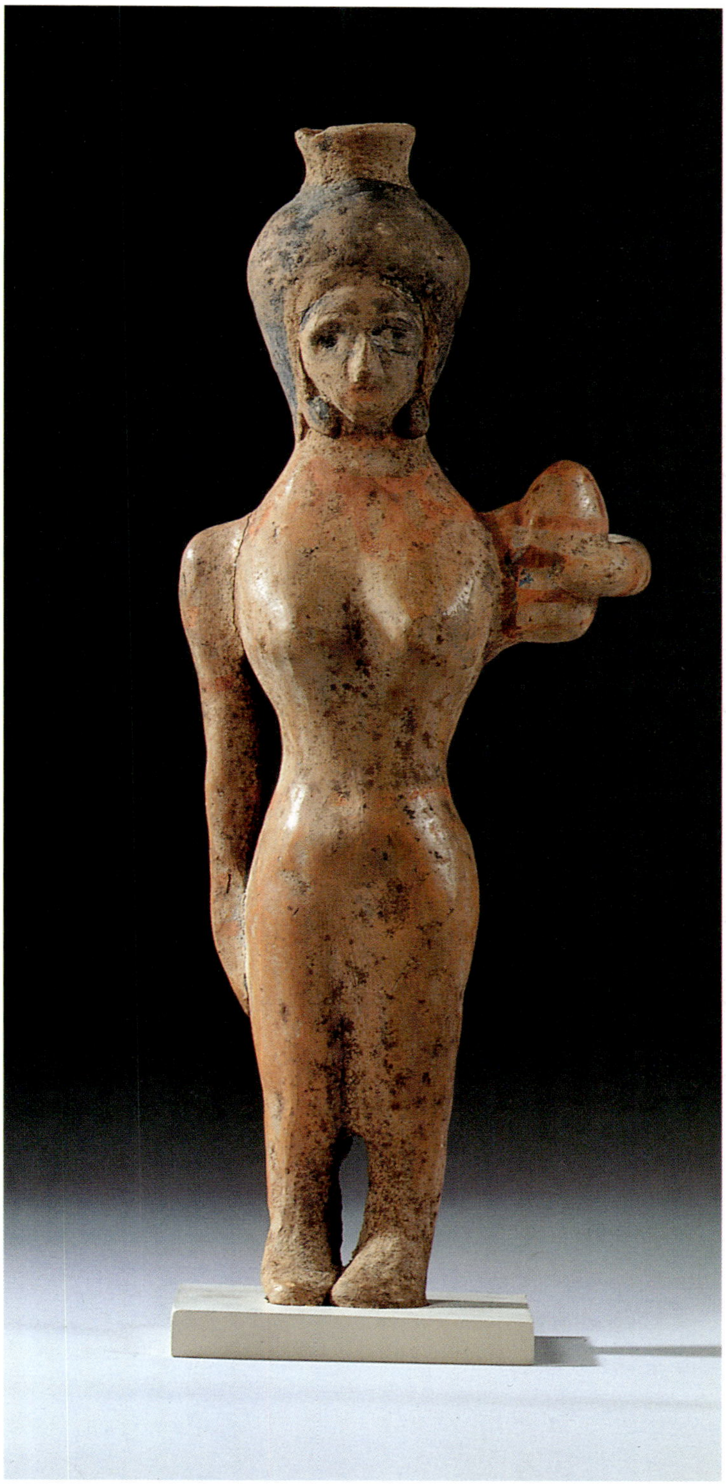

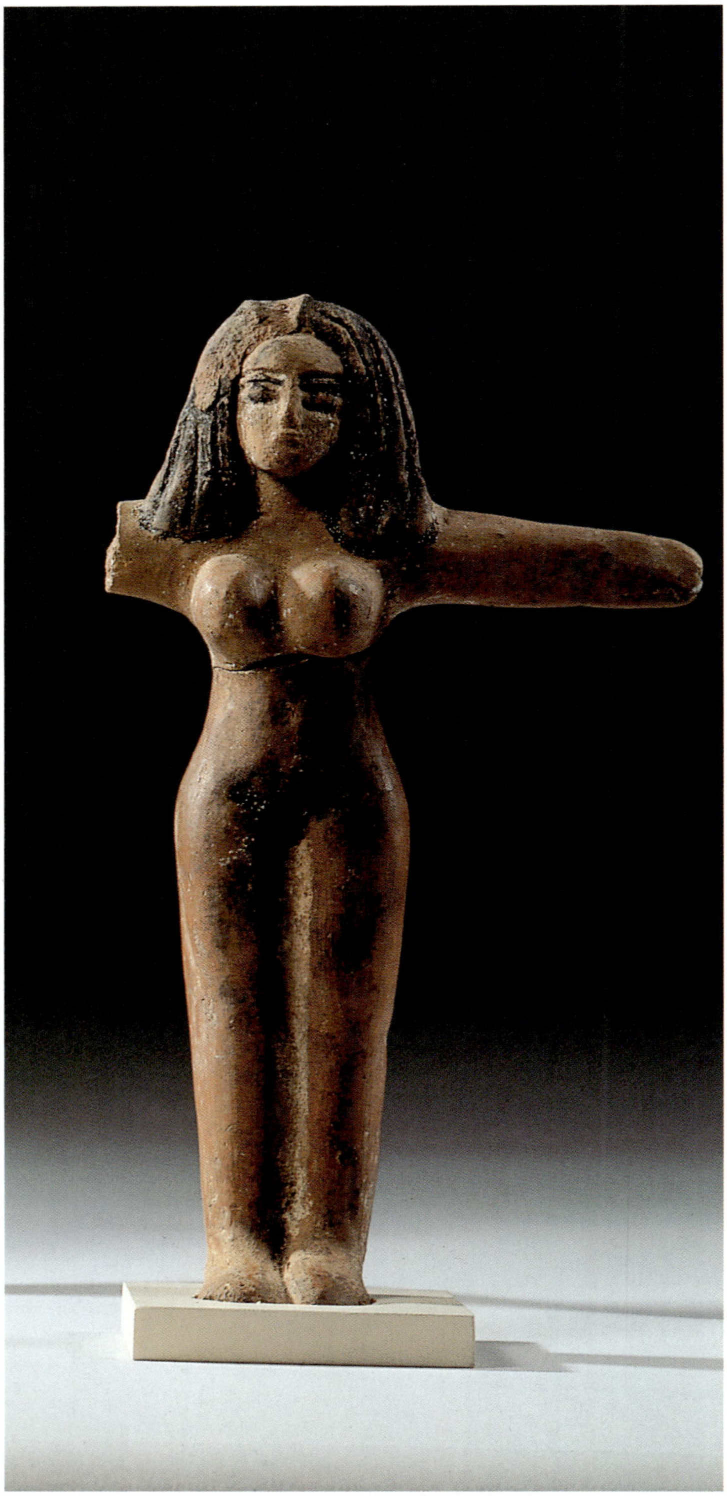

bly served as a cosmetic container.[5] Among surviving items of jewelry are two carnelian and four lead earrings, a pair of faience scarabs, a collection of unworked mussel and cowrie shells pierced for stringing,[6] and several strands of faience beads and amulets. The assemblage also includes a bronze figurine of the lotus god Nefertum, whose presence facilitated the soul's rebirth in the afterlife.[7]

The most distinctive items in the burial inventory are the two terracotta female figures. One—in the form of a hollow vase with its mouth emerging from the head—depicts the standing figure of a woman holding a vessel or wickerwork basket in her outstretched left arm. Outfitted with a black-painted wig, she is nude and completely unadorned except for a pair of large ear plugs, a pendent collar, and a belt or hip girdle (indicated by two painted bands around the waist). The other, smaller figure depicts a standing nude female with shoulder-length hair, her arms outstretched horizontally.

The female-shaped vessel is relatively unusual.[8] In general type, however, it may be compared with a feminoform vase of late Eighteenth Dynasty date from Abydos, which also depicts a female attendant with ear plugs and long black wig, cradling a basket in her left arm.[9] The second, smaller figure from Tomb D229 is characterized by a painted pubic triangle and thus may have served as a fertility figurine.[10]

The inclusion of these two female pottery figures clearly identifies the tomb owner as a woman. This fact is confirmed by the *shabti*, which is inscribed for *Aset-bity*, an abbreviated form of *Aset-em-akh-bity* ("Isis is in Chemmis"), a common woman's name of the Third Intermediate Period.[11] GEM

Published: Peet and Loat, *Abydos*, 3: 33 and pls. 11, no. 6; 12, nos. 5, 7, 8.

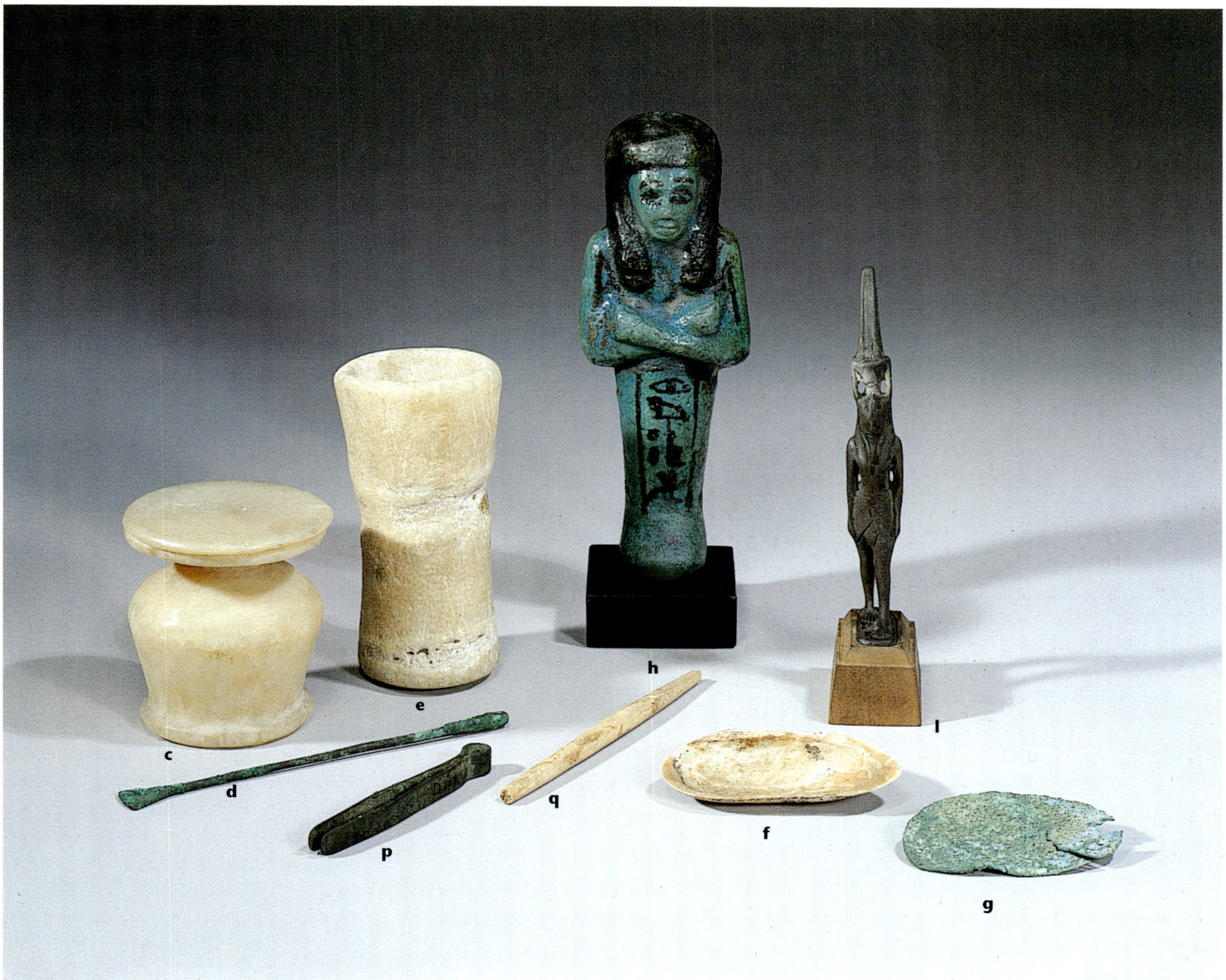

h
e
l
c
d
q
f
p
g

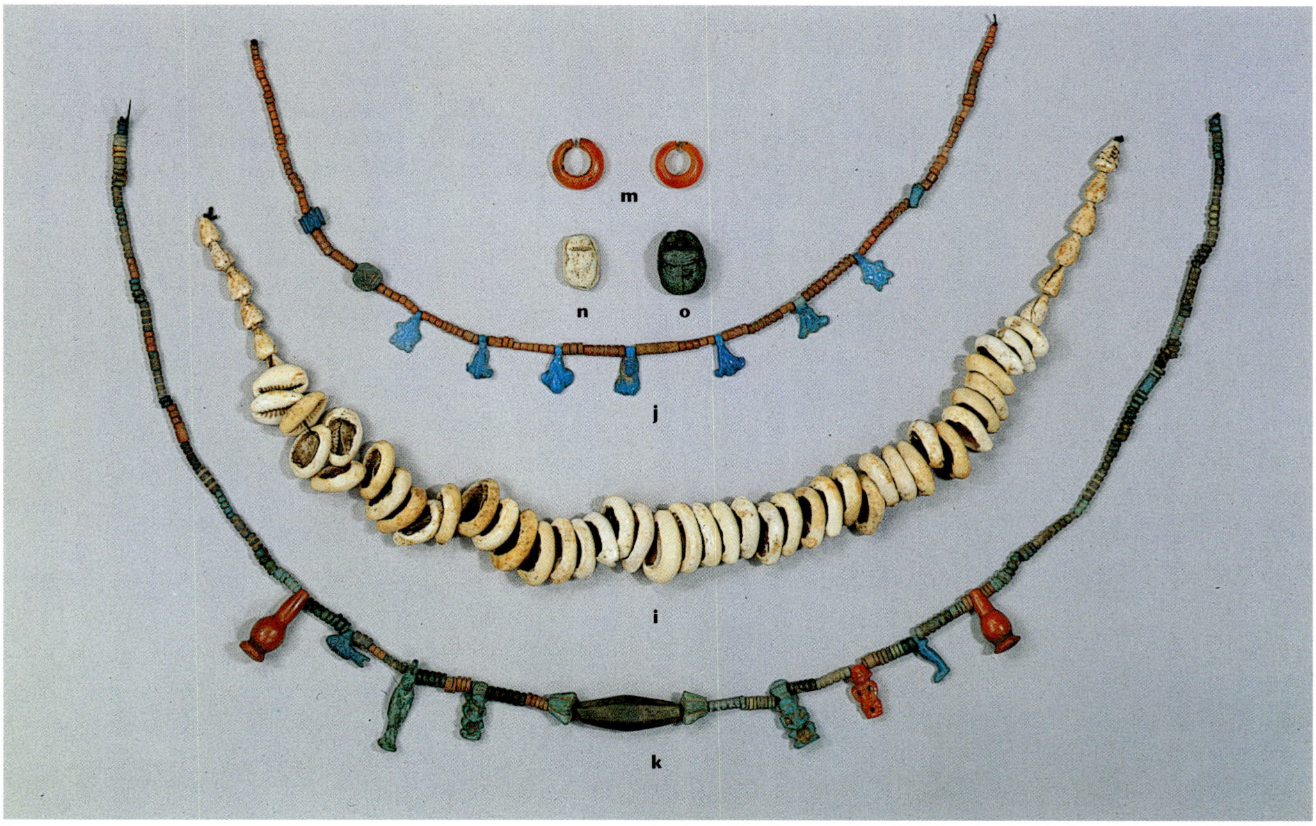

m
n
o
j
i
k

Shabtis

In the final centuries of the third millennium B.C., during the First Intermediate Period, small, rather crude wax figures representing the deceased as a miniature mummy laid out in a coffin were placed in tombs. Known later in ancient Egyptian as *shabtis*, *shawabtis*, or *ushabtis*, depending on their date,[1] these mummiform statuettes enjoyed a long and widespread use in the ancient Egyptian funerary cult, extending over a period of some two thousand years. The *shabti's* primary function, in its more developed stages, was to serve as a laborer for the deceased who could be called upon to perform manual agricultural tasks for the owner.[2]

Beginning in the Twelfth or Thirteenth Dynasty, *shabtis* were inscribed with a spell instructing them to obey the commands of the deceased.[3] The standard New Kingdom text (drawn from Chapter 6 of the Book of the Dead) reads as follows:

> O shabti, allotted to me, if I be summoned or if I be detailed to do any work which has to be done in the God's Domain; if indeed obstacles are implanted for you therewith as a man at his duties, you shall detail yourself for me on every occasion of making arable the fields, of flooding the banks, or of conveying sand from east to west; "Here am I," you shall say.[4]

From their first occurrence, *shabtis* were associated with both male and female burials. In fact, some of the earliest examples, associated with women's burials of the Herakleopolitan period (Dynasties 9–10), are female-shaped. Four such figures (two in wax and two in mud) from the Eleventh Dynasty tomb of Queen Nofru at Deir el-Bahri bear the sinuous form of a nude female with long hair and prominent breasts, her arms extended at the sides.[5]

By the Twelfth Dynasty, however, gender distinction in *shabtis* had largely disappeared—the result of a trend toward standardization. The arms and legs were no longer differentiated; the figure was no longer that of a nude body, but of a fully bandaged mummy with a tripartite wig featuring a heavy mat of hair on the back and two lappets on the front. (With a few minor variations, this form remained standard until the disappearance of the *shabti* in the Ptolemaic Period.) Thus, in the Middle Kingdom, women's *shabtis* became indistinguishable in outward appearance from those of men. The accompanying inscription alone provided clues as to its gender association. Aside from the name itself, the owner's female identity was often indicated by the presence of feminine pronouns and by her divine association with the goddess Isis (rather than the male deity Osiris).[6]

During the early New Kingdom, *shabtis,* both male and female, retained a generalized mummiform appearance. On a double *shabti* of the period of Thutmose III (cat. no. 4), for example, the royal architect Bener-merut and his wife, the Mistress of the House Ikhem, are virtually indistinguishable in their mummiform state. The only clear distinction in physical appearance is the presence of the long Osirian beard worn by Bener-merut; Ikhem is rendered beardless.[7] A more subtle distinction may be seen in Ikhem's somewhat softer and fuller facial features—the Egyptian craftsman's understated manner of indicating gender. In typical fashion, the text on each figure is the same, except for the scribe's use of feminine forms in referring to the deceased and her *shabti.*[8]

As the New Kingdom evolved, *shabtis,* while retaining their traditional mummy-like pose, became increasingly individualized in appearance. Since the beginning of Dynasty 18, female examples were often distinguishable by their earrings and by their coiffure, which consisted of a tripartite wig extending down the back and over the breasts, often with a lotus-flower fillet at the brow. On more elaborate examples in the Ramesside Period, curled bangs framed the forehead, while coiled tresses lay beside the cheeks. Moreover, the upper part of the body was now shown in daily attire (rather than in mummy wrappings), with the breasts fully modeled and accentuated.[9]

The trend toward feminization reached a peak in the Ramesside Period.[10] The painted wooden *shabti* of Lady Maya (cat. no. 76) provides an excellent example of the elaborate coiffure of the period, with its finely delineated strands of hair, inserted locks at the back of the wig, and the fine, wispy bangs of Maya's own hair (which extend over the forehead beneath the wig). In a similar vein, the elegant figure of a young woman adorned with a long, filleted wig and jewelry is delicately represented by the bronze mountings for a wooden *shabti* of the Nineteenth Dynasty in the Metropolitan Museum of Art.[11]

A pair of Amarna-Period *shabtis* made for an affluent Egyptian and his wife, likewise in the Metropolitan Museum of Art, reveal clear attempts at individualizing male and female types. The husband wears the false beard, curly wig, and pleated shirt and kilt fashionable in the late Eighteenth Dynasty; his spouse appears beardless and completely mummiform and wears a crinkled, filleted wig.[12] Distinctions between *shabtis* of husbands and wives were also underscored by differences in use of materials and colors, particularly for the wig.[13]

In the development of the *shabti,* the New Kingdom formed a period of transition. Through the early Eighteenth Dynasty, examples were usually large, custom-made, and few in number, suggesting that they were personally commissioned by the owner.[14] By the later Ramesside Period, however, this individualized type in limestone and wood was replaced increasingly by *shabtis* that were mass-produced in molded faience or pottery. These were frequently grouped in sets of eleven: ten workers and a *reis,* or overseer, distinguishable by his whip of authority and his daily dress.

By the beginning of the Third Intermediate Period, or Twenty-first Dynasty, such funerary figures (which were now identified by the term *ushabti)*[15] were produced by the thousands according to standardized models. Members of royalty and the priestly aristocracy were regularly provided with four hundred or more figures: one worker for each day of the year plus the requisite number of foremen.[16] Mass production and replication in molded faience reached a peak in the Twenty-sixth Dynasty, when numerous examples with finely modeled features were manufactured.[17]

73 *Shabti* of Kai-neferu

Wood with pigment; from Deir el-Medina; New Kingdom, late Dynasty 18, reign of Akhenaten or later; H: 27.4 cm; max. W: 5 cm

Museum of Fine Arts, Boston. Hay Collection. Gift of C. Granville Way, 1872. 72.4088

This graceful figurine represents the only known *shabti* of the Mistress of the House, Kai-neferu, a member of the family of Setau, who figured prominently among the workmen at the Theban village of Deir el-Medina.[18] Although Kai-neferu's *shabti* is without recorded provenance, its assignment to the Setau family at Deir el-Medina is indicated clearly by the position of the winnowing basket held along the right upper arm. This was a short-lived but distinctive feature characteristic of *shabtis* of the Setau family.[19] Like many others of the Setau clan, Kai-neferu's *shabti* is distinguished by its excellent craftsmanship—perhaps reflecting the skills and taste of Setau himself; the facial features are particularly delicate and well modeled. In coloring, Kai-neferu's *shabti* is typical of funerary figures of the late Eighteenth and early Nineteenth Dynasty from Deir el-Medina: white body, blue wig, and polychrome necklace. As with a few other female *shabtis* from the site, the face is executed in red rather than yellow, the standard coloration for females.[20] The diminutive features and slender proportions of this *shabti* also reveal its female identity. GEM

Published: Spanel, in *Mummies and Magic*, no. 95.

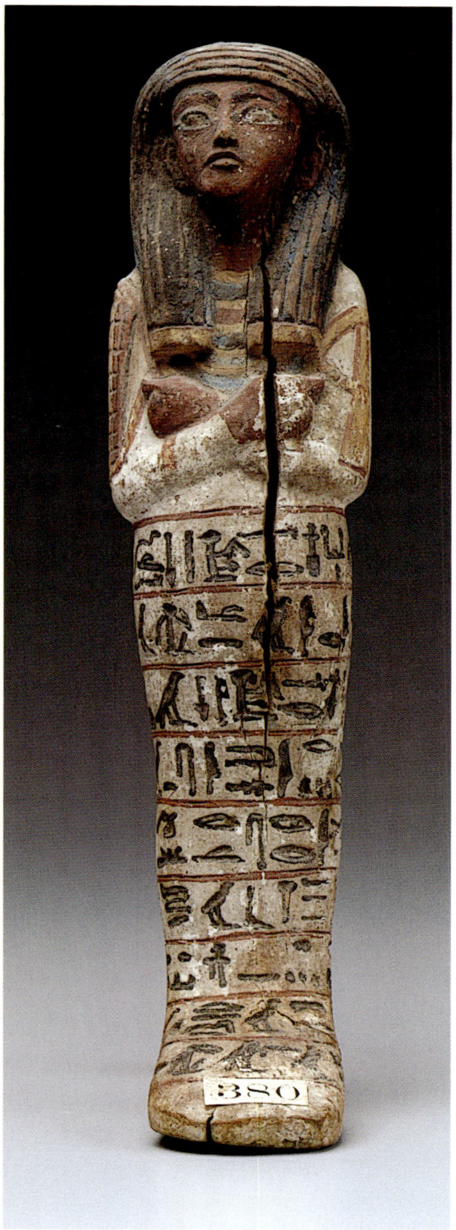

74 *Shabti* of Henut-wedjebu

Wood, with blue paste inlays and black pigment; probably from Sheikh Abd el-Qurna, Thebes, tomb of Hatiay; New Kingdom, Dynasty 18, reign of Amenhotep III; H: 27.8 cm

The Toledo Museum of Art. Gift of The Apollo Society. 1993.52

As its inscription records, this beautifully carved wooden *shabti* belonged to Henut-wedjebu ("Lady of the River Banks"), whose coffin is represented by catalogue number 91. In its elegance and refinement, this figurine reflects the high quality of *shabti* production during the reign of Amenhotep III. The crossed hands of Henut-wedjebu's *shabti* hold a pair of hoes, agricultural implements that enabled the *shabti* to perform its requisite labors in the field.[21] The conventional lappet, or three-part, striated wig, hangs down the back and over both shoulders.[22] Around the neck is a pectoral with scarab emblem, and a *usekh* collar with multiple rows of flowers, beads, and seeds sewn onto a papyrus backing. GEM

Published: *Toledo Annual Report* 1992/93.

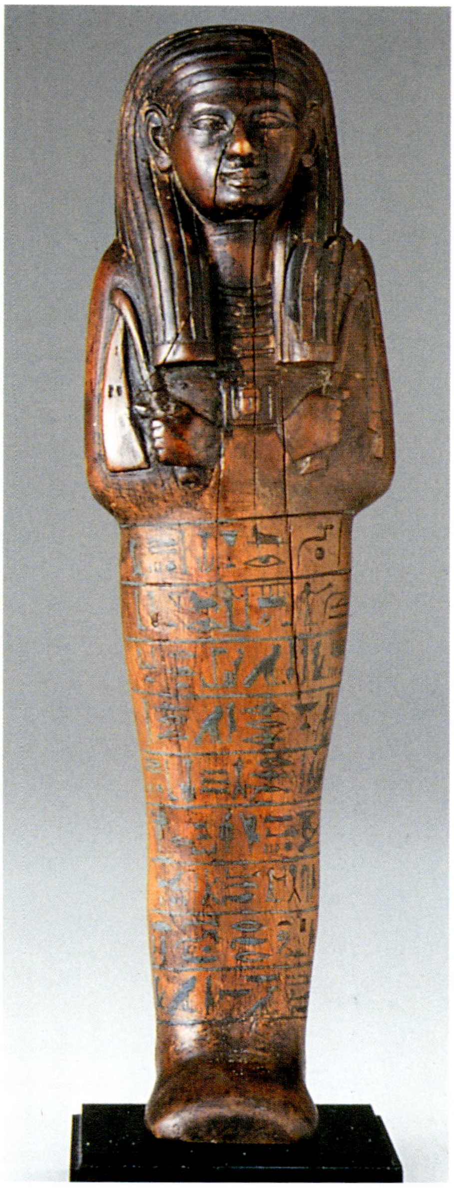

75 *Shabti* of Sati

Faience; provenance unknown; possibly from Saqqara; New Kingdom, late Dynasty 18, reign of Amenhotep III or later; H: 25 cm; W: 8 cm

The Brooklyn Museum. Charles Edwin Wilbour Fund. 37.123E

One of two identical examples in the Brooklyn Museum, this *shabti* of the Mistress of the House Sati is one of

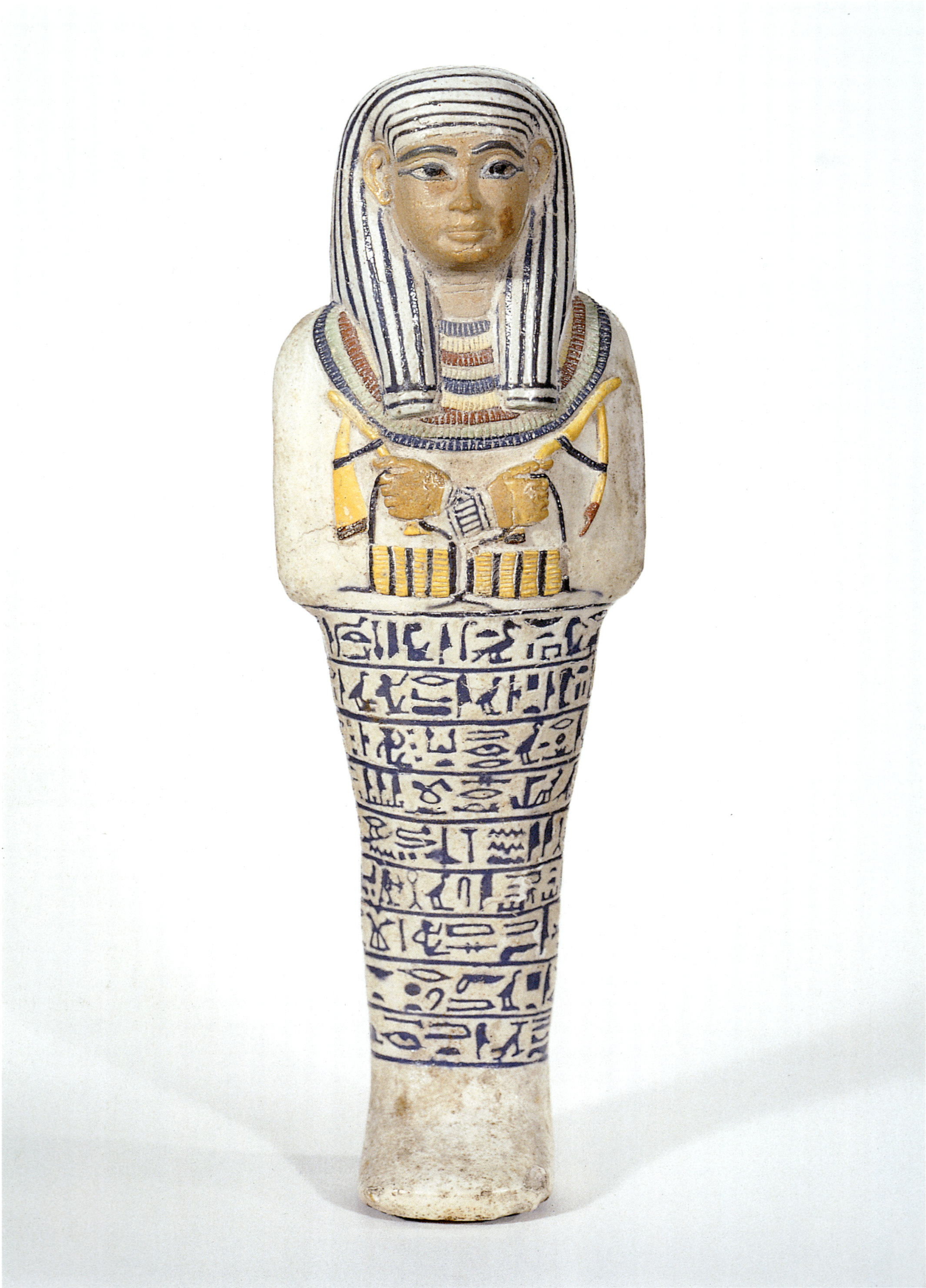

the finest funerary figures known from ancient Egypt, equaled only by the contemporary *shabti* of Ptahmose, High Priest of Amen.[23] The polychrome technique of both Sati's and Ptahmose's *shabtis* is both distinctive and unusual: it entails a painstaking procedure that involved glazing with at least six different colors, each applied separately to prevent mixing. Due to the time-consuming nature of this technique, only a few *shabtis* were apparently executed in this way. Under the circumstances, it is indeed remarkable that Sati, whose only recorded title is "Mistress of the House" *(nebet per)*, was accorded two such figures—a possible indication of her rank or social standing.[24] In place of yellow, the conventional color for female skin in ancient Egypt, Sati's face is glazed, most unusually, in a true flesh tone.[25] Like other *shabtis* produced with this technique, her eyes are enhanced by the cosmetic lines (which curve down and up from the outer eye) often worn by both males and females of the upper classes. The soft, sensuous modeling of the face and the fold lines of the neck are characteristic of the art of Amenhotep III's reign.
GEM

Published: Fazzini et al., *Ancient Egyptian Art,* no. 47; *Egypt's Dazzling Sun,* no. 70 and color plate 37; Thomas et al., *American Discovery,* 83–84, no. 5.

76 *Shabti* of Maya

Wood with pigment; provenance unknown; New Kingdom, Dynasty 19; H: 24 cm

The University of Pennsylvania Museum of Archaeology and Anthropology, Philadelphia. Gift of Mrs. Dillwyn Parrish, 1914. E 12615a

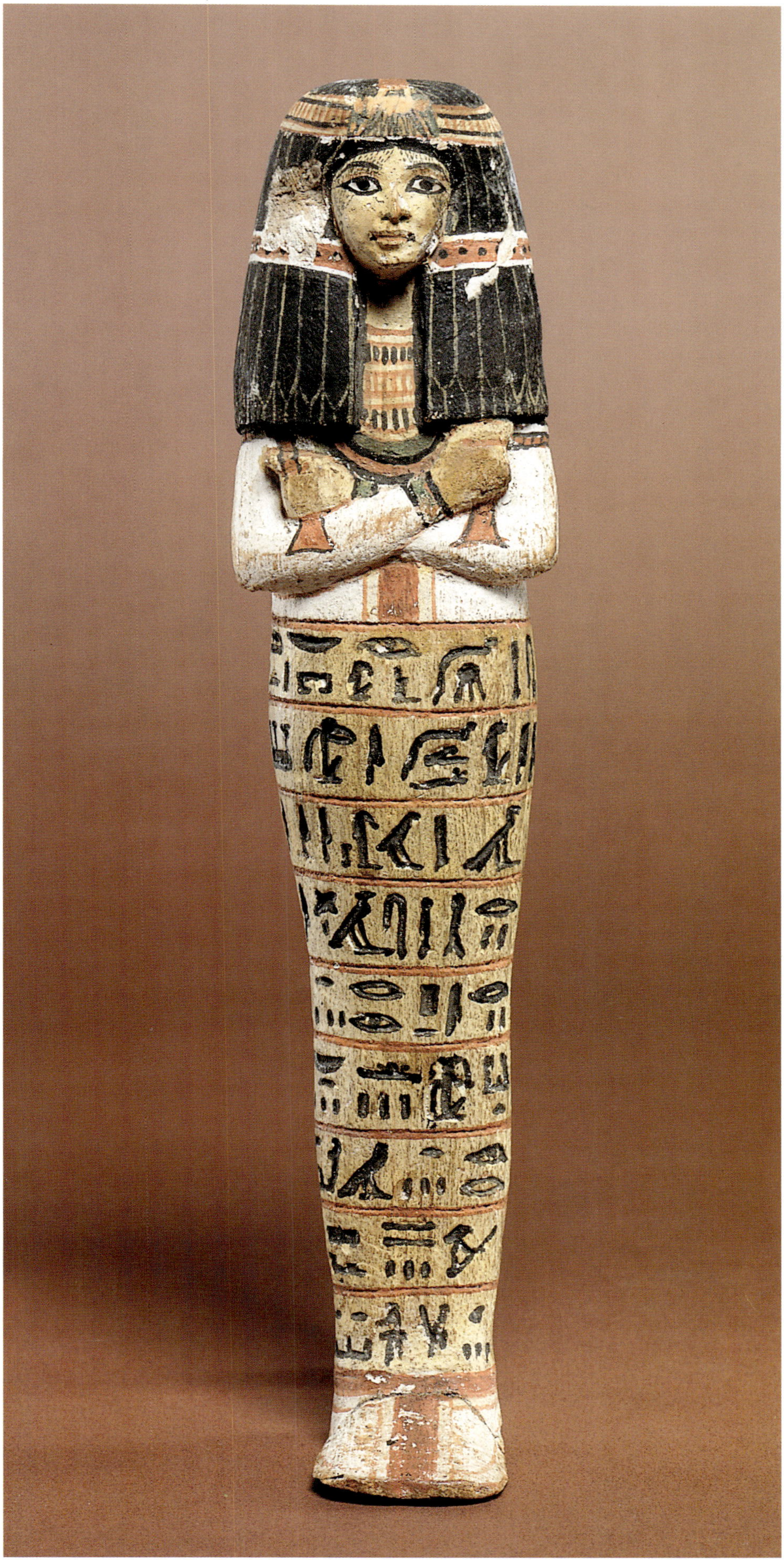

First attested in the Herakleopolitan Period and the Eleventh Dynasty, funerary figurines were produced through the end of ancient Egyptian history.[26] Like other essential components of burial equipment, they were made for both sexes. Nonetheless, disparities exist. Figurines for women were much less common in all periods. The difference in numbers does not reflect the vagaries of survival. Next to scarabs, amulets, and pottery, funerary figurines are the most plentifully attested of all ancient Egyptian antiquities. Furthermore, although certain details, such as the coiffure and facial modeling, were often modified for women, both the production and the typology of funerary figurines favored men.

To elaborate, the text most frequently inscribed on funerary figurines was Chapter 6 of the Book of the Dead. In at least two passages, the dead person makes self-reference in the third person. The correct gender is frequently observed, but the masculine pronoun is written just as often in certain phrases on figurines belonging to women ("he says," "a man at his task"). The incorrect gender is especially conspicuous on Maya's figurine. The heavy coiffure and the facial modeling are clearly feminine, and the scribe who copied the text was informed that the figurine was destined for a woman because her title—*nebet per* ("Mistress of the House," "Housewife")—is specified correctly. Nonetheless, the masculine gender appears in the phrase "he says."[27] The implication is that Chapter 6 of the Book of the Dead was intended primarily for men.

As for typology, the more common of the two categories of figurines was accessible to women as well as men. This was the mummiform figurine, which was prevalent from the Middle Kingdom through the Ptolemaic Period. In the late Eighteenth or early Nineteenth Dynasty a new type sporting the so-called dress of the living appeared. Characterized by a loose-fitting, billowed-sleeve fine linen garment that ended at the knee or just below, figurines of this type were made more often for men.

For the earlier part of their history, funerary figurines were made in restricted numbers for each burial. *Shabti* is the much more common spelling in the Middle Kingdom and the Second Intermediate Period, although *shawabti* appears occasionally. Funerary figurines made for women are certainly attested—some of the earliest examples are known from burials of women—but they are not common until the Eighteenth Dynasty, when both the numbers and the types for either sex increased dramatically.[28] The term *shabti* prevailed, but *shawabti* appeared increasingly in Chapter 6 of the Book of the Dead, primarily at Deir el-Medina. A third designation for funerary figurines, *ushabti*, does not appear until the Twenty-first Dynasty.[29]

As home to the workmen and artists who built and decorated the royal tombs in the Valley of the Kings, Deir el-Medina was an unsurpassed atelier for funerary figurines. Although Maya's figurine has the spelling *shabti*, not *shawabti*, several other characteristic features suggest that Deir el-Medina is the provenance: the careful modeling and painting; the elaborate wig and collar; the use of white paint for the body, particularly for the background of the text; and the palaeography of the hieroglyphs.[30] DBS

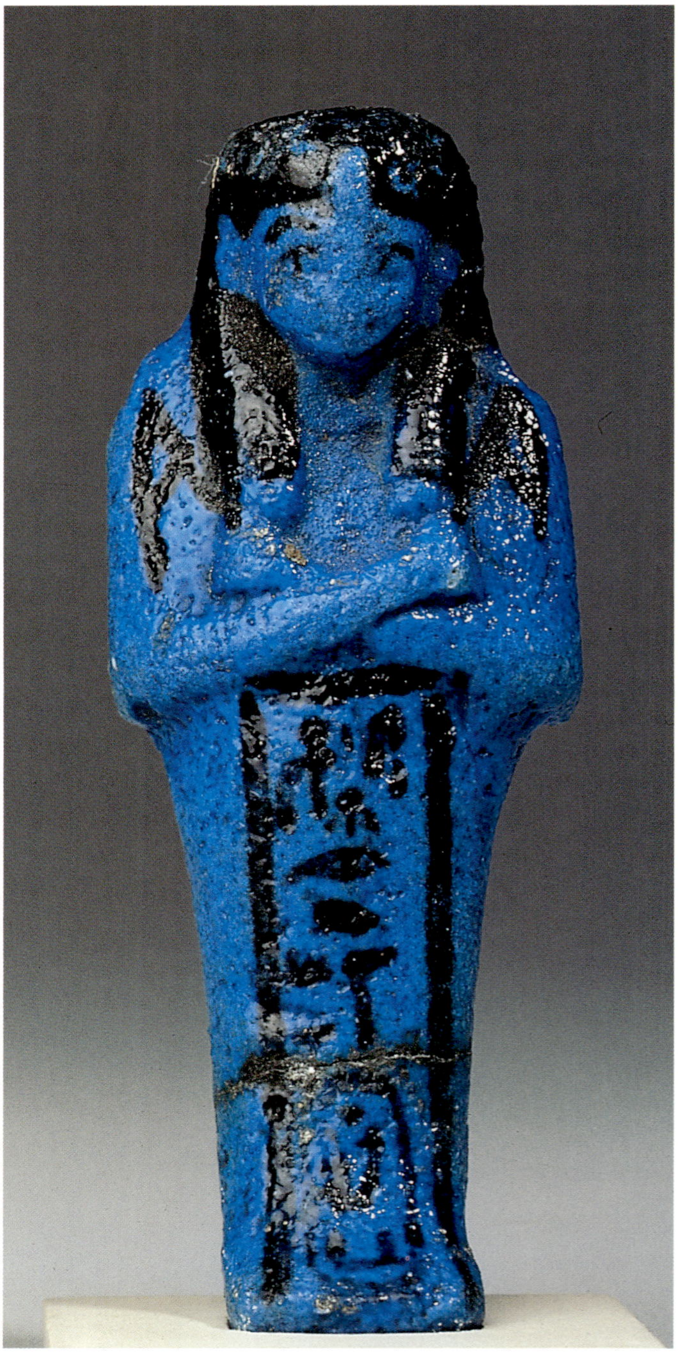

77 a *Shabti* inscribed for Queen Henuttawey

Blue-glazed composition; from Thebes, Deir el-Bahri; Royal Cache; Third Intermediate Period, Dynasty 21, reign of Pinedjem I; H: 12 cm

Cincinnati Art Museum. Gift of the Heirs of John W. Bookwalter. 1919.463.

77 b *Shabti* inscribed for Princess Maatkara

Blue-glazed composition; from Thebes, Deir el-Bahri; Royal Cache; Third Intermediate Period, Dynasty 21, reign of Psusennes I; H: 11.4 cm

Cincinnati Art Museum. Gift of the Heirs of John W. Bookwalter. 1919.464.

Shabtis were an essential component of the burial equipment for female royalty as they were for members of the aristocracy. The two examples exhibited here were made for two royal women of the Twenty-first Dynasty, Queen Henuttawey and her daughter Maatkara. Although they lack excavated contexts, both pieces almost certainly derived from the Great, or Royal, Cache at Deir el-Bahri, a massive tomb group that contained the collective burials of twenty kings and queens of the New Kingdom and ten royal persons,

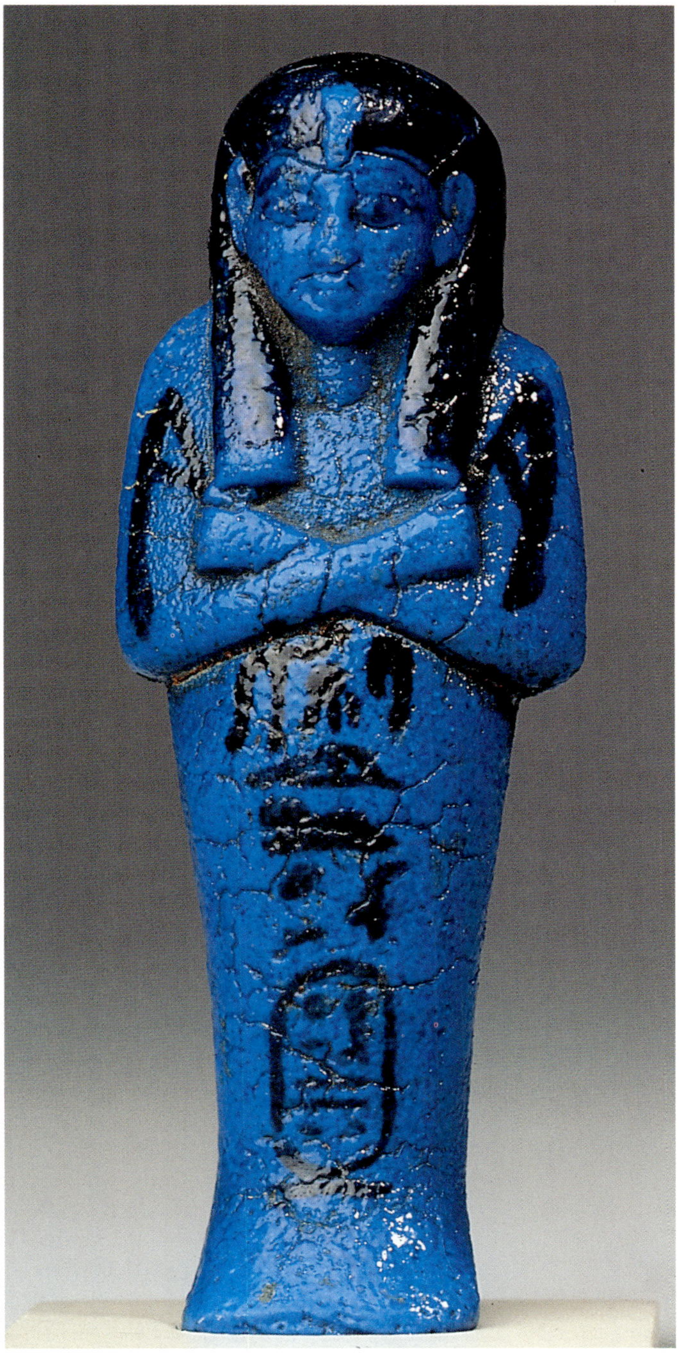

priests, and priestesses of the Twenty-first Dynasty.[31]

This dynasty, in fact, marked a quantifiable change in the conception of *shabtis*.[32] Large "gangs" of workers now served the deceased: one for each day, organized in groups of ten, each group placed under an overseer. The grand total thus came to 401 (365 workers and 36 overseers) and sometimes more. The present examples probably derived from such massed groups, which typically were deposited in one or more wooden *shabti* boxes.[33]

Both Henuttawey's and Maatkara's *shabtis* exhibit the vivid "royal blue" faience glaze introduced at this time by the Theban priesthood of Amen.[34] They also illustrate another important change in the nature of the *shabti:* they depict female workers, clearly distinguished in physiognomy. In addition to modeled breasts, female *shabtis* tend to display more rounded facial features and body contours than their male counterparts. They are also distinguished by a prominent black wig ornamented with a central *uraeus*.

A good deal is known about the identities of these two royal personages. Queen Hennutawey, the daughter of Ramesses XI (who ruled from Tanis in the Nile delta), was the wife of Pinedjem I, high priest of Amen at Thebes. Her marriage to Pinedjem, in fact, was the first in a series of such diplomatic unions between the kings of Tanis and the Theban high priesthood of Amen.[35] As recorded by various inscriptions on her *shabti*, Hennutawey's titles included "Adoratrice of Hathor," "Queen," "Royal Wife," and "Royal Mother."[36] This last is a reference to Hennutawey's offspring with Pinedjem I: Princess Maatkara, the owner of the second *shabti*. As the Divine Wife and Adoratrice of Amen, Maatkara occupied an even more imposing position in the Theban priesthood than her mother. In her various ritual capacities, she often appeared on an equal footing with the pharaoh himself in various royal rites and ceremonies.[37] The enlarged breasts of Maatkara's mummy reveal that she probably died in childbirth.[38] GEM

78 Tomb painting of mourning women

Paint on gesso over mud plaster; from Thebes, Tomb 181 ("The Tomb of Two Sculptors"); New Kingdom, Dynasty 18, reign of Amenhotep III; H: 23 cm; W: 33 cm

The Museum of Fine Arts, Boston. William Francis Warden Fund. 68.555

The funerary procession and entombment of the mummy was attended by a large group of female, and sometimes male, mourners.[1] Some of the mourning women were, of course, relatives of the deceased. Others, however, were professionals who were reimbursed for their services (see also cat. no. 31). The present fragment depicts a group of such women portrayed in the act of bereavement. Those in the foreground kneel and touch the ground and their heads in sorrow.

This fragment originally formed part of a larger grouping of thirteen standing and kneeling women shown mourning at the funerary rituals[2] enacted for Nebamen and Apuki, two high-ranking sculptors buried in the same tomb at Thebes.[3] This scene, depicted on the north wall of the burial chamber,[4] was part of a procession before the two anthropoid coffins bearing the deceased men. The scene continues in the lower register with two funerary boats transporting the tomb furnishings

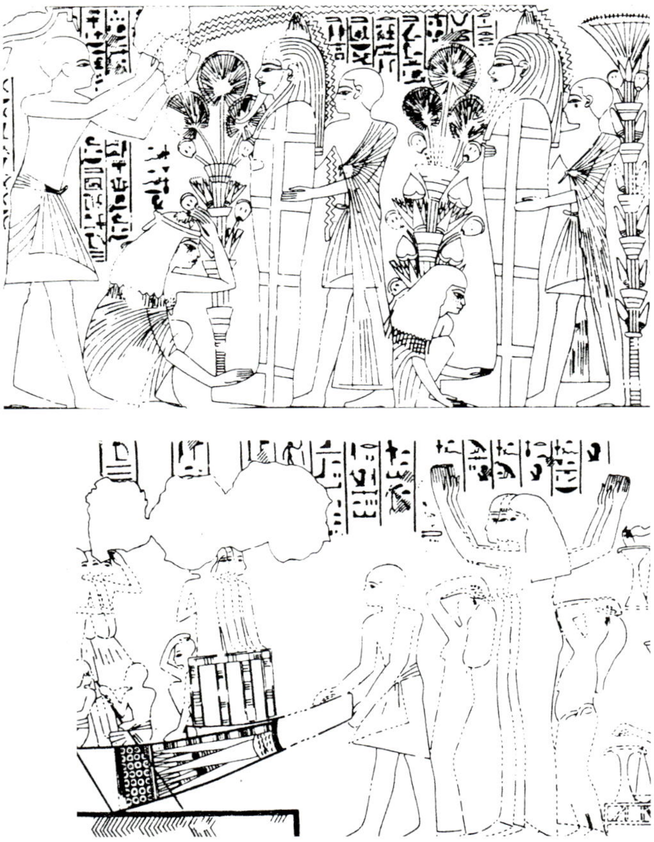

Fig. 10 Henut-nefer before anthropoid sarcophagi of Nebamen and Apuki; women mourning before light kiosks. Detail from north wall of burial chamber, Tomb 181 ("The Tomb of Two Sculptors"), Thebes. Drawing from N. de G. Davies, *The Tomb of Two Sculptors at Thebes* (New York, 1925), pl. 19.

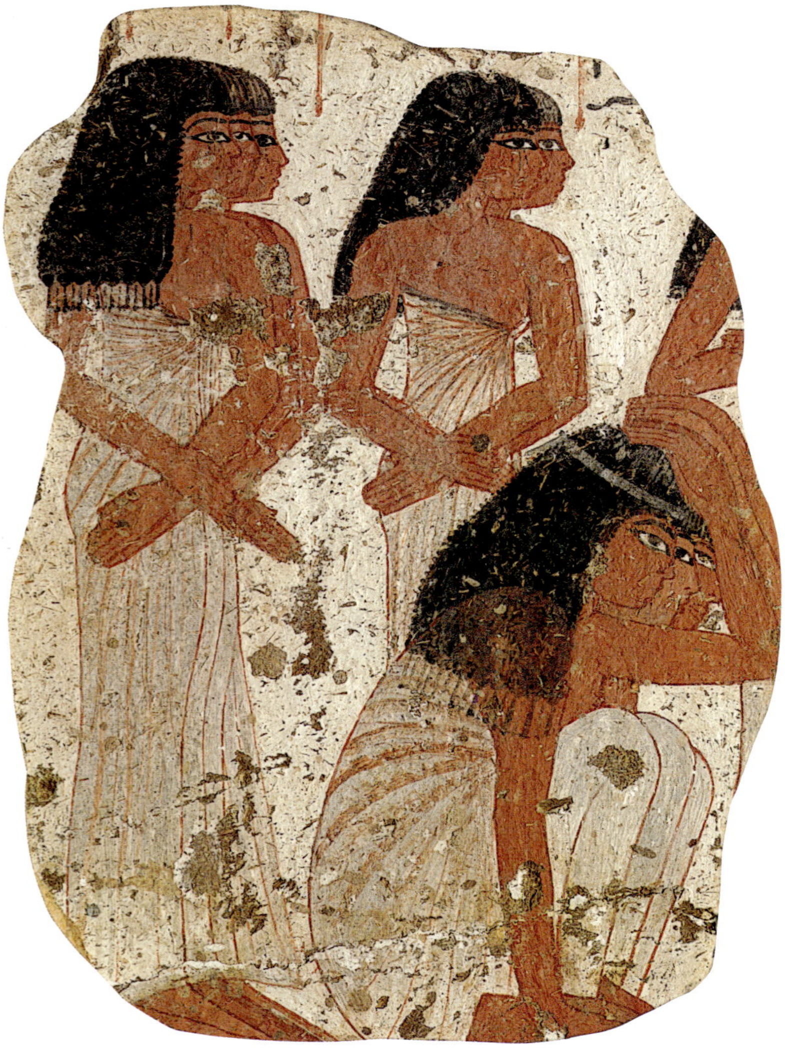

of Nebamen and Apuki. Five women mourn before the light kiosks sheltering wine jars (see also cat. no. 79), which would have been placed before the doorway of the tomb chapel (fig. 10, bottom).

Before each of the two anthropoid coffins of the deceased men is a woman, Henut-nefer, who touches the foot of each mummy case in a farewell gesture (fig. 10, top). The scenes and texts in this tomb suggest that Henut-nefer was first married to Apuki.[5] After his death, she married his colleague, Nebamen. With the death of her second husband, she had the tomb decorated[6] in such a way as to memorialize both of her deceased husbands and guarantee the continued existence of both men in the afterlife. Another woman who figures prominently in this tomb is Henut-nefer's mother-in-law, Tjepu (cat. no. 6), the mother of Nebamen.[7]

Each of the mourners in this scene wears a long wig with the ends fringed in tiny ringlets. The women wear gowns[8] tied under their breasts. These garments are colored gray-blue, perhaps to indicate the dust that the women have thrown over their heads to express their grief.[9] Dashed lines on the cheeks indicate the tears shed by the mourners.[10] AKC

Published: Davies, *Tomb of Two Sculptors*, pl. 19; *Gazette des Beaux-Arts (Suppl.)* (February, 1971), 53, fig. 23).

79 Libation vase with lid

Terracotta with pigment; provenance unknown; New Kingdom, Late Dynasty 18–early Dynasty 19; H with lid: 94.5 cm

The University of Pennsylvania Museum of Archaeology and Anthropology, Philadelphia. Gift of Miss Sophia Cadwalader in memory of Eckley B. Coxe, Jr. E14368a,b

Along with funerary furnishings and texts, *shabti* figurines, and servant figures depicted either in the form of statues or painted on the walls of tombs, a deceased person also required the items of everyday life—clothing, food, and beverages—that would make the eternal afterlife comfortable and pleasant. This tall, elegant vase, one of a pair, originally held wine for the

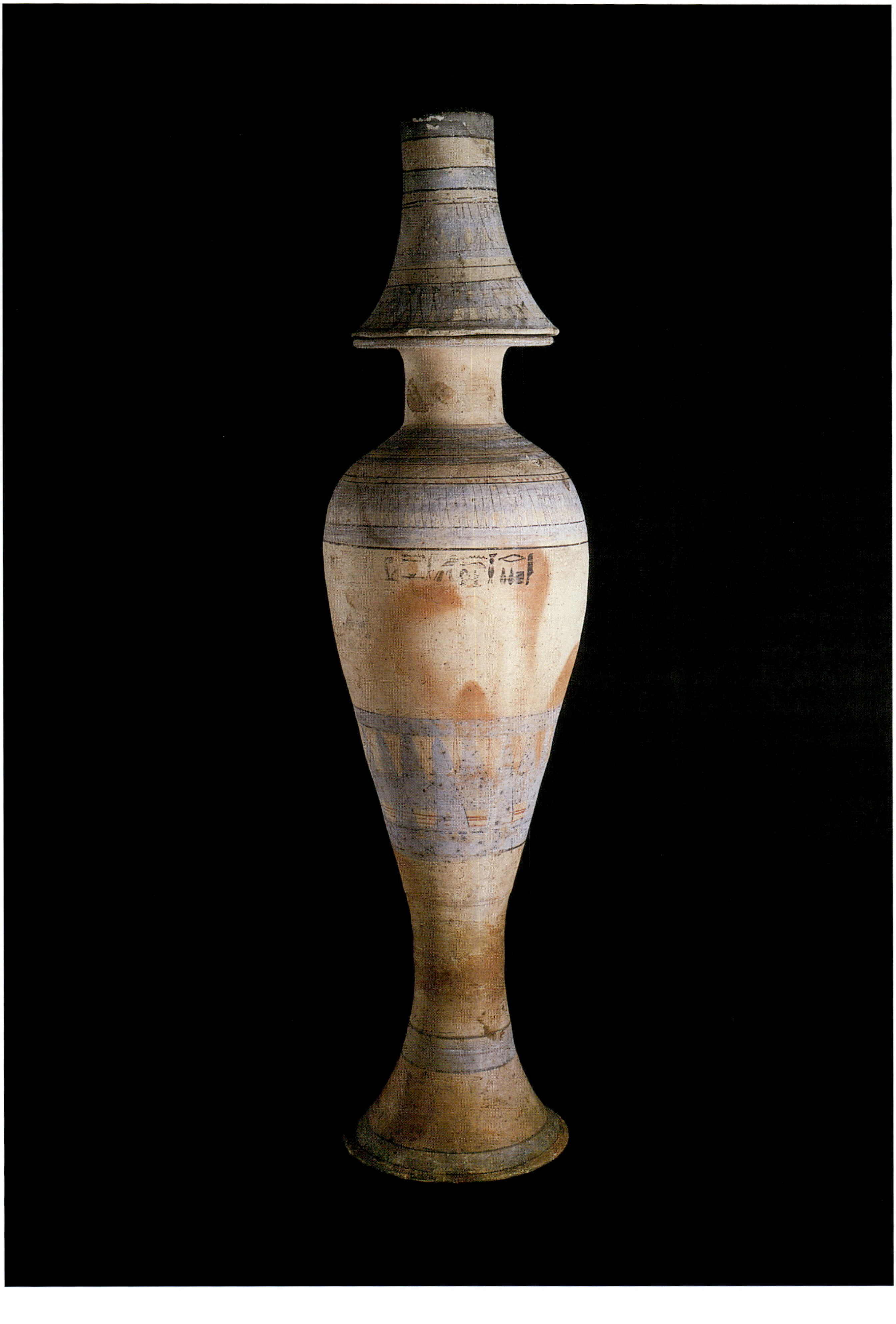

deceased woman, Menedjem, whose name is included in the inscription painted on the vessel: "Sweet wine[1] for the Osiris, Menedjem." The mate bears the dedication, "*Hamu*-wine[2] for the Osiris, Menedjem." A second, smaller pair of vessels from the same tomb, and now in the British Museum,[3] held "Northern wine for the Osiris, Menedjem."

This vessel is of a type known as blue-painted pottery, which was popular in the late Eighteenth and early Nineteenth Dynasties.[4] As blue-painted pottery has been found in domestic, temple, and tomb contexts, and was made in a variety of shapes, it seems to have been used for numerous purposes. The painted decoration, with the colors blue, black, and red predominating, imitates the wreaths of fresh flowers that were draped about the necks of large serving jars during banquets. Although linear and floral motifs are most common, elaborate examples may include human figures, birds, animals, and representations of the gods Bes and Hathor.

This vessel was made in the shape known in ancient Egyptian as the *hes*.[5] This type of vase was frequently used in religious ritual to pour libations[6] and thus is frequently depicted in vignettes from the Book of the Dead (cat. no. 83) on tomb and temple walls and on funerary stelae. Similar, though smaller, wine jars have been found at Amarna, and those discovered in the tomb of King Tutankhamen have spouts to facilitate pouring.[7] This example has a lid in the form of an inverted lotus blossom, which would have been sealed in place with clay.[8] The rarity of *hes* vases and this vessel's large size suggest that Menedjem was a woman of high status.[9] Perhaps in the future archaeologists will rediscover the tomb from which these jars came,[10] and we may learn more about Menedjem and her status in ancient Egyptian society.
AKC

Published: Hermann Ranke, "The Egyptian Collections of the University Museum," *University Museum Bulletin* 15 (1950): 67, fig. 41; Colin A. Hope, in *Egypt's Golden Age*, 90-91 (for previous bibliography).

80 Headrest inscribed for Irwt

Travertine; provenance unknown;
Old Kingdom, late Dynasty 5 or Dynasty 6; H: 19.5 cm; W: 18.8 cm
The Cleveland Museum of Art. Gift of the John Huntington Art and Polytechnic Trust. 14.626

This woman's headrest illustrates the typical "pillow" used by both men and women in an ancient Egyptian household. Headrests such as this are known from at least the period of the Old Kingdom through the end of the New Kingdom. The present example, with its three-part arrangement consisting of curved headpiece, fluted pillar, and rectangular base, is typical of the variety in use during the Old Kingdom. Although they look uncomfortable to the modern eye, headrests of this type were probably quite comfortable as well as efficient; their form was sculpted carefully to fit the curve of the owner's head just above the ears and was at times padded with a folded cloth. In the hot climate of Egypt, this arrangement allowed air to circulate freely around the head and neck while keeping the head above the level of creeping insects.[1]

Beginning in the Old Kingdom, headrests were placed beneath the head of the deceased in both men's and women's sarcophagi, where they served a protective as well as a practical function; they elevated the head so that the face was aligned with the "eye panel" on the coffin's side. The magical function of headrests is evident in their later appearance as amulets placed within the mummy wrapping, beginning in the New Kingdom.

The present example belonged to a woman named Irwt,[2] who chose, for reasons unknown, to have her name and title inscribed on the edge of the support below the headpiece rather than on the front of the stem—in the reserved panel already prepared for the vertical inscription. Her title, *špst nisw*, "Noblewoman of the King," is commonly attested among nonroyal women of rank or standing of the later Old Kingdom. Like other women's titles of the period, it formed the feminine

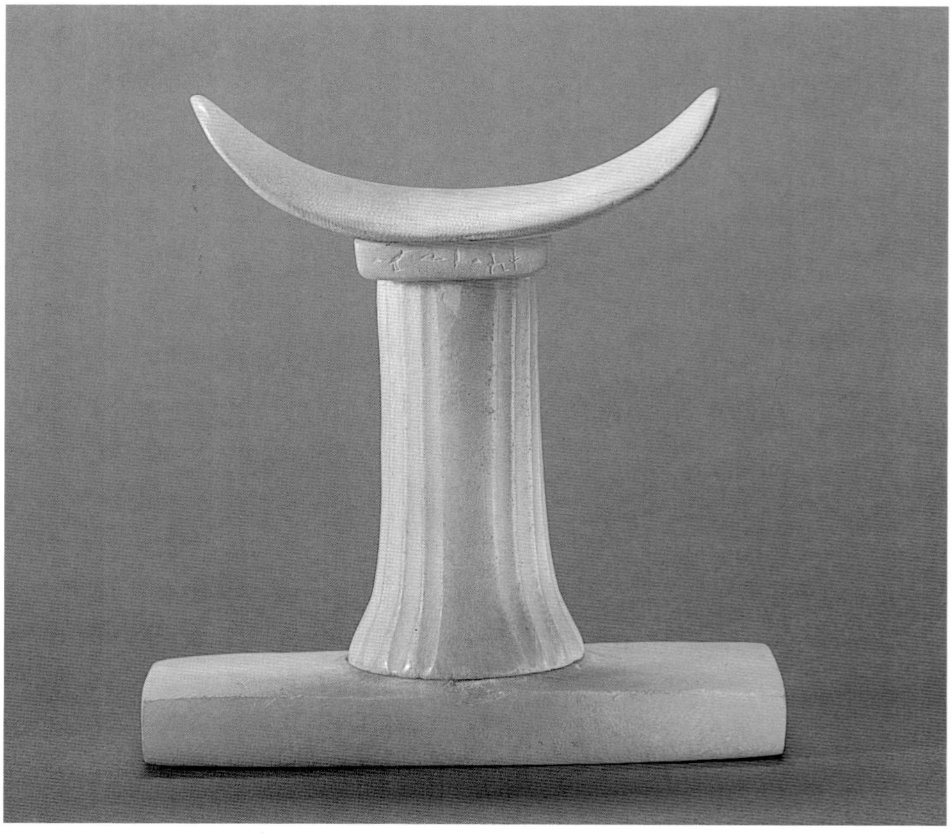

counterpart of a formerly male designation: *šps nisw*, "Nobleman of the King."[3] (In contrast to the male title, which is attested in ancient Egypt's capital city Memphis, nearly all occurrences of the feminine title, curiously, come from outlying provinces of Egypt.) As H.L. Fischer observes, feminine administrative titles such as this were bestowed only by direct relationship to the king.[4] Irwt thus must have been an individual of some social standing. GEM

Published: C.R. Williams, "The Egyptian Collection in the Museum of Art at Cleveland, Ohio," *JEA* 5 (1918): 169–70, and pl. 26, no. 5.

81 Heart scarab inscribed for Nub-ity

Green talc; provenance unknown; New Kingdom, Dynasties 18–20; H. 2.5 cm; L: 5.5 cm

Yale University Gallery of Art, New Haven, Connecticut. Anonymous Gift. 1937.155

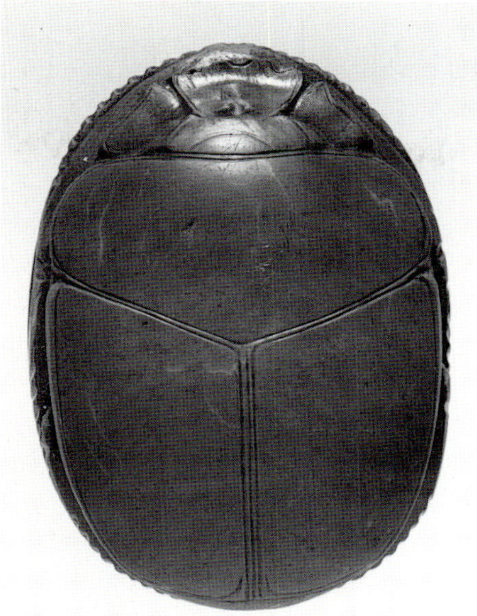

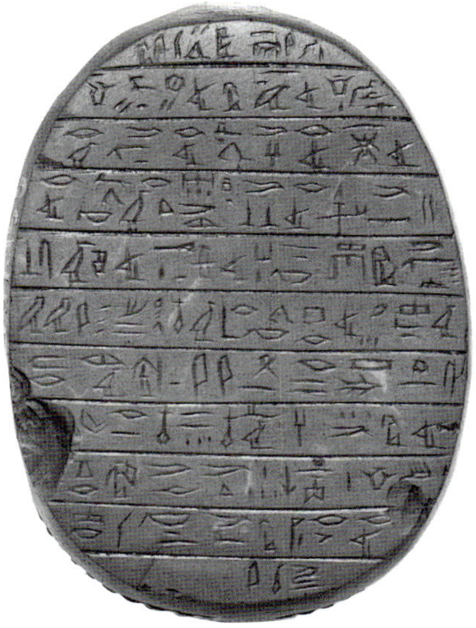

During mummification, most of the internal organs were removed and embalmed separately. The heart, however, because it was considered the seat of all knowledge, was left in place inside the body. A special amulet, known as the "heart scarab," was placed within the mummy's wrappings near the heart, either in the cavity itself or suspended from a cord around the neck.[1] The heart scarab's flat underside typically was inscribed with Chapter 30B of the Book of the Dead, a spell designed to prevent the heart from testifying against its owner during the divine ritual of the weighing of the heart. Rendered in eleven horizontal lines, the text of the spell reads:

> O my heart which I had from my mother! O my heart which I had from my mother! O my heart of my different ages! Do not stand up as a witness against me, do not be opposed to me in the tribunal, do not be hostile to me in the presence of the Keeper of the Balance, for you are my *Ka* which was in my body, the protector who made my members hale. Go forth to the happy place whereto we speed; do not make my name stink to [the] Entourage who make men. Do not tell lies about me in the presence of the god; it is indeed well that you should hear![2]

The spell refers to the journey of the deceased to the Hall of Judgment in the underworld. There the heart of the deceased was balanced against the feather of Maat, the goddess of truth and justice. If the heart was judged virtuous (as the illustrated texts uniformly depict), the deceased was admitted into the realm of the resurrected dead as one "true of voice" or "justified."

The present example was inscribed for a woman named Nub-ity,[3] whose name appears in the uppermost register of the text. Ready-made for the mortuary trade, scarab and text were prepared in advance and the owner's name was inserted after the object was purchased. This explains why a feminine determinative appears in the first line following Nub-ity's name, while a masculine determinative appears throughout the remainder of the text. Similarly, the inscription begins with the feminine third-person singular pronoun *s*, while the masculine *f* appears throughout the body of the text.[4] Like other items of funerary equipment, a woman's heart scarab was often a feminized adaptation of an object designed and intended for a man. GEM

Published: Scott, *Egyptian Art at Yale*, no. 62.

82 Canopic jar of Iny

Limestone with painted decoration; probably from Deir el-Bahri, Thebes; New Kingdom, Dynasty 18, period of Amenhotep III; H: 38 cm; Diam: 16 cm

The Metropolitan Museum of Art. Gift of Helen Miller Gould, 1910. 10.130.1003A,B

Beginning in the Old Kingdom, the body of a deceased, whether male or female, was buried with a fairly standardized assortment of funerary equipment directly associated with mummification. One essential component of this assemblage was the set of canopic jars designed to hold the viscera of the deceased.

The present jar originally belonged to a set of four such containers specifically identified with the Four Sons of Horus—Imset, Hapi, Duamutef, and Qebehsenuef—who served as protectors of the internal organs. The dedicatory inscription shows that this jar was designated for the protection of Hapi and Nephthys (the corollary protective goddess), who served as guardian divinities of the lungs.[1] The inscription, arranged in three vertical columns and highlighted in blue pigment, reads as follows:

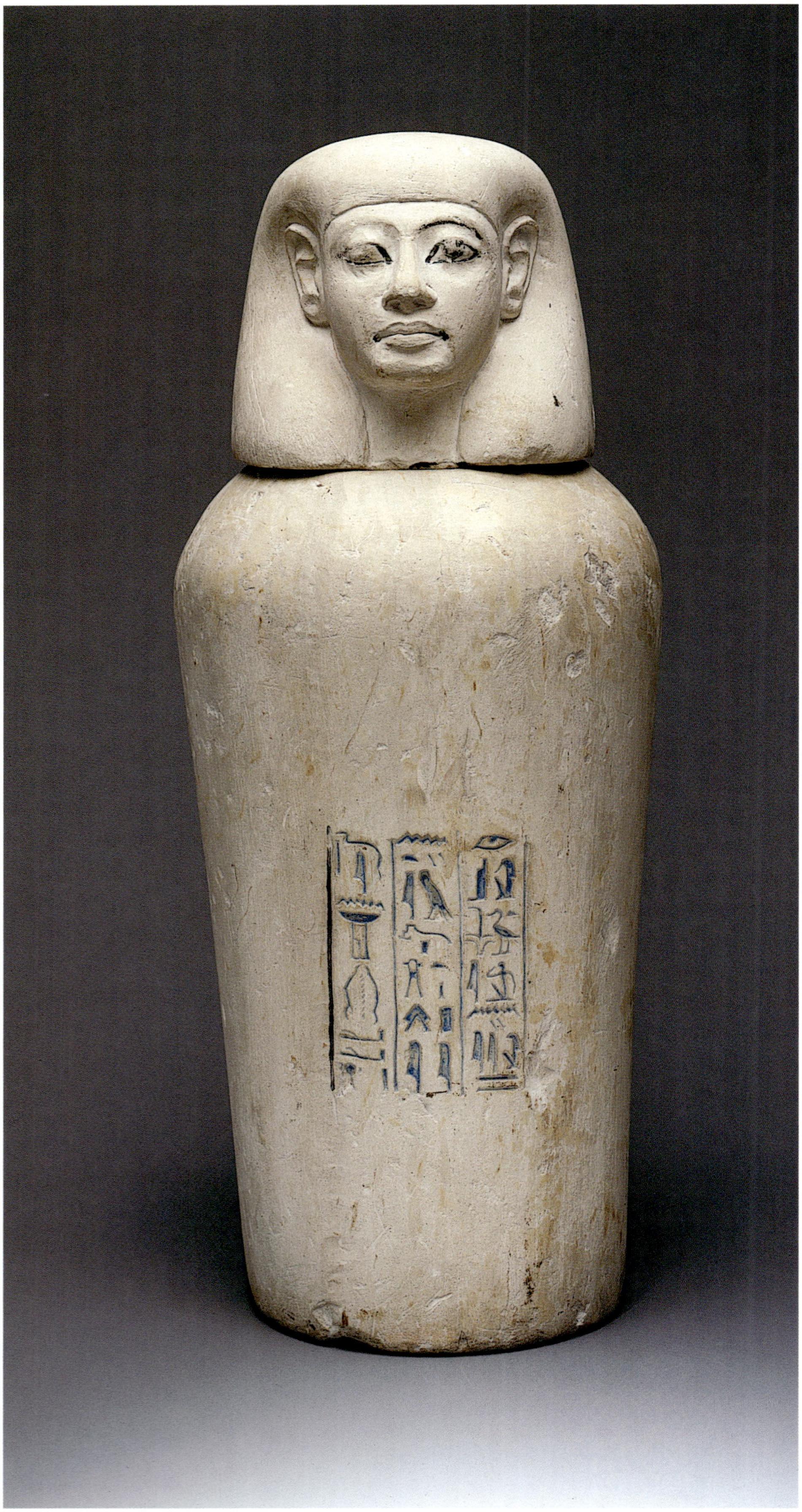

Words spoken by Nephthys. I embrace in my two arms that which is within me, giving protection to Hapi, [and to] the Osiris, the daughter of the king, Iny, justified.

In the inscription, the owner of the vessel is identified as Iny, "Daughter of the King."[2] On the basis of its collection history and style, Iny's jar, in fact, may be associated with a group of canopic vessels belonging to members of the family and household of Amenhotep III, who were buried in a tomb or group of tombs in the cliffs west of Deir el-Bahri.[3]

The canopic jar of Iny is distinguished by its exceptionally fine quality and delicacy of carving.[4] The quality and care invested in the carving may reflect Iny's elevated status or standing within the royal family.

With its human-headed lid, Iny's jar is typologically indistinguishable from the conventional jar associated with male burials of the period.[5] Even its formulaic inscription identifies the deceased with Osiris; because this deity had no true female equivalent, women prefixed their name with that of the male god.[6]

In all likelihood, the stopper of Iny's jar formed part of a set of four canopic jars with beardless, human-headed lids. The precise correlation between the use of beardless-headed stoppers and female burials remains unclear, however.[7] In typical fashion, the eyes and mouth of Iny's canopic jar stopper were originally highlighted in black.[8] Like other canopic jars of the period, it was probably stored in the compartment of a wooden chest that served as a coffin for the mummified internal organs. GEM

83 Fragment from a woman's Book of the Dead

Papyrus and ink; provenance unknown;
Late Period, Ptolemaic era, 1st century B.C.
Cincinnati Art Museum. Gift of the Heirs of John W. Bookwalter. 1919.483

From Egypt's early history, the burial of the deceased was customarily accompanied by a series of inscribed ritual spells and incantations to protect and guide him or her in the passage from this world to the next. The oldest funerary inscriptions, the so-called Pyramid Texts, date from the

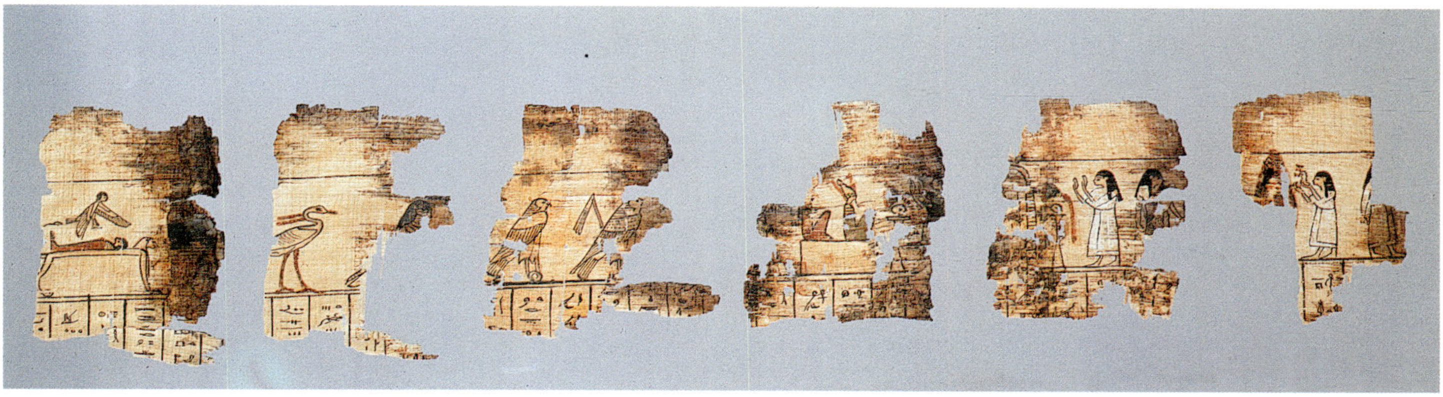

Old Kingdom. The strict prerogative of royalty, they were carved on the walls of pyramid burial chambers of both kings and queens, beginning in the late Fifth Dynasty. Queen Wedjebten, whose tomb relief fragment is featured in this volume (cat. no. 38), was among the first of the Old Kingdom queens to have such texts carved on the wall of her burial chamber.

During the New Kingdom, the genre of funerary texts was greatly enlarged. In addition to the collection of writings known as the *Amduat* (which describes the physical aspects of the netherworld) and the texts of the "Opening of the Mouth Ceremony" (which restored to the deceased power over his or her physical senses), the New Kingdom saw the development of the Book of the Dead (known in Egyptian as the "Book of Coming Forth by Day"). Most of its spells (which number about two hundred) come either from the Pyramid Texts or from their Middle Kingdom descendants, the Coffin Texts.[1] Such Books of the Dead were almost always written on papyrus scrolls[2] and were accompanied by vignettes illustrating the various spells or incantations selected.

Surviving examples show that Books of the Dead belonged to women as well as men. The texts were the same for both sexes, underscoring the parity with men that women enjoyed in the funerary realm.[3]

Although some copies of the Book of the Dead were clearly custom-made, by the later periods of Egyptian history (from which the present document derives) most funerary papyri were mass-produced—with generic male or female subjects, and with blank spaces reserved for the name of the deceased. The surviving illustrations and their sequence reveal that this Book of the Dead fragment came from an abbreviated text in which various chapters were excerpted from the total body of spells.[4]

There is evidence to suggest that an educated woman might have produced her own copy of the Book of the Dead for her tomb. The Greenfield Papyrus may have been executed by Nesitanbetisheru, daughter of Pinedjem II, the Twenty-first Dynasty Priest of Amen. One of the religious titles Nesitanbetisheru claimed was "Worker on the Scrolls of Amen-Ra."[5]

The present fragment formed part of a Book of the Dead prepared in the late Ptolemaic Period[6] for a woman whose name is no longer preserved. She appears in the vignettes dressed in a long, white, transparent gown.

A series of vignettes illustrating ten spells are preserved. (The vignettes and the accompanying hieroglyphic texts read from right to left.) The most important figures—the sacred birds and the two seated deities—face toward the right. The deceased faces both to the right and to the left; her figure often serves to divide the separate scenes.

On the far right is a fragmentary depiction of the deceased facing right. A careful comparison of this document with others of similar date indicates that this vignette represents either Spell 54, Spell 56,[7] or an abbreviated version combining the two. In the papyrus's original state, the deceased would have held the hieroglyphic sign for air in her left hand, indicating that she had received the "sweet breath of Atum." In the next vignette, which represents Spell 59,[8] the deceased stands before a sycamore tree sacred to the sky goddess Nut. The deceased pours water from a libation vase, thus ensuring that she will never be deprived of water in the afterlife. On the damaged right-hand side of the next fragment, the figure of the deceased faces right, with her right arm at her side. This vignette illustrates Spell 64, the "Chapter of Knowing All the Chapters of Going Forth by Day in a Single Chapter."[9]

The concept of "going forth" is continued in the next vignette in which the deceased raises her arms in a gesture of worship before an offering table draped with a lotus flower and a fragmentary shrine in which a goddess stands. This vignette depicts Spell 68,[10] the "Chapter of Coming Forth by Day." In this important spell, the deceased states her mastery over her heart, mouth, hands, and feet. This spell therefore allows the deceased to move about freely in the afterlife and to partake of funerary offerings. As the text states: "As for whoever knows this spell, it means . . . [s]he shall do what the living do. . . . "

In the next vignette, the mummy of the deceased is lying on a funerary bed in the form of a lion, a symbol of resurrection. Above the mummy is the *ba,* or animated aspect of the soul, of the deceased in the form of a human-headed bird. The claws of the bird clutch a *shen* sign, the symbol of eternity. This vignette illustrates Spell 89, "The Chapter of Causing the *ba* to Be United to Its Body in the Underworld":

> Oh deities . . . grant that my *ba* may return to me from wherever it may be—may (my *ba)* look upon its material body—may its body neither perish nor suffer corruption [i.e., decay] forever.[11]

According to ancient Egyptian religious belief, the deceased person's *ba* must return to its body to receive nourishment from the offerings left at the tomb. This spell ensured the deceased's control over his or her *ba.*

The next vignette depicts two deities seated upon a platform; one wears the double crown of Upper and Lower Egypt. These deities represent Osiris and the obscure deity Rekem. Chapter 72 of the Book of the Dead[12] was another spell that magically allowed the deceased to "go forth by day," to leave the tomb in any form he or she chose, and to partake of foods and beverages.

In the next vignette is a partial figure of a hawk holding a flail, symbolic of power. This image illustrates Spell 77, the

"Chapter of Making the Transformation into a Golden Falcon."[13] This spell allowed the deceased to assume the falcon's form and to fly the length of the country. According to the spell, all the deities were in awe of the powers of the deceased while occupying the form of a falcon of gold. Another divine bird, standing behind the first, depicts Spell 78,[14] which states the hope of the deceased to be transformed into a divine falcon and to obtain the divine *nemes* headdress, the "passport for the journey through the Netherworld."[15]

Though the next vignette is heavily damaged, a human-headed bird, the *ba*, can still be detected. This vignette represents Spell 85, the "Chapter of Making the Transformation into a Living *Ba*." The last preserved vignette, depicting a phoenix, represents Spell 83, the "Chapter of Making the Transformation into a *Bennu* Bird." Both of these spells associate the deceased's *ba* with the powerful *ba* of the sun god Ra, as they traversed the sky by day and the underworld by night in the solar boat of the god.[16] AKC

84 Reserve head of a woman

Limestone; from Giza, Western Cemetery, Tomb G4540; Old Kingdom, mid–late Dynasty 4; H: 26.3 cm

Museum of Fine Arts, Boston. Harvard University–MFA Expedition, 1914. 21.328

This white limestone portrait of a woman belongs to a category of object commonly termed a "reserve" head. More than thirty examples survive from Egyptian antiquity, all of them dated to the Fourth and early Fifth Dynasties of the Old Kingdom. The present example is one of approximately twenty found during the early part of this century in the royal cemetery complex located west of the Great Pyramid of Khufu at Giza.[1] The massive size of the tombs, or *mastabas,* from which these reserve heads derive, as well as their proximity in setting to Khufu's pyramid, strongly suggest that many of the finest examples were royal gifts to influential members of the court.[2] One female head in the series (now in the Cairo Museum) may be identified as that of Meret-ites, daughter of Khufu, on the basis of the associated slab stela that bears the name and titles of this princess.[3]

Given the prominent position occupied by royal women in the early Old Kingdom, the strong representation of female subjects within the sequence of heads from Giza (ten out of the approximately twenty identifiable portraits) comes as no surprise. This fact is confirmed by the number of substantial tombs for women (some of them pyramidal in form) built in close proximity to the king's pyramid. In the exceptional case of the Queen Mother Khentkawes, a monumental tomb was erected between the causeways of kings Khafra and Menkaura. As she was an ancestress of Dynasty 5, a royal cult and estate were established in her honor and maintained throughout the Fifth Dynasty.[4]

Like the portrait of Prince Sneferu-seneb from neighboring *mastaba* G4240, the features of the head are remarkably delicate and refined. In the fashion of the prince, her face is fine-boned and marked by aquiline features: deep-set eyes and sharply pointed nose. In physiognomy, she presents a striking contrast with the portrait of Meret-ites, whose broader nose and heavier bone structure suggest a more southerly, perhaps Nubian, origin. This marked variation in facial types among female portraits of the period has led to speculation about the ethnic makeup of royal women in Dynasty 4. While there is no firm evidence at present for the later royal custom (adopted in the New Kingdom) of accepting daughters of foreign rulers in marriage, the possibility of occasional intermarriage between the royal houses of Egypt and Nubia at this time should not be excluded. Indeed, Egypt's commercial ties with Nubia are clearly attested under Khufu and his successors.[5]

While the royal associations of this portrait and other reserve heads are clear, the precise context and function of these sculptures are not. The fact that all were found in tombs and are uniformly cut away at the base of the neck has led to the suggestion that they were designed to be placed in the burial chamber alongside the mummy.[6] It has been hypothesized that such heads functioned as substitutes for the complete statues of the tomb owners or their actual bodies, hence the name "reserve head." However, this is only one of several theoretical interpretations that have been offered.

Although no trace of pigment remains, the head of this woman may originally have been painted, as studies of other examples of this type indicate.[7] Despite the head's shaven appearance, the sculptor probably meant to indicate that she wore her hair short, a popular hairstyle for women at that period of Egyptian history.[8] GEM

Published: W.S. Smith, *HESPOK* (London, 1946), pl. 7; Smith, *Ancient Egypt as Represented in the Museum of Fine Arts, Boston* (Boston, 1960), 35, fig. 12; PM, 1^2, 100–131; F. Junge, "Hemiunu, Ancha-ha-ef und die sog. 'Ersatzköpfe,'" *Kunst des Alten Reiches* 107, pl. 39d; R. Tefnan, *Art et magie au temps des pyramides. L'énigme des têtes dites "de remplacement"* (Brussels, 1991), 103–4, pls. 9a–b.

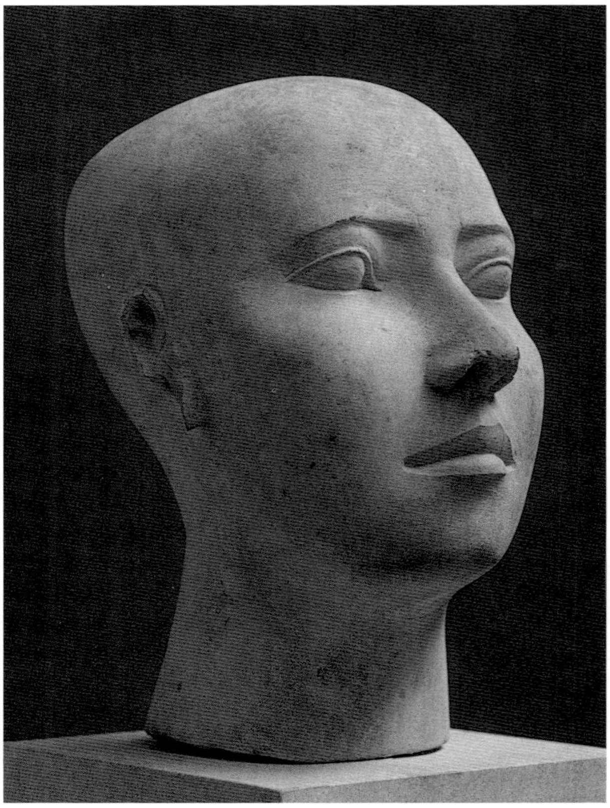

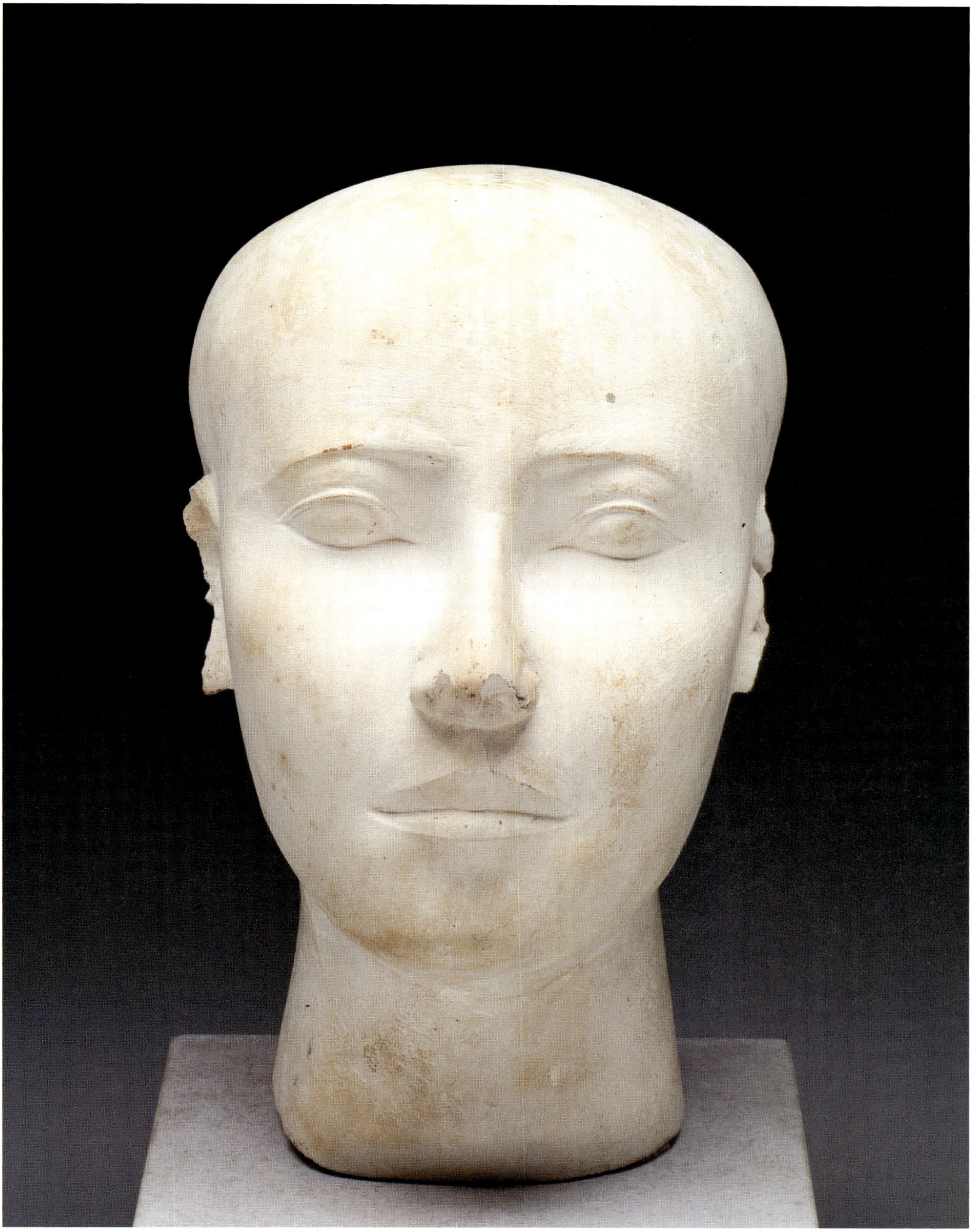

85 Funerary statue of Intekes

Painted limestone; from Giza, Far Western Cemetery G1200, *Mastaba* 1039; Old Kingdom, late Dynasty 5–early Dynasty 6; H: 32 cm

Phoebe Hearst Museum of Anthropology, University of California at Berkeley. 6–19773

This statue depicting a seated woman by the name of Intekes was found together with a statue of a seated man sealed in the *serdab* (an enclosed chamber designed for the *ka* statues of the tomb owners) of their *mastaba* tomb. Presumably the male statue depicted Intekes' husband; however, it bears no inscription—a curious omission considering the importance of the name in ancient Egypt.[1] The inscription on Intekes' statue provides her title: "Priestess of Hathor, Mistress of Dendara."

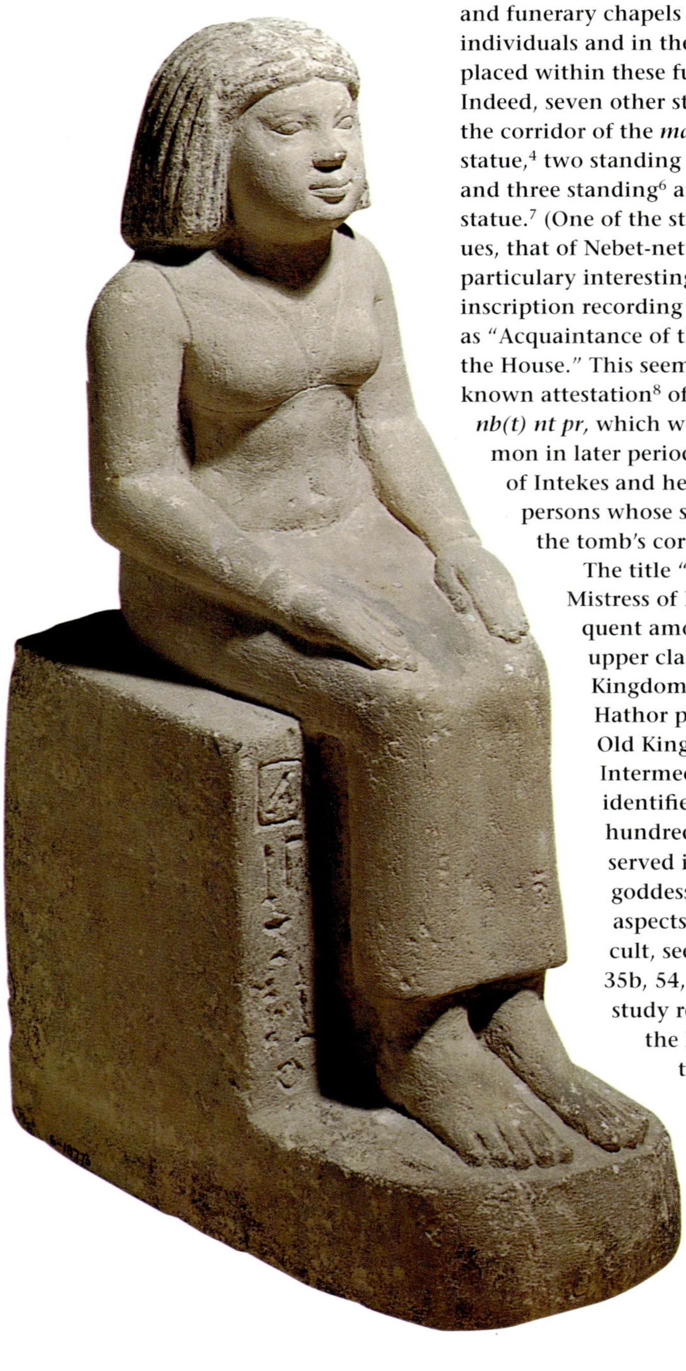

Intekes' round, open face and blocky proportions are typical of statuary of the late Fifth or early Sixth Dynasty. She is depicted in the conventional attitude for seated women of the period: positioned with legs together and hands placed on the thighs, palms down.[2] She wears a simple sheath dress with shoulder straps that cover the breasts. The heavy shoulder-length wig, painted black, strengthens the statue at the neck, a point where it might otherwise be vulnerable to damage. For the same reason, her arms are engaged tightly to her body, and her legs to the seat.

The late Fifth and early Sixth Dynasties, when Intekes' statue was made, witnessed a great increase in the number of tombs and funerary chapels erected for private individuals and in the quantity of statues placed within these funerary monuments. Indeed, seven other statues[3] were found in the corridor of the *mastaba:* one family statue,[4] two standing female statues,[5] and three standing[6] and one seated male statue.[7] (One of the standing female statues, that of Nebet-net-ka, Cairo 37718, is particulary interesting because it bears an inscription recording this woman's titles as "Acquaintance of the King, Mistress of the House." This seems to be the earliest known attestation[8] of the second title, *nb(t) nt pr,* which would become so common in later periods.) The relationship of Intekes and her husband to those persons whose statues were found in the tomb's corridor is unclear.[9]

The title "Priestess of Hathor, Mistress of Dendara" was frequent among women of the upper classes in the Old Kingdom. One study of Hathor priestesses of the Old Kingdom and the First Intermediate Period has identified more than two hundred such women who served in the cult of the goddess.[10] (For the various aspects of Hathor and her cult, see cat. nos. 20c, 22a, 35b, 54, and 55.) The same study reports that men held the higher administrative positions in the cult, and that these offices could be inherited.[11] The

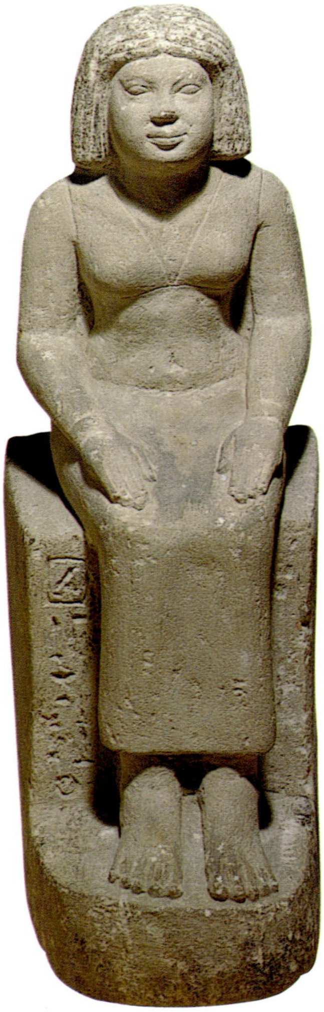

less lofty cultic positions in the priestly hierarchy were held overwhelmingly by women.[12] Their titles could not be passed on to their children,[13] although evidence of families' participation in the cult, and of marriages linking these families, suggests that titles associated with the cult of Hathor may have carried desirable religious, social, and political implications.[14]

The women who served as Hathor priestesses might perform as musicians, singers, or dancers during the worship of the goddess.[15] Others shook sistra and *menats* to placate the deity.[16] At least one woman is recorded as performing "purification" services for Hathor; she received the same payment as the men who acted in this capacity.[17] The title *hemet-netjer* ("Priestess") remained common for women during the Middle Kingdom. By the New Kingdom, however, priestly titles for women are attested only rarely; at that period women served in the capacities of *shemayit, hesyt* ("Chantresses" or "Songstresses"), or *khenerut* ("Musicians") in the cult of Hathor and other deities.[18]

As stated above, the statues of Intekes and her husband were originally placed in the *serdab* of their *mastaba* tomb.[19]

Like other *serdab* statues of the period, they were positioned so that Intekes and her husband could gaze through the opening in the wall of the *serdab*, which faced the adjoining offering chapel. The slot allowed them to witness and partake of the periodic offerings made on their behalf by family members and *ka* priests. AKC

Published: Lutz, *Egyptian Statues*, pls. 26b, 27a; PM 3, pt. 1, p. 54.

86 Funerary stela for Lady Nefer

Limestone with pigment; Giza, Western Field, Cemetery 1200, *Mastaba* G1207; Old Kingdom, Dynasty 4, reign of Khufu; H: 50.8 cm

Phoebe Hearst Museum of Anthropology, University of California at Berkeley. 6–19801

Women figured prominently in a variety of contexts during the Old Kingdom. This phenomenon is most apparent in the cemeteries at Giza, which contain many *mastabas* and tomb chapels belonging not only to female royalty but also to nonroyal women of rank and standing. This funerary stela was originally set into the wall of the brick *mastaba* of one such lady, named Nefer.[1] Nefer's *mastaba* was located in a cemetery in the Western Field at Giza, which contained ten tombs of the same variety, each bearing a tomb chapel with a funerary stela recessed into its western face.[2] Eight of these slab-stelae survive intact; Nefer's stela is one of three that depict women. In all, five of the thirteen classifiable slab-stelae from Giza that may be identified with a known individual belong to women; three are princesses, and two (including Nefer) are nonroyal women of standing.[3]

Lady Nefer's title *rẖt nỉsw* (Acquaintance of the King) is characteristic of ranking nonroyal women in the Old Kingdom.[4] Like its masculine counterpart, *rẖ nỉsw* (and in contrast to its later usage in the New Kingdom) this title appears to have been conferred directly by the king himself, indicating the designate's direct relationship with the royal house. The size and layout of Lady Nefer's *mastaba* as well as its proximity to the pyramid complex of Khufu affirm this relationship.

As G. Reisner originally observed, the entire block of tombs to which Nefer's *mastaba* belonged was carefully planned and developed, probably by royal architects under Khufu's administration. The slab-stelae—the work of royal craftsmen—

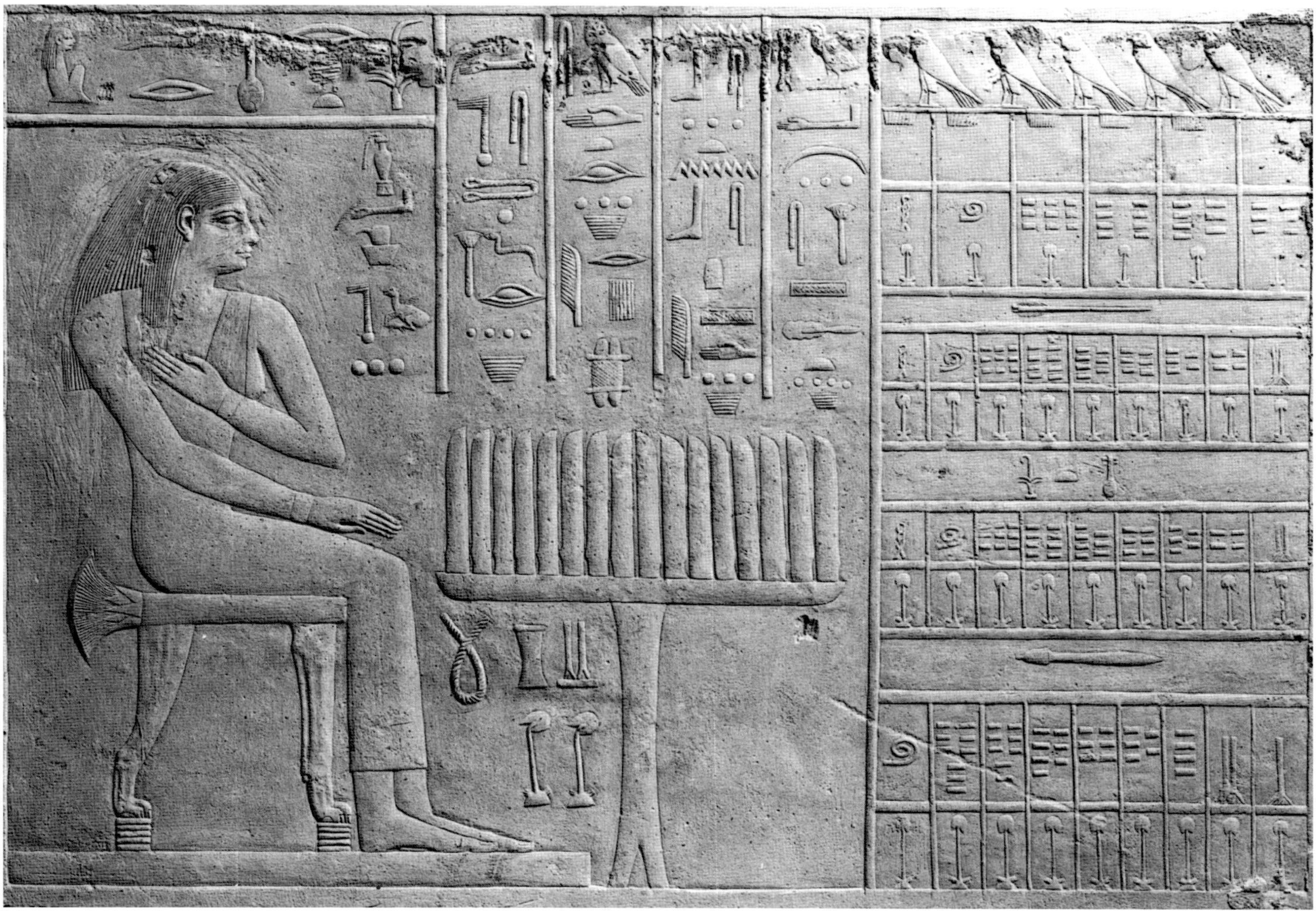

were almost certainly granted by Khufu himself and presented as marks of favor.[5]

Like Sety-hekenet, the other nonroyal woman in Nefer's funerary grouping, Nefer must have occupied a prominent position within the royal circle. Unfortunately, little else is known about her; in keeping with period protocol, no genealogy or husband's name is provided on the identifying inscription. The fact that Nefer was accorded her own tomb complex, however, reveals much about her elevated administrative or social standing.[6] Unlike Old Kingdom royal females, who were regularly provided with their own tombs, nonroyal women typically occupied a subordinate role in the chapels of their husbands.[7]

The quality of Lady Nefer's slab-stela, as previously mentioned, indicates its royal workmanship. The subtly modeled low relief decoration closely resembles surviving relief work from the central chapel (GIb) of the three pyramids belonging to Khufu's queens.[8] The stela apparently formed the sole decoration of the tomb, marking the offering niche of the burial chapel.[9] This scene, representing the deceased seated at a table, accompanied by offering lists, corresponds to that depicted on early false doors and niche stones of the early Old Kingdom.[10] On her stela, Nefer is depicted in the same manner as a man: seated on a lion-legged chair before an offering table, her left hand on her breast and her right arm extended.[11] Her dress, consisting of a V-necked, ankle-length garment with shoulder straps, is conventional for women of the Old Kingdom. Nefer's hair is combed behind the ears, falling on either side of her shoulder. According to convention, her facial features appear slightly fleshier and more rounded than those of a man.

The stela contains offering lists grouped in three different forms. Above the offering table is the short list of offerings enumerating items of food and drink. On the right side of the stela is the "linen" list, an inventory of linen offerings in the tomb presented in descending order of fabric quality. An abbreviated list in ideographic form also appears under the table.[12] GEM

Published: Reisner, *Giza Necropolis* 1: pl. 18b; C. Keller in *American Discovery*, no. 38 (for a complete bibliography and text translation).

87 Funerary stela for Ta-sheryt-akhet

Wood, with paint over gesso; from Thebes, excavations at the Ramesseum; Third Intermediate Period, Dynasty 22; H: 24.7 cm; W: 19 cm

The University of Pennsylvania Museum of Archaeology and Anthropology, Philadelphia. E 2043

The present stela is one of a dozen related wooden stelae of Twenty-second Dynasty date discovered within burials in the Theban Ramesseum.[1] All depict the dedicant standing in adoration before Ra-Horakhty (Ra-Horus-of-the-Horizon), a syncretized form of the gods Ra and Horus. This stela is one of eight depicting women; all are either Chantresses of Amen or Daughters of Priests of Amen.[2]

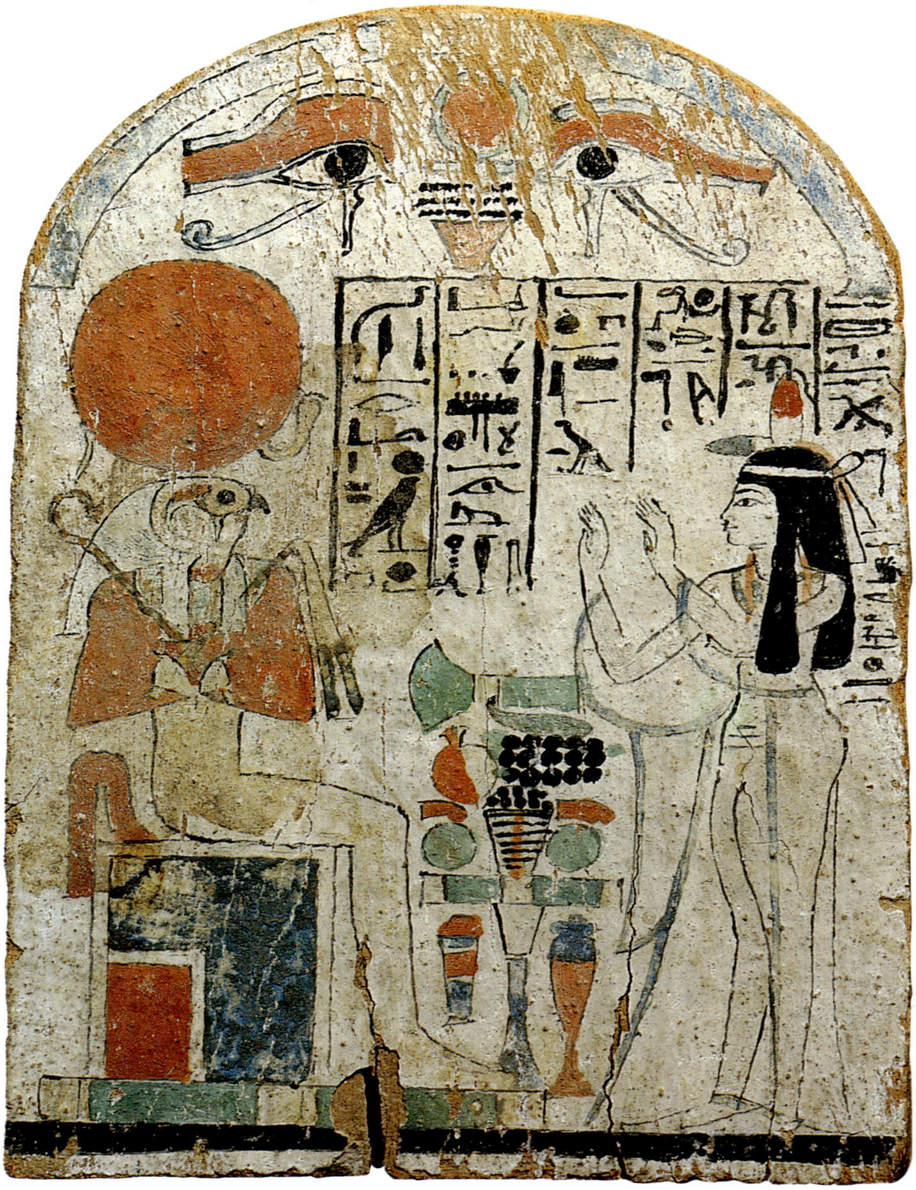

In the present stela, the dedicant, identified as Ta-sheryt-akhet ("the Young One of the Horizon"), Chantress of Amen, approaches the falcon-headed Ra-Horakhty, who is seated before an offering table holding a crook and flail. As on other stelae of this variety, the deceased confronts the sun god directly, associating herself with the solar cycle of birth, death, and rebirth.[3] The god, who wears the conventional sun disc with *uraei,* is situated on a mat of green rush bound with yellow cross-ties. Ta-sheryt-akhet stands with hands upraised in prayer and is dressed in a long, transparent robe; her elaborate wig bears an incense cone of unguent and a small lotus flower. In the arch above is a central *sn* ring over a water symbol and a vase; the whole is flanked by *udjat* eyes.[4]

Above the main scene is a vertical inscription in six columns:

> Words spoken by Ra-Horakhty that he might give incense and linen (to) [the] Osiris songstress of the house of Amen Ta-sheryt-akhet, daughter of one whom the god loves, the scribe of the stable(?) of [ ] of Nespanetjer *(n) djr* [ ], justified.

As observed above, Ta-sheryt-akhet's title "Chantress of Amen" was typical for women of standing in the New Kingdom and Third Intermediate Periods. (Amen, in fact, was the divinity worshipped most commonly by such women, followed by Hathor.[5]) Here, Ta-sheryt-akhet bears the generic designation *hesyt* rather than *shemayit,* as employed by Neskhonsu-pakhered and Henut-wedjebu (cat. nos. 90 and 91). The distinction between the two terms is not entirely clear.[6]

Although Ta-sheryt-akhet's burial was not discovered intact, the inscriptions from associated burials at the Ramesseum reveal that all the tombs equipped with this type of stela belonged to ranking members of the Theban priesthood of Amen under Osorkon I.[7] In some instances a royal lineage is indicated clearly, as in the case of Sheb-en-Sepdet, daughter of Osorkon's son Nemarat.[8] GEM

Published: J.E. Quibell, *The Ramesseum* (London, 1898), pl. 20, 2; *Egyptian Mummy,* 57, no. 57.

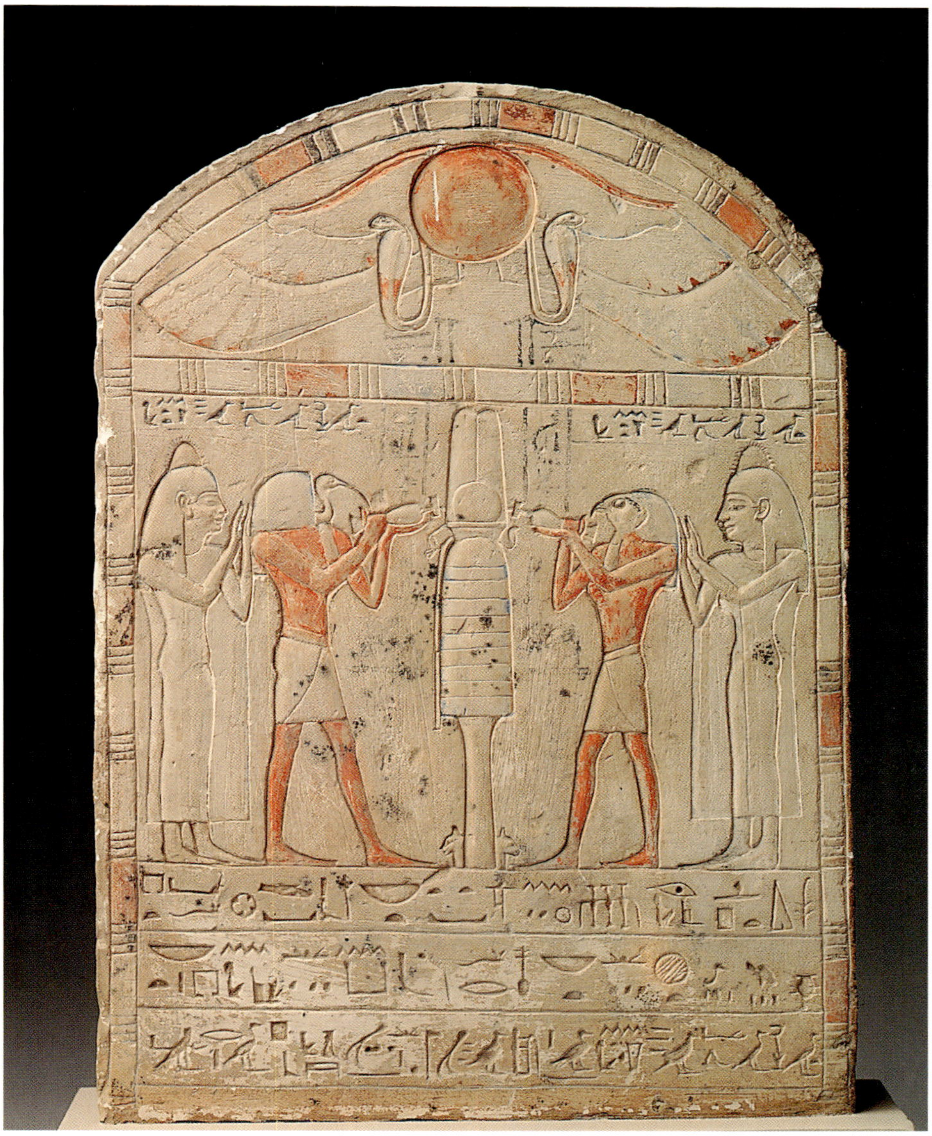

88 Round-topped (funerary) stela of Ta-Khaa-en-Bastet

Limestone with pigment; probably from Abydos; Late Period, Dynasty 25–early Dynasty 26; H: 33 cm; W: 24 cm

Cincinnati Art Museum. Gift of Millard F. and Edna F. Shelt. 1947.392

This funerary stela of the Twenty-fifth or early Twenty-sixth Dynasty was prepared for a woman named Ta-Khaa-en-Bastet.[1] She is depicted twice in the stela's main scene, her hands raised in reverence behind the figures of Horus and Thoth who pour water libations before a central *djed* pillar with *atef* crown, sacred symbol of the god Osiris.[2] The presence of the *djed* pillar, fetish of Osiris, indicates that the stela probably came from Abydos, Osiris's cult center, and was intended for placement in his temple there. By having this stela made for this purpose, Ta-Khaa-en-Bastet hoped to share in the cult of the deity in perpetuity. In conventional fashion, the dedicatory inscription below the central scene records the various food offerings that the king made to Osiris on behalf of Ta-Khaa-en-Bastet's *ka:*

> An offering which the king gives (to) Osiris, Foremost of Westerners, Lord of Abydos, (that) he may grant funerary offerings of bread and beer, cattle and fowl, and all good and pure things for the *ka* of the lady, the Mistress of the House Ta-Khaa-en-Bastet, daughter of the Scribe of the Divine Scrolls of Onuris, Pabarema.

Ta-Khaa-en-Bastet's only recorded title is "Mistress of the House," a designation commonly found among Egyptian women of the middle and upper classes (cf. cat. nos. 2, 4, 35a, 75, 90, and 91). The inscription also tells us that her father, Pabarema, was employed as scribe of the god Onuris, the divine huntsman in Egyptian mythology. Because Onuris's cult center was located at the city of This in Middle Egypt, it is likely that Ta-Khaa-en-Bastet and her father lived in that city, which lies close to Abydos, the probable site of the stela's dedication. From the inscription, it is impossible to tell whether Ta-Khaa-en-Bastet was married. If she was unmarried and her father widowed, her title "Mistress of the House" may indicate that she supervised her father's household in This.

Several lines of inscription (in a quite competent hand) have been added beneath the central *uraei* at the top of the stela and before the faces of Horus and Thoth. The painted texts below the winged *uraei* refer to the Behdetite, the winged solar Horus;[3] those before Horus and Thoth read, respectively: "Words Spoken by Horus" and "Words Spoken by Thoth."[4] The fact that these inscriptions were painted rather than carved indicates that they were added after the initial completion of the stela.

On her stela, Ta-Khaa-en-Bastet is garbed, according to conventional fashion, in a close-fitting dress and a loose, transparent overgarment. On her head she wears a perfumed cone of wax; this item of headdress is depicted frequently in contemporary scenes of worship, perhaps to symbolize the pleasure that one experienced in the presence of the gods.[5]

Extensive traces of the original painted decoration remain: red on the solar disc and *uraei,* on the bodies of Thoth and Horus, and on the ornamental border; and blue on the *djed* and the headdresses of the deities and Ta-Khaa-en-Bastet, as well as the inscription itself. AKC/GEM

Published: *Sculpture Collection,* 23.

89 Panel of a coffin made for a woman

Wood with pigment; provenance unknown, probably from Asyut; Middle Kingdom, late Dynasty 11 or 12;
L: 178.8 cm
The Brooklyn Museum. Charles Edwin Wilbour Fund. 1995.112

Recently acquired by the Brooklyn Museum, this panel from the west (left) side of a coffin makes its debut here. Although the archaeological context of the panel is not recorded, the distinctive decorative pattern and the selection of texts indicate that it is from the central Egyptian city of Asyut, which was the most important center for coffin production during the First Intermediate Period and the Middle Kingdom.[1] The coffin panel displays the two most significant innovations of this workshop—the layout of the texts and the depiction of various funerary items on the outside—not the interior—of the coffin.

Throughout the Old Kingdom and the First Intermediate Period, the external texts on coffins from all sites, including some from Asyut, were confined to a single row along all four sides of the rectangular box. A magical spell that promised the gift of certain funerary offerings to the deceased by the king and a god (Osiris or Anubis), this text—the so-called invocation-offering formula—was the most frequently duplicated of all the countless inscriptions from ancient Egypt.[2] At some point in the First Intermediate Period, the complex configuration represented by this coffin panel appeared.[3] Two or more rows spanned the long sides (the east and west sides). The short sides (north and south or head and foot) generally had two or three rows. More significant, however, was the addition of four groups of columns on the long sides; each column consisted of one or more units. Here each column is a doublet.

The bold new decoration on the exterior of the coffins generally featured persons bearing offerings,[4] the offerings alone, or a combination of the two patterns.[5] The second arrangement appears on the present panel. From left to right, the offerings depicted are jars of unguent and bags of linen on a table, a canopic chest, a prism-shaped garden pool, and a sieve or jar stopper underneath, a mirror in a slipcase,[6] and a pair of sandals. These items are not gender specific; they are among the commodities represented in the so-called *frises d'objets* on the inside and the outside of coffins for both men and women.[7]

The depiction of the funerary equipment on the exterior of the coffin reverses the practice at most other sites.[8] Normally, decoration and important spells from the Coffin Texts and the Pyramid Texts appear on the interior for greater proximity to the dead, just as paintings and reliefs cover the walls of a tomb. In fact, the coffin with interior decoration is a microenvironment of the tomb. The bold inversion of tradition and the playful innovations that characterize the Asyut ateliers necessitate a reexamination of the frequent claims about cultural stagnation during the First Intermediate Period.

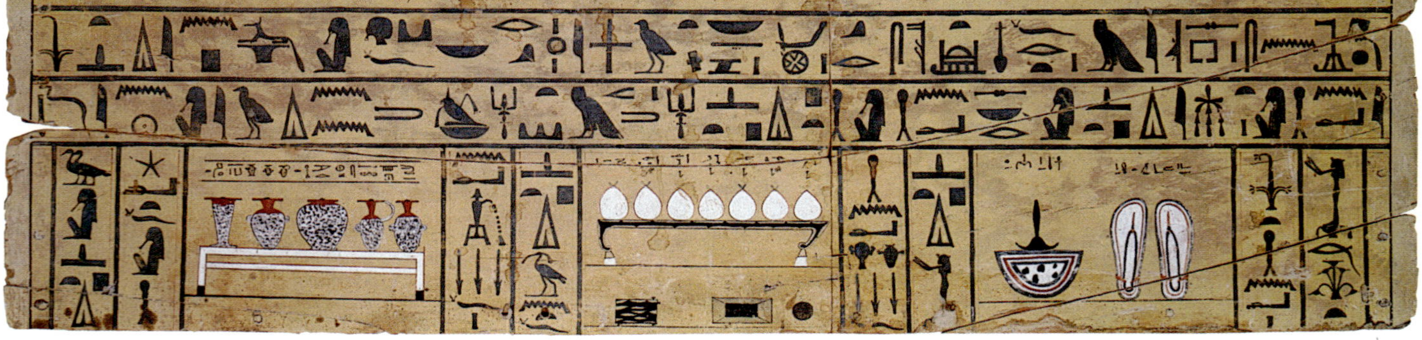

Perhaps forgetting that the coffin was intended for a woman, the scribe who drew the blue hieroglyphs of the inscription used a masculine grammatical reference and then quickly corrected his mistake. In the second line of the horizontal text, the pronoun of the datival phrase "to you" is written in the feminine form over the masculine, which is now barely visible in red outline.[9] In the only other gender-specific passage, which occurs a few signs later, the scribe correctly wrote the feminine in the phrase "at your right [*sic*] side."[10]

A distinctive feature of Asyut coffins that is well represented on this panel is the specification of obscure deities in the invocation-offering formula, such as Akhenitef (*3ḫnit.f*) and Heryibsenuef (*Ḥriibsnw.f*), who were probably local deities.[11] Less commonly attested on Asyut coffins but much better known elsewhere is the musician goddess Meryt, who is associated on the panel with Upper and Lower Egypt.[12] DBS

Published: Sylvia Schoske and Dietrich Wildung, *Entdeckungen: Ägyptische Kunst in Süddeutschland* (Mainz, 1985), 31, no. 21a, and endpapers.

90 Cartonnage (mummy case) of Neskhonsu-pakhered

Cartonnage; probably from Thebes; Third Intermediate Period, Late Dynasty 22; L: 1.7 m

Phoebe Hearst Museum of Anthropology, University of California at Berkeley. 6–19929

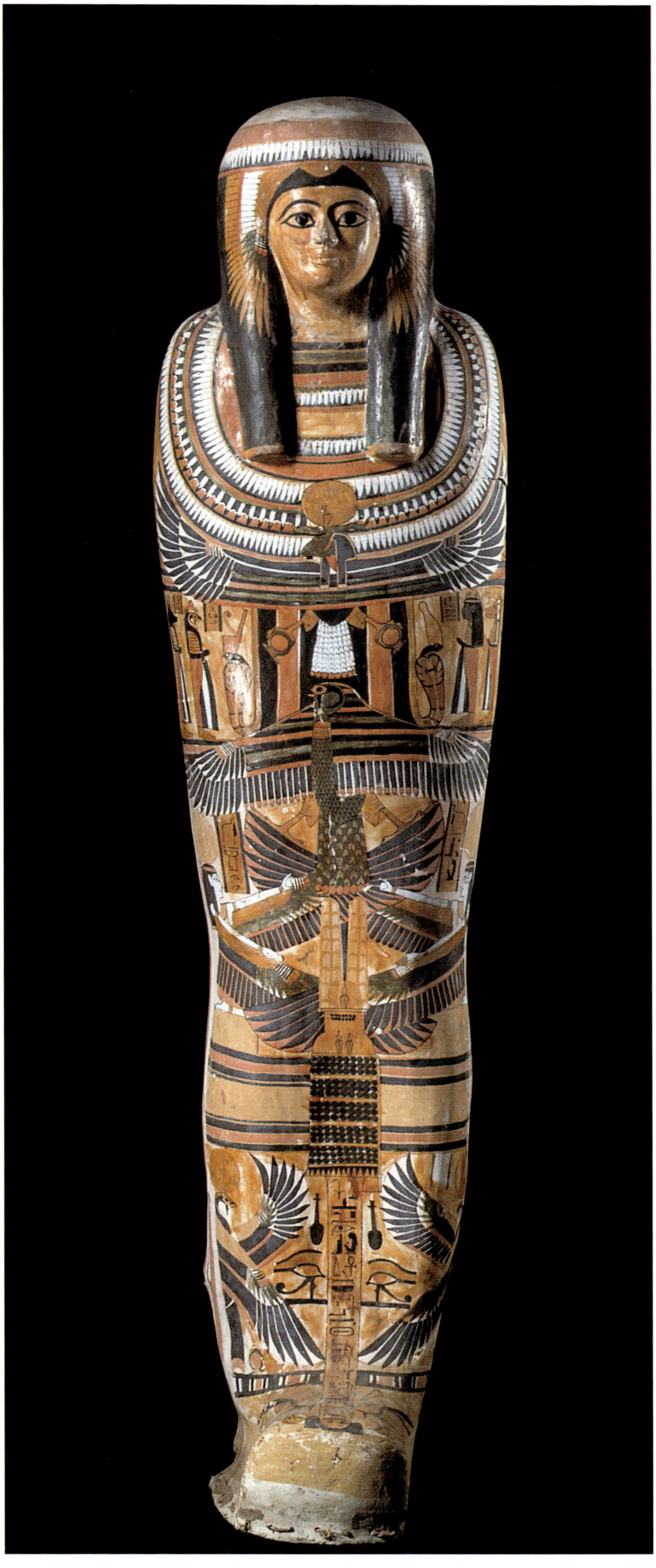

As recorded in the dedicatory inscription above the foot, the occupant of this mummy case was Neskhonsu-pakhered (literally, "she belongs to Khonsu-the-child").[1] Like Henut-wedjebu, whose outer coffin is included in this volume (cat. no. 91), she is designated by inscription as "Mistress of the House" and "Chantress of Amen," a pairing of titles not uncommon among Theban women of the upper and middle classes. Although the precise context of Neskhonsu-pakhered's tomb and the circumstances of its discovery are not recorded,[2] some definite conclusions can be drawn: the inscriptions on both her inner and outer coffins identify her as the wife[3] of Nespernub, whose cartonnage and outer coffin are housed in the British Museum.[4] In style and decoration, both Neskhonsu-pakhered's and Nespernub's coffins are typical of the Twenty-second Dynasty at Thebes.[5] According to the titles on Nespernub's coffin, he (like his father, Ankhefenkhonsu) was a Theban priest at Karnak. In all likelihood, Neskhonsu-pakhered was buried in her husband's tomb at Thebes.

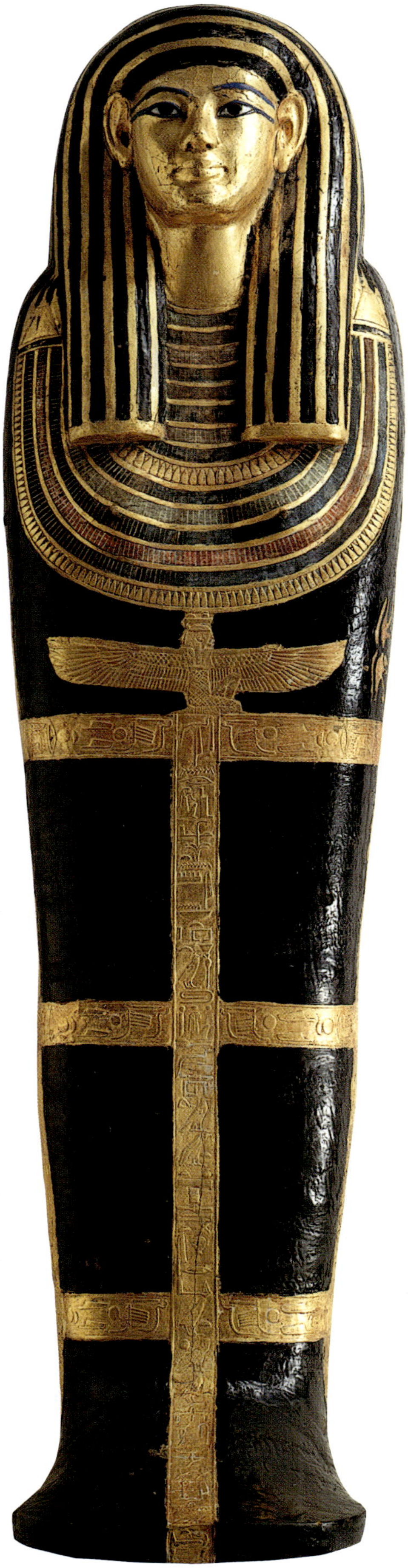

Neskhonsu-pakhered's age and precise identity must remain a mystery; unlike her father—whose mummy lies intact within its cartonnage—she no longer survives in the flesh. Her cartonnage was ripped open and her mummy removed from its case before its acquisition by the Hearst Museum. Neskhonsu-pakhered's outer wooden coffin, however, survives;[6] like her cartonnage, it is virtually identical in style to her husband's, suggesting that both had been commissioned at the same time.[7]

On her mummy case, Neskhonsu-pakhered wears the vulture cap over her wig (see cat. no. 52). An ancient headdress previously reserved for goddesses and queens, it symbolized the vulture goddess Nekhbet, patron deity of Upper Egypt. In the style of the early Third Intermediate Period, Neskhonsu-pakhered's mummy cover is replete with images of protective winged deities: three falcons[8] and a winged ram-headed deity, together with Isis and Nephthys, grace the exterior, while the underside of the outer coffin is occupied by the sky goddess Nut (symbolizing the heavens across which the deceased passed from this world to the next). GEM

Published: Fazzini, *Images*, no. 102.

91 Coffin of Henut-wedjebu

Painted, gilded, and inlaid wood; excavated at Sheikh Abd el-Qurna, Thebes, tomb of Hatiay; New Kingdom, Dynasty 18, reign of Amenhotep III; H: 64.5 cm; W: 52.5 cm; L: 1.8 m

Washington University Gallery of Art, St. Louis. Gift of Charles Parsons, 1896. 2292

This beautifully decorated coffin of the period of Amenhotep III belongs to the lady Henut-wedjebu,[1] "Mistress of the House" and "Chantress of Amen." The coffin's lavish gilded decoration and its find context—from the tomb of Hatiay, Scribe and Granary Overseer of the Mansion of the Aten—identify the occupant as a woman of aristocratic standing. Although her precise relationship to Hatiay is unclear, her title, *nebet per,* and the size and quality of her coffin suggest that she was his wife; the two remaining occupants of the tomb, both women, possessed coffins and mummies that were far less well prepared.[2] By contrast, Henut-wedjebu's coffin closely resembles Hatiay's in decoration and differs only in minor inscriptional variations.[3]

Henut-wedjebu's title of "Chantress" *(shemayit)* was associated frequently with women at the upper levels of Egyptian society. The precise meaning of the term remains unclear, but music and musicianship clearly played important roles in ancient Egyptian religion.[4] Musicians, both male and female, were frequently shown playing a harp, a lyre, or a reed instrument similar to an oboe.[5] Cultic instruments of a percussive nature also were a common feature of performance: on her tomb statue, Meryt, wife of Maya (Tutankhamen's treasurer), is depicted with a *menat* (cat. no. 35c); Henuttawey, the Chantress of Isis, shakes two sistra in honor of Amen on her own metal sistrum.[6]

A painting from the Theban tomb of Kynebu,[7] dating to the Twentieth Dynasty, is a graphic illustration of a funerary banquet procession involving Singers of Amen. In the primary scene, the tomb owner's four daughters—two dancers, a lyrist, and an oboist—are identified clearly as Songstresses of Amen. The wall text also refers to "singing to the *ksks*," an ancient Egyptian acrobatic dance.[8] As other tomb depictions show, temple songstresses often performed in groups or choruses of three or more, frequently under the guidance of a musical leader or chorister.

Henut-wedjebu's coffin bears twenty-three hieroglyphic texts, excerpted mainly from contemporary Books of the Dead. The kneeling figure of the sky goddess Nut adorns the coffin lid beneath the collar, while Nephthys and Isis adorn the head and the foot of the coffin, respectively. The coffin's eight side panels depict the Four Sons of Horus, shown in pairs between the flanking figures of the jackal-headed Anubis, god of embalming. GEM

Published: *Egypt's Dazzling Sun*, no. 61.

92 Bust of a noblewoman

Indurated limestone with traces of pigment; provenance unknown, probably from Asyut; New Kingdom, late Dynasty 18–early Dynasty 19; H: 49.5 cm; W: 34.6 cm; D: 26.8 cm

Cincinnati Art Museum. Given by his friends in memory of Joseph David Nelson, Jr. 1966.266

This near-life-size bust fragment is from a pair statue that depicted a noblewoman together with another person, probably her husband. The woman's left arm was originally placed around the shoulders of her husband in a typical protective gesture. It is not possible to determine whether the couple was depicted seated or standing, since the lower edge of the breakage occurs above the level of the hips.

The woman wears a very large, heavy, elaborately plaited wig that covers her shoulders. Traces of black pigment remain in the carved plaiting.[1] The tightly crimped strands of hair extend in front to the level of the woman's breasts with a border of

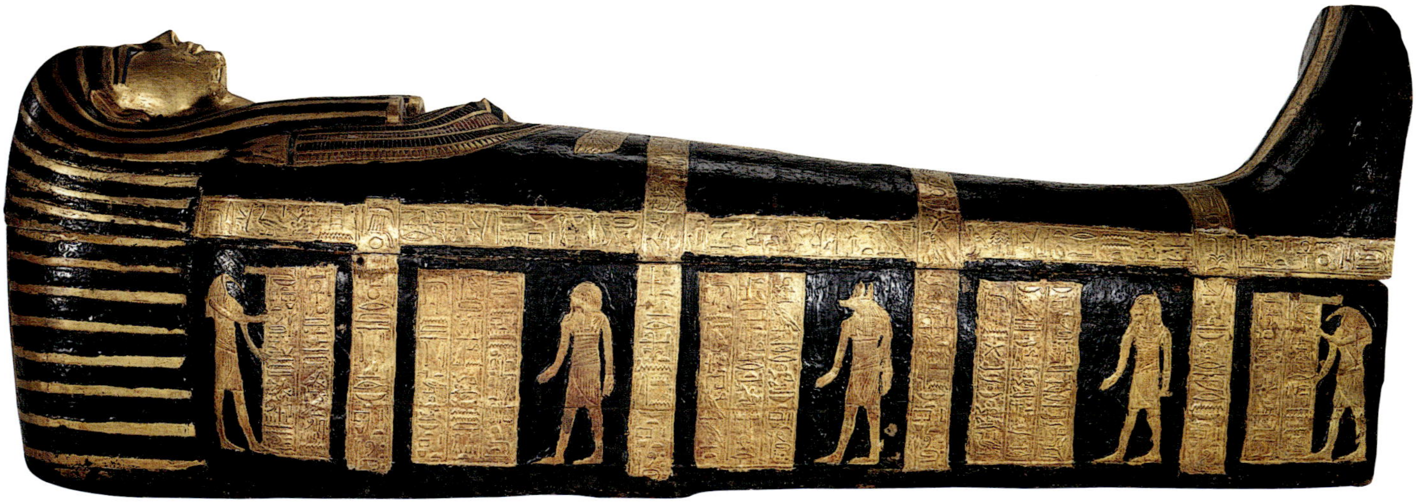

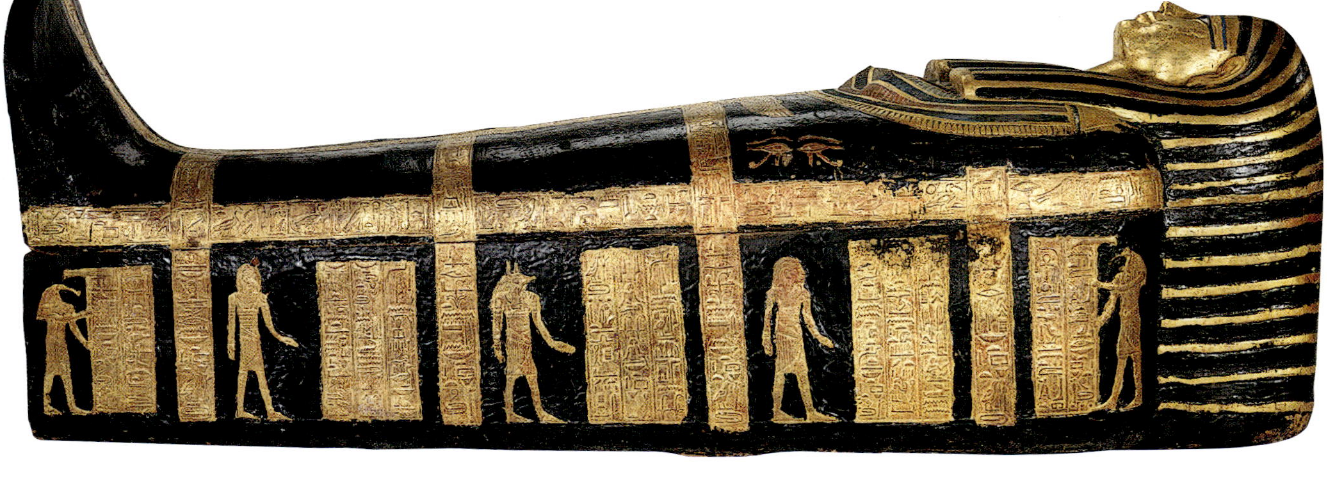

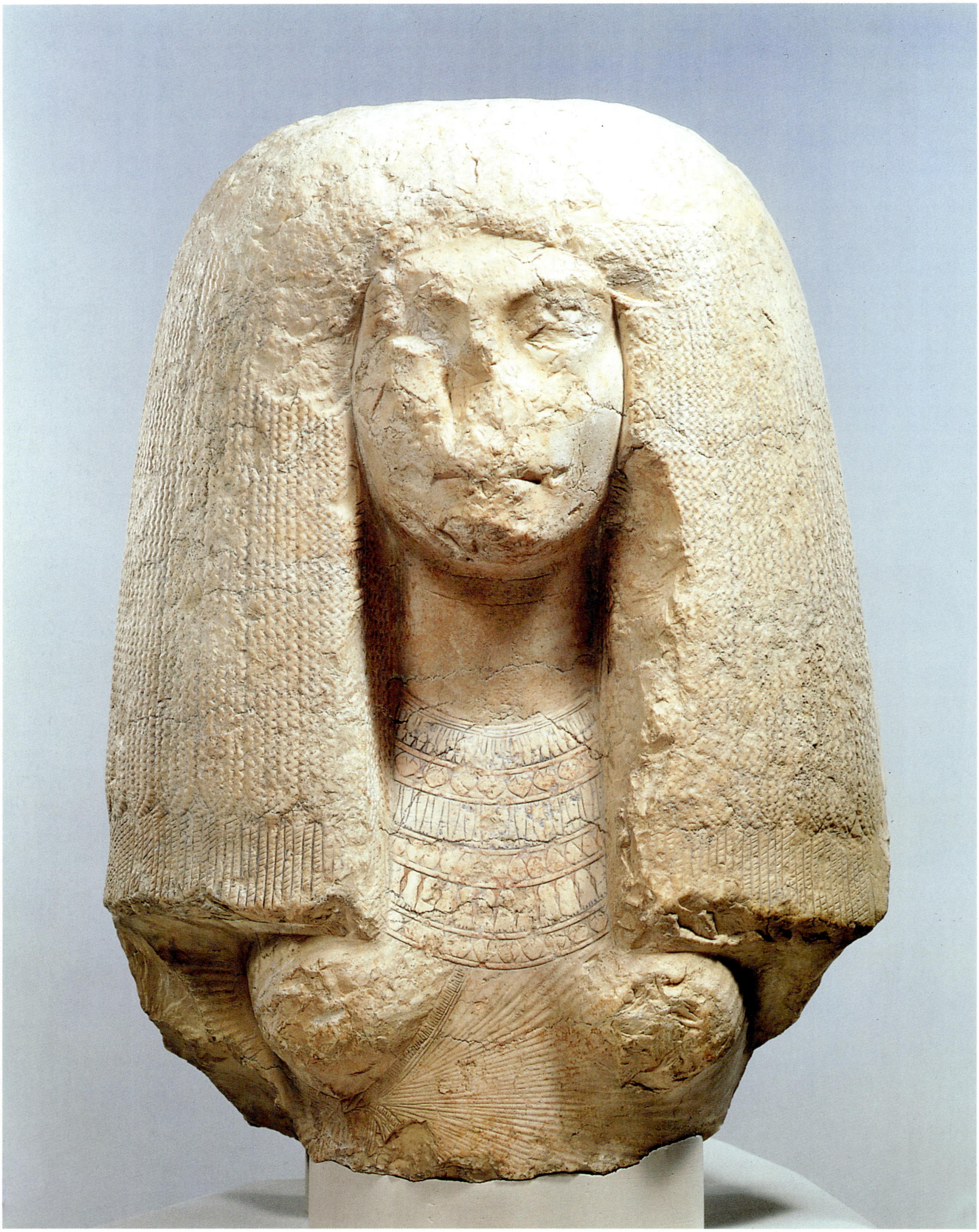

multiple curls at the lower edge of the wig. Just above the eyebrows, a band decorated in a floral motif extends around the circumference of the wig.

A delicately pleated gown drapes over the noblewoman's shoulders and is fastened with a narrow tied band under the proper right breast. Across her chest she wears a broad collar consisting of six bands of floral elements. Traces of red and blue pigment remain in the tracings of the collar. Another unadorned band is carved high on the neck.

Heavy damage has been inflicted on the face and breasts; the pattern of the damage suggests that it was done intentionally in antiquity. The mutilation of the eyes, nose, and mouth of a person's *ka* statue was believed by the ancient Egyptians to destroy the deceased's abilities to see, speak, eat, drink, and breathe in the afterlife.[2] The destruction of the breasts would have prevented the woman from nourishing children born to her in the realm of the blessed dead. In spite of this abuse, the sensitive modeling of the planes of the face are still readily apparent; the outer corners of the lips, for example, preserve an extraordinarily lifelike appearance.[3]

Six vertical columns of inscription are partially preserved on the back of the statue. The hieroglyphs retain traces of blue pigment. Since only one figure of the pair has been preserved, it is likely that at least six additional lines of inscription were carved on the part of the statue now lost. The columns of text read as follows:[4]

| 4 | 5 | 6 | 3 | 2 | 1 |

1 An offering which the king gives, and Hathor, Mistress of Medjedney, Mistress of Heaven, Mistress of the Gods . . .

2 . . . in praise of that which I did for Wepwawet, son of Isis-[Hathor] . . .

3 . . . to Hathor, Mistress of Medjedney, by all the praised ones . . .

4 . . . which was done for him because . . .

5 . . . a good life, praying for him old age, adoring . . .

6 . . . Upper Egypt, the overseer of priests of all the gods of Asyut, Djefau- . . .

Unfortunately, the name of the noblewoman depicted here is not preserved, although at least one part of her husband's name, Djefau-, and one of his priestly titles is recorded. This title hints at the high social position of Djefau . . . and his wife.

Although no provenance for the statue has been recorded, the title "Overseer of Priests of All the Gods of Asyut," the references to Wepwawet and Hathor, Mistress

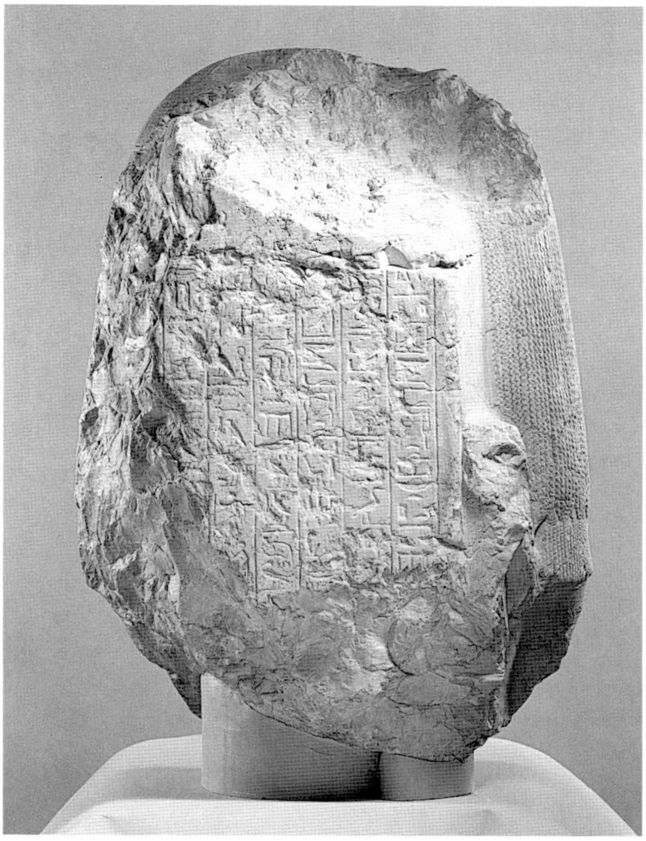

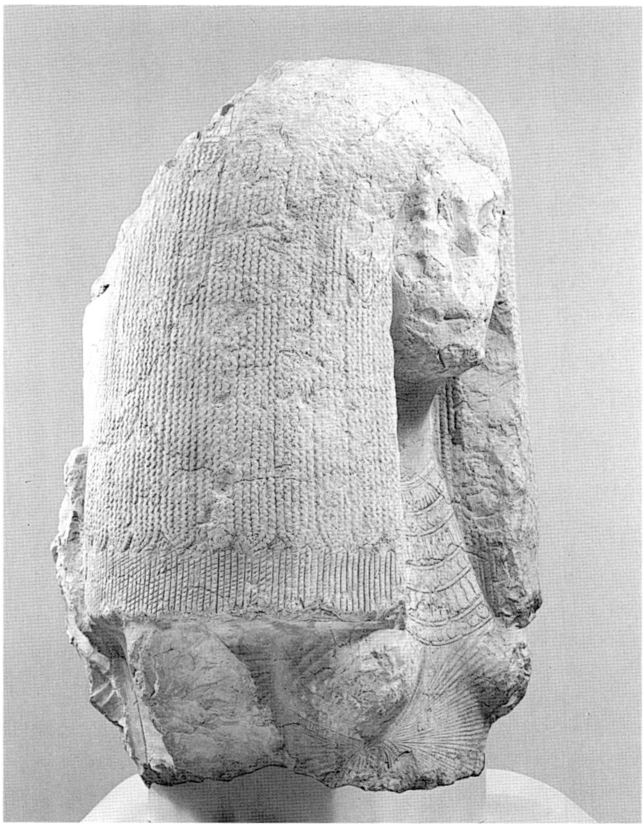

of Medjedney, and the name Djefau . . . , which was a common element in the names of the Middle Kingdom monarchs of Asyut,[5] strongly suggest that it came from that location. Furthermore, scholars who have examined this statue have remarked on its stylistic similarity to the Yuni and Renenutet pair statue (cat. no. 93), particularly in the attention to detail evident in the wigs and costumes.[6] This and the sensual portrayal of the woman's face and body suggest that the bust is contemporary with that of Yuni and Renenutet, which dates to the beginning of the Nineteenth Dynasty, when provincial craftsmen were producing sculptures of much higher quality than those in the administrative centers of the country.[7] The very existence of this statue fragment suggests that another tomb lies undiscovered at the Asyut necropolis. Perhaps in the future this tomb will be found, or further attestation discovered of the man Djefau-, and we may learn more about this enigmatic woman and her family. AKC

Published: *Sculpture Collection,* 16–17; J.D. Cooney, "Treasures from the Ancient World," *Apollo* (April, 1971): 10, 12 (illus.); Vandier, *Manuel* 3, 442, 486–87, 491, 498, 500, and pl. 144.3.

93 Statue depicting Yuni and Renenutet

Limestone with pigment; from Asyut Necropolis,[1] tomb of Amenhotep; New Kingdom, Dynasty 19, reign of Sety I;[2]
H: 84.5 cm
The Metropolitan Museum of Art. Rogers Fund, 1915. 15.2.1

This statue came from the tomb of Amenhotep,[3] whose titles include "Royal Scribe, Chief Lector Priest, Chief of Physicians, and Overseer of Priests." The relief depictions that lined its tomb walls[4] show Amenhotep, his wife, Renenutet (fig. 11) and other family members in the presence of deities. In addition to her duties as Mistress of the House, Renenutet also served as Chantress of Wepwawet and of Amen-Ra.

Two other statues were also found in Amenhotep's tomb. One is a life-size depiction of Amenhotep's son, Yuni.[5] The second, approximately half-life-size, portrays Yuni together with his wife, who also bore the name Renenutet. Both wear elaborately plaited wigs and pleated garments similar to those of the bust in catalogue number 92. The quality of the carving of this statue and of the noblewoman bust is remarkable, for at this period—the early Nineteenth Dynasty—there was a decline in artistic standards. As Cyril Aldred observes:

> The private stone statuary of the Nineteenth Dynasty, most of which has been recovered from the Theban area, shows a steady decline in quality and range. Tomb statues of a man and his wife, in the tradition of those of the late Eighteenth Dynasty, continue to be produced during the reign of Sethos I and in the earlier years of Ramesses II, though there is a falling off in size and excellence. There are, however, exceptions, and a high degree of skill is shown in the carving of the statues, both in limestone and wood, which have been recovered from the necropolis of Deir Durunka, near Asyut, and which date to the earlier part of the dynasty.[6]

Yuni held numerous titles,[7] including those of *wab* and *sem* Priest, and "Overseer of the Priests of Sekhmet." His wife,

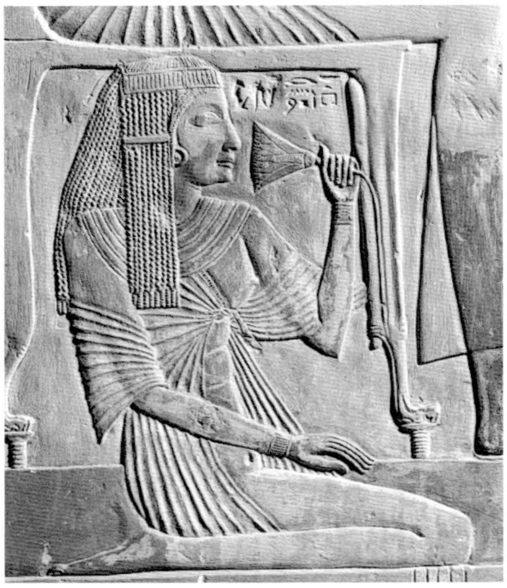

Fig. 11 Renenutet with lotus flower. Detail from wall relief depicting Renenutet beside her husband, Amenhotep. From the tomb of Amenhotep at Deir Durunka, Asyut. Gift of Edward Drummond Libbey. 62.24. Photo courtesy of the Toledo Museum of Art.

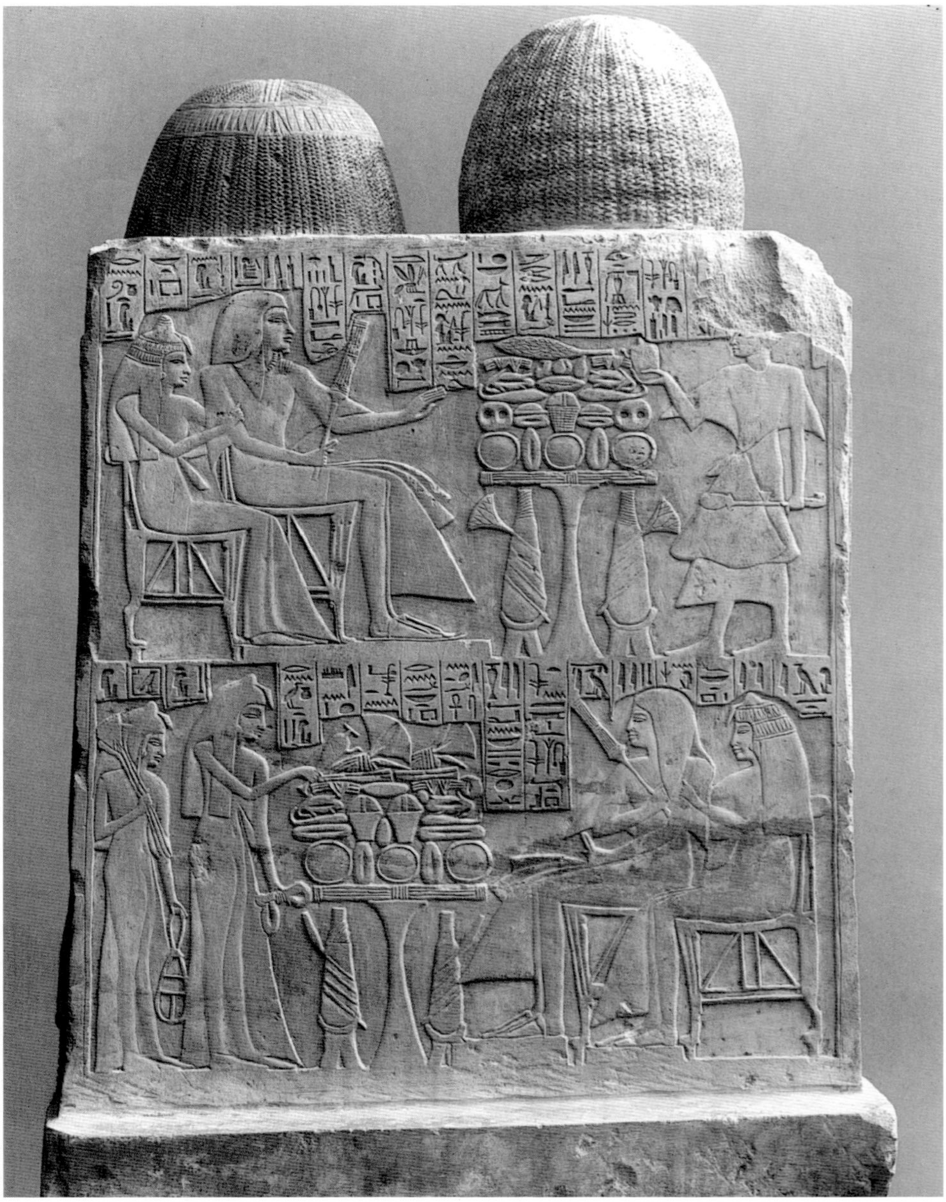

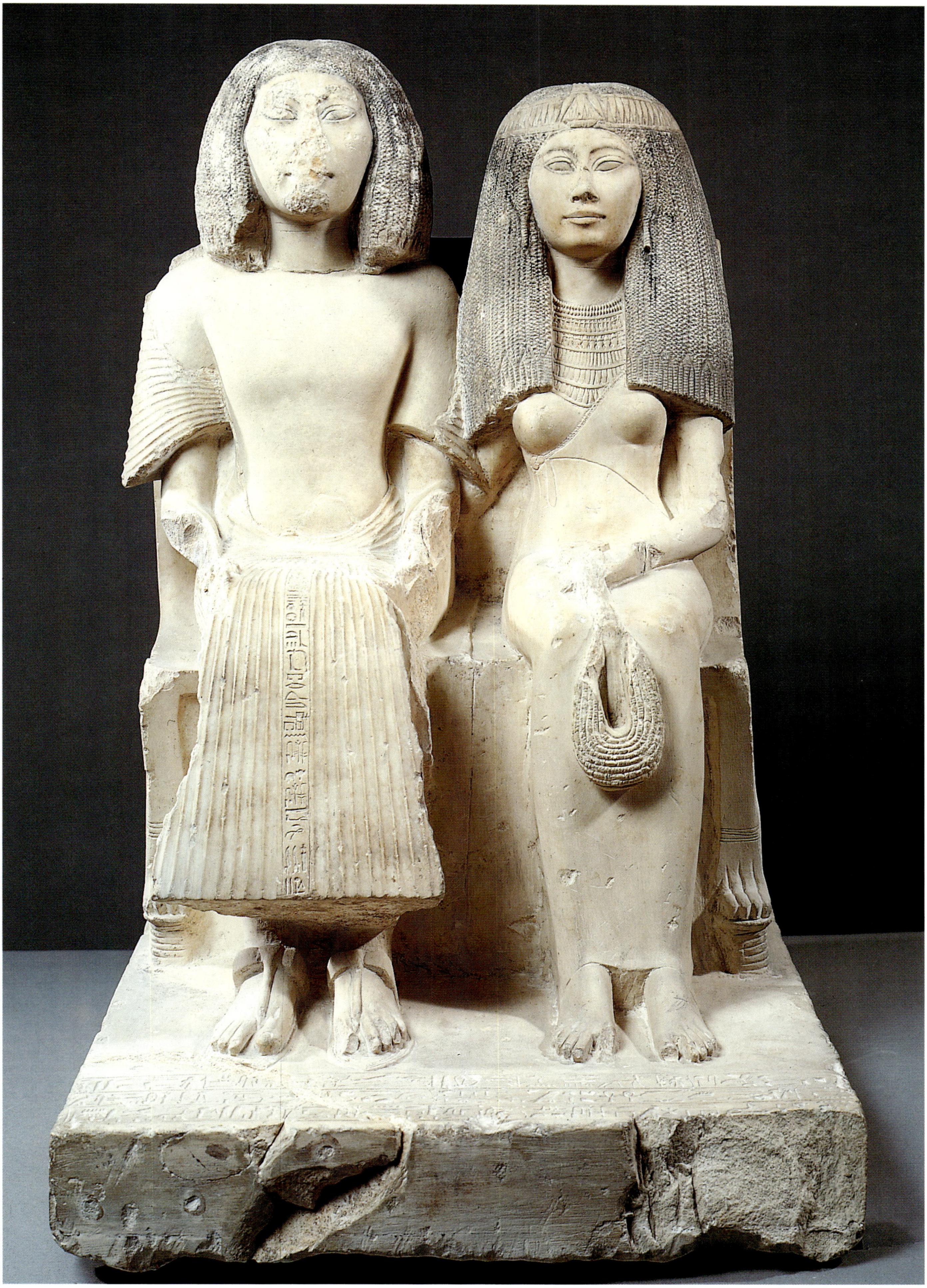

Renenutet, Mistress of the House, was also active in Asyut's temples, serving as Chantress of Amen-Ra and Great One of the Women's Company of Hathor,[8] Mistress of Medjedney. In her left hand she holds a *menat* necklace, which was shaken by priestesses during religious rituals.[9]

The back of this statue is carved and inscribed as a stela, divided into two registers. In the upper scene, Yuni and Renenutet are seated in two chairs that have legs in the form of a lion's paws. Before them is a table laden with funerary offerings. Facing the seated couple from the other side of the table is a priest with a libation vase in his right hand and a censer in his left.

The lower part of the "stela" honors Renenutet's parents, Metiay and Yia, who are seated before their own offering table. The inscription provided Metiay's titles: "Acquaintance of the King, Royal Scribe, and Keeper of Stores." Yia's only title here is "Mistress of the House"; likewise, this is the sole title mentioned for Renenutet in the register above. One suspects that other titles were omitted due to considerations of space, and that Yia, like her daughter and other upperclass women of the period, served as a chantress in one of the local temples. Renenutet libates before her parents' offering table and carries a *menat* necklace in her left hand. Behind her is her servant, Hathor, who assists by carrying flowers for the offering table and a mirror in its case. All of the women wear diaphanous gowns and long wigs topped by incense cones. The honor demonstrated on this statue toward Renenutet's parents, rather than toward those of Yuni, leads one to wonder if Renenutet herself was responsible for commissioning the sculpture.[10] AKC

Published: H.E. Winlock, "The Statue of Iny and Rennut," *BMMA* 14, no. 2 (1919): 32–34; Hayes, *Scepter*, 2: 349–52, fig. 220. For the inscription, see Ahmed Bey Kamal, "Fouilles à Deir Dronka et à Assiout, 1913–1914," *ASAE* 16 (1916): 86–89, no. 74.

94 Pair Statue of Djehuty-em-heb and Iay

Red sandstone; provenance unknown, probably from Asyut; New Kingdom, Dynasty 20, reign of Ramesses III or later; H: 48.2 cm

Yale University Gallery of Art, New Haven, Connecticut. Gift of Ludlow Bull, '07, and Assoc. in Fine Arts 1947.81

This statue represents a continuation of the group of *ka* statues known, or believed, to have come from the necropolis at Asyut. Depicted here is the General, Royal Scribe, and Acquaintance of the King, Djehuty-em-heb, together with his wife, the Mistress of the House and Chantress of Wepwawet, Iay.[1] In Iay's left hand, the handle of a sistrum, an object used in temple ritual (cat. no. 35b), is preserved. Unfortunately, the head, neck, and shoulders of Iay's figure have been broken away and are lost.

In spite of the difficulty in achieving fine modeling in a coarse-grain sedimentary rock such as sandstone,[2] the sculptor had admirably captured the elaborate pleating of Iay's gown and Djehuty-em-heb's sleeves and kilt, as well as the undulating waves of the latter's wig. The sandstone of this sculpture may have been chosen for its red color, which resembles the red pigment normally used to represent the skin of males.[3] In fact, this sculpture was coated (except in the areas representing the surface of the skin) with a thin wash in preparation for the painted details. Black pigment was employed by the artist to highlight and add definition to the modeling of the figures.

The woman Iay continued in the custom of her predecessors, Renenutet (cat. no. 93) and the unnamed noblewoman depicted in catalogue number 92, as a chantress in the temple of Wepwawet and other deities.[4] It is this title associated with Wepwawet that allows the statue to be accurately dated, since a Djehuty-em-heb associated with the Asyut Wepwawet temple is mentioned in the Harris Papyrus, which enumerates temple endowments made by Ramesses III.[5]

Iay lived and served the gods of Asyut approximately one hundred years later than her counterparts depicted in the New York and Cincinnati statues. Perhaps she visited their tombs in the Asyut necropolis. Indeed, her name *ỉ3ỉỉ*[6] is so similar to that of the mother of Yuni's wife, Renenutet, Yia, *ỉỉỉ3*,[7] one wonders if she might have been a descendant of that couple.[8] As is the case with Cincinnati's bust of a noblewoman, the existence of this statue of Djehuty-em-heb and Iay hints at the possibility that their tomb still lies hidden at Asyut. AKC

Published: Scott, *Egyptian Art at Yale*, no. 73.

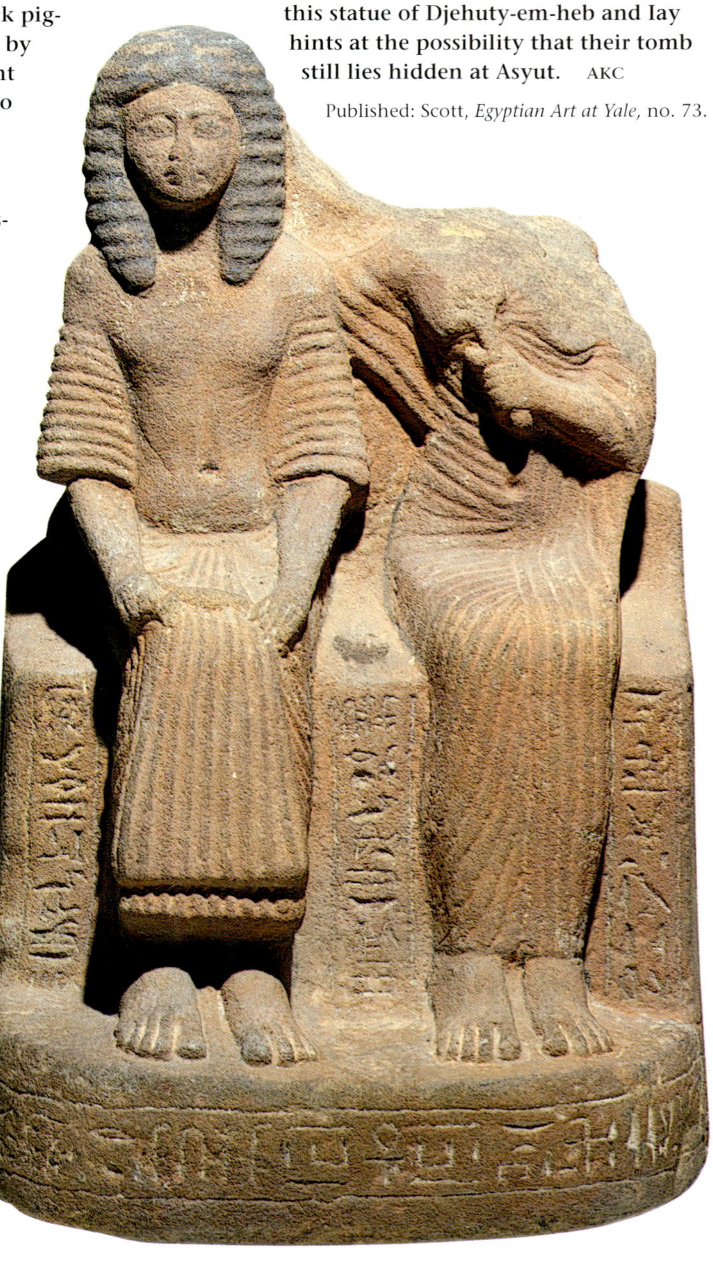

The legal status of women in ancient Egypt[1]

JANET H. JOHNSON
Professor of Egyptology, Oriental Institute, University of Chicago

From our earliest preserved records (Old Kingdom), the formal legal status of Egyptian women (unmarried, married, divorced, or widowed) was identical with that of Egyptian men. Differences in social status between individuals are evident in almost all products of this ancient culture: its art, its texts, its archaeological record. In the textual record, men are distinguished by the type of job they held,[2] from which they derived status, clout, and income.[3] Most women, however, did not hold jobs outside the home and consequently were usually referred to by more generic titles such as *nbt pr* ("Mistress of the House") or *ʿnḫ.t nt niwt* ("Citizeness").[4] Women were also identified frequently by the name and titles of their husband or father, from whom presumably they derived their social status. Thus, the New Kingdom "Instructions of Any" state, "A woman is asked about her husband, a man is asked about his rank."

In the legal arena, however, both women and men could act on their own and were responsible for their own actions.[5] Criminals, whether male or female, lost their freedom, and a small number of persons, male and female, were legally tied somehow to others. Some, especially in the New Kingdom, were prisoners of war; some bound themselves (and their children) to an individual or, more frequently, to a temple because of debts or to secure protection.[6] Yet, in general, Egyptian women, like Egyptian men, were legally responsible for their own actions and personally accountable to both civil and criminal law. They were able to acquire, own, and dispose of both real and personal property. They could enter into contracts in their own names; they could initiate civil court cases and likewise could be sued; they could serve as witnesses in court cases; they could sit on juries; and they could witness legal documents. That women very rarely *did* serve on juries or as witnesses to legal documents is a result of *social*, not legal, factors.

The great disparity between women's social and legal status can be observed in both documentary and literary materials. In "The Instructions of the (Vizier[7]) Ptahhotep," for instance, preserved in Middle Kingdom and later copies, a man's wife is viewed basically as a dependent, whom he must care for well and lovingly:

> When you prosper and found your house and love your wife with ardor, fill her belly, clothe her back; ointment soothes her body. Gladden her heart as long as you live; she is a fertile field for her lord. Do not contend with her in court. Keep her from power, restrain her—her eye is her storm when she gazes. Thus will you make her stay in your house.

The jarring reference to contending with her in court shows clearly that women had legal rights and were willing to fight for them. This distinction between women's legal status in ancient Egypt and their public or social status is of major importance in understanding how the Egyptian system worked.

Criminal law

Criminal law involves "state" intervention to punish an individual who has done something that harms the "state." This harm can be direct (e.g., treason, theft of government property) or indirect (e.g., murder). Some offenses that we regard today as involving criminal law (e.g., theft of personal property, rape) were treated in ancient Egypt as matters of civil law. That is, the "state" did not intervene to bring the malefactor to justice; a suit had to be brought to court by the aggrieved party. We have few records dealing with people in prison. One Middle Kingdom papyrus gives a list of escaped criminals; most are men, but a few seem to be women.[8] A New Kingdom ostracon[9] recording a trial of a woman for theft refers for precedent to an earlier case in which a woman was found guilty of theft and remanded to the vizier for punishment. Two types of criminal cases attested from ancient Egypt involved women: so-called harem conspiracies, in which women were involved in plots to kill a reigning monarch, and thefts from royal tombs and temples, in which a few women seem to have played the role of "accessory after the fact."

Although an Old Kingdom reference exists, which has been interpreted as reflecting the trial of a queen for treason,[10] the best-attested "harem conspiracy" dates from the reign of Ramesses III, in the later part of the New Kingdom. A special tribunal was set up to investigate the conspiracy and bring the guilty to punishment. According to the tribunal's report,[11] various officials "had been in collusion with (Queen) Tiy[e] and the women of the harem. [They] had made common cause with them. [They] had begun to take their words outside to their mothers and their brothers who were there, saying: 'Gather people and stir up enemies to make rebellion against their lord!'" The persons arrested and found guilty were executed. Members of the royal family who had been involved in the conspiracy, including the prince in whose name the conspiracy was undertaken, were also arrested and tried, but they were allowed to take their own lives instead of being executed. Among the others who were examined and executed were "the wives of the men of the gate of the harem, who had joined the men who plotted the matters, . . . six women." Although this tribunal did not deal with the fate of Queen Tiye, one can assume that she did not escape unscathed.[12]

In the records of the investigation (also by special tribunal) of the thefts, especially of items made of gold and other valuable metals, from the royal tombs in the Valley of the Kings, the wives of several suspected thieves were brought in for questioning. These women were interrogated "by beating with the stick" or by having their feet and hands "twisted." Further, they were made to swear an "oath by the Ruler on pain of mutilation not to speak falsehood" and to testify how they (as simple working people) came into possession of a servant/slave. All denied knowledge of the husband's acquiring silver through division of the spoils of the tomb robberies. Some women said their husband had acquired the servant/slave without their knowing the details; other women claimed to have purchased the servant/slave with their own money (earned from growing crops in their gardens or, elsewhere, from weaving cloth). When the wife of the gold worker who melted down gold and silver for the robbers was interrogated, she swore he never did such work "while he was in my house." She stated that her husband had been married four times[13] and suggested that perhaps he had carried out these illegal acts while married to a different wife. The vizier, however, had her held in custody "until there be found a thief to accuse her." In another, more intriguing, case, a woman claimed that when her father learned that her husband was robbing the tombs, the father forbade the husband to enter the father's home,[14] so the husband stashed his loot at another workman's home.

Overall, the treatment received by the women, in which they were made to testify against employers, neighbors, and family, was the same treatment handed out to men who were brought in as witnesses. The punishments meted out in these texts (execution for treason, cutting off ears and noses for violating public trust, severe beatings, and incarceration for theft of government property) were sometimes adjusted to fit the status of the guilty party (execution versus suicide), but there is no evidence that women received better or worse treatment than men.

Civil law

The Egyptian word that corresponds most closely to our word *law* (of which a possible definition is a system of rights—that is, individual claims—which are enforced by the "state" if they conform to certain conditions) is *hp*. This word can also connote custom, order, justice, or right, according to its usage. In ancient Egypt all law was given from above; there was no "legislature" or any concept of "legislation."

In a New Kingdom court case,[15] a man cites the "law of Pharaoh" as precedent; in another,[16] when citing the law, a man says, "The King said. . . . " Thus "law" is the King's word.[17] The only preserved compilation of laws from ancient Egypt is the so-called Hermopolis Legal Code. This text is a third (?)-century-B.C. copy of a mid–first-millennium-B.C. compilation.[18] It is not an actual "law code" but a collection of "case law"[19] dealing with specific (and sometimes quite minute) details. One section is concerned with leases of real property, another with "annuity contracts," and another with inheritance law. The latter sections are an important source for family law (discussed below). It is probably only fortuitous that we do not have preserved similar collections from earlier periods.

Contracts were written copies of oral agreements in which Party A spoke to Party B in the presence of witnesses[20] and a (professional) scribe who copied down (and put into legalese) the words of Party A. Although only Party A spoke, Party B had the right to accept or refuse the contract, thus making these agreements bilateral and binding on both parties.[21] Copies of contracts concerning real property were filed in the local records office, under the ultimate jurisdiction of the vizier.[22] These public records enabled the state to know who was responsible for paying taxes on the land; the documents were also available for consultation in any subsequent lawsuit.

Civil lawsuits involved an oral petition[23] to the court by a private individual. Egyptian judges based their decisions on traditions and precedent[24] and kept copies of their decisions.[25] We do not know enough about courts in the Old and Middle Kingdoms to discuss their composition or functioning. In the New Kingdom there was a "great court" under the vizier (in which the vizier served as appellate judge); there were special ad hoc courts, such as those already mentioned, which were set up to investigate the harem conspiracies and tomb robberies; and there were local courts, also apparently ad hoc, of which the best-known example is the court at Deir el-Medina. (This New Kingdom village is located on the West Bank at modern Luxor, ancient Thebes, and was inhabited by the workmen who carved and decorated the royal tombs in the Valley of the Kings.) Both the great court and the special courts were composed of high officials; the local courts were composed of local people, usually the relatively important local citizens. At Deir el-Medina the *qnbt* included scribes and crew chiefs, but also some simple workmen and, even more rarely, women.[26]

Just as women and men apparently received identical treatment with reference to criminal law, so women functioned equally with men in the realm of civil law. Beginning in the Old Kingdom, women were able to acquire,[27] own, and dispose of[28] property (both real[29] and personal) in their own names.[30] The Egyptians not only had the concept of private property; they also developed a concept of "joint property," property acquired by a married couple during their marriage.[31] The husband had use of the joint property; that is, he could dispose of joint property without his wife's permission. Yet if a husband sold or otherwise disposed of a piece of joint property (or of any of his wife's property which she had brought to the marriage), he was legally liable to provide his wife with something of equal value. That the husband had use of joint property reflects the *social* fact that men normally participated in the public sphere, whereas women did not.

The earliest contracts of which we have record are *imyt pr* documents, literally, "that which is in the house." These contracts frequently have been identified as wills, but this is incorrect. Rather, they are documents used to transfer property to someone *other than* the person(s) who would inherit that property if the owner died intestate. It is not clear that the transfer took place only at the death of the person making the document. For this reason, they are more properly called (land) transfer documents.[32] These documents were sealed and filed or recorded in a central government office, as noted above.[33] One of the earliest land-transfer documents to which reference has been preserved (in the late Third Dynasty tomb of the nobleman Metjen) was made by Metjen's mother, Nebsenet, on behalf of his children, her grandchildren. She made this contract to transfer the land not to her immediate heir,

---

P BOULAQ 10 (NEW KINGDOM)

[1]"List of objects . . . [2]which he[A] gave to the Lady Tagemy, his mother: 1 burial-place [3]after he had given her coffin to . . . , makes 40 *dbn*.
[4]Again: what he gave to her: 1 coffin for her burial, while he had (also) made the burial-place [5]for Huy-nefer, his father.
But see, the children of the Lady Tagemy [6]contest this today, in order to claim her possessions. [7]But they are not those who buried their father, nor did ⟨these⟩ children of hers [8]bury (her). (Still) it is her property which they claim [9]today, although they did not bury together with my [10]father, when he buried his father and his mother.
"Let the possessions [11]be given to him who buries,' says the Law of Pharaoh.
My Good Lord, [12]see, I am in the presence of the officials; cause that the right thing be done.
[13]See, the landed property of Tay-nehsy was given to Sa-wadjy when she was buried, [14]while he gave her his coffin. One gave him her share in the presence of the officials, [15]for it was King Amenhotep who gave it to him in the court."

A The father of the man who is making the petition.

---

her son, but directly to her grandchildren.[34]

Two Middle Kingdom *ỉmyt pr* documents[35] written only a few years apart illustrate both the legal and the social aspects of such contracts. In year 44 of King Amenemhat III, a man made a transfer document for his brother, giving him "everything in field or in town" and "all my dependents." In year 2 of the succeeding king, that brother made a transfer document for his own wife "consisting of everything which my brother . . . gave to me together with all the possessions at his place, being everything which he gave to me." He also transferred to his wife the right to live in the "houses which my brother . . . built for me" and the right to be buried in his tomb with him. In addition, he gave his wife the right "to give [these possessions] to any one she desires among her children whom she will bear to me." Thus, with this one document, the second man provided for his wife while entailing property for his children. She became legal owner of the property, with all the rights and responsibilities involved therein. But because the property had been the husband's private property,[36] not the joint property of the couple, the husband also had the legal right to entail it as he pleased, in this case for their joint children. He granted his wife, however, the right to "inherit" or "disinherit" from among their children.[37]

The difference between women's legal and social positions is made clear by the final line of the transfer document:[38] "It is the Deputy Geb who will educate my children." Although the husband is fully confident of his wife's ability to handle the property and raise the children, and thus transfers the property to her without reservation, he also realizes that his children will go further in life if they have a male to intervene on their behalf in the public world of education and, from that point, in the job market. For this *social* reason, and not for any legal or economic reason, the husband names a male advocate for his children.

A fair amount of Old Kingdom evidence shows women in the economy or the "public sphere," including women working as merchants in market scenes and women acting as priestesses, especially for the goddess Hathor. Much of the New Kingdom evidence comes from documents[39] reflecting women's economic dealings with other women and with men.[40] The government was also perfectly willing to deal with women, as indicated by Papyrus Wilbour, a long text recording "taxes" due on farmland. Each piece of land is identified by owner and by the person working the land (if that person is different from the owner). Of the 2,110 parcels of land for which the name of the owner is preserved, women are listed as owners of 228, just over 10 percent;[41] the land frequently is described as worked by their children. However these women originally acquired this land,[42] the significant point is that they hold the title and bear responsibility for assessments due.

The legal independence and identity of Egyptian women is reflected not only in the fact that they could deal with property on the same terms as did men and that they could make the appropriate contracts in their own names, but also in the fact that they themselves were held accountable for economic transactions and contracts into which they had entered. For instance, someone brought charges against a woman named Iry-nefret, claiming that she had illegally used silver and a tomb belonging to a woman named Bak-Mut to help pay for the purchase of a servant girl. Iry-nefret was brought to court; she told in her own words how she acquired the girl, listing all the items she had given the merchant as price for the girl and identifying the individuals from whom she had bought some of the items used in this purchase.[43] She had to swear an oath before the judges in the names of Amen and the Ruler. The judges then asked the complainant to produce the witnesses who would attest that she had used stolen property to purchase the girl. These witnesses comprised three men and three women, including the older brother of Iry-nefret's husband and the older sister of the woman Bak-Mut, from whom the property allegedly was stolen. The end of the papyrus record of the court case is lost, but it is clear that the woman Iry-nefret acted on her own in purchasing the servant girl and was held solely liable for her actions. The testimony of both women and men was held by the judges to be equally admissible.

Civil law in ancient Egypt includes several offenses that we consider mat-

---

P KAHUN I, 1 (MIDDLE KINGDOM)

Label (on the verso)

"*Ỉmyt pr* which the *wꜥb*-priest and overseer of the phyle Wah made."

Contract (on the recto)

[1/1]"Copy of the *ỉmyt pr* which the Sealbearer and Trusted One of the Controller of Works 'Ankh-ren made.

[1/2]"Year 44, 2nd month of Summer, day 13. [1/3]The *ỉmyt pr* which the Sealbearer and Trusted One of the Controller of Works of the Northern District Shepses's son Ihi-sonb, who is called 'Ankh-ren, made:

[1/4]"All my property in the country or in town belongs to my brother, the *wꜥb*-priest and overseer of the phyle of Sopdu, Lord of the East, Shepses's son Ihi-sonb, who is called Wah. [1/5]All my dependents belong to this brother of mine." This was put as a copy at the office of the Second Reporter of the South in Year 44, 2nd month of Summer, day 13."

[1/6]"Year 2, 2nd month of Inundation, day 18. [1/7]The *ỉmyt pr* which the *wꜥb*-priest and overseer of the phyle of Sopdu, Lord of the East, Wah made:

"I am making an *ỉmyt pr* for my wife, [1/8]the woman of 'Left-Side,'[A] Sopdu's daughter Shefet, who is called Teti, consisting of everything which my brother gave to me, [1/9]the Sealbearer and Trusted One of the Controller of Works 'Ankh-ren, together with all the possessions at his place, being everything which he gave to me. She will give ⟨them⟩ [1/10]to any one she desires among her children whom she will bear to me. I am giving to her the three Asiatics [1/11]whom my brother, the Sealbearer and Trusted One of the Controller of Works 'Ankh-ren gave to me. She will give ⟨them⟩ to any one she desires among her children.

[1/12]As for my tomb, let me be buried in it together with my wife, without letting any man at all interfere.

[1/13]As for the structures which my brother, the Sealbearer and Trusted One of the Controller of Works 'Ankh-ren built for me, she shall be therein without letting anyone expel her therefrom.'"

Added in a different handwriting

[1/14]"It is the Deputy Geb who will educate my children."

Added as a second column

[2/1]"List of the people in whose presence this was done:

[2/2]The Decorator of Pillars Kemni

[2/3]The Door-keeper of the Temple 'Ankh-tifi's son Ipu

[2/4]The Door-keeper of the Temple Sonb's son Sonb"

A The name of the town from which the wife came.

ters for criminal law, including theft of personal property. One New Kingdom ostracon[44] lists the property that a female servant had stolen and the associated penalty for each object, usually triple the value of the item stolen. In another New Kingdom document,[45] one woman accuses another of having stolen a chisel from a workman; the second woman denied the charge under oath, but later produced the chisel and two other stolen objects. She was judged as deserving death for swearing a false "great oath in [the name of] the lord" (i.e., the king) and was left for sentencing by the vizier.[46]

Although private individuals had to bring the charges in cases of theft, the government was responsible for carrying out punishment; the same is true in cases of rape and/or adultery.[47] Papyrus Salt 124 contains a list of charges brought by a workman from Deir el-Medina against one of his superiors, including theft from the royal tombs and temples, appropriating government workmen to work on his own projects, fighting with and beating up other workmen, and rape and/or adultery. The workman claimed that this superior's own son took an oath charging his father with sleeping with various married women and charging that both his father and his brother slept with the daughter of one of the women with whom the father had slept. The workman bringing charges also mentioned another case in which his superior "violated" (?) another woman. We do not know the outcomes of these charges.

In another case involving rape/adultery, a relatively powerful individual was able to behave unethically for some time before a responsible official stepped into the case.[48] Here a simple laborer told how a workman of the crew was caught sleeping with the laborer's wife. When the laborer complained "to the officials," however, the officials gave him one hundred blows for his audacity in complaining. Finally the crew chief came to the laborer's aid, and the workman was forced to swear an "oath (in the name of) the lord saying, 'As Amen endures, as the Ruler endures, if I speak with the woman, I shall have . . . my nose and ears cut off and I shall be given to the land of Kush.'" Yet enforcement seemingly was lax at best, because the workman subsequently made the woman pregnant. On this occasion the workman's father, also a member of the crew, took his son before the officials and the scribe and "caused that he take an oath (in the name of) the lord again, saying, 'If I go to the place where the daughter of Payom is, I shall be put as a stonecutter at the mountain of Elephantine.'" We do not know whether the second oath was any more effective than the first.

Family law

Marriage in ancient Egypt was a totally private affair in which the state took no interest and of which it kept no record. There is no evidence for any legal or religious ceremony establishing the marriage, although probably a party was held. The preserved portion of the first story of Setne Khaemwast from the Late Period tells how Ahure and Na-nefer-ka-Ptah fell in love and wanted to marry. Their parents agreed, so Ahure was taken to Na-nefer-ka-Ptah's house, people (especially the bride's father) gave presents, a big party was held, the two slept together, and then they lived together and had a child.[49] Basically marriage was an agreement by two people and their families that they would live together *(ḥms irm)*, establish a household *(grg pr)*,[50] and have a family. The same vocabulary was used for both women and men. Before the marriage, the man gave a gift to his prospective father-in-law; this gift has been interpreted as serving to break the woman's bonds with her biological family, so that the new couple could establish their own family as the center of their life and loyalty. (For a discussion of the ties between the new couple and their parents, see the comments and suggestions at the end of this essay.)

Although women were legally men's equals and could deal with property on equal terms with men, their social and public roles were vastly different from those of men, as noted above. Although in some cases the wife in a couple is stronger or more important than the husband (by family, fortune, or personality),[51] most Egyptians tended to marry a person from their own social class; thus a woman frequently married a man in the same (or a similar) profession as her father and brother(s). In

---

O NASH 1 (NEW KINGDOM)

[1]"Year 6, 3rd Month of Summer, day 10. On this day the workman Neb-nefer, son of Nakhy, reached [2]the Tribunal of judges. He brought suit against the citizeness Herya. The Workman Neb-nefer said:

"As for [3]me, I hid a chisel of mine in (my) house after the enemy. Someone took it away. [4]I had all people who were in the place swear an oath about my chisel. After [5]a few days the citizeness Nubemnehem came and said to me: 'The anger of God happened to me. I saw [6]Herya take your chisel.' So she said."

Then the Tribunal said to Herya: [7]"In truth, are you the one who took Neb-nefer's chisel, or not?" Herya answered: [8]"No, I am not the one who took it." The Tribunal said to her: "Can you swear a great oath [9]in (the name of) the lord about the chisel and say 'I am not the one who took it'"? Then the citizeness Herya said: [10]"As Amen endures, as the Ruler (whose anger is worse than death, namely Pharaoh) endures, if one finds out [11]that I am the one who took this chisel ⟨then I shall be punished⟩."

[12](An hour) after the Tribunal heard her, a servant of the [13]Tribunal, Pashed, was sent with her. She brought the chisel, it having been [14]hidden by her together with a *wšb*-vessel of the god Amen, Beautiful of Face. [15]She hid them in her house. She had also taken the *ʿn*[16]of the *wšb*-vessel of Amen. ⟨Nevertheless⟩ she took a [17]great [oath] by the lord saying [vo 1]"I am not the one who took the chisel."

Then the Tribunal [vo 2]said: "The citizeness Herya is a great liar, [vo 3]worthy of death. The workman Neb-nefer is in the right." [vo 4]Her words were put down until the Vizier came. The Tribunal [vo 5]on this day: . . .[A]

[vo 7](This is) the crime of this village in which copper [vo 8]was stolen, even if by a widow, in order to let my lord know the plan [vo 9]of the place (in) which the citizeness Tanedjem-heset stole a . . . (worth) 1½ *dbn* here [vo 10]formerly. The Vizier Nefer-renpet was mad (because) she was the wife of Pashed, [vo 11]son of Heh. The Vizier sent the scribe Hay and he had her taken to Riverbank.[B] [vo 12]May my lord have the woman who stole the copper, [vo 13]and likewise the *wšb*-vessel, punished so that another woman like her not repeat acting likewise. [vo 14]See, I have caused that my lord know. For it is the Vizier [vo 15]who knows. May he do any [vo 16]plan he wishes. May it be known!"

A The two chief workmen, three scribes, the chief of police, a guard, and the work crew as a whole.

B *Mryt* with "city" determinative; for discussion, see A.G. McDowell, *Jurisdiction in the Workmen's Community of Deir El-Medina* (Leiden, 1990), 221–22.

---

some instances where a woman married several times, all her husbands followed the same profession. Some were even members of the same guild. This resulted not from formal laws or restrictions but simply, we presume, from the fact that this was the group of people with whom one had the most contact and was most comfortable.

Women sometimes helped their husbands with their jobs (whether they worked in the equivalent of the modern mom-and-pop store or the wife filled in for her husband when he was "on the road")[52] and had ways of acquiring some wealth by their own initiative, especially through textile production. Yet they needed some assurance that the father of their children would provide for their own and the children's material future. Thus there developed what have been called "marriage contracts," although such documents are purely economic and embody no social expectations at all. These documents were not designed to legitimize the marriage; they were not a prerequisite for marriage nor did they have to be contracted at the time of the union, because some refer to children who already had been born to the couple. They were not intended to establish the social/personal rights and responsibilities of either party toward the other.[53] Such concepts certainly existed; they are presented in wisdom literature of the Old Kingdom.[54] Also, in a New Kingdom letter,[55] a man spells out what he considered a man's obligations to his wife: fidelity,[56] (loving) attention, the responsibility to provide well for her and their children, to take care of her medically, to take pride in her, and not to treat her as a master treats a servant. These so-called marriage contracts, however, concern only economic matters—the husband's responsibility to feed and clothe his wife (and their children), and their children's right to inherit his wealth[57]—and are more appropriately called "annuity contracts." As such, they were extremely advantageous to the wife, and one may assume that the woman and her family exerted as much pressure as they could to ensure that the husband made such a contract.

Such contracts originally may have documented an agreement between the groom and his (future) father-in-law.[58] This is the case for the earliest preserved annuity contracts, all dating post–New Kingdom, and for the system seemingly underlying the Hermopolis Legal Code, which envisions one man making such a contract with another man "for" or "on behalf of" a specific woman; the first man used all his (current and future) possessions as security for his promise to provide food and clothing for the woman.[59] The great majority of actual annuity contracts,[60] however, were made by the husband directly with the wife, not with her father.[61] Already in Old through New Kingdom Egypt, as we have seen, women are full participants in the legal system, not dependent on a man to handle their legal concerns.[62]

In the evidence for family law preserved from the Late Period (generally post–New Kingdom and sometimes specifically Egypt under the Persians, Ptolemies, and Romans), especially the Demotic[63] evidence, many of the underlying social and legal assumptions of the system reconstructed for Old through New Kingdom Egypt are spelled out more fully, and some of the social implications of this system become visible. Modern scholars often treat Egypt in the Late Period as a strange phenomenon; Egyptologists consider it so "decadent" and so much "polluted" by foreign contacts (Persian and especially Greek) as to be no longer "really" Egyptian. Indeed, during much of this time, the ruler of Egypt did not speak Egyptian.[64] Yet throughout this period Egyptian culture remained vital and vibrant,[65] and, until Egypt was incorporated into the Roman Empire, the ruling dynasty encouraged[66] local culture and involved "Egyptians" in the civil administration.[67]

One of the boons of the Late Period is the great number of documents, both literary and otherwise,[68] that have been preserved. The literary texts display some concerns and some types of presentation that reflect contemporary non-Egyptian literature, but they clearly derive from earlier Egyptian literary genres. Similarly, the private documentary materials clearly originate in an Egyptian milieu. At the same time, they spell out in much greater detail aspects of social and economic life that were attested already in earlier periods. Therefore, these texts have great value for understanding Egypt during the Late Period and also may be used, with care, to suggest possible reconstructions for earlier periods.

One valuable development of the Late Period is the tendency of contracts to include more and more details. The law, precedent, or custom underlying earlier documents was spelled out more precisely.[69] The spelling out of what, in earlier times, had been assumed standards may have been, at least partly, an effort to close loopholes by applying the law strictly.[70] It also may have been due in part to the professionalization of legal scribes: even people who could read and write themselves would tend to go to a specialist scribe who knew standard legal format and the proper legal phrases.

Representative examples of two very similar[71] annuity contracts are found in the so-called Family Archive from Siut (a town in Middle Egypt). In one case we have the actual contract,[72] in which the man addresses the woman. He lists the value of all the expensive property that she brought to the marriage, he notes that he will give her an amount of money as a "bridal gift," and he declares that all his property is security for her money. He acknowledges that if they divorce (and whether the divorce was instigated by him or by her), he must give her money equivalent to the full value of everything he had listed; if he does not give her all the money, he must (continue to) feed and clothe her until he *does* give her the full amount in silver. The amounts of grain, oil, and money for clothing that he must provide every month are spelled out. If he defaults on his payments, she remains legally entitled to any and all arrears. By implication, if they divorce, once he has paid her the full amount of silver specified in the contract, she will return the contract to him, and all obligations will be canceled. As in earlier Egyptian marriages, the wife "owned" the property but the husband had use of it.[73] Thus, in case of divorce, the husband had to repay the value, not return the specific items. It has been suggested that the bridal gift (in this case, twenty pieces of silver) served the same purpose as the earlier fine imposed on a husband who divorced his wife:[74] it would have had to be paid out by the husband only in case of divorce. The contract is confirmed by the husband's father, a point to which we return later.

The other annuity contract is quoted in the transcript of a court case.[75] Here a man is marrying for the second time and using one-third of his property as security for the contract. (The other two-thirds are entailed for the children of his first wife.)[76] In this case the man lists the value of items of clothing that the woman brought to the marriage, including the total amount of money she contributed. He commits himself to providing her with specific annual amounts of grain and money and acknowledges that she remains legally entitled to any and all arrears in payment. As in the first contract, the husband agrees to return to the wife the full amount of money whenever she requests it. In addition, he formally spells out the restriction that he cannot simply return her money to her and cancel his obligation; he must continue to support her until *she* asks for the money. The man who made the second contract also goes a step further in declaring that one-third of all his property ("everything which I have and everything which I shall acquire") is entailed not merely for his wife's support but to be passed along to their children. In this case, because the contract involves a second marriage, the man's eldest son by his first wife is called on to confirm the contract, which he does "in his own handwriting."

This latter fact, that the eldest son agreed to his father's actions, is one of the crucial points of a long, involved court case. This case provides quite a bit of evidence about women's actual legal status in Ptolemaic Egypt. Here a woman tried unsuccessfully to wrest property from her husband's younger half-brother. Her main argument was that her father-in-law had first pledged all his property as security for his own wife's annuity contract and then had confirmed her husband's pledge of all his property as security for her own annuity contract. (This property included what little he might actually have had at the time of the marriage and, more important, what he would inherit from his father when his father died.) She claimed that, by the law of Pharaoh, he did not therefore have the legal right to make a second annuity contract for a second wife. Because that

STATUE OF NAKHT-MUT (THIRD INTERMEDIATE PERIOD)

On the stela held by Nakht-mut

[1]"Praising Amen-Ra, King of the Gods, Lord of Heaven, Lord of the Land, Lord of the Water, Lord of the Mountains, Lord of the Oceans, . . . by the Fourth Prophet of Amen [2]Nakht-mut, who says:

"I . . . tell about your brilliance and your excellence . . . You are Shu who illumines the sun-folk, Aten [3]who gives light, . . . You cause all people to live through seeing your beauty . . . No one can live without you. . . . [6]How beautiful is the sight of your face, . . . more pleasing than (other) gods, without his equal. . . .

[9]I say this to you as praise and prayer that you come to me [10]quickly. I call on behalf of my daughter . . . who is in my heart, she being excellent for me, . . . Tasheren-mut, who is called [11]Shepen-ese, born to Nes-mut, . . . in order that you make permanent for her the *imyt pr* of everything which I gave to her . . . in city and in country, consisting of servants, [12]cattle, household goods, and all valuable objects . . . No other son or daughter shall say "Give me the like!" You shall not allow her to lose any extra (property) which (comes) [13]into my house after today . . . [14]like the Great God said: "Let every man make the determination[A] of his (own) property!" I am the possessor of property from my father and my mother and what I [acquired [15]with my own] hands. The rest is as a favor of the King for my service in my time. No evil (deed) of mine was found; . . . [16]You are the good protector of the trusted one, who answers the call of the sleeping.[B] Thus you should fight against the one who will fight against him in the future.[C] Send your arrow . . . [17]against them in order to wipe out their breath. . . . It will be against all great people, all brothers, all people who will trespass against her in the future, concerning everything which [18]I gave her and everything which I gave her children. . . . [19]For I am . . . a pure person who committed no sin [20]in your service; I gave *M3ʿt* to you; lying is my abomination. . . . [21]I am a great one of my city, a leader of my people. . . . I know that the [22]outcome of good deeds is a storehouse which descendants will find afterwards. . . . [24]There is none like me. . . . May you cause that those who come in the future say "How beautiful it is to walk [25]straightforwardly on the path of God! . . . "

On the right side

[1]The Lady of the House Nes-mut, who says: "Amen, you are the molder of gods and men. You are the strength of [2]those who live and the protection of those who are dead. . . . [4]Come to me, I am your servant! Act excellently for [5]our daughter Shepen-ese! Let her seize this property and kill anyone who will trespass against her! You are the protector of the future."

On the left side

[1]The daughter Tasheren-mut, who is called Shepen-ese, who says:

"What is [2]the God of a person except his father and his mother? . . . [3]The one who handed over to me is one [4]who loved me, my Khnum[D] and my Meskhenet.[E] I seized everything they [5]made for me for they are justified before God. May the [6]gods act according as you (plural) testified forever!"

A *Sẖr.*

B I.e., the dead.

C I.e., in the afterlife.

D The god who fashioned mankind on his potter's wheel; thus the father.

E The goddess of birth; thus the mother.

second annuity contract (on behalf of the mother of her husband's younger brother) was legally null and void by her account, then the younger brother should not have inherited anything from the father when the father died. She admitted that her husband had written a "division document" for his half-brother, granting him one-third of all their father's property, but she claimed that the document had been made under duress and should be given no legal weight.

The woman pointedly acts on her own in filing suit against the younger half-brother; her husband never appears. Although the younger brother refers to him (as the man through whom she is bringing suit), he is never brought or sought as a party or as a witness. This is probably the case because at an earlier date, when the husband himself had contested his younger brother's right to inherit from their father, he had lost in court and had had to write a "quit claim deed" transferring the one-third share to the younger brother. Also, he had been forced to swear that if he ever brought up the matter again, he would incur a whopping fine of three thousand silver pieces, and the younger brother would still have legal ownership of the one-third share.

After the statements by the complainant, the defendant, and any witnesses they chose to call, relevant contracts were read into the court record, including the annuity contract made to the second wife. The judges' decision cited the legal precedents ("law of Pharaoh," "law of year 21") on which their decision was based. The law as quoted by the judges, however, differed significantly from the law as quoted by the complainant. The full version of the law stated that a man could not legally make an annuity contract for a second wife *unless his first wife or his eldest son by that first wife agreed to his doing so.* Because the older brother had, indeed, "signed at the bottom [of his father's annuity contract on behalf of the father's second wife] . . . in his own handwriting," all the contracts were legal and binding. The earlier judgment—that the older brother had to write the "cession" for the younger brother—was reaffirmed, and the younger brother was awarded control of the disputed property.

The documents that make up this archive contain clear examples of the extra details found in Late Period contracts, which can be understood as spelling out the cultural, social, or legal background assumed by earlier contracts. They can best be understood as a direct development from that earlier system. Thus the annuity contracts reveal a system nearly identical with that which has been reconstructed for New Kingdom Egypt, but with property rights and various contingencies spelled out in detail. Even the fact that the eldest son by the first marriage had to confirm his father's new annuity contract (here "in his own handwriting") reflects a formal solution to an ongoing problem already evident in New Kingdom documentation.[77] Divorce and remarriage were common in Egypt at all periods; contention between siblings and between half-siblings was frequent. A somewhat pragmatic expedient was adopted: it became incumbent on the father to secure the permission of his older children, who stood to lose part of their inheritance. As we shall see below, men, even full-grown men, remained economically dependent on their parents, and especially on their fathers, until the parents died. Thus it would also be in the son's best interests to agree to his father's remarriage (and not risk rupture and complete disinheritance). In this way, everybody's wants or needs were satisfied by persuading everyone to agree to what at least some people wanted. It is reasonable to assume that this system of economic support for wife and children, which we see in written contracts made for wealthy women, reflected normal standards of behavior and spelled them out in some detail. These standards may also have held true even for those with less property; even a poor man's wife wanted assurances that he would not throw away what little they had.[78]

Although either party could divorce the spouse on any grounds or virtually on no grounds,[79] the economic responsibilities spelled out in the annuity contracts made this a serious step. Thus a married woman normally was supported by her husband for as long as they remained married,[80] and his property was entailed for their children.[81] Because even remarriage after a first wife's death could lead to wrangling over property and inheritance rights,[82] a bitter divorce and remarriage could lead to major legal contests. It will probably never be known whether such a social situation prompted the woman who denounced her father for using property belonging to her as security for economic pledges to the father's second wife and went to court to demand restitution.[83]

If a man divorced his wife, he had to return her dowry (if she had brought one) and pay her a fine; if she divorced him, there was no fine. A spouse divorced for fault[84] (including adultery) forfeited his or her share of the couple's joint property. After divorce, both were free to remarry. Yet it seems clear that until the husband returned his wife's dowry and paid her the fine, or until she accepted it,[85] the husband remained liable for supporting her, even if they were no longer living together.[86] Some ex-husbands, then as now, tried to avoid supporting their ex-wives,[87] and there are several examples where a woman's biological family steps in to support or assist her when her husband cannot or will not do so.[88]

Both sons and daughters could inherit property from either parent;[89] both mothers and fathers retained the right to take action to disinherit any child.[90] The best-known example of the latter is probably the will of Nau-nakht, a "free woman[91] of the land of Pharaoh." She married twice. Her first husband had died, and she had retained possession of her share of their joint property. She was married again, to a simple workman of the Deir el-Medina crew, by whom she had eight children. As she grew old, she decided that four of the children were not taking care of her properly, so she went to court in year 3 of Ramesses IV and disinherited those four children from all of her own personal property (inherited, acquired while married to the first husband, or acquired while married to the second husband). Meanwhile she noted that they would still inherit equally from their father (and his two-thirds share of their joint property). The husband and children appeared in court a year later, agreeing to abide by Nau-nakht's disposition of her property.

In the inscriptions on the slightly later statue of Nakht-mut, the father specifically disinherits any other sons and daughters whom he might have had, saying, "No other son or daughter shall say 'Give me the like!'" because "like the Great God said: 'Let every man make the determination[92] of his (own) property!'"

When persons died intestate, their property went to their children or, if they had no children, to their parents and/or siblings. If they wanted their property to go to someone other than their children, or if they wanted to give special (favorable or unfavorable) treatment to one or more children, they had to write a document and have it witnessed or make a deposition in court, witnessed and recorded by the court. The earliest such documents preserved are the *imyt pr* documents discussed above, whereby an individual transferred property to someone other than a normal heir—for example, grandchildren rather than children, or wife (and children) rather than children directly. From the New Kingdom we have an example of a man legally adopting his own wife so that she would inherit his property like a daughter, taking precedence over the man's siblings or any other relatives. The woman, in turn, adopted the three children of the slave-woman who had worked in their home.[93] Childless individuals were encouraged to adopt children, who would become their legal heirs.[94]

We also have evidence for some (residual) "rights of primogeniture."[95] Very frequently the eldest son inherited his father's position, and younger sons (or sons of second marriages) often bore titles different from their fathers and older brothers. Yet numerous exceptions exist, presumably the result of differences in children's abilities and differences in relationships between parents and children. In addition, the child called eldest son bore responsibility for taking care of his parents' funerals and received some of their property in recompense. An Old Kingdom man called himself his mother's "eldest son," "heir," and possessor of her property because he had buried her and acted as her mortuary priest. In turn he passed

ADOPTION PAPYRUS (NEW KINGDOM)

[1]"Year 1, 3rd month of Summer, day 20, under the Majesty of the King of Upper and Lower Egypt, Ramesses . . . (XI). [2]On this day, proclamation to Amen of the shining forth of this noble god, he arising and shining forth and [3]making offering to Amen. Thereupon Neb-nefer, my husband, made a writing for me, the musician [4]of Seth Nanefer, and made me a daughter of his, and wrote down for me all he possessed, having no [5]son or daughter apart from myself. 'All profit that I have made with her, I will bequeath [6]it to Nanefer, my wife, and if ⟨any of⟩ my own brothers or sisters arise to confront her at my death tomorrow [7]or thereafter and say "Let my brother's share be given (to me)—." Before many and numerous [8]witnesses: . . .[A] [10]Behold, I [11]have made the bequest to Ren-nefer, my wife, this day before Hu-irymu, my [12]sister.'

[13]Year 8, 1st month of Inundation, day 10, under the Majesty of the King of Upper and Lower Egypt, Ramesses . . . (XI). [14]On this [15]day, declaration made by the stable-master Neb-nefer and his wife the musician of Seth of Spermeru[B] Ren-[16]nefer, to wit:

"We purchased the female slave Dini-huiry and she gave birth to these [17]three children, one male and two female, in all three. And I[C] took them and [18]nourished them and brought them up, and I have reached this day with them [19]without their doing evil towards me, but they dealt well with me, I having no son or daughter [20]except them. And the stable-master Padiu entered my house and took Taamon-niu [21]their elder sister to wife, he being related to me and being my younger brother. And I accepted him [22]for her and he is with her at this day. Now behold, I have made her a freewoman[D] of[23]the land of Pharaoh, and if she bears either son or daughter, they shall be free[24]men of the land of Pharaoh in exactly the same way, they being with the stable-master Padiu, [25]this younger brother of mine. And the children shall be with their elder sister in the [26]house of Padiu, this stable-master, this younger brother of mine, and today I make him a son [vo 1]of mine exactly like them."

And she said:

"As Amen endures, and the Ruler [vo 2]endures, I (hereby) make the people whom I have put on record freemen [vo 3]of the land of Pharaoh, and if any son, daughter, brother, or sister of their mother and [vo 4]their father should contest their rights, except Padiu this son of mine—for [vo 5]they are indeed no longer with him as servants, but are with him as younger siblings, [vo 6]being freemen of the land ⟨of Pharaoh⟩—may a donkey copulate with him and a donkey with his wife, whoever it be that shall [vo 7]call any of them a servant. And if I have fields in the country, or [vo 8]if I have any property in the world, or if I have merchants (?), these shall be divided among [vo 9]my four children, Padiu being one of them. And as for these matters of which [vo 10]I have spoken, they are entrusted in their entirety to Padiu, this son of mine who dealt well with me [vo 11]when I was a widow and when my husband had died.'

Before many and numerous witnesses: . . ."[E]

A Mostly men, but including the wife of one of the men.

B The town from which Ren-nefer came.

C Feminine.

D *Nmḥ*.

E Both men and women.

DOOR ARCHITRAVE OF TJENTI (OLD KINGDOM)

[1]"As for the funerary offerings [2]which come to me [3]via the King, [4–5] consisting of grain and [6]clothing, [7]it is my wife, the King's Acquaintance Tepem-nefret [8]who brings forth [9]funerary offerings for me therefrom, [10–11]for she is a revered one for me.

[12]As for the (one of the) [13]two plots [14–15]of land [[16]for the funerary offerings] [17]of my mother, [18]the King's Acquaintance [19]Bebi, [20]it belongs to [21]my wife, the King's Acquaintance [22]Tepem-nefret. [23]She is the one who makes [24]funerary offerings therefrom [25]for me and my mother, [26]the King's Acquaintance [27]Bebi. [28]I am the one who requests it [29]from the King [30]in order to be revered. [31]I am her [32]eldest son and her heir; [33]I am the one who buried her [34]in the necropolis."

There follows a list of four mortuary priests and the amount of land and grain each gets.

[39]"(It) comes to them [40]from the possessions of [41]Tepem-nefret [42]while I endow her with a small plot of land [43]for these mortuary priests. [44]If they do not [45]remain [46]in the mortuary chapel, [47]which is in the possession of my wife [[48]the King's Acquaintance Tep]em-nefret, [49](it[A]) reverts [50]to the possession of my wife, Tepem-nefret."

A The property and income.

the property, and the attached responsibilities for serving as his mortuary priest, to his wife, who used income from the donated land to hire men to carry out the actual ceremonies.[96] Other Old Kingdom inscriptions either name a woman as mortuary priest[97] or use both a seated man and a seated woman as determinative after the word,[98] implying that both men and women are included in the group. In such cases it is assumed that the women were equal recipients of the income involved, although they may not have carried out the ritual themselves. The New Kingdom yields examples of an individual who undertook the expense of burying a deceased person but whose child was forced to defend in court his claim to property inherited on that basis.[99] The Late Period Hermopolis Legal Code spells out clearly that any child, son or daughter, could fulfill the "responsibility of the eldest son to bury his parent(s)," thereby acting as "eldest son" and receiving the "eldest son's" extra share of the inheritance as recompense. Although individual children might inherit specific items from their parents, real property (whether buildings or fields) tended to remain undivided;[100] all siblings had a share interest in the property. In such cases, one sibling frequently acted on behalf of the group in managing the property. Here, too, the sibling who acted for the group was frequently called the "eldest son," but needed to be neither the eldest nor a son. In a New Kingdom case,[101] for example, the complainant's mother was acting as "eldest son," managing property on behalf of her siblings.

Also, because children could inherit from both parents, but women could not (with rare exceptions) hold public office, men often inherited positions through their mothers and ultimately held the same positions and the same titles as their maternal grandfathers or uncles. Several influential nomarchs from the Middle Kingdom[102] acquired office in this way, and early in the New Kingdom a man acquired the position of Governor of El-Kab when his maternal uncle died without children.[103] Thus, whatever rights of primogeniture existed in earliest Egyptian society, Egypt quickly moved to a system of modified primogeniture: the eldest son was likely to receive preferential treatment unless he proved himself unable or unwilling, and the language of primogeniture was retained for a potentially very different situation.

This "potentially very different situation" has several other implications that deserve fuller study. The annuity contracts of the Ptolemaic Period spell out most clearly the economic rights provided to married women within the legal system, and the legal independence of Egyptian women is clear from both contractual and court evidence. As noted at the beginning of this essay, however, the legal system cannot be understood apart from the Egyptian social system, and there is one aspect of the social system that may not have received sufficient attention. Daughters might receive their inheritance as a dowry at the time they married. If a woman's husband wrote her an annuity contract, it recorded the amount of the dowry, which was hers to reclaim whenever she wanted. If this was a common practice, daughters received their share of the family wealth at the time of their marriage—that is, when they "reached maturity" and turned their allegiance from their biological family to their new nuclear marital family. Sons, by contrast, apparently did not receive their inheritance until their parents died, in most cases long after they reached "maturity" and married. This is why so many annuity contracts were confirmed by the groom's father (as in the first example we examined)—because the son would not actually come into ownership of the property to be inherited from his father until his father's death. The father had to confirm that he approved of his son's marriage and would not use this marriage as an excuse to disown his son (thereby leaving the son's new wife high and dry).[104] Thus a son and his family remained dependent on his parents. Some aging parents may willingly have transferred decision making and control to their sons, but others certainly pulled the strings, controlling their sons for as long as they could.[105]

This situation could have put men and women on very different footings in relation to their families and (in practice if not in theory) to society at large. Women may have been more independent and judged capable of making major decisions affecting themselves, their property, and their families; men were not. Although the men functioned in the public sphere and the women normally remained at home and raised families, women may have been freer to act independently and make decisions in some arenas than were their husbands. A woman usually could count on her family to come to her assistance in case of trouble, but day to day, on average, because of the husband's relationship to his parents, the nuclear family was more dependent on the husband's family than on the wife's.

This hypothesis must be checked by looking carefully at the large number of documents that can tell us about the time of life at which women and men normally acquired inherited property. If it is correct, then, aside from differences in personality between husband and wife, the wife may have had more "freedom" and "independence" (because she could always count on her family to help) and may have entered the marriage in the stronger economic and social position in the family itself. Since women seem frequently to have received a house or at least part of a house as their "dowry/wedding gift," at least in the Late Period, the generic title *nbt pr*, "Mistress of the House," may imply more than we normally assume.

Egyptian texts quoted

ABBREVIATIONS USED FOR TYPES OF TEXT

I	Inscription
O	Ostracon
P	Papyrus
S	Stela or Statue

ABBREVIATIONS USED FOR DATES

OK	Old Kingdom
MK	Middle Kingdom
NK	New Kingdom
LP	Late Period
1 IP	First Intermediate Period
3 IP	Third Intermediate Period

LITERARY

Instructions of Ptahhotep, MK, page 175, notes 47, 54, 89	Lichtheim, *Ancient Egyptian Literature,* I/61–80
Instructions of King Amenemhat I for His Son, MK, note 10	Lichtheim, *Ancient Egyptian Literature,* I/135–39
Instructions of 'Any, NK, page 175, note 89	Lichtheim, *Ancient Egyptian Literature,* II/135–46
Instructions of 'Onchsheshonqy LP, notes 47, 89	Lichtheim, *Ancient Egyptian Literature,* III/159–84

DOCUMENTARY

Adoption Papyrus, NK, notes 6, 20, 23, 91, 93, translation page 183	A.H. Gardiner, *JEA* 26 (1940): 23–29
I Ahmose, Son of Abana, NK, note 51	Sethe, *Urkunden* 4: 1–11
I Amenemhat, MK, note 56	Lichtheim, *Ancient Egyptian Autobiographies,* 1988, ch. 6
I Amenemhat, NK, note 56	A.H. Gardiner, *ZÄS* 47 (1910): 87–99
O Ashmolean 1945.39, NK, note 86	S. Allam, *Hieratische Ostraka und Papyri,* 1973, 24–26, no. 4
O Berlin 10627, NK, note 94	Wente, *Letters,* 149–50, no. 206
P Berlin 8523, NK, note 51	Wente, *Letters,* 209, no. 339
P Bibliothèque Nationale 215 LP, note 17	W. Spiegelberg, *Die sogenannte Demotische Chronik des Pap. 215 der Bibliothèque nationale zu Paris* (1914)
O Bodleian 253, NK, note 31	S. Allam, *Hieratische Ostraka und Papyri,* 1973, 157, no. 18
P Boulaq 10, NK, notes 15, 23, 24, 99, translation page 177	J.J. Janssen and P.W. Pestman, *JESHO* 11 (1968): 137–70
P BM 10591, LP, page 181, note 75	H. Thompson, *A Family Archive from Siut,* 1934
P BM 10593, LP, page 181, note 72	H. Thompson, *A Family Archive from Siut,* 1934
P Brooklyn 35.1446, MK, note 8	Hayes, *Papyrus;* Parkinson, *Voices,* 99–101, no. 33c
P Brooklyn 35.7476, NK, note 83	A. Théodorides, *RIDA* 7 (1960): 55–145
O Cairo 49866, NK, note 51	J. Černý, *ASAE* 27 (1927): 183–210
P Cairo 65739, NK, page 178, notes 40, 43	J.A. Wilson, in J.B. Pritchard, *ANET,* 1955, 216–17
O Deir el-Medina 587, NK, note 86	Wente, *Letters,* 154, no. 219
P Deir el-Medina 27, NK, page 179, note 48	S. Allam, *Hieratische Ostraka und Papyri,* 1973, 301–2, no. 272
I Djefahapy, MK, notes 2, 3	G.A. Reisner, *JEA* 5 (1918): 79–98

O Gardiner 150, NK, note 26	S. Allam, *Hieratische Ostraka und Papyri,* 1973, page 181, no. 180
Hermopolis Legal Code, LP, pages 177, 180, 184; notes 18, 62, 95	G. Mattha, ed. by G.R. Hughes, *Demotic Legal Code of Hermopolis West,* 1975
Hekanakhte Papers, 1 IP, note 105	T.G.H. James, *Hekanakhte Papers,* 1962
I Iti, 1 IP, note 56	Lichtheim, *Ancient Egyptian Literature,* 1: 89
S Juridique, NK, note 103	P. Lacau, *Stèle juridique,* 1949
P Kahun I, MK, page 178; notes 22, 35, 90; translation page 178	F. Ll. Griffith, *Petrie Papyri: Hieratic Papyri from Kahun and Gurob,* 1898; Parkinson, *Voices,* 108–10, no. 36
I Kheti, MK, note 102	H. Brunner, *Texte aus den Gräbern der Herakleopolitenzeit von Siut,* 1937
I Khnumhotep, MK, note 102	P.E. Newberry, *Beni Hasan,* 1893
Late Ramesside Letters, NK, note 52	Wente, *Letters,* ch. 10
P Leiden 352, NK, note 44	J. Černý, *JEA* 23 (1937): 186–89
P Leiden 371, NK, note 55	Wente, *Letters,* 216–17, no. 352
I Metjen, OK, page 177, note 34	Sethe, *Urkunden* 1, 1–7
Moscow Bowl 3917, NK, note 87	Wente, *Letters,* 96–97, no. 128
S Nakht-mut, 3 IP, page 183, notes 3, 89; translation page 182	E. Otto, *Die biographischen Inschriften der ägyptischen Spätzeit,* 1954, 139–43, no. 6
O Nash 1, NK, page 177; notes 9, 23, 24, 45; translation page 179	S. Allam, *Hieratische Ostraka und Papyri,* 1973, 214–17, no. 217
Will Naunakht, NK, page 183, note 89	J. Černý, *JEA* 31 (1945): 29–53
I Nikauankh, OK, note 37	Sethe, *Urkunden* 1: 161–62
O Petrie 16, NK, note 99	J.J. Janssen and P.W. Pestman, *JESHO* 11 (1968): 137–70
O Petrie 18, NK, note 84	S. Allam, *Hieratische Ostraka und Papyri,* 1973, 234–35, no. 233
O Petrie 61, NK, note 88	Wente, *Letters,* 1990, 147, no. 199
I Qedes, 1 IP, note 51	Lichtheim, *Ancient Egyptian Literature,* 1: 90
P Salt 124, NK, page 179	S. Allam, *Hieratische Ostraka und Papyri,* 1973, 281–87, no. 266
I Senmose, NK, notes 22, 37, 89	A. Théodorides, *RIDA* 17 (1970): 117–216
I Tjenti, OK, note 96, translation page 184	Sethe, *Urkunden* 1, 163–65
P Tomb Robberies, NK, page 175, notes 13, 14	T.E. Peet, *Great Tomb-Robberies,* 1930, 135–75
P Turin Judicial, NK, note 11	J.A. Wilson, in J.B. Pritchard, *ANET,* 1955
P Turin 2021, NK, notes 16, 25, 31, 77, 78, 82	J. Černý and T.E. Peet, *JEA* 13 (1927): 30–39
O Varille 30, NK, note 31	S. Allam, *Hieratische Ostraka und Papyri,* 1973, 254, no. 257
I Vizier, MK/NK, notes 22, 32	van den Boorn, *Duties of the Vizier,* 1988
I Weni, OK, note 10	Lichtheim, *Ancient Egyptian Literature,* 1: 18–23

Notes

Women's work: Some occupations of nonroyal women as depicted in ancient Egyptian art

1 Although these texts are often quite repetitive, they give far more information about the individual tomb owner than any texts provide about the women depicted in a tomb.

2 In the New Kingdom, it would have included the female relatives of artisans such as those from Deir el-Medina, who were able to construct and decorate their own tombs.

3 The provenance of Enehy's statue is unknown, but the style suggests that it came from the New Kingdom cemetery at Saqqara. It is most likely that the statue was originally in her husband's tomb and that a statue of this husband, of similar size and pose, once existed.

4 Some women have their own tomb chapels, but these chapels are usually part of the funerary complex of a husband or son (for example, the chapel dedicated to Wa'tetkhethor in the *mastaba* of her husband, Mareruka, at Saqqara) or were provided by a male relative (such as the Theban tomb of Senet, TT 60, which initially was identified as belonging to her son, Antefoker).

5 Private statuary that renders the woman absurdly smaller than her husband is the exception, not the rule, in Egyptian art. Most of the examples date to the late Old Kingdom.

6 Madjet is modern Deir Durunka, a site near Asyut.

7 The family group often includes daughters and sons as well.

8 Henry G. Fischer, "Women in the Old Kingdom and the Heracleopolitan Period," in Lesko, ed., *Women's Earliest Records,* 11–12.

9 For an extensive catalogue and discussion of mourners, see Werbrouck, *Les pleureuses;* Fischer, *Egyptian Studies,* 1: 39–50.

10 Because two mourners are shown, one is tempted to associate them with the *ḏryt*-mourners of old, now replaced by members of the family.

11 Several of the male workers are also identified by name and occupation.

12 For a woman (or a man) who was not from an upperclass family, this might well have been a high reward, on a par with allowing an official to dedicate a statue of himself at Karnak or in another temple.

13 This is recorded in "The Instructions of 'Any." See Lichtheim, *Ancient Egyptian Literature,* 2: 141.

14 First published by A.M. Moussa and H. Altenmüller, *Das Grab des Nianchchnum und Chnumhotep* (Mainz, 1977), pl. 23; also appears in Fischer, in Lesko, ed., *Women's Earliest Records,* 13, fig. 2.

15 One example from the Saqqara tomb of Kagemni is illustrated in Smith, *HESPOK,* fig. 155, p. 301; originally published by Cicil M. Firth and Battiscombe Gunn, *Teti Pyramid Cemeteries,* 2 (Cairo, 1926), pl. 53.1. A second example, also from Saqqara, appears in Fischer, in Lesko, ed., *Women's Earliest Records,* 14, fig. 10a. In this same tomb, as noted by Fischer, women are also shown steering such boats.

16 Perhaps a princess, but more likely a provincial noblewoman.

17 Because all of these images probably come from a funerary context, they can be given a ritual interpretation connected with the rebirth of the spirit. They also present something of the reality of normal life, however.

18 Published in Davies, *Kurnah,* pl. 35 (bottom).

19 This suggests that at least some spinning was done at home as a cottage industry.

20 Davies, *Kurnah,* 50.

21 Several examples are published in Smith, *HESPOK,* figs. 124, 125, pl. 54b.

22 The Hatshepsut scenes, which are repeated by Amenhotep III, are published in Edouard Naville, *The Temple of Deir el Bahari* (London, 1896), pl. 53.

23 For two examples, see Smith, *HESPOK,* figs. 153, 154, p. 300.

24 Nurses undoubtedly served the royal family in other periods of Egyptian history, but they are never singled out as a privileged group until the Eighteenth Dynasty. For a discussion of royal nurses and their male counterparts, see Roehrig, "Eighteenth Dynasty Titles."

25 The coffin and probably the body of Sitra, nurse of Hatshepsut, were found in KV 60 near Hatshepsut's tomb in the Valley of the Kings. Burial equipment of Senetnay, nurse of Amenhotep II and wife of Sennefer, the mayor of Thebes, was found in KV 42.

26 Hatshepsut's feet rest on what seems to be a ceremonial stool projecting from the side of Sitra's chair. This might lead to the conclusion that Sitra is to be understood as holding a statue of the king. One would expect a royal statue to be held facing forward, however, as in the kneeling naophorous statues in which a man is shown presenting a *naos* with the image of a god inside.

27 They even appear to be exchanging a glance, though this may be reading too much into the angle of the eyes.

28 In the scenes depicting the divine birth of Hatshepsut, she appears as an infant, not as a miniature king. These scenes, however, are meant to commemorate what was supposed to be an actual event. Hatshepsut, also, is interacting with beings in the divine realm, not with a mere human, as is the case with Sitra.

29 Now in the British Museum, London (BM 174).

30 Now in the Egyptian Museum, Cairo (CG 42116).

31 Three are in the Egyptian Museum, Cairo (CG 42114, 42115, and JE 47278); one in Berlin (2296); an unfinished statue carved in bedrock stands above Senenmut's tomb chapel (TT 71); two fragmentary statues were found at Karnak and are now in storerooms there.

32 Both kings hold crooks in their right hands, but Amenhotep II reaches out with his left hand, while Thutmose IV holds an *ankh* in his.

33 In representations of a male guardian holding a young child, whether prince or princess, the child always reaches out to the man. As a prince grows older, this gesture toward the guardian ceases. This may be seen on the stela of Meryra (Kunsthistorisches Museum, Äg.-or. Slg. Inv. Nr. 5814), where the owner is shown holding a prince on his lap. The prince, Si-Amen, wears a sidelock but is dressed for a banquet and does not appear to be a young child. He makes no gesture toward Meryra.

34 In his tomb at Thebes (TT 109) a man named Mery was depicted in both of these roles. In one scene he is represented as the "guardian," holding Amenhotep II as a young prince on his lap. In this scene the child reaches out to touch the man's shoulder. In the second scene, Mery is shown in his role as "mentor," teaching the prince to shoot a bow and arrow.

35 This is documented in various letters and legal documents from the Middle and New Kingdoms. See, for example, Wente, *Letters,* 59, 63, 144, 151.

36 A Fifth Dynasty tomb found at Gebelein contained three mummified bodies and several bolts of cloth, including one twenty-one meters long (see Roveri, ed., *Egyptian Civilization,* 199–200). The Middle Kingdom burial of Wah contained at least thirty-eight folded lengths of cloth that had been laid inside the coffin around the mummified body (see Winlock, *BMMA* Part 2 [1921]: 32). Wooden chests in the early Eighteenth Dynasty tomb of Hatnofer and Ramose contained seventy-six folded sheets; another dozen or more were used as packing in the baskets or as palls over the coffins. Hatnofer's coffin held an additional eighteen shawls and sheets, which surrounded her mummified body (see Ambrose Lansing and William C. Hayes, *BMMA* Part 2 [1937]: esp. 18–28). The mid-Eighteenth Dynasty tomb of Kha contained more than fifty loincloths, several fringed shawls, numerous sheets and bedcovers, two tapestry-weave textiles with rows of pile on one side, and more than forty shirts and tunics (Rosalind M. Hall, *Egyptian Textiles* [Aylesbury, 1986], 35–39; Roveri, ed., *Egyptian Civilization,* 203–5).

37 Wah's body was wrapped in approximately 450 square yards of linen; see Winlock, *Deir el-Bahri,* 226. It was then surrounded with another 550 square yards of linen sheets (see previous note).

38 The bowl is now in the Petrie Museum, University College, London (UC 9547), and was first published in Guy Brunton and Gertrude Caton-Thompson, *The Badarian Civilization and Predynastic Remains near Badari* (London, 1928), pl. 38. The earliest fragment of linen fabric (UC 2943) was found in the Fayum and is dated to the fourth millennium B.C.; see Gertrude Caton-Thompson and E.W. Gardner, *The Desert Fayum* (London, 1934), 46.

39 For the titles, see Fischer, *Egyptian Studies,* 1: 69–79. Also see Fischer, in Lesko, ed., *Women's Earliest Records,* 16–17.

40 Fischer, in Lesko, ed., *Women's Earliest Records,* 10 and n. 75.

41 Only five wall paintings have been documented. These include three at Beni Hasan (tombs 3, 15, and 17), published in Percy E. Newberry, *Beni Hasan* 1, 2 (London, 1893); one at el-Bersha (tomb 2) published in Percy E. Newberry, *El-Bersheh* 1 (London, 1893); and one at Thebes (TT 103), published in Davies, *Five Theban Tombs.*

41 Many more models than wall paintings have been preserved. Several are listed in Breasted, *Servant Statues,* 52–55, pls. 47–48; Angela M.J. Tooley, "Middle Kingdom Burial Customs: A Study of Wooden Models and Related Materials," PhD dissertation, University of Liverpool, 1989, 51–57. Two others were found in the tomb of Djehutynakht (Deir el-Bersha tomb 10A); see *Mummies and Magic,* 113 and fig. 61.

43 Both men and women are seen harvesting flax. Possibly the women harvested the younger plants, which were of the right maturity for the manufacture of cloth, and the men harvested the older plants with heavier fibers, used for making nets, rope, and mats. These items traditionally were made by men.

44 It is assumed that women also were responsible for making the finished clothing and for mending worn cloth and garments, but scenes of these activities have not been preserved. At least they have not been recognized as such.

45 Hackling separates the unwanted stem fibers from the usable bast fibers. Roving is the process of splicing the bast fibers loosely together in preparation for spinning. For a detailed description of the Egyptian process of preparing and spinning flax fibers, see Elizabeth J.W. Barber, *Prehistoric Textiles: The Development of Cloth in the Neolithic and Bronze Ages* (Princeton, 1991), 44–51.

46 For example, evidence of nonindustrial manufacture of linen cloth was found in the settlement area at Lisht North. The settlement material will be published by Dieter and Felix Arnold in the series of volumes on the excavations at Lisht conducted by the Metropolitan Museum of Art.

47 Susan Allen has kindly allowed me to use a copy of her article on spinning bowls, which will be published in the Martha Bell Festschrift.

48 Men are also shown spinning, but male spinners are always associated with scenes showing other men knotting nets, twisting rope, or weaving mats. This suggests that male spinners prepared the heavier fibers used for the industries that were traditionally men's work.

49 In another scene of weavers in the Middle Kingdom Theban tomb of Dagi, the weaver on the left-hand side of the loom seems to be in the act of weaving this fringe. See Davies, *Five Theban Tombs,* pl. 37. For a more complete description of this scene, see Louisa Bellinger, "Craft Habits, Part 1: Loom Types Suggested by Weaving Details," in *Textile Museum Workshop Notes* (1959), esp. 2–3.

50 The models belonging to the chancellor Meketra were discovered in 1920 by the Egyptian Expedition of the Metropolitan Museum of Art. When the models were divided, the weavers' shed went to the Egyptian Museum, Cairo (JE 46723).

51 This is seen easily in the drawing of the looms published in Winlock, *Models,* pls. 66, 67.

52 The woman's name appears in several of the Hekanakhte Papers, which currently are being retranslated by James Allen of the Department of Egyptian Art at the Metropolitan Museum of Art.

53 See Hayes, *Papyrus,* 105–7. Hayes makes other references to female weavers on p. 105, n. 380. Although most of these women have Asiatic names, the fact remains that they are all women and that cloth manufacture is regarded as women's work.

54 These are found in the tomb of Neferhotep (TT 49), the tomb of Djehutynefer (TT 104), and the tomb of Neferrenput (TT 133). It is quite possible that others exist but have yet to be recognized or documented.

55 See, for example, Hayes, *Scepter* 2: 265. I am indebted to Nobuko Kajitani, Conservator in Charge of the Department of Textile Conservation at the Metropolitan Museum of Art, for discussing various types of looms with me and for sharing her vast knowledge of ancient Egyptian textiles.

56 The scene is published in a drawing in Davies, *Kurnah,* pl. 37, and is described on 49–51.

57 For example, Jaroslav Černý, "Papyrus Salt 124 (Brit. Mus. 10055)," *JEA* 15 (1929): 246, ll. 19–20.

58 The fact that only depictions of upright looms are recorded for the New Kingdom may be an accident of preservation. It also may be a function of the novelty of the new upright loom, which may have been something of a status symbol.

59 Heddle-jacks are blocks of wood used to support the heddle bar of a horizontal loom. Their use is explained by Barber, *Prehistoric Textiles,* 86–88, where she includes and refines a description by Herbert Winlock.

60 For a summary of the existing evidence, see ibid., 88–89.

61 Textiles with decoration rendered in tapestry weave also appear for the first time in the later Eighteenth Dynasty, and it has been suggested that the loom was adopted because of this weaving technique. Yet because so few examples of tapestry-woven fabric have been preserved, it seems more likely that the vertical loom was adopted as a more efficient way of manufacturing traditional plain-weave Egyptian textiles than as a method of producing something entirely new.

62 Bellinger, *Textile Museum Workshop Notes* (1959): 3–4.

63 This inlaid fringe seems always to occur along the left-hand side from the weaver's point of view.

64 The sheet in question is MMA 36.3.111. It contains an average of 46 warp threads and 30 weft threads per sq. cm.

65 The greatest width is recorded as 160 cm, the greatest length as 515 cm, the weight as 140 grams.

66 This length of cloth contains roughly 7,300 warp threads. These had to be measured and placed on the loom, where alternate threads could be attached to the heddle, to be raised and lowered as the weaving progressed.

67 Both fragments are now in the Metropolitan Museum of Art, MMA 31.3.62 and MMA 27.3.616.

68 This piece is now in the Egyptian Museum, Cairo (JE 56279). All three pieces were used as mummy wrappings.

69 Noted briefly in Lansing and Hayes, *BMMA* Section 2 (1937): 28.

70 My description is based on an examination of the photographs and on information from excavation notes in the archives of the Department of Egyptian Art at the Metropolitan Museum of Art.

71 This fringe extends about nine inches on either end of the pad.

72 Kha was an architect from the workmen's village of Deir el-Medina. He lived in the later part of the dynasty sometime around the reigns of Amenhotep II–Amenhotep III. This textile and a second similar example from the same tomb are now in the Egyptian Museum in Turin, Italy. In the original publication of this tomb, a photograph shows the pad draped across the seat of a chair, rather like a cushion. In this photograph, the pad appears to be about the same size as the one found by the Metropolitan Museum (Ernesto Schiaparelli, *Relazione sui lavori della missione archeologica italiana in Egitto (anni 1903–1920),* 2 [Turin, 1927], 15, fig. 15). An excellent new photograph appears in Roveri, ed., *Egyptian Civilization,* 213, fig. 301.

73 In a quick survey of scenes listed in PM 1^1, there are thirteen scenes of carpenters, eleven of jewelry makers, ten of metalworkers, and nine of stone-vessel makers in the New Kingdom tombs, but only three of spinners and weavers.

In women good and bad fortune are on earth

1 Robins, *Women,* 15.

2 Michael Heltzer, *The Internal Organization of the Kingdom of Ugarit: Royal Service-System, Taxes, Royal Economy, Army, and Administration)* (Wiesbaden, 1982); Barbara Lesko, ed., *Women's Earliest Records from Ancient Egypt and Western Asia* (Atlanta, Ga., 1989); Piotr Michalowski, *Letters from Early Mesopotamia* (Atlanta, 1993), especially pp. 38–39, 78–81.

3 For a discussion of early Celtic society, see V. Muller, "Kin Reproduction and Elite Accumulation in the Archaic States of Northwest Europe," in Thomas C. Patterson and Christine W. Gailey, eds., *Power Relations and State Formation* (Washington, D.C., 1987), 81–97. For early Japan, see *From Court to Capital: A Tentative Interpretation of the Origins of the Japanese Urban Tradition* (Chicago, 1978).

4 The summary here is based on the work of Sarah M. Nelson, summarized in "Gender Hierarchy and the Queens of Silla," in *Sex and Gender Hierarchies* (Cambridge, England, 1993), 297–315. It is supplemented with fuller studies, in particular by Chong-Sun Kim, "The Kolp'um System: Basis for Sillan Social Stratification," *Journal of Korean Studies* 1, no. 2 (1977): 43–69; and James H. Grayson, "Some Structural Patterns of the Royal Families of Ancient Korea," *Korea Journal* 16, no. 6 (1976): 27–32.

5 Nelson, *Hierarchies,* 302.

6 Grayson, *Korea Journal* 16, no. 6 (1976): 28. Cited (page number incorrect) by Nelson, *Hierarchies,* 302.

7 Quoted by Nelson, *Hierarchies,* 301, from Kim, *Journal of Korean Studies* 1, no. 2 (1977): 43–69.

8 Nelson, *Hierarchies,* 311, argues that the king lists, edited by later Confucian and Buddhist scholars, might have suppressed the fact of queens ruling jointly with their husbands and might have left in only the female rulers without consorts. She offers no evidence for this suggestion, however, other than an unidentified royal burial containing males and females of equal affluence.

9 Mertz, *Certain Titles.*

10 Robins, *Women,* 26–27; Robins, "A Critical Examination of the Theory That the Right to the Throne of Ancient Egypt Passed through the Female Line in the 18th Dynasty," *GM* 62 (1983): 67–77. The most interesting aspect of the heiress theory is the difficulty of finding a proposed definition. For the data relating to royal women of the Old, Middle, and New Kingdoms, see Schmitz, *Untersuchungen.*

11 Robins, *Women,* 27.

12 In the period after Akhenaten's reign, it was in such disgrace that it might have profited little in any case.

13 Ahmose: his full sister Ahmose-Nefertari
Thutmose II: his half-sister Hatshepsut
Thutmose III: his half-sister Nefrura
Thutmose IV: his sister or daughter Iaret
Amenhotep III: his daughters Sitamun and perhaps Henuttaneb
Amenhotep IV/Akhenaten: his daughter Meretaten and perhaps Ankhesenpaaten
Tutankhamun: Akhenaten's daughter Ankhesenpaaten/Ankhesenamen
For royal women of the period, see Robins, *Women,* 29; Bryan, *Thutmose IV* (Baltimore, 1991), 93–140. Also see Schmitz, *Untersuchungen.*

14 Robins, *Women,* 29.

15 Nelson, *Hierarchies,* 301.

16 In the New Kingdom the usage was less extensive but could apply to royal family members who were not the king's offspring. See Aidan Dodson and Jac. J. Janssen, "A Theban Tomb and Its Tenants," *JEA* 75 (1989): 125–38.

17 See Schmitz, *Untersuchungen,* 124–25, for a discussion of this point in particular. The wife of Teti I, founder of the Sixth Dynasty, might be construed as an exception. She carried the singular title "Daughter of the King of Upper and Lower Egypt." Schmitz (ibid., 137, n. 1) considers her to be nonroyal with a deliberately variant cultic title; see also pp. 182–96 and 288–96. On the Eighteenth Dynasty usage of the title, also see Robins, *Women,* 26.

18 Kent Flannery, "The Cultural Evolution of Civilizations," *Annual Review of Ecology and Systematics* 3 (1972): 399–426; Bruce Trigger, "Generalized Coercion and Inequality: The Basis of State Power in Early Civilization," in H. Claessen, P. Van de Velde, and M.S. Smith, eds., *Development and Decline in the Evolution of Sociopolitical Organization* (South Hadley, Mass., 1985), 46–61.

19 Nelson, *Hierarchies,* 310–11.

20 Naguib, *Le clergé féminin,* 49–71. On p. 50 she specifically notes the ascendancy of Hathor even over Isis. Despite Isis's presence in the Pyramid Texts as the consort of Osiris, and her equation even there with the goddess Sothis (the star Sirius), it was largely in the Late Period that Isis took over the role of fertility goddess associated with the Nile inundation—a role intrinsic to Hathor (Naguib, *Le clergé féminin,* 42–44). Also see Philippe Derchain, "Les pleurs d'Isis et la crue du Nil," *CdE* 45 (1970): 282–84.

21 Robins, *Women,* 38; Parkinson, *Voices,* 38, 40–41; Lichtheim, *Ancient Egyptian Literature,* 1: 116 [building inscription of Senusert I]. As a result, kings felt connected to one another: see the Instruction for King Merikara, which expresses a somewhat reflective view: "A goodly office is kingship, it has no son, no brother to maintain its memorial, but one man provides for the other; a man acts for him who was before him, so that what he has done is preserved by his successor" (Lichtheim, *Ancient Egyptian Literature,* 1: 105).

22 On the specific role of Mother-Wife played by the goddesses and assumed by the queens, see Jan Assmann, "Muttergattin," *LÄ* 4: 264–66; Assman, "Muttergöttheit," *LÄ* 4: 266–71. Also see, among the voluminous citations, Herman te Velde, "Some Remarks on the Structure of Egyptian Divine Triads," *JEA* 57 (1971): 80–86; Te Velde, "Mut the Eye of Re," *Akten des Vierten Internationalen Ägyptologen Kongresses München 1985, SAK* Beihefte 3 (1989): 395–403.

23 Intrinsic to the mythological models is the concept of Egyptian creation that first brought into being a creator god, self-generated by one of several means (masturbation, thought, speech). The agents of this creator were of his making, including the male and female diversity of the cosmos. See on this subject, for example, Allen, *Egyptian Genesis.*

24 In general see Christine Meyer, "Regent(in)," *LÄ* 5: 206–7.

25 For the question of whether the queen in the first two dynasties bore the title "She Who Sees Horus" or "She Who Sees Horus and Seth," see Kaplony, *Inschriften,* 1: 373–74. Cf. Helck, *Untersuchungen,* 119–21.

26 Kaplony, *Inschriften,* 1: 588–92; for the sealing, Kaplony's no. 22, see pl. 54, fig. 201. See Wolfgang Helck, "Neith-hotep," *LÄ* 4: 394–95; Hoffman, *Egypt before the Pharaohs,* 322–24, on the dynastic union of Upper and Lower Egypt. Spencer, in *Early Egypt,* 61, believes she is the mother of Aha.

27 Spencer, *Early Egypt,* 67–69.

28 Kaplony, *Inschriften,* 1: 495; 3: pl. 122, no. 730. Possibly this is intended as the *mr* sign, but it is too uncertain to assert. Compare the variety of signs resembling the "hoe" in Werner Kaiser, "Zur Entstehung des gesamtägyptischen Staates," *MDAIK* 46 (1990): 287–99. See Abb. 2 b–d.

29 Kaplony, *Inschriften,* 1: 493–96; Wolfgang Helck, "Meret-Neith," *LÄ* 4: 93; Günter Dreyer, "Ein Siegel der frühzeitlichen Königsnekropole von Abydos," *MDAIK* 43 (1987): 33–43. The seal shows the names of the Horuses Narmer, Aha, Djer, Djet (or Wadj), Den, and the king's mother Mer-Neith, along with the signs normally read for the god Khenty-amentiu (recumbent jackal) and Enduring (Men) before the names of the first three. These may be intended to indicate that these were deceased rulers. Also see Werner Kaiser, "Zum Siegel mit frühen Königsnamen von Umm el-Qaab," *MDAIK* 43 (1987): 115–19.

30 See Kaplony, *Inschriften,* 1: reference nos. 3, 6 (pp. 494–95), which were found in the Djer tomb complex. Also numbers 7–8 from Saqqara *mastaba* tomb 3503 dated to Djer's reign.

31 Kaplony, *Inschriften,* 1: 496, referring to his no. 10, p. 494.

32 A photograph of the Palermo Stone with the partial writing of her name appears in Gardiner, *Egypt of the Pharaohs,* pl. 3. The best study, even now, is Kurt Sethe, *Beiträge zu ältesten Geschichte Aegyptens,* 2: "Die auf den Denkmälern der ältesten geschichtlichen Dynastieen vorkommenden Könige" (Leipzig, 1905), 30, 47. Also see Ludwig Borchardt, *Die Annalen und die zeitliche Festlegung des alten Reiches der ägyptischen Geschichte* (Berlin, 1917), 36, n. 1, where he considers Mer-Neith to be the mother of Den rather than his wife, as did Sethe.

33 Ibid., 31, n. 1.

34 Borchardt believed that a fragmentary horizontal band entry in row 6 of the Cairo fragments preserves the title *špst-njswt,* "Royal Noblewoman." He considers it probable evidence of a queen's regency (ibid., 34). This perhaps would correspond to Dynasty 2–3. Also, the late excerptors of the king lists, dependent on the work of Manetho discovered a record of a female ruler in this approximate time. Africanus's list includes Binothris in the Second Dynasty Thinite rulers: "In his reign it was decided that women might hold the kingly office" (quoted from Gardiner, *Egypt of the Pharaohs,* 431). Neither of these intriguing pieces of information can be placed into a clearer context.

35 See note 34.

36 Christiane Zivie, "Nitokris," *LÄ* 4: 513–14.

37 For example, Manetho's statement that Nitocris built the third pyramid at Giza (Menkaura's) stems from the fact that that complex was remodeled during the reigns of Merenra and Pepy II (Zivie, *LÄ* 4: 513 and n. 19).

38 Von Beckerath, "Pepi I" and "Pepi II," *LÄ* 4: 926–29.

39 Jequier, *Les pyramides,* especially the erased cartouche before her name, pl. 4–5; the obelisks on p. 4; the decree in favor of the queen and Ankhnesmeryra, p. 5. Also daughter of Pepy I by Ankhnesmeryra I. She was titled in the queen's pyramid "King's eldest daughter of his body of Men-nefer is Meri-Ra" (Schmitz, *Untersuchungen,* 110, 342). She was also "King's Wife, She Who Sees Horus and Seth, Greatest of the *Hts* Scepter, King's Mother, and Countess." The fact that she would have been buried eventually in a queen's pyramid of the reign of Merenra is consistent with the type of burial given Neith-hotep. See the argument cited against this identification in Zivie, *LÄ* 4: 514.

40 Jürgen von Beckerath, "Sobeknofru," *LÄ* 5: 1050–51. The monuments are gathered and discussed in Labib Habachi, "Khata'na-Qantir: Importance," *ASAE* 52 (1952): 458–70.

41 A granite block from Hawara has the common formula "[she made it as] her monument for her father, living forever." See W.F.M. Petrie, *Hawara, Biahmu and Arsinoe* (London, 1889), pl. 27, 12. Also see Matzker, *Die letzten Könige,* 96. Argument must continue as to whether there is a monument that

names her as princess before her rulership: a statue socle from Gezer naming a "king's daughter Sobeknefru" could belong to a daughter of Senusert I, whom Amenemhat III apparently emulated more than once in naming children. The best-attested princess of Amenemhat III's time was Nofru-Ptah, who was buried at Hawara. Senusert I also had a daughter of that name. See Matzker, *Die letzten Könige,* 25–26.

42 See Gardiner, *Egypt of the Pharaohs,* 439.

43 Matzker, *Die letzten Könige,* 95–97.

44 Some believe that the uninscribed brick pyramids at Mazghuna belong to Amenemhat IV and Sobeknefru. See Matzker, *Die letzten Könige,* 174 and notes.

45 Paris, Louvre E 27135. See Delange, *Statues égyptiennes,* 30–31.

46 Habachi, *ASAE* 52 (1952): 464–65, pl. 15.

47 For a brief description see T.G.H. James, "Egypt: From the Expulsion of the Hyksos to Amenophis I," *CAH* 2, part 1, ch. 8.

48 Stela of Tetishery from Breasted, *Ancient Records,* II, 36; Petrie, *Abydos,* 3: pl. 52.

49 *Urk.* IV, 22–23; James, *CAH,* ch. 8, 302–3.

50 Stela of Kares, chief steward of Ahhotep (limestone stela Dira abu el-Naga). See Breasted, *Ancient Records,* II, 49; Cairo CG 34003, Lacau, *Stèles,* pl. 4, pp. 7–9. *Urk.* IV, 45–49.

51 See Robins, *Women,* 44.

52 The so-called Donation Stela remains a point of debate with regard to the Second Priesthood of Amen. This is my understanding of the text. See discussions in Bernadette Menu, "La stèle d'Ahmes Nefertary dans son contexte historique et juridique," *BIFAO* 77 (1977): 89–100; Michel Gitton, "La résiliation d'une fonction religieuse: Nouvelle interprétation de la stèle de donation d'Ahmes Nefertary," *BIFAO* 76 (1975): 65–89; Gitton, "Le rôle des femmes dans le clergé d'Amon à la 18e dynastie," *BSFE* 75 (1976): 31–46.

53 Robins, *Women,* 44–47, 149–50. Michel Gitton, "Gottesgemahlin," *LÄ* 2: 791–812.

54 Gay Robins, "The Relationships Specified by Egyptian Kinship Terms of the Middle and New Kingdoms," *CdE* 54 (1979): 197–217.

55 Robins, *Women,* fig. 2.

56 Blocks in the Musée Plein Air in Karnak, and in the block field north of the Hypostyle Hall, studied by Luc Gabolde of the Centre Franco-Egyptien of Karnak. Although Peter Dorman has doubted their date from the reign of Thutmose II, it seems far less complicated to accept that Hatshepsut's role as God's Wife of Amen was displayed prominently within the precinct of her functioning. The building, complementing one of Amenhotep I in which Ahmose-Nefertari figured, very likely was associated with the chapels for royal ancestry cults. See Dorman, *Senenmut,* 43, n. 131.

57 Dorman, *Senenmut,* 18–45. No one could have prepared a more thorough and careful analysis. The date of her accession remains uncertain; perhaps a methodology that accepts dates at face value rather than as a means of recording "history for posterity" (i.e., manipulative) is unhelpful.

58 *BAR,* 2: 341–42; *Urk.* IV, 59–61.

59 Dorman, *Senenmut,* 204–6.

60 Wilfried Seipel, "Hatschepsut I," *LÄ* 2: 1046, after the obelisk text of *Urk.* IV, 361, 4. The feminization of Hatshepsut's titles varied throughout her inscriptions.

61 Seipel, *LÄ* 2: nn. 29–31.

62 Ibid., nn. 32–37. The scenes of eastern military expeditions were so badly damaged that they were recognized only in the 1960s by Donald Redford.

63 Dorman, *Senenmut,* 126–27; Richard Fazzini, "Report on the 1983 Season of Excavation at the Precinct of the Goddess Mut," *ASAE* 70 (1985): 287–307.

64 Dorman, *Senenmut,* 51–65.

65 Ibid., 22–28.

66 PM 2^2: 260.

67 Information collected for a catalogue of nonroyal women's titles records eleven Singers of Amen *(shemayit)* for Hatshepsut compared with eight for Thutmose III, a sole ruler, despite the larger body of material for the latter.

68 Seipel, *LÄ* 2: 1047 and nn. 62–63.

69 Dorman, *Senenmut,* 201–11.

70 For example, see Charles van Siclen, "The Date of the Granite Bark Shrine of Tuthmosis III," *GM* 79 (1984): 53.

71 For example, the prince Amenemhat, named as overseer of cattle in a year 23 inscription of Thutmose III, is posited to have been the son of Nefrura. See Dorman, *Senenmut,* 79. Another prince, Si-amen, is known from a statue of the treasurer under Hatshepsut, Sennefer (CG 1112).

72 Dorman, *Senenmut,* 65.

73 Evidence that Peribsen's monuments were disgraced is spotty at best. A cult of the king is attested at a later date. See W. Helck, "Peribsen," *LÄ* 4: 937–38.

74 Lichtheim, *Ancient Egyptian Literature,* 1: 137. This text was popular throughout the New Kingdom, possibly because of its subject matter, palace intrigue. Richard Parkinson's recent translation ("Had any woman previously raised troops? Is tumult raised in the Residence? Is water which destroys the earth let forth? Are commoners deceived by what they have done?") and his accompanying footnote to the passage inform us that he believes the conspiracy was planned by a woman (Parkinson, *Voices,* 51). Although this is a clear possibility, Lichtheim's translation, on the whole, is more faithful to the language, particularly in the last line. She reads, "Does one release water that destroys the soil and deprives people of their crops?" *(iryt* = produce). Still, one should consider the likelihood that Eighteenth Dynasty revisions with a particularly antifemale flavor might have been added, possibly even in the wake of Hatshepsut's reign. The passage mentions nothing of a source in the women's royal apartments.

75 King Khufu was presented as power hungry in the Papyrus Westcar (Lichtheim, *Ancient Egyptian Literature,* 1: 215–19), and King Neferkara (Pepy II?) was ridiculed for nightly homosexual encounters with a general (Parkinson, *Voices,* 55–56).

76 See Lise Manniche, "Some Aspects of Ancient Egyptian Sexual Life," *Acta Orientalia* 38 (1977): 21–22; Romer, *People of the Nile,* 156–59; quote from Edward Wente, "Some Graffiti from the Reign of Hatshepsut," *JNES* 43 (1984): 47.

77 The authors in question include the absence of royal iconography as part of the political satire by suggesting that the "absence of an uraeus on the crown may be part of the pictorial commentary 'on the ambiguity of the queen/king's role.'" Wente, *JNES* 43 (1984): 53.

78 Ibid., 53.

79 Extracted from *BD,* ch. 42. See Faulkner, *Book of the Dead.*

80 Paul Barguet, *Le livre des morts des anciens Égyptiens* (Paris, 1967), 236; illustrated in *Egypt's Dazzling Sun,* 217, fig. 8.5.

81 See Robins, *Women,* 53–55, for a clear and balanced overview; for the argument in favor of Nefertiti's rule, see J.R. Harris, "Nefertiti Rediviva," *Acta Orientalia* 35 (1973): 5–13; Harris, "Nefernefruaten," *GM* 4 (1973): 15–17; Samson, *Amarna.*

82 Gardiner, *Egypt of the Pharaohs,* 277–79. The tomb of Tauseret has recently been restored and studied by Hartwig Altenmüller, "Bemerkungen zu den neu gefundenen Daten im Grab der Königen Twosre (KV 14) im Tal der Könige von Theben," in C.N. Reeves, ed., *After Tutʿankhamun* (London, 1992), 141–64.

83 EA 26 from Tushratta. See Moran, *Amarna Letters.*

84 James, *Hekanakhte Papers;* Wente, *Letters,* 58–64.

85 Translation is after both Lichtheim, *Ancient Egyptian Literature,* 1: 69, and Parkinson, *Voices,* 70.

86 Lichtheim, *Ancient Egyptian Literature,* 2: 143.

87 Wente, *Letters,* 147; Ostracon Petrie 61.

88 Wente, *Letters,* 148.

89 Robins, *Women,* 57–75, on marriage, divorce, adultery.

90 Schmitz, *Untersuchungen,* 140.

91 Ibid., 290.

92 Ibid., 33, 37, 117–33, for the Old Kingdom. In many cases the title "King's Daughter" became a rank at court and was given to numerous women whose genealogical attachments to the king's family are unidentifiable. This phenomenon was most apparent in Dynasties 5 and 6 but may have grown out of the extension of "Prince" and "Princess" titles in Dynasties 3 and 4 to persons other than king's sons and daughters. It was also common in the Second Intermediate Period for women with princess rank to marry high officials. See Anthony J. Spalinger, "Remarks on the Family of Queen *Ḫʿ.s-nbw* and the Problem of Kingship in Dynasty XIII," *RdE* 32 (1980): 103–15.

93 Ibid., 114.

94 Breasted, *Ancient Records* I, sec. 628, Khnumhotep II of Beni Hasan.

95 Iti of Gebelein stated: ibid., sec. 459; CG 20001. Lichtheim, *Ancient Egyptian Literature,* 1: 88–89.

96 Instruction of Ptahhotep, Lichtheim, *Ancient Egyptian Literature,* 1: 69.

97 Robins, *Women,* 30–36, especially 32.

98 Geoffrey T. Martin, "The Tomb of Tia and Tia: Preliminary Report on the Saqqâra Excavations, 1983," *JEA* 70 (1984): 5–12.

99 Lichtheim, *Ancient Egyptian Literature,* 2: 200–203.

100 Ibid., 201.

101 Ibid., 200–201.

102 Ibid., 201.

103 Spalinger, *RdE* 32 (1980).

104 Lichtheim, *Ancient Egyptian Literature,* 2: 184–85.

105 Ibid., 188.

106 Henry G. Fischer, "Administrative Titles of Women in the Old and Middle Kingdom," in *Egyptian Studies,* 1: 69–79; Fischer, "Women in the Old Kingdom and the Heracleopolitan Period," in Lesko, ed., *Women's Earliest Records,* 5–24; Fischer, *Egyptian Women;* William A. Ward, "Non-Royal Women and Their Occupations in the Middle Kingdom," in Lesko, ed., *Women's Earliest Records,* 33–43; Ward, *Essays;* Ward, *Index.* On the last, see Fischer, *Egyptian Titles;* Robins, *Women,* 114–17.

107 See Fischer in *Egyptian Studies,* 1: 76, nn. 42–43. The wife of Khnumhotep II at Beni Hasan was both *ḥ3tt-ʿ* and *rpʿtt,* as was his mother, who was the daughter of a monarch. The wife of Khnumhotep I was "female patrician," while the wife of Wahkai at Qau and a woman at Bersheh were both "countess."

108 Graefe, *Untersuchungen,* 2: 47–50.

109 CG 1578, a stela from Abydos, shows Nebet opposite a man named Khui. Her titulary was that of "the patrician woman, daughter of Geb, the

countess, daughter of Merhu, the one of the curtain, judge, vizier, daughter of Thoth, female companion of the King of Lower Egypt, daughter of Horus" *(rpʿtt s3t Gb ḥ3tt s3t Mrḥw ṯ3yt t3t s3t Ḏḥwt smrt b?t s3t Ḥr)* (Fischer in *Egyptian Studies,* 1: 74, nn. 31–41). Nebet was the probable (step?)mother of Djau and Idi, and presumably of the queen Ankhnesmeryra. The strongest likelihood is that the stela was a later commemoration for Nebet. Fischer first believed that there were indications that it was a post–Old Kingdom monument (ibid., 74–75, nn. 34, 38). For a mention of the female vizier, also see Robins, *Women,* 115.

110 Similar titles appear in CG 42205. The sculptor carved *ṯ3tt,* rather than *t3tt,* after the title "judge" *(s3b)* (Fischer in *Egyptian Studies,* 1: 74, n. 32). The error suggests that the sculptor expected a title containing the word "daughter."

111 See W.K. Simpson, *Papyrus Reisner* I. *Accounts of the Dockyard Workshop at This in the Reign of Sesostris I* (Boston, 1963). In the Berlin Lahun Papyri (P. Berlin 10016), also see a request for women workers as substitutes in the mortuary temple of Senusert II at Lahun: "Half of them have been removed from the mortuary temple 'Powerful is Senwosret, the deceased.' Please send women substitutes for them" (Wente, *Letters,* 76).

112 Parkinson, *Voices,* 100–101; other bibliography, 158, no. 33; W.C. Hayes, *A Papyrus of the Late Middle Kingdom in the Brooklyn Museum* (Brooklyn, 1955).

113 Parkinson, *Voices,* 143; 160, no. 56.

114 Hekanakhte Letter, No. 1. Parkinson, *Voices,* 104; James, *Hekanakhte Papers,* pl. 24; Wente, *Letters,* 60.

115 Wente, *Letters,* 92.

116 Antonio Loprieno, "L'esclave," in *L'homme égyptien* (Paris, 1992), 227–66, discusses the notion of slavery throughout Egyptian history. He also includes household dependents in his survey.

117 Robins, *CdE* 54 (1979): 197–217.

118 Wente, *Letters,* 93.

119 P. Gurob 3, 1, recto; Wente, *Letters,* 36.

120 Roehrig, "Institution of Royal Nurses"; Bryan, *Thutmose IV,* chs. 3, 5.

121 The will of Ni-ka-ankh perhaps is suggestive but is difficult to interpret.

122 Marianne Galvin, "The Hereditary Status of the Titles of the Cult of Hathor," *JEA* 70 (1984): 42–49.

123 Hans Hickmann wrote numerous papers on music. See, for example, "La chironomie dans l'Égypte pharaonique," *ZÄS* 83 (1958): 96–127; "Dieux et déesses de la musique," *Cahiers d'histoire égyptienne* 6 (1954): 31–59.

124 Del Nord, "The Term *ḫnr:* 'Harem' of 'Musical Performers'?" in W.K. Simpson and W.M. Davies, eds., *Studies in Ancient Egypt, the Aegean, and the Sudan* (Boston, 1981), 137–45. Betsy Bryan, "The Etymology of *ḫnr:* 'Group of Musical Performers,'" *BES* 4 (1982): 35–54.

125 On the spelling, see Bryan in *BES* 4 (1982): 35–54.

126 All statistics are taken from a collection of nonroyal women's titles now in progress.

127 E. Wente et al., *The Tomb of Kheruef. Theban Tomb 192.* The Epigraphic Survey (Chicago, 1980).

128 Robins, *Women,* 142–56; Henry Fischer, "Priesterin," *LÄ* 4: 1100–1105.

129 Late Ramesside Letter No. 35. Dynasty 20, year 10 of the Herihor Renaissance. Wente, *Letters,* 183–84.

130 Late Ramesside Letter No. 34. Wente, *Letters,* 183.

131 For Nodjme and her religious titles, see Naguib, *Le clergé féminin.*

132 P. Lacau and H. Chevrier, *Une chapelle d'Hatshepsout à Karnak* (Cairo, 1979), pls. 18–19.

133 If Leclant's reading of a stela from North Karnak is correct; see "Gotteshand," *LÄ:* 813–15, and n. 15; Gitton, *Ahmès Néfertary,* 100–110. Gitton believes that the "Divine Adoratrice" and "God's Wife" already were synonymous in the Eighteenth Dynasty, at least as to function, and he states that "God's Wife" appeared in Luxor Temple. It was not a god's wife represented in Luxor Temple in Amenhotep III's reign, however, but a god's hand, possibly Tiye (?). So, too, Naguib, *Le clergé féminin,* 213–14.

134 So, too, Naguib, *Le clergé féminin,* 157–60, and J. Yoyotte, "Les vierges consacrées d'Amon thébain," *CRAIBL* (1961): 43–52.

135 Gitton, "Gottesgemahlin," *LÄ* 4: 797–98.

136 See Bryan, *Thutmose IV,* ch. 3.

137 Graefe, *Untersuchungen,* 2: 13–59. The list is very long, but some of it is clearly personal to the God's Wives—for example, the funerary cult attendants.

138 Or, alternatively, masturbated and spewed out first male and then female. This Heliopolitan version is an old one but by no means only creation form. See, for example, Allen, *Egyptian Genesis.*

139 Coffin Texts 6, 191, Spell 576.

140 Coffin Texts 6, 89, Spell 503.

141 The texts cited here my be found in Dieter Mueller, "Die Zeugung durch das Herz in Religion und Medizin der Ägypter," *Orientalia* N.S. 35 (1966); for the discussion of *ib* "heart" and its behaviors, see A. Piankoff, *Le coeur dans les textes égyptiennes* (Paris, 1930).

142 Lichtheim, *Ancient Egyptian Literature,* 3: 191–92. The religious texts from which the particular associations for Hathor and Mut stem may be studied in Constant de Wit, *Le rôle et le sens du lion dans l'Égypte ancienne* (Leiden, 1951); and P. Germond, *Les invocations à la Bonne Année au temple d'Edfou* (Geneva, 1986).

Public and Private Lives

FAMILY

1 Statue of Rerem

1 According to correspondence dated Jan. 19, 1954, from William Stevenson Smith, Museum of Fine Arts, Boston, to Mr. Frank Gallo of Toledo, Ohio, several other statues were found in this uninscribed tomb, including: Toledo 49.21, depicting Rerem and his wife, Ankhet; Richmond, Virginia 39.1.19, which depicts Ka-her-set-f and provides his nickname, Ked-nes; and Cairo 39.1.18, depicting two adult men (both Rerem?) and the son, here also referred to by his nickname, Ked-nes.

2 For royal cults, and the hierarchy of the priests who served in them, see Ann Macy Roth, "The Organization and Functioning of the Royal Mortuary Cults of the Old Kingdom in Egypt," in McGuire Gibson and Robert D. Biggs, eds., *The Organization of Power: Aspects of Bureaucracy in the Ancient Near East* SAOC 46 (Chicago, 1991 [2nd ed. with corrections]), 133–40.

3 *wꜥb nisw, ḥm nṯr ḫwfw, rrm; rḫ nisw n pr-ꜣ, iry-ḫt [?] ḫntyw-š, rrm.*

For *ḫntyw-š* titles in the cult of Khufu during the Fifth and Sixth Dynasties, see Zahi Hawass, "The Programs of the Royal Funerary Complexes of the Fourth Dynasty," in David O'Connor and David P. Silverman, eds., *Ancient Egyptian Kingship*, Probleme der Ägyptologie, Bd. 9 (Leiden, New York, Cologne, 1995), 242–43.

4 See essay in this volume by Janet Johnson.

5 See B.G. Trigger et al., *Ancient Egypt: A Social History* (Cambridge, Mass., 1983, 1984), 192–94, 226–27.

6 Studies of the title *ḫnty-š* include: H. Kees, *Kulturgeschichte des Alten Orients* (Munich, 1933), 30; H. Junker, *Giza VI* (Vienna, 1943), 15–19; W. Helck, *Untersuchungen zu den Beamtiteln* (ÄF 18), (1954), 107–9, and "Bemerkungen zu den Pyramidenstädten im Alten Reich," *MDAIK* 15 (1957): 98, 102–3; K. Baer, *Rank and Title*, 272–73; and S. Schott, "Aufnahmen vom Hungersnotrelief," *RdE* 17 (1965): 9–12. For studies of this title as it occurs in the Middle and New Kingdoms, see: William C. Hayes, *A Papyrus of the Late Middle Kingdom in The Brooklyn Museum (Papyrus Brooklyn 35.1446)* (Brooklyn, 1995).

7 Trigger, *Social History*, 227.

8 Hayes, *A Papyrus of the Late Middle Kingdom*, 129–34.

9 Fischer, *Egyptian Studies*, 72, which includes mention of the statue discussed here.

10 For a brief mention of this gradual decline in the wealth of administrators at the end of the Old Kingdom, see Naguib Kanawati, *Akhmim in the Old Kingdom, Part I: Chronology and Administration*, The Australian Centre for Egyptology: Studies 2 (Sydney, 1992), 294.

2 Family group: Couple with granddaughter

1 For a brief discussion of the representation of grandchildren in tomb reliefs, see Whale, *Family*, 280–81. Whale suggests that grandchildren appear in these tomb scenes only when they serve some specific function, such as offering to the deceased grandparent.

2 Smith, *Art and Architecture*, 113, 115.

3 Thanks to James Allen, Associate Curator of Egyptian Art, the Metropolitan Museum of Art, for providing translations of the inscriptions on this statue.

4 An inscription on the proper right side of the statue repeats the request for offerings: "A royal offering of Osiris, king of the living, giving an invocation offering of bread and beer, beef and fowl, and every good and pure thing for the Hall-Keeper of Amen, Ked-Amen." Dr. Allen (see note 3) noted the unusual reference here to Osiris as king of the *living*.

5 The inscription on the left proper side of the statue reads: "A royal offering of Hathor, resident in Thebes, giving everything that comes from her offering-table for the *ka* of the Mistress of the House, Nebet-Yunet."

6 At least in some cases, however, the rendering of an offspring as a child on a funerary statue does not necessarily indicate that the person did not achieve adulthood. For example, see Lutz, *Egyptian Statues*, 25–26, pl. 37, for the lower part of a statue in which a son is depicted in small scale beside his father's legs. The son is depicted with the artistic conventions of infancy: nude, with sidelock, and finger to mouth. The inscription, however, names him as "His eldest son, the scribe Sennu." A statue of the adult Sennu and his wife is known: see ibid., 24, pls. 34, 35a.

7 See Wilkinson, *Jewellery*, pl. 1a. Also see Janssen and Janssen, *Growing Up*, 37–41, for a discussion of children's hairstyles.

8 See, for example, Lichtheim, *Ancient Egyptian Literature*, 2: 136, "The Instructions of Any."

9 G. Pinch, "Childbirth and Female Figurines at Deir el-Medina and el-'Amarna," *Orientalia* 52, no. 3 (1983): 408.

10 In the account of the creation of the world by Atum in the Pyramid Texts (see, for example, 447a,b), sets of male/female twins were born, forming the Great Ennead—a recognition that the female element is as necessary and important as the male. For the powers of the primeval female deity, see Fekri A. Hassan, "Primeval Goddess to Divine King: The Mythogenesis of Power in the Early Egyptian State," in Friedman and Adams, *Followers of Horus*, 307–22.

11 Jaroslav Černý, "The Will of Naunakhte and the Related Documents," *JEA* 31 (1945): 29–53.

12 See, for example, J.J. Janssen and P.W. Pestman, "Burial and Inheritance in the Community of the Necropolis Workmen at Thebes (Pap. Bulaq X and O. Petrie 16)," *JESHO* 11, no. 2 (1968): 137–70.

13 See Sadek, *Popular Religion*, 77–78.

14 Černý, *JEA* 31 (1945); also see cat. no. 1.

15 It was certainly in her best interests to inter her parents in a fitting manner. For laws of inheritance, see Janssen and Pestman, *JESHO* 11, no. 2 (1968): 137–70; and Janet Johnson in the present volume.

16 See essay by Janet Johnson.

3a Pair statue

3b Seated statue of Sabu

1 The frequent claim that the woman is Memy-Sabu's wife is not unreasonable because in many cases in which the connection between the man and the woman is specified, it is one of marriage. Where no familial tie is specified, the woman obviously could have been any other relative. Although the statue is usually assigned to the late Fifth Dynasty or to the Sixth Dynasty, the reign of Niuserre (earlier in the Fifth Dynasty) has recently been suggested; see Cherpion in *Kunst des Alten Reiches*, 37. For the reading of the name Memy-Sabu, see n. 15 below.

2 Henry G. Fischer, "Rechts und Links," *LÄ* 5: 187, 190 with reference to Reginald Engelbach, "Some Remarks on *Ka*-Statues of Abnormal Men in the Old Kingdom," *ASAE* 38 (1938): 295. In the New Kingdom, however, the man indeed normally appears on the proper right; see Fischer, "More Emblematic Uses from Ancient Egypt," *MMJ* 11 (1976): 128. Several exceptions to the New Kingdom arrangement exist, perhaps occasioned by symmetrical pairs that would "mirror" each other; see Robins, *Women*, 172, 174, fig. 76.

3 For an important discussion of the position and height of women in sculpture and relief during the Old Kingdom, see Fischer, *Egyptian Women*, 2–9.

4 She also stands to the right of her husband: Hildesheim, Pelizaeus-Museum, 17; see Martin-Pardey, *Plastik des Alten Reiches*, 1. CAA (Mainz, 1977), 1,39–1,46. The significance of the woman's height and her position at the proper right is not certain. Although she may in fact have been taller than her husband, another possibility exists: she may have received the double emphasis for some other (nonbiological) reason such as her husband's affection or his gratitude for burial in her tomb. Of the very rare Old Kingdom group statues in which the man embraces the woman or holds her hand (see note 9 below), the majority render the woman's height as equal to the man's. In none of these does the woman also stand at the right. Still, the equal stature may have a symbolic value.

5 For example, Brooklyn 49.215: "family" statue of Nykare, limestone, provenance not known but probably from Saqqara; see John D. Cooney, "Three Egyptian Families of the Old Kingdom," *BMB* 13 (1952): 1–9 and cover illus.; Robins, *Women*, 165, fig. 71.

6 Cairo, Egyptian Museum, JE 51280, limestone, from Giza; see Saleh and Sourouzian, *Egyptian Museum*, no. 39; and Edna R. Russmann, *Egyptian Sculpture: Cairo and Luxor* (Austin, 1989), 39–41, 214–15, n. 14.

7 W.K. Simpson, "Amor Dei: *nṯr mrr rmṯ m tꜣ wꜣ*," in *Fragen an die altägyptischen Literatur: Studien zum Gedanken an Eberhard Otto*. ed. Jan Assmann et al. (Wiesbaden, 1977), 493–98. See also Heinrich Schäfer, *Principles of Egyptian Art*, ed. Emma Brunner-Traut, trans. John Baines (Oxford, 1974), 174.

8 Old Kingdom group statues of kings and deities have more complex configurations. In the famous Mycerinus triads, when the king occupies the central position, he is sometimes embraced or has his hand held by two flanking deities, usually female, such as Hathor and a personified nome; see George A. Reisner, *Mycerinus: The Temples of the Third Pyramid at Giza* (Cambridge, Mass., 1931), pls. 38c–d, 43a–d. Nonetheless, sometimes only Hathor touches the king; ibid., pl. 45a–d. When the king stands at the proper left in a triad and Hathor is in the center, she still clasps him. Positioned at the proper right, the nome deity remains passive because the reach would have been much too far; ibid., pls. 38a, 39–40. All these arrangements accord with the hierarchy of sentiment.

Significant anomalies exist. In at least one triad, the king, who is in the center, goes completely unembraced; Reisner, *Mycerinus*, pls. 41–42. That the nome deity is male is probably coincidental. More important is the dyad in which the king is embraced by his wife, Khamerernebty II, who stands at the proper left; ibid., pls. 56–60. This arrangement parallels the reversals predominant in nonroyal pair statues of the Old Kingdom.

9 See Cherpion in *Kunst des Alten Reiches,* 33–47 and pls. 2–8. Pertinent here are Leipzig 3155 (ibid., pl. 4c); a group statue from Balat (ibid., pl. 7a); possibly Leipzig 3684 (pl. 7d); and Boston 30.1456 (pl. 8d). To this roster add Museum of Fine Arts, Boston, 13.3164a–c: uninscribed statue group, limestone, from Giza (2353 B); see Smith, *HESPOK,* 57 and pl. 25f. To be distinguished are the reciprocal embrace, as in the Memy-Sabu statue and Boston 13.3164a–c; the unrequited hug, as in the Hetepheres II–Meresankh III composition in Boston (cat. no. 37); and handholding by the man, as in Leipzig 3155.

Of uncertain status is Berlin, Egyptian Museum (Charlottenburg), 12547: statue group of Tjenti and Imeretef, limestone, provenance not known; see Biri Fay, *Egyptian Museum Berlin* (Berlin, 1985), 16; and cf. Fischer, "Quelques prétendues antiquités de l'Ancien Empire," *RdE* 30 (1978): 78–89, wherein the authenticity of the sculpture is questioned. In this group statue the man holds the woman's hand.

10 Fischer, *MMJ* 8 (1973): 14; Fischer in *Kunst des Alten Reiches,* 86; Simpson in *Studien zum Gedanken an Eberhard Otto,* 496.

11 If the embrace indeed involved decorum or etiquette, then "affection," "intimacy," and other similar terms may be inappropriate. A handshake does not necessarily indicate friendship or admiration; often it is no more than a courtesy. An embrace very similar to Memy-Sabu's, however, which is found on the famous Hetepheres II–Meresankh III group statue in the Museum of Fine Arts, Boston (cat. no. 37), may convey more than one sentiment. Hetepheres was the mother of Meresankh. Hetepheres extends her left arm around Meresankh's shoulders and places her palm on her daughter's left breast. The gesture is at least one of affection between mother and daughter, and very likely also appreciation. Although Hetepheres was buried in Meresankh's tomb, the mother had built the tomb for the daughter, who died first. Therefore a reciprocal embrace would be expected, as (for example) in the uninscribed engaged statue group, presumably of the two, on the west wall of the west room of the tomb; see Dows Dunham, "A Statue of Two Egyptian Queens," *BMFA* 34 (1936): 3–5; and Dunham and Simpson, *Mersyankh III,* pls. 11, 17a–b.

The meaning of the embrace may have been determined by the context and the persons involved. In certain situations, the gesture may have denoted physical intimacy, conveying ideas of procreation and rebirth in the next life. Although this interpretation does not work in the case of Hetepheres and Meresankh, wherein ideas of maternal affection, protection, or appreciation are more obvious, it may be valid for pair statues of husbands and wives. Pertinent here is a relief from Deir el-Bahri, now in the Staatliche Sammlung Ägyptischer Kunst, Munich (1621); Nebhepetra Montuhotep embraces a woman in a manner not so dissimilar from Memy-Sabu's intimate hug; see Cherpion in *Kunst des Alten Reiches,* 36 and pl. 7c.

12 See the sculptures cited in n. 9 above.

13 Scott, *BMMA* 7 (1948–49): 95, see also 99–100. The quoted location of the tomb is not precise because it does not specify whether the burial lay in the western, central, or eastern part of the cemetery along the northern edge. Sara Detweiler of the registrar's office at the Philadelphia Museum of Art kindly provided information about the sculpture, and Dorothea Arnold checked the records in the Department of Egyptian Art, the Metropolitan Museum of Art, for evidence about the same provenance for the two statues. No substantiating documentation is on file.

14 Somewhat different in style from both the New York and the Philadelphia statues is a sculpture of the woman Isran in the Phoebe Hearst Museum, University of California, Berkeley (6-19802), which was excavated at Giza in a pit of tomb G1402 with a larger work belonging to the overseer of craftsmen Sabu. G1402 lies near the northern edge of the western limit of the western cemetery. This location may be the same original context of both the New York and the Philadelphia sculptures, although they do not necessarily derive from the same tomb. Even if they did so, the proximity of its exact position on the northern edge to the western limit is not specified (see preceding note). Likewise, the relation of Sabu of G1402 to the (Memy-)Sabu of the two statues is not clear, but the attestation of the name in other contexts perhaps indicates that more than one Sabu existed. For the Berkeley sculpture, see C. Keller, "Statue of the Lady Isran," in Thomas et al., *American Discovery,* 130, no. 42. For the location of G1402, see Reisner, *Giza Necropolis,* 1: map 2.

15 This suggestion was proposed to me by Anne Capel. Dorothea Arnold and James P. Allen kindly examined the inscription on the Memy-Sabu statue and reported that the titles *rḫ nsw* and *Mmy* are written somewhat larger than *S3bw,* as noted by Fischer in *MMJ* 8 (1973): 14, n. 18. This distinction may imply that the woman's name was Memy and that the man was known as Sabu. The name Memy is not attested for a woman, however, before the Middle Kingdom (ibid.). Furthermore, the difference in the size of the hieroglyphs may indicate nothing more than inadequate space, if we assume that the scribe chose to restrict the inscription to the front of the statue base. If Memy is the woman's name, then the immediate juxtaposition with Sabu is very odd. A title or epithet between the two names would be expected. As Anne Capel has suggested in a personal communication, possibly the title *rḫ nsw* serves for both; on the Philadelphia statue, Sabu has this designation. Nonetheless, the double-duty title would seem to be unusual.

16 Fischer, *Egyptian Studies,* 1: 70.

17 The first of the examples that Fischer cites (see previous note) does not have the feminine ending.

18 Fischer, *MMJ* 8 (1973): 14.

19 For other examples of the averted glance, see Fischer in *Kunst des Alten Reiches,* 84–85.

20 Fischer, "Varia Aegyptiaca: 1. Yellow-Skinned Representations of Men in the Old Kingdom," *JARCE* 2 (1963): 19–20.

21 On gender distinctions of skin color in Egyptian art, see ibid.; and Elisabeth Staehelin, "Hautfarben," *LÄ* 2: 1068–72. On color symbolism and other color values in Egyptian art, see Hermann Kees, "Farbensymbolik in ägyptischen religiösen Texten," *NAWG,* Phil.-Hist. Kl. 11, pp. 413–79; Wolfgang Schenkel, "Die Farben in ägyptischer Kunst und Sprache," *ZÄS* 88 (1963): 131–47; Emma Brunner-Traut, "Farben," *LÄ* 2: 124–25; John Baines, "Color Terminology and Color Classification: Ancient Egyptian Color Terminology and Polychromy," *American Anthropologist* 87 (1985): 282–97.

4 Double *shabti* of Bener-merut and Ikhem

1 For a partial listing, see Schneider, *Shabtis,* 1: 212–14; 2: 89–90; 3: pls. 33–35.

2 Cf. Schneider, *Shabtis,* 1: 213 (*shabti* of Meny and Henut-iunu). Here, Henut-iunu's left arm is positioned on Meny's left shoulder, while her right hand is placed on his right arm.

3 The similar mummiform appearances of Ikhem and Bener-merut typify the *shabti* style of the period of Thutmose III. Double *shabtis* of the later Eighteenth Dynasty, beginning in the reign of Amenhotep III, clearly distinguish male from female through the varying use of color, wig type, and physiognomy; see Schneider, *Shabtis,* 2: 89 (*shabti* of Amenemhat and Bengay).

4 Ikhem's text translates as follows: "Oh you *shawabti* of the house-mistress Ikhem! If Tekh-em-sha is called or assigned by name to do the work that is done in the necropolis, even though she has been exempted from it, as a woman to her duty—to dig fields, to irrigate banks, and to transport sand from east to west—'I will do it: here I am,' you [feminine] shall say." (Translation by James Allen.)

5 For a list of Bener-merut's monuments, see Helck, *Zur Verwaltung,* 401, 509. A limestone ostracon lists him as assistant director or codirector (under the vizier Rekhmira) of Thutmose III's building activities at Deir el-Bahri; see W.C. Hayes, "A Selection of Tuthmoside Ostraka from Dēr El-Bahri," *JEA* 46 (1960), 46.

6 See Helck, *Zur Verwaltung,* 401 (Cairo statue 42171).

5 Statuette of a noblewoman

1 Hayes, *Scepter,* 1: 215.

2 Ibid.

3 Russmann, *Egyptian Sculpture,* 55, 57.

4 Hayes, *Scepter,* 1: 240 and fig. 202.

5 Pinch, *Votive Offerings,* 135–36, pl. 32c,d.

6 For a discussion of the scroll wig, see Pinch, *Votive Offerings,* 335–36, who also speculates that the wig may have derived from similar hairstyles worn by Near Eastern goddesses; see E. Brunner-Traut, *Die altägyptischen Scherbenbilder* (Wiesbaden, 1956), 27. Prior to this time, the scroll wig appears to have been reserved for female deities, especially Bat and Hathor. A more common headdress worn by women of the early Middle Kingdom was a heavy flaring wig with tresses bobbed off square below the shoulders; see Hayes, *Scepter,* 1: 216.

7 Strouhal, *Life,* 84. For the alternate suggestion that royal fashion influenced the representation of deities, see Pinch, *Votive Offerings,* 135–36.

8 Ranke, *Personennamen,* 1: 50, 13.

9 The possessive pronoun is the masculine *f.* The ambiguity or carelessness of the inscription is not uncommon in Middle Kingdom sculpture; see S. Goldstein in *The St. Louis Art Museum Bulletin* 19: 4 (1990): 11.

10 Cf. the pair statue of Hetepheres and Meresankh (cat. no. 37).

6 Painting of the woman Tjepu

1 James, *Corpus,* 1: 112, no. 252e. In front of Tjepu's head are partially preserved signs for the Egyptian words "the indestructible [i.e., semipolar] stars," which served as celestial symbols of continuity and rebirth.

2 For a full account of the tomb, see Davies, *Tomb of Two Sculptors;* for Tjepu's title as Mistress of the House, see ibid., 29.

3 Ibid., 29–31, pls. 3, 5, 8. This scene occupied the west bay of Tomb 181, where it flanked the west side of the entrance. For the ritual of The Beautiful Feast of the Valley, see Schott, *Das schöne Fest.* A portion of the funerary banquet scene (with female attendants), which occupied the tomb wall immediately behind Tjepu, is preserved in a fragment in the Nelson-Atkins Museum of Art; *Handbook,* 1, *Art of the Occident,* 5th ed. (Kansas City, 1973), 28.

4 The stylized manner in which Tjepu's mantle is pinned, exposing her right breast, represents the painter's artistic license; Davies, *Tomb of Two Sculptors,* 30–31. As Davies (p. 30, n. 2) notes, however, the hanging armlet between the wrist and the elbow is a comparatively rare addition.

5 Tjepu, in fact, accompanies Nebamen in the only two scenes where the names of both mother and son are preserved.

6 As Davies (*Tomb of Two Sculptors,* 10 and n. 1) notes, the substitution of mother for wife in such scenes is infrequent and unexplained.

7 Ibid., 11.

8 Ibid., 12. Henetnofret's role as Apuki's wife is clear from the pictorial contexts in which she appears in the tomb (ibid., 7, 9). As Davies observes, the only clear instance of Henetnofret's connection to Nebamen is her appearance before him with a cup (ibid., pl. 5). In this context Davies draws attention to Theban Tomb 78, where the tomb owner's wife offers the cup while his mother sits with him (ibid., 9, n. 1).

7 Lady with a large wig

1 Robins, *Women,* 181–83.

2 Bothmer et al., *ESLP,* no. 92, 116–17.

3 Ibid., 117.

4 The British Museum 37901, with fillet but no *uraeus:* Seipel, *Gott Mensch Pharao,* 406–7 (illus.), notes that, lacking an inscription, it could be a goddess, a queen (might one expect a queen's fillet, or even that of a goddess, to bear a *uraeus*?), or "another person." Ägyptisches Museum, Berlin, 21763, with fillet and *uraeus:* K.-H. Priese et al., *Staatliche Museen zu Berlin. Ägyptisches Museum und Papyrussammlung* (Mainz, 1991), no. 110, p. 187 (illus.): "30. Dynastie(?), um 380–350 v. Chr(?)."

5 Most notably Berlin, Verein zur Förderung des Ägyptischen Museums (Berlin-Charlottenburg), Inv.-Nr. 9–79: B. Fay, *Egyptian Museum Berlin,* 4th ed., enlarged and rev. (Berlin, 1990), 132–33 (illus.), with reference to its original publication by K.-T. Zauzich, "Die Berliner Unbekannte," in *Den Mitgliedern des Vereins zur Förderung des Ägyptischen Museums Berlin-Charlottenburg.*

6 Bothmer et al., *ESLP,* xxxvii, 116–17 and 118–19.

7 T.G.H. James, review of Bothmer et al., *JEA* 48 (1962): 170.

8 Robins, *Women,* 157.

9 Cairo, Egyptian Museum CG 42035, 42134, 42135, and 42228; and CG 42118, 42126, and 42133 respectively: G. Legrain, *Service des antiquités de l'Egypte.* CG. *Statues et statuettes de rois et de particuliers* (Cairo, 1906, 1909, 1914), vol. 1 (42001–42138); vol. 2 (42139–42191); vol. 3 (42192–42250).

10 Cairo, Egyptian Museum 18/6/24/2. I owe knowledge of this statue and those cited in the next note to the Corpus of Late Egyptian Sculpture developed by Bernard Bothmer and Herman de Meulenaere.

11 Cairo, Egyptian Museum JE 37026 (K.179), JE 37027 (K.241), and JE 38017 (K.649). The inscriptions on these three statues attest to the mainly late use of the term "the Hathor" or "the Osiris-Hathor," not simply "the Osiris," in reference to their deceased owners. Not all related sculptures use this term, however.

MOTHERHOOD

8a Statuette of woman dressing hair of nursing mother

8b Relief of a woman and child between trees (Tomb of Mentuemhat)

1 See Emma Brunner-Traut, "Die Wochenlaube," *MIO* 3 (1955): 11–30; and Barry J. Kemp, "Wall Paintings from the Workmen's Village at el-'Amarna," *JEA* 65 (1979): 47–53.

2 The purification period lasted for fourteen days, according to Papyrus Westcar. See Lichtheim, *Ancient Egyptian Literature,* 1: 221.

3 See also cat. no. 39 for hairdressing as a part of religious purification.

4 Strouhal, *Life,* 16–17, figs. 12–13. The goddess of childbirth, Meskhenet, was sometimes depicted as a human-headed brick; *LÄ* 4: 107.

5 Pinch, *Magic,* 128–30. See also Bulté, *Talismans.*

6 Ebbell, *Papyrus Ebers,* 109–10, XCIV.

7 See note 1 above.

8 See Florence D. Friedman, "Aspects of Domestic Life and Religion," in *Pharaoh's Workers: The Villagers of Deir el Medina,* ed. Leonard H. Lesko (Ithaca, 1994), 97–111. It seems likely that these enclosed, bedlike structures might also have been used much like modern cribs or playpens by blocking the stairway entrance.

9 This scene, and the fragmentary one on the upper register depicting one girl pulling a thorn from the foot of another, was copied from the Eighteenth Dynasty tomb of Menna (TT 69). See Manuelian, *Living in the Past,* 18–19.

10 Ebbell, *Papyrus Ebers,* 39–40, XXVI.

11 Ibid., 71, LIX; 73, LX; 74–75, LXII.

12 Ibid., 82, LXIX.

13 Ibid., 105, XC–XCI.

14 Berlin 3038. W. Wreszinski, *Der Grosse Medizinische Papyrus* (Leipzig, 1909), 47, no. 199; see also Robins, *Women,* 79.

15 See Pinch, *Magic,* 82–83; and Strouhal, *Life,* 22.

16 Ebbell, *Papyrus Ebers,* 113, XCVII.

17 Ibid., 109, XCIII, XCIV.

18 Lichtheim, *Ancient Egyptian Literature,* 2: 141.

19 Strouhal, *Life,* 23–24. Strouhal (p. 24) also discusses containers interpreted as cups for weaning children.

9 Statuette of Princess Sobek-nakht nursing a prince

1 For this title, see Fischer, *Egyptian Women,* 76, n. 43; Troy, *Patterns of Queenship,* 83, 133; Ward, *Essays,* 45.

2 Cairo CG 20537; Hans O. Lange and Heinrich Schäfer, CG, nos. 20001–20780, *Grab- und Denksteine der Mittleren Reichs* (Berlin, 1902), 2: 144–45, pl. 39.

3 Cairo JE 75039; Georg Steindorff, "Skarabäen mit Namen von Privatpersonen der Zeit des Mittleren und Neuen Reiches aus der Sammlung S.M. Königs Fuâd I," *ASAE* 36 (1936): 164 [3], pl. 1, 3; Geoffrey T. Martin, *Egyptian Administrative and Private Name Seals* (Oxford, 1971), 109, no. 1409, pl. 19,1.

4 Berlin 14078; *Ägyptisches Museum Berlin* (Berlin, 1967), 37–38 (illus.).

5 The two works are not *exactly* the same. The Berlin Isis, for example, lacks both fillet and *uraeus.* Three-dimensional depictions of deities from this period, however, almost never wear these trappings, which were associated with royalty.

10a Vessel in form of a kneeling woman

10b Figure vase: Woman holding a swaddled infant

1 Some scenes depict the birth of a god or king, but they belong to the divine realm and may have little relation to the birthing practices of most ancient Egyptian women; see, for example, a Ptolemaic relief at Armant illustrated in C.R. Lepsius, *Denkmaeler aus Aegypten und Aethiopien* 4 (Geneva, 1973 [reprint]), pl. 60b. The hieroglyphic determinative used in words associated with birth, particularly *ms,* often takes the form of a kneeling woman at the precise moment of delivery, when the baby's head and arms first emerge from her body; e.g., London BM 61062, Miriam Stead, *Egyptian Life* (London, 1986), 19, fig. 24. For a commentary on such scenes, see Paul Ghalioungui, *The House of Life;* Per Ankh, *Magic and Medical Science in Ancient Egypt* (Amsterdam, 1973 [2nd edition]), 114–16 (with references).

2 These are the so-called maternity bower scenes on ostraca from Deir el-Medina; see Emma Brunner-Traut, "Die Wochenlaube," *MIO* 3 (1955): 11–30; Barry J. Kemp, "Wall Paintings from the Workmen's Village at El-Amarna," *JEA* 65 (1979): 51–53; Alan R. Schulman, "A Birth(?) Scene from Memphis," *JARCE* 22 (1985): 97–103; and Geraldine Pinch, "Private Life in Ancient Eypt," in Jack M. Sasson et al., eds., *Civilizations of the Ancient Near East* (New York, 1995), 376–77.

3 John D. Cooney, "Some Persian Influence in Late Egyptian Art," *JARCE* 4 (1965): 47.

4 Elizabeth Riefstahl, *Ancient Egyptian Glasses and Glazes in The Brooklyn Museum,* Wilbour Monographs 1 (Brooklyn, 1965), 100–101.

5 H. Rand, "Figure-Vases in Ancient Egypt and Hebrew Midwives," *IEJ* 20 (1970): 210–12; cf. Emma Brunner-Traut's comments in a letter to the editor of the *IEJ* 22 (1972): 192.

6 Berlin 3038; translation from Reeves, *Egyptian Medicine,* 54. This book contains a useful overview of the ancient Egyptians' gynecological practices. See also, among others, Dorothea Cole, "Obstetrics for Women of Ancient Egypt," *DiE* 5 (1986): 27–33.

7 H. Rand, *IEJ* 20 (1970): 212. Although this thesis remains problematic, the object held in the figure's left hand might support the idea that the Brooklyn vessel had some gynecological, or at least medical, association. The object resembles horn-shaped containers discovered in women's tombs and thought to have held either medicine or oil. Like those horns, the Brooklyn detail has a spoon-shaped spout.

8 According to Bourriau, "It would seem that the body [of such a vessel] was built up in horizontal sections, and that the sections were modelled using moulds (perhaps the clay was simply pressed against the body of a finished vase) helped out with fingers and tools." From "Pottery Figure Vases of the New Kingdom," in Pascale Ballet, ed., *Cahiers de la céramique égyptienne* 1 (Cairo, 1987), 96.

9 To use the terminology of Janine Bourriau; ibid., 92. The once-popular rubric "mother and child bottles" presumes the woman's identity and is less acceptable than Bourriau's term; e.g., Hans D. Schneider, in *Ägyptens Aufstieg,* 173, no. 88.

10 Ibid., 90–91; Bourriau, *Umm el-Ga'ab,* 36.

11 E.g., Emma Brunner-Traut, "Das Muttermilchkrüglein: Ammen mit Stillumhang und Mondamulett," *WO* 5 (1970): 145–64; and Janine Bourriau, in *Cahiers* I (1987), 94.

12 J. Sainte Fare Garnot, "Deux vases égyptiens représentant une femme tenant un enfant sur ses genoux," in *Mélanges d'archéologie et d'histoire offerts à Charles Picard* (Paris, 1949), 905–16.

13 Christiane Desroches-Noblecourt, "Pots anthropomorphes et recettes magico-médicales dans l'Egypte Ancienne," *RdE* 9 (1952): 51–67.

14 Brunner-Traut, *WO* 5 (1970): 145–64.

15 Ebbell, *Papyrus Ebers,* 95. For another example of the curative powers of this milk see the prescription cited in Reeves, *Egyptian Medicine,* 49.

11 Jar in the form of a woman

1 For the identification of this stone, see James A. Harrell, "Misuse of the Term 'Alabaster' in Egyptology," *GM* 119 (1990): 37–42; D. and R. Klemm, "Calcit-Alabaster oder Travertin?" *GM* 122 (1991): 57–70; and Barbara G. Aston, *Ancient*

Egyptian Stone Vessels: Materials and Forms, Studien zur Archäologie und Geschichte Altägyptens 5 (Heidelberg, 1994), 47–51.

2 A red polished Naqada I vessel, for example, has the distinctive form of a goat's udder (Toronto, Royal Ontario Museum 900.2.11). The piece almost certainly held goat's milk; Michael Allen Hoffman, *The First Egyptians,* exh. cat. (Columbia, S.C., McKissick Museum, USC, 1988), 62, no. 7.

3 The seminal study on this group of containers is Emma Brunner-Traut, "Gravidenflasche: Das Salben des Mutterleibes," in *Archäologie und altes Testament: Festschrift für Kurt Galling* (Tübingen, 1970), 35–48.

4 Ibid., 40.

5 Ibid., 40–41. One of these containers represents a woman whose legs, like those of Taweret, take the form of a lion's hind paws; Copenhagen, Ny Carlsberg Glyptotek AEIN 1646, Maria Møgensen, *La collection égyptienne; la Glyptothèque Ny Carlsberg* (Copenhagen, 1930), 223, pl. 68.

6 Brunner-Traut, *Festschrift K. Galling,* 46–47.

7 E.g., Susan K. Doll in *Egypt's Golden Age,* 293, no. 404 (Boston MFA 02.525); and Caris-Beatrice Arnts, in *Ägyptens Aufstieg,* 173, no. 89.

8 John Garstang, "Excavations at Abydos, 1909: Preliminary Descriptions of the Principal Finds," *University of Liverpool, Annals of Archaeology and Anthropology* 2 (1909): 129, pl. 16. For the dating of the pottery group, see Bourriau, *Umm el-Ga'ab,* 36.

12 Magic (apotropaic) wand

1 G. Steindorff, "The Magical Knives of Ancient Egypt," *JWAG* 9 (1946): 42, n. 4, where he observes that, according to Ludwig Keimer, hippo ivory has a more solid structure than elephant ivory. Steindorff also notes the magical properties accorded the teeth, tusks, and talons of wild animals.

2 British Museum 20778. See F. Legge, "The Magic Ivories of the Middle Empire," *PSBA* (May, 1905): pl. 12, fig. 27 for a line drawing of this relief-carved wand.

3 Cairo 9433, of ebony, is mentioned by Steindorff, *JWAG* 9 (1946): 42, n. 3.

4 Ibid., 47, n. 8.

5 Janssen and Janssen, *Growing Up,* 9.

6 An example in Cairo, 9434, has a jackal head carved separately from acacia wood, with a hole for inserting the narrow tip of the ivory wand. See Legge, *PSBA* (May, 1905): 141, pl. 7, fig. 10.

7 An example in University College, London, is an exception in that no jackal head is depicted at the narrow end. An upright cobra is depicted on both the obverse and the reverse of the tip. See Legge, *PSBA*: 159, pl. 1, no. 49. This wand also exhibits ancient repair.

8 The narrow tip of the Walters wand has been lost; on the reverse, however, traces of the right side of the jackal's face may be detected above the break.

9 Altenmüller, *Apotropaia.*

10 One example, excavated from a tomb at Abydos, is inscribed with the name of a little-known Second Intermediate Period king, Sobekkay. Steindorff, *JWAG* 9 (1946): 51, suggests that this king occupied the throne as a child and thus was equipped with an apotropaic wand.

11 See Coffin Texts, Spell 1146.

12 Ibid., 45.

13 Ibid. Steindorff notes the rare occurrence of symmetry in the decoration on the reverse side of the Walters wand.

14 For Aha and Bes-images, see Romano, *Bes-Image.* For a discussion of the fascinating group of objects found together in a box—including a statue of the female Aha and fragments of four apotropaic wands—during excavations at the Ramesseum, see Ritner, *Mechanics,* 222–33.

15 Gardiner's Sign List, O6.

16 Ibid., R7.

17 Ibid., Q7.

18 Legge, *PSBA* (May, 1905): 301–2, no. 48, pls. 3–4. Altenmüller, *Apotropaia,* 45–46, no. 50. Altenmüller gives the woman's name as "Sechtj-Re."

19 Hayes, *Scepter,* 1: 249.

20 See note 7 above.

21 Robins, *Women,* 87.

13 Fertility figurine

1 See cat. no. 14, n. 4.

2 Ibid., n. 10.

3 If the abbreviation of the limbs is analogous to the "mutilation" of hieroglyphs, perhaps it is significant that "there is no definite evidence for the ritual breaking of votive offerings in Egypt"; see Pinch, *Votive Offerings,* 214.

4 See, for example, the figurines of both sexes illustrated in Needler, *Predynastic,* 336–47; and Joan Crowfoot Payne, *Catalogue of the Predynastic Objects in the Ashmolean Museum* (Oxford, 1993), figs. 3, 7–12, 81.

5 Pinch, *Votive Offerings,* 214, pl. 52b.

14 Paddle-shaped female figure with bead-hair

1 Bourriau, *Pharaohs and Mortals,* 127; Pinch, *Votive Offerings,* 198.

2 Theban area: Winlock, *Deir el Bahri,* pl. 38; Saleh and Sourouzian, *Egyptian Museum,* no. 81 (JE 56274); Jean-Pierre Corteggiani, *The Egypt of the Pharaohs at the Cairo Museum,* trans. Anthony Roberts (London, 1987), 66, no. 31 (same item); Bourriau, *Pharaohs and Mortals,* 126–27, no. 121 (Edinburgh, Royal Museum of Scotland, 1911.284). Beni Hasan: John Garstang, *The Burial Customs of Ancient Egypt as Illustrated by Tombs of the Middle Kingdom, Being a Report of Excavations Made in the Necropolis of Beni Hassan during 1902–3–4* (London, 1907), 152, fig. 150; Piotr Bienkowski and Angela M.J. Tooley, *Gifts of the Nile: Ancient Egyptian Arts and Crafts in Liverpool Museum* (London, 1995), 49, fig. 65 (Liverpool, 55.82.15).

3 In addition to the references in Pinch, *Votive Offerings,* 214, see Saleh and Sourouzian, *Egyptian Museum,* no. 81; Corteggiani, *Egypt of the Pharaohs,* 66, no. 31.

4 On hair: Philippe Derchain, "La perruque et le cristal," *SAK* 2 (1975): 55–74; Derchain, "Symbols and Metaphors in Literature and Representations of Private Life," *RAIN* 15 (August, 1976): 9. On tattoos: L. Keimer, *Remarques sur le tatouage dans l'Egypte ancienne,* MIÉ 53 (Cairo, 1948); R.S. Bianchi, "Tattoo in Ancient Egypt," 21–28, in *Marks of Civilization: Artistic Transformations of the Human Body,* ed. Arnold Rubin (Los Angeles, 1988), 23; Bianchi, "Tätowierung," *LÄ* 6: 145. In some contexts, however, tattoos may have an apotropaic function; see Pinch, *Votive Offerings,* 217.

5 Ibid., 214.

6 Ibid.

7 Ibid., 217; see also Pinch, *Magic,* 127, fig. 67.

8 Bourriau, *Pharaohs and Mortals,* 127.

9 Corteggiani, *Egypt of the Pharaohs,* 66.

10 G. Pinch, "Childbirth and Female Figurines at Deir el-Medina and el-'Amarna," *Or* 52 (1983): 405–14. See also Bourriau's astute comments in *Pharaohs and Mortals,* 125.

11 Paul Barguet, "L'origine de la signification du contrepoids de collier-menat," *BIFAO* 52 (1953): 103–11; see also Pinch, *Votive Offerings,* 279.

12 Garstang, *Burial Customs,* 153, fig. 151. A related "doll" from the same tomb (420) at Beni Hasan is now in the collection of Eton College; see Nicholas Reeves and Stephen Spurr, "Ancient Egypt at Eton," *Egyptian Archaeology* 6 (1995): 22.

13 G. Elliot Smith, *The Royal Mummies,* vol. 1. CG 61051–61100 (Cairo, 1912), 8–14 and pls. 5–8 (CG 61053–61055).

14 The best example is Cairo, Egyptian Museum, JE 56274, cited in note 2.

15 For example, The Brooklyn Museum 07.447.505 and 07.447.502; see Needler, *Predynastic,* 336–38, nos. 267–68; Fazzini et al., *Ancient Egyptian Art,* no. 1.

16 See note 4.

15 Nude female figure

1 *Mummies and Magic,* 109–17.

2 Breasted, *Servant Statues,* pl. 90b,d; Pinch, *Votive Offerings,* pls. 49a, 50a–b, 51c; Bourriau, *Pharaohs and Mortals,* 124–25, no. 118; 125, no. 119; 126, no. 120. Some fertility figures have one arm on the chest; see Pinch, *Votive Offerings,* pls. 48b, 49b, 51b. Many fertility figures, such as the example from the tomb of Djehutynakht cited in note 6, below, have no arms at all.

3 For example, the wooden statuette of a standing woman, MFA, Boston, 21.882; *Mummies and Magic,* 115, fig. 70, and 116, n. 77.

4 *Mummies and Magic,* 115, fig. 170 (right).

5 Dunham, *Egyptian Department,* 72, fig. 45; Smith, *Ancient Egypt,* 96, fig. 58; Terrace, *BMFA* 66 (1968): 6–7, figs. 2–3; Terrace, *American Connoisseur* 678, no. 178 (1968): 269, fig. 10; A.M. Roth and C.H. Roehrig, "The Bersha Procession: A New Reconstruction," *Journal of the Museum of Fine Arts, Boston* 1 (1989): 32–33, figs. 1–2.

6 Dunham, *Egyptian Department,* 70, 72 (fig. 46b); Terrace, *American Connoisseur* 678, no. 178 (1968): 270, fig. 11 (left).

7 See cat. nos. 13 and 14 and Breasted, *Servant Statues,* 95 and pl. 90a; Smith, *Ancient Egypt,* 97, fig. 60 (right); Terrace, *BMFA* 66 (1968): 19, fig. 18; Terrace, *American Connoisseur* 168, no. 678 (1968): 270, fig. 11 (left).

8 See cat. nos. 13 and 14.

16 a Stela: Woman and boy adoring Taweret

16 b Female figurine with model bed

1 A second model bed, now in Cairo (Peet and Woolley's General Object Catalogue No. 12/425), was also found with the other objects in the cabinet. Other objects found in the house were a yellow faience flower pendent, a blue faience Bes amulet, and several pieces of pottery. See T. Eric Peet and C. Leonard Woolley, *The City of Akhenaten, Part I: Excavations of 1921 and 1922 at El-'Amarneh* (London, 1923), 24–25.

2 Ibid., pl. I, for plan.

3 Ibid., 24.

4 The child clearly is male, and not female, as the presence of the long white kilt indicates. This misinterpretation is present in the initial publication of the stela (ibid., 25) and has been repeated in several subsequent publications.

5 Kemp, *Ancient Egypt,* 308–9. The rough edges on the Cincinnati figurine indicate that the excess clay was not carefully trimmed after it was removed from the mold, providing additional evidence for mass-production.

6 Robins, *Women,* 76.

7 Pinch, *Votive Offerings,* 232–33, List 6.

8 See also cat. no. 1.

9 See Jac. J. Janssen and P.W. Pestman, "Burial and Inheritance in the Community of the Necropolis Workmen at Thebes (Pap. Bulaz X and O. Petrie 16)," *JESHO* 11, no. 2 (1968): 137–70.

10 For domestic ancestor worship, see Sadek, *Popular Religion,* 77–78.

11 See Robins, *Women,* 63, for discussion.

12 Ibid., 77–78, and references therein.

17 Plaque with Bes image

1 The most comprehensive effort to distinguish the individual gods was made by Franz Ballod, *Prolegomena zur Geschichte der zwerghaften Götter in Ägypten* (Moscow, 1913).

2 For a discussion of changes in the gods' physical appearance, see Romano, "The Bes-image," passim.

3 It is impossible to date precisely the earliest appearance of this form of the Bes-image. At the site of Tell Abu Hawām in present-day Israel, R.W. Hamilton found a faience amulet of a Bes-image in a context contemporary with the late New Kingdom through Dynasty 22 in Egypt (ca. 1100–925 B.C.); R.W. Hamilton, "Excavations at Tell Abu Hawām" *Quarterly of the Department of Antiquities in Palestine* 4 (1935): 27, no. 143, pl. 35. Thus this new type of Bes-image may have begun as early as Dynasty 20.

4 This body type began in Dynasty 18 around the time of Amenhotep II; see, for example, Edinburgh, Royal Museum of Scotland 1956.113 (wooden cosmetic box inscribed with the name of Amenhotep II), Aldred, *New Kingdom Art,* 56, no. 22. Previously the Bes-image had been shown as a "lion-man"—that is, with a human head and a lion's mane, limbs, and tail. Perhaps in response to an increased infant mortality rate, Eighteenth Dynasty artisans "remade" the Bes-image, combining the traditional lion's head and tail with a body showing the primary features of an achondroplastic dwarf. Achondroplasts have an exceedingly high infant mortality rate; thus, to the Egyptians, any dwarf who survived early childhood would have been a charmed, even magical being that had overcome the very danger the birth gods were supposed to vanquish. By giving these deities a new body type, the artisans were reinforcing the link between the gods' appearance and their protective function. For dwarfs in ancient Egypt, see Véronique Dasen, *Dwarfs in Ancient Egypt and Greece* (Oxford, 1993), passim.

5 The association between the Bes-image and the protection of children is evident at least as early as the Middle Kingdom. See, for example, the presence of multiple Bes-images on an infant's feeding bottle in the Metropolitan Museum of Art, MMA 44.4.4; Hayes, *Scepter,* 1: 247; and Henry G. Fischer, *Ancient Egyptian Representations of Turtles,* Metropolitan Museum of Art Papers 13 (New York, 1968), 33, pl. 20. Many more examples of the Bes-image as guardian of infants and new mothers can be cited from the New Kingdom. Ostraca from Deir el-Medina, for example, show women nursing their babies on special beds with legs carved in the form of Bes. These ostraca depict the so-called birth arbor, a lightly constructed room or canopy where a woman and her child were secluded from the rest of the village immediately after delivery; see Emma Brunner-Traut, "Die Wochenlaube," *MIO* 3 (1955): 11–30.

6 Jeanne Bulté has assembled a corpus of eighty-six examples, both complete and fragmentary, of these plaques; Bulté, *Talismans Égyptiens,* 17–33. To her list should be added three unpublished examples: Berlin 9067, Cairo 14/1/19/2, and Philadelphia 29–83–495 as well as Leiden A.1188C, Willem Pleyte, *Chapitres supplémentaires du* Livre des Morts, 2. *Traduction et Commentaire 162, 162,* 163* (Leiden [1881]), plates between pp. 118 and 119. Several scholars have suggested that on some of these plaques the god holds a small anthropomorphic figure. These miniature images are often quite indistinct, but none of those examined by this author appears to be human.

7 Bulté suggests that the tail and buttocks of the Philadelphia figure have been skillfully designed to resemble a palm tree; *Talismans,* 23. The resulting composition is believed to recall the common Egyptian theme of monkeys climbing the trunk of a date palm; e.g., on a wooden cylindrical cosmetic box of the Eighteenth Dynasty, Ludwig Borchardt, "Eine Holzschachtel mit Darstellung einer ländichen Szene in Nubien," in *Studies Presented to F. LL. Griffith* (London, 1932), 257–62, pl. 25; on several New Kingdom ostraca from Deir el-Medina, J. Vandier d'Abbadie, *Catalogue des ostraca figurés de Deir el Médineh (Nos. 2256 à 2722),* Documents de fouilles publiés par les membres de l'Institut Français d'Archéologie Orientale du Caire, vol. 2, no. 2 (Cairo, 1937), nos. 2001–3 and 2009 (pl. 1), 2004 and 2005 (pl. 2), 2007–8, and perhaps 2012 (pl. 3).

8 Bulté, *Talismans,* 97.

9 Bulté believes that this monkey is feeding the diminutive Bes-image; *Talismans,* 23. An examination of the Philadelphia piece clearly shows the larger Bes-image holding the food (a date?) between the thumb and forefinger of his right hand.

10 This composition is extremely rare; it can be documented on only one other plaque (Paris, Louvre E 17339; Bulté, *Talismans,* 24, pl. 7a–b). Normally the area on the back of the god's headdress is occupied by a bound oryx or ibex.

11 See above, n. 5.

12 Gérard Santolini, "Thot, le babouin et la palmier doum," in *Mélanges Adolphe Gutbub* (Montpellier, 1984), 211–18.

13 The oryx and the ibex found on most of these plaques, but not on the Philadelphia example, were denizens of the desert and linked inextricably to Seth. By showing them bound and harmless, the artisans emphasized the Bes-image's dominance over malignant powers.

14 Bulté, *Talismans,* 18–19, docs. 3–6.

15 All of the plaques have lost their rings. Two unpublished faience statuettes of the late Third Intermediate Period still have nose rings, however (London BM 37401; New York MMA 23.6.36).

18 Vessel in form of Bes-image

1 The "type piece" for this new form of the Bes-image is Berlin 22200, a faience plaque found at the Assyrian city of Ashur in modern Iraq; PM 7 (1951): 397. The curvilinear quality of the Richmond example is accentuated by its great "Falstaffian" belly and by the leopard skin, with hundreds of spots, draped over the shoulders. The leopard skin first appeared on Bes-images of the Third Intermediate Period; e.g., Cairo CG 38718, Georges Deressey, CG, Nos. 38001–39384, Statues des divinités (Cairo, 1906), 184, pl. 40.

2 See previous note.

3 For example, Brooklyn 34.1191 (unpublished); Leiden A.1114, Willem Pleyte, *Chapitres supplémentaires du* Livre des Morts 2. *Traduction et Commentaire 162, 162,* 163* (Leiden [1881]), pl. between pp. 112 and 113; Paris, Louvre E 10929, Jean Leclant, "Egypt, Land of Africa," in Jean Vercoutter et al., *The Image of the Black in Western Art* (New York, 1976), 1: 278, fig. 380. A related vessel in blue frit recently appeared on the New York art market; Antiquarium, Ltd. Fine Art Gallery (sale catalogue), *Myth and Majesty: Deities and Dignitaries of the Ancient World* (New York, 1992), illustrated on front and rear covers. This piece may be slightly later than the faience examples.

4 Emma Brunner-Traut, "Die Wochenlaube," *MIO* 3 (1955): 11–30; Barry J. Kemp, "Wall Paintings from the Workmen's Village at El-ʿAmarna," *JEA* 65 (1979): 51–53; Alan R. Schulman, "A Birth (?) Scene from Memphis," *JARCE* 22 (1985): 97–103; Geraldine Pinch's most useful observations appear in *Votive Offerings,* 219–21, and in "Private Life in Ancient Egypt," in Jack M. Sasson et al., eds., *Civilizations of the Ancient Near East* (New York, 1995), 376–77. Some scholars contend that birth took place in these bowers; Wenig, *Woman,* 26.

5 E.g., J. Vandier d'Abbadie, *Catalogue des ostraca figurés de Deir el Médineh (Nos. 2256 à 2722),* Documents de fouilles publiés par les membres de l'Institut Français d'Archéologie Orientale du Caire, vol. 2, no. 2 (Cairo, 1937), nos. 2335 (pl. 49), 2337–38 and 2340 (pl. 50), 2343 (pl. 51), 2344–46 (pl. 53), 2339, 2341, and 2347–48 (pl. 52), 2349–51, 2359–63 (pl. 54), and 2353 (pl. 57). A Middle Kingdom limestone statuette from Lisht, today in the Metropolitan Museum of Art, seems to be an earlier, three-dimensional version of a maternity arbor scene; MMA 22.2.35, Hayes, *Scepter,* 1: 222, fig. 138.

6 Kemp, *JEA* 65 (1979): 51–53.

Amulets

1 As Andrews, *Amulets,* 6, notes, three of the four ancient Egyptian terms for amulet—*meket, nehet,* and *sa*—derive from verbs meaning "to guard" or "protect."

2 Ibid., 9. See drawings in Wilkinson, *Jewellery,* 14–16 and figs. 5–7. It should be noted that, while the *Bat*-amulet was later identified with Hathor, this association is not at all clear for the early Dynastic period; see H.G. Fischer, "The Cult and Nome of the Goddess Bat," *JARCE* 1 (1962); 11–13.

3 Andrews, *Amulets,* 63–64, 66.

4 Ibid., 67.

5 Ibid., 12.

6 Ibid., 10.

7 See under cat. no. 25, note 8.

8 See under cat. no. 25.

9 Andrews, *Amulets,* 43; Wilkinson, *Jewellery,* 60–61. It should be noted, however, that oyster-shell amulets are not exclusively associated with women.

10 Andrews, *Amulets,* 12.

11 For an inscribed depiction of Mut in this guise wearing the double crown, see ibid., 22, fig. 18c.

12 Ibid., 45.

13 See under cat. no. 19, note 13.

14 Andrews, *Amulets,* 33, fig. 29c,d.

15 The inventory of the Treasure of the Three Wives of Thutmose III included, for example, cylindrical amulet cases of gold and silver, gold and silver bivalve shells, three gold Hathor cow plaques, crouching cat ornaments in gold and carnelian, hollow gold figures of Taweret and Bes, and acacia seed-shaped beads; see Hayes, *Scepter,* 2: 130–37.

16 Andrews, *Amulets,* 34 and fig. 30, 3.

17 For Sekhmet's other aspects, see discussion in cat. no. 65.

18 Andrews, *Amulets,* pl. 19a,c.

19 Cylindrical amulets

1 See Andrews, *Catalogue,* 92 for a listing and brief description of cylindrical amulets.

2 These cylindrical amulets also occur occasionally through the New Kingdom. The Third Intermediate Period amuletic cases of similar shape, which contained spells inscribed on papyrus, are not included in this discussion.

3 See Christine Lilyquist, "Granulation and Glass: Chronological and Stylistic Investigations at Selected Sites, ca. 2500–1400 B.C.E." *BASOR* 290–91 (1993): 37–38, for a discussion of the granulation on these cylinders.

4 See the examples in notes 7 (Janssen) and 11 (Lilyquist) below.

5 Andrews, *Amulets,* 42, mentions examples with silver-covered cores, and stone bead segments of feldspar, lapis lazuli, carnelian, turquoise, or rock crystal. Andrews, *Jewellery,* 173, mentions an example of a solid stone cylinder that belonged to Sithathor.

6 Ibid.

7 Jac. J. Janssen and Rosalind M. Janssen, "A Cylindrical Amulet Case: Recent Investigations," *Gegengabe: Festschrift für Emma Brunner-Traut,* eds. Ingrid Gamer-Wallert and Wolfgang Helck (Tübingen, 1992), 157–65.

8 Ibid., 163 and n. 33.

9 Borghouts, *Magical Texts,* 42–43; and Janssen and Janssen in *Gegengabe,* 162–63.

10 A possible exception is the amulet case in University College London, U.C. 6482, excavated at el-Haraga by Engelbach in 1913 and published by both the excavator and by Petrie in the 1920s. As discussed by Janssen and Janssen in *Gegengabe,* 157, 164–65, with reference to the above-mentioned publications, there is confusion regarding the identification of the tomb in which this cylindrical amulet was found.

11 Lilyquist, *BASOR* 290–91 (1993): 38, 60, n. 36.

12 Andrews, *Amulets,* 44, 102.

13 Faulkner, *Book of the Dead,* pl. 32, ch. 156.

14 Andrews, *Amulets,* 105.

15 For example, see Andrews, *Amulets,* 42.

16 Ibid., 102–5.

17 Janssen and Janssen in *Gegengabe,* 162–63.

20 a–v Amulets

1 The frog hieroglyph functioned as the cryptogram for the phrase *wehem ankh* ("repeating life"), an epithet applied to the deceased from the Middle Kingdom onward.

2 For the frog's association with Heket, see L. Kákosy, "Heqet," in *LÄ* 2: 1123–24.

3 In this connection, attention may be drawn to a frog amulet in Brooklyn inscribed with a protective spell to the goddess Mut: *Egypt's Golden Age,* no. 353. For frogs and their symbolism, see E.T. Riefstahl, *Ancient Egyptian Glass and Glazes in the Brooklyn Museum* (Brooklyn, 1968), no. 25; and Hornung and Staehelin, *Skarabäen,* 112–13.

4 Andrews, *Amulets,* 20. See discussion under cat. no. 55.

5 For the goddess, see W. Gugliemi, "Nebet-hetepet," *LÄ* 4: 362–63. In the Pyramid Texts, Hetepet is listed as a cult site north of Heliopolis (Pyramid Texts 1210).

6 Ibid.

7 For Nebet Hetepet as "Lady of Contentment," see A. Gardiner, *Ancient Egyptian Onomastica,* 2 (London, 1947), 146; for "Mistress of Offerings," see Hornung, *Conceptions of God,* 280.

8 For Hathor as "Lady of the Vulva," see, most recently, Roberts, *Hathor Rising,* 138; see also Bleeker, *Hathor and Thoth,* 39–41; Pinch, *Votive Offerings,* 153–54, 243–44; and Hornung, *Conceptions of God.*

9 For Hatmehit and her cult, see I. Gammer-Wallert, "Hatmehit," in *LÄ* 2: 1042–43; also H. de Meulenaere, "Cults and Priesthoods of the Mendesian Nome," in H. de Meulenaere and P. MacKay, *Mendes* 2 (Warminster, 1976), 178.

10 For its dolphin identity, see D. Meeks, "Le nom de dauphin et le poisson de Mendès," *RdE* 25 (1973): 209–16; for its identification as the Schilbe, see R. Engelbach in "Notes on the Fish of Mended," *ASAE* 24 (1924): 161–68. For a more recent discussion, see I. Gamer-Wallert, *Fische und Fischkulte im alten Ägypten* (Wiesbaden, 1970), 98–101.

11 De Meulenare, *Mendes* 2, 178ff.

12 See ibid., 178 and n. 8.

13 For an inscribed example in the British Museum, see Andrews, *Amulets,* 21, fig. 17 right; for Hatmehit in her fish form, see Engelbach, *ASAE* 24 (1924): pl. 3.

14 See Andrews, *Amulets,* 66–67 and fig. 71; also Fazzini et al., *Egyptian Art,* no. 54 and n. 3. The monkey is depicted in private tombs of the New Kingdom where it appears under the owner's chair, presumably as a symbol of future sexual fulfillment in the next life. For the erotic imagery of the monkey, see G. Robins, "Ancient Egyptian Sexuality," *DiE* 11 (1988): 63.

15 For a comparable example, see Andrews, *Amulets,* pl. 64m and fig. 71b. As Andrews (66) notes, the squatting posture with head resting on paws dates back to Middle Kingdom prototypes.

16 See, for example, F. Daumas, *Les mammisis des temples égyptiens* (Paris, 1958). See also cat. no. 59 in this volume.

17 For similar lion-headed aegis amulets in gold and silver, cf. *Egypt's Golden Age,* no. 354, and Andrews, *Amulets,* pl. 40.

ADORNMENT

21 Hair ornaments and accessories

1 Hayes, *Scepter,* 2: 64, fig. 33.

2 See Davies in *Egypt's Golden Age,* 189–90. The information in this essay has been excerpted from that article.

3 See Freed in *Egypt's Golden Age,* 195.

4 E.g., eyelashes and beards; for an analysis, see ibid., 193–94.

5 *Egypt's Golden Age,* 197.

6 For one such example found in a tomb in the "Tety Pyramid Cemeteries" at Sakkara, see Hayes, *Scepter,* 2: 402, fig. 253.

7 See Freed in *Egypt's Golden Age,* 197 and no. 230.

8 Bruyère, *Deir el Médineh,* 80.

9 See E. Riefstahl, "Two Hairdressers of the Eleventh Dynasty," *JNES* 15 (1956): pls. 9, 13, 14c. As Riefstahl (17) observes, the pin appears to be associated exclusively with scenes of hairdressing and does not occur as an ornament in a finished coiffure. For the hieroglyphic derivation of the hairpin, see ibid., 16–17.

10 Petrie, *Objects of Daily Use,* 24 and pl. 19, fig. 1.

11 *Egypt's Golden Age,* no. 231. The head of the *uraeus* serpent was also commonly found; see Hayes, *Scepter,* 1: 240.

12 For pins with Taweret finials, see Hayes, *Scepter,* 1: 240. For the motif of the suckling calf, see *Egypt's Golden Age,* no. 232.

22 a,b Mirrors

1 For an example with a Hathor head of nearly identical style and proportions, see Hayes, *Scepter,* 2: 63, fig. 32.

2 For an example in the Oriental Institute, Chicago, inscribed with the name of Queen Ahmose Nefertari, see G. Hughes, "The Cosmetic Arts in Ancient Egypt," *Journal of the Society of Cosmetic Chemists* 10, no. 3 (1959): fig. 8.

3 For similar mirrors datable to the period of Hatshepsut-Amenhotep III, see Lilyquist in *Egypt's Golden Age,* no. 215.

4 The representation of women of foreign (Nubian) extraction in such contexts would support such a hypothesis because foreign women were often imported to work as servants or household attendants; see Lilyquist in *Egypt's Golden Age,* 187–88.

5 For discussion of these figures as reflections of idealized feminine beauty, see R. Bianchi in *Source Notes in the History of Art* 4, nos. 2–3 (1985): 10–18.

23 Cosmetic vessels

1 A portion of the material presented in this catalogue entry also appears in the Cincinnati Art Museum's *Interactive Video—The Egyptian Collection* and appears here courtesy of Anne K. Capel and the Cincinnati Art Museum.

2 Green eye paint, for example, acquired symbolic meaning, as attested in the Pyramid Texts; see Baumgartel, *Prehistoric Egypt,* 2: 52–53.

3 Lesko, *LED,* 1: 244.

4 Lesko, *LED,* 1: 104–5.

5 As Brovarski (*Egypt's Golden Age,* 216) observes, this feature was characteristic of the end of Dynasty 3 and the beginning of Dynasty 4. Both green and black eye paints are mentioned in the offering lists in the Old Kingdom. Although green eye paint continued to be used during the Middle Kingdom, it was supplanted by kohl, or black eye paint, in the New Kingdom.

6 *Egypt's Golden Age,* 30 and n. 32.

7 Theophrastus, *Concerning Odours.* For an excellent survey of ancient Egyptian cosmetics and unguents, see Manniche, *Herbal.*

8 Jar labels from First Dynasty royal tombs already mention the seven sacred oils; see Shaw and Nicholson, *Dictionary,* 210.

9 Hayes, *Scepter,* 1: 117, 243 and n. 14.

10 Green malachite, a copper ore pulverized for eye paint, is the most commonly preserved substance, although galena and red ochre are also attested. See Shaw and Nicholson, *Dictionary,* 72–73.

11 Cf. *Egypt's Golden Age,* nos. 267, 268. The traditional shape of the kohl pot continued into the New Kingdom; as a time-saving measure, kohl vessels were now drilled with a simple tubular hole rather than a fully hollowed-out interior.

12 *Egypt's Golden Age,* 217, n. 32.

24 a–d Woman's burial assemblage

1 As C. Lilyquist observes, the present example has a close parallel in an example from Buhen; see Lilyquist, *Mirrors,* 40, n. 455. Mirrors of this variety are frequently found in sets of "dressing table" accessories; cf. Hayes, *Scepter,* 2: 64, fig. 33.

2 For a list of examples, see Lilyquist, *Mirrors,* 35, n. 397. For similar silver wire torques from Abydos and Mostagedda, see Andrews, *Jewellery,* 64, figs. 49b and 117; Andrews, *Catalogue,* no. 565 and pl. 39; no. 675 and pl. 47.

3 Lilyquist, *Mirrors,* 35, n. 397.

4 Cf. Peet and Loat, *Abydos,* 3, pl. 9, nos. 5, 11, 21, 22.

25 Woman's burial assemblage

1 Herbert E. Winlock, "Excavations at Thebes in 1912–13, by the Museum's Egyptian Expedition," *BMMA* 9, no. 1 (1914): 16, fig. 8.

2 See Wilkinson, *Jewellery,* 50–55, for a discussion of those women's jewelry and the circumstances of the cache discoveries. For the jewelry of Queen Weret, wife of Senusert II, discovered in November 1994, see Adela Oppenheim, "A First Look at Recently Discovered 12th Dynasty Royal Jewelry from Dahshur," *KMT* 6, no. 1 (1995): 10–11.

3 Andrews, *Jewellery,* 140; note, however, the presence of a gold-plated "belt" on the body of "a daughter" of Khafra, mentioned by Wilkinson, *Jewellery,* 46.

4 See note 2 above.

5 Winlock and Mace, *Tomb of Senebtisi,* 18–19, 68–71, pls. 22, 23, 27, 31C. This element of royal costume is currently being studied by Diana Craig Patch, "A 'Lower Egyptian' Costume: Its Origin, Development, and Meaning," *JARCE* 32 (1995): 93–116; esp. pp. 103–5, and n. 47.

6 Andrews, *Jewellery,* 141–42 fig. 156.

7 Ibid., 141.

8 Wilkinson, *Jewellery,* 81; and Andrews, *Amulets,* 42, though Aldred, *Jewels,* 15–16, interpreted the shape of the cowrie shell as a "half-closed but ever watching eye," and thus as protection against the evil eye.

9 For examples in English translation, see Ebbell, *Papyrus Ebers,* 111–12. Page 108 of the same reference translates a recipe using acacia to prevent pregnancy.

10 Manniche, *Herbal,* 66.

11 L. Keimer (review of H.E. Winlock, *The Treasure of Three Egyptian Princesses* [New York, 1948]) in *BiOr* 6, no. 5 (1949): 138, and n. 8.

12 Ebbell, *Papyrus Ebers,* 111–12; Manniche, *Herbal,* 65–67; and Watterson, *Women,* 84–85.

13 For a brief description of Middle Kingdom jewelry incorporating acacia-seedpod amulets, see Wilkinson, *Jewellery,* 81.

14 Keimer, *BiOr* 6, no. 5 (1949): 138, n. 8.

15 Andrews, *Amulets,* 43, pl. 43d. See also Wilkinson, *Jewellery,* 60, regarding actual oyster shells engraved with royal names and interpreted as "military decorations."

16 Aldred, *Jewels,* 196, pl. 45; shell pendent of Queen Mereret.

17 Wilkinson, *Jewellery,* 60.

18 Ibid., pl. 1b.

19 Ibid., 60.

20 Shell pendent, Munich, Staatliche Sammlung Ägyptischer Kunst, AS 5301. For publications of this object, see ibid., 61; and Andrews, *Jewellery,* 181, fig. 166.

21 Andrews, *Amulets,* 28.

22 Hayes, *Scepter,* 2: 308.

23 Examples from the New Kingdom and the Third Intermediate Period are engraved with the name of the deceased. See Andrews, *Amulets,* 99.

24 MMA accession cards 13.180.5a, 13.180.5b, and 13.180.5A–B.

25 For a similar example, see Hornung and Staehelin, *Skarabäen,* no. 854, pl. 95.

26 Necklace

1 The present example was presented by its discoverer, Theodore Davis, to the Metropolitan Museum of Art in 1915. For a recent review of the tomb's find context, see C.N. Reeves, *The Valley of the Kings* (London, 1990), 131–33.

2 The cornflower, an annual herb that grows wild in eastern Europe and Asia, was a frequent decorative component on New Kingdom jewelry and was often included in mummy garlands. The decoction has a mildly astringent effect and was used in antiquity for eye irritations and menstrual disorders. As the herb's Egyptian name has not yet been identified, the precise aspects of its use remain obscure. See Manniche, *Herbal,* 85; Renate Germer, *Flora des pharaonischen Ägypten,* DAIK Sonderheft 14 (Mainz am Rhein, 1985), 173.

3 Information extracted from Andrews, *Jewellery,* 126.

4 For the proposed identification with Tauseret, see Hayes, *Scepter,* 2: 360; and, more recently, H. Altenmüller, *SAK* 10 (1983): 58ff. The associated finds in Tomb 56 included a circlet, earrings, several finger rings, bracelets, a pair of silver "gloves," and a silver sandal. For the contents of the tomb, see T. Davis et al., *The Tomb of Siptah* (London, 1908), 35ff.

5 In all likelihood, Tauseret assumed the trappings of kingship either as coregent with Siptah or after his death; her relationship to Siptah, however, is unclear. See S. Quirke, *Who Were the Pharaohs?* (London, 1990), 65; and Partridge, *Faces of Pharaohs,* 168. Tauseret's sepulcher numbers among the most elaborate of tombs in the Theban Valley of the Kings.

6 For this suggestion, see Reeves, *Valley of the Kings,* 132. See ibid., 131–33 for a summary of the evidence.

27 Jewelry

1 For Predynastic beaded jewelry, see Needler, *Predynastic,* nos. 234–37 and pl. 53; for the stringing of pierced, unworked shells, see ibid., nos. 236, 238.

2 The earliest intact woman's jewelry set from Dynastic times comes from a burial of Dynasty 1 at Nag ed-Deir. Its contents, which may have typified the burial of an upper-class female, included a sheet-gold diadem, a string collar with gold pendents in the form of mollusk shells, two gold-foil finger rings, ten gold barrel beads with reed-bundle markings, three large gold amulets, stone and metal bangles, and multiple beaded strands in stone, faience, and gold; see Andrews, *Jewellery,* 18–19 and fig. 11.

3 Andrews, *Jewellery,* 43, fig. 31 and 102.

4 Cf. the openwork diadems of the Twelfth Dynasty princesses Senebtisi and Khnumet, with their intricate interwoven designs; Andrews, *Jewellery,* 97, fig. 75, and 103, fig. 82; or the elaborate ornamented sheet-gold circlet of Sithathoryunet (ibid., 104, fig. 83).

5 See *Egypt's Golden Age,* 234 and no. 307.

6 See remarks of M. Eaton-Krauss in *Egypt's Golden Age,* 234. Another form of neck ornament worn by men and women beginning in the New Kingdom was the *shebyu* collar composed of multiple rows of solid gold rings strung on cords; the earliest known example is found in the late Seventeenth Dynasty burial of a woman from Qurna; see Andrews, *Jewellery,* 23, figs. 14 and 181.

7 See discussion under cat. no. 25.

8 For a survey of bracelets, see Andrews, *Jewellery,* 145–48; for Predynastic bangles, see Needler, *Predynastic,* nos. 240–44 and pl. 54.

9 See Andrews, *Jewellery,* 123. The jewelry assemblage of a young peasant girl from a Twelfth Dynasty burial at Abadiyeh in the Metropolitan Museum of Art consisted of four beaded strands of varying length, which served respectively as a girdle, an armlet, and two bracelets; see Hayes, *Scepter,* 1: 237–38.

10 Unpublished excavation notes, Egypt Exploration Society. I would like to thank Dr. Patricia Spencer of the EES for this information.

11 As revealed in the X ray of the mummy of Meryet, wife of Kha; see Curto and Mancini in *JEA* 54 (1968): 79b, fig. 3, pl. 13:2.

12 Wainwright and Whittemore, *Balabish,* 54–55 and pl. 19, 2.

13 Ibid., 57–58 and pl. 21. Cleft hoops of this variety were described previously as hair rings because of the narrowness of their cleft openings. There is no archaeological evidence, however, that the Egyptians wore such rings in their hair.

14 Davies, *Tomb of Two Sculptors,* pl. 29. Thausing and Goedicke, *Nofretari,* pl. 37.

15 See M. Eaton-Krauss, in *Egypt's Golden Age,* 232.

16 Winlock, *Deir el Bahri,* pl. 87. For a solid faience ear plug with a 6.5-cm diameter, see *Egypt's Golden Age,* no. 301.

17 Cf. tomb group B101 at Balabish; Wainwright and Whittemore, *Balabish,* pl. 20. For ancient Egyptian rings and their various types, see M. Eaton-Krauss, in *Egypt's Golden Age,* 244–50.

OCCUPATIONS

28 Servant statues

1 See Catharine Roehrig's essay in this volume; also Fischer, *Egyptian Women,* 10–11.

2 Fischer, *Egyptian Women,* 11 and nn. 91–94. The winnowing and sieving of grain was always performed by women, apparently in groups of five; see ibid., 11, n. 95. For the statue type depicting squatting women sifting grain or flour from a wicker sieve into a large flat basket or tray, see Breasted, *Servant Statues,* 25–26 (Type 5); and Smith, *HESPOK,* 98,e. Attention may also be drawn to the Old Kingdom depictions of women (and men) tending open charcoal fires or simple ovens in which bread pots or molds are sometimes indicated; see Smith, *HESPOK,* 97–98, esp. D2 (Cairo 37822; from the Giza *serdab* of Zasha). As Fischer observes, while women assist in the breadmaking process, only men are officially documented as "bakers" *(rtḥ); Egyptian Women,* 11 and n. 93.

3 For an inventory of examples, see Breasted, *Servant Statues,* 17–20 (Type 2); and Smith, *HESPOK,* 96. In some examples of the type, a grain sack lies at the upper end or a receptacle is situated at the lower to receive the grain.

4 For this cloth covering, see Lutz, *Egyptian Statues,* 28 and 31, fig. 30.

5 For the type, cf. Smith, *HESPOK,* 96–97,b. This straining activity apparently represents the only part of the beer-making process in which women were involved. Men are additionally shown cleaning and sealing beer jars; for examples, see ibid., 97. The present figure was identified as male by Lutz (*Egyptian Statues,* 28) and Smith (*HESPOK,* 65 and 97, b4). The round face, ankle-length garment, and hairstyle suggest a woman, however. This identification was confirmed, upon visual inspection, by A. Capel.

6 Cf. the short coiffure worn by a companion grain-grinding figure from the same tomb: Elsasser and Frederickson, *Ancient Egypt,* 43 (6–19812).

7 Smith, *HESPOK,* 96, a12 and 97, b7. Ni-Inpw-kau's statue represents a very early attestation of the title "Mistress of the House."

8 Ibid., 65.

29 Tomb model

1 *Mummies and Magic,* 102–3. See Vandier, *Manuel,* 3: 147 for the suggestion that such female offering-bearers symbolized real or imaginary estates that served as repositories of provisions for the deceased.

2 Breasted, *Servant Statues,* 60; see also comments of C. Roehrig in *Mummies and Magic,* 102–3.

3 Its placement on the Cincinnati figure is clearly indicated by the presence of a hole with remains of a dowel pin.

4 For other representations of the statue and garment type, see Breasted, *Servant Statues,* pl. 56; G. Robins, ed., *Beyond the Pyramids. Egyptian Regional Art from the Museo Egizio, Turin* (Atlanta, 1991), nos. 24, 25. The Cincinnati figure's affinities with the aforementioned examples suggest that it shared a similar provenance from Asyut. (The author acknowledges E.R. Russmann for this suggestion.)

5 These are rendered simply by two nipples represented in dark paint. The figure's slender form and tiny waist also suggest adolescence.

6 The author acknowledges Anne Capel for this suggestion.

30 Statuette of a serving girl

1 British Museum: *Art Treasures of the British Museum* (New York, 1957), no. 32. Petrie Museum, University of London: W.M.F. Petrie, *Illahun, Kahun and Gurob* (London, 1891), pl. 19, 43. Berlin Museum, 13244: Breasted, *Servant Statues,* 88 and pl. 83b. Auction market: Sotheby's, London, *Egyptian and Middle Eastern Antiquities,* July 10–11, 1989, no. 95. Other examples, unpublished, reside in the Metropolitan Museum of Art and the Clarence Day collection.

2 These arms, which are simple rolls of clay with little or no attempt at modeling a hand, may hang at the side or curve around to the midsection.

3 The head of one such figure was found at Abydos, Tomb D8; see D. Randall-MacIver and A.C. Mace, *El Amrah and Abydos, 1899–1901* (London, 1902), pl. 51.

4 On several examples, the triangular pubic area is delineated in black paint; compare the examples in the Petrie Museum of Egyptian Archaeology, University of London; the British Museum; and the Ägyptisches Museum, Berlin.

5 Petrie Museum, University of London. Published Petrie, *Illahun, Kahun and Gurob,* 19 and pl. 19, 43. The aforementioned examples in the British Museum and Berlin bear similar decoration.

31 Relief of mourners and funerary repast

1 For ancient Egyptian kilts and skirts, see Vogelsang-Eastwood, *Pharaonic Egyptian Clothing,* 53–71. Note that the Detroit fragment is an exception to Vogelsang-Eastwood's statements on pages 70–71, for here the kilt of the central female mourner is clearly pleated, fringed, and curved at the front edge.

2 For a discussion of the other public roles available to women, see Robins, *Women,* 111–26.

3 Tyldesley, *Daughters of Isis,* 132.

4 Werbrouck, *Les pleureuses;* and Henry George Fisher, "Representations of *ḏryt*-mourners in the Old Kingdom," *Egyptian Studies,* 1: 39–50.

5 M. Tosi and A. Roccati, *Stele e altre epigrafi di Deir el-Medina n. 50001–n. 50262* (Turin, 1972), no. 50053; and Robins, *Women,* 164.

6 Werbrouck, *Les pleureuses,* 120–21; and Fischer, *Egyptian Studies,* 1: 39–50, especially 45–49, n. 36, where the use of *ḏryt* as a professional title is discussed.

7 Ibid., 45–49, n. 36.

8 Svetlana Hodjash and Oleg Berley, *The Egyptian Reliefs and Stelae in the Pushkin Museum of Fine Arts, Moscow* (Leningrad, 1982), 121–23.

9 Fischer, *Egyptian Studies,* 1: 121.

10 It was at one time hoped that the Detroit and Pushkin reliefs would prove to be from the Memphite tomb of Horemheb; see ibid., 121–22. For the mourning scenes from Horemheb's Memphite tomb, see Martin, *Hidden Tombs,* 79, 83–84.

32 Relief: Female attendants clapping hands

1 See Winlock, *Deir el Bahri,* 101–4, for the excavation report. An informative and more recent discussion of the archaeological remains is found in Ward, *Essays,* 103–5.

2 For a discussion of this king, see L. Habachi, "King Nebhepetra Menthuhotp: His Monuments, Place in History, Deification and Unusual Representations in the Form of Gods," *MDAIK* 19 (1963): 16–52.

3 This fragment, along with others from the same tomb, is discussed in Elizabeth Riefstahl, "Two Hairdressers of the Eleventh Dynasty," *JNES* 15 (1956): 10–17; plate 9A is a reconstruction of the scene made during excavations.

4 This entry owes much to the research of Manniche, *Music and Musicians.*

5 Ibid. Manniche includes examples and discussion of all these instances.

6 Ibid., Ch. 4, "Music for the Gods," 57–73.

7 For discussions of these terms, see Betsy M. Bryan, "The Etymology of *HNR,* 'Group of Musical Performers,'" *BES* 4 (1982): 35–54; Ward, *Essays,* 69–80; Fisher, *Egyptian Women,* 14; William A. Ward, "Non-Royal Women and Their Occupations in the Middle Kingdom," in Lesko, ed., *Women's Earliest Records,* 39–43, and comments, 44–45.

8 Manniche, *Music and Musicians,* 123, fig. 74.

9 Ibid., 120–21, fig. 73.

10 The chapel was decorated in raised relief; the corridor was rendered in sunk relief.

11 See cat. nos. 34 and 39 for more information on hair and hairstyles.

12 Riefstahl, *JNES* 15 (1956): 15.

13 Winlock, *Deir el Bahri,* 224, pl. 32.

14 Ibid., 46, pl. 11.

15 For a recent discussion of the burials of Mayet and others in the mortuary temple of Nebhepetra Mentuhotep, see Ward, *Essays,* 102–14.

16 See notes 13 and 14 above.

33 Relief depicting Hap-iu's lady musicians

1 See Manniche, *Music and Musicians,* 40, 56.

2 The relief in Berlin (2301) was originally published by A. Scharff in *ZÄS* 74 (1938): 42ff., pl. 3; see also Smith, *Art and Architecture,* 252 and 287, n. 63; and Bothmer in Bothmer et al., *ESLP,* 103–4.

3 Manniche, *Music and Musicians,* 54–55. The barrel drum usually had a wooden body with two membranes laced into position. For surviving examples, see ibid., 74–75 and pl. 2; for another female drummer on a contemporary banquet relief, see Bothmer et al., *ESLP,* no. 86 and pl. 82, fig. 217.

4 For this garment and possible Persian influence from Asia Minor, see C.R. Williams, "The Egyptian Collection in the Museum of Art at Cleveland, Ohio," *JEA* 5 (1918): 283.

5 For the hairstyle, see Bothmer et al., *ESLP,* 104; for the insert, see Williams, *JEA* 5 (1918): 283.

6 For the *seweret* bead, see discussion under cat. no. 25.

7 Williams, *JEA* 5 (1918): 283–84; for the possible Sudanese origin of the costume and jewelry, see Bothmer et al., *ESLP,* 104.

8 Manniche, *Music and Musicians,* 47.

9 Her coiffure is typical of the style of fourth-century reliefs; see Bothmer et al., *ESLP,* 104.

10 See Williams, *JEA* 5 (1918): 282 and n. 1.

11 Cf. Bothmer et al., *ESLP,* 110.

12 See discussion of Bothmer et al., *ESLP,* 110. For reliefs with similar theme and style, cf. ibid., no. 87; for the Tha-nefer reliefs, see Williams, *JEA* 5 (1918): 281–84 and pl. 40.

13 Bothmer et al., *ESLP,* 109–10.

34 Relief of the hairdresser Inu

1 For comments on this topic, see Baer, *Rank and Title,* 300–301; and David P. Silverman, "The Nature of Egyptian Kingship," in O'Connor and Silverman, *Ancient Egyptian Kingship,* 64. For a recent discussion regarding the divinity of the queen, see Robins, *Women,* 23–25.

2 John Baines, "Egyptian Twins," *Orientalia* 54 (1985): 461–82, esp. 469–70, though these "overseers of royal manicurists" served in the Old, not the Middle, Kingdom.

3 Ward, *Index,* references titles such as "overseer of the king's bathroom" (no. 367 [a typographical error—should read 362]:46); "chief of the king's clothing in the private chamber" (no. 1086:127); and "keeper of royal sandals" (no. 552:67).

4 Ibid., "chief physician of the king" (no. 732:88).

5 See Helck, *Untersuchungen,* 36, 43, 65–66; and Aylward M. Blackman, "The House of the Morning," *JEA* 5 (1918): 148–65, esp. 148–52, 164.

6 Winlock, *Meryet-Amun,* 9–10, pls. 13, 33.

7 Ibid.

8 Partridge, *Faces,* reproduces photographs of many mummies that retain the natural hair.

9 Ebbell, *Papyrus Ebers,* 79.

10 Ibid., 78.

11 Ibid., 79.

12 Ibid., 80.

13 Ward, *Essays,* 23.

14 This is Merit-ites, a woman of the Fifth Dynasty, whose statue in Leiden provides her titles: "Royal Acquaintance, Royal Ornament, Mistress of Festivals, and Overseer of the Wig Workshop." See Smith, *HESPOK,* 79 (no depiction of the statue or Leiden catalogue number is provided).

15 Ewa Laskowska-Kusztal, "Un atelier de perruquier à Deir el-Bahari," *Travaux de Centre d'Archéologie Méditerranéenne de l'Académie Polonaise des Sciences,* 20. *Études et Travaux 10* (1978), 83–120.

35 Seated statue of Enehy

1 Georg Steindorff, "Two Egyptian Statues of the Ramessid Period," *JWAG* 5 (1942): 11.

2 Correspondence dated August 27, 1976, from Norio Oyama, acting director of the Matsuoka Museum of Art, to the Walters Art Gallery.

3 Steindorff, *JWAG* 5 (1942): 9–10, fig. 2.

4 For the recent discovery of the tomb of Maya and Meryt, see Martin, *Hidden Tombs,* esp. 147–88.

5 The author acknowledges Betsy Bryan for assistance with and commentary on this inscription, which inspired the title of this exhibition.

6 Maspero, *Recueil de travaux,* 4: 141.

7 No. 2297. See Fechheimer, *Plastik,* 66; and Roeder, *Aegyptische Inschriften,* 2: 6–8. The small, standing daughter is Enehy. Here she is not given the title "Chantress"; she holds an arched, Hathor-headed sistrum in her hand, however.

8 Lesko, *LED,* 3: 151.

9 Robins, *Women,* 148.

10 Several members of the Fifth Dynasty family of Kaha were employed in these positions; see Manniche, *Music and Musicians,* 122.

11 Ibid., 122.

12 Fischer, *Egyptian Studies,* 1: 71; Fischer, *Egyptian Women,* 10.

13 There seems to be only one known instance of a woman serving as a *weret khener* for a female divinity, namely the goddess Bastet. Male deities who were served by a female Great One of the Musical Troupe include Amen, Sobek, Min, Ra, and Onuris. This information is courtesy of Betsy Bryan.

14 Barbara S. Lesko, "Researching the Role of Women in Ancient Egypt," *KMT* 5, no. 4 (Winter, 1994): 18–20.

15 Robins, *Women,* 149, poses other important questions concerning the role of women in cultic activity.

16 See, for example, cat. no. 39; and Aylward M. Blackman, "On the Position of Women in the Ancient Egyptian Hierarchy," *JEA* 7 (1921): 27–28.

17 For reference to certain items of apparel sacred to Hathor, see Bleeker, *Hathor and Thoth,* 58–59.

18 See also cat. nos. 22a and 36.

19 A travertine sistrum inscribed for King Tety of Dynasty 6 is of this early type. See N. de G. Davies, "An Alabaster Sistrum Dedicated to King Teta," *JEA* 6 (1920): 69–72.

20 Christian Tutundjian de Vartavan, "The Origin, Evolution and Function of the *Shm,* Known as the *Naos*-Sistrum. Preliminary Researches," *Wepwawet* 2 (Summer, 1986): 26–29. A *sekhem* scepter is a wand frequently depicted held by the king or high officials, or employed during the ritual of presenting funerary or votive offerings; see Shaw and Nicholson, *Dictionary,* 257.

21 See also cat. no. 55.

22 The *menat* originally was specific to the cult of Hathor, though it came to be used in the worship of other gods; see Sheldon Lee Gosline, "The *MNJT* as an Instrument of Divine Assimilation," *DiE* 30 (1994): 41–42.

23 The incised line around the outer edges of some counterpoises is probably an artistic remembrance of the earlier double-counterpoise style; see Aldred, *Jewels,* 227, no. 114; and Hayes, *Scepter,* 2: 45.

24 For example, by a dancing girl (Aldred, *Jewels,* 160, fig. 37); and by King Amenemhat III (ibid., pl. 151).

25 Ibid., 45, fig. 11. For an example of a rather curious necklace held horizontally in this manner, see A. St. G. Caulfield, *The Temple of the Kings at Abydos* (London, 1902), pl. 16, no. 8.

26 Pinch, *Votive Offerings,* 190–97, 352.

27 Gosline, *DiE* 30 (1994): 41, notes that "the presentation of the counterpoise was the final step in the ritual process toward obtaining direct access to the deity."

28 Lichtheim, *Ancient Egyptian Literature,* 1: 232, 235, n. 22.

29 Blackman, *JEA* 7 (1921): 22.

30 See, for instance, Davies, *The Tomb of Rekh-Mi-Re at Thebes,* 1 (Metropolitan Museum Egyptian Expedition Publications, Vol. 11; New York, 1943), pl. 63.

31 Gosline, *DiE* 30 (1994): 46.

32 Betsy Bryan observes that his wig style is precisely that worn by Queen Tiye, from whose husband's reign this object dates; see *Egypt's Dazzling Sun,* 364. This counterpoise was excavated at Semna in Upper Nubia, near the temple at Sedeinga, where Queen Tiye (cat. no. 44) was worshipped in the form of Hathor.

33 Alternately, this may represent Hathor's protection of the young Horus during his sojourn in the papyrus marshes while hiding from Seth. Note, too, that a festival held in honor of Hathor was called *sšš wꜣḏw n ḥt-ḥr,* "shaking papyrus for Hathor"; see Bleeker, *Hathor and Thoth,* 86.

34 Gosline, *DiE* 30 (1994): 39; and Blackman, *JEA* 7 (1921): 23, fig. 5.

35 Gosline, *DiE* 30 (1994): 39.

36 Blackman, *JEA* 7 (1921): 9, 14.

37 Ibid., 23.

36 Hand wands

1 Early examples with tips in the form of a gazelle's head are mentioned in Elsasser and Fredrickson, *Ancient Egypt,* 68.

2 Hayes, *Scepter,* 1: 247.

3 For a discussion of the magical properties of the objects found in this tomb, see Ritner, *Mechanics,* 222–32.

4 Pinch, *Votive Offerings,* 222.

5 Pinch, *Magic,* 121–22, fig. 63.

6 Pinch, *Votive Offerings,* 222.

7 Hayes, *Scepter,* 1: 247 and 2: 316.

8 N. Reeves, *The Complete Tutankhamen* (London, 1995), 163, reproduces a scene from the Middle Kingdom tomb of Inyotef-iker (Thebes, no. 60) in which each of two people manipulates two pairs of wands strung together with cords.

9 See ibid., and Manniche, *Music and Musicians,* 87, pl. 15.

10 OIM 5518, ivory.

11 A similar set in the Metropolitan Museum is described by Hayes, *Scepter,* 2: 316.

12 For a recent discussion of this type of sistrum, see Christian Tutundjian de Vartavan, "The Origin, Evolution and Function of the *Shm,* Known as the *Naos*-Sistrum: Preliminary Researches," *Wepwawet* 2 (Summer, 1986): 26–30.

13 Pinch, *Magic,* 84.

14 See, for instance, Bleeker, *Hathor and Thoth,* 68.

15 Pinch, *Magic,* 84.

16 H. Hickmann, "La danse aux miroirs: Essai de reconstitution d'une danse pharaonique de l'ancien empire," *BIE* 37 (1954–55): 151–90.

17 Manniche, *Music and Musicians,* 87.

Female Royalty

37 Pair statue of Hetepheres II and her daughter Meresankh III

1 Wilfried Seipel, "Hetepheres II," *LÄ* 2: 1173–74.

2 William Kelly Simpson, "Meresanch I–III," *LÄ* 4: 78–79.

3 For references to Kawab's Giza *mastaba* (G7120), see PM 3[1], 187.

4 Technically, Meresankh was not a King's Daughter, since her father Kawab had died before attaining the throne. She was considered as such, however, because she was the granddaughter of Khufu as well as the niece and stepdaughter of Djedefra.

5 Troy, *Patterns of Queenship,* 153–54.

6 Ibid., 154. The reference to Hathor associated with Ra at Heliopolis reflects the growing devotion to the solar deity. Noteworthy, too, is the earliest use of the title "Son of Ra" by a king during the reign of Djedefra, Meresankh's stepfather. See Grimal, *History,* 71.

7 G. Reisner, "The Tomb of Meresankh, A Great-Granddaughter of Queen Hetep-Heres I and Sneferuw," *BMFA* 25, no. 151 (1927): 64.

8 Ibid., 64, fig. 1.

9 Dunham and Simpson, *Mersyankh III.*

10 Reisner, *BMFA* 25, no. 151 (1927): 78.

11 Ibid., pls. 6a,b.

12 Dunham and Simpson, *Mersyankh III,* 21, and fig. 14. Also see William S. Smith, "Inscriptional Evidence for the History of the Fourth Dynasty," *JNES* 11 (1952): 127, 119, fig. 7.

13 Reisner, *BMFA* 25, no. 151 (1927): 74, states that the skeleton is of a small female about fifty years of age at death—an opinion later confirmed by Dr. Douglas E. Derry in Dunham and Simpson, *Mersyankh III,* 21–22. The skeletal remains seem to have been placed in Cairo; see ibid., 23, no. 27-6-19, and pls. 16a–d.

14 For the statues and fragments (including early servant statues) found in G7530, see Smith, *HESPOK,* 42–44. For the report on the reconstruction of BMFA 30.1456, see Dows Dunham, "A Statuette of Two Egyptian Queens," *BMFA* 34, no. 201 (1936): 3–5.

15 Ibid., 5.

16 The present author believes that the presence of the name Sabu on the statue from the Philadelphia Museum of Art (cat. no. 3b) depicting the same woman (and, apparently, from the same tomb) indicates that the two names on the Metropolitan Museum of Art's pair statue refer to the separate individuals depicted and are not a compound name referring to the male.

17 See cat. no. 3a.

18 Reisner, *BMFA* 25, no. 151 (1927): 74; and Dunham and Simpson, *Mersyankh III,* 8, pls. 2a,b, fig. 2.

19 See, for example, Zaki Iskander's suggestion regarding the use of natron in solution mentioned in J.E. Harris and Kent R. Weeks, *X-Raying the Pharaohs* (New York, 1973), 83.

20 See Christine El Mahdy, *Mummies, Myth and Magic* (London, 1989), 59.

21 Reisner, *BMFA* 25, no. 151 (1927): 74.

22 See PM 3[1], 197–99 for references.

23 Reisner, *BMFA* 25, no. 151 (1927): 67.

24 Smith, *Art and Architecture,* 100.

25 Reisner, *Giza Necropolis* 1, 116; and PM 3[1], 193.

26 Philip Watson, *Egyptian Pyramids and Mastaba Tombs* (Aylesbury, 1987), 30. See also Porter and Moss III. 1, 1–3.

27 Dunham and Simpson, *Mersyankh III,* 3.

28 Ibid., 8.

29 Yvonne Harpur, *Decoration in Egyptian Tombs of the Old Kingdom: Studies in Orientation and Scene Content* (London, 1987), 244. Grimal, *History,* 72, 75, also notes the possibility that Neferhetepes, Hetepheres II's daughter by Djedefra, may have been the mother of Userkhaf, the first king of the Fifth Dynasty.

30 PM 3[1], 198, nos. 7–8.

38 Relief: Queen Wedjebten with lotus

1 Jequier, *Oudjebten.*

2 Ibid., 13.

3 Ibid., 13, fig. 6.

4 For a discussion of diadems of this type, see Wilkinson, *Jewellery,* 40–41.

5 Troy, *Patterns of Queenship,* 156, no. 6.11.

6 For the importance of this title in the Sixth Dynasty, and the implications of the king's taking a nonroyal wife, see Baer, *Rank and Title,* 285–86; and Trigger, *Social History,* 79–80.

7 Jequier, *Neit et Apouit.*

8 Grimal, *History,* 118–19, Table 3.

9 Jequier, *Oudjebten,* 4–5, fig. 2; see also Badawy, *History,* 1: 150–51, fig. 99.

10 Ibid., 4–5, 18, fig. 15.

11 Ibid., 18–19; Badawy, *Egyptian Architecture,* 1: 150–51.

12 Jequier, *Oudjebten,* pl. 3.

13 Ibid., pl. 3, depicts wall fragments in situ.

14 See note 7 above.

15 But see Grimal, *History,* 126, who notes the possibility that the Pyramid Texts may have appeared in the pyramids of the queens of Pepy I.

16 In the reign of Nynetjer (Binothris) of Dynasty 2, it was determined that females could rule Egypt. See W.G. Waddell, *Manetho* (London, 1971), 100ff.

17 Quirke, *Religion,* 155.

39 Relief: Queen Nefru and the Hairdresser Henut

1 See L. Habachi, "King Nebhepetre Menthuhotp: His Monuments, Place in History, Deification and Unusual Representations in the Form of Gods," *MDAIK* 19 (1963): 16–52.

2 Herbert E. Winlock suggested that both she and Nebhepetra Mentuhotep were offspring of King Sankhib-tawey and Queen Iah (Winlock, *Rise and Fall,* 27). This theory is questioned by Ward, *Essays,* 104 and n. 112, 145–46.

3 See Ward, *Essays,* 104–5, fig. 9. Nefru may have been the mother of Nebhepetra Mentuhotep's eldest son, the Prince Inyotef, who predeceased his father, and whose tomb lies between Nefru's and that of the king. See Winlock, *Rise and Fall,* 44, 64.

4 Hayes, *Scepter,* 1: 158–59. Hayes also mentions the new entrance to the tomb constructed in the reign of Hatshepsut of the Eighteenth Dynasty.

5 *Shabtis,* a necklace, and fragments of beautifully pleated linen belonging to the queen were found, however, by the 1925–26 Metropolitan Museum Expedition. See Hayes, *Scepter,* 1: 229–327; and Winlock, *Deir el-Bahri,* 101, pl. 36. Nefru's necklace included *seweret* beads; see cat. no. 25.

6 Winlock, *Deir el-Bahri,* 102–3.

7 For a discussion of this hairpin and others, see E. Riefstahl, "Two Hairdressers of the Eleventh Dynasty," *JNES* 15 (1956): 16–17.

8 For examples of hairpieces and the method by which they were attached to the natural hair, see Winlock, *Meryet-Amun,* 9–10, pls. 13, 33.

9 See M. Gauthier-Laurent, "Les scènes de coiffure féminine dans l'ancienne Égypte," *Mélanges Maspero* 1 (Cairo, 1935–38), 674–78, for examples of this date, excluding the Nefru scene and another fragment from the tomb of Nefru depicting a woman with a pinned-up lock of hair. For the latter, see Riefstahl, *JNES* 15 (1956): 17, pl. 14c, and 16, n. 27 for additional hairdressing scenes not in Gauthier-Laurent.

10 Naville, *Deir el-Bahari,* 1: pls. 19B, 20.

11 Gauthier-Laurent, *Mélanges Maspero,* 1: 675, fig. 2.

12 Naville, *Deir el-Bahari,* 3: pl. 3.

13 As on the sarcophagus of *Int-it.s,* see G. Steindorff, *Grabfunde des Mittleren Reich in den Königlichen Museen zu Berlin II. Der Sarg des Sebk-o. —Ein Grabfund aus Gebelêin* (Berlin, 1901), 22–24 and pl. 5.

14 As in the tomb of Kemsit; see Naville, *Deir el-Bahari,* 3: pl. 3.

15 On her sarcophagus, Kawit holds a mirror in her left hand and lifts a bowl to her lips with her right hand, while an attendant pours additional refreshment for her. See Naville, *Deir el-Bahari,* 1: pl. 20.

16 Philippe Derchain, "La perruque et le cristal," *SAK* 2 (1975): 55–74.

17 Riefstahl, *JNES* 15 (1956): 17.

18 Neither the titles nor the name of the woman whose hair is being dressed on the stela of *[ ]-merer* (see Gauthier-Laurent, *Mélanges Maspero,* 1: 675, fig. 2) have been preserved; in the scene, however, she wears a prominent *menat* necklace, certainly a sacred symbol in the cult of Hathor. Likewise, Queen Nefru is nowhere, to my knowledge, termed a "Priestess of Hathor." Her position as wife and daughter of kings would identify her strongly with the goddess herself, rather than as a priestess of the goddess. See Troy, *Patterns of Queenship,* 53–54. Nebhepetra Mentuhotep was especially devoted to Hathor; he built a chapel for her at Dendara (see Winlock, *Rise and Fall,* 28). On a block of relief from his mortuary temple, the goddess stands behind him, saying, "I have united for you the Two Lands according to the command of the ancient spirits . . . " (see Hayes, *Scepter,* 1: 157–58, fig. 94). The same king referred to himself as "Son of Hathor, Lady of Denderah" (see Bleeker, *Hathor and Thoth,* 51).

19 See cat. nos. 20 and 36.

20 Philippe Derchain, "Snefrou et les Rameuses," *RdE* 21 (1969): 19–25, esp. 21–25.

21 Georges Posener, "La légende de la tresse d'Hathor," *Egyptological Studies in Honor of Richard A. Parker,* ed. L.H. Lesko (Hanover and London, 1986), 111–17.

22 Aylward Blackman, "The House of the Morning," *JEA* 5 (1918): 149–65.

23 Ibid., 155–56.

24 Beer was offered because Hathor was the goddess of inebriation (Bleeker, *Hathor and Thoth,* 1, 44, 51, 56, 83–84) rather than milk, as suggested by Naville, *Deir el-Bahari,* 2: 9. Sadhe is offered beer, clearly labelled *Hnkt* in the inscription, in a depiction from her shrine; see ibid., pl. 13; and Kemsit is offered wine, *snw* (Faulkner, *CDME,* 231); see Naville, *Deir el-Bahari,* 2: pl. 20.

25 This item also was closely associated with the cult of Hathor. See H. Hickmann, "La danse aux miroirs," *BIE* 37 (1954–55): 151–90.

26 Emma Brunner-Traut, "Die Wochenlaube," *MIO* 3 (1955): 11–30.

27 Likewise, they wore a special hairstyle; see ibid.

28 Barry J. Kemp, "Wall Paintings from the Workmen's Village at el-'Amarna," *JEA* 65 (1979): 53. See also Ashraf Iskander Sadek, "Les fêtes personnelles au Nouvel Empire," *BSAK* 3 (1988): 357–58, for a list of items required for a woman's personal holiday, possibly the celebration of the end of the ritual purification period.

29 Brunner-Traut, *MIO* 3 (1955): 29–30, Abb. 11.

40 Head of a queen or princess

1 For an excellent discussion of the royal sculpture of this period, see Biri Fay, *The Louvre Sphinx and Royal Sculpture from the Reign of Amenemhat II* (Mainz, 1996), passim.

2 Paris, Louvre AO 13075; M.E.L.R. du Mesnil du Buisson, "L'ancienne Qatna, ou les ruines d'el-Mishrifé au N.-E. de Homs (Emèse), deuxième campagne de Fouilles (1927)," *Syria* 9 (1928): 10–11, pl. 12. For the Brooklyn and Qatna sculptures and other Middle Kingdom sphinxes, see Fay, *Louvre Sphinx,* 28–30 and 30–32, respectively.

3 Joachim Winkelmann, *Geschichte der Kunst des Alterthums* (Dresden, 1764), 58.

4 Wolfgang W. Helck, "Ägyptische Statuen im Ausland—ein chronologisches Problem," *Ugarit-Forschungen* 8 (1976): 101–15.

41 Head of a female sphinx

1 For a brief treatment of this protective flame- and poison-spitting cobra, often found on the brows of deities and royalty (including some members of female royalty), see K. Martin, "Uräus," *LÄ* 6: 864–68. Although the *uraeus* has a number of divine associations that include links to the Lower Egyptian goddess Wadjet and the eye of Horus and of the sun, it was perhaps as the Eye of Ra and Daughter of Ra that many goddesses came to be considered as *uraei.* Eventually almost all goddesses could be likened to the *uraeus.*

2 I owe this suggestion to Jack A. Josephson.

3 Wildung, *Sesostris und Amenemhet,* 88.

4 For a detailed discussion of the question of portraiture in ancient Egyptian art, see Spanel, *Through Ancient Eyes.*

5 E.g., Johnson, *Cobra Goddess,* drawings on 248–49.

6 E.g., Evers, *Staat,* 97, mentions the numerous windings of the *uraeus* in sculptures of Senusert I (early Dynasty 12) as well as their far less frequent appearance in sculptures as late as Senusert II; L. Keimer, "Sur un fragment de statuette en calcaire ayant la forme d'un oiseau (vautour?) à tête de reine," *ASAE* 35 (1935): 182–91 and pls. 1–2, illustrates here, in what may be a royal woman shown with a vulture's body, that *uraei* sometimes have numerous windings even later in Dynasty 12; B.V. Bothmer, "The Philadelphia-Cairo Statue of Osorkon II (Membra Dispersa III)," *JEA* 46 (1960): 5, n. 4; C. Aldred, "Some Royal Portraits of the Middle Kingdom in Ancient Egypt," *MMJ* 3 (1970): 31–37, with figs. 5–16, which are heads attributed to kings from Mentuhotep II of Dynasty 11 to Senusert I. For related *uraei* in relief, see Aldred, *Middle Kingdom Art,* pl. 18 (Montuhotep III of Dynasty 11) and pl. 21 (Senusert I).

7 E.g., Aldred, *MMJ* 3 (1970): 32, fig. 5 (reattributed, on a correction slip, from Mentuhotep III [?] to Senusert I); 33, fig. 9 (attributed to Dynasty 11 or 12); 35, fig. 13 (Amenemhat I); and 36–37, figs. 14–16 (attributed to Amenemhat I).

8 Fay *(Louvre Sphinx)* attributes it to early Dynasty 12; the writer thanks Biri Fay for providing him a copy of this part of her monograph prior to its publication. Wildung, *Sesostris and Amenemhet,* 88, suggests that it might represent the wife of Amenemhat I or Senusert I.

9 For Egyptian sphinxes, see C. Coche-Zivie, "Sphinx," *LÄ* 5: 1139–47. For sphinxes throughout history, see Demisch, *Die Sphinx,* with a chapter on Egyptian sphinxes on pp. 16–39.

10 Fay, *Louvre Sphinx,* 63 (n. 1, with pl. 83, a–d), where the author disputes the not uncommon identification of a head (probably of King Radjedef) as part of a sphinx.

11 Martin-Pardey, in *Nofret-di Schöne,* 46; Seipel, *Gott Mensch Pharao,* 156. See G. Robins, "A Critical Examination of the Theory That the Right to the Throne of Ancient Egypt Passed through the Female Line in the 18th Dynasty," *GM* 62 (1983): 67–77 for an argument against this theory, at least for Dynasty 18; also see B. Bryan's comments in this volume.

12 Troy, *Patterns of Queenship,* 64.

13 C. Traunecker, "Aménophis IV et Néfertiti: Le couple royal d'après les talatates du IXe pylône de Karnak," *BSFE* 107 (1986): 17–43, with fig. 2a on p. 21.

14 E.g., Robins, *Women,* 52–54; R. Morkot, "Violent Images of Queenship and the Royal Cult," *Wepwawet* 2 (1986): 109.

15 E.g., Morkot, *Wepwawet* 2 (1986); Troy, *Patterns of Queenship,* 66.

42 Kneeling statue of Hatshepsut

1 The vessel is embellished with a *djed* pillar, symbol of "stability." For a synopsis of the various interpretations of this vessel, see Tefnin, *Statuaire d'Hatshepsout,* 91.

2 Hayes, *Scepter,* 2: 97.

3 Marianne Eaton-Krauss, "The *Khat* Headdress to the End of the Amarna Period," *SAK* 5 (1977): 21–39, esp. 35, nos. 12–19.

4 Tefnin, *Statuaire d'Hatshepsout,* 90–91.

5 For a recent discussion of these inscriptions, and past interpretations, see Gae Callender, "Problems in the Reign of Hatshepsut," *KMT* 6, no. 4 (1995–96): 18–19.

6 Ibid., 20.

7 A title that is known from the Middle Kingdom but did not become prominent until the beginning of the New Kingdom; see Gay Robins, "The God's Wife of Amun in the 18th Dynasty in Egypt," in Cameron and Kuhrt, eds., *Images of Women,* 70–71. Also see cat. no. 48.

8 Robins, *Women,* 46.

9 Grimal, *History,* 207. See also Redford, *History and Chronology,* 73 and n. 83.

10 Other evidence suggests her accession to the throne in Thutmose III's year 2. For a discussion of this evidence, see Callender, *KMT* 6, no. 4 (1995–96): 24–27, 79; and Dorman, *Senenmut,* 18–45.

11 See Callender, *KMT* 6, no. 4 (1995–96): 22.

12 Though mutilation of Hatshepsut's monuments did occur late in the reign of Thutmose III; see Dorman, *Senenmut,* 46–65.

13 Murnane, *Coregencies.*

14 For further discussion, see ibid., 239–65.

15 During the reign of the Second Dynasty King Nynetjer, it was decided that females could sit on Egypt's throne. W.G. Waddell, *Manetho* (London, 1971), 100 ff.

16 Christiane M. Zivie, "Nitokris," *LÄ* 4: 513–14.

17 Jürgen von Beckerath, "Sobeknofru," *LÄ* 5: 1050–51.

18 Kenneth A. Kitchen, "Tausret," *LÄ* 6: 244–45.

19 Robins, *Women,* 50.

20 Callender, *KMT* 6, no. 4 (1995–96): 23–24.

21 Redford, *History and Chronology,* 80.

22 Ibid., 57–60.

23 PM 2[2]: 344–47.

24 Grimal, *History,* 209; and Redford, *History and Chronology,* 87.

25 KV 20; see Theodore M. Davis et al., *The Tomb of Hâtshopsîtû* (London, 1906).

43 Statue of Senenmut holding Nefrura

1 Robins, *Women,* 46.

2 Ibid., 48–49. Gitton, *Ahmès Néfertary,* 65–66, 71, cites evidence suggesting that Hatshepsut and Nefrura held the title jointly for a short period of time.

3 Robins, *Women,* 151–52; and see Dennis C. Forbes, "Princess Neferure: Hatshepsut's Intended Successor?" *KMT* 5, no. 4 (1994–95): 41–42, where another possible depiction of Nefrura—a statuette in the Museum of Fine Arts, Boston (52.347)—is discussed. For that object see also Spanel, *Through Ancient Eyes,* cat. no. 21, 81–83.

4 These scenes are described by Robins in *Women,* 151–52. See also M. Gitton, "Le rôle des femmes dans le clergé d'Amon à la XVIIIe dynastie," *BSFE* 75 (1976): 31–46.

5 See Dorman, *Senenmut,* 165–69, for Senenmut's family.

6 Ibid., 169–71.

7 Ibid., passim.

8 According to Appendix 2 in Dorman, *Senenmut,* 188–97.

9 Aldred, *New Kingdom Art,* 52.

10 For a line drawing of another depiction of Nefrura carrying the *hetes* scepter, and a discussion of this ritual object, see Troy, *Patterns of Queenship,* 84, fig. 55.

11 Berlin 2296, a block statue. According to Dorman, *Senenmut,* 123, the similarity in the inscriptions suggests that the texts for these statues were drafted at the same time.

12 This translation is from ibid., 123–24, with minor changes by the current author.

13 Exactly when Senenmut's downfall and death occurred is uncertain; see the discussion in ibid., 141–64, 177–81.

14 Grimal, *History,* 209.

15 Dorman, *Senenmut,* 78–79; Robins, *Women,* 49–50.

16 Dorman, *Senenmut,* 79.

17 Robins, *Women,* 150, 152.

44 Head of Queen Tiye

1 See Robins, *Women,* 42–55 ("Queens, Power and Kingship") for a discussion of these women.

2 *ḏd mdw in,* "words spoken by. . . ." Above the line of vertical registers are the word *bḥdt* and a pendent *uraeus,* a reference to Horus the Behdetite.

3 See Bryan, in *Egypt's Dazzling Sun,* 141 and n. 63, 152, for a list of the statues included in this group.

4 W. Raymond Johnson, "Images of Amenhotep III in Thebes: Styles and Intentions," in Berman, ed., *Art of Amenhotep III,* 26–46.

5 For references to scenes from the first *Heb Sed* of Amenhotep III, see Bryan, in *Egypt's Dazzling Sun,* 39–40; for scenes from the third *Heb Sed,* see also *The Tomb of Kheruef: Theban Tomb 192* (University of Chicago, Oriental Institute Publication 102; Chicago, 1980), pls. 49–63 for scenes from the third *Heb Sed.*

6 Bryan, in *Egypt's Dazzling Sun,* 176.

7 But see Aldred, *Akhenaten,* 152, where he states that Tiye was "the Heiress in the line of descent of the deified queen, Ahmose-Nefertari"; see also ibid., 219–20.

8 Ibid., 146.

9 Berman, in *Egypt's Dazzling Sun,* 67–69, n. 2.

10 Ibid. For the titles of Yuya and Thuya and their other offspring, see Aldred, *Akhenaten,* 219–20.

11 See Baines and Malek, *Atlas,* 109, 118–19.

12 Two hundred examples of five types are known.

13 Green, *Queens and Princesses,* 498.

14 Aldred, *Akhenaten,* 193.

15 Ibid., 443–49.

16 Robins, *Women,* 52.

17 Davies, *Rock Tombs,* 3: 18, pl. 19.

18 Bryan, in *Egypt's Dazzling Sun,* 110.

19 Ibid., and see 443, fig. 123b. She also appears as a sphinx trampling foreign enemies on the side of her throne in a scene from the tomb of Kheruef: see *Tomb of Kheruef,* pl. 47. See cat. no. 41 for a Middle Kingdom example of a royal female in the form of a sphinx.

20 Bryan, in *Egypt's Dazzling Sun,* 43.

21 Ibid., 176.

22 No Egyptian source for this stone is known. See comments and mention of other Egyptian statuary of the same material by Bryan, in *Egypt's Dazzling Sun,* 175–76.

23 Ibid., 175–77, fig. 15a.

45 Relief: Nefertiti offering to the Aten

1 Redford, *Akhenaten,* 137.

2 Petrie, *El Amarna,* 5–6; Davies, *El Amarna,* 5: 19–28 and plates.

3 Ibid., pl. 33 for reconstruction.

4 A frequently updated bibliography compiled by Edward K. Werner appears regularly in the *American Research Center in Egypt, Newletter (NARCE)* beginning with vol. 95 (Fall 1975–Winter 1976): 15–29. This bibliography is divided into topics that include "The Role of Nefertiti."

5 Redford, *Akhenaten,* 71–78, figs. 6–7.

6 It has been suggested that the *ḥwt-bnbn* was part of another building, the *gmt-pꜣ-itn* intended for Nefertiti's private use. See J.O. Gohary, "Nefertiti at Karnak," in *Glimpses of Ancient Egypt: Studies in Honour of H.W. Fairman,* ed. John Ruffle, G.A. Gaballa, and Kenneth A. Kitchen (Warminster, 1979), 30–31.

7 Redford, *Akhenaten,* 79. This translation of Nefertiti's epithet is Redford's.

8 Though Nefertiti is always depicted in the rear rather than the forward position, "behind" Akhenaten, in only one of these scenes (Davies, *El Amarna,* 2: pls. 37–38) is a face preserved—that of Akhenaten. It is unclear whether there was a second line to indicate the face of Nefertiti.

9 Enthroned, on the east wall of the tomb of Meryra II, see Davies, *El Amarna,* 2: pls. 37 and 38; riding on a palanquin, on the west wall of Huya's tomb, see Davies, *El Amarna,* 3: pl. 13.

10 Offering at the temple, on the west wall of the tomb of Panehsy; see Davies, *El Amarna,* 2: pl. 18.

11 An elaborate *atef,* see Davies, *El Amarna,* 2: pl. 8. It has been suggested that Nefertiti wears other kingly crowns as well; see Julia Samson, "Nefertiti's Regality," *JEA* 63 (1977): 88–89, 92, figs. 1–3 (though the present author sees no evidence to indicate "the Queen's red crown" mentioned by Samson, 89). See also Earl L. Ertman, "The Cap-Crown of Nefertiti: Its Function and Probable Origin," *JARCE* 13 (1976): 63–67.

12 Samson, *JEA* 63 (1977): 90–91.

13 Cooney, *Amarna Reliefs,* no. 51, 82–85. See also Robert Morkot, "Violent Images of Queenship and the Royal Cult," *Wepwawet* 2 (Summer, 1986): 1–9.

14 Ray Winfield Smith and Donald B. Redford, *The Akhenaten Temple Project, 1: Initial Discoveries* (Warminster, 1976), pl. 23:2. For Tiye as sphinx, see cat. no. 44, note 19.

15 In the tomb of Panehsy: Davies, *El Amarna,* 2: 31–32, pls. 9, 21.

16 See Samson, *JEA* 63 (1977) for a synopsis of the theory and evidence.

17 John A. Wilson, "Akh-en-Aton and Nefert-iti," *JNES* 32 (1973): 235–41.

18 See Redford, *Akhenaten,* 76, fig. 6.

19 Wilson, *JNES* 32 (1973): 240–41; Tawfik, "Aton Studies: 3. Back Again to Nefer-nefru-Aton," *MDAIK* 31 (1975): 162–63, 165.

20 Prayers were also addressed to Queen Tiye, mother-in-law to Nefertiti. See cat. no. 44, note 14.

21 See cat. no. 44 regarding Queen Tiye's divinity.

22 For an example of the latter, see Aldred, *Akhenaten and Nefertiti,* 22, fig. 6.

23 For a discussion of Amarna art and its evolution, see ibid., 48–66. The art of the Amarna period is a topic in Werner's bibliography, cited above, note 4.

24 See, for instance, in Aldred, *Akhenaten and Nefertiti,* figs. 1, 25, 59, 99, 100 (though not all are inscribed for Nefertiti); see cat. no. 46.

25 See Ertman, *JARCE* 13 (1976): 63–67.

26 Petrie, *El Amarna,* 6; Aldred, *Akhenaten and Nefertiti,* 114.

27 Nefertiti is often seen shaking sistra at Karnak; see Smith and Redford, *Akhenaten Temple Project,* 1: 80–82. She appears with sistra less frequently at Amarna (Aldred, *Akhenaten and Nefertiti,* 127; Davies, *El Amarna,* 6: pl. 14), where the princesses seem to have taken over this function. Perhaps her increasingly divine status made it inappropriate for her to employ this cultic item.

28 Petrie, *El Amarna,* 6; Davies, *El Amarna,* 5: 25, pl. 33.

46 Relief of Queen Nefertiti kissing daughter

1 The ancient name of the city was Akhetaten, "Horizon of the Aten."

2 This relief was discovered at Hermopolis, where it had been reused in the construction of a temple by Ramesses II. See Cooney, *Amarna Reliefs,* 1–3, for a history of the reliefs.

3 The Aten was represented as a solar disc, wearing a *uraeus,* with rays ending in human hands.

4 Janssen and Janssen, *Growing Up,* 37–41, for a discussion of children's hairstyles in ancient Egypt.

5 Aldred, *Akhenaten and Nefertiti,* 165.

6 On a fragmentary stela in the Ägyptisches Museum, Berlin, No. 14511. See Aldred, *Akhenaten and Nefertiti,* 69, fig. 45.

7 On a fragmentary stela now in the Louvre, Paris, E. 11624. See ibid., 134, no. 56.

8 Part of a fragmentary painting in the Ashmolean Museum, Oxford, no. 1893.1–41 (267). See ibid., 38–39, figs. 20–21.

9 Davies, *El Amarna,* 3: pl. 4.

10 See Salima Ikhram, "Domestic Shrines and the Cult of the Royal Family at El-'Amarna," *JEA* 75 (1989): 89–101, for a study of private shrines at Amarna devoted to the worship of the royal family.

11 For a discussion of these compositions, see Whitney Davis, "Two Compositional Tendencies in Amarna Relief," *AJA* 82, no. 3 (1978): 387–93.

12 Silverman, *Religion,* 85.

13 See cat. no. 45 for a discussion of Nefertiti's status.

14 Davies, *El Amarna,* 2: 31–32.

15 Silverman, *Religion,* 82–83.

16 For a brief discussion of the suppression of the old gods, especially Amen, see Redford, *Akhenaten,* 140–42.

17 Gay Robins, "The Role of the Royal Family in the 18th Dynasty up to the Reign of Amenhotep III: 2. Royal children," *Wepwawet* 3 (1987): 16–17.

18 See Claude Traunecker, "Aménophis IV et Nefèrtiti: Le couple royal d'après les talatattes du IXe pylône de Karnak," *BSFE* 107 (1986): 17–44, for the theory that Akhenaten and Nefertiti assumed the creative roles of Ra and Hathor.

19 B. Schmitz, in *Ägyptens Aufstieg,* no. 141.

47 Standard bearing statue of queen

1 For these New Kingdom robes, see G. Robins, "Problems in Interpreting Egyptian Art," *DiE* 17 (1990): 45–47.

2 E.g. Troy, *Patterns of Queenship,* 116–19. The projection at the front of the figure's headdress appears to be the remains of a vulture's head rather than a *uraeus,* the common alternative. Although the vulture headdress is not restricted to queens, there is no reason to maintain the occasional interpretation of the Harer statue as that of a private woman: Vandier, *Manuel,* 3: 665.

3 For Mut and the vulture headdress, see also cat. no. 61, note 2. There is no compelling reason to accept an interpretation of this bust as an "Osiris-Reliquiar": H. Satzinger, "Der heilige Stab als Kraftquelle des Königs: Versuch einer Funktionsbestimmung der ägyptischen Strabträger-Statuen," *Jahrbuch der Kunsthistorischen Sammlung in Wien* 77 (1981): 33, Dok. B4.

4 J. Pijoan, *El Arte Egipcio hasta la Conquista Romana* (Madrid, 1932), 278, fig. 363, who suggested it might represent Queen Tiye; C. Chadefaud, *Les statues portes-enseignes de l'Egypte ancienne (1580–1085 avant J.-C.): Signification et insertion dans le culte du Ka royal* (Paris, 1982), 98, no. PE C.4, quotes Pijoan's suggestion; H. Satzinger, review of Chadefaud, *Les statues,* in *BiOr* 41 (1984): col. 380, said, "Teje?"; Vandier, *Manuel,* 3: 491, dated it to Dynasty 18 but to the post-Amarna period.

5 G. Scott, III, *Temple, Tomb and Dwelling: Egyptian Antiquities from the Harer Family Trust Collection,* exh. cat., University Art Gallery, California State University, San Bernardino (San Bernardino, 1992), 132.

6 Ibid., 132 and 134, where Scott notes that the text continues either "beloved of Amen-Ra . . ." or "beloved of [the goddess] Amenet, lady of. . . ."

7 C. Desroches-Noblecourt, "Touy, mère de Ramses II, la reine Tanedjmy et les reliques de l'expérience amarnienne," *L'Egyptologie en 1979, axes prioritaires de recherches* 2 (Paris, 1982), 238–39, with fig. 65; Desroches-Noblecourt, "Abou Simbel, Ramses et les dames de la couronne," in Bleiberg and Freed, eds., *Shattered Visage,* 129. According to Desroches-Noblecourt, during her lifetime Mut-Tuya would have been viewed as the incarnation of Mut, a reflection of the emphasis Ramesses II placed on his divinity and divine origins.

8 G. Botti and P. Romanelli, *Le sculture del Museo Gregoriano Egizio* (Vatican City, 1951), pls. 19, 20.

9 Scott, *Temple, Tomb and Dwelling,* 134, who suggests that queens Nefertiry and Merit-Amen are more likely candidates. Aldred, *Egyptian Art in the Days of the Pharaohs, 3100–320 B.C.* (London, 1980), 186, considers the statue an image of Queen Nefertiry. For Ramesses II's queens, see Desroches-Noblecourt in Bleiberg and Freed, *Shattered Visage,* 127–66.

10 G. Scott, III, *Dynasties: The Egyptian Royal Image in the New Kingdom,* exh. checklist, San Antonio Museum of Art (San Antonio, 1995), no. 38. A more definite identification of the statue as an image of Nefertiry was proposed: see *In the Tomb of Nefertari: Conservation of the Wall Paintings,* exh. cat., the J. Paul Getty Museum and the Getty Conservation Institute (Malibu, 1992), 76–77, no. 23.

11 The statue of a woman often cited as a standard bearer may rather be sistrum-bearing: H. Satzinger, rev. of Chadefaud, *Les statues,* col. 380; H. Satzinger, in "Der heilige Stab," 14–15, notes that queens can appear in small scale in relief or half in the round on standard-bearing statues of Ramesses II, but as in a private pair statue of a male standard-bearer and woman on the same scale (illustrated by Satzinger as fig. 9 on p. 14), they do not themselves also bear the standard.

12 See, e.g., C. Chadefaud, *Les statues;* H. Satzinger, "Der heilige Stab," 16–28; M. Eaton-Krauss, "Concerning Standard-Bearing Statues," *SAK* 4 (1976): 69–73; R. Caminos, rev. of Chadefaud, *Les statues, JEA* 72 (1986): 216–21.

13 *Important Classical, Western Asiatic and Egyptian Antiquities,* sale cat., Christie's, New York, Thursday, June 14, 1979, 61.

14 For the main resting place of the standards, see H. Satzinger, "Der heilige Stab," 26. Perhaps particularly likely West Bank Theban provenances would be Ramesses II's funerary temple (PM 2^2: 431–43) and its subsidiary temple, seemingly related to the queens Tuya and Nefertiry: C. Desroches-Noblecourt, "Le mammisi de Ramses au Rameseum," *Memnonia* 1 (1990–91): 25–46; E. Uphill, "Where Were the Funerary Temples of the New Kingdom Queens?," *Sesto Congresso Internazionale di Egittologia, Atti* 1 (Turin, 1992), 613–18.

48 Statue of Amenirdas I, God's Wife of Amen

1 See Kitchen, *Third Intermediate Period.*

2 Gay Robins, "The God's Wife of Amun in the 18th Dynasty in Egypt," in Cameron and Kuhrt, eds., *Images of Women,* 70.

3 See Gitton, *Ahmes Néfertary,* esp. 7–12; and note 2, above.

4 Robins, *Women,* 149–50.

5 The God's Wife of Amen, Aset, daughter of Ramesses VI, may have been the first celibate holder of this office; see Robins, *Women,* 153–54.

6 Ibid., 154.

7 See Kitchen, *Third Intermediate Period,* Table 11, p. 478, for the genealogy.

8 See Kendall, *Kush,* 7–11, for a concise discussion of the Kushite kingdom and its conquest of Egypt.

9 For Osorkon III and Shepenwepet I, see Kitchen, *Third Intermediate Period,* para. 312, pp. 351–52; and para. 317–18, pp. 356–57.

10 Shabako also installed his son, Horemakhet, as High Priest of Amen and stripped the office of its military and political influence; see ibid., para. 344, p. 382.

11 For a list of Amenirdas' titles and epithets, see Troy, *Patterns of Queenship,* 177.

12 Kendall, *Kush,* 8–9.

13 Ibid., 9; see also Grimal, *History,* 332, 334.

14 See Trigger, *Social History,* 294–95.

15 R.A. Caminos, "The Nitocris Adoption Stela," *JEA* 50 (1964): 99.

16 Kitchen, *Third Intermediate Period,* para. 321, pp. 359–60; Grimal, *History,* 335.

17 Ibid., para. 344, p. 382; para. 347, p. 386.

18 Caminos, *JEA* 50 (1964): 71–101.

19 Ibid., 99–100.

20 For these examples and references, see Fazzini, *Egypt,* 20; see also Robins, *Women,* 156.

21 Fazzini, *Egypt,* 20.

22 The prenomen of Amenirdas was Kha-Neferu-Mut; see Kitchen, *Third Intermediate Period,* Table 13, p. 480.

23 E.R. Russmann, "Two Royal Heads of the Late Period in Brooklyn," *BMA* 10 (1968–69): 89–90.

24 Robins, *Women,* 151, states that this is typical apparel for the God's Wife of Amen, and that sometimes it is worn belted at the waist.

25 Bothmer et al., *ESLP,* 1–2, observes that the strands of hair have not been indicated, with additional comments.

26 For information on the use of the lily in ancient Egypt, see Manniche, *Herbal,* 50–51, 166.

27 See note 16 above.

28 Kitchen, *Third Intermediate Period,* para. 347, pp. 386–87, and Table 13, p. 480.

49 *Shabti* of Nebseni

1 Ranke, *Personennamen,* 1: 186, 14 (and variant *neb sen:* 186, 13).

2 For the type, cf. Schneider, *Shabtis,* 2: 199–200 ("Classical" mummy with beard, hands empty, VC2). It finds a particularly close stylistic parallel in the *shabti* of the Chief Steward Sen-yu in New York: Hayes, *Scepter,* 2: 59, fig. 2.

3 For the genealogy of God's Wives, see G. Robins, "The God's Wife of Amun in the 18th Dynasty in Egypt," in Cameron and Kuhrt, eds., *Images of Women,* 86, fig. 5.1. Ahmose-Nefertari, Hatshepsut, and Nefrura are the most likely candidates, since all left a large number of attestations in which frequent and exclusive use was made of the title "God's Wife" (ibid., 71). The succeeding God's Wives of the latter half of the Eighteenth Dynasty are less frequently attested and rarely make prominent use of the title.

4 For a review of the evidence relating to the various functions of this position, see ibid., 70–78. Her cultic duties were apparently diverse and included

possible oversight of temple construction as well as participation in temple ritual. See ibid., 72–73; and Gitton, *Ahmès Néfertary,* 32–42.

5 Little, however, is known about the personnel associated with this office. The Donation Stela of King Ahmose indicates that Ahmose-Nefertari's personnel consisted of both male and female workers *(hsby, hsbyt).*

6 See Robins in Cameron and Kuhrt, eds., *Images of Women,* 73, 75–76.

7 See ibid., 74, 77.

50 Ostracon: Ramesses II suckled by a goddess

51 Goddess suckling a queen

1 For the genealogy of Dynasty 25, see Kitchen, *Third Intermediate Period,* 478, Table 11. See also pp. 358–59, where Kitchen expresses uncertainty about the mother(s) of Piankhy and Abar.

2 For a brief discussion of marriage within the royal family, see Robins, *Women,* 26–27, 29.

3 See Baines and Malek, *Atlas,* 84–107.

4 For the titles and epithets of Khensa, see Troy, *Patterns of Queenship,* 176, no. 25.4.

5 Kendall, *Kush,* 26.

6 These tombs measure between 6 and 7 meters square. Those of the Twenty-fifth Dynasty kings at El-Kurru range from 8 to 11 meters square. See ibid., 21.

7 For Upper Nubia, see Baines and Malek, *Atlas,* 186.

8 For royal women depicted in this and other scenes formerly reserved for the king, see Fazzini, *Egypt,* 20–21.

9 For a list of those goddesses who suckle the king, see Jean Leclant, "Sur un contrepoids de Menat au nom de Taharqa: Allaitement et 'apparition' royale," *Mélanges Mariette,* Bibliothèque d'Études 32 (1961): 275.

10 Ibid., 265.

11 Much like the pose of the statue of Memy and Sabu (cat. no. 3a) and of Hetepheres and Meresankh (cat. no. 37).

12 Kendall, *Kush,* 27.

13 During the later Meroitic Period, this Kushite ideal of feminine plumpness was exaggerated to the point of obesity. See ibid., 14, figs. 13–14.

14 Leclant, *Mélanges Mariette* 32 (1961): 251–84, pls. 1–2.

15 Kendall, *Kush,* 27.

16 But inscribed for his father; see ibid., 41.

17 Ibid., 41.

18 Ibid., 27.

19 Ibid.

20 Ibid.

52 Bust of a queen

1 As L. Troy observes (*Patterns of Queenship,* 117), the first certain evidence for the association of the vulture headdress and queenship may be found at the transition to the Fifth Dynasty, when it is found outlined on the royal female determinative of Khentkawes I. The first clear representation of a queen wearing the vulture cap is that of the Sixth Dynasty queen Iput I, wife of Tety; see ibid.

2 Robins, *Women,* 23.

3 For the association of the vulture headdress with the cult of Hathor, see Troy, *Patterns of Queenship,* 78; as the author notes, the vulture cap appears on the Middle Kingdom mummy of a woman who was a *ẖkrt nisw.*

4 The bust was originally assigned an earlier dating—to the Middle Kingdom (Steindorff, *Catalogue,* 23) and to the beginning of the Eighteenth Dynasty (Vandier, *Manuel,* 3: 224, 315). This early dating was rejected by Muller and others in favor of a dating to the Late Period; see E. Lillesø, "Two Wooden Uraei," *JEA* 61 (1975): 141; and H. Sourouzian, "Une tête de la reine Touy à Gourna," *MDAIK* 37 (1981): 454, n. 54.

5 E.R. Russman, personal correspondence, Nov. 11, 1995. Cf. Bothmer's comments (*ESLP,* no. 92) concerning the female bust in Richmond (cat. no. 7). Equally diagnostic for dating is the exaggerated detailing of the headdress.

6 Both exhibit a diminutive mouth with ends upturned in a "smile," a feature first introduced in sculpture of the Twenty-sixth Dynasty. See Bothmer et al., *ESLP,* xxxviii.

7 This sense of restraint indicates a date later than the Twenty-sixth Dynasty and antecedent to the Ptolemaic era, when the female form was rendered in a more sensuous manner; see Bothmer, in *ESLP,* 116. As in the Richmond bust, the nipples on the Baltimore fragment are not indicated; see ibid. Acknowledgment to Anne K. Capel for providing this theory and the reference.

8 For the distinction between "archaizing" and "archaistic" tendencies of the Twenty-sixth and Thirtieth Dynasties, respectively, see Bothmer et al., *ESLP,* 38.

9 The Hathor headdress is particularly rare in the Late Period; see Sourouzian, *MDAIK* 37 (1981): 454–55.

Goddesses

53 a Female figurine with incurving arms

53 b Jar with female and attendants on boat

1 The other is Brooklyn 07.447.505.

2 H. de Morgan, "Report on Excavations Made in Upper Egypt," *ASAE* 12 (1912): 32.

3 Needler, *Predynastic,* publishes five of the sixteen: nos. 269–73, pp. 339–43.

4 For the dating of these objects, see Needler, *Predynastic,* 92, 206, 337.

5 One of the sides is quite worn. It is not clear whether the female is accompanied by one or two attendants. Two males are present in each of the other two boat scenes.

6 Needler, *Predynastic,* 92, 337.

7 Brooklyn, 07.447.505.

8 For example, see Emma Swan Hall, "Some Ancient Egyptian Sculpture in American Museums," *Apollo* (July, 1968): 6, 7, fig. 6.

9 Westendorf, *Painting,* 13.

10 Spanel, in Fazzini et al., *Ancient Egyptian Art,* no. 1, where various theories are discussed.

11 Müller, *Aegyptische Kunst,* no. 4.

12 See, for example, Fekri A. Hassan, "Primeval Goddess to Divine King: The Mythogenesis of Power in the Early Egyptian State," in Friedman and Adams, eds., *Followers of Horus,* 314.

13 G.D. Hornblower, "Predynastic Figures of Women and Their Successors," *JEA* 15 (1929): 34.

14 See H. Wild, *Les danses sacrées de l'Égypte ancienne,* Sources Orientales 6 (Paris, 1963), 36–117, esp. 40–41; for a labeled depiction of the *ib3* dance, see Wenig, *Woman,* pl. 14.

15 Needler, *Predynastic,* 342, pl. 66; 343–44.

16 Boston, MFA B15557. Published as plate 29d in Rice, *Egypt's Making.*

17 London, BM 50687. Hornblower, *JEA* 15 (1929): 36–37, pl. 6, no. 5.

18 F.A. Hassan in Friedman and Adams, eds., *Followers of Horus,* 307–22.

19 Needler, *Predynastic,* 337.

54 a Fragment of statue of bovine-headed Hathor

54 b Statuette of bovine-headed Hathor

1 Bleeker, *Hathor and Thoth,* 34–37. Pinch, *Votive Offerings,* 177, observes that the tree goddess is sometimes depicted with the head of a cow; see J.E. Quibell, *The Ramesseum* (London, 1898), pls. 20, 24.

2 Bleeker, *Hathor and Thoth,* 48–51.

3 Mariette, *Abydos,* 1: pl. 39b, and *Denderah,* 3: pl. 179 and 5, pl. 338.

4 For depictions, see Aldred, *Egypt,* ill. 113; and Smith, *HESPOK,* pl. 13.

5 Henry George Fischer, "The Cult and Nome of the Goddess Bat," *JARCE* I (1962): 7–18. Also see Troy, *Patterns of Queenship,* 54, 82.

6 Bleeker, *Hathor and Thoth,* 31–33; and Pinch, *Votive Offerings,* 175.

7 Ibid., 33. Also see Michel Malaise, "Histoire et signification de la coiffure hathorique à plumes," *SAK* 4 (1976): 220.

8 See Ramadan el Sayed, "Les sept vaches célestes, leur taureau et les quatre gouvernails d'après les données de documents divers," *MDAIK* 36 (1980): 357–90. For a depiction of the seven sacred cows, see Faulkner, *Book of the Dead,* pl. 35, Ch. 148.

9 Bleeker, *Hathor and Thoth,* 42–45; and Pinch, *Votive Offerings,* 181.

10 See, most recently, Christian Leblanc, *Ta Set Neferou: une nécropole de Thebes-Ouest et son histoire.* I: *Géographie-toponyme historique de l'exploration scientifique du site* (Cairo, 1989), pl. 77 (VQ 40, Hathor as cow), pl. 126 (VQ 52, Hathor as cow), pl. 150 (VQ 60, cow-headed Hathor), pls. 180 and 181,A (VQ 7k, cow-headed Hathor), pl. 189 (VQ 73, Hathor as cow), and pl. 117 (VQ 74, Hathor as cow). [Editor's note: VQ no. is a tomb designation in the Valley of the Queens.]

11 Faulkner, *Book of the Dead,* pl. 37, Ch. 186.

12 Cairo JE 38574; see Lange and Hirmer, *Egypt,* pls. 146–47; also depicted in Roberts, *Hathor Rising,* 49–51, ills. 61–62. A similar statue in Cairo (C.G. 784), dated to the Twenty-sixth Dynasty, depicts the Overseer of Sealers, Psamtik, standing under the head of the bovine Hathor. Psamtik does not, however, drink the divine milk of the goddess. See Edward L.B. Terrace and Henry G. Fischer, *Treasures of Egyptian Art from the Cairo Museum,* exh. cat. (London, 1970), 165–68, no. 38.

13 Jocelyne Berlandini, "La déesse bucéphale: Une iconographie particulière de l'Hathor memphite," *BIFAO* 83 (1983): 33–49, pls. 1–2.

14 For Ptah, see H. te Velde, "Ptah," *LÄ* 4: 1177–80.

15 Brooklyn Museum object files, 37.356E, formerly New-York Historical Society Abbott Collection 789.1A.

16 Berlandini, *BIFAO* 83 (1983): 34.

17 See note 15, above. Williams notes that two of the statuettes in Cairo, 39134 and 39137, also have the counterpoise at the rear of the crown.

18 See note 15, above. This example depicts Hathor with Isis and "other goddesses."

19 See note 15, above; C.R. Williams does not provide the Cairo catalogue number.

20 Translation by J.D. Cooney, with additions by the present author.

55 a Sistrum fragment with Hathor mask

55 b Hathor mask

1 For the *naos* sistrum as a development of the *sekhem* wand, see Christian Tutundjian de Vartavan, "The Origin, Evolution and Function of the *SHM*, Known as the *Naos*-Sistrum: Preliminary Researches," *Wepwawet* 2 (1986): 26–30.

2 See, for instance, Aldred, *Egypt*, 43. For a different interpretation of this creature, see W.A. Fairservis, Jr., "A Revised View of the Na'rmr Palette," *JARCE* 28 (1991): 7.

3 Andrews, *Amulets*, 20.

4 Pinch, *Votive Offerings*, 145.

5 Ibid., 153–59.

6 For a discussion of those objects dating from the Second Intermediate Period and New Kingdom, see Pinch, *Votive Offerings*, 148–53.

7 Ibid., 155.

56 Votive stela to Hathor

1 For the goddess Bat and her relationship to Hathor, see H.G. Fischer, "The Cult and Nome of the Goddess Bat," *JARCE* 1 (1962): 7–23.

2 For this (unfortunately) very fragmentary Dynasty 11 relief of Hathor as a cow, see R. Drenkhahn, *Ägyptische Reliefs im Kestner-Museum Hannover* (Hannover, 1989), no. 18, 62–63 (illus). For Nebhepetra in relation to Hathor at Thebes and elsewhere, see D. Arnold, *Der Tempel des Königs Mentuhotep von Deir el-Bahri*. 1, *Architektur und Deutung*, AVDAIK 8 (Mainz am Rhein, 1974), 83–84; L. Gestermann, "Hathor, Harsomtus und Mnṯw-ḥtp.w II.," *Studien zu Sprache und Religion Ägyptens. Zu Ehren von Wolfhart Westendorff überreicht von seinen Freunden und Schülern*. II, *Religion* (Göttingen, 1984), 763–76; H. Goedicke, "Hathor's Cult at Deir el-Bahari," *Hathor. Estudios de egiptologia* 1 (1989): 11–31; R. Gillam, "Priestesses of Hathor: Their Function, Decline, and Disappearance," *JARCE* 32 (1995): 231–33; L. Habachi, "King Nebhepetre Mentuhotp: His Monuments, Place in History, Deification and Unusual Representations in the Form of Gods," *MDAIK* 19 (1963): 16–52. Important women of Nebhepetra's court (see cat. no. 39) were associated with the cult of Hathor.

3 On Hathor, see, e.g., cat. nos. 20c, 22a, 35b, 54, and 55 and Allam, *Hathorkult;* Bleeker, *Hathor and Thoth;* F. Daumas, "Hathor," *LÄ* 2: 1024–33; Derchain, *Hathor quadrifons;* Naguib, *Le clergé féminin*, 23–74; Pinch, *Votive Offerings;* Troy, *Patterns of Queenship;* E. Wente, "Hathor at the Jubilee," *Studies in Honor of John A. Wilson, September 12, 1969*, SAOC 35 (Chicago, 1969), 83–91.

4 For Hathor's association with the ancient celestial cow goddesses in Egyptian mythology, see Daumas, *LÄ* 2: 1025.

5 For Nut as the Milky Way, see R. Wells, "The Mythology of Nut and the Birth of Re," *SAK* 19 (1992): 305–21; and A. Kozloff, "Star-Gazing in Ancient Egypt," in C. Berger, G. Clerc, and N. Grimal, eds., *Hommages à Jean Leclant*. 4, *Varia*, *BdE* 106,4 (Cairo, 1994), 169–76.

6 E.g., Wente, *Studies in Honor of John A. Wilson*, 90.

7 E.g., C. Traunecker, "Amenophis IV et Néfertiti: le couple royal d'après les talatates du IXe pylône de Karnak," *BSFE* 107 (1986): 17–43.

8 Troy, *Patterns of Queenship*.

9 For Hathor's visual iconography and its basic significance, see Hornung, *Conceptions of God*, 109–17.

10 For a recent hypothesis suggesting that a grotto associated with Hathor near the Valley of the Queens at Thebes symbolized a giant uterus from which deceased royalty were reborn, see C. Desroches-Noblecourt, "Le message de la Grotte Sacrée," *Egypte: Vallée des Reines, Vallée des Rois, Vallée des Nobles. Les Dossiers d'Archéologie*, 149–50 (May–June, 1990): 4–21.

11 Pinch, *Votive Offerings*.

57 Statue of winged Isis and Osiris

1 For the role of Isis in the various traditions of the Osirian myth, see Hart, *Egyptian Myths*, 29–41; and S.T. Hollis, "Five Egyptian Goddesses in the Third Millennium B.C.," *KMT* 5, no. 4 (1994–95): 82–83.

2 Fazzini, *Egypt*, 11–12.

3 For bronze groups of the type, see Roeder, *Aegyptische Bronzefiguren*, 495–97 and pl. 67. For an earlier two-dimensional image of winged Isis protecting Osiris, see, for example, A. Calverley, M. Broome, and A. Gardiner, *The Temple of King Sethos at Abydos I. The Chapels of Osiris, Isis, and Horus* (London and Chicago, 1933), pl. 13. In the text associated with this scene, Isis states that she has spread her wings protectively around Osiris; for the text and translation, see Münster, *Isis*, 201 and n. 2162. Protective winged images of Isis, Nephthys, Neith, and Selket may be found on royal sarcophagi (e.g., that of Tutankhamen). For indications of the date of the present statuette, cf. a seated Isis figure in Hildesheim inscribed for Psamtik I (Pelizaeus-Museum, no. 1203: H. Müller, *Münchner Jahrbuch des bildenden Kunst* 14 [1963]: 10, fig. 2). For the style of the inscription, cf. seated statuettes of Isis in Stockholm (Medelhavsmuseet E 14956: P. Reuterswärd, *Studien zur Polychromie der Plastik*. 1, *Ägypten* [Stockholm, 1958], pl. 10) and Paris (Louvre N3992: unpublished).

4 Translation from Lichtheim, *Ancient Egyptian Literature*, 2: 83. For the Great Hymn to Osiris, see also Münster, *Isis*, 2–3.

5 The author acknowledges the assistance of A. Capel in translating this inscription.

6 See PM 2^2: 289 (British Museum 1162) with bibliography; recently illustrated in Quirke, *Religion*, 12, fig. 4.

58 Bust fragment of a goddess, probably Isis

1 A portion of the material presented in this catalogue entry appears in the Cincinnati Art Museum's *Interactive Video—The Egyptian Collection* and appears here courtesy of Anne K. Capel and the Cincinnati Art Museum.

2 Although she is one of the longest-lived and most prominent of Egyptian goddesses, very little is known about Isis's early history; in fact, there are no certain attestations of the goddess before the Fifth Dynasty, when she is first mentioned in the *Pyramid Texts*. On the antiquity of the Isis cult, see Münster, *Isis;* and Jan Bergman, "Isis," *LÄ* 3: 188–89.

3 Bergman, *LÄ* 3: 189–91.

4 For a Thirteenth Dynasty copper statuette of Isis and Horus in Berlin, see *Ägyptisches Museum Berlin* (Berlin, 1967), 37–38, and discussion under cat. no. 9.

5 Isis's association with her sister Nephthys is an ancient one, dating back to the *Pyramid Texts;* see S.T. Hollis, "Five Egyptian Goddesses in the Third Millennium B.C.," *KMT* 5, no. 4 (1994–95): 82.

6 This has traditionally been interpreted as the origin of the name of the goddess *3st;* however, there is no scholarly consensus on the derivation and meaning of the name. For the suggestion that it derives from the word *was*, "to have power," see Bergman, *LÄ* 3: 186–88, and Quirke, *Religion*, 67 (following J. Osing).

7 See S.K. Heyob, *The Cult of Isis among Women in the Greco-Roman World* (Leiden, 1975); R.E. Witt, *Isis in the Greco-Roman World* (London, 1971). The worship of Isis was among the first of Egyptian cults to spread throughout the Mediterranean world—to Greece and Italy, among other localities.

8 L. Green, "Isis, the Egyptian Goddess Who Endured in the Greco-Roman World," *KMT* 5, no. 4 (1994–95): 62–63.

9 G. Haeny, "A Short Architectural History of Philae," *BIFAO* 85 (1985): 197–235. See also W. MacQuitty, *Island of Isis: Philae, Temple of the Nile* (New York, 1976). As Haeny observes, the remains of a kiosk of Psamtik II are the earliest clear evidence for a cult establishment to Isis at Philae.

10 Green, *KMT* 5, no. 4 (1994–95): 64. C. Favard-Meeks, *Le temple de Behbeit el-Higara. Essai de reconstitution et d'interpretation*, BSAK 6 (Hamburg, 1991).

11 Procopius, *De Bello Persico* I, 19, 36–37.

12 See M. Müller, "Zwei Bildwerke aus der dritten Zwischenzeit," *BSEG* 9–10 (1984–85): 199–222; also M. Jørgensen, "Ein aegyptisk bronzefigur," *Mededelser fra Ny Carlsberg Glyptothek* 49 (1993): 85–94. A Third Intermediate Period date for the Cincinnati bust fragment was first suggested by E. Russmann.

59 a Isis nursing Horus

59 b Isis nursing Horus

59 c Horus the Child

1 A portion of the material presented in this catalogue entry appears in the Cincinnati Art Museum's *Interactive Video—The Egyptian Collection* and appears here courtesy of Anne K. Capel and the Cincinnati Art Museum.

2 This account is based upon one of several versions of the myth of Osiris, Isis, and Horus. For a discussion, see Hart, *Egyptian Myths*, 29–41; see also J. Gwyn Griffiths, *Plutarch's De Iside et Osiride* (Cardiff, 1970); and Münster, *Isis*.

3 For Isis's role in the Osiris myth, see Susan T. Hollis, "Five Egyptian Goddesses in the Third Millennium B.C.," *KMT* 5, no. 4 (1994–95): 82–83. For remarks concerning Horus's conception from the reassembled body of Osiris, see, recently, Lisa Manniche, "Divine Reflections of Female Behavior," *KMT* 5, no. 4 (1994–95): 54–55.

4 For a discussion of Isis's magical curative powers, see Ritner, *Mechanics*, esp. pp. 81, 86.

5 This effort led her to open conflict with Seth before the divine tribunal of forty-two presiding deities. See J. Gwyn Griffiths, *The Conflict of Horus and Seth from Egyptian and Classical Sources* (Liverpool, 1960).

6 Pinch, *Magic*, 29–31.

7 In the Pyramid Texts, it is stated that the king drinks divine milk from the breasts of his mother Isis (Pyramid 707a: Mercer, *Pyramid Texts*, 1: 137). As Fazzini (*Egypt*, 10) observes in connection with a much later image, "As Horus is the divine model for the pharaoh, [the scene] may also be viewed as a mythicized depiction of a king receiving divine sustenance for his 'birth' into office. . . . "

8 For the growth of the cults of Isis and Harpokrates in the Late Period, see Fazzini, *Egypt*, 9–11. The motif became increasingly important ideologically from Dynasty 21 onward; cf. cat. no. 66. As Fazzini observes, such sculptures of Isis with Horus did not begin to become common until the Kushite Period; see ibid. For a historical review of Isis as nursing mother, see Hans Wolfgang Müller, "Isis mit dem Horuskinde. Ein Beitrag zur Ikonographie der stillenden Gottesmutter im hellenistischen und römischen Ägypte," *Münchner Jahrbuch des bildenden Kunst* 14 (1963): 7–38. For bronzes of Isis nursing Horus, see Roeder, *Aegyptische Bronzefiguren*, 245–59, 264.

9 For the rise in popularity of Isis and Harpokrates in the Third Intermediate Period, see also D. Redford, "Notes on Ancient Buto," *BES* 5 (1983): 82–83; Redford, *Pharaonic King-Lists*, 328–29. For the small chapel J at Karnak, see PM 2^2: 203–4, and D. Redford, *Or* 55 (1986): 1–15, where it is identified as "The House of Isis of the Great Mound-of-the-God of Wese (Thebes)."

10 On *mammisis* in general, see F. Daumas, "Geburtshaus," *LÄ* 2: 462–76; and Daumas, *Les mammisis des temples égyptiens* (Paris, 1958).

11 *Mammisis* are normally viewed as an innovation of Dynasty 30. However, inscriptional and other evidence suggests that one of the temples of the Mut precinct at Karnak came to function as a *mammisi* in the Third Intermediate Period. (See R. Fazzini and W. Peck, *SSEAJ* 11 [1981]: 122–25; and H. De Meulenaere, in J. Quaegebeur, ed., *Studia Paulo Naster Oblata. 2. Orientalia Antiqua.* OLA 13 [Louvain, 1982], 27–29.) The temple in question is the structure labeled A in the northeast corner of the precinct most often identified as a temple of Khonsu-pa-khered ("Khonsu-the-Child"), son of Amen and Mut. For inscriptional evidence for a *mammisi* of Isis at Abydos, beginning in Ramesside times, see ibid., 25–27.

12 See J. Berlandini, in *Hommages à la mémoire de Serge Sauneron. 1927–1976.* 1, *Égypte pharaonique*, BdE 81 (Cairo, 1979), 102–9. For feminine clerical titles of the era, see also Naguib, *La clergé feminin*, esp. 207–11 and 225–32 on the various meanings of *mwt nṯr* ("Mother of the God") and *mn't* ("nurse"), including of a child god.

13 See L. Green, "Isis, the Egyptian Goddess Who Endured in the Greco-Roman World," *KMT* 5, no. 4 (1994–95): 62. Although such figurines are typically referred to as Isis-Hathor, precise identification is difficult. For seated amulets of the type, see Andrews, *Amulets*, 20 and fig. 18a.

14 For a discussion of the vulture headdress, see cat. no. 52.

15 Isis is first depicted with Hathor's headdress by the early Eighteenth Dynasty. Isis appropriated many aspects of Hathor's worship; the Hymns to Isis on the walls of her temple at Philae contain many references that first occur in relation to Hathor in the second millennium B.C. See Hollis, *KMT* 5, no. 4 (1994–95): 83; also see L. Žakbar, *Hymns to Isis in Her Temple at Philae* (Hanover, N.H., 1988), esp. p. 195. Such figurines of Isis with the horned disc crown are conventionally identified as "Isis-Hathor." For seated amulets of the type, see Andrews, *Amulets*, 20 and fig. 18a.

16 For a similar bronze statuette of Isis complete with base in the Royal Ontario Museum, Toronto, see Green, *KMT* 5, no. 4 (1994–95): 63 (illus.).

60 Isis/Scorpion nursing infant Horus

1 Selket is mentioned on the funerary stela of Merka at Saqqara; cf. W.B. Emery, *Excavations at Saqqara. Great Tombs of the First Dynasty*, 3, EESM 47 (London, 1958), 830–31, nn. 830–33, and pls. 23, 39. For a summary of evidence for Selket (who originated in the delta, probably at Kedem), see F. von Känel, "Selqet," *LÄ* 5: 830–33; also idem, "La nèpe et le scorpion, une monographie sur la déesse Serket" (thesis, University of Paris III, Sorbonne, n.d.); and Känel, *Les prêtres-ouâb de Sekhmet et les conjurateurs de Serket*, Bibliothèque de l'École des Hautes Études, Section des Sciences Religieuses 87 (Paris, 1984), 163–64 and 289–91. Although Selket is associated early on with the Nepa, or water scorpion, her name does not incorporate the land scorpion as a determinative until the Nineteeth Dynasty. From this time forward, Selket assumes the form of a scorpion goddess.

2 Along with Isis, Nephthys, and Neith; see Pyramid Texts 605a–606d; 1373–1375c; 1427c–d; 1468d–1469a. Among her later kingly functions, she assisted in the *Sed* Festival and the birth of the king; see Känel, *LÄ* 5: 832, nn. 21, 22.

3 See references in note 2, above. Here she generally served with Qebehsenuf as guardian of the intestines; see Känel, *LÄ* 5: 833, n. 20. Selket's epithet "Lady of the Beautiful House" alludes to her association with the place of embalming; see Hart, *Dictionary*, 192.

4 In the earliest versions of the Osiris myth, the young Horus miraculously defeated snakes sent against him; late tradition had him poisoned by snakes or scorpions.

5 See Pinch, *Magic*, 29–30.

6 See Jean-Claude Goyon, "Hededyt: Isis-Scorpion et Isis au scorpion en marge du papyrus de Brooklyn 47.218.50-III," *BIFAO* 78 (1978): 441, figs. 1–3; also see A. Calverley, M. Broome, and A. Gardiner, *The Temple of King Sethos I at Abydos. 4, The Second Hypostyle Hall* (London and Chicago, 1958), pl. 68, scene SE.

7 For a review of the evidence, see Dimitri Meeks, "Hededet," *LÄ* 2: 1076–78. As Jean-Claude Goyon argues, the cult of Isis-Hededet may be traced back historically to at least the Middle Kingdom; see Goyon, *BIFAO* 78 (1978): 446. For the earliest attestations of the name in the Coffin Texts, see Meeks, *LÄ* 2: 1077, nn. 1–4; as Meeks notes, Hededet is not associated here with the scorpion.

8 The clergy of Isis-Hededet is attested at Edfu beginning in the Saitic Dynasty; ibid., 1077, n. 12. Hededet, who is assigned the epithet "brilliant," shared solar iconography with Isis. Outside of Edfu, Hededet was worshipped at Sais, where she formed the counterpart to the local Selket. For an examination of Isis as Scorpion goddess, see Goyon, *BIFAO* 78 (1978): 439–57.

9 See Meeks, *LÄ* 2: 1076–77 and references. At Edfu, she appears under the name "Isis Who Is Hededet in Edfu." Isis-Hededet served as a protective deity not only for Horus but for Osiris as well; see Goyon, *BIFAO* 78 (1978): 451.

10 Both Selket and Hededet were identified with Isis in Ptolemaic Period cult centers, such as Edfu and Dendera. For the association of Isis and Selket, see Känel, *LÄ* 5: 832, n. 27. For the interrelationship of Selket and Hededet, see Meeks, *LÄ* 2: 1077.

11 For a comparable seated figure in green porphyry of Hededet or Isis-Scorpion in suckling pose with two scorpions on her head, see Fazzini, *Egypt*, 12, 33, and pl. 23; and S. Schoske and D. Wildung, *Gott und Götter im Alten Ägypten* (Mainz, 1992), no. 38.

61 Statuette of the goddess Mut

1 See, e.g., O. Goelet, "Nudity in Ancient Egypt," *Source Notes in the History of Art* 12, no. 2 (1993): 20–31; G. Robins, "Problems in Interpreting Egyptian Art," *DiE* 17 (1990): 45–47.

2 Here and in the bust of Mut (cat. no. 47), Mut does not wear the vulture headdress. Mut sometimes has been erroneously called a vulture goddess, in part because she is often shown wearing the vulture headdress (hardly original to her) and in part because her name, which probably means "mother," is written with a vulture hieroglyph, the phonetic sign used for the word "mother": H. te Velde, "Towards a Minimal Definition of the Goddess Mut," *JEOL* 26 (1979–80): 4.

3 For a seemingly unique and unexplained image of a God's Wife and Divine Adoratrice of Amen wearing two double crowns, see G. Legrain, "Le temple et les chapelles d'Osiris à Karnak: Le temple d'Osiris-Hiq-Djeto," *RecTrav* 22 (1900): 131 (with sketch). This scene is one of the chapel's three Dynasty 23 reliefs of Shepenwepet I being suckled by a goddess (an element of iconography long known for kings but not for queens) that foreshadow the image of a Sudanese queen being suckled by a goddess (cat. no. 51): e.g., Fazzini, *Egypt*, 20–21. For a reference to a royal High Priest of Dynasty 22 being suckled by a goddess, see R. Caminos, *The Chronicles of Prince Osorkon*, Analecta Orientalia 37 (1958): 19.

4 E.g., the image of Sekhmet wearing the double crown on a Memphite relief of the reign of King Siamun in Dynasty 21: W.M.F. Petrie, *The Palace of Apries (Memphis II)*, *BSAE* 15 (1909): pl. 19, where only the back of Sekhmet's crown is visible at the far left of the photograph; a number of Third Intermediate Period amulets with leonine-headed goddesses normally identified as Sekhmet or Bastet (e.g., Quirke, *Religion*, 32, fig. 16). For some Ptolemaic–Roman Period examples, see M.T. Derchain-Urtel, *Synkretismus in ägyptischen Ikonographie: Die Göttin Tjenenent*, GOF 4, Aegypten, vol. 8 (Wiesbaden, 1979), 54–63; and S. Cauville, "Les statues cultuelles de Dendera d'après les inscriptions pariétales," *BIFAO* 87 (1987): 89 and pls. 18–19.

5 H. te Velde, "Mut and Other Ancient Egyptian Goddesses," in Jacqueline Phillips (ed.), *Ancient Egypt, the Aegean and the Near East: Studies in Honor of Martha Rhoads Bell* (San Antonio, 1996). The writer is grateful to Herman te Velde for furnishing him with a copy of this manuscript.

6 J. Yoyotte, "Hera d'Héliopolis et le sacrifice humain," *Annuaire. Ecole Pratique des Hautes Etudes. Ve Section—Sciences religieuses* 89 (Paris, 1980–81), 29–102. For some other destructive aspects of Mut, see, e.g., A. Leahy, "Death by Fire in Ancient Egypt," *JESHO* 27 (1984): 196–206.

7 For a popular article on the precinct and recent work there, see R. Fazzini and W. Peck, "Excavating at the Temple of Mut," *Archaeology* 36 (1983): 16–23.

8 G. Martin et al., *The Tomb of Ḥetepka and Other Reliefs and Inscriptions from the Sacred Animal Necropolis, North Saqqara, 1964–1973*, Egypt Exploration Society. Texts from Excavations, Fourth Memoir (London, 1979), 64, no. 227, and pl. 54 (drawing of text on back pillar). The writer thanks Patricia Spencer, Secretary of the Egypt Exploration Society, for furnishing him with photographs of this statuette.

9 Niche stela, Cairo, Egyptian Museum JE 36728: P. Vernus, "Inscriptions de la Troisième Période Intermédiaire (III)," *BIFAO* 76 (1976): 3–15 and pls. 5–6; pair statue, Paris, Louvre A89: B.V. Bothmer, "Apotheosis in Late Egyptian Sculpture," *Kêmi* 20 (1970): 44, no. 10 and pls. 11, 18, which, however, barely show the female half of the pair. Bothmer's publication includes a reference to C. Boreaux, *Musée du Louvre. Antiquités égyptiennes, Catalogue-Guide* (Paris, 1932), 463–64, who described the figure of the woman as Old Kingdom in style.

10 R. Fazzini, "Several Objects and Some Aspects of the Art of the Third Intermediate Period," in T.G.H. James (ed.), *Chief of Seers. Some Studies in Memory of Cyril Aldred* (London, forthcoming). On archaizing, see two recent studies and their references to earlier literature: Manuelian, *Living in the Past;* and S. Neureiter, "Eine neue Interpretation des Archaismus," *SAK* 21 (1994): 219–54. In R. Fazzini et al., *Neferut net Kemit*, no. 60, R. Bianchi characterized Brooklyn's Mut statuette as displaying a restrained version of an often-postulated Nubian tradition of the full-figured woman. For the present writer, however, certain aspects of that figure are archaizingly Egyptian in origin. Moreover, no likely link to a Nubian influence can be traced for a different female full-figured style that began sometime in Dynasty 21 (e.g., A. Piankhoff and N. Rambova, *Mythological Papyri* [New York, 1957], pls. 1–2: papyri of Herubekhet) and is known in Dynasty 22 in both Theban art (e.g., cat. no. 87 and Munro, *Totenstelen*, 8 and pl. 1, 1–2) and Lower Egyptian art (e.g., T.G.H. James, *Ancient Egypt*, 31, fig. 15, a temple relief of Queen Karamama).

11 For references to Mut in numerous guises, including as *uraeus*, see H.M. Stewart, "A Crossword Hymn to Mut," *JEA* 57 (1971): 87–104. A Dynasty 18 image of a cobra normally identified as the goddess Renenutet could be an image of Mut (Cairo, Egyptian Museum CG 935: PM 2^2: 262). For the feline and leonine aspects of Mut, see H. te Velde, "The Cat as Sacred Animal of the Goddess Mut," in *Studies in Egyptian Religion Dedicated to Professor Jan Zandee = Studies in the History of Religions* 43 (Leiden, 1982), 127–37. Equally relevant here is H. te Velde, "Mut, the Eye of Re," *BSAK* 3 (1988): 395–403.

62 Votive stela with Taweret and Mut

1 MMA accession card, 47.105.4; see also L. Keimer in *BiOr* 6, no. 5 (1949): 138. This stela is mentioned by R. Gundlach, "Thoeris," *LÄ* 6: 497.

2 Restored as "Sculptor" by Hayes, *Scepter*, 2: 386.

3 The precinct of Mut at Karnak; for the dating of this precinct, see Fazzini's comments in cat. no. 65. Some see in the face of Mut a likeness to Queen Tiye, wife of Amenhotep III; see Kozloff, in *Egypt's Dazzling Sun*, 403.

4 Andrews, *Amulets*, 40–41.

5 But see Hart, *Dictionary*, 212, where he refers to Ipet as the antecedent of Taweret.

6 Anna Maria Donadoni-Roveri, "Fouilles dans le Musée de Turin: Une statuette de Tiyi-Toueris, des cartons de tissage copte," *Acts, First International Congress of Egyptology, Cairo, October 2–10, 1976*, ed. Walter F. Reineke (Schriften zur Geschichte und Kultur des Alten Orients, no. 14; Berlin, 1979), 181–85; Hayes, *Scepter*, 2: 385–86; Kozloff, in *Egypt's Dazzling Sun*, 403.

7 R.A. Fazzini notes that Mut does sometimes appear with the hippopotamus goddess Ipet (personal correspondence, Aug. 12, 1996).

8 Ibid., 182; and Dimitri Meeks, "Ipet," *LÄ* 3: 174.

9 Hayes, *Scepter*, 2: 385.

10 For examples of these medical remedies in English translation, see Ebbell, *Papyrus Ebers*, 111–12.

11 Manniche, *Herbal*, 65–67.

12 Watterson, *Women*, 84–85, and 187, n. 26, cites estimates of deaths of newly delivered mothers—twenty-five maternal deaths for every one thousand births—based on calculations from sixteenth-through eighteenth-century England.

13 See cat. no. 25; and L. Keimer's review of Winlock, *Three Egyptian Princesses*, in *BiOr* 6, no. 5 (1949): 138 and n. 8.

14 John M. Riddle, *Contraception and Abortion from the Ancient World to the Renaissance* (Cambridge [Mass.] and London, 1992), 69–70. Riddle also cites evidence that ingesting acacia seeds or leaves reduced pregnancies in mice and rats from 87.5 to 100 percent.

15 Acknowledgments to James P. Allen, Associate Curator of Egyptian Art, Metropolitan Museum of Art, for his reading of this inscription.

16 Hayes, *Scepter*, 2: 386.

17 The traces of the hieroglyphs at the damaged proper right side of the inscription should be restored as Gardiner's Sign List M27, rather than Gardiner's Sign List D40. The fronds extending from the lower left side of the sedge-plant hieroglyph are clearly discernible upon examination of the stela's inscription. The partially preserved hieroglyph at the proper left end of the inscription should be restored as a seated woman determinative (Gardiner's Sign List B1) with the addition of a flower or scepter in the hand.

18 For several instances of the name "Khonsu" for females, see Ranke, *Personennamen*, 1: 270, no. 16.

63 a Statue of Taweret

63 b Statuette of Ipet/Taweret

1 For a recent discussion of Taweret and her protection of royals and commoners alike, see Gay Robins, "Women and Children in Peril: Pregnancy, Birth and Infant Mortality in Ancient Egypt," *KMT* 5, no. 4 (1994–95): 29–32.

2 For an interesting occurrence of the head of a hippopotamus written inside the *hwt*-sign, see F. Legge, "The Magic Ivories of the Middle Empire, Part II," *PSBA* (Dec., 1905): 298, pl. 1.

3 Robins, *KMT* 5, no. 4 (1994–95): 24–35; and Andrews, *Amulets*, 40–41.

4 Pinch, *Votive Offerings*, 351, and references therein.

5 If these elements of the headdress were originally present in another material, the attachment must have fit over and around the *modius* and *uraeus*, for no insertion hole is present in the top of the headdress.

6 Steindorff, *Catalogue*, 141, n. 1.

7 Anna Maria Donadoni-Roveri, "Fouilles dans le Musée de Turin: Une statuette de Tiyi-Toueris, des cartons de tissage copte," *Acts, First International Congress of Egyptology, Cairo, October 2–10, 1976*, ed. Walter F. Reineke (Schriften zur Geschichte und Kultur des Alten Orients, no. 14; Berlin, 1979), 181–85; and Dimitri Meeks, "Ipet," *LÄ* 3: 174.

8 Mercer, *Pyramid Texts* 1: 91, no. 381a; 2: 176.

9 The figure of Ipet may have represented the constellation Draco; see *Egypt's Dazzling Sun*, 403.

10 E. Hornung, *The Tomb of Seti I* (Zurich and Munich, 1919), 172–77, pls. 160, 161.

11 Ibid.

12 Pinch, *Magic*, 162.

13 See, for example, Barry J. Kemp, "Wall Paintings from the Workmen's Village at El-'Amarna," *JEA* 65 (1979): 47–48, fig. 1.

14 H.S. Baker, *Furniture in the Ancient World: Origins and Evolution 3100–475 B.C.* (London, 1966), 65, fig. 70; 67, fig. 72.

15 Pinch, *Votive Offerings*, 302, 313, 318.

16 For other examples of votive female figurines, see ibid., 127, 208, 217.

17 *Egypt's Dazzling Sun*, 402–3, no. 105, and fig. 105b.

18 Pinch, *Magic*, 162.

64 Standing figures of Neith

1 On a late Predynastic vase from Diaspolis Parva, the goddess's standard bears this symbol; see S.T. Hollis, "Five Egyptian Goddesses in the Third Millennium B.C.," *KMT* 5, no. 4 (1994–95): 47 (illus. from Petrie, *Diaspolis Parva*, pl. 20, 11). The crossed arrow-and-shield symbol as well as the sign of two bows bound in a package served to identify her; the latter made up the hieroglyph of her name. Her later epithets—"Mistress of the Bow . . . Ruler of Arrows"—further underscore her combative aspect as a huntress.

2 For the Nag ed-Deir amulet and an Old Kingdom woman's necklace of coleoptera-shaped pendents, see Wilkinson, *Jewellery*, 14–15, with fig. 5, and p. 26, with fig. 17; also Andrews, *Jewellery*, 175–76, with fig. 162. For Neith and the coleoptera, see El-Sayed, *Neith*, 1: 23–24; and 2: 226–27 (Doc. 75).

3 Cf. an ebony tablet with *serekh* of the First Dynasty King Aha; and an engraved diorite vase of *Nynetjer* of the early Second Dynasty; see Hollis, *KMT* 5, no. 4 (1994–95): 47–48. See also El-Sayed, *Neith*, 2: 225–26 (Doc. 73) and pl. 1 (Aha tablet); and 227 (Doc. 76) and pl. 2 (*Nynetjer* vase).

4 As Hollis (ibid., 46) observes, nearly 40 percent of such theophoric names relate to Neith; see Kaplony, *Inschriften* (Wiesbaden, 1963). Also see El-Sayed, *Neith*, 1: 183–84; and 2: 209–38.

5 See essay by Betsy Bryan in this volume for a more in-depth discussion of these two First Dynasty queens.

6 Hollis, *KMT* 5, no. 4 (1994–95): 48; see also essay by Bryan in this volume.

7 Hollis, *KMT* 5, no. 4 (1994–95): 49; and El-Sayed, *Neith*, 2: 266 (Doc. 191) and pl. 4. Attention may also be drawn to Queen Neith of Dynasty 6: see Troy, *Patterns of Queenship*, 156, no. 6.9.

8 See note 3, above.

9 A head from the sun temple of Userkaf at Abu Ghurob has often been cited as early evidence for Neith's association with the Red Crown; see El-Sayed, *Neith*, 1: 92–93; and 2: 262–63 (Doc. 183). This interpretation, however, has not been universally accepted. For evidence in the Old Kingdom linking Sais with the Red Crown, see ibid.

10 For the epithet, see El-Sayed, *Neith*, 1: 60; and Westendorf in *LÄ* 2: 634. An allusion to Neith as "Father and Mother of the Gods" already occurs in Dynasty 19 (ibid., 2: Doc. 389b).

11 For a listing of Late Period texts presenting Neith as creatress, see El-Sayed, *Neith*, 1: 57. For a discussion of Neith as demiurge, see ibid., 61–65; for Neith's association with the Nile's floodwaters, see ibid., 58 (Coffin Texts).

12 Neith is already attested as mother of Sobek in the Old Kingdom *Pyramid Texts* (Pyramid 510a); see El-Sayed, *Neith*, 1: 52, 270 (Doc. 197). In the Ramesside period, she appears as a woman with the head of a crocodile; see El-Sayed, *Neith*, 2: 360 (Doc. 351). Neith's association with Mehet-weret is well attested in the Middle Kingdom Coffin Texts and in documents of the Ptolemaic and Roman Periods; see ibid., 53–57.

13 See essay by Catharine Roehrig in this volume. As the mythical inventor of weaving, Neith was linked with mummy bandages; see El-Sayed, *Neith*, 1: 76–80.

14 For Neith's association with Hathor, see El-Sayed, *Neith*, 1: 142–43.

15 An early anthropomorphic depiction may be found on an engraved diorite vase of Nynetjer; there she wears a double bow on her head and carries the *was* scepter. For Neith's aspect as primordial cow, see El-Sayed, *Neith*, 1: 51, 53, 60–61. For a review of the iconography of the goddess, ibid., 3–12.

16 The scrolling frontal element of the crown is lost on both examples.

17 For standing figures of Neith, see Roeder, *Aegyptische Bronzefiguren*, 217–21; for seated and squatting bronze figurines of the goddess, see ibid., 221–22.

18 For a statuette with a movable *ankh* amulet in this hand, see J. Capart, *Worcester Art Museum Annual* 1 (1935–36): 20 and fig. 2.

19 For a seated figure in Berlin with similar inlaid gold *usekh* and crown with inlaid gold vertical stripes, see Wenig, *Woman*, no. 90.

20 For similar dedicatory inscriptions, see Capart, *Worcester Art Museum Journal* 1 (1935–36): 20–22.

65 Bust from a statue of the goddess Sekhmet

1 For some of Amenhotep III's statues of deities, see Bryan, in *Egypt's Dazzling Sun*, 125–84, 215–18.

2 E.g., PM 2^2: 12, 80, 201, 245, 257–60, 262–68, 271, 275, 289–90, 334, 338, 443, 451–52, 485, 526, 535; J. Yoyotte, "Une monumentale litanie de granit: Les Sekhmet d'Aménophis III et la conjuration permanente de la déesse dangereuse," *BSFE* 87–88 (1980): 46–75. Although not all Sekhmet statues had their final surface carving, much less a final polishing or inscription, most of the seated

statues at least are certainly (or most probably) of the reign of Amenhotep III, whose inscriptions are the earliest on any of the statues. Kozloff, in *Egypt's Dazzling Sun,* 226, suggests that the standing Sekhmets may date to Dynasty 26, but even if some may be later than Amenhotep III's reign, others are dated to his era by inscription; see G. Haeny, in H. Ricke, L. Habachi, and G. Haeny, *Untersuchungen im Totentempel Amenophis III.* Beiträge Bf 11 (Wiesbaden, 1981), 98–99 and pls. 21, 34–35.

3 In the temple of Mut is a significantly larger and often illustrated seated statue of Sekhmet crowned with a circlet of *uraei:* e.g., J. Yoyotte, *BFSE* 87–88 (1980): 46, fig. 1 (H: 275 cm). Also in the Mut Temple are parts of at least one other colossal statue of Sekhmet; its epithet connects her with Ptah, whose consort she had become at Memphis and Thebes. For a nearly four-foot-tall head crowned with sun disc and *uraeus* from a fourteen- to sixteen-foot-tall Sekhmet, see M. Benson and J. Gourlay, *The Temple of Mut in Asher* (London, 1899), 37–38, and pl. 10 opposite p. 122.

4 *Egypt's Dazzling Sun,* 226.

5 Ibid., 36, fig. 2,2.

6 Although they were surely incorrect in believing that Amenhotep III's statues of Sekhmet were once entirely painted, Benson and Gourlay were correct in noting that certain details were painted; *Temple of Mut,* 29, 33.

7 For Sekhmet's epithets, especially on the statues of Amenhotep III's reign, see, e.g., the works cited in PM 2^2: 262–63; Hoenes, *Sachmet,* 232–42; Yoyotte, *BFSE* 87–88 (1980): 46–75; G. Haeny, in *Untersuchungen,* 90–99 and pls. 22, 34, 35; Germond, *Sekhmet,* 387–90, 414–17; and R. Fazzini and W. Peck, "The 1982 Season at Mut," *NARCE* 120 (Winter, 1982): 40, 52.

8 E.g., Eggebrecht, in *Nofret—di Schöne,* no. 138; Grimal, *History,* 225.

9 For Sekhmet and her emissaries and the physician-priests of Sekhmet, see, e.g., Hoenes, *Sachmet,* 35–53; Germond, *Sekhmet,* 286–309; F. von Känel, *Les prêtres-ouâb de Sekhmet et les conjurateurs de Serket,* Bibliothèque de l'Ecole des Hautes Etudes. Section des Sciences Religieuses 87 (Paris, 1984), 1–160, 235–305.

10 Grimal, *History,* 225.

11 Quirke, *Religion,* 31.

12 Yoyotte, *BFSE* 87–88 (1980): passim; the quotation is from p. 52.

13 E.g., ibid., 49–51.

14 Cairo, Egyptian Museum CG 648: PM 2^2: 261. Cf. H. te Velde, "Mut, the Eye of Re," *BSAK* 3 (1988): 395–403, where he cites (pp. 397–98) this statue's inscription as part of the evidence that the cult of Mut at South Karnak was associated with the ideological complex of *uraeus,* lion, eye, and crowns relevant to many goddesses.

15 E.g., ibid., 397, 400.

16 On Isheru lakes, see Gessler-Löhr, *Die heiligen Seen ägyptischer Tempel: Ein Beiträg zur Deutung sakraler Baukunst im alten Ägypten,* HÄB 21 (1983): 401–24, with references to the earlier and important discussions by J. Yoyotte in *RdE* 14 (1962): 101–10, and S. Sauneron in *BIFAO* 62 (1964): 50–57. As Gessler-Löhr notes (p. 401), the enclosing form for Isherus is certain only for the temple of Mut at Karnak and the temple of Bastet at Bubastis. For a reconstruction of the latter, see Arnold, *Lexikon,* 44. Because these lakes could be associated with the primordial ocean called Nun, the temples rising from them on mounds were also dramatic symbols of creation and ongoing re-creation.

17 H. te Velde, *BSAK* 3 (1988): 400, states that Mut was not called "Eye of Ra" until Ramesside times. However, he has since kindly informed me of a recent publication of a late–Dynasty 18 image of Mut labeled "Eye of Ra": The Epigraphic Survey, *Reliefs and Inscriptions at Luxor Temple.* I: *The Festival Processsion of Opet in the Colonnade Hall,* OIP 112 (Chicago, 1994), pl. 119.

18 Ibid., 400–401.

19 H. te Velde, "The Cat as Sacred Animal of the Goddess Mut," *Studies in the History of Religions (Supplements to Numen)* 43 (Leiden, 1982), 127–37. For a Late Period bronze cat inscribed with invocations to both Mut and Bastet, see H. Schlögl, *Archäologische Sammlung der Universität Zurich. Stiftung Koradi/Berger* (Zurich, 1989), 14–15, 66–67. Cats can be adept at fighting snakes, and, as te Velde notes, the Eye and Daughter of Ra can also appear as a cat to help defeat the enemies of Ra who appear as serpents.

20 Te Velde, *BSAK* 3 (1988): 401–3, where he also notes texts referring to music, dancing, eating, and drinking at the site every day. For other comments on this and other texts of the gateway relating to appeasement through music and dance, see S. Sauneron et al., *La porte ptolémaïque de l'enceinte de Mout à Karnak, MIFAO* 107 (1983): 20 (part of a reprint of an article by S. Sauneron that appeared in *BIE* 45 for 1963–64). Playing sistra became part of the cults of some gods as well because goddesses were not the only divine powers who could be dangerous: cf. Robins, *Women,* 18.

21 Te Velde, *BSAK* 3 (1988): 401–2, with reference to a translation and commentary on these texts: J. van Dijk, "Hymnen uit het dagelijks tempelritueel voor de Egyptische godin Moet," in K. Veenhof, ed., *Schrijvend Verleden = MVEOL* 24 (Leiden-Sutphen, 1983), 233–46.

22 *Sḫm.t dmḏ.t m Mwt,* which may distinguish this union from Sekhmet's other syncretizations with other goddesses on these statues, written with the simple juxtaposition of two divine names.

23 Sauneron et al., in *MIFAO* 107 (1983): 21.

24 Te Velde, in *Studies in the History of Religions* 43: 137.

66 Aegis and *menat* with head of lion-headed goddess

1 For an examination of the aegis, see Bonnet, *Reallexikon,* 8–9.

2 C.R. Clark, "An Egyptian Bronze Aegis," *BMMA* 12, no. 3 (1953): 78–80; D. Dunham, "An Egyptian Bronze Aegis," *BMFA* 29, no. 176 (1931): 104–9.

3 See E. Staehelin, "Menit," *LÄ* 4: 52–54.

4 See Germond, *Sekhmet,* 323–27.

5 Numerous bronze *menat* counterpoises also bear dual male and female heads, which have been traditionally identified as Shu and Tefnut; for examples, see J.-L. Chappaz, "Un contrepoids de collier 'Menat' au Musée d'art et d'histoire," *Genava* 31 (1983): 9–13; and Roeder, *Aegpytische Bronzefiguren,* 468–69, figs. 709–12. Gods can also be associated with the aegis; see Andrews, *Amulets,* pl. 40, b); and J. Quaegebeur, "Apis et la Menat," *BSFE* 98 (1983): 17–39.

6 Her identity is not certain; other alternatives may include Bastet or Mut. In this regard, it may be noted that the lion-headed aegis was closely associated with the cult of Bastet, in which it served to appease the violent side of the goddess; see Germond, *Sekhmet,* 326–27; see also cat. no. 65.

7 For Sekhmet's protective nature, see ibid.

8 At 7 cm, it is substantially larger than similar gold and silver amulets, which are normally 3 cm or less in height. A comparably sized example in gold or electrum in the Louvre is inscribed for Osorkon IV, furnishing a probable indication of date for the present example; see J. Berlandini, "Petits monuments royaux de la XXIe à la XXVe dynastie," in J. Vercoutter, ed., *Hommages à Serge Sauneron,* 1, *Égypte pharaonique* (Cairo, 1979), 98–101 and pl. 16. For smaller silver amulets of this variety, see cat. no. 20; and Andrews, *Amulets,* pl. 40 b,e.

9 See Canby (*Jewelry,* 22) for the suggestion that it was designed as an object to be placed in the hand of a cult statue of the goddess. Extant large-scale bronze inlaid aegises with hinged counterpoises from the Third Intermediate and Late Periods may have been used as cult objects; see note 2, above. Most examples are surmounted by the fully human head of the goddess Isis-Hathor; see Clark, *BMMA* 12, no. 3 (1953): 80, for the suggestion that these may have been carried by female members of the royal family in ceremonies connected with the worship of Isis-Hathor; see Germond, *Sekhmet,* 326, n. 2, for the suggestion that Hathor here represents Sekhmet appeased.

67 Statuette of lion-headed goddess

1 On such "mixed-form" images of deities, see, e.g., Hornung, *Conceptions of God,* 109–25.

2 E.g., Fakhry, *Monuments of Sneferu,* 126–27, with fig. 141 and frontispiece; and Hoenes, *Sachmet,* 20–23, with fig. 21. On the reconstruction of the latter relief's text, see H. Sternberg, "Sachmet," *LÄ* 5: n. 37 on 330–31.

3 E.g., an early Dynasty 22 bronze of Mut who once had a figure of Khonsu on her lap: M. Jørgensen, "En aegyptisk bronzefigur," *Meddelelser fra Ny Carlsberg Glyptotek* 49 (1993): 85–94 (with English summary). This is one of the earliest-known three-dimensional images of an enthroned goddess with a divine child rather than a child-king on her lap; possibly it predates the figure of Isis and Horus (not in bronze) published by M. Müller in "Zwei Bildwerke aus der Dritten Zwischenzeit," *BSEG* 9–10 (1984–85): 199–222.

4 For Third Intermediate Period bronzes, most of which are of humans, see C. Ziegler, "Les arts du métal à la Troisième Période Intermédiaire," in *Tanis,* 85–101. For Dynasty 25 royal bronzes, see Russmann, *Representation.* For Egyptian bronzes in general, see Roeder, *Aegyptische Bronzefiguren.*

5 Egyptologists do not agree whether the ruff is that of a lion (e.g., E. Varin, "A propos d'une figurine de bronze léontocéphale au Musée d'Art et d'Histoire de Genève," *BSEG* 14 [1990]: 81–82) or a lioness (e.g., Kozloff, in *Egypt's Dazzling Sun,* 225), even when it appears on statues of goddesses, including Sekhmet (cat. no. 65), or on bronzes such as this.

6 M. Malaise, "Histoire et signification de la coiffure Hathorique à plumes," *SAK* 4 (1976): 215–36; J. Quaegebeur, "Reines ptolémaïques et traditions égyptiennes," in H. Maehler and V. Strocka, eds., *Das ptolemaïsche Ägypten: Akten des internationalen Symposions 27–29. September 1976 in Berlin* (Mainz am Rhein, 1978), 245–62. For this headgear worn by the Divine Adoratrices of Amen, see J. Leclant, *Recherches sur les monuments thébains de la XXVe dynastie dite éthiopienne,* BdE 36 (1965), 355: To the monuments he cites, add a statue of Amenirdas I in the British Museum: Robins, *Women,* 114, fig. 43.

7 Kindly provided by A. Capel.

8 Translated from C. Traunecker, *Que sais-je? Les dieux de l'Egypte* (Paris, 1992), 55. For the almost forty goddess with leonine associations, see C. de Wit, *Le rôle et le sens du lion dans l'Egypte ancienne* (Leiden, 1951), 285–368. They are Bastet, Matit, Mehit, Hathor, Shesemtet, Sekhmet, Neseret, Tenenet, Tefnut, Wepset, Sebeqet, Sementet, Tasentnefret, Djedet, Werethekaw, Pakhet, Nekhbet, Taweret, Isis, Wadjet, Mut, Menhit, Mentet, Merseger, Ipet, Wenut, Menat, Mehenet, Nebetuu, Repit, Renenutet, the lioness of Athribis, and some foreign goddesses venerated in Egypt, most notably Qadesh and Astarte.

9 Saleh and Sourouzian, *Egyptian Museum,* no. 254.

10 The attribution of most such bronzes to Wadjet is owed originally to B.V. Bothmer, who believed that all such bronzes could be so identified and considered the Mut figure's text a "scribal error": "Statuettes of *W3ḏ.t* as Ichneumon Coffins," *JNES* 8 (1949): 121–23.

11 J. Vandier, "Ouadjet et l'Horus léontocéphale de Bouto: A propos d'un bronze du Musée de Chaalis," *MonPiot* 55 (1967): 7–75, esp. p. 58; T.G.H. James, "A Wooden Figure of Wadjet with Two Painted Representations of Amasis," *JEA* 68 (1982): 156–65, esp. pp. 159–60. James adds to Vandier's discussion the suggestion that Sekhmet may be the source common to representations of many leonine-headed goddesses and cites J. Yoyotte's 1980 study of Sekhmet statues (see cat. no. 65), which deals in part with "the diffusion of the conception of the 'dangerous goddess' in the theology of the Late Period."

12 For an English summary of these myths, see Pinch, *Votive Offerings,* 191–92.

13 Bothmer, *JNES* 8 (1949): 121–23.

14 Vandier, *MonPiot* 55 (1967): 53–59; James, *JEA* 68 (1982): 160; H.-W. Fischer-Elfert, "Uto," in *LÄ* 6: 906–11; and R. Parkinson and S. Quirke, "An Egyptian Bronze Figure: The Goddess Wadjyt from the King Bequest," *Annual Review: National Art Collections Fund. Annual Reports and Accounts for the Year Ended 31st December 1992,* 52–56. As Parkinson and Quirke note (p. 55), related bronzes of Wadjet have been found at a number of sites, including Bubastis, the reported provenance of this figure.

68 a Bastet cat

68 b Standing figure of Bastet

1 The cat is generally thought to have been domesticated in Egypt in the period between the Old and Middle Kingdoms. Cf. Malek, *Cat,* 56–57; but see reservations expressed by Strouhal, *Life,* 114. There were two indigenous feline species: the jungle cat *(Felis chaus)* and the African wild cat *(Felis silvestris libyca).* As Strouhal notes, the cat's popularity as a house pet probably arose from its ability to rid the house of rodents and vermin (ibid.). The Egyptian onomatopoeic word for cat *(miw)* is first clearly attested on an Old Kingdom inscription, which mentions a lady named *Miw-t* (Ranke, *Personennamen,* 1: 420, 19). For recent studies on the Egyptian cat, see Malek, *Cat;* Delvaux and Warmenbol, eds., *Les divins chats,* 1991.

2 For the possible erotic connotations of cats and kittens in ancient Egyptian art, see P. Derchain, "Symbols and Metaphors in Literature and Representations of Private Life," *Royal Anthropological Institute News* 15 (1976): 9; also Pinch, *Votive Offerings,* 193.

3 H.G. Fischer, "Marginalia," *GM* 122 (1991): 23–25.

4 Other female deities associated with the cat included Hathor and Mut (see cat. nos. 54 and 61). The male or tom cat, it may be noted, was sacred to the sun god Ra.

5 The Egyptian name of her city, Bast, means "the Place of Ointment," which has led to speculation that Bastet may originally have been an ointment goddess. Indeed, the name of Bastet, as that of her city, is written with the hieroglyphic sign representing an ointment jar; see H. Kees, *Der Gotterlaube im alten Aegypten* (Leipzig, 1941), 3. For an overview of the goddess, see E. Otto, "Bastet," *LÄ* 1: 628–30.

6 The goddess's name and reference to her priest are first attested on stone vessels of Hetepekhemy at Saqqara. See N.E. Scott, "The Cat of Bastet," *BMMA* 17, no. 2 (1958): 3.

7 In his cartouche, King Osaorkon II calls himself "the son of Bastet." For Bubastis and the Libyan dynasts, see Kitchen, *Third Intermediate Period,* 303–4, 351.

8 Scott, *BMMA* 17:2 (1958), 6.

9 See Pinch, *Votive Offerings,* 192–93 for Sekhmet and Bastet as polar expressions (fierce and gentle) of a single deity, here called "the Distant Goddess." The close interrelationship of the two goddesses is evidenced by the fact that both deities shared the same consort (Ptah) and son (Nefertum). Indeed, the two were often paired or referenced together in ancient inscriptions and texts.

10 See H. Junker, *Der Auszug der Hathor-Tefnut aus Nubien* (Berlin, 1911), 32.

11 Herodotus II, 67.

12 For ornate examples of the seated cat, see Quirke, *Religion,* 33; and Shaw and Nicholson, *Dictionary,* 62. As Scott *(BMMA* 17, no. 2 [1958]: 3) notes, the sacred animals of Bastet may have been selected for their special markings, which may have included a scarab-shaped spot between the ears (the presence of the scarab associated the cat with the solar realm). See N. Langston and B. Langston, *The Cat in Ancient Egypt* (Cambridge, England, 1940), 54. In this context, attention may be drawn to the *maat* pattern in the ears of the Detroit cat; cf. Malek, *Cat,* 91.

13 For life-sized cat coffins in bronze and wood, respectively, see N. Scott, "Bastet," 1–7; E. Riefstahl, "A Sacred Cat," *BMB* 12, no. 2 (1952): 1–15; and *Mummies and Magic,* no. 191. The practice of interring cats in temple precincts was especially prominent in the Ptolemaic Period; the presence of a major precinct at Bubastis would suggest that the cats interred there were sacred to Bastet. It is by no means clear, however, that all cat mummies were sacred to Bastet, or that all cat burial grounds were necessarily associated with temple precincts; see discussion of Alain-Pierre Zivie in *Mummies and Magic,* 232–33. For a list of cat necropolises, see A. Charron and L. Ginsburg, in Delvaux and Warmenbol, *Les divins chats,* 137–39. Bronze cat coffins were normally hollow-cast in two pieces to facilitate insertion of the cat mummy or bones.

14 The earliest depictions of Bastet as a lion-headed woman date to the Old Kingdom; see Scott, *BMMA* 17, no. 2 (1958): 3.

15 Cf. the Morgan statuette of Bastet in the Metropolitan Museum of Art (ibid.). As Scott notes, the striped material may recall the natural markings of the animal. This patterned, fringed garment may also be of foreign, Syrian origin; see L. Delvaux, in Delvaux and Warmenbol, *Les divins chats,* 131.

16 Bronze statuettes of Bastet's female votaries are frequently equipped with the same two implements. Cf. a statuette in Brooklyn; Riefstahl, *BMB* 12, no. 2 (1952): 11, fig. 9; also J. Quaegebeur, "Apis et la menat," *BSFE* 98 (1983): 17–39. Both the votary and the goddess may additionally carry the figures of Horus or the lotus god Nefertum, Bastet's son; see Riefstahl, *BMB* 12, no. 2 (1952): 11, figs. 9, 10.

17 For Bastet's association with Hathor, see Scott, *BMMA* 17, no. 2 (1958): 5; for Bastet as the pacified manifestation of a violent goddess, see H. te Velde, "The Cat as Sacred Animal of the Goddess Mut," in M. Heerma von Voss, E.J. Sharpe, and R.J.Z. Werblowsky (eds.), *Studies in Egyptian Religion Dedicated to Professor Jan Zandee* (Leiden, 1982), 129–37. For the sistrum as reference to Bastet's fearsome aspect, see Andrews, *Amulets,* 34. Reclining cats are often depicted on Hathoric sistra; see cat. no. 35b.

18 See Andrews, *Amulets,* 32; Scott, *BMFA* 17, no. 2 (1958): 8.

19 Andrews, *Amulets,* 32 and fig. 29 c, d; for votive bronzes depicting a cat with kittens in Brooklyn and London, respectively, see Riefstahl, *BMB* 12, no. 2 (1952): 6, fig. 5; and Shaw and Nicholson, *Dictionary,* 50 (illus.).

69 Maat

1 Although Maat is widely represented in the sanctuaries of other deities, only one temple dedicated to the goddess herself has survived—at Karnak in the precinct of Montu (PM 2^2: 11–13). On the goddess, see W. Helck, "Maat," *LÄ* 3: 1110–19.

2 See Grimal, *History,* 47. Alternately, rather than as an active force, Maat may be seen as the embodiment of a prearranged divine plan that ensured the harmonious coexistence of the universe's constituent parts; see S. Sauneron, "Maat," in Georges Posener et al., *A Dictionary of Egyptian Civilization,* trans. Alix MacFarlane (London, 1959), 155.

3 In a similar vein, it was through his responsibility to Maat that the vizier, who controlled the law courts of Egypt, served as supreme judge. The vizier, in fact, held the honorary title of "Priest of Maat"; see Helck, *Beamtentitel* 74, n. 53. For Late Period depictions of a vizier wearing a necklace with a pendent of Maat, see B. Grdseloff, "L'insigne du grand juge égyptien," *ASAE* 40 (1940): 185–202.

4 From the literary composition titled "King as Priest of the Sun," see J. Assmann, "Der König als Sonnenpriester," *ADAIK* 7 (1970). The English translation is taken from Quirke, *Religion,* 38.

5 In this capacity, she sometimes stands behind the king with wings outstretched in a protective embrace. This pose is also assumed by other goddesses; cf. cat. no. 57.

6 Emily Teeter, "The Presentation of Maat: the Iconography and Theology of an Ancient Egyptian Offering Ritual," (Ph.D. dissertation, University of Chicago, 1990). The divine recipient may vary, depending upon the context.

7 Grimal, *History,* 222; see also Troy, *Patterns of Queenship,* fig. 34 (tomb of Kheruef).

8 See Hayes, *Scepter,* 2: 97.

9 S. Tawfik, "Aton Studies," *MDAIK* 29 (1973): 85–86 and pl. 29 b,c.

10 Robins, *Women,* 156; see J. Leclant, "Recherches sur les monuments thébains de la XXVe dynastie dite éthiopienne," *BdE* 36 (1965): pls. 9, 67 A,B.

11 For this suggestion, see Friedman, *Rhode Island School of Design. Museum Notes* 77, no. 1 (1990): 10. It should be noted, however, that none of the images of Maat in such offering scenes is depicted on such an altar-shaped base; cf. Teeter, "Presentation," 81–83.

12 For the iconography of the Hathor mask, see cat. no. 55 and Pinch, *Votive Offerings,* 138.

13 See Friedman, *Rhode Island School of Design. Museum Notes* 77, no. 1 (1990): 10.

70 Relief of the goddess Seshat

1 For an overview of Seshat, see W. Helck, "Seschat," *LÄ* 5: 884–88.

2 In this capacity, Seshat is shown recording the name while Thoth carves the years in the notched palm branch symbolizing years; see Helck, *LÄ* 5: 885 and n. 16. The identification of the *jšd* tree with the Persea remains a matter of dispute; see L. Kákosy, "Ishedbaum," *LÄ* 3: 182; and R. Germer, "Persea," *LÄ* 4: 942.

3 Priests of Seshat are attested in the delta and Memphite region; see Rossini and Schumann-Antelme, *Nétèr,* 172. Amulets depicting the goddess are very rare; see Andrews, *Amulets,* pl. 66j.

4 See R. Engelbach, "A Foundation Scene of the Second Dynasty," *JEA* 20 (1934): 183–84, pl. 24. It should be noted that Seshat already appears as a divine symbol in Dynasty 1; see Helck, *LÄ* 5: 885 and n. 9.

5 Pyramid Texts 616b; Coffin Texts VI, 410, Spell 778; see also Helck, *LÄ* 5: 886.

6 In contrast to the masculine form *sesh* ("scribe"), the female equivalent *seshet* occurs rarely as a

title and is attested only in the Middle Kingdom; see Robins, *Women,* 111–13. Moreover, as Robins observes, it is not always certain that *seshet* in this context means "female scribe."

7 Ibid., 113–14. On the question of women's literacy in ancient Egypt, see cat. no. 88.

8 This block was excavated at the pyramid temple of Senusert I at Lisht by the Egyptian Expedition of the Metropolitan Museum of Art and was originally in the collection of that museum (MMA 39.1.6).

9 See L. Borchardt, *Das Grabdenkmal des Königs Saȝhu-Re,* 2. *Die Wandbilder* (Leipzig, 1913), pl. 1; and D. Valbelle, "Les récensements dans l'Egypte pharaonique des troisième et deuxième millenaires," *CRIPEL* 9 (1987): 36, no. 7, and 37, fig. 3.

10 For the relief's inscriptions, see James, *Corpus,* 1: no. 92 and pl. 33; for Seshat's epithets, see Helck, *LÄ* 5: 885–86.

11 The origin of Seshat's headdress remain obscure; see Helck, *LÄ* 5: 884. In the present relief Seshat does not appear to be wearing the panther-skin robe.

12 For the full context of the scene, see the reconstructed reliefs of the temple of Pepy II at Saqqara: Fazzini, *Images,* cat. 36b.

71 Statuette of cobra goddess

1 For comparison, see the Eighteenth Dynasty example in the Brooklyn Museum, illustrated in *Egypt's Golden Age,* 302–3. Two serpent goddesses with human female heads were found in 1992 at Qantir in a small sanctuary. Probably dating to the Ramesside Period, the figures were identified as either Hathor or Renenutet. See J. Leclant and G. Clerc, "Fouilles et travaux en Egypte et au Soudan, 1993–1994," *Or* 64, no. 3 (1995): 242, pl. 8. The limestone figures were painted and apparently wore crowns similar to that worn by the figure in Philadelphia. For a color reproduction, see A. Eggebrecht, *Pelizaeus Museum Hildesheim: The Egyptian Collection,* transl. by R. Bianchi (Mainz: Philipp von Zabern, 1996), fig. 139.

2 For a discussion of crowns, see Abd el Monem Joussef Abubakr, *Untersuchungen über die ägyptischen Krönin* (New York, 1937), 44–45. See also comments by Saleh and Sourouzian, *Egyptian Museum,* nos. 208, 244, and 250.

3 For reliefs, see for example, Anna Maria Donadoni Roveri, ed., *Religious Beliefs* (Milan, 1988), pls. 224 and 236; see also the example in *Egypt's Golden Age,* 302. This last example and one now in the Brooklyn Museum (Bernard V. Bothmer and Jean L. Keith, *The Brooklyn Museum Guide,* no. 5 [New York, 1974], p. 44) are also cryptographic writings in three dimensions of Queen Hatshepsut's name. A large coiled snake (presumably Hathor) is also part of a royal statue of Amenhotep now in Cairo (listed N.E. 4 in Vandier, *Manuel,* 3: 309 and 629). The latter two examples are full serpents; they do not have human heads. For further information on cryptographically written names, see H.G. Fischer, *L'écriture et l'art de l'Egypte ancienne* (Paris, 1986), 39–43 and 138–39; H.G. Fischer, "Hieroglyphen," *LÄ* 2: 1196; and David P. Silverman, "Cryptographic Writing in the Tomb of Tutankhamun," *SAK* 8 (1980): 233–36.

4 For information on Meretseger, consult B. Bruyère, *Meret Seger à Deir el Médineh* (Cairo, 1932); and the synopsis and further literature listed by Dominique Valbelle, "Merseger," *LÄ* 4: 79–80.

5 For further information on Renenutet, consult Jan Broekhuis, *De Godin Renenwetet* (Groningen, 1971), and the synopsis and literature listed by Christine Beinlich-Seeber, "Renenutet," *LÄ* 5: 234–36.

6 See, for example, those of Renenutet listed by Broekhuis, *Die Godin Renenwetet,* 11–55.

7 For the iconography of Meretseger and Renenutet, see the sources listed above in notes 4 and 5. For a further discussion of human-headed serpents, see also H.G. Fischer, "Iconographic and Literary Comparisons," in Assmann, Feucht, and Grieshammer, *Altägyptische Literatur,* 155–58. A cobra with the head of a king now in the Walters Art Gallery (see ibid., n. 8, and Steindorff, *Catalogue,* pl. 23, no. 143) apparently dates to the Twenty-fifth Dynasty.

8 See, for example, Alexander Piankoff, *The Tomb of Ramesses VI* (New York, 1954), pl. 5; on p. 16, the author identifies the figure as Nekhbet that appears on the soffit of the doorways between the different sections of the entrance corridor. A winged vulture grasping *shen* signs in her claws and identified as Nekhbet appears over the doorways of the tomb of Nofretari (Edmund Dandelinger, *Der Genseitsweg der Nofretari* (Graz, 1973), pls. 9 and 11; without identification on pls. 11, 18, and 19). For other tombs with similar decoration, see Erik Hornung, *The Valley of the Kings* (New York, 1990), 29, 189, and 208. On p. 189, the author also notes that the tomb of Sennefer is the only private tomb with this decoration. Fourteen repetitions of a similar image occur as well on the roof of the small golden shrine of Tutankhamen (I.E.S. Edwards, *The Treasures of Tutankhamun* [London, 1972], 24–25). On the upper part of the back of the "ecclesiastical throne" of Tutankhamen, the vulture is depicted with both the *shen* and the feather, as in our example, in its claws (I.E.S. Edwards, *Tutankhamun: His Tomb and Its Treasures* [London, New York, 1976], 224). The same image is repeated several times on the ceiling in the hypostyle hall of Ramesses II's temple at Abu Simbel (Rita Freed, *Ramses II: The Great Pharaoh and His Time* [Denver, 1987], 66ff.)

9 See note 13, below.

10 For a discussion and references to further literature on this deity, see Hans-Werner Fischer-Elfert, "Uto," *LÄ* 6: 906–11.

11 Several versions of the Horus of Gold name are listed by Henri Gauthier, *Le livre des rois d'Egypte* 4 (Cairo, 1907–17), 66–81, but none has writing similar to this one. Ordinarily the falcon without plumes is perched atop the hieroglyphic sign for gold, and Kenu is spelled out rather than indicated by an ideogram.

12 As is the case on the other side, some peculiarities exist. The word *dj* on either side appears without an indication of its form. It is not followed by *t(j)* (for either a feminine participle or an old perfective) or *s* for the third-person feminine suffix, the *sḏm.f.* It is also possible that the passive *sḏm(w)* noun was understood. In any case, no *n* is indicated before the name(s) of the king. In addition, on the left side, *nb* is written without its proper feminine ending, and, on the right side, Nekhbet has no epithets.

13 See M. Heerma van Voss, "Nekhbet," *LÄ* 4: 366–68, for a brief discussion and further literature on the deity. Vultures wearing the *atef* crown adorn the ceiling of the hypostyle hall of Ramesses II's temple at Abu Simbel (see above, note 8). On a pendent of Tutankhamen (D.P. Silverman, *Treasures of Tutankhamun* [New York, 1976], 108–9), Wadjyt wearing a Red Crown is on one side of the *udjat* eye, while Nekhbet wearing the *atef* crown is on the other. Another pendent from the same tomb depicts a vulture wearing an *atef* crown (Edwards, *Tutankhamun, His Tomb and Its Treasures,* 169), and it is identified by the author as Nekhbet.

14 See Gardiner, *Egyptian Grammar,* signs M15 and M16. See also Henry G. Fischer, *Ancient Egyptian Calligraphy* (New York, 1979), 34ff.

15 See Winfried Barta, "Horus von Edfu," *LÄ* 3: 33–36, for a discussion of this deity and further references.

16 Heerma van Voss, *LÄ* 4: 367 and Fischer-Elfert, *LÄ* 6: 907–8.

17 See François Daumas, "Hathor," *LÄ* 2: 1024–33, for this designation (p. 1024), a detailed description of the goddess, and further references.

18 Ibid. Note the different positions of the *uraeus* in representations of Isis and Hathor in Saleh and Sourouzian, *Egyptian Museum,* nos. 250 and 251. Note also the *uraeus* of Atem in no. 205.

19 See above, note 16, and Wolfgang Schenkel, "Horus," *LÄ* 3: 14–25.

20 I am indebted to Edna Russmann for this observation. See her remarks in "Kushite Headdresses and 'Kushite' Style," *JEA* 81 (1995): 231

Afterlife

72 Woman's burial assemblage

1 Peet and Loat, *Abydos,* 3: 30; for a published list (incomplete) of objects found in D229, see ibid., 33.

2 The incised ivory inlay strips found on the floor of the tomb offer a hint of the more precious items in the burial that were taken by thieves.

3 The wooden headrest was not given to the Cincinnati Art Museum and consequently is not included in the exhibition; Peet and Loat, *Abydos,* 3: 33, no. 6.

4 For the pottery vessels, see ibid., pl. 5, figs. 31–46; pl. 10, fig. 8.

5 Beginning in the Predynastic Period, such shells were used to prepare eye pigment; a number have preserved traces of ground malachite and galena; see Needler, *Predynastic,* no. 231; and cat. no. 23w in the present volume. This type of shell may have served, alternatively, as a scoop or ladle; no traces of pigment were found inside.

6 The shells are of two varieties: *Columbella rustica,* a Mediterranean species, and *Cypraea* (cowrie). Both varieties are attested in jewelry from Predynastic times; see Needler, *Predynastic,* nos. 236, 238.

7 Such bronze figures of Nefertum are first attested in the Third Intermediate Period; see Andrews, *Amulets,* 18; also Petrie, *Amulets,* no. 175.

8 Leiden, Rijksmuseum van Oudheden, AT 75. The piece is nearly identical in type and detail, although slightly smaller in scale (21 cm in height); it clearly derived from the same workshop. Unprovenanced, it was acquired in 1828 from the collection of Giovanni d'Anastasi; see Leemans, *Description Raisonée* (Leiden, 1840), D 132. My acknowledgments to E. Russmann for bringing this piece to my attention, and to Martin Raven for providing documentation on this piece.

9 Ashmolean Museum, Oxford E2431 (pub. *Egypt's Golden Age,* no. 90). This vase was found in an apparently intact burial of a young girl, datable to the reign of Amenhotep III or slightly later. Beneath her hip girdle is a black semicircle representing an enlarged pubic triangle, a feature clearly preserved on the aforementioned example in Leiden. A more general parallel may be drawn with a type of female-headed flask of uncertain function datable to the reign of Thutmose III; see *Egypt's Golden Age,* no. 84.

10 Such figures were also associated with women's burials; see *Mummies and Magic,* no. 52.

11 Ranke, *Personennamen* 1: 4, 3; 3: 46. Chemmis, a town in the extreme north of the delta, was the site where Isis gave birth to Horus; see Mercer, *Pyramid Texts,* 1214b, 1703c, 1877d, 2190a. The author gratefully acknowledges the assistance of Anne Capel in translating the *ushabti* inscription.

73–77 *Shabtis*

1 For these terms, see Spanel in cat. no. 76. The author thanks Dr. Spanel for his helpful input in the writing of this entry. The term *shabti* is used here as a generic designation for this category of funerary figurine.

2 The later term *ushabti* literally means "answerer" or "respondent."

3 As Spanel notes, Chapter 6 did not become a standard feature on *shabtis* until the beginning of Dynasty 18. During the Middle Kingdom, *shabtis* were often uninscribed or simply bore the name and title of the deceased; see Spanel, in *Mummies and Magic,* 126; "Two Unusual Eighteenth-Dynasty Shabtis in the Brooklyn Museum," *BES* 10 (1989/90): 149.

4 Translation from Faulkner, *Book of the Dead,* 101.

5 Hayes, *Scepter,* 1: 326–27 and fig. 215.

6 See for example, the Eleventh Dynasty *shabti* of the House Mistress Mer(yet)-soneb, who is identified by inscription as "the one in honor with Isis, the goddess"; see Hayes, *Scepter,* 1: 328.

7 Female *shabtis* invariably were represented beardless, but male *shabtis* were rendered both bearded and beardless. The *shabtis* of Yuya, for example, included both bearded and beardless examples; J.E. Quibell, *Catalogue général des antiquités du Musée du Caire. Tomb of Yuaa and Thuiu* (Cairo, 1908), pl. 18. Cf. the lid of a late Eighteenth Dynasty double *shabti* in Boston, on which both husband and wife are rendered beardless; *Mummies and Magic,* no. 98.

8 See the comments of Hayes, *Scepter,* 2: 130.

9 Schneider, *Shabtis,* 1: 165–66; cf. ibid. 3: no. 3.1.3.1 (pl. 16).

10 Ibid., 165–66, 204–5.

11 Hayes, *Scepter,* 2: 427–28 and fig. 273. Clear attempts at feminization are also evident in the extremely delicate facial features and the slender, almost emaciated arms upraised and crossed over her chest.

12 The woman holds a pair of Hathor-headed sistra, thus associating herself with the maternal goddess of love and childbirth (ibid., 2: 325).

13 See, for example, the Ramesside-Period *shabtis* of Sen-nedjem and his wife, Iy-neferty. His is carved in limestone, hers from wood, while the wigs are rendered in blue and in black, respectively; see ibid., 425–26.

14 In the Middle Kingdom, both men's and women's *shabtis* normally were issued singly or in small multiples. Beginning in the reign of Amenhotep II, the number of figurines per burial expanded greatly; see Spanel, *BES* 10 (1989/90): 150.

15 The term *ushabti* originated in Dynasty 21 and remained standard thereafter.

16 Schneider, *Shabtis,* 1: 320.

17 Ibid., 321–22, 338ff.

18 Spanel in *Mummies and Magic,* 151–52.

19 *Shabtis* belonging to two individuals whose names are recorded on Setau's funerary stela exhibit the same distinctive basket position, which represents a brief transitional stage in the movement of the container from the front of the figure to its back. In fact, the same basket position may be seen on two of the three extant *shabtis* of the House Mistress Werel, another female in the Setau family. For a general discussion, see Spanel, in *Mummies and Magic,* 151–52.

20 Cf. the red facial coloration of the *shabti* of Nedjmet-behedet, wife of the workman Pashedu at Deir el-Bahri (BMFA 72.755).

21 Ibid., 168ff. As Spanel notes, hoes first appear on *shabtis* in the reign of Thutmose IV; *Mummies and Magic,* 125–26.

22 Ibid., 165–67.

23 Egyptian Museum, Cairo CG 48406. *Egypt's Dazzling Sun,* 310, fig. 10.7. On the quality of the Sati figurines, see Spanel, in Fazzini et al., *Ancient Egyptian Art,* no. 47.

24 In fact, all other surviving examples in this technique belonged either to royalty or to high-ranking officials under Amenhotep III: Ptahmose (vizier and high priest of Amen), Huy (royal scribe), and Queen Tiye.

25 See Bryan, in *Egypt's Dazzling Sun,* 328.

26 A complex issue, the terminology for funerary figurines involves chronological and typological considerations. Because none of the popular terms—*shabti, shawabti, ushabti*—was used consistently throughout the long history of funerary figurines, none is suitable as a comprehensive designation. Furthermore, some figurines either have a very simple formula consisting of a column or two down the front or completely lack a text. Thus the designation "funerary figurines" is the more appropriate term, albeit quaint and cumbersome. See Donald B. Spanel, "Notes on the Terminology for Funerary Figurines," *SAK* 13 (1986): 249–53.

27 Because this version of Chapter 6 of the Book of the Dead is abbreviated, the expression "as a man (or woman) at his (or her) task" is omitted. Denise Doxey, Stacie Olsson, and Ellen Morris kindly supplied this information.

28 Spanel, "Two Unusual Eighteenth-Dynasty *Shabtis* in the Brooklyn Museum," *BES* 10 (1989–90): 145–67. Dating to the Herakleopolitan Period and Dynasty 11, the small wax images that are prototypes of funerary figurines belonged to women; Spanel, *SAK* 13 (1986): 251, nn. 2–3.

29 Ibid., 252, n. 17; 253, n. 20.

30 For excellent color illustrations of the type, see the *shawabti* of the Deir el-Medina workman Sennedjem in the Kunsthistorisches Museum, Vienna (ÄS 6614); see Elfriede Reiser-Haslauer, *Kunsthistorisches Museum, Wien, Ägyptisch-Orientalische Sammlung,* 5: *Uschebti,* 1. CAA (Mainz, 1990), 97–100; Reiser-Haslauer, "Uschebti für Sennedjem," in *Götter • Menschen • Pharaonen: 3500 Jähre ägyptische Kultur. Meisterwerke aus der Ägyptisch-Orientalischen Sammlung des Kunsthistorischen Museums, Wien,* ed. Meinrad Maria Grewenig and Wilfried Seipel, exh. cat., Historisches Museum der Pfalz, Speyer (Speyer, 1993), 192, no. 105.

31 For a description of this First or Royal Cache, which was discovered in 1881, see Maspero, "Les momies royales," *MMAF* 1 (1889): 511ff. It contained some 3,700 *ushabtis* deposited in at least twenty boxes or on the floor.

32 Schneider, *Shabtis,* 1: 319–23.

33 Cf. the burial of Henuttawey, daughter of Pinedjem, which contained 411 *shabtis* placed in two boxes (containing 189 and 222 figures, respectively). For an account of the tomb setting, see C. Roehrig in *Mummies and Magic,* 163. One hundred fifty *shabtis* of Maatkara were found scattered over the floor in Cache 1. For an example of a nearly identical type as well as a list of other known examples, see Schneider, *Shabtis,* 1: 118 (4.3.0.5) and 3: pl. 47; cf. also *Tanis,* no. 4. For a general inventory of finds from the cache, see PM 1^2: 658–67. The mass production and the concomitant reduction in status of royal *shabti* figures in the Twenty-first Dynasty help to account for the inferior artistic quality and modeling of these figures in comparison with earlier examples. As Schneider (*Shabtis,* 1: 323) observes, the multiplication in the number of figurines caused a tendency toward uniformity in shape, material, and even text during this period, which persisted in *shabtis* of later periods.

34 Schneider, *Shabtis,* 1: 245. For an illustrated survey of royal *shabtis* of Twenty-first Dynasty date, see *Tanis,* cat. nos. 1–28.

35 For Queen Henuttawey, see Kitchen, *Third Intermediate Period,* par. 46; para. 47, no. 268. For Maatkara, see ibid., para. 48. As observed by Watterson (*Women,* 158), the advantage to the Tanite kings lay in placing their daughters in positions in which they could exert considerable influence on the kings' behalf.

36 X-rays of Hennutawey's mummy indicate that her age at time of death was between 35 and 40. The queen's natural hair has been supplanted with artificial plaited strands, which completely frame the face. Her skin was painted with yellow ochre; her cheeks and lips were highlighted in red and the eyebrows detailed in black. For an account, see Partridge, *Faces of Pharaohs,* 190–94.

37 J. Yoyotte, "Les adoratrices de la IIIe période intermédiare. A propos d'un chef d'oeuvre rapporté par Champollion," *BSFE* 64 (1972): 39–42, 45.

38 The packing of the body cavity also indicated that she had given birth just before death. X-ray examination has revealed that the small mummy placed at her head, presumed to be that of her baby, is actually that of a female hamadryas baboon. The child's fate is unknown, as are the reasons for including the animal mummy. The latter remains a matter of great speculation; see Partridge, *Faces of Pharaohs,* 195–99.

78 Tomb painting of mourning women

1 For mourners, see Werbrouch, *Les pleureuses.*

2 For a description of a New Kingdom funerary procession and the accompanying rituals, see Strouhal, *Life,* 264–66.

3 Davies, *Tomb of Two Sculptors.*

4 Ibid., pl. 19.

5 Ibid., 9–10.

6 Ibid., 11.

7 Ibid., 10.

8 For the wraparound dresses frequently worn by mourners, see Vogelsang-Eastwood, *Pharaonic Egyptian Clothing,* 109, 111, and fig. 7: 15.

9 Werbrouch, *Les pleureuses,* 130–31.

10 Ibid., 152.

79 Libation vase with lid

1 For a discussion of this type of wine, see Colin A. Hope, in *Egypt's Golden Age,* 90.

2 Ibid. Possibly a type of wine from one of Egypt's oases.

3 BM 59774 and 59775; see ibid., 91, for references.

4 The information in this paragraph is taken largely from ibid., 88–89.

5 See Gardiner, *Egyptian Grammar,* 529, Sign List W14–18.

6 For the faience *hes* vases found in the tomb of Tutankhamen, see I.E.S. Edwards, *Tutankhamun: His Tomb and Its Treasures* (New York, 1976), 234–35.

7 For the wine jars found in Tutankhamen's tomb, see L.H. Lesko, *King Tut's Wine Cellar* (Berkeley, 1977). Also see Nicholas Reeves, *The Complete Tutankhamun* (London, 1990), 202–3.

8 A. Lucas, *Ancient Egyptian Materials and Industries,* 4th ed. (London, 1962), 18–19.

9 Hope, in *Egypt's Golden Age,* 90.

10 Possibly located on the West Bank at Thebes.

80 Headrest inscribed for Irwt

1 Petrie, *Objects of Daily Use,* 33.

2 Ranke, *Personennamen,* 1: 41, 21.

3 For a brief discussion of the title, see Fischer, *Egyptian Women,* 15–16. As Fischer states, the title is first known from the Sixth Dynasty, thus revealing the probable usage date of the Cleveland headrest. In contrast to the other two nonroyal women's titles prevalent in the Old Kingdom—*rḫt nisw* ("Royal Acquaintance") and *ḫkrt nisw* ("Ornamented of the King")—*špswt nisw* is far more restricted in its usage. See also Robins, *Women,* 116.

4 Fischer, *Egyptian Women,* 17.

81 Heart scarab inscribed for Nub-ity

1 Andrews, *Amulets,* 56–59; Petrie, *Amulets,* 24, no. 90.

2 Translation from Faulkner, *Book of the Dead,* pl. 15. The word *the* inserted in line 11 represents an editorial change on the part of the present authors.

3 Ranke, *Personennamen,* 1: 190, 7.

4 For an analysis of this text, see Scott, *Egyptian Art at Yale,* 112, no. 62.

82 Canopic jar of Iny

1 The inside of the present jar is lined with pitch and still contains the viscera wrapped in linen.

2 Ranke, *Personennamen,* 1: 33, 16. The name is variously attested in the New Kingdom.

3 As Hayes notes, all of the occupants are otherwise unidentified. As for Iny, no daughter of Amenhotep III is known by that name. For the complex, see Hayes, *Scepter,* 2: 262; PM 1^2: 2: 770.

4 In this respect, it stands out not only among the remaining canopic jars from the Amenhotep III household complex but also among the majority of such vessels belonging to female royalty of the Eighteenth Dynasty. For the canopic jars from Deir el-Bahri associated with the household of Amenhotep III, see Hayes, *Scepter,* 2: 262; and Winlock, *Three Egyptian Princesses,* 47–48. The crude quality of these jars is a surprising and unexplained feature, given the otherwise richly endowed tomb contexts from which they derive; see the comments of Winlock, ibid., 47.

5 As for gender identification, color alone distinguishes male from female on the terracotta examples of the Thutmoside Period: yellow was employed for female skin and red for males; see Hayes, *Scepter,* 2: 227.

6 Robins, *Women,* 175.

7 All of the above-mentioned stoppers from the Amenhotep III household complex were beardless. Although a number of complete sets of beardless-headed canopic jars belonging to women are known from the Middle and New Kingdom, the evidence is not conclusive. Men as well as women could have beardless sets; other assemblages show a mixture of bearded and beardless stoppers.

8 Traces of pigment survive on the eyes, eyelids, and corners of the mouth.

83 Fragment from a woman's Book of the Dead

1 For the Pyramid and Coffin Texts, respectively, see Mercer, *Pyramid Texts,* and Faulkner, *Coffin Texts.*

2 For the substitute use of a mummy's linen bandages as a writing surface for spells from the Book of the Dead, see *Mummies and Magic,* no. 181.

3 Only the owner's name and the use of feminine pronouns (in the text) and the depiction of the female form (in the vignettes) distinguish the feminine version from the masculine.

4 The author gratefully acknowledges Malcolm Mosher for his generous assistance in identifying the extant vignettes and suggesting their reconstructed sequence. Many thanks also to Cecile Mear, Assistant Paper Conservator at the Cincinnati Art Museum, for her diligent work in cleaning and restoring the present fragment.

5 For a discussion, see, most recently, L.H. Lesko, "Some Remarks on the Books of the Dead Composed for the High Priests Pinedjem I and II," in Silverman, ed., *For His Ka,* 183–84.

6 This fragment has been dated to the first century B.C. by Malcolm Mosher (personal correspondence, Dec. 11, 1994).

7 Faulkner, *Coffin Texts,* pl. 15; for additional commentary on Ch. 56 (Theban recension), see 105.

8 Ibid., pl. 16.

9 Ibid., 106–7.

10 Ibid., 107.

11 Ibid., pl. 17.

12 Ibid., rubric, pl. 6.

13 Ibid., pl. 25.

14 Ibid., pls. 25–26.

15 Ibid., 166, for commentary on this spell.

16 For Spells 85 and 83, see ibid., pl. 27 and commentary on p. 166.

84 Reserve head of a woman

1 W.S. Smith, *HESPOK,* 25–26.

2 Ibid., 23–25.

3 For the head of Meret-ites, see *Art and Architecture,* fig. 103. The slab stela is in Boston (MFA 12.1510). For an account of the discovery of these pieces, see G.A. Reisner in *BMFA,* 13, no. 76 (1915): 29ff.

4 For the *pr*-estates of Khentkawes, see B.G. Trigger et al., *Ancient Egypt: A Social History* (Cambridge, 1983), 79, 90.

5 See ibid. 123–26.

6 As A.L. Kelley *(Newsletter of the Society for the Study of Egyptian Antiquities* 5, no.1 [1974]:7) observes, however, only a few of the surviving thirty-one reserve heads can be securely associated with the tomb chamber, thus raising serious doubt over Reisner's original assumption of their placement in the burial chamber. The fact that more than half of the examples (including the present one) were found in the burial shaft rather than in the chamber itself has led others to suggest that they were originally displayed at the entrance to the tomb chamber rather than within; see ibid., 7.

7 The male head from tomb 4140 at Giza (MFA 14.718) bears considerable traces of red paint on the surface, suggesting that it was originally painted a uniform red; see *Mummies and Magic,* 83.

8 Cf. the afore-mentioned reserve heads of Meret-ites and Sneferu-seneb in Cairo, where the hair is clearly depicted as a close-fitting cap; see *Art and Architecture,* figs. 103–4.

85 Funerary statue of Intekes

1 For the importance of an individual's name in ancient Egypt, see "names" in Shaw and Nicholson, *Dictionary,* 194.

2 Her husband exhibits the typical male hand position, with right hand closed in a fist resting on the thigh.

3 See Smith, *HESPOK,* 63, G1039 for a listing of the nine statues.

4 Hearst 6–19763, "Acquaintance of the King, One Revered before the Great God, Overseer of the Treasury, Meretash; His Eldest Son, Senenu."

5 Hearst 6–19800, "Acquaintance of the King, Int-es-ka"; and Cairo 37718, "Acquaintance of the King, Mistress of the House, Nebet-net-ka."

6 Cairo 37715, "Overseer of Masons, One Revered before the Great God, Ikha"; Cairo 37721, "It is his son who made [it] for him, Ikha"; Hearst 6–19799, "Instructor of Masons, Ipi-wer."

7 Hearst 6–19809, uninscribed and apparently unfinished.

8 Fischer, *Egyptian Studies* 1: 76, n. 42, presents a brief overview of early examples of the title *nbt pr;* none of those discussed, however, are as early as this example dating to the late Fifth or early Sixth Dynasty.

9 Smith, *HESPOK,* 63, however, states that Nebet-net-ka (Cairo 37718) is the wife of Ikha (Cairo 37715 and 37721) but does not state his reason for believing this.

10 M. Galvin, "Addendum," in Lesko, ed., *Women's Earliest Records,* 29.

11 Ibid., 30; and Galvin, "The Hereditary Status of the Titles of the Cult of Hathor," *JEA* 70 (1984): 42–49.

12 Robins, *Women,* 144.

13 Galvin in Lesko, ed., *Women's Earliest Records,* 30; and Galvin, *JEA* 70 (1984): 42–49.

14 Ibid., 45–46.

15 For references, see H. Fischer, "Priesterin," *LÄ* 4: 1100–1105.

16 Ibid.

17 Ibid., and Robins, *Women,* 144.

18 For an overview of the titles, see Robins, *Women,* 148–49; also see cat. nos. 35a, 87, and 90.

19 Smith, *HESPOK,* 63. The *serdab* (modern Arabic for "cellar") was introduced in private tombs during the Fourth Dynasty of the Old Kingdom.

86 Funerary stela for Lady Nefer

1 For the name, see Ranke, *Personennamen,* 1: 201, 10. For a description and plan of Nefer's *mastaba,* see Reisner, *Giza Necropolis,* 1: 190, no. 11 and fig. 99.

2 For a general discussion of these *mastabas* and their classification, see Reisner, *Giza Necropolis,* 1: 184–91.

3 Female royalty: Nefert-yabet (G1225); Meret-ites (G4140); Weneshet (G4840). Female nonroyalty: Sethy-hekenet (G1227); Nefer (G1207). Altogether, the emplacement of just over three dozen slab-stelae is evidenced in the various *mastabas* at Giza (C. Keller, in Thomas et al., *American Discovery,* 125; Reisner, *Giza Necropolis,* 1: pls. 17–20).

4 See Fischer, *Egyptian Women,* 15.

5 Reisner, *Giza Necropolis,* 1: 64. As Reisner observes, this conclusion seems assured by their original placement within the brickwork cores of the *mastabas.*

6 The *mastabas* of Lady Nefer (8.64 sq. m) and Sethy-hekenet (9.73 sq. m) are roughly comparable to that of Princess Nefert-yabet (8.96 sq. m) in the same complex; and to those of men (royal and nonroyal) with the notable exception of Prince Wepemnofret. See Reisner, *Giza Necropolis,* 1: 113–14.

7 Fischer, *Egyptian Women,* 2–3.

8 Pyramid GIb. See Smith, *HESPOK,* 160.

9 As Reisner *(Giza Necropolis,* 1: 305) observes, the *mastabas* conceivably might have been decorated with painted scenes, but no evidence of any such decoration has survived.

10 Reisner, *Giza Necropolis,* 1: 321–22, 330ff; Smith, *HESPOK,* 159.

11 As Smith (*HESPOK,* 159) observes, the right arm is always provided with a left hand and both feet are left, a convention that endures until the close of Dynasty 18.

12 Smith, *HESPOK,* 159.

87 Funerary stela for Ta-sheryt-akhet

1 See J.E. Quibell, *The Ramesseum* (London, 1898), 9, 17; also Munro, *Totenstelen,* 6, 11. For excavations in the area of the Ramesseum, see PM 1 2², 678–84. Stela Philadelphia E2043 is listed on 680.

2 Neskhonsu-pakhered, whose cartonnage is cat. no. 90, represents one of these individuals; her funerary stela is in the Museum of Fine Arts, Boston *(Mummies and Magic,* no. 118).

3 Cf. the stela of Neskhonsu-pakhered; ibid.

4 The remaining stelae bear the crowning ornament of the winged sun disc, symbolizing the celestial sphere.

5 Manniche, *Music and Musicians,* 124.

6 Ibid.

7 See F. Hassanien et al., in S. Schoske, ed., *Aktan der Viertan Internationalen Ägyptologen Kongresses München 1985,* BSAK 2 (Hamburg, 1989), 185. Cf. the burial chapel of Zed-mut-as-ankh, daughter of the fourth prophet of Amen, Nakht-ef-Mut (whose tomb and coffin survive), and that of Zed-Khensu-af-ankh, fourth prophet of Amen; see Quibell, *Ramesseum,* 10–12.

8 Ibid., 11–12 (inscription on a large alabaster basin). Nakht-ef-Mut's cartonnage contained the stamped leather *menat* counterpoise bearing the name of Osorkon I (ibid., 10).

88 Round-topped (funerary) stela of Ta-Khaa-en-Bastet

1 For the name, see Ranke, *Personennamen* 1: 366, 11. For a close stylistic parallel, see stela B.M. 809 from Abydos (Munro, *Totenstelen,* 283, pl. 36, fig. 133).

2 At the base of the *djed* pillar emerge two feline heads, probably symbolizing the two-headed sphinx Aker, who guarded the eastern and western entrances to the underworld ruled by Osiris. For Aker, see Shaw and Nicholson, *Dictionary,* 19–20.

3 Thanks to Richard A. Fazzini, who assisted in the reading of these signs.

4 The formula, "Words spoken by . . . ," appended to Horus and Thoth indicates that they were the recitants of the prayer to Osiris on the dedicant's behalf.

5 During the New Kingdom, these cones were worn regularly by guests in banqueting scenes. As the party progressed, the wax melted, causing the perfumed oil to flow onto the guests' hair (wigs) and skin.

89 Panel of a coffin made for a woman

1 For studies of the coffins from Asyut, see Günther Lapp, *Typologie der Särge und Sargkammern von der 6. bis 13. Dynastie,* SAGA 7 (1993): 121–46 (para. 272–324); Diana Magee, "Asyût to the End of the Middle Kingdom: A Historical and Cultural Study" (PhD dissertation, University of Oxford, 1989), 29–66; Harco O. Willems, *Chests of Life: A Study of the Typology and Conceptual Development of Middle Kingdom Standard Class Coffins,"* MVEOL 25 (1988), 102–4; Donald B. Spanel, "Beni Hasan in the Herakleopolitan Period," PhD dissertation, University of Toronto, 1985, 161–82; and Edward Brovarski, "The Inscribed Material of the First Intermediate Period from Naga-ed-Dêr," PhD dissertation, University of Chicago, 1989, 1060–67.

2 The protocol of the giving changed over time; see Ronald J. Leprohon, "The Offering Formula in the First Intermediate Period," *JEA* 76 (1990): 163–64. The most important study of the invocation-offering formula is Günther Lapp's *Die Opferformel des Alten Reiches unter Berücksichtigung einiger späterer Formen,* SDAIK 21 (1986).

3 Although the textual layout may have evolved in the First Intermediate Period, the panel itself may date to the Twelfth Dynasty. With complete coffins, the best indicator of date is the version of the invocation-offering formula found on the east side; see Donald B. Spanel, "Palaeographic and Epigraphic Distinctions between Texts of the So-Called First Intermediate Period and the Early Twelfth Dynasty," *Studies in Honor of William Kelly Simpson,* ed. Peter Der Manuelian (Boston, 1996), in press. Because the west side lacks this critical information, the only evidence is the refined style of the hieroglyphs and of the painting, which seems to suggest a date in the Twelfth Dynasty.

4 As, for example, on the coffin of Wepwawetnakht in the Pelizaeus-Museum, Hildesheim (6000); see *Ägypten. Geheimnis der Grabkammer: Suche nach Unsterblichkeit,* ed. Arne Eggebrecht (Mainz, 1993), 94–96, no. 35.

5 On the combination types, the offerings predominate; see Emile Chassinat and Charles Palanque, *Une campagne de fouilles dans la nécropole d'Assiout,* MIFAO 24 (1911): 228–33 and pls. 37–39 (now Louvre 12035).

6 The label above the mirror describes it as a "mirror of silver."

7 For similar items on the exterior of Asyut coffins, see Chassinat and Palanque, *Une campagne de fouilles,* pl. 37. For convenient line drawings of the commodities included in the *frises d'objets,* see Pierre Lacau, *Sarcophages anterieurs au Nouvel Empire,* 1 (Cairo, 1904), pls. 30–54.

8 At Akhmim and Gebelein, however, coffins of an equally experimental design were produced, some with extensive offering lists, others with scenes resembling wall paintings; see ibid., CG, Nos. 28001–28086, vol. 1, 1–5 (28001), 10–19 (28004–28006), 22–24 (28008), 30–32 (28013) and pls. 1–3, 6–7; vol. 2, 93–96 (28115–28116); On CG 28001, see also Naguib Kanawati, *The Rock Tombs of El-Hawawish: The Cemetery of Akhmim,* vol. 5 (Sydney, Australia, 1986), 63–64 and pl. 16.

9 The erasure of the masculine pronoun appears to indicate nothing more than a scribal error. It does not mean that the coffin was originally intended for a man but appropriated for the unknown woman. If the coffin had been constructed for a man, traces of the masculine pronoun would be expected in both passages. The red outline around many of the other blue hieroglyphs provides the telltale clue about what happened. The scribe's method was to draw the entire text carefully in red, then fill it in with blue pigment. Having written the masculine in red, the scribe must have recognized his error immediately—or had it pointed out to him—because he erased the sign without painting it blue. Having made the correction, he proceeded to the next gender-specific passage with no problems.

10 The incorrect specification of the right (eastern) side results from confusion over two hawk-shaped deities—Horus-Sopdu and Ha—who are often mentioned at the beginning of the so-called speech of Ra. On the right panel, the text usually reads, "Words spoken by Ra, 'I have placed [literally, given] for you, Horus-Sopdu, lord of the east, at your eastern [i.e., right] side.'" On the left panel, the inscription begins, "Words spoken by Ra, 'I have placed for you, Ha, at your western [i.e., left] side.'" The hieroglyphs for these two gods were quite similar and could be mistaken easily. The scribe should have specified Ha and the west (left). For the correct positions, see Lapp, *Särge* para. 290. On Horus-Sopdu, see Inke W. Schumacher, *Der Gott Sopdu der Herr der Fremdländer,* OBO 79 (1988): 245–47. On Ha, see ibid., 83, 90, 93, 97, 142, 154–55, 229–30, 293; and Dietrich Wildung, "Ha," *LÄ* 2: col. 923.

11 These two deities are barely mentioned in the scholarly literature; see Lapp, *Särge,* 128; and Winifried Barta, *Aufbau und Bedeutung der altägyptischen Opferformel,* ÄF 24 (1968): 38. The name Heryibsenuef is probably a miswriting for Herytepsenuef (*Ḥritpsnw.f*), which occurs slightly more often than Akhenitef. As on the Brooklyn panel, both names are found only on the west side of Asyut coffins: for example, Chassinat and Palanque, *Une campagne des fouilles,* 9 and n. 1, 13, 16, 19, 25, 27, 54, 115, 124, 126, 136, 144, 170, 187, 192, 219, 234; and Henri Gauthier and Gustave Lefebvre, "Sarcophages du moyen empire provenant de la nécropole d'Assiout," *ASAE* 23 (1923): 5, 8, 15, 18, 21, 30.

12 Waltraud Guglielmi, *Die Göttin Mr.t: Entstehung und Verehrung einer Personifikation,* PÄ 7 (1991).

90 Cartonnage (mummy case) of Neskhonsu-pakhered

1 Ranke, *Personennamen,* 1: 178, 22.

2 The coffin was not excavated scientifically but was acquired for the University of California by Dr. George Reisner from the Cairo Museum in 1900–1901.

3 The word employed is *ḥsbyt*. For the interpretation of this term as "wife," see J.J. Janssen in Demarée and Janssen, *Gleanings,* 127, n. 37.

4 Attention may be drawn to a contemporary round-topped stela in Boston inscribed for Neskhonsu-pakhered, Mistress of the House and Chantress of Amen, who is identified here as the wife of Nes-pa-her-an, Entrance Priest of Amen; see *Mummies and Magic,* 164–65, no. 118.

5 For the cartonnage of Nespernub in the British Museum (BM 30720), see Andrews, *Egyptian Mummies,* 46, fig. 51. Although unprovenanced, his coffin clearly derived from Thebes. As Andrews observes, Nespernub's titles *(mr-ntr, wn 'wy pt m Ipt-swt,* and *qbhw Hnsw n Bn(b)n)* on both his inner and outer coffins identify him as a Theban priest based at Karnak (Carol Andrews, personal correspondence, July 24, 1995). For two mummy cases of similar style and decoration originating in the same Theban workshop, see the cartonnages of Penu and Tabes in Boston *(Mummies and Magic,* nos. 120, 121). The date of Neskhonsu-pakhered's cartonnage is also confirmed by her name, which is attested variously in the Twenty-second Dynasty; see Ranke, *Personennamen,* 1: 178, 22.

6 Phoebe Hearst Museum of Anthropology, University of California at Berkeley, 6–19931, unpublished.

7 Both outer coffins exhibit the artistic style characteristic of the late Twenty-second Dynasty, with decoration limited to the head and collar and to the bands of text that run down the center and along both sides.

8 From inscriptions on other examples, the upper two falcon deities may be identified as "the Behdetite," i.e., the solar Horus; see *Mummies and Magic,* 170.

91 Coffin of Henut-wedjebu

1 See Ranke, *Personennamen,* 1: 243, 2. Names beginning with *ḥnwt* ("Mistress") are common in Dynasty 18, although the particular combination Henut-wedjebu occurs more frequently in the Ramesside Period; see Bryan, in *Egypt's Dazzling Sun,* 314 and n. 11.

2 These belonged to the ladies Siamen and Huy. Their relationship to Hatiay is also unclear; the present location of both coffins is unknown. In size and quality of decoration, Henut-wedjebu's coffin and mummy are distinguished clearly from

theirs. On Siamen's coffin lid, for example, yellow paint substitutes for the gilding applied to Henut-wedjebu's coffin, while her mummy lacks both the mask and the pectorals found on the latter; moreover, her shroud lacks the vertical decorative band characteristic of Henut-wedjebu's cartonnage. These traits suggest a clear differentiation in social standing within the household. For the burial contexts of Siamen and Huy, see G. Daressy, "Rapport sur la trouvaille de [Hatiay]," *ASAE* 2 (1901): 8–9. Curiously, despite its elaborate coffins and accompanying jewelry, Hatiay's tomb structure is singularly unprepossessing, consisting of little more than a cave sealed off by a mud-brick wall; see Bryan's remarks in *Egypt's Dazzling Sun,* 312.

3 Daressy, *ASAE* 2 (1901): 8. As Daressy (ibid.) notes, the two are obviously products of the same workshop. Like that of Hatiay, Henut-wedjebu's mummy wears a necklace with two pectorals.

4 One question involves the extent to which the role of chantress involved actual singing or simply the chanting of hymns. Clearly, substantial training was involved, as tomb depictions indicate.

5 A painted oboe case bears the name of a *shemayit* of the goddess Mut; Manniche, *Music and Musicians,* 124.

6 Ibid., 63 and 126, fig. 75 (Louvre E 11201). Hand clapping was another common form of percussive accompaniment (see cat. no. 32).

7 Ibid., 52–53 and fig. 30.

8 Ibid., 52–53.

92 Bust of a noblewoman

1 When Stephen D. Bonadies, Chief Conservator at the Cincinnati Art Museum, began work to remove areas of poorly executed restoration on the statue, it was discovered that the bust had previously been covered with a coat of lacquer. Removal of the lacquer and the grime that it had trapped revealed the original bright quality of the pigments.

2 See Ritner, *Mechanics,* 148–53.

3 Note the similarity to the modeling of the lips of Nakht-Min's wife; see Russmann, *Egyptian Sculpture,* 136–38, no. 63. Dr. Russmann noted this similarity in the two statues during a May 1991 visit to the Cincinnati Art Museum.

4 The inscription was originally translated (undated correspondence) by Klaus Baer from a photograph. In July 1992 E.R. Russmann examined the statue and was able to read additional signs in line 6. A careful examination by Geoffrey T. Martin and the present writer in July 1995 revealed further hieroglyphs and allowed correction of earlier misinterpretations of some of the signs, all of which are incorporated here.

5 For the name Djefaihapi, see Horst Beinlich, "Djefaihapi," *LÄ* 1: 1105–7; PM 4: 261–62, 264; and see Ranke, *Personennamen,* 1: 406, nos. 16–17, 20.

6 This comparison was noted in remarks by Klaus Baer, which were included with an undated translation of the inscription in the museum's archives. E.R. Russmann also noted such similarities in correspondence dated August 4, 1992.

7 Hayes, *Scepter,* 2: 350, 352.

93 Statue depicting Yuni and Renenutet

1 Henri Wild, "Note concernant des antiquités trouvées, non à Deir Dronka, mais dans la nécropole d'Assiout," *BIFAO* 69 (1971): 307–9.

2 K.A. Kitchen, "Encore la famille de Iouny," *RdE* 28 (1976): 156–58.

3 For a discussion of the tomb, which was not properly recorded at the time of excavation, see Joachim Selim Karig, "Die Kultkammer des Amenhotep aus Deir Durunka," *ZÄS* 95 (1968): 27–34.

4 For the reliefs from the tomb, see ibid.; and Robert D. Gempeler, *Werke der Antike im Kunsthaus Zürich* (Zurich, 1976), 16–20.

5 Hayes, *Scepter,* 2: 349–50.

6 Cyril Aldred, *Egyptian Art in the Days of the Pharaohs 3100–320* BC (New York and Toronto, 1980), 195–96.

7 For Yuni's titles, see Winlock, *BMMA* 14, no. 2 (1919): 34; and Hayes, *Scepter,* 2: 349.

8 *Wrt ẖnr* is the title translated here. The inscription has been translated by John Gee and James Allen.

9 See cat. no. 35b for more information on *menat* counterpoises and necklaces.

10 Other women are known to have commissioned statues; see, for example, cat. no. 2.

94 Pair Statue of Djehuty-em-heb and Iay

1 Much of the following discussion derives from Scott, *Egyptian Art at Yale,* 128–31.

2 For the use of sandstone in ancient Egypt, see A. Lucas, *Ancient Egyptian Materials and Industries,* 4th ed. (London, 1962), 55–57, 419.

3 Russmann, *Egyptian Sculpture,* 6.

4 For Wepwawet, see E. Greafe, "Upuaut," *LÄ* 6: 862–64.

5 Scott, *Egyptian Art at Yale,* 128, believes that the statue dates to one of the immediate successors of Ramesses III; see 130, n. 4 for Harris Papyrus references.

6 Ranke, *Personennamen,* 1: 6, 2.

7 Ibid., 8, 8, with the addition of the vulture, Gardiner's Sign List G1.

8 The ancient Egyptians are well known for passing favorite family names through one generation after another. For a general discussion of names, see Tyldesley, *Daughters of Isis,* 77; unfortunately, the sources for this material are not referenced.

The legal status of women in ancient Egypt

1 All texts are cited by common abbreviations; all texts quoted are listed at the end of this essay, together with the bibliographic reference for their original publication or for a subsequent translation or study of the text.

2 E.g., in the Middle Kingdom contracts made by a man named Djefahapy, the author distinguished between senior-level (nationally appointed?) government officials *[ḥ3ty-ʿ]*, (local) government officials *[sr]*, "commoners" *[nḏs*, lit., "small people"], and peasants *[iḥwty]*.

3 The men of the upper classes, about whom we have the most information, held jobs in the "public sector" and frequently received both wages and income-producing property; they held the latter as a result of their position. Although many individuals were especially careful to distinguish such property held by virtue of employment from personal property (e.g., Djefahapy, mentioned in the previous note, and Nakht-mut, from the Third Intermediate Period, translation page 182), many also tried to convert "professional" holdings into personal ones and pass them along to their heirs.

4 Literally, "living woman of the city."

5 This situation contrasts sharply with that of some other ancient societies. In ancient Greece, for example, women did not have their own legal identity, were not allowed to own (real) property, and, to participate in the legal system, always had to work through a male. Usually this was their closest male relative (father, brother, husband, son), who was called their κύριος, "lord." This basic distinction between Egyptian and Greek society led classical authors to several, sometimes rather severe, misunderstandings of Egyptian society. For example, Diodorus Siculus (27, 2) referred to marriage contracts in which the husband agreed to obey his wife in all things, although (as we shall see) there were no Egyptian "marriage contracts" referring to the social or marital rights or duties of either party. See Pestman, *Marriage*, 136. Similarly, Herodotus (2, 35) claimed that sons had no legal responsibility to support their parents, but daughters did; this claim is not reflected in the documentation. Thus, it is necessary to concentrate on Egyptian sources themselves, not on secondary material, in discussing the legal status of Egyptian women.

6 The exact status of such people does not fit any modern (or classical) category. Although they were bought and sold and thus "owned" by someone else, and although they were bound to work for their "owner" at whatever location the "owner" desired, they retained many aspects of personal freedom: for example, they could marry and own or dispose of property. Perhaps the closest modern analogy is with professional athletes. We (the general public, newscasters, and such) speak often about teams "buying" and "selling" their players; the players are not free to work for any team they want; they cannot move away from the location where their "owner" wants them to play (although modern athletes, unlike ancient Egyptian servants/slaves, retain the right to quit). The teams, however, are actually buying and selling the athlete's *work*, not the athlete himself, who retains his full personal independence. For an example of the "manumission" of a slavewoman and her children, see the Adoption Papyrus, translation page 183.

7 The highest official in the land below the king himself.

8 One such is Teti, the [daught]er of Sainhur; she is described as a "woman (who escaped from) the scribe of the farmland of Thi[nis]" (a city in Upper Egypt north of modern Luxor/ancient Thebes). When a prisoner escaped, family members were forced to serve in the escapee's place. When Teti was caught, an administrative order was issued "to release (her people) in the law-court, being (an order) issued in order to execute against her the law pertaining to one who flees without doing his labour-duty." In a later review by the vizier's office, it was noted that the case of Teti was "Closed. Statement by the Scribe of the Vizier, Deduamen: It is closed." (P. Brooklyn 35.1446, l. 63)

9 O. Nash 1, translation page 179.

10 Thus Weni says in his self-laudatory autobiography: "When there was a secret charge in the royal harem against Queen Weret-yamtes, his majesty made me go in to hear (it) alone. No chief judge and vizier, no official was there, only I alone. . . . Only I put (it) in writing together with one other senior warden of Nekhen, while my rank was (only) that of overseer of ⌈royal tenants⌉. Never before had one like me heard a secret of the king's harem . . . " (ll. 10–12); see Sethe, *Urkunden*, 1: 100/13–101/4. The Middle Kingdom "Instructions of King Amenemhat I for His Son" also contain a passage that has been interpreted as referring to a harem conspiracy: "Had women ever marshaled troops? Are rebels nurtured in the palace?" (ll. 7–8)

11 Judicial P. of Turin.

12 In addition, the official record of this investigation records the punishment (by cutting off their noses and their ears) of several officials who had been part of the original investigating team. They were so punished "because they had abandoned the good instructions given to them [i.e., the instructions of the king in constituting the court]. The women had gone. They had reached them at the place where they were. They had caroused [literally, made a beer hall] with them and with Pay-is" (one of the defendants, who had been commander of the army and who had been allowed to commit suicide for his part in the conspiracy).

13 "I am one of four wives, two being dead and another still alive." There is no good evidence for "bigamy" in ancient Egypt, but abundant evidence for "serial monogamy." Thus one assumes that the woman being interrogated is the former wife, passing off the blame to the current wife (or vice versa).

14 Does this imply that the couple had been living with her parents?

15 P. Boulaq 10, translation page 177.

16 P. Turin 2021.

17 *Wḏ-nswt*, lit., "command of the king." Actual examples have been preserved from the Old Kingdom on. Diodorus Siculus (1, 94–95) preserved the tradition that six Egyptian kings, from Menes at the beginning of the First Dynasty through the Persian Darius, were renowned as lawgivers. This seems to reflect an Egyptian tradition because a Demotic text written in the second or third century B.C. records Darius as bidding the soldiers, priests, and scribes of Egypt to write down *p3 hp n Km.t*, "the law of Egypt" (P. Bibliothèque Nationale 215 vo, c/10). See Wilhelm Spiegelberg, *Die sogenannte Demotische Chronik des Pap. 215 der Bibliothèque National zu Paris nebst den auf der Rückseite des Papyrus stehenden Texten*, Demotische Studien vol. 7 (Leipzig, 1914). Here *hp* can mean "body of law, regulations."

18 For discussion of the date of composition of the text, see Janet Johnson, "The Persians and Continuity of Egyptian Culture," in *Achaemenid History*, vol. 8: *Continuity and Change* (Leiden, 1994), p. 157, n. 36. Since Diodorus Siculus (see preceding note) said of King Bocchoris (Dynasty 24, ca. 720 B.C.) that he "gave precision to the law of contracts," it is tempting to date the original of the Hermopolis Law Code to that period. A book of case law (if that is what this document is, rather than a theoretical document defining a system that may never actually have existed as such) could be copied long after it was out-of-date; this is made clear by the early Roman Period translation of this very collection of case law into Greek.

19 The same is true of other ancient Near Eastern documents (e.g., the Mesopotamian "Code of Hammurabi"), which are frequently referred to as law codes.

20 Usually men, but occasionally women also served as witnesses; for example, both parts of the New Kingdom Adoption Papyrus (translation page 183) were witnessed before groups that included women.

21 It seems that, originally, if a dispute arose about a contract, the witnesses would be asked to testify in court concerning what Party A had said, to which Party B had agreed. Through time, the written document itself became legal evidence in a legal case. Although few Egyptians could read and write, Egyptian society worked through written documents and precedents; these could cover a geographical and temporal range that human witnesses could not.

22 The "Instructions of the Vizier" contains the statement "It is to him [i.e., the vizier] that every transfer document *[imyt pr]* shall be brought. It is he who shall seal it." This statement has been interpreted by G.P.F. van den Boorn in *Duties of the Vizier*, 180–83, no. 7, as referring only to those transfer documents concerning property held by virtue of government employment. Yet it is clear from Papyrus Kahun I, 1/5 (translation page 178) that other transfer documents were also recorded. The early New Kingdom *imyt pr* made by a man named Senmose on behalf of his wife and children states, "[It was sealed] by the Vizier's registry office today, before the Overseer of the City, Vizier . . . , [and it was registered (?) . . .] by the scribe Hori."

23 See, for example, the passages from P. Boulaq 10 (translation page 177) and O. Nash 1 (translation page 179).

24 See, for example, P. Boulaq 10 (translation page 177) and O. Nash 1 (translation page 179).

25 For example, at the end of P. Turin 2021, a New Kingdom document concerning inheritance following a second marriage, it is stated: "And the vizier gave an order to the priest and scribe of the mat [literally, *tm3*] of the Tribunal of the Temple of [King] Ramesses III, Ptahemheb, saying: 'Let this arrangement which I made be written in the Registry of the Temple of Ramesses III!' And a copy was made for the Grand Tribunal of Thebes before numerous witnesses."

26 The court mentioned in O. Gardiner 150, for example, included three workmen and two women with the title "Citizeness."

27 They made these acquisitions through purchase, lease, foreclosure on a mortgage, "wages" (e.g., for weaving or other work in their home as well as for a formal "job" outside the home), gift, or inheritance.

28 They disposed of property through sale, foreclosure on a mortgage, gift, or "quit claim."

29 Many modern scholars have argued that Egyptians could not really "own" real estate because (in theory) everything belonged to the king, and the king could confiscate property awarded by himself or could remove someone from office and give the property belonging to that office to the new holder of the office. In addition, Egyptians had to pay taxes even on property that they claimed. Twentieth-century Americans claim to "own" real estate, although we must pay annual taxes to a higher-level authority; that authority retains the right of "eminent domain" to confiscate property "for the public good," and government retains the right to tell people what they can and cannot do with their property. Egyptians made a clear legal distinction between possession/use (transfer by lease or within a marriage) and ownership

(transfer only by sale, inheritance, foreclosure on a mortgage, and the like) and used different legal forms and contracts for each situation. Thus, when an Egyptian claimed that he owned property, he owned it; he did not merely have possession of it.

30 An early example of women's acquiring and owning property is found in the inscription of Prince Nikaura, a son of King Khufu of the Fourth Dynasty, who transferred landed property to his wife and son and daughter. (Sethe, *Urkunden,* 1: 16–17.)

31 For example, in O. Bodleian 253 and O. Varille 30 (both from the New Kingdom), men take oaths not to beat their wives again; if they do so, they will receive 100 blows and forfeit to her all their joint property. Sometimes the division was half and half; more frequently it was one-third for the wife and two-thirds for the husband, as in P. Turin 2021. Also, either partner to the marriage could continue to acquire or dispose of his or her own private property during the marriage, without any involvement by the spouse.

32 For a summary of discussions of the legal meaning of these documents, see van den Boorn, *Duties of the Vizier,* 180–83, no. 7.

33 See note 22.

34 "Fifty arouras of (farm)land belonging to his mother Nebsenet were given to him, she making an *imyt pr* thereof for my (i.e., Metjen's) children, (the arouras) being put in their possession in a royal document [valid in] all places" (Sethe, *Urkunden,* 1, 2/14–16).

35 Preserved in Papyrus Kahun I (translation page 178).

36 I.e., transferred from his brother.

37 The entailing of property for one's children is seen already in the Old Kingdom. For example, the Fifth Dynasty noble Nikauankh transferred his house to his children but denied them the legal right to transfer it further "in an *imy.t pr* or as a gift [?] to anyone except to his [child's own] son." Such a clause is found in many transfer documents, such as the New Kingdom *imyt pr* made by Senmose, in which property goes to his wife and then a son and three daughters. It becomes a standard part of Late Period annuity contracts, which are discussed below.

38 This line was written in a different hand.

39 These include many that are not formal contracts or court records; for example, they may or may not be dated and do not have witness lists. Rather, they served as aides-mémoires recording details of a transaction, series of transactions, or (impending) lawsuit.

40 In P. Cairo 65739, for example, a woman provided a detailed list of the items she had given to a merchant in payment for a purchase, including cloth that she herself had woven and metal vessels that she had bought from various men and women.

41 See Sally L.D. Katary, *Land Tenure in the Ramesside Period* (London, 1989), 72, gl.

42 Whether by inheritance as widows or daughters of men who had acquired the land as payment for military service or by some other means. For the former suggestion, see Bernadette Menu, *Le régime juridique des terres et du personnel attaché à la terre dans le Papyrus Wilbour* (Lille, 1970).

43 P. Cairo 65739.

44 P. Leiden 352.

45 O. Nash 1, translation page 179.

46 Capital cases normally were left to the decision of the king or vizier.

47 In the cases we have, we cannot be certain whether the woman was a willing participant or not—that is, whether it was a case of rape or adultery. Apparently there were no strictures against sex between "consenting adults" as long as neither was married to someone else, and it was as offensive for a married man to have sex outside marriage as for a married woman. Beginning with the earliest wisdom literature, men were warned to take appropriate care in dealing with women outside their family. In "The Instructions of Ptahhotep," for example, we find this advice: "If you want friendship to endure in the house you enter as master, brother, or friend, in whatever place you enter, beware of approaching the women! Unhappy is the place where it is done, unwelcome is he who intrudes on them. A thousand men are turned away from their good: a short moment like a dream, then death comes for having known them." The Late Period "Instructions of 'Onchsheshonqy" contains the following advice: "If you find your wife with her lover, get yourself a bride to suit you" (13/12), "A woman lets herself be loved according to the character of her husband" (20/19), and "Do not make love to a married woman. He who makes love to a married woman is killed on her doorstep" (23//6–7). Egyptian texts contain no evidence of any concern with virginity at marriage.

48 P. Deir el-Medina 27.

49 See Lichtheim, *Ancient Egyptian Literature,* 3/125–38. That a marriage was celebrated by a party given by the parents is also suggested by a New Kingdom ostracon; see J.J. Janssen, "An Allusion to an Egyptian Wedding Ceremony?" *GM* 10 (1974): 25–28.

50 On *ḥms irm* and *grg pr,* see J.J. Clère, "Un mot pour 'mariage' en égyptien de l'époque ramesside," *RdE* 20 (1968): 171–75. Clère also noted that various goddesses (Tauseret, Rennet) were called *nbt ḥms* and *nbt/ḥnwt grgt,* "Mistress of Marriage, Mistress of the Dowry."

51 P. Berlin 8523, for example, is a New Kingdom letter from one man to another in which the writer indicates that his wife has overturned his decision on renting out his fields. O. Cairo 49866 contains journal entries listing workmen absent from work; for the first month of winter, day 21, two men were absent at "birthday parties" *(ḥbw),* two were sick *(mr),* and one had not shown up for work because he had had a fight with his wife. Perhaps more significant are examples of individuals who, using the standard name formula "A, son/daughter of B," gave their mother's name in position B rather than their father's without necessarily trying to denigrate their father. A representative example is Ahmose, son of Abana, who lived during the early Eighteenth Dynasty. Ahmose followed his father into the military and became something of a hero during the "wars of liberation" from the Hyksos. Also intriguing are examples such as that of the man named Qedes, who lived during the First Intermediate Period and served as a soldier in his home district of Gebelein. On his funerary stela he is shown with his mother and his son (who is named for Qedes' father), and he credits his success to his mother: "I was a worthy citizen who acted with his arm, the foremost of his whole troop. I acquired oxen and goats. I acquired granaries of Upper Egyptian barley. I acquired title to a [great] field. I made a boat of 30 (cubits) and a small boat that ferried the boatless in the inundation season. I acquired these in the household of my father Iti; (but) it was my mother Ibeb who acquired them for me." Although this scenario could reflect a strong, "aggressive" mother overshadowing the father, or a widowed mother raising her son on her own, it is more likely that Qedes was the son of his father's second marriage, that he had an older half-brother who inherited the father's position and influence, and that he depended on his mother for "backing." See H.G. Fischer, "The Nubian Mercenaries of Gebelein during the First Intermediate Period," *Kush* 9 (1961): 54–55. Several contemporary Naga el-Deir stelae say that a woman brought up her children "from the back of the house," perhaps indicating a strong-willed second wife who pushed her children to success. See Dows Dunham, *Naga-ed-Der Stelae of the First Intermediate Period* (Oxford, 1937, stelae nos. 69 and 78). Also see notes 102 and 103 below.

52 For example, Henut-tawy, the wife of Nesamenope, in the Late Ramesside Letters; see Deborah Sweeney, "Hennuttawy's Guilty Conscience," *JEA* 80 (1994): 208–12; and J.J. Janssen, "On Style in Egyptian Handwriting," *JEA* 73 (1987): 167 and n. 25.

53 As did both Greek and Aramaic Jewish marriage contracts preserved from first millennium Egypt; also see note 62 below.

54 See, for example, the passage from "The Instructions of Ptahhotep" quoted in note 47.

55 P. Leiden I, 371.

56 Similar claims of fidelity are found, for example, in the First Intermediate Period inscription of Iti ("I was a worthy citizen who acted with his arm. I was a great pillar in the Theban nome, a man of standing in the Southland. I nourished Imyotru [his capital city] in years of misery. Though 400 men were in desperation as a result of it [the years of misery], I did not seize a man's daughter, nor did I seize his field"); in the Middle Kingdom inscription of the Nomarch Amenemhat ("There was no citizen's daughter whom I shamed, no widow whom I oppressed, no farmer whom I drove away, no herdsman whom I turned back"); and in the New Kingdom inscription of the similarly named High Priest Amenemhat ("I did not know the servant girl in my father's house; I did not copulate with his maid-servant").

57 And, by implication, the associated status and clout.

58 As Pestman, *Marriage,* 124ff.

59 The woman was allowed to intervene directly only when the man to whom the contract had been made, and who was to be acting on her behalf, had died without appointing another man to watch over her interests. Most of the scenarios presented are legal debates between the two men about whether the money that one man was supposed to give to the other had been paid and whether the man who was supposed to pay the annuity had done so or owed arrears and interest. That these annuity contracts were actually about support of a woman is made clear from the section in which the man who originally made the contract claims that he no longer is required to pay the annuity because the woman for whom it was made has died.

60 Which date from the Ptolemaic Period.

61 Or any other man on her behalf.

62 There occur to me two possible explanations for the apparently subordinate legal status of women in these earliest annuity contracts and in the section of the Hermopolis Legal Code referring to such contracts. In the Third Intermediate Period, Egypt was dominated politically by Libyan tribesmen. It is possible that the system reflected in these earliest documents reflects a Libyan or "tribal" modification of the original Egyptian system, a system that had returned in full force by the Ptolemaic Period. Very little is known, however, about women or marriage during the Libyan Period; therefore such a reconstruction remains an unsupported suggestion. It is also possible that as Egypt contended with Babylonian and Assyrian policies and eventually became incorporated into the Persian Empire, she came into direct contact with "cuneiform law," in which contracts of all kinds were regularly made between men. It is possible that as the Egyptians struggled to present legal conventions in formal language, they may have borrowed formats or formulae that eventually were modified to fit the actual Egyptian social and legal situation. The strong similarity between Persian Period Demotic

Egyptian and Aramaic contracts concerning real estate, in which individual phrases or clauses apparently were translated from one language to the other, may reflect the intervention of the state in setting proper formats for documents that had to be registered with the state. For a discussion of the similarity or identity of the phrases, see Bezalel Porten, "Aramaic-Demotic Equivalents: Who Is the Borrower and Who the Lender?" in *Life in a Multi-Cultural Society: Egypt from Cambyses to Constantine and Beyond,* ed. Janet H. Johnson (Chicago, 1992), 259–64. The marriage documents of the two groups are quite different, however; the Aramaic documents, for example, include statements concerning the rights and duties of the husband and wife. Presumably they reflect the two different social systems and the lack of interest on the part of the state in such matters.

63 The name of a very cursive script and that stage of the Egyptian language used during the Late Period for personal documents (e.g., letters, contracts) as well as many literary and some religious documents.

64 The Persian kings spoke Persian and used Aramaic as their administrative language; the Ptolemies spoke Greek and used it as their administrative language; the Romans spoke Latin and used Greek as their administrative language.

65 By whatever standards used to measure such things—art, literature, religion.

66 Or at least the rulers did nothing to discourage it.

67 As pure Egyptians at the local level and as bicultural individuals in the higher levels of administration.

68 In both Egyptian and (especially) Greek.

69 See Bernadette Menu, "Les actes de vente en Egypte ancienne, particulièrement sous les rois kouchites et saïtes," *JEA* 74 (1988): 165–81.

70 Ibid.

71 But not identical.

72 P. BM 10593.

73 As noted above; see notes 27–30. P.W. Pestman, *The New Papyrological Primer,* 5th ed. (Leiden, 1990), 52, shows how a man could even refer to himself as the "owner" of property belonging to his wife.

74 See below.

75 P. BM 10591.

76 See note 31, above.

77 P. Turin 2021 deals with exactly the same situation, a man whose first wife had died and who had remarried. There, as here, the children of the first wife inherited two-thirds of their father's property (in addition to their mother's property). That text, however, is a record of a court appearance by the father, the second wife, and the children of the first wife, in which the children of the first wife attest that indeed they have received the two-thirds of their father's property and that they have no objections to their father's endowing his second wife with the remaining one-third.

78 That every woman had some right to communal property may be the meaning of the statement made by the husband/father in P. Turin 2021: "Pharaoh said: 'Give every woman's *sfr* to her.'"

79 They could do so without any interest on the part of the state. The vocabulary for divorce, like that for marriage, reflected the fact that marriage basically was living together; a man "left, abandoned" (*ḫ3ᶜ*) a woman; a woman "went (away from)" (*šm*) or "left, abandoned" a man.

80 The word *ḥbswt,* attested by the First Intermediate Period or early Middle Kingdom, means literally "covered or clothed female" but has been suggested to mean "bride." See Hans Goedicke, *Studies in the Hekanakhte Papers* (Baltimore, 1984), 35. If this is so, it, too, would imply that society held a man responsible for proper support (food and clothing) of his wife.

81 Assumed in Old through New Kingdom cases (see note 37, above) and spelled out specifically in Ptolemaic annuity contracts.

82 As implied by P. Turin 2021.

83 P. Brooklyn 35.7476.

84 For example, the woman mentioned in O. Petrie 18, who not only abandoned her husband when he was sick but took and sold some of his or their (joint) property. The husband went to court and swore an oath saying she had no rights to his property; rather, his son, who took care of him when he was sick, would get everything. The woman then was forced to swear that she would not try to claim anything.

85 To judge by the the Late Period annuity contracts.

86 Examples that have been interpreted in this way include O. Deir el-Medina 587 and O. Ashmolean 1945.39.

87 In one New Kingdom letter (Moscow Bowl 3917), for example, a man asks his superior to chastise his ex-wife, claiming that the share that the ex-wife took is really his own.

88 In the New Kingdom O. Petrie 61, for example, a man promises his daughter that if her husband banishes her, she can live in the storeroom that he built; that is, because he built it himself, it belongs to him, not to the state, and no one can force her to leave it. Also see note 31, above, for examples in which a man forces his son-in-law to take an oath (on pain of forfeiture of joint property) not to beat the man's daughter again.

89 This is illustrated, for example, in the inscriptions of Senmose and Nakht-mut (the latter translation page 182). The literary texts stress that one should not be greedy and turn against one's siblings for the sake of a greater inheritance. Thus "The Instructions of Ptahhotep" advise: "Do not be greedy in the division; do not covet more than your share. Do not be greedy toward your kin; the mild has a greater claim than the harsh. Poor is he who shuns his kin; he is deprived of ⌈interchange⌉." The New Kingdom "Instructions of 'Any" exhort: "Do not rely on another's goods; guard what you acquire yourself; Do not depend on another's wealth lest he become master in your house. Build a house or find and buy one; shun ⌈contention⌉. Don't say 'My mother's father has a house; "⌈a house that lasts⌉," one calls it.' When you come to share with your brothers, your portion may be a storeroom." The Late Period "Instructions of 'Onchsheshonqy" advise: "Do not dislike one who says to you 'I am your brother.' If my share in my father's house is small, it will not increase." The New Kingdom text of 'Any, in advocating self-sufficiency, specifically envisages inappropriate help from one's mother—the inheritance of a house via the mother from the maternal grandfather.

90 See, for example, P. Kahun I, translation page 178.

91 *Nmḥ,* the same term as used in the Adoption Papyrus (translation page 183) for the new "free" status of the adopted children.

92 *Sḥr.*

93 Of whom it is generally assumed that her husband had been the father (Adoption Papyrus, translation page 183). For a discussion of the "social context" of the Adoption Papyrus, see C.J. Eyre, "The Adoption Papyrus in Social Context," *JEA* 78 (1992): 207–21.

94 In O. Berlin 10627 one man taunts another: "You are not a man since you are unable to make your (successive) wives pregnant like your fellowmen. A further matter: You abound in being exceedingly stingy. You give no one anything. As for him who has no children, he adopts an orphan instead [to] bring him up."

95 The strongest arguments, however, come from the Hermopolis Legal Code, in which siblings, including daughters, must take the initiative to get their "fair share" away from the eldest brother. It has been noted above (note 62) that the Hermopolis Legal Code may reflect a more "tribal" system than that found in earlier and later Egypt; therefore such evidence must be used very carefully.

96 The Door Architrave of Tjenti, translation page 184.

97 Sethe, *Urkunden,* 1/35.

98 Ibid., 36.

99 Preserved examples (e.g., P. Boulaq 10, translation page 177, and O. Petrie 16) may reflect a young person defending his inheritance from a grandparent via a parent against the parent's siblings (or half-siblings?). Perhaps these documents reflect the tendency of the older and more powerful to pick on the younger and more vulnerable, especially if there is a history of family infighting and/or valuable property to be contested.

100 Examples would include a house that is occupied jointly, agricultural land that is worked jointly, fruit trees from which the crop is owned jointly, etc. Usually this happened when the property involved was too small to be divided successfully, as in the case of siblings owning 1/16 shares of a house or a date tree, or land already divided into parcels so small as to become almost uncultivatable if subdivided further. In cases of agricultural land, and the like, the land could be worked jointly or could be administered by one sibling on behalf of the group.

101 Inscription of Mes, published by Alan H. Gardiner, *The Inscriptions of Mes: A Contribution to the Study of Egyptian Judicial Procedure, UGAÄ,* 4, no. 3 (1905).

102 Examples include Khnumhotep of Beni Hasan ("The Majesty of King Amenemhat [II] appointed me to be Hereditary Prince, Count, Overseer of the Eastern Desert Lands, Stolist of Horus and Pakhet, to the inheritance of the father of my mother in Menat-Khufu") and Kheti II of Asiut, who even noted that his mother ruled the nome until he came of age. For the latter, see Hellmut Brunner, *Die Texte aus den Gräbern der Herakleopolitenzeit von Siut mit Übersetzung und Erläuterungen,* vol. 5 (Glückstadt, 1937).

103 "There exists my office of Governor of El-Kab, it having come to me as the office of my father, the Governor of El-Kab Iy-mery, it having come to my father as property of his mother's brother, the Governor of El-Kab Iy-the-younger, who died without children" *(Stèle juridique,* ll. 5–6; also see ll. 25–26).

104 Also note that among the earliest "annuity contracts" are parallel contracts made by a father and son to the woman the son was going to marry; I would argue that these contracts represent a stage when the legal system was trying to come to grips with the basic social situation (man economically dependent on father guaranteeing to take care of future wife). For discussion of these texts, see Janet Johnson, "'Annuity Contracts' and Marriage," in Silverman, ed., *For His Ka,* 113–32.

105 A prime example is Hekanakhte, of the Eleventh Dynasty, published by James, *Hekanakhte Papers*

Chronology

PREDYNASTIC PERIOD	to 2920 B.C.
EARLY DYNASTIC PERIOD	
Dynasty 1	2920–2770 B.C.
Dynasty 2	2770–2649 B.C.
OLD KINGDOM	
Dynasty 3	2649–2575 B.C.
Dynasty 4	2575–2465 B.C.
Dynasty 5	2465–2323 B.C.
Dynasty 6	2323–2150 B.C.
Dynasties 7–8	2150–2134 B.C.
FIRST INTERMEDIATE PERIOD	
Dynasties 9–11	2134–2040 B.C.
MIDDLE KINGDOM	
Dynasty 11	2040–1991 B.C.
Dynasty 12	1991–1783 B.C.
Dynasty 13	1783–after 1640 B.C.
SECOND INTERMEDIATE PERIOD	
Dynasties 15–17	1640–1550 B.C.
NEW KINGDOM	
Dynasty 18	
Ahmose	1550–1525 B.C.
Amenhotep I	1525–1504 B.C.
Thutmose I	1504–1492 B.C.
Thutmose II	1492–1479 B.C.
Thutmose III	1479–1425 B.C.
Hatshepsut	1473–1458 B.C.
Amenhotep II	1427–1401 B.C.
Thutmose IV	1401–1391 B.C.
Amenhotep III	1391–1353 B.C.
Amenhotep IV (Akhenaten)	1353–1335 B.C.
Smenkhkara	1335–1333 B.C.
Tutankhamen	1333–1323 B.C.
Ay	1323–1319 B.C.
Horemheb	1319–1307 B.C.
Dynasty 19	
Ramesses I	1307–1306 B.C.
Seti I	1306–1290 B.C.
Ramesses II	1290–1224 B.C.
Merenptah	1224–1214 B.C.
Seti II	1214–1204 B.C.
Amenmesses	(usurper)
Siptah	1204–1198 B.C.
Tauseret	1198–1196 B.C.
Dynasty 20	
Sethnakht	1196–1194 B.C.
Ramesses III	1194–1163 B.C.
Ramesses IV–XI	1163–1070 B.C.
THIRD INTERMEDIATE PERIOD	
Dynasty 21	1070–945 B.C.
Dynasty 22	945–712 B.C.
Dynasty 23	ca. 828–712 B.C.
Dynasty 24	ca. 724–712 B.C.
Dynasty 25	ca. 712–657 B.C.
LATE PERIOD	
Dynasty 26	664–525 B.C.
Dynasty 27	525–404 B.C.
Dynasty 28	404–399 B.C.
Dynasty 29	399–380 B.C.
Dynasty 30	380–343 B.C.
Late Persian Period	343–332 B.C.
GRECO-ROMAN PERIOD	332 B.C.–A.D. 395

Based on Baines and Málek, *Atlas* (New York, 1980), pp. 36–37.

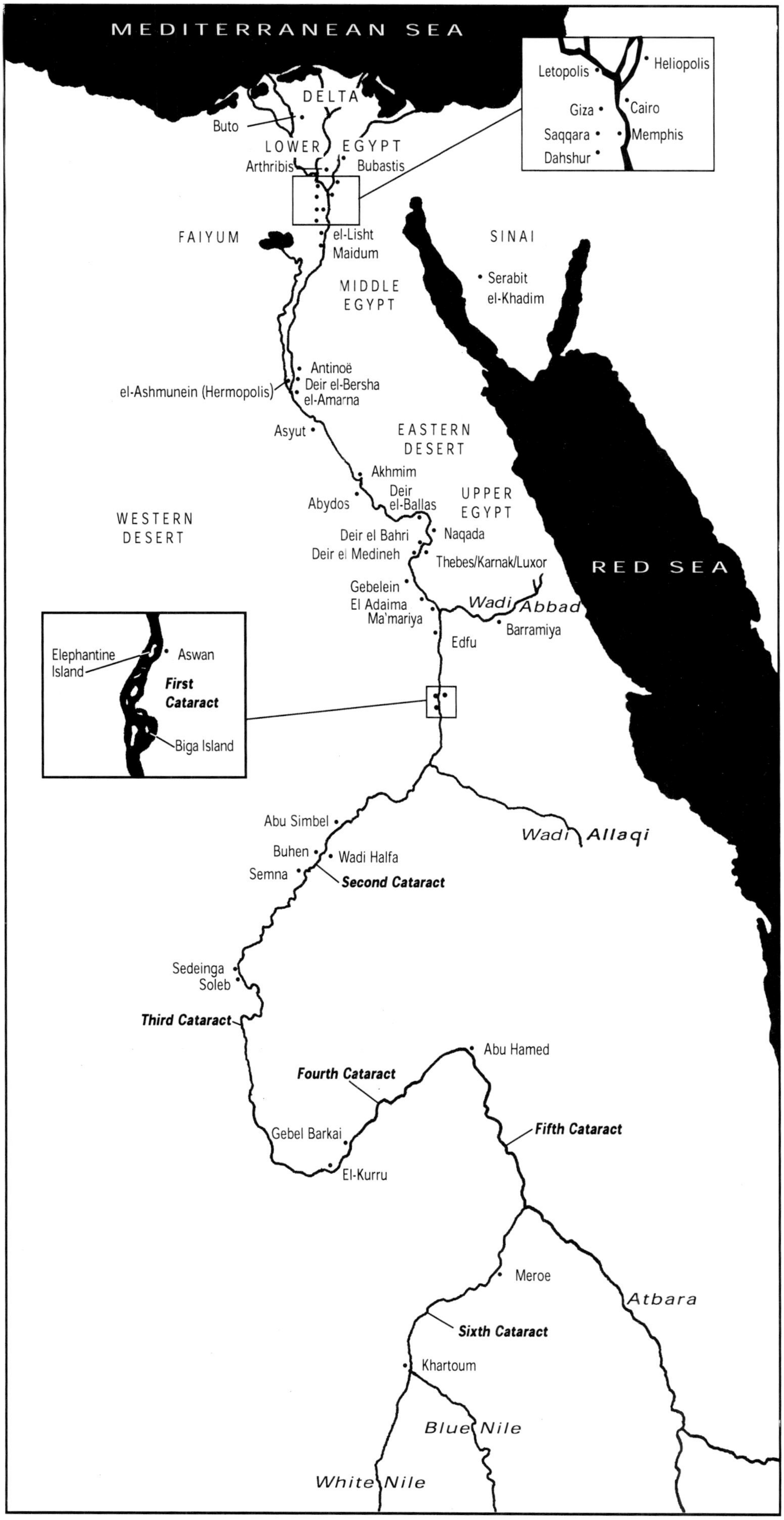

MEDITERRANEAN SEA
DELTA
Buto
LOWER EGYPT
Arthribis
Bubastis
Letopolis
Heliopolis
Giza
Cairo
Saqqara
Memphis
Dahshur
FAIYUM
el-Lisht
Maidum
SINAI
Serabit el-Khadim
MIDDLE EGYPT
Antinoë
Deir el-Bersha
el-Ashmunein (Hermopolis)
el-Amarna
Asyut
EASTERN DESERT
Akhmim
Abydos
Deir el-Ballas
UPPER EGYPT
WESTERN DESERT
Deir el Bahri
Naqada
Deir el Medineh
Thebes/Karnak/Luxor
RED SEA
Gebelein
El Adaima
Wadi Abbad
Ma'mariya
Barramiya
Edfu
Elephantine Island
Aswan
First Cataract
Biga Island
Abu Simbel
Wadi Allaqi
Buhen
Wadi Halfa
Semna
Second Cataract
Sedeinga
Soleb
Third Cataract
Abu Hamed
Fourth Cataract
Gebel Barkai
Fifth Cataract
El-Kurru
Meroe
Atbara
Sixth Cataract
Khartoum
Blue Nile
White Nile

Bibliography

Aldred, C. *Akhenaten: King of Egypt* (London, 1988)

———*Jewels of the Pharaohs* (New York, 1971)

———*Egypt to the End of the Old Kingdom* (London, 1984)

———*Akhenaten and Nefertiti.* Exh. cat. The Brooklyn Museum (Brooklyn, 1973)

———*Middle Kingdom Art in Ancient Egypt, 2300–1590 B.C.* (London, 1956)

———*New Kingdom Art in Ancient Egypt during the Eighteenth Dynasty, 1570 to 1320 B.C.* Rev. ed. enlarged (London, 1961)

———*Old Kingdom Art in Ancient Egypt* (London, 1949)

Allam, S. *Beiträge zum Hathorkult (bis zum Ende des Mittleren Reiches), MÄS* 4 (Berlin, 1963)

Allen, J. *Egyptian Genesis,* 2nd ed. (San Antonio, 1995)

Altenmüller, H. *Die Apotropaia und die Götter Mittelägyptens: eine typologische und religionsgeschichte Untersuchung der sogenannten "Zaubermesser" des Mittleren Reich* (Munich, 1965)

Andrews, C.A.R. *Egyptian Mummies* (London, 1984)

———*Amulets of Ancient Egypt* (Austin, 1994)

———*Catalogue of Egyptian Antiquities in the British Museum 6: Jewellery 1* (London, 1981)

———*Ancient Egyptian Jewellery* (London, 1990)

Arnold, D. *Lexikon der ägyptischen Baukunst* (Zurich, 1994)

Assmann, J., E. Feucht, and R. Grieshammer, eds. *Fragen an die altägyptische Literatur: Studien zum Gedenken an Eberhard Otto* (Wiesbaden, 1977)

Badawy, A. *A History of Egyptian Architecture 1. From the Earliest Times to the End of the Old Kingdom* (London, 1990)

Baer, K. *Rank and Title in the Old Kingdom* (Chicago, 1960)

Baines, J., and J. Málek. *Atlas of Ancient Egypt* (New York, 1980)

Baumgartel, E.J. *The Cultures of Prehistoric Egypt.* Rev. ed., 2 vols. (Oxford, 1960)

Berman, L., ed. *The Art of Amenhotep III: Art Historical Analysis* (Cleveland, 1990)

Bleeker, C.J. *Hathor and Thoth.* Studies in the History of Religions 26 (Leiden, 1973)

Bleiberg, E., and R. Freed, eds. *Fragments of a Shattered Visage: The Proceedings of the International Symposium of Ramesses the Great.* Memphis State University. Monographs of the Institute of Egyptian Art and Archaeology 1 (Memphis, 1991)

Bonnet, H. *Reallexikon der Ägyptischen Religionsgeschichte* (Berlin, 1952)

Boorn, G.P.F. van den. *The Duties of the Vizier: Civil Administration in the Early New Kingdom* (London, 1988)

Borchardt, L. *Das Grabdenkmal des Königs Sa3hu-Re* 2 (Leipzig, 1913)

Borghouts, J.F. *Ancient Egyptian Magical Texts.* Nisaba 9 (Leiden, 1978)

Bothmer, B.V., et al. *ESLP.* Exh. cat. The Brooklyn Museum (Brooklyn, 1960)

Bourriau, J. *Pharaohs and Mortals: Egyptian Art in the Middle Kingdom.* Exh. cat. The Fitzwilliam Museum (Cambridge, 1988)

———*Umm el-Ga'ab: Pottery from the Nile Valley before the Arab Conquest.* Exh. cat. Fitzwilliam Museum (Cambridge, 1981)

Breasted, J.H. *Egyptian Servant Statues* (Washington, D.C. 1948)

———*Ancient Records of Egypt.* 5 vols. (New York, 1962)

Bruyère, B. *Rapport sur les fouilles de Deir el Médineh* 2, FIFAO 15 (Cairo, 1937)

Bryan, B. *The Reign of Thutmose IV* (Baltimore, 1991)

Bulté, J. *Talismans égyptiens d'heureuse maternité: "Faience" bleu vert à pois foncés* (Paris, 1991)

Cameron, A., and A. Kuhrt, eds. *Images of Women in Antiquity* (London and Canberra, 1980)

Capart, J. *L'art égyptien* 4 (Paris, 1947)

———*Documents pour servir à l'étude de l'art égyptien* 1 (Paris, 1927)

Cooney, J.D. *Amarna Reliefs from Hermopolis in American Collections* (Brooklyn, 1965)

———*Five Years of Collecting Egyptian Art, 1951–1956.* Exh. cat. The Brooklyn Museum (Brooklyn, 1956)

Davies, N. de G. *The Rock Tombs of El Amarna*

———1. *The Tomb of Meryra* (London, 1903)

———2. *The Tombs of Panehesy and Meryra II* (London, 1905)

———3. *The Tombs of Huya and Ahmes* (London, 1905)

———4. *Tombs of Penthu, Mahu, and Others* (London, 1908)

———5. *Smaller Tombs and Boundary Stelae* (London, 1908)

———6. *Tombs of Parennefer, Tutu, and Ay* (London, 1908)

———*The Tomb of Two Sculptors at Thebes* (New York, 1925)

———*The Tomb of Nakht at Thebes* (New York, 1917)

———*The Tomb of Nefer-hotep at Thebes* (New York, 1933)

———*Seven Private Tombs at Kurnah* (London, 1948)

———*Five Theban Tombs* (London, 1913)

———*The Tomb of Rekh-mi-Re' at Thebes* (New York, 1935)

Delange, E. *Catalogue des statues égyptiennes du Moyen Empire* (Paris, 1987)

Delvaux, L., and E. Warmenbol, eds. *Les divins chats d'Égypt: Un air subtil, un dangereux parfum* (Louvain, 1991)

Demarée, R.J., and J.J. Janssen. *Gleanings from Deir el-Medina* (Leiden, 1982)

Demisch, H. *Die Sphinx. Geschichte ihrer Darstellung von den Anfängen bis zur Gegenwart* (Stuttgart, 1977)

Derchain, P. *Hathor quadrifons: Récherches sur la syntaxe d'un mythe égyptien.* Publications de l'Institut historique et archéologique de Stamboul 28 (Istanbul, 1972)

Dorman, P. *Monuments of Senenmut* (London, 1988)

Duell, P., et al. *The Mastaba of Mereruka.* 2 vols. (Chicago 1938)

Dunham, D. *The Royal Cemeteries of Kush* 1. *El Kurru* (Cambridge, 1950)

Dunham, D., and J.J. Janssen. *Second Cataract Forts* 1. *Semna Kumma* (Boston, 1960)

Dunham, D., and W.K. Simpson. *The Mastaba of Queen Mersyankh III (G7530–7540). Giza Mastabas* 1 (Boston, 1974)

Ebbell, B. *The Papyrus Ebers: The Greatest Egyptian Medical Document* (London, 1937)

Eggebricht, A., ed. *Ägyptens Aufsteig zur Weltmacht.* Exh. cat. Roemer und Pelizaeus Museum, Hildesheim (Mainz, 1987)

The Egyptian Mummy: Secrets and Science. University Museum Handbook 1 (Philadelphia, 1980)

Egypt's Dazzling Sun: Amenhotep III and His World (Bloomington, Ind., 1992)

Egypt's Golden Age: The Art of Living in the New Kingdom, 1558–1085 B.C. Exh. cat. Museum of Fine Arts (Boston, 1982)

Elsasser, A.B., and V.M. Frederickson. *Ancient Egypt.* Exh. cat. Robert H. Lowie Museum of Anthropology, University of California, Berkeley (Berkeley, 1966)

El-Sayed, R. *La déesse Neith de Sais.* 2 vols. *BdE* 86, nos. 1–2 (1982)

Evers, H.G. *Staat aus dem Stein: Denkmäler, Geschichte und Bedeutung der ägyptischen Plastik während des Mittleren Reichs.* 2 vols. (Munich, 1929)

Fakhry, A. *The Monuments of Sneferu at Dahshur.* 2 vols. (Cairo, 1961)

Faulkner, R.O. *The Ancient Egyptian Coffin Texts.* 3 vols. (Warminster, 1973)

———*The Egyptian Book of the Dead* (San Francisco, 1994)

———*Concise Dictionary of Middle Egyptian [CDME]* (Oxford, 1976)

Fay, B. *The Louvre Sphinx and Royal Sculpture from the Reign of Amenemhat II* (Mainz, 1996)

Fazzini, R.A. *Egypt, Dynasty XXII–XXV.* Iconography of Religions 16:10 (Leiden, 1988)

———*Images for Eternity: Egyptian Art from Brooklyn and Berkeley.* Exh. cat. The Brooklyn Museum and The Fine Arts Museums of San Francisco (Brooklyn, 1975)

Fazzini, R.A., et al. *Ancient Egyptian Art in The Brooklyn Museum* (New York, 1989)

———*Neferut net Kemit: Egyptian Art from The Brooklyn Museum.* Exh. cat. (Tokyo, 1983)

Fechheimer, H. *Die Plastik der Ägypter* (Berlin, 1920)

———*Kleinplastik der Ägypter* (Berlin, 1922)

Fischer, H.G. *Egyptian Studies* 1. *Varia* (New York, 1976)

———*Egyptian Titles of the Middle Kingdom* (New York, 1985)

———*Egyptian Women of the Old Kingdom and of the Heracleopolitan Period* (New York, 1989)

Frankfort, H. *Kingship and the Gods* (Chicago and London, 1948)

Friedman, R., and B. Adams, eds. *The Followers of Horus: Studies Dedicated to Michael Allen Hoffman, 1944–1990.* Egyptian Studies Association Publication No. 2, Oxbow Monograph 20 (Oxford, 1992)

Gardiner, A.H. *Egypt of the Pharaohs* (Oxford, 1961)

———*Egyptian Grammar.* 4th rev. ed. (Oxford, 1973)

Germond, P. *Sekhmet et la protection du monde.* Aegyptiaca Helvetica 9 (Basel and Geneva, 1981)

Gitton, M. *Les divines épouses de la 18e dynastie* (Paris, 1984)

———*L'épouse du dieu Ahmès Néfertary.* 2nd ed. (Paris, 1981)

Graefe, E. *Untersuchungen zur Verwaltung und Geschichte der Institution der Gottesgemahlin des Amun vom Beginn des Neuen Reiches bis zur Spätzeit* 1 (Wiesbaden, 1981)

Greene, L. "Queens and Princesses of the Amarna Period: The Social, Political, Religious and Cultic Role of the Women of the Royal Family at the End of the 18th Dynasty," Ph.D. diss. (University of Toronto, 1988)

Grimal, N. *A History of Ancient Egypt* (Cambridge, Mass., and Oxford, 1994)

Grose, D.F. *Early Ancient Glass.* Hudson Hills Press, in association with The Toledo Museum of Art (New York and Toledo, 1989)

Hart, G. *A Dictionary of Egyptian Gods and Goddesses* (London, 1986)

———*Egyptian Myths* (London and Austin, 1990)

Hayes, W. *The Scepter of Egypt* 1. *From the Earliest Times to the End of the Middle Kingdom.* 5th rev. ed. (New York, 1990); 2. *The Hyksos Period and the New Kingdom (1675–1080 B.C.).* 4th rev. ed. (New York, 1990)

———*A Papyrus of the Late Middle Kingdom in The Brooklyn Museum* (Brooklyn, 1955)

Helck, W. *Zur Verwaltung des Mittleren und Neuen Reichs* (Leiden, 1958)

———*Untersuchungen zu den Beamtentiteln des ägyptischen Alten Reichs* (Glückstadt, 1954)

Heyob, S.K. *The Cult of Isis among Women in the Graeco-Roman World* (Leiden, 1975)

Hoenes, S.E. *Untersuchungen zu Wesen und Kult der Göttin Sachmet* (Bonn, 1976)

Hoffmann, M.A. *Egypt before the Pharaohs: The Prehistoric Foundations of Egyptian Civilization* (Austin, 1979)

Hornung, E. *Conceptions of God in Ancient Egypt: The One and the Many,* J.R. Baines, tr. (Ithaca, 1982)

Hornung, E., and E. Staehelin. *Skarabäen und andere Siegel-Amulette aus Basler Sammlungen* (Mainz, 1976)

James, T.G.H. *Corpus of Hieroglyphic Inscriptions in The Brooklyn Museum* 1. *From Dynasty I to the End of Dynasty XVIII.* Wilbour Monographs 6 (Brooklyn, 1974)

———*Ancient Egypt: The Land and Its Legacy* (London, 1988)

———*The Hekanakhte Papers and Other Early Middle Kingdom Documents* (New York, 1962)

Janssen, R.M., and J.J. Janssen. *Growing Up in Ancient Egypt* (London, 1990)

Jéquier, G. *Les pyramides des reines Neit et Apouit* (Cairo, 1933)

———*La pyramide d'Oudjebten* (Cairo, 1928)

Johnson, S. *The Cobra Goddess of Ancient Egypt: Predynastic, Early Dynastic, and Old Kingdom Period* (London and New York, 1990)

Junker, H. *Giza.* 5 vols. (Vienna and Leipzig, 1938–55)

Kaplony, P. *Die Inschriften der ägyptischen Frühzeit* 1 (Wiesbaden, 1963)

Kemp, B.J. *Ancient Egypt: Anatomy of a Civilization* (New York, 1991)

Kendall, T. *Kush: Lost Kingdom of the Nile* (Boston, 1982)

Kischkewitz, H. *Egyptian Drawings* (London, 1972)

Kitchen, K.A. *The Third Intermediate Period in Egypt (1100–650 B.C.).* 2nd rev. ed. (Warminster, 1986)

Kunst des Alten Reiches: Symposium im Deutschen Archäologischen Institut Kairo am 29. und 30. Oktober 1991. Deutsches Archäologisches Institut, Abteilung Kairo, Sonderschrift 28 (Mainz am Rhein, 1995)

Lacau, P. *Stèles du nouvel empire.* 2 vols. (Cairo, 1909, 1926)

Lange, K., and M. Hirmer. *Egypt: Architecture-Sculpture-Painting in Three Thousand Years* (London and New York, 1968)

Lesko, B.S., ed. *Women's Earliest Records from Ancient Egypt and Western Asia* (Atlanta, 1989)

Lesko, L.H., ed. *Egyptological Studies in Honor of Richard A. Parker: Presented on the Occasion of His Seventy-eighth Birthday, December 10, 1983* (Hanover, N.H., 1986)

Lesko, L.H., and B.S. Lesko, eds. *LED* (Berkeley and Providence, 1982, 1984)

Lhote, A. *Les chefs-d'oeuvre de la peinture égyptienne* (Paris, 1954)

Lichtheim, M. *Ancient Egyptian Literature.* 3 vols. (Berkeley, Los Angeles, London, 1976)

Lilyquist, C. *Egyptian Mirrors from the Earliest Times through the Middle Kingdom* (Berlin, 1979)

Lutz, H.F. *Egyptian Statues and Statuettes in the Museum of Anthropology of the University of California.* University of California Publications, Egyptian Archaeology 5 (Leipzig, 1930)

Mace, A.C., and H.E. Winlock. *The Tomb of Senebtisi at Lisht* (New York, 1916)

Malek, J. *The Cat in Ancient Egypt* (London, 1993)

Manniche, L. *Music and Musicians in Ancient Egypt* (London, 1991)

———*An Ancient Egyptian Herbal* (Austin, 1993)

———*Sexual Life in Ancient Egypt* (London, 1987)

Manuelian, P. *Living in the Past: Studies in Archaism of the Egyptian Twenty-sixth Dynasty* (London and New York, 1994)

Mariette, A. *Abydos.* 2 vols. (Paris, 1869, 1880)

———*Denderah.* 6 vols. (Paris, 1870–75)

Martin, G.T. *The Hidden Tombs of Memphis* (London, 1991)

Maspero, G. *Les momies royales de Deir el-Bahari. MMAF* 1 (Paris, 1889)

Matzker, I. *Die letzten Könige der 12. Dynastie* (Frankfurt am Main, 1986)

Mekhitarian, A. *Egyptian Painting* (New York, 1954)

Mercer, S.A.B. *The Pyramid Texts.* 4 vols. (New York, London, Toronto, 1952)

Mertz, B. "Certain Titles of Egyptian Queens and Their Bearing on the Hereditary Right to the Throne." Ph.D. diss. (University of Chicago, 1952)

Moran, W. *The Amarna Letters* (Baltimore, 1994)

Müller, H.W. *Ägyptische Kunst* (Frankfurt, 1970)

Mummies and Magic: The Funerary Arts of Ancient Egypt. Exh. cat. Museum of Fine Arts, Boston (Boston, 1988)

Munro, P. *Die spätägyptische Totenstelen* (Glückstadt, 1973)

Münster, M. *Untersuchungen zur Gottin Isis vom Alten Reich bis zum Ende des Neuen Reiches. MÄS* 2 (1978)

Murnane, W.J. *Ancient Egyptian Coregencies. SAOC* 40 (1977)

Naguib, S.-A. *Le clergé féminin d'Amon thébain. OLA* 38 (1990)

Naville, E. *The XIth Dynasty Temple at Deir el Bahari.* 3 vols., Egypt Exploration Fund, 28th, 30th, and 32nd Memoir (London, 1907–13)

Needler, W. *Predynastic and Archaic Egypt in The Brooklyn Museum,* Wilbour Monographs 9 (Brooklyn, 1984)

Nofret-die Schöne: Die Frau im Alten Ägypten: "Wahrheit" und Wirklichkeit. Exh. cat. Roemer und Pelizaeus Museum, Hildesheim (Mainz, 1985)

O'Connor, D., and D.P. Silverman, eds. *Ancient Egyptian Kingship, PÄ* 9 (1995)

Parkinson, R. *Voices from Ancient Egypt: An Anthology of Middle Kingdom Writings* (Norman, Okla., 1991)

Partridge, R.B. *Faces of Pharaohs: Royal Mummies and Coffins from Ancient Thebes* (London, 1994)

Peck, W.H. *Egyptian Drawings* (New York, 1978)

Peet, T.E., and W. Loat. *The Cemeteries of Abydos,* 2, 3 (London, 1913–14)

Peet, T.E., and C.L. Woolley. *The City of Akhenaten.* 1. *Excavations of 1921 and 1922 at El-'Amarneh* (London, 1923)

Pestman, P.W. *Marriage and Matrimonial Property in Ancient Egypt. A Contribution to Establishing the Legal Position of the Woman* (Leiden, 1961)

Petrie, W.M.F. *Abydos* 1 (London, 1902)

———*Amulets* (London, 1914)

———*Tell El-Amarna* (London, 1894)

———*Medum* (London, 1892)

———*Objects of Daily Use* (London, 1927)

Petrie, W.M.F., and G. Brunton. *Sedment* 1 (London, 1924)

Phillips, T., ed. *Africa: The Art of a Continent.* Exh. cat. The Royal Academy (London, Munich, and New York, 1995)

Pinch, G. *Votive Offerings to Hathor* (Oxford, 1993)

———*Magic in Ancient Egypt* (Austin, 1995)

Porter, B., and R.L.B. Moss. *Topographical Bibliography of Ancient Egyptian Hieroglyphic Texts, Reliefs, and Paintings.* 7 vols. (Oxford, 1960–72)

Quirke, S. *Ancient Egyptian Religion* (London, 1992)

Ranke, H. *Die Ägyptischen Personennamen.* 3 vols. (Glückstadt, 1935–77)

Redford, D.B. *Akhenaten: The Heretic King* (Princeton, 1984)

———*History and Chronology of the Eighteenth Dynasty of Egypt: Seven Studies* (Toronto, 1967)

———*Pharaonic King-Lists, Annals and Day-Books: A Contribution to the Study of the Egyptian Sense of History. SSEA* Publication 4 (Mississauga, Ont., 1986)

Reeves, C. *Egyptian Medicine.* Shire Egyptology (London, 1992)

Reisner, G.A. *A History of the Giza Necropolis.* 2 vols. (Cambridge, Mass., 1955)

Rice, M. *Egypt's Making: The Origins of Ancient Egypt, 5000–2000* B.C. (London and New York, 1990)

Ritner, R.K. *The Mechanics of Ancient Egyptian Magical Practice. SAOC* 54 (1993)

Roberts, A. *Hathor Rising: The Serpent Power of Ancient Egypt* (Devon, 1995)

Robins, G. *Women in Ancient Egypt* (Cambridge, Mass., 1993)

Roeder, G. *Ägyptische Inschriften aus den Königlichen Museen zu Berlin* 2 (Leipzig, 1924)

———Staatliche Museen zu Berlin. Mitteilungen aus der Aegyptischen Sammlung 6. *Ägyptische Bronzefiguren* (Berlin, 1956)

Roehrig, C.H. "The Eighteenth Dynasty Titles Royal Nurse *(mn't nswt),* Royal Tutor *(mn' nswt),* and Foster Brother/Sister of the Lord of the Two Lands *(sn/snt mn'n nb t3wy).*" Ph.D. diss. (University of California at Berkeley, 1990)

Romano, J. "The Bes-Image in Pharaonic Egypt." Ph.D. diss. (New York University, 1989)

Rossini, S., and R. Schumann-Antelme. *Nétèr: Dieux d'Egypte* (Paris, 1992)

Roveri, A.M.D., ed. *Egyptian Civilization: Daily Life* (Milan, 1987)

Ruffle, J.G., A. Gaballa, and K.A. Kitchen, eds. *Glimpses of Ancient Egypt: Studies in Honour of H.W. Fairman* (Warminster, 1979)

Russmann, E. *The Representation of the King in the XXVth Dynasty.* Monographies Reine Elisabeth 3 (Brussels and Brooklyn, 1974)

———*Egyptian Sculpture: Cairo and Luxor* (Austin, 1989)

Sadek, A.I. *Popular Religion in Egypt during the New Kingdom,* Hildesheimer Ägyptologische Beiträge 27 (Hildesheim, 1987)

Saleh, M., and H. Sourouzian. *Official Catalogue of the Egyptian Museum, Cairo* (Mainz, 1987)

Samson, J. *Amarna, City of Akhenaten and Nefertiti: Nefertiti as Pharaoh* (Warminster, 1978)

Sasson, J.M., et al., eds. *Civilization of the Ancient Near East.* 1 (New York, 1995)

Schmitz, B. *Untersuchungen zum Titel S3-Njswt "Königsohn"* (Bonn, 1976)

Schneider, H.D. *Shabtis.* 3 vols. (Leiden, 1977)

Schott, S. *Das schöne Fest vom Wustenhale; Festbrauche einer Totenstadt* (Wiesbaden, 1953)

Scott, G.D. *Ancient Egyptian Art at Yale* (New Haven, 1986)

Sculpture Collection of the Cincinnati Art Museum (Cincinnati, 1970)

Seipel, W. *Gott, Mensch, Pharao: Viertausend Jahre Menschenbild in der Skulptur des alten Ägypten.* Exh. cat. Kunsthistorisches Museum, Wien (Vienna, 1992)

Sethe, K., ed. *Urkunden des Alten Reichs, Urkunden des ägyptisches Altertums.* Vol. 1 (Leipzig, 1903)

———*Urkunden der 18. Dynastie, Historisch-biographische Urkunden,* Urkunden des ägyptisches Altertums 4 (Leipzig, 1906)

Shafer, B.E. *Religion in Ancient Egypt: Gods, Myths, and Personal Practice* (Ithaca and London, 1991)

Shäfer, J.H. *Principles of Egyptian Art.* J.R. Baines, tr. (Oxford, 1974)

Shaw, I., and P. Nicholson. *The Dictionary of Ancient Egypt* (London, 1995)

Silverman, D.P., ed. *For His Ka: Essays Offered in Memory of Klaus Baer* (Chicago, 1994)

Smith, W.S. *HESPOK.* 2nd ed. (Oxford, 1949)

———*The Art and Architecture of Ancient Egypt.* 2nd ed. (Baltimore, 1981)

Spanel, D.B. *Through Ancient Eyes: Egyptian Portraiture.* Exh. cat. Birmingham Museum of Art (Birmingham, Ala., 1988)

Spencer, G. *Early Egypt: The Rise of Civilisation in the Nile Valley* (London, 1993)

Steindorff, G. *Catalogue of the Egyptian Sculpture in the Walters Art Gallery* (Baltimore, 1946)

Strouhal, E. *Life of the Ancient Egyptians* (Norman, Okla., 1992)

Teeter, E. "The Presentation of Maat: The Iconography and Theology of an Ancient Egyptian Offering Ritual." Ph.D. diss. (University of Chicago, 1990)

Tefnin, R. *La statuaire d'Hatshepsout* (Brussels, 1979)

Thausing, G., and H. Goedicke. *Nofretari: A Documentation of Her Tomb and Its Decoration* (Graz, 1971)

Thomas, N., et al., eds. *The American Discovery of Ancient Egypt.* Exh. cat. Los Angeles County Museum of Art (Los Angeles, 1995)

Trigger, B.G., et al. *Ancient Egypt: A Social History.* 2 vols. (Cambridge, Eng., 1983, 1984)

Troy, L. *Patterns of Queenship in Ancient Egyptian Myth and History* (Uppsala, 1986)

Tyldesley, J. *Daughters of Isis: Women of Ancient Egypt* (London, 1994)

Vandier, J. *Manuel d'archéologie égyptienne.* 6 vols. (Paris, 1952–78)

Vogelsang-Eastwood, G. *Pharaonic Egyptian Clothing* (Leiden, New York, and Cologne, 1993)

Wainwright, G.A., and T. Whittemore. *Balabish, EES* Memoire 37 (London, 1920)

Ward, W.A. *Index of Egyptian Administrative and Religious Titles of the Middle Kingdom* (Beirut, 1982)

———*Essays on Feminine Titles of the Middle Kingdom and Related Subjects* (Beirut, 1986)

Watterson, B. *Women in Ancient Egypt* (New York, 1991)

Wenig, S. *The Woman in Egyptian Art* (New York, 1969)

Wente, E.F. *Letters from Ancient Egypt* (Atlanta, 1990)

Werbrouck, M. *Les pleureuses dans l'Egypte ancienne* (Brussels, 1938)

Westendorf, W. *Painting, Sculpture, and Architecture of Ancient Egypt* (New York, 1968)

Whale, S. *The Family in the Eighteenth Dynasty of Egypt: A Study of the Representation of the Family in Private Tombs* (Sydney, 1989)

Wildung, D. *Sesostris und Amenemhet. Ägypten im Mittleren Reich* (Munich, 1984)

Wilkinson, A. *Ancient Egyptian Jewellery* (London, 1971)

Winlock, H.E. *Excavations at Deir el Bahri, 1911–1931* (New York, 1942)

———*Models of Daily Life in Ancient Egypt* (New York, 1955)

———*The Rise and Fall of the Middle Kingdom in Thebes* (New York, 1947)

———*The Treasure of the Three Egyptian Princesses* (New York, 1948)

———*The Tomb of Queen Meryet-Amun at Thebes* (New York, 1932)

Yoyotte, J., et al. *Tanis: L'or des pharaos* (Paris, 1987)

Journal and Monograph Series Abbreviations

AEO A.H. Gardiner, *Ancient Egyptian Onomastica*, 3 vols. Oxford

ÄF *Ägyptologische Forschungen.* Glückstadt

AJA *American Journal of Archaeology.* Baltimore

ASAE *Annales du Service des antiquités de l'Egypte.* Cairo

AVDAIK *Archäologische Veröffentlichungen, Deutsches Archäologisches Institut, Abteilung Kairo.* Berlin

BAR J.H. Breasted, *Ancient Records of Egypt.* 5 vols. 1906. Reprint, London. 1988

BD *Book of the Dead*

BBf *Beiträge zur ägyptischen Bauforschung und Altertumskunde.* Cairo

BdE *Institut français d'archéologie Orientale, Bibliothèque d'étude.* Cairo

BES *Bulletin of the Egyptological Seminar.* New York

BIE *Bulletin de l'Institut d'Egypte.* Alexandria and Cairo

BIFAO *Bulletin de l'Institut français d'archéologie Orientale.* Cairo

BiOr *Bibliotheca Orientalis.* Leiden

BMB *The Brooklyn Museum Bulletin.* Brooklyn

BMFA *Bulletin of the Museum of Fine Arts, Boston.* Boston

BMJ *The Brooklyn Museum Journal.* Brooklyn

BMMA *Bulletin of the Metropolitan Museum of Art.* New York

BSAE *British School of Archaeology in Egypt.* London

BSAK *Studien zur Altägyptischen Kultur, Beihefte.* Hamburg

BSEG *Bulletin de la Société d'égyptologie de Genève.* Geneva

BSFE *Bulletin de la Société française d'égyptologie.* Paris

CAA *Corpus Antiquitatum Aegyptiacarum.* Mainz

CAH *Cambridge Ancient History.* Cambridge

CdE *Chronique d'Egypte.* Brussels

CDME Faulkner, *Concise Dictionary of Middle Egyptian.* Oxford

CG *Catalogue général des antiquités égyptiennes du musée du Caire.* Cairo

CRAIBL *Compte rendus de l'Académie des inscriptions et belles-lettres.* Paris

CRIPEL *Cahiers de recherches de l'Institut du papyrologie et d'égyptologie de Lille.* Lille

DiE *Discussions in Egyptology.* Oxford

EES *Egypt Exploration Society.* London

ESLP B.V. Bothmer et al., *Egyptian Sculpture of the Late Period: 700 B.C. to A.D. 100.* Brooklyn, 1960

FIFAO *Fouilles de l'Institut français d'archéologie Orientale.* Cairo

GM *Göttinger Miszellen.* Göttingen

GOF *Göttinger Orientforschungen.* Wiesbaden

HÄB *Hildesheimer Ägyptologischen Studien.* Hamburg

HESPOK W.S. Smith, *A History of Egyptian Sculpture and Painting in the Old Kingdom.* Oxford

IEJ *Israel Exploration Journal.* Jerusalem

JARCE *Journal of the American Research Center in Egypt.* New York

JE *Journal d'entrée, catalogue général des antiquités égyptiennes du musée du Caire.* Cairo

JEA *Journal of Egyptian Archaeology.* London

JEOL *Jaarbericht van het Vooraziatisch-Egyptisch Genootschap (Gezelschap) Ex Oriente Lux.* Leiden

JESHO *Journal of the Economic and Social History of the Orient.* Leiden

JNES *Journal of Near Eastern Studies.* Chicago

JPK *Jahrbuch Preussischer Kulturbesitz.* Berlin

JWAG *Journal of the Walters Art Gallery.* Baltimore

Kêmi *Kêmi. Revue de Philologie et d'Archéologie égyptiennes et coptes.* Paris

LÄ *Lexikon der Ägyptologie.* Eds. H.W. Helck and W. Westendorf. 6 vols. Wiesbaden, 1975–86

LED L.H. Lesko and B.S. Lesko, eds., *A Dictionary of Late Egyptian,* 1–2. Berkeley and Providence

MÄS *Münchner Ägyptologische Studien.* Munich and Berlin

MDAIK *Mitteilungen des Deutschen Archäologischen Instituts, Abteilung Kairo.* Wiesbaden

MIE *Mémoires de l'Institut d'Egypte.* Cairo

MIFAO *Mémoires publiés par les membres de l'institut français d'archéologie Orientale du Caire.* Cairo

MIO *Mitteilungen der Instituts für Orientforschung.* Vienna

MMAF *Mémoires publiés par les membres de la mission archéologique français au Caire.* Cairo

MMJ *Metropolitan Museum Journal.* New York

MonPiot *Fondation Eugène Piot, Monuments et mémoires publiés par l'Académie des inscriptions et belles-lettres.* Paris

MVEOL *Mededelingen en Verhandelingen van het Vooraziatisch-Egyptisch Genootschap (Gezelschap) Ex Oriente Lux.* Leiden

NARCE *Newsletter of the American Research Center in Egypt.* New York

NAWG *Nachrichten von der Akademie der Wissenschaften in Göttingen.* Göttingen

OBO *Orbis Biblicus et Orientalis.* Freiburg and Göttingen

OLA *Orientalia Lovaniensia Analecta.* Louvain

Or *Orientalia.* Rome

PÄ *Probleme der Ägyptologie.* Leiden

PM B. Porter and R.L.B. Moss, *Topographical Bibliography of Ancient Egyptian Hierographic Texts, Reliefs, and Paintings.* 7 vols. Oxford, 1927–51

PSBA *Proceedings of the Society of Biblical Archaeology.* London

RAIN *Royal Anthropological Institute News.* London

RdE *Revue d'Égyptologie.* Cairo and Paris

RIDA *Revue internationale des droits de l'antiquité,* 3rd series, Brussels

RT *Recueil de travaux rélatifs à la philologie et à l'archéologie égyptiennes et assyriennes.* Paris

SAGA *Studien zur Archäologie und Geschichte Altägyptens, Deutsches Archäologisches Institut, Abteilung Kairo und Ägyptologisches Institut, Universität Heidelberg.* Heidelberg

SAK *Studien zur Altägyptischen Kultur.* Berlin

SAOC *Studies in Ancient Oriental Civilization.* Chicago

SDAIK *Sonderschrift des Deutschen Archäologisches Institut, Abteilung Kairo.* Berlin

SSEA *Society for the Study of Egyptian Antiquities.* Toronto

UGAÄ *Untersuchungen zur Geschichte und Altertumskunde Ägyptens.* Leipzig, Berlin, and Hildesheim

WO *Welt des Orient.* Wuppertal

ZÄS *Zeitschrift für Ägyptische Sprache und Altertumskunde.* Leipzig

Index

Page numbers in *italics* refer to illustrations.

Abar, 117
Abu Roash, 104
Abydos, 27, 28, 30, 31, 63, 74, 75, 84, 87, 88, 145, 146, 165, 166, 195 n. 10, 199 n. 3
acacia seed, 85, 130, 198 n. 9, 207 n. 14; jewelry, 85, *85,* 86
administrative titles, women's, 39–40
adoption, 67, 115, 183
Adoption Papyrus, 183, 215, 217
adornment, 75–90, 197–98; cosmetics and cosmetic vessels, 79–87, *79–86,* 197; hair adornments and accessories, 75–79, *75–78,* 197, 198; jewelry, 85–90, *84–90,* 197, 198
adultery, 179, 183, 216 n. 47
aegis, 74, *74,* 136, 140, *140;* and *menat* with head of lion-headed goddess, 74, 135, *136, 137,* 139, 140, 208
afterlife, 44, 51, 65, 67, 70, 92, 94, 102, 105, 118, 125, 132, 145–74, *145–74,* 210–14; Book of the Dead fragment, 156, 158–59, *159,* 160, 212; canopic jar, 157, 158, *158;* coffins, 166–69, *166–69,* 213–14; funerary statues, 162, *162,* 163, 169–74, *170–74,* 210–14; funerary stelae, 163–66, *163–65,* 212–13; headrest, 156, *156,* 157, 211–12; heart scarab, 157, *157,* 212; libation vase with lid, 154, *155,* 156, 211; reserve head, 160, *160, 161,* 212; *shabtis,* 54, 134, 145, 146, 148–53, *149–53,* 154, 211; tomb painting of mourning women, 93, 153, 154, *154,* 211; women's burial assemblages, 84–89, *84–87,* 145–46, *145–47,* 197–98, 210–11; *see also* coffins; mummification; statues, funerary; stelae, funerary; tombs
agriculture, 15, 16, *16,* 19, 20, 26, 38, 40, 49–50, 92, 94, 148, 149, 188, 217 n. 100
Ägyptisches Museum, Berlin, 61, 199, 203 n. 6, 205 n. 4
Aha, 27, 28, 64, 67, 132, 195 n. 14
Ahhotep, 30, 31
Ahmose, 26, 30, 31, *31,* 32, 44, 109, 117, 204 n. 5; coffin of, 14, *14;* Donation Stela of, 31, *31,* 44, 190 n. 52
Ahmose-Nefertari, 26, 30, 31, *31,* 44, 115, 117, 202 n. 7, 203 n. 3, 204 n. 5; Donation Stela of, 31, *31,* 44, 190 n. 52
Amarna, 17, 66, 67, 73, 111–14, 148, 156, 202 n. 23, 204; beaded jewelry, 88, *88*
Amduat, 159
Amen, 32, 33, 51, 55, 58, 114, 115, 116, 118, 124, 126, 128, 130, 141, 153, 164, 165, 169, 178, 199 n. 13; cult of, 42, 43, *43,* 50, 98, 115
Amenemhat, 190 n. 71; tomb of, *42*
Amenemhat I, 20
Amenemhat II, 107
Amenemhat III, 29, 30, 37, 40, 178, 190 n. 41, 208 n. 2
Amenemhat IV, 29, 30
Amenemopet, 18, *18*
Amenhotep, 172, *172*
Amenhotep I, 26, 31
Amenhotep II, 18, *18,* 26, 34, 42, 123, 187 nn. 32–34, 188 n. 72, 196 n. 4, 211 n. 14
Amenhotep III, 17, 26, 42, 43, 62, 63, 80, *81,* 108, 111, 114, 123, 134–36, 141, 149, 151, 158, 168, 188 n. 72, 191 n. 133, 193 n. 3, 210 n. 9, 211 n. 24, 212 nn. 3–4
Amenhotep IV/Akhenaten, 26, 35, 36, 73, 108, 111, 112–14, 141, 189 nn. 12–13, 202
Amenirdas I, 43, *43,* 115–17; statue of, God's Wife of Amen, 43, 115–16, *116,* 117, 203
Amenirdas II, 43, 44
Amen-Ra, 31, 33, 42, 43, 129, 136
Amen Temple, Karnak, 58, 115, 126
Amessis, 36
amulets, women's, 35, 45, 59, 60, 68, 70–74, *70–74,* 85, *85,* 127, 130, 132, 136, 140, 151, 156, 196–98, 206 n. 13, 207 n. 18, 208 n. 8; with Bes-image, 73, *73,* 196 n. 3; burial, 70, 74, *74,* 85, *85,* 86, 87, *87,* 88, 90, 130, 145, 146, *147,* 197–98; cylindrical, 70–71, *71,* 196–97; favored by women, 70, 73, *73;* frog, 71, *71,* 72, 197; Hathor head on pillar, 72, *72,* 125, 197; Hatmehit, 72, *72,* 197; heart scarab, 157, *157;* seated monkey, 72, *72;* Taweret, 71, *71,* 87, *87,* 88, 130
An, 124, 125
Ankhnesmeryra, 17, *17,* 29, *29,* 189 n. 39, 191 n. 109
Ankhnesneferibra, 43, 126
annuity contracts, 177, 180–83, 184, 215–17
Anubis, 35, 166, 169
Anuket, 118
apotropaic wand, 64; magic (apotropaic) wand, 64, *64,* 68, 101, 132, 195
Apuki, 153, 154, 194 n. 8
Arsinoe II, 126
artisan class, 37, 39–40
Aset, 203 n. 5
Aspelta, 118
Asyut, 166, 171, 172, 174, 199 n. 4; coffin, 166, *166,* 167, 213
Aten, 35, 112, 113, 114, 203 n. 3; relief: Nefertiti offering to the Aten, 112–13, *113,* 202
Atenism, 35
Athribis, 58
attendants clapping hands, female (relief), 42, 94, *94,* 95, 98, 105, 199
attendants on boat, jar with female and, 121, *121,* 122, *122,* 204
Atum, 128, 192 n. 10
Ay, 37

Badari, cemetery, 19
Badarian Period, 19, 87
baking, 14, 16
Balabish, 80, 87, 88, 89
baldness, 96
Banebdjed, 72
banquet scenes, 93, *93,* 94, 95, *95,* 169, 193 n. 3, 213 n. 5
Bapef, 103
Bastet, 70, *73,* 74, *74,* 99, 136, 139–40, 199 n. 13, 208; cat, 135, 136, 139, *139,* 140, 209; standing figure of, 139, 140, *140,* 209
Bat, 51, 70, 122, 123, 124, 193 n. 6
bathing, 79
beaded jewelry, 84–88, *84–88, 94,* 95, *95,* 196–98; from Amarna, 88, *88;* burial assemblages, 84–88, *84–85,* 145, 146, *147; menat* necklace, 13, 41, 57, 66, 85, 94, 99, 100, *100,* 200, 201 n. 18
Beautiful Feast of the Valley, 32, 33, 42, 55, 193 n. 3
beds, model, 67, 195 n. 1; female figurine with model bed, 66, 67, *67,* 121, 195–96
beer, 105, 198 n. 5, 201 n. 24; makers, female, 91, *91,* 92, 198
Beit el-Wali, 148
Bener-merut and Ikhem, double *shabti* of, 54, *54,* 148, 193
Beni Hasan, 39, 41, 65, 66, 187 n. 41, 190 n. 107, 195 n. 12; tomb of Khnumhotep at, 20, *20*
Berlin, 58, 62, 95, 98, 110, 123, 193 n. 9, 194 n. 5; Papyri, 71, 191 n. 111
Bersheh, 39
Bes, 65, 67, 70, 73, 76, 132, 156
Bes-image, 67–70, 195 n. 14, 196; amulets with, 73, *73,* 196 n. 3; plaque with, 67, 68, *68,* 196; vessel in form of, 68, *69,* 70, 196
bird-headed cosmetic palette, double, *79,* 80
birth arbor, 59, 68, 105, 196 n. 5
birth-houses, *mammisis,* 73, 127
Book of the Dead, 35, *35,* 45, 54, 70, 71, 117, 148, 151–52, 156, 157, 159, 169; fragment from a woman's, 156, 158–59, *159,* 160, 212
bovine-headed Hathor: fragment of statue of, 55, 74, 122, *122,* 123, 204; statuette of, 55, 74, 122, 123, *123,* 204

bracelet, 87, *87,* 88, 93, 102, *102,* 198
breast milk, 16, *16,* 59–60, 62, 63; divine, 118, 205 n. 7; *see also* suckling
brewing, 91–92, 105
Bubastis, 70, 138–39, 140, 208 n. 16, 209
burial assemblages, women's, 70, 76, 80, 84–89, *84–87,* 145–46, *145–47,* 197–98, 210–11; female terracotta figures, 145, *145,* 146, *146;* group of amulets from a woman's burial, 70, 74, *74;* hair accessories, 75, 79; jewelry, 84–89, *84–87*
Buto, 144

canopic jar, 128, 157–58; of Iny, 157–58, *158,* 212
cat, 70, *73,* 75, 129, 136, 139–40, *139–40,* 208 n. 19, 209; Bastet, 135, 136, 139, *139,* 140, 209; coffins, 140, 209 n. 13; fragmentary hairpin with seated, 75, 76, *76;* standing figure of Bastet, 139, 140, *140*
celibacy, 43, 115
chantress, 13, 14, 15, 98, 162, 164, 165, 167, 168, 169, 173, 174; seated figure of Enehy, 96, *97,* 98, *98,* 199–200
Chemmis, 125, 126, 128
Chief of the *khener* of Amen, 42, 43
childbirth, 17, 43, 44, 45, 51, 59, 61–68, 70, 72, 75, 85, 102, 105, 122, 125, 126, 127, 130, 153, 194–97, 207 n. 12; *see also* motherhood
child-gods, 73, 85, 99, 126–28, *126–28,* 139
citizeness, 175, 215 n. 26
civil law, 175, 176–79, 215
cobra, 64, 107, *107,* 108, 117, 120, 123, *123,* 125, 129, 134, *135,* 138, *138,* 139, 142–44, 201 nn. 1, 6, 210; statuette of cobra goddess, 142–44, *143–44,* 210
coffins, 66, 74, 105, 134, 153, 154, *154,* 156, 158, 166–69, 187 n. 36, 213–14; cartonnage (mummy case) of Neskhonsu-pakhered, 126, 165, 167, *167,* 168, 213; cat, 140, 209 n. 13; of Henut-wedjebu, 42, 126, 165, 167, 168, *168,* 169, *169,* 213–14; panel of, made for a woman, 166, *166,* 167, 213; Theban, 14, *14*
Coffin Texts, 128, 159, 166, 206 n. 7, 207
coiffure, *see* hairstyles
coleoptera beetle, 132
comb, 75; double-sided, 75, 76, *76;* fragmentary, 75, 76, *76*
conception, 65–67, 70, 126
concubine figures, *see* fertility figurines
contraception, 130, 198 n. 9, 207 n. 14
co-regency, 109, 110, 112
cornflower, 86, 198 n. 2
corvée system, 26, 40, 50
cosmetic vessels and cosmetics, 68, 70, 75, 79–87, *79–86,* 120, 142, 145, 146, *147,* 151, 197–98; cosmetic and unguent vessels, 82, *82,* 83, *83,* 197; kohl, 80, *81,* 84, *85,* 86, 145, *147,* 197; palettes, 79, *79,* 80, *80*
cosmological texts, female characteristics in, 44–46
counterpoise, *menat,* 41, 57, 66, 85, 94, 99, 100, 101, *101,* 123, *123,* 124, 200, 208 n. 5
cow, 122–25, *122–24,* 126, 204, 205
cowrie shell, 70, 85; burial assemblages, 84, *84,* 85, *85,* 87, *87,* 145, *147,* 198 n. 8; girdle, 85, *85,* 87
creator god, 189 n. 23
creator goddesses, 44, 45, 134, 192 n. 10; *see also* goddesses, nurturing role
criminal law, 175–76, 215
cylindrical amulets, 70–71, *71,* 196–97
Cynopolis, 27

Dagi, tomb of, 188 n. 49
daughter, 13, 14, 51; legal rights of, 181–84; *see also* King's Daughter
Deir Durunka, 172, 187 n. 6
Deir el-Bahri, 17, 32, 33, *33,* 34, 96, 108, 124, 141, 148, 158, 193 n. 11, 212 n. 4; Royal Cache, 152
Deir el-Bersheh, 39, 66
Deir el-Medina, 36, 37, 59, 68, 75, 94, 124, 130, 149, 152, 179, 183, 187 n. 2, 188 n. 72, 194 n. 2, 196 n. 5; court at, 177
Den, 28, 29
Dendera, 206 n. 10; Hathor's temple at, *45,* 101, 124, 140, 162
diadem, 87, 88, 104, 111, 118, 130, 143
Divine Adoratrice, 43, *43,* 44, 191 n. 133
Divine Child, 66
divorce, 37, 67, 175, 181, 182, 183, 217
Djari, tomb of, 14, *14*
Djedefra, 103, 104, 200 n. 6
Djehuty-em-heb and Iay, pair statue of, 174, *174,* 214
Djehutynakht, tomb of, 66, 188 n. 41, 195 n. 2
Djer, 27, 28; seal of, *28*
Djeserkarasonb, tomb of, 15, *15*
donation stela of Ahmose and Ahmose-Nefertari, 31, *31,* 44, 190 n. 52
"The Doomed Prince" (story), 38
door architrave of Tjenti, 184
double crown, 128, 144, 159, 196 n. 11, 206
double Hathor face, mirror with, 76, *77,* 79, 84, 102, 124
double *shabti* of Bener-merut and Ikhem, 54, *54,* 148, 193
dress, women's, 22, *22,* 30, 50, 51, 54, 57, 66, 67, 85, 96, 104, 114, 148, 159, 162, 164, 166, 171, 172, 174, 199 n. 1; of goddesses, 118, *188,* 121, *121,* 128, 129, *129, 133,* 134, *134,* 136, 140, *140,* 141, 142, *142;* of mourners, *93,* 94, 154, *154;* of musicians, *94,* 95; of royalty, 30, *30,* 32, 112, 114, 117, 120; of servants, 91, *91,* 92, *92,* 93; *shabti,* 152
Duat-nefret, 51
dwarfs, 196 n. 4

Early Dynastic Period, 79, 82, 90, 132
ear plug in the form of a rosette, openwork, 90, *90*
earring, 95, *95,* 140, *140,* 145, 146, *147,* 148, 198; lotus-flower, 89, *89;* penannular, 89, *89,* 90
ear stud in the form of a papyrus column, 90, *90*
Ebers Papyrus, 59, 62, 85, 96, 130
Edfu, 128, 144, 206; stela, 60, 61
education, 142, 178
El-Assassif, 84
elite women, 13, 15, 16, 17, 25, *25,* 30, 37, 39, 55, 96, 128; family statues, 49–58, *49–58;* marriage, 37–39; nurturing role, 17, 60; roles and offices of, 39–46; *see also* nonroyal women
El-Kurru, 117
El Ma'mariya, 121
embryotomy, 61
Enehy, 13, 96, 98, 99, 101, 187 n. 3; seated statue of, 13, 22, 42, 96, *97,* 98, *98,* 199–200; statue of, 96, *96*
episiotomy, 61
erotic imagery, 34, *34,* 35, 65, 66, 70, 102, 105
Esna cosmology, 134
estates, women's, 44, 49, 50
eye paint, *see* cosmetic vessels and cosmetics; kohl

falcon pendent, crowned, 85, *85*
family, 13, 49–58, *49–58,* 67, 162, 192–94; divine, 125–28, *125–28;* law, 177, 179–85, 215–17; of Pahery, 38, *38;* royal, 25–36, 37, 38, 113–14, 189, 190, 200–204; statues, 49–58, *49–58,* 169–74, *170–74,* 192–94; structure, 36–37; women within the, 36–39
Fayum, 30, 187 n. 38
fertility, 59, 65–67, 70, 72, 75, 79, 112, 114, 122, 125, 139, 194–97
fertility figurines, 65, *65,* 66, 85, 121, 146, *146,* 195; female figurine with incurving arms, 121, *121,* 122, 204; nude female figure, 66, *66,* 195; paddle-shaped female figure with bead-hair, 65, *65,* 66, 195; statuette of a serving girl, 93, *93*
figure, nude female, 66, *66,* 195
flax, 19, 20, *20,* 21, 22, 188
food preparation, 14, *14,* 15, *15,* 16, 24, 37, 51, 91, *91,* 92, 93, *93,* 164, 198
foreign women, 111, 160, 197 n. 4
frog, 64, 68, 70, 71–72, 197; amulet, 71, *71,* 72, 197
funerary art, *see* afterlife; coffins; mummification; *specific works;* statues, funerary; stelae, funerary; tombs
funerary repast, relief of mourners and, 15, 93, *93,* 94, 153, 199

Geb, 125
gender distinctions, 13, 52, 53, 109, 112, 122, 164, 167, 187 n. 5; amulets, 70; height, in group statues, 52, 53, 192 nn. 3–4; in legal status, 175–84; in *shabtis,* 148, 151–52, 153, 211 n. 7; skin color, 53, 174, 193 n. 21, 212 n. 5
genitalia, 65, 66, 70, 72, 85, 102
girdle, 70, 87, 88, *145,* 146, 198, 210 n. 9; cowrie-shell, 85, *85,* 87; of Isis *(tyet),* 70
Giza, 53, 91, 92, 103, 104, 140, 160, 163–64, 189 n. 37, 193 n. 14; reserve head, 160, *160, 161*
goddesses, 13, 44–46, 55, 57, 94, 108, 114, 121–44, *121–44,* 204–10; amulets, 70–74, *71–74,* 127, 130, 196, 197; appeased, 100, 129, 135, 136, 139, 140; cat, 70, *73,* 129, 136, 139–40, *139–40,* 208; cobra, 64, 107, *107,* 108, 120, 125, 129, 134, *135,* 138, *138,* 139, 142–44, *143–44,* 201 nn. 1, 6, 210;

cosmology, 44–45, *45*, 46, *46;* cow, 122–25, *122–24*, 126, 204, 205; cults, 13, 42, 76, 98–102, 125–28, 132, 140, 162, 199–200, 205; dress of, 118, *118*, 121, *121*, 128, 129, *129*, *133*, 134, *134*, 136, 140, *140*, 141, 142, *142;* dual nature of, 100, 122, 125, 128, 134, 136, 139, 140, 209 n. 9; fish, 72, 197; frog, 64, 68, 70, 197; hippopotamus, 63, 64, 70, 125, 130, *130*, 132, 207; kite, 125–26, *125–26;* leonine, 63, 64, *73*, *74*, 108, 122, 125, 129, 130, 135–39, *134–38*, 208–9; male usurpation of power, 122; nurturing role, 16, 17, *17*, 18, 70–74, 75, 77, 86, 99, 116, 117–18, *118*, 122–28, *127–28*, 129, 130, *131–32*, 134, 136, 139, 140, 189 n. 20, 194–97, 204–7, 211 n. 12; priestesses of, 96–102, *96–102*, 162, *162*, 178, 199–200; of records, 142, *142;* royalty suckled by, 117, 118, *118*, 123, 124, 136, 204, 206; scorpion, 128, *128*, 206; tree, 125, 126, 130, 204; vulture, 114, 118, 143; *see also specific goddesses*
God's Wife of Amen, 29, 31, 32, 33, 43, *43*, 44, 109, 110, 115–17, 190 n. 56, 191 nn. 133, 137, 203; statue of Amenirdas I, 115–16, *116*, 117, 203
graffito, erotic, 34, *34*, 35
Great Hymn of Osiris, 125
Greenfield Papyrus, 159
gynecology, 61–62, 67, 85, 194 nn. 6–7

hair accessories and ornaments, 75–79, *75–78*, 87, *94*, 95, 96, *96*, 197–98, 201
hairdressing, 16, 55, 75, 96, 105, 197–98, 199, 201; purification rituals, 105; relief: Queen Nefru and the hairdresser Henut, 72, 75, 105, *105*, 201; relief of the hairdresser Inu, 72, 75, 96, *96*, 105, 199; statuette of woman dressing hair of nursing mother, 59, *59*, 60, 72, 75, 96, 194
hairpin, 75, 197 nn. 9, 12, 201 n. 7; fragmentary, with seated cat, 75, 76, *76;* with pomegranate-shaped terminal, 75, 76, *76*
hairstyles, women's, 51, 55, 57, 58, 60, 63, 75, 92, 96, 104, 148, 151, 160, 164, 193 n. 6, 198 nn. 5–6, 199, 201; adolescent, 93, *93*, 113, 203 n. 4; hairpieces, 96, *96;* Hathoric, 55, *55*, 70, 105, 111, 120, *120;* of mourners, *93*, 94; of musicians, *94*, 95, *95;* paddle-shaped female figure with bead-hair, 65, *65*, 66, 195; *shabti*, 148, 149, *149*, 151, 152, 153; *see also* hairdressing; headdress; wigs
handclapping, 98; relief: female attendants clapping hands, 42, 94, *94*, 95, 98, 105, 199
hand wand, 98, 99, 101–2, *102*, 200; pair, 98, 101, 102, *102*, 200
Hapi, 157, 158
Hap-iu's lady musicians, relief depicting, 42, 95, *95*, 199
Hapu, 14, *14*
Hapuseneb, 33, 38, 43, 135
harem conspiracies, 176, 177
Hathor, 13, 18, 27, *27*, 32, 35, 41, 42, 45, 46, 50, 51, 55, 66, 70, 72, *73*, 74, *74*, 79, 85, 95, 112, 122–25, 127, 128, 130, 134, 138, 140, 143, 144, *144*, 156, 162, 165, 171, 178, 189 n. 20, 191 n. 142, 192 nn. 5, 8, 193 n. 6, 194 n. 11, 196, 197, 200 n. 6, 201, 205, 208 n. 9, 209 n. 4, 210 n. 18, 211 n. 12; as anthropomorphized counterpoise, 101, *101;* bovine-headed statues, 55, 74, 122, *122*, 123, *123*, 124, 125, 134, 204; cult, 42, *42*, 95, 96, 98, 99–102, *99–102*, 103, 105, 108, 120, 125, 162, 199–200, 201 n. 18, 205; Festival of, 100; headdress, 70, 111, 122, 123, 127, 132, 141, 143, 206 n. 15; head on pillar, 72, *72*, 125, 197; as lion-headed snake goddess, 45, *46;* mask, 41, 55, 74, 123, *123*, 124, *124*, 141, 205; mirror with double Hathor face, 76, *77*, 79, 84, 102, 124, 197; sistrum fragment with Hathor mask, 41, 55, 74, 123, *123*, 124, 205; sistrum with Hathor head, 13, 41, 85, 94, 99, *99*, 125, 140, 174; temple of, *45*, 101, 124; votive stela to, 74, 108, 124, *124*, 125, 205
Hathoric wig, *see* scroll wig
Hatiay, tomb of, 168, 169, 213–14 n. 2
Hatmehit amulet, 72, *72*, 197 n. 9
Hatnofer and Ramose, tomb of, 21, *21*, 22, 23, *23*, 24, *24*, 187 n. 36
Hatshepsut, 17, *17*, 18, 25, 29, 30–35, 36, 38, 40, 42, 43, 87, 109, 110, 111, 115, 117, 124, 135, 141, 187 nn. 25–28, 190 nn. 56, 74, 197 n. 3, 201 n. 4, 202, 203 n. 18, 210 n. 3; cult of, 32, 33; kneeling statue of, 108, *108*, 109, 201–2; shrine of, 43, *43*, 109
Hawara, 30, 190 n. 41
Hayet, 67
headdress, 166, 193 n. 6; Hathoric, 70, 111, 122, 123, 127, 132, 141, 143, 206 n. 15; of Isis, 126–28, *125–28*, 143, 206 n. 15; *nemes*, 30, *30*, 160; vulture, 44, 101, *101*, 114, *115*, 118, *118*, *119*, 120, *120*, 127, *127*, *167*, 168, 203, 204 nn. 1, 3, 206 n. 2; *see also* wigs
headrest, 156; inscribed for Irwt, 156, *156*, 157, 211–12
heart scarab, 157; inscribed for Nub-ity, 45, 157, *157*, 212
Hededet, 128, 206
heiresses, 26
Hekanakhte, 21, 36, 40
Hekareshu, 18, *18*
Hekarneheh, tomb of, 18, *18*
Hekat, 64, 68, 72
Hekenu, 94
Heliopolis, 95, 101, 128, 197 n. 5
Henetnofret, 57, 194 n. 8
Henut, Queen Nefru and the hairdresser (relief), 72, 75, 105, *105*, 201
Henut-demit, 98
Henutnofret, 14, *14*, *154*
Henuttawey, 169, 211; *shabti* inscribed for, 152, *152*, 153, 211
Henut-wedjebu, 167; *shabti* of, 149, *149*, 211; coffin of, 42, 126, 165, 167, 168, *168*, 169, *169*, 213–14
Herakleopolis, 30
Hereditary Noblewoman, 60, 61, 104
Herihor, 42
Hermopolis Legal Code, 177, 180, 184, 215, 216, 217
hes vases, 156
hesyt, 42, 98, 165
Hetepheres II, 132; and her daughter Meresankh III, pair statue of, 103, *103*, 104, 193 n. 11, 200; tomb of, 104, 132
hippopotamus, 63, 64, 70, 125, 130, *130*, 132, 207; cosmetic palette in the shape of, 80, *80;* ivory, 64, *64*, 195 n. 1
homosexuality, 35
Horemheb, tomb of, 199 n. 10
Horus, 16, 17, 27, 28, 30, 34, 61, 70, 72, *73*, 122, 124, 125–28, 136, 139, 143, 144, 157, 164, 165, 166, 169, 200 n. 33, 205–6, 208 n. 3, 210 n. 11; the child, 126, 127, *127*, 205–6; Isis nursing, 16, 17, 126, 127, *127*, 128, *128*, 205–6; jewelry, 85, *85*, 86, *86*
House of the Morning, 105
human sacrifice, 128

Ihy, 99, *101*
Ikhem, 54, *54*, 148, 193
Imiu, 40
imy-pr, position of, 53
imyt pr documents, 177–78, 183, 215, 216
incense cone, 32, 67
Ineni, 32
infant mortality, 67
infertility, 67
inheritance, 49–50, 51, 67, 115, 162, 177, 178, 181–85, 192 n. 15, 215–17
"The Instructions of Any," 60, 175
"Instructions of Ptahhotep," 36–37, 38, 175, 216 n. 47, 217 n. 89
"The Instructions of the Demotic Insinger" Papyrus, 46
instruments, musical, 14, 94, 95, *95*, 98, 169
Intekes, funerary statue of, 96, 162, *162*, 163, 212
intimacy, expressions of, 52–53, 54, 193 n. 11
Inu, relief of the hairdresser, 72, 75, 96, *96*, 105, 199
Iny, canopic jar of, 157–58, *158*, 212
Inyotef-iker, tomb of, 200 n. 8
Ipet, 130–32, 207 n. 7
Ipet/Taweret, statuette of, 63, 67, 130, 132, *132*, 207
Iput, 104, 105, 204 n. 1
Irwt, headrest inscribed for, 156, *156*, 157, 211–12
Isheru, 135, *135*, 136, 208 n. 16
Isis, 14, 16, 17, 27, *43*, 61, 70, *73*, 74, *74*, 94, 125–28, 130, 143, 148, 168, 169, 189 n. 20, 205–6, 208 n. 9, 210 n. 18; blood of, 70, 71; bust fragment of a goddess, probably Isis, 70, 126, *126*, 205; cult of, 126–28, 205–6; girdle of *(tyet)*, 70, *73;* nursing Horus, 16, 17, 126, 127, *127*, 128, *128*, 205–6; statue of winged Isis and Osiris, 125, *125*, 126, *126*, 129, 205
Isis-scorpion, 128; nursing infant Horus, 70, 126, 128, *128*, 206
Ita, 107
Itef, 54–55, *55*
Iti, 94
Iutenheb, 40

jewelry, women's, 70, *74*, 85–90, *84–90*, 95, *95*, 104, 124, 136, 148, 197–98; aegis and *menat* with head of lion-headed goddess, 74, 135, 136, *136, 137;* assorted, 87, *87,* 88; beaded, 84–88, *84–88, 94,* 95, *95,* 99, 100, *100,* 145, 146, *147,* 196, 197, 198; beaded, from Amarna, 88, *88;* burial assemblage, 84–89, *84–87,* 145, 146, *147,* 197–98; ear stud in papyrus column form, 90, *90;* finger rings, 90, *90;* lotus-flower earrings, 89, *89; menat* necklace, 13, 41, 57, 66, 85, 94, 99, 100, *100,* 125, 169, 174; necklace, 86, *86,* 87, *87,* 88, 198; openwork ear plug in the form of a rosette, 90, *90;* penannular earrings, 89, *89,* 90; shell, 84, *84,* 85, *85,* 87, *87,* 88, 90

Ka-her-set-f, 49
Kai-neferu, *shabti* of, 149, *149*
Kamose, 30
Kares, 31
Karnak, 31, 32, 33, 34, 43, *43,* 44, 109, 112, 115, 128, 130, 132, 135, 144, 167, 187 n. 12, 190 n. 56, 202, 206 n. 11, 208 n. 14; Amen Temple, 58, 115, 126
Kashta, 43, 115, 117
Kawab, 103, 104, 200 n. 4
Ked-Amen, 50, *50,* 51
Kenamen, tomb of, 18, *18*
Kha and Meryt, tomb of, 24, 198 n. 11
Khafra, 103, 140, 160, 198 n. 3
Khasekhemwy, 142
Khasnebu, 37; stela of, 37, *37*
Khemernebty, *27*
kheneru, see musical troupe
Khensa, 117, 118
Khentkawes, 160, 204 n. 1
Khnumhotep, 190 n. 107; tomb of, 20, *20*
Khnumhotep II, 37–38, 190 n. 107
Khonsu, 37, 114, 129, 130, 136, 208 n. 3
Khufu, 49, 50, 103, 160, 163, 164, 190 n. 75, 192 n. 3, 200 n. 4, 216 n. 30
Khuyt, 58
king, 26, 102, 108, 111, 113, 114, 115, 128, 177, 189; divinity of, 126, 127, 129, 140; double crown, 128; nurtured by goddess, 117, 118, *118,* 123, 124; nurtured by nonroyal women, 16, 17, 18, *18,* 19; succession, 26, 27, 36, 37, 109, 126, 127, 189; *see also specific kings*
King's Acquaintance, 52, 53, 162, 163, 184
King's Daughter, 26, 27, 31, 37, 38–39, 60, 64, 103, 104, 105, 109, 158, 189 n. 17, 190 n. 92
King's Mother, 26, 27, 28, 29, 31, 43, 104
King's Principal Wife, 26, 27, 28, 29, 35, 36, 37, 103, 105, 109
kinship principles, royal, 26, 27, 28, 30, 36, 37, 38, 109–12, 189, 190
kohl, 75, 79, 80, *81,* 83, 197; pots, 80, *81,* 84, *85,* 86, 145, *147,* 197
Kom el-Hisn, 94
Kynebu, tomb of, 169

lactating-woman vessels, *see* nursing-woman vases
legal rights, women's, 13, 49–50, 51, 60, 175–85, 215–17
linen, *see* textile production
lion, 159, 196 n. 4, 208; aegis and *menat* with head of lion-headed goddess, 74, 135, 136, *136, 137,* 139, 140, 208; statuette of lion-headed goddess, 108, 138, *138,* 139, 208–9
Lisht, 188 n. 45, 196 n. 5
looms, 19, 20, *20,* 21, 22, 23, 188
lotus flower, 105, 130, 146, 148, 156, 165; earrings, 89, *89;* Queen Wedjebten with (relief), 104, *104,* 105, 159, 200–201; Renenutet with, 172, *172*
lovemaking, *see* sexuality
love marriages, 38–39
Luxor Temple, 17, 33, 43, 191 n. 133

maat, 43, 116, 141
Maat, 125, 135, 140–41, 157, 209; bronze statuette, 124, 135, 140–41, *141,* 209; relief figure, 141, *141*
Maatkara, 43, 141, 152, 153; *shabti* inscribed for, 43, 152, 153, *153,* 211
magic (apotropaic) wand, 64, *64,* 68, 101, 132, 195
Maketaten, 112, 113
marriage, 36–39, 162, 175, 176, 179; contracts, 180–83, 184, 215–17; intermarriage, 160; legal rights, 177–78, 179–84, 215–17; politics and choice in, 37–39; royal succession, 26, 27, 28, 37
mask, Hathor, 41, 55, 74, 123, *123,* 124, *124,* 141, 205
masturbation, 102, 189 n. 23, 191 n. 138
Maya, 96, 169; *shabti* of, 148, 151, *151,* 152
Mayet, tomb of, 95
Medinet Habu Chapel, 33, 43, *43,* 44, 116, 124
Mehet-weret, 122, 123, 134, 207 n. 12
Meketra, tomb of, 20, *20,* 21
Memphis, 96, 123, 128, 136, 157
Memphite cults, 42
Memy-Sabu statue, *51,* 52, 53, 104, 128, 192–93
menat, 13, 41, *56,* 57, 66, 74, *74,* 85, 94, 98, 99, 136, 162, 200 n. 22; and aegis with head of lion-headed goddess, 74, 135, 136, *136, 137,* 139, 140, 208; counterpoise, 41, 57, 66, 85, 94, 99, 100, 101, *101,* 123, *123,* 124, 200, 208 n. 5; necklace, 13, 41, 57, 66, 85, 94, 99, 100, *100,* 125, 169, 174, 200, 201 n. 18
Mendes, 72
Mendesian triad, 72
Menedjem, 156
Menkaura, *27,* 104, 122, 160, 189 n. 37
Menna, tomb of, 16, *16,* 194 n. 9
menstruation, 70
Mentuemhat, tomb of, 16; relief of woman and child between trees, 59, 60, *60,* 194
Mentuhotep, tomb of, 84
Mentuhotep II, 124
Merenra, 29, 39
Meresankh III: tomb of, 103; pair statue of Queen Hetepheres II and, 103, *103,* 104, 193 n. 11, 200
Meret-ites, 160, 199 n. 14
Meretseger, 143
Meritaten, 102, 112, 113
Mer-Neith, 28–29, 132; seal of, *28*
Meryt, *25,* 96, 167, 169, 198 n. 11
Meryt-Amen, 54, 96
Meskhenet, 194 n. 4
Metiay, 174
Metjen, 177
midwives, 59, 61
mirrors, 75, 76–79, 82, 84, *84,* 102, 105, 166, 197; with double Hathor face, 76, *77,* 79, 84, 102, 124, 197; with handle in form of a woman, 76, *78,* 79, 84
Mistress of the House, 13, 36, 50, 54, 55, 64, 92, 149, 151, 152, 162, 166, 167, 168, 172, 174, 175, 185, 192 n. 5
model servant figures, 92, *92,* 93, 198–99
monarchs, female, 29–36, 87, 109–12, 132, 141, 176, 189, 190, 200, 201, 202; in nurturing role, 16, 17, *17,* 29, *29,* 109, *109,* 110, *110*
monkey, seated, 72, *72*
motherhood, 13, 15, 16–19, 37, 59–74, *59–74,* 194–97; amulets, 70–74, *70–74,* 196–97; fertility, 65–67, 70, 72, 75, 79, 112, 114, 122, 125, 194–97; goddesses, 16, 17, *17,* 18, 70–74, 75, 77, 86, 99, 116, 117–18, *118,* 122, 123, 124, 125–28, *127–28,* 129, 130, *131–32,* 134, 136, 139, 140, 189 n. 20, 194–97, 204–7, 211 n. 12; nonroyal women, 16–19, *16–18,* 59–60, 194–97; postpartum purification ritual, 59, 60, 61, 68, 70, 85, 105, 130, 194 n. 2; royal women, 16, 17, *17,* 29, *29,* 60, *60,* 61, *103,* 104, 109, *109,* 110, *110,* 113, 114, *114,* 129, 200–204; suckling, 16, *16,* 17, 18, *18,* 41, 59, *59,* 60, *60,* 61, 62, 63, 66, 70, 117–18, *118, 127–28,* 171; *see also* childbirth; pregnancy
mourners, 14, 15, 93, *93,* 94, 122; *dryt-,* 14, 94, 187 n. 10, 199; relief of funerary repast, 15, 93, *93,* 94, 153, 199; tomb painting of mourning women, 93, 153, 154, *154,* 211
mummification, 19, 45, 66, 85, 89, 90, 96, 109, 126, 153, *154,* 156, 157, 159, 160, 187 n. 36, 199 n. 8, 211 nn. 36, 38; of animals, 139, 140; of internal organs, 157, 158; process, 104, 157; *see also* coffins
mummiform statuettes, *see shabtis*
musical troupe *(kheneru),* 42, *42,* 98, 101, 199–200
musicians, 14, 15, *15,* 41–42, *42,* 43, 58, 87, 94–98, *94–98,* 136, 162, 169, 199–200; relief: female attendants clapping hands, 42, 94, *94,* 95, 199; relief depicting Hap-iu's lady musicians, 42, 95, *95,* 199; seated statue of Enehy, 13, 22, 42, 96, *97,* 98, *98,* 199–200
Mut, 35, 45, 46, 114, 115, 116, 118, 128–30, 135, *135,* 136, 138, 191 n. 142, 196 n. 11, 197 n. 3, 203 nn. 3, 7, 206–9; in Book of the Dead vignettes, 35, *35;* Sekhmet and, 134–35, *135,* 136; statuette of, 70, 114, 128–29, *129,* 135, 138, 139, 206–7; votive stela with Taweret and, 130, *130,* 132, 207
Mut-nefret, 50, *50,* 51
Mutnofret, 31, 37
Mut precinct and Temple (Thebes), 135, *135,* 136; Sekhmet statue at, *135*

Nagada, 27
Nag ed-Deir, 70, 132, 198 n. 2
naked adolescent girl motif, 93, *93*
Nakht-mut, statue of, 182, 183
Narmer Palette, 123

Nau-nakht, 183
Nebamen and Apuki, 55, 57, 153, 154; tomb of, 14, *14*, 57, 153, 154, *154*, 193–94
Nebet, 39, 190–91 n. 109
Nebet Hetepet, 72, 197 nn. 5, 7
Nebet-net-ka, 162
nebet per, see Mistress of the House
Nebet-Yunet, 50, *50*, 51, 192 n. 5
Nebhepetra Mentuhotep, 94, 95, 105, 124, 201
Nebsenet, 177
Nebseni, 117; *shabti* of, 117, *117*, 203–4
Nefer, Lady, funerary stela for, 163, *163*, 164
Nefernefervaten-Tasherit, 113
Neferrenput, tomb of, 16, 21, 188 n. 54
Nefertari, 89, 203
Nefertiti, 35, *35*, 36, 108, 112–14, 141; relief: Nefertiti offering to the Aten, 112–13, *113*, 202; relief of Queen Nefertiti kissing daughter, 17, 112, 113, 114, *114*, 203; smiting the enemy, 112, *112*
Nefertum, 146, 209; bronze figurine of, 146, *147*
Nefru, 105; relief: Queen Nefru and the hairdresser Henut, 72, 75, 105, *105*, 201; tomb of, 94, *94*, 95, 96, *96*, 105
Nefrukakashta, 117, 118, *118*
Nefru-Ptah, 37
Nefrura, 18, 32, 33, 34, 41, 44, 109, 110, 115, 117, 190 n. 71, 203 n. 18; statue of Senenmut holding Nefrura, 18, 33, 41, 109, *109*, 110, 115, 202
Neith, 28, 29, 35, 70, *73*, 104, 105, 128, 132–34, 207; cult of, 132, 134; standing figure of, 132, *133*, 134, 207
Neith-hotep, 27–28, 29, 132, 189 n. 39; seal of, *28*
Nekhbet, 27, 45, 64, 114, 118, 143, 144, 168, 210
Nemarat, 165
nemes headdress, 30, *30*, 160
Nephthys, 14, 70, 72, *73*, 94, 125, 126, 128, 157, 168, 169, 205
Nesitanbetisheru, 159
Neskhonsu-pakhered, cartonnage (mummy case) of, 126, 165, 167, *167*, 168, 213
Nespernub, 167, 168
Neterikhet (Djoser), 27
Niankhkhnum and Khnumhotep, tomb of, 16
Ni-Inpw-kauw, 92
Nikaura, 94, 216 n. 30
Nitocris, 116, 189 n. 37
Nitokret (Neith-ikret), 25, 29, 43, 44, 109
Niuserra, 104, 192 n. 1
Nodjme, 42, 43
Nofru, tomb of, 148
nonroyal women, 13–24, 32, 37, 53, 54, 85, 156; adornment, 75–90, *75–90*, 197–98; burial practices, 13–24, 53, 57, 70, 76, 84–89, *84–87;* family statues, 49–58, *49–58*, 192–93; lowerclass, 13, 14, 15, 16, 88, 96; nurturing role, 15, 16–19, *16–18*, 59–60, 194–97; occupations, 13–24, 39–41, 43, 91–102, *91–102*, 187–88, 198–200; textile production, 15, 19–24, *20–24;* tombs, 13–24, 53, 57, 85, 145–46, 156, 162, 163–74, 187–88, 192–93; upperclass, 13, 14, 15, 16, 17, 79, 89, 96, 98, 151, 156–57, 162, 163, 166, 169; *see also* elite women; *specific occupations*
Nubia, 32, 33, 112, 116, 160, 197 n. 4, 206 n. 10
Nub-ity, heart scarab inscribed for, 45, 157, *157*, 212
nude female figure, 66, *66*, 195
nudity, 63, 65, 66, 76, 79, 93, 128, 146, 148; goddess, 128
nursing, *see* royal nurse; suckling
nursing-woman vases, 62, *62*, 63, 194, 195
nurturing role of women, *see* childbirth; motherhood; suckling
Nut, 45, *45*, 73, *73*, 124, 125, 159, 168, 169, 205 n. 5
Nynetjer, 27, 29, 201 n. 16, 202 n. 15, 207 n. 15

occupations, women's, 39–41, 51, 91–102, *91–102*, 178, 180, 184, 198–200; hairdressers, 96, *96*, 199; mourners, 93, *93*, 94, 199; musicians, 94–98, *94–98*, 199–200; of nonroyal women, 13–24, 39–41, 43, 91–102, *91–102*, 187–88, 198–200; priestesses, 96–102, *96–102*, 162, 178, 199–200; of royal women, 25–36, 42, 43, 44, 87, 109, 115–17, 132, 189, 201; servants, 91–95, *91–94*, 198–99; textile production, 19–24, *20–24*, 188
Onuris, 166, 199 n. 13
Opet Festival, 33
Osiris, 27, 35, 51, 55, 72, 94, 117, 122, 126, 127, 128, 148, 154, 158, 159, 165, 166, 192 n. 4, 194 n. 11, 205–6; statue of winged Isis and, 125, *125*, 126, *126*, 129, 205
Osorkon I, 165
Osorkon III, 43, 115
oyster shell, 70, 85, 196 n. 9, 198 n. 15; pendent, 85, *85*

paddle doll, 65; paddle-shaped female figure with bead-hair, 65, *65*, 66, 195
Pahery, family of, 38, *38*
Paiankh, 42
Palermo Stone, 28
palette, 79–80
Papyrus Reisner I, 40
Papyrus Salt, 124, 179
Papyrus Wilbour, 178
Payshuweben, 42
Pebatma, 117
Peksater, 117
Pepy I, 29, 189 n. 39, 200 n. 15
Pepy II, 17, *17*, 29, *29*, 39, 104, 105, 189 n. 37, 210 n. 12
Philae, 126, 140, 206 n. 15
Piankhy, 115, 116, 117
Pinedjem I, 153
Pinedjem II, 159
Piye, 43
political marriages, 37–39
postpartum purification rituals, 59, 60, 61, 68, 70, 85, 105, 130, 194 n. 2
pregnancy, 59, 61, 62, 63, 65, 66, 67, 70, 71, 125, 126, 130, 179, 198 n. 9
priestesses, 96–102, *96–102*, 199–200; of Hathor, 41, 99–102, 162, *162*, 178; sacred cult objects of, 99–102, *99–102*, 200
priests, women, 41–44
princess, 26, 27, 38, 108, 113, 114, 190 n. 92; head of queen or, *106*, 107, *107*, 108, 201; marriage, 38–39; nurtured by nonroyal women, 17, *17; see also* royal women; *specific princesses*
property rights, women's, 13, 49, 50, 177–78, 179, 181–85, 215–17
Psamtik I, 43, 44, 68, 142, 143, 144, 204 n. 12
Psamtik II, 43, 58, 205 n. 9
Ptah, 98, 123, 136, 208 n. 3
Ptah-may, 98
Ptahmose, 151
Ptolemy Philadelphos, 126
puberty rituals, 65, 102, 132
Punt, 32, 72, 109
Puyemra, 33
Pyramid Texts, 27, 105, 132, 140, 158–59, 166, 189 n. 20, 192 n. 10, 197, 200 n. 15, 205

queen: bust of a, 118, *119*, 120, *120*, 168, 204; divinity of, 29, 108, 112, 115, 120, 124–25, 128, 132, 141; goddess suckling a, 117, 118, *118*, 204; or princess, head of, *106*, 107, *107*, 108, 201; regent, 27–29, 30, 32, 109, 128, 189 n. 34; standard bearing statue of, 114–15, *115*, 135, 203; *see also* royal women; *specific queens*

Ra, 27, 34, 64, 101, 122, 124, 125, 128, 141, 143, 160, 164, 199 n. 13, 200 n. 6, 213 n. 10; Eye of, 102, 108, 122, 124, 129, 135, 136, 139, 201 n. 1, 208, 209 n. 4
Radjedef, 108
Ra-Horakhty, *43*, 164, 165
Ramesses II, 21, 29, 38, 89, 101, 114, 115, 135, 136, 172, 203, 210; ostracon: Ramesses II suckled by a goddess, 17, 117, 118, *118*, 204
Ramesses III, 176, 215 n. 25
Ramesses IV, 183
Ramesses VI, 203 n. 5; tomb of, *45*
Ramesses XI, 153
Ramesseum, 21, 101, 164–65, 195 n. 14
Ram of Mendes, 35
rape, 179, 216 n. 47
razor, 75, *75*, 82
Red Crown, 132, 134, 143, 207 n. 9
Rekem, 159
religious service, women in, 41–44, 96–102
Renenutet, 13, 15, 100, 143; with lotus flower, 172, *172;* statue depicting Yuni and, 13, 14, 15, 22, 87, 100, 172, *172, 173*, 174, 214
Rerem, statue of, 49, *49*, 50, *50*, 192
reserve head, 160, 212 nn. 6–8; of a woman, 160, *160, 161*, 212
royal guardian, 18, *18*, 19, 187 nn. 33–34
royal nurse, 17, *17*, 18, *18*, 19, 41, 187 nn. 24–26
royal women, 25–36, 37, 38, 39, 44, 55, 57, 85, 96, 103–20, *103–20*, 127, 132, 152, 163, 164, 189, 200–204; family, 25–36, 37, 38, 113–14, 189, 190, 200–

204; harem conspiracies, 176, 177; kinship principles, 26, 27, 28, 30, 36, 37, 38, 109, 189, 190; marriage, 37–39, 160; as monarchs, 29–36, 87, 109–12, 132, 141, 176, 189, 190, 200, 201, 202; nurturing role, 16, 17, *17*, 29, *29*, 60, *60*, 61, *103*, 104, 109, *109*, 110, *110*, 113, 114, *114*, 129, 200–204; occupations, 25–36, 42, 43, 44, 87, 109, 115–17, 132, 189, 201; purification rituals, 105; *shabtis* for, 152–53, *152–53;* suckled by goddesses, 117, 118, *118;* tombs, 29, 36, 38, 39, 85, 87, 94, 103–10, 115, 117, 143, 152–54, 158–60, 163, 164, 179, 197 n. 8; *see also* King's Daughter; King's Mother; King's Principal Wife; princess; queen; *specific royal women*

Sabu, seated statue of, 51, 52, *52*, 53, *53*, 192–93, 200
sacred cult objects, 99–102, *99–102*, 199–200
Sahura, 142
Sais, 132, 134, 206 n. 8
Saqqara, 30, 38, 62, 104, 128, 187 n. 3, 197, 209 n. 6
Sati, *shabti* of, 149, *150*, 151
Satiah, 110
scorpion goddesses, 128, *128*, 206
scribe, 117, *117*, 142, 152, 167, 173, 174, 177, 181, 213 n. 9; relief of the goddess Seshat, 142, *142*, 209–10
scroll wig, 55, *55*, 105, 120, *120*, 124, *124*, 193 n. 6
Sedeinga, 112
sed festival, 102, 111, 116, 124, 202 n. 5, 206 n. 2
Sekenenra, 30
Sekhat-Hor, 122
Sekhmet, 70, *73*, 134–36, 138, 140, 206 n. 4, 207–9; bust from a statue of, 108, 134, *134*, 135–36, 138, 139, 140, 207–8; Mut Temple depictions, 134, 135, *135*, 136
Selket, 70, 128, 206 n. 1
Semna, 71, 200 n. 32
Seneb and family, statue of, 52
Senebtisi, 85, 198 n. 4
Senenmut, 18, 22, 23, 32, 33, 34, 35, 41, 109–10; statue of Senenmut holding Nefrura, 18, 33, 41, 109, *109*, 110, 115, 202
senet, 57
Senisonb, 33, 43
Sennefer, Mayor of Thebes, *25*
Senusert I, 40, 100, 190 n. 41, 201 n. 6; funerary temple of, 142, *142*
Senusert II, 191 n. 111, 198 n. 2, 201 n. 6
serdab statues, 162, *162*, 163
servant figures, female, 66, 91–94, *91–93*, 198–99; female figurine with incurving arms, 121, *121*, 122; servant statue: woman grinding grain, 15, 91, *91*, 92, 198; servant statue: woman straining mash for beer, 15, 40, 91, *91*, 92, 198; statuette of a serving girl, 93, *93*, 121, 199; tomb model: female servant or offering-bearer, 92, *92*, 93, 121, 198–99
Servant Priestess, 42
servants, female, 14, *14*, 15, 25, 39–41, 57, 70, 79, 87, 91–95, *91–94*, 96, 176, 178, 179, 191, 197 n. 4, 198–99; clothmakers, 21
Seshat, 142, 209–10; relief of, 142, *142*, 209–10
Setau family, 149, 211 n. 19
Seth, 28, 35, 85, 125, 126, 196 n. 13, 200 n. 33, 205 n. 5
Sethos I, 172
Setnakhte, 36, 87
Sety I, 140; tomb of, 132
Sety II, 35, 41, 87
Sety-hekenet, 164
seweret beads, 85, *85*, 94, *95*
sexuality, 34, *34*, 35, *35*, 39, 44–45, 57, 65, 70, 102, 105, 125, 139, 179, 197 n. 14, 216 n. 47; and fertility, 65–66, 70
Shabako, 115, 203 n. 10
shabtis, 54, 134, 145, 146, 148–53, *149–53*, 154, 201 n. 5, 211; double *shabti* of Benet-merut and Ikhem, 54, *54*, 148, 193; of Henut-wedjebu, 149, *149;* inscribed for Princess Maatkara, 43, 152, 153, *153;* inscribed for Queen Henuttawey, 152, *152*, 153; of Kai-neferu, 149, *149;* of Maya, 148, 151, *151*, 152; of Nebseni, 117, *117*, 203–4; of Sati, 149, *150*, 151
shaving, 75, *75*, 82, 96
Sheb-en-Sepdet, 165
shebyu collar, 198 n. 6
shell, 82, 83, 210 nn. 5–6; cosmetic, 82, *82*, 83, 145, *147;* cowrie, 70, 84, *84*, 85, *85*, 87, *87*, 145, *147*, 198 n. 8; jewelry, 84, *84*, 85, *85*, 87, *87*, 88, 90; oyster, 85, *85*, 196 n. 9, 198 n. 15
shemayit, 42, 98, 101, 165
Shepenwepet I, 43, 115, 116, 206 n. 3
Shepenwepet II, 117, 143, *143*
Shepseskhaf, 104
Sheshonq, 126
Shu, 44
Si-Amen, 187 n. 33
Silla culture, Korea, 26, 27, 28, 29, 30
Sinai, 32
singers, *see* chantress
Siptah, 35, 36, 198 n. 5
sistrum, 13, 41, 85, 94, 98, 99, 100, 113, *135*, 136, 140, *140*, 162, 169, 200 nn. 19–20, 202 n. 27, 208 n. 20; fragment with Hathor mask, 41, 55, 74, 123, *123*, 124, 205; with Hathor head, 13, 41, 85, 94, 99, *99*, 125, 140, 174, 199, 200; *naos*, 99, 102
Sitra, 17, *17*, 187 nn. 25–26
Siut, 181
skin color, 53, 174, 193 n. 21, 212 n. 5
slaves, 41, 176, 191 n. 116
Sneferu-seneb, 160
Sobek, 134, 199 n. 13, 207 n. 12
Sobek-nakht nursing a prince, statuette of Princess, 16, 60, *60*, 61, 194
Sobeknefru, 25, 29–30, 32, 109, 190 nn. 41, 44; wearing king's headdress and kilt, 30, *30*
sphinx, 108, 112, 201, 202 n. 19; head of a female, 107, *107*, 108, 135, 139, 201
stelae, funerary, 14, 39, 53, 94, 105, 110, 112, 156, 163–66, 212–13
suckling, 16, *16*, 17, 18, *18*, 41, 59, *59*, 60, *60*, 61, 62, 63, 66, 68, 70, 116, 117–18, 171, 194–97; goddess suckling a queen, 117, 118, *118*, 204; Isis nursing Horus, 16, 17, 126, 127, *127*, 128, *128*, 205–6; ostracon: Ramesses II, suckled by a goddess, 17, 117, 118, *118*, 204; statuette of Princess Sobeknakht nursing a prince, 16, 60, *60*, 61, 72, 194; statuette of woman dressing hair of nursing mother, 16, 59, *59*, 60, 72, 75, 96, 194; *see also* motherhood
Sudan, 44, 112

Taharqa, 43, 44
Ta-Khaa-en-Bastet, round-topped (funerary) stela of, 165, *165*, 166, 213
Tanis, 153
tannin, 85, 130
Ta-sheryt-akhet, funerary stela for, 42, 164, *164*, 165, 213
tattoos, 65, 66
Tauseret, 25, 29, 35–36, *36*, 87, 109, 198 nn. 4–5; tomb of, 36, *36*, 87
Taweret, 63, 64, 65, 67, 70, 74, *74*, 75, 86, 87, 130–32, 195 n. 5, 196 n. 15, 197 n. 12, 207; figurine of, 71, *71;* statue of, 63, 67, 130, *131*, 132, 207; statuette of Ipet/Taweret, 63, 67, 130, 132, *132*, 207; stela: woman and boy adoring Taweret, 66, 67, *67*, 73, 195–96; votive stela with Mut and, 130, *130*, 132, 207
Tefnut, 44, 112, 136
temple statues, 58
tenant landholders, *ḫnyt-š*, 49, 50
Tetetenu, 67
Teti I, 189 n. 17
Tetishery, 30, 31; stela of, 30, *30*, 31
Tety, 40, 200 n. 19
textile production, 14, 15, 16, 19–24, *20–24*, 41, 51, 91, 124, 134, 164, 180, 187 nn. 19, 36–38, 188 nn. 43–73
Tey, 40
theft, 176–79
Theset, 49, 50, *50*
Thinis, 40
This, 166
Thoth, 68, *141*, 165, 166, 209 n. 2
Thutmose I, 26, 30, 31, 34, 37, 109
Thutmose II, 26, 30, 31, 32, 34, 37, 109, 190 n. 56
Thutmose III, 17, 26, 32, 33, 34, 42, 54, 62, 63, 109, 110, 124, 148, 190 nn. 67, 71, 193 n. 3, 196 n. 15, 202 nn. 10–11, 210 n. 9
Thutmose IV, 18, *18*, 26, 42, 44, 134, 187 n. 32
Thutmoside, 42
Tia, 38
Tiaa, 44
Tiye, 36, 43, 80, *81*, 89, 102, 108, 110, 114, 132, 141, 176, 200 n. 32, 207 n. 3, 211 n. 24; head of, 111, *111*, 112, 202
Tjaroy, 42
Tjasep, 103
Tjepu, 154; painting of, 55, *56*, 57, 154, 193–94
toilet implements, 75–79, *75–78*, 145, 146, *147;* with horse-shaped handle, 75, 76, *76;* with papyriform blade, 75, 76, *76*

tree goddess, 125, 126, 130, 204
Turin, 98
Turin Canon, 29, 30
Tutankhamen, 26, 96, 102, 156, 169, 205 n. 3, 210 nn. 8, 10
Tuya, 114, 203 n. 14
tweezers, 75, 145, *147;* blunt-edged, 75, *75, 76*

uadjet eye, 74, *74*
Unas, 105
unguent vessels, 82, *82,* 83, *83,* 197; glass, 83, *83*
uraeus, see cobra
usekh, 87, 136
Userhat, tomb of, 22, *22*

Valley of the Kings, 17, 36, 86, 87, 109, 152, 176, 177, 187 n. 25
vessels, cosmetic, 79–87, *79–86,* 197
vizier, 39, 40, 177, 209 n. 3, 215
vulture headdress, 44, 101, *101,* 114, *115,* 118, *118, 119,* 120, *120,* 127, *127, 167,* 168, 203, 204 nn. 1, 3, 206 n. 2

Wadjyt, 139, 143, 144, 201 n. 1, 209 nn. 10, 14, 210 n. 13
Wah, tomb of, 95, 187 nn. 36–37
wand, hand, 98, 99, 101–2, *102,* 200
wand, magic (apotropaic), 64, *64,* 68, 101, 132, 195
weaving, *see* textile production
Wedjebten, 104, 159; relief: Queen Wedjebten with lotus, 104, *104,* 105, 159; tomb of, 104–5
Wepwawet, 35, 171, 172, 174
Weret, 198 n. 2
wet nurse, 17, *17,* 18, 41, 60, 62
widows, 40, 175, 181, 182, 216 n. 42
wife, 13, 14; *see also* God's Wife of Amen; King's Principal Wife; Mistress of the House; queen; women
wigs, 34, *34,* 50, 55, *55,* 57, 58, 60, 67, 75, 79, 94, *94,* 95, *95,* 96, *103,* 104, *106,* 107, *107,* 111, *111,* 148, 154, 162, *162,* 165, 169, *170,* 171, 172, 174; goddess, 123, 124, *124,* 128, 134, *134,* 138, *138,* 141, 142, *143;* lady with a large wig, 57, *57,* 58, 120, 194; lappet, 134, *134,* 138, *138;* scroll, 55, *55,* 105, 120, *120,* 124, *124,* 193 n. 6; *shabti,* 148, 149, *149,* 152, 153; *see also* hairdressing; hairstyles, women's
women: administrative titles of, 39–40; foreign, 111, 160, 197 n. 4; legal rights of, 13, 49–50, 51, 60, 175–85, 215–17; literacy, 142; nurturing role of, *see* motherhood; priestly titles of, 29, 31–33, 41–44, 109, 162, 163, 189; property rights of, 13, 49, 50, 177–78, 179, 181–85, 215–17; in religious ideology, 44–46; status and roles of, 25–46, 175; *see also* daughter; elite women; goddesses; nonroyal women; occupations, women's; royal women; wife

Yia, 174
Yuni and Renenutet, statue depicting, 13, 14, 15, 22, 87, 100, 172, *172, 173,* 174, 214

Photograph credits

The Art Institute of Chicago, Chicago, cat. nos. 21d, 49

Photos courtesy of Dr. Betsy Bryan, figs. 1, 8, 10, 13, 16, 17, 18, 19, 20, 21

The Brooklyn Museum, New York, cat. nos. 6, 8b, 9, 10a, 13, 14, 19, 22b, 27w, 27x, 27y, 34, 39, 40, 41, 46, 53a, 53b, 54b, 56, 61, 70, 75, 89; comparative figs. 4, 6, 7, 8; Bryan figs. 2a, 6; and Roehrig fig. 8

Cairo Museum, Egypt, Bryan fig. 2a

California State University Art Gallery, San Bernardino, cat. no. 47

Cincinnati Art Museum, Cincinnati, cat. nos. 16a–b, 20a–c, 20e–u, 20v1–v10, 21a–c, 21f–i, 22a, 23a–d, 23f–j, 23n–v, 23x–y, 24a–d, 27a–v, 27aa–dd, 29, 32, 35b, 38, 58, 59b–c, 64b, 65, 67, 68b, 72a–q, 77a–b, 83, 88, 92; comparative fig. 9; and Bryan figs. 3, 4, 5

Copyright, The Cleveland Museum of Art, Cleveland, cat. nos. 30, 33, 50, 80, 91

The Detroit Institute of Arts, Detroit, cat. nos. 20d, 21e, 31, 68a

Field Museum of Natural History, Chicago, cat. nos. 43, 60, 63a

Drawing by B. Girsh from the Metropolitan Museum of Art tomb card 4886, Roehrig fig. 18

Joslyn Art Museum, Omaha, cat. no. 48

Copyright of Ibrahim Harari, Bryan fig. 9

Matsuoka Museum of Art, Tokyo, comparative fig. 1

The Metropolitan Museum of Art, New York, cat. nos. 2, 3a, 4, 8a, 25, 26, 35c, 42, 54a, 62, 82, 93; and Roehrig figs. 1, 2, 3, 5, 6, 7, 8, 9, 10, 11, 12, 13, 14, 15, 16, 17a–b

Miami University Art Museum, Oxford, Ohio, cat. no. 27z

Copyright Maurice and Pierre Chuzeville, Musée du Louvre, Bryan figs. 7, 14

Museum of Art, Rhode Island School of Design, Providence, cat. no. 69

Courtesy, Museum of Fine Arts, Boston, cat. nos. 10b, 15, 35d, 37, 44, 51, 73, 78, 84; comparative figs. 3, 5; and Bryan figs. 2b, 3

The Nelson-Atkins Museum of Art, Kansas City, Missouri, cat. no. 45

Courtesy of The Oriental Institute of The University of Chicago, Chicago, cat. no. 11

Courtesy of the Petrie Museum, University of London, Roehrig fig. 4

Philadelphia Museum of Art, Philadelphia, cat. no. 3b

Phoebe A. Hearst Museum of Anthropology, University of California at Berkeley, cat. nos. 23k, 28a, 28b, 36b, 76, 85, 90

The Saint Louis Art Museum, St. Louis, cat. nos. 5, 55b

The Toledo Museum of Art, Toledo, Ohio, cat. nos. 1, 23e, 23m, 23z, 23aa, 23bb, 36a, 74; and comparative fig. 11

The University of Pennsylvania Museum of Archaeology and Anthropology, Philadelphia, cat. nos. 17, 23, 59a, 64a, 71, 76, 79, 87

Copyright of Virginia Museum of Fine Arts, Richmond, cat. nos. 7, 18

Washington University Gallery of Art, St. Louis, cat. no. 91

The Walters Art Gallery, Baltimore, cat. nos. 12, 35a, 52, 55a, 57, 63b, 66

Yale University Art Gallery, New Haven, Connecticut, cat. nos. 23w, 81, 94